GALATIANS

Baker Exegetical Commentary on the New Testament

ROBERT W. YARBROUGH
AND ROBERT H. STEIN, EDITORS

Volumes now available

Matthew *David L. Turner*

Mark *Robert H. Stein*

Luke *Darrell L. Bock*

John *Andreas J. Köstenberger*

Acts *Darrell L. Bock*

Romans *Thomas R. Schreiner*

1 Corinthians *David E. Garland*

2 Corinthians *George H. Guthrie*

Galatians *Douglas J. Moo*

Ephesians *Frank Thielman*

Philippians *Moisés Silva*

1–2 Thessalonians *Jeffrey A. D. Weima*

James *Dan G. McCartney*

1 Peter *Karen H. Jobes*

1–3 John *Robert W. Yarbrough*

Jude and 2 Peter *Gene L. Green*

Revelation *Grant R. Osborne*

Douglas J. Moo (PhD, University of St. Andrews) is Kenneth T. Wessner Professor of New Testament at Wheaton College Graduate School. Before coming to Wheaton, he taught for more than twenty years at Trinity Evangelical Divinity School in Deerfield, Illinois. He has written commentaries on Romans, Colossians and Philemon, James, and 2 Peter and Jude and chaired the Committee on Bible Translation for the New International Version revision.

GALATIANS

DOUGLAS J. MOO

Baker Exegetical Commentary on the New Testament

Baker Academic
a division of Baker Publishing Group
Grand Rapids, Michigan

© 2013 by Douglas J. Moo

Published by Baker Academic
a division of Baker Publishing Group
P.O. Box 6287, Grand Rapids, MI 49516-6287
www.bakeracademic.com

Printed in the United States of America

Library of Congress Cataloging-in-Publication Data

Moo, Douglas J.
    Galatians / Douglas J. Moo.
      p. cm. — (Baker exegetical commentary on the New Testament)
    Includes bibliographical references and index.
    ISBN 978-0-8010-2754-3 (cloth)
    1. Bible. Galatians—Commentaries. I. Title.
  BS2685.53.M65 2013
  227′.4077—dc23
                                                              2013018569

17   18   19   20   21   22   23   9 8 7 6 5 4 3

For
Jenny, συνεργάτις

Contents

Series Preface

The chief concern of the Baker Exegetical Commentary on the New Testament (BECNT) is to provide, within the framework of informed evangelical thought, commentaries that blend scholarly depth with readability, exegetical detail with sensitivity to the whole, and attention to critical problems with theological awareness. We hope thereby to attract the interest of a fairly wide audience, from the scholar who is looking for a thoughtful and independent examination of the text to the motivated lay Christian who craves a solid but accessible exposition.

Nevertheless, a major purpose is to address the needs of pastors and others involved in the preaching and exposition of the Scriptures as the uniquely inspired Word of God. This consideration directly affects the parameters of the series. For example, serious biblical expositors cannot afford to depend on a superficial treatment that avoids the difficult questions, but neither are they interested in encyclopedic commentaries that seek to cover every conceivable issue that may arise. Our aim, therefore, is to focus on those problems that have a direct bearing on the meaning of the text (although selected technical details are treated in the additional notes).

Similarly, a special effort is made to avoid treating exegetical questions for their own sake, that is, in relative isolation from the thrust of the argument as a whole. This effort may involve (at the discretion of the individual contributors) abandoning the verse-by-verse approach in favor of an exposition that focuses on the paragraph as the main unit of thought. In all cases, however, the commentaries will stress the development of the argument and explicitly relate each passage to what precedes and follows it so as to identify its function in context as clearly as possible.

We believe, moreover, that a responsible exegetical commentary must take fully into account the latest scholarly research, regardless of its source. The attempt to do this in the context of a conservative theological tradition presents certain challenges, and in the past the results have not always been commendable. In some cases, evangelicals appear to make use of critical scholarship not for the purpose of genuine interaction but only to dismiss it. In other cases, the interaction glides over into assimilation, theological distinctives are ignored or suppressed, and the end product cannot be differentiated from works that arise from a fundamentally different starting point.

The contributors to this series attempt to avoid these pitfalls. On the one hand, they do not consider traditional opinions to be sacrosanct, and they are certainly committed to doing justice to the biblical text whether or not it supports such opinions. On the other hand, they will not quickly abandon a long-standing view, if there is persuasive evidence in its favor, for the sake of fashionable theories. What is more important, the contributors share a belief in the trustworthiness and essential unity of Scripture. They also consider that the historic formulations of Christian doctrine, such as the ecumenical creeds and many of the documents originating in the sixteenth-century Reformation, arose from a legitimate reading of Scripture, thus providing a proper framework for its further interpretation. No doubt the use of such a starting point sometimes results in the imposition of a foreign construct on the text, but we deny that it must necessarily do so or that the writers who claim to approach the text without prejudices are invulnerable to the same danger.

Accordingly, we do not consider theological assumptions—from which, in any case, no commentator is free—to be obstacles to biblical interpretation. On the contrary, an exegete who hopes to understand the apostle Paul in a theological vacuum might just as easily try to interpret Aristotle without regard for the philosophical framework of his whole work or without having recourse to those subsequent philosophical categories that make possible a meaningful contextualization of his thought. It must be emphasized, however, that the contributors to the present series come from a variety of theological traditions and that they do not all have identical views with regard to the proper implementation of these general principles. In the end, all that matters is whether the series succeeds in representing the original text accurately, clearly, and meaningfully to the contemporary reader.

Shading has been used to assist the reader in locating salient sections of the treatment of each passage: introductory comments and concluding summaries. Textual variants in the Greek text are signaled in the author's translation by means of half-brackets around the relevant word or phrase (e.g., ⌜Gerasenes⌝), thereby alerting the reader to turn to the additional notes at the end of each exegetical unit for a discussion of the textual problem. The documentation uses the author-date method, in which the basic reference consists of author's surname + year + page number(s): Fitzmyer 1992: 58. The only exceptions to this system are well-known reference works (e.g., BDAG, LSJ, *TDNT*). Full publication data and a complete set of indexes can be found at the end of the volume.

Robert W. Yarbrough
Robert H. Stein

Author's Preface

I am very grateful to Baker Publishing Group and to the editors of this series to have been given the opportunity to write a commentary on Galatians. Studying the Greek text of a NT book, making my own decisions about its meaning (in conversation with many other scholars), and then putting those decisions into English prose that will (it is hoped!) communicate successfully with an audience—all this is one of the chief delights of my life. I have learned a lot during the years of my work on Galatians; and I trust that my thinking and therefore my living are more closely aligned with Christ and his purposes as a result of this study.

Many people have helped me produce this commentary. Colleagues and students at Wheaton College and in the wider academic community have had an immense impact on my understanding of the letter. Providing special assistance in this process were four PhD students, each of whom wrote dissertations with me that focused on aspects of Galatians: Matt Harmon, Chee-Chiew Lee, Chris Bruno, and Dane Ortlund. Also very helpful were three other students who assisted with bibliography collection, proofreading, and formatting: Keith Williams, Mike Kibbe, and Paul Cable. I am privileged to teach at an institution that enables students to work with faculty on scholarly projects.

The careful editorial work by Baker personnel and by the series editor, friend and former colleague Robert Yarbrough, has immeasurably improved the commentary. I am also thankful for the patience of publisher and editor as they waited long past the initial deadline for my work to reach its conclusion (a delay largely due to my extensive, unexpected, but delightful work on the updated NIV, released in 2011).

As always, I am especially grateful for the support in many, many ways of my children, their spouses, and especially my wife, Jenny. She has not only been a wonderful, understanding wife, but she is a true "fellow worker," having read the entire manuscript, noted the far too many typos and grammatical errors, and offered insightful suggestions for improvement. It is to her that I dedicate this volume.

November 2011
Doug Moo

A Note to the Reader

The series preface to the book explains many of the formal features of the commentary. I want to add here a few words about some features that are particular to this volume.

First, I have chosen to cite regularly only nine of the many commentaries on Galatians. Interrupting my own argument about the meaning of the text with long lists of commentaries makes it difficult to follow what I am saying. Moreover, citing a large number of commentaries is usually not very helpful, since there is so much repetition among them. I have therefore chosen to cite regularly only a handful of commentaries, which I have singled out for their general exegetical excellence and/or for a distinctive view of the letter that they embody. These commentaries are those written by J. B. Lightfoot, Ernest deWitt Burton, Hans Dieter Betz, F. F. Bruce, Franz Mussner, Richard Longenecker, James Dunn, Louis Martyn, and Martinus de Boer. Naturally, I include references to other commentaries when they make a contribution not represented by these nine or when I considered it important to give readers a wider view of the spectrum of opinion on a particular issue.

Second, the reader will quickly see that I consistently refer to English translations to illustrate exegetical options. I do so not simply because I am a translator myself (although I am sure that is one reason!), but because the translations are important representations of the exegetical tradition. Translations are the product of many scholars working cooperatively, and they therefore provide a useful filter of the bewildering variety of exegetical options found in the academy. They also reflect in (usually!) accessible English the various options for interpreting the Greek text. The preacher or teacher can then use a rendering found in the translations to express a particular option in the understanding of the Greek text and can usefully refer listeners to a particular translation for a semiofficial endorsement of the option being argued for.

Third, the translations of Galatians, including those at the beginning of every "Exegesis and Exposition" section, are my own. They are attempts to reflect in English as much of the form of the underlying Greek as possible. (Of course, it is impossible fully or even significantly to reproduce the form of the Greek in English.) As such, they are far from being good translations of the Greek; they are designed only to provide an English basis for the commentary on the Greek text. Translations of other Scripture within the commentary are from the NIV (2011) unless otherwise noted.

Abbreviations

Bibliographic and General

§/§§	section/sections
//	textual parallels
ABD	*The Anchor Bible Dictionary*, edited by D. N. Freedman et al., 6 vols. (New York: Doubleday, 1992)
AD	*anno Domini*, in the year of the Lord
ad loc.	*ad locum*, at the place
ANRW	*Aufstieg und Niedergang der römischen Welt*, edited by H. Temporini and W. Haase, Part 2: *Principat* (Berlin: de Gruyter, 1972–)
AT	author's translation
BC	before Christ
BDAG	*A Greek-English Lexicon of the New Testament and Other Early Christian Literature*, by W. Bauer, F. W. Danker, W. F. Arndt, and F. W. Gingrich, 3rd ed. (Chicago: University of Chicago Press, 2000)
BDF	*A Greek Grammar of the New Testament and Other Early Christian Literature*, by F. Blass and A. Debrunner, translated and revised by R. W. Funk (Chicago: University of Chicago Press, 1961)
BDR	*Grammatik des neutestamentlichen Griechisch*, by F. Blass, A. Debrunner, and F. Rehkopf (Göttingen: Vandenhoeck & Ruprecht, 1984)
CEB	Common English Bible
cf.	*confer*, compare
chap./chaps.	chapter/chapters
e.g.	*exempli gratia*, for example
esp.	especially
ESV	English Standard Version
frg./frgs.	fragment/s
GKC	*Gesenius' Hebrew Grammar*, edited and enlarged by E. Kautzsch, revised by A. E. Cowley, 2nd English ed. (Clarendon: Oxford, 1910)
HALOT	*The Hebrew and Aramaic Lexicon of the Old Testament*, by L. Koehler, W. Baumgartner, J. J. Stamm, and M. E. Richardson, 5 vols. (Leiden: Brill, 2000)
HCSB	Holman Christian Standard Bible
Heb.	Hebrew
Institutes	John Calvin, *Institutes of the Christian Religion*, edited by John T. McNeill, translated by Ford L. Battles, 2 vols., Library of Christian Classics 20–21 (Philadelphia: Westminster, 1960)
KJV	King James Version

LEH	*Greek-English Lexicon of the Septuagint*, compiled by J. Lust, E. Eynikel, and K. Hauspie, rev. ed. (Stuttgart: Deutsche Bibelgesellschaft, 2003)
lit.	literally
LN	*Greek-English Lexicon of the New Testament: Based on Semantic Domains*, by J. P. Louw and E. A. Nida, 2nd ed. (New York: United Bible Society, 1999)
LSJ	*A Greek-English Lexicon*, by H. G. Liddell, R. Scott, and H. S. Jones, 9th ed. (Oxford: Oxford University Press, 1940)
LXX	Septuagint (the Old Testament in Greek)
𝔐	majority text
MM	*The Vocabulary of the Greek Testament: Illustrated from the Papyri and Other Non-literary Sources*, by J. H. Moulton and G. Milligan (repr., Grand Rapids: Eerdmans, 1976)
MS/MSS	manuscript/manuscripts
MT	Masoretic Text
NA[28]	*Novum Testamentum Graece*, edited by Eberhard Nestle, Erwin Nestle, B. Aland, K. Aland, J. Karavidopoulos, C. M. Martini, and B. M. Metzger, 28th ed. (Stuttgart: Deutsche Bibelgesellschaft, 2012)
NAB	New American Bible
NASB	New American Standard Bible
NET	New English Translation
NETS	*A New English Translation of the Septuagint*, by the International Organization for Septuagint and Cognate Studies (New York: Oxford University Press, 2007)
NewDocs	*New Documents Illustrating Early Christianity*, edited by G. H. R. Horsley and S. R. Llewelyn (North Ryde, NSW: Ancient History Documentary Research Centre, Macquarie University, 1976–)
New Pauly	*Brill's New Pauly: Encyclopedia of the Ancient World*, edited by H. Cancik, H. Schneider, and M. Landfester, 20 vols. (Leiden: Brill, 2002–11)
NIDB	*The New Interpreter's Dictionary of the Bible*, edited by K. D. Sakenfeld, 5 vols. (Nashville: Abingdon, 2009)
NIDNTT	*New International Dictionary of New Testament Theology*, edited by C. Brown, 4 vols. (Grand Rapids: Zondervan, 1975–85)
NIV	New International Version
NJB	New Jerusalem Bible
NKJV	New King James Version
NLT	New Living Translation
NPNF[1]	*Nicene and Post-Nicene Fathers of the Christian Church*, edited by P. Schaff, 1st series, 14 vols. (repr., Grand Rapids: Eerdmans, 1952–57)
NRSV	New Revised Standard Version
NT	New Testament
OT	Old Testament
OTP	*The Old Testament Pseudepigrapha*, edited by J. H. Charlesworth, 2 vols. (Garden City, NY: Doubleday, 1983–85)
𝔓	papyrus
RSV	Revised Standard Version

Str-B	*Kommentar zum Neuen Testament aus Talmud und Midrasch*, by H. L. Strack and P. Billerbeck, 6 vols. (Munich: Kessinger, 1922–61)
s.v.	*sub verbo*, under the word
TDNT	*Theological Dictionary of the New Testament*, edited by G. Kittel and G. Friedrich, translated and edited by G. W. Bromiley, 10 vols. (Grand Rapids: Eerdmans, 1964–76)
TDOT	*Theological Dictionary of the Old Testament*, edited by G. J. Botterweck, H. Ringgren, and H.-J. Fabry, translated by J. T. Willis, G. W. Bromiley, D. E. Green, and D. W. Stott, 14 vols. (Grand Rapids: Eerdmans, 1974–)
TLG	Thesaurus Linguae Graecae, online digital library (Irvine: University of California, 2001–)
TNIV	Today's New International Version
UBS[4]	*The Greek New Testament*, edited by B. Aland et al., 4th rev. ed. (Stuttgart: Deutsche Bibelgesellschaft, 1993)
v./vv.	verse/verses
v.l.	*varia lectio*, variant reading
vs.	versus
x	number of times a form occurs

Hebrew Bible

Gen.	Genesis	2 Chron.	2 Chronicles	Dan.	Daniel
Exod.	Exodus	Ezra	Ezra	Hosea	Hosea
Lev.	Leviticus	Neh.	Nehemiah	Joel	Joel
Num.	Numbers	Esther	Esther	Amos	Amos
Deut.	Deuteronomy	Job	Job	Obad.	Obadiah
Josh.	Joshua	Ps(s).	Psalm(s)	Jon.	Jonah
Judg.	Judges	Prov.	Proverbs	Mic.	Micah
Ruth	Ruth	Eccles.	Ecclesiastes	Nah.	Nahum
1 Sam.	1 Samuel	Song	Song of Songs	Hab.	Habakkuk
2 Sam.	2 Samuel	Isa.	Isaiah	Zeph.	Zephaniah
1 Kings	1 Kings	Jer.	Jeremiah	Hag.	Haggai
2 Kings	2 Kings	Lam.	Lamentations	Zech.	Zechariah
1 Chron.	1 Chronicles	Ezek.	Ezekiel	Mal.	Malachi

Greek Testament

Matt.	Matthew	Eph.	Ephesians	Heb.	Hebrews
Mark	Mark	Phil.	Philippians	James	James
Luke	Luke	Col.	Colossians	1 Pet.	1 Peter
John	John	1 Thess.	1 Thessalonians	2 Pet.	2 Peter
Acts	Acts	2 Thess.	2 Thessalonians	1 John	1 John
Rom.	Romans	1 Tim.	1 Timothy	2 John	2 John
1 Cor.	1 Corinthians	2 Tim.	2 Timothy	3 John	3 John
2 Cor.	2 Corinthians	Titus	Titus	Jude	Jude
Gal.	Galatians	Philem.	Philemon	Rev.	Revelation

Other Jewish and Christian Writings

Arist.	Aristides the Apologist	Jdt.	Judith
2 Bar.	2 Baruch (Syriac Apocalypse)	Jub.	Jubilees
		L.A.B.	Liber antiquitatum biblicarum (Pseudo-Philo)
Comm. Gal.	John Chrysostom, Commentary on the Epistle of St. Paul the Apostle to the Galatians	Lam. Rab.	Lamentations Rabbah
		Lev. Rab.	Leviticus Rabbah
		1–4 Macc.	1–4 Maccabees
Comm. Jo.	Origen, Commentary on the Gospel of John	Midr. Teh.	Midrash Tehillim (Midrash on Psalms)
Dial.	Justin Martyr, Dialogue with Trypho	Num. Rab.	Numbers Rabbah
		Pesiq. Rab.	Pesiqta Rabbati
1 En.	1 Enoch	Pirqe R. El.	Pirqe Rabbi Eliezer
1 Esd.	1 Esdras (in the Apocrypha)	Pr. Man.	Prayer of Manasseh
		Pss. Sol.	Psalms of Solomon
2 Esd.	2 Esdras (4 Ezra)	Sib. Or.	Sibylline Oracles
Exhort.	Clement of Alexandria, Exhortation to the Greeks	Sir.	Sirach (Ecclesiasticus)
		T. Sol.	Testament of Solomon
Gen. Rab.	Genesis Rabbah	Tob.	Tobit
Idol.	Tertullian, On Idolatry	Wis.	Wisdom of Solomon
Ign. Magn.	Ignatius, To the Magnesians		

Josephus

Ag. Ap.	Against Apion
Ant.	Jewish Antiquities
J.W.	Jewish War

Philo

Contempl.	On the Contemplative Life	Moses	On the Life of Moses
		Prelim. Studies	On the Preliminary Studies
Creation	On the Creation of the World	Somn.	De somniis (On Dreams)
Decalogue	On the Decalogue	Spec. Laws	On the Special Laws
Heir	Who Is the Heir?	Virtues	On the Virtues
Leg.	Legum allegoriae (Allegorical Interpretation)		
Migr.	On the Migration of Abraham		

Rabbinic Tractates

The abbreviations below are used for the names of the tractates in the Mishnah (indicated by a prefixed m.), Tosefta (t.), Babylonian Talmud (b.), and Palestinian/Jerusalem Talmud (y.).

'Abot	'Abot	Šabb.	Šabbat
B. Qam.	Baba Qamma	Sanh.	Sanhedrin
Ber.	Berakot	Soṭah	Soṭah
Mak.	Makkot	Ta'an.	Ta'anit
Qidd.	Qiddušin		

Targumim

Sam. Tg.	Samaritan Targum	Tg. Onqelos	Targum Onqelos
Tg.	Targum	Tg. Ps.-J.	Targum Pseudo-Jonathan

Qumran/Dead Sea Scrolls

CD	Damascus Document, from the Cairo Genizah
8HevXIIgr	Greek Minor Prophets Scroll, from Cave of Horror in Nahal Hever
PYadin 19	Papyrus Yadin 19, from Cave of Letters in Nahal Hever
1QpHab	Pesher Habakkuk
1QS	Rule of the Community
4Q266	Damascus Document[a] (later called 4Q268)
4QFlor	4QFlorilegium (4Q174)
4QMMT	Miqṣat Maʿaśê ha-Torah (4Q394–4Q399)
4QPNah	Pesher Nahum (4Q169)
11QPs[a]	11QPsalms[a] (11Q5)
11QT[a]	Temple Scroll[a] (11Q19)

Classical Writers

Ages.	Xenophon, *Agesilaus*
Cic.	Plutarch, *Cicero*
Hist.	Polybius, *Universal History*
Is.	Dionysius of Halicarnassus, *De Isaeo*
Mem.	Xenophon, *Memorabilia*
Pericles	Plutarch, *Life of Pericles*
Rhet.	Aristotle, *Rhetoric*
Tox.	Lucian of Samosata, *Toxaris*

Transliteration

Hebrew

א	ʾ		בָ	ā	qāmeṣ
ב	b		בַ	a	pataḥ
ג	g		הַ	a	furtive pataḥ
ד	d		בֶ	e	segôl
ה	h		בֵ	ē	ṣērê
ו	w		בִ	i	short ḥîreq
ז	z		בִ	ī	long ḥîreq written defectively
ח	ḥ		בָ	o	qāmeṣ ḥāṭûp
ט	ṭ		בוֹ	ô	ḥôlem written fully
י	y		בֹ	ō	ḥôlem written defectively
כ/ך	k		בוּ	û	šûreq
ל	l		בֻ	u	short qibbûṣ
מ/ם	m		בֻ	ū	long qibbûṣ written defectively
נ/ן	n		בָה	â	final qāmeṣ hēʾ (בָה = āh)
ס	s		בֵי	ê	segôl yôd (בֶי = êy)
ע	ʿ		בֵי	ê	ṣērê yôd (בֵי = êy)
פ/ף	p		בִי	î	ḥîreq yôd (בִי = îy)
צ/ץ	ṣ		בֲ	ă	ḥāṭēp pataḥ
ק	q		בֱ	ĕ	ḥāṭēp segôl
ר	r		בֳ	ŏ	ḥāṭēp qāmeṣ
שׂ	ś		בְ	ĕ	vocal šĕwāʾ
שׁ	š				
ת	t				

Notes on the Transliteration of Hebrew

1. Accents are not shown in transliteration.
2. Silent *šĕwāʾ* is not indicated in transliteration.
3. The spirant forms בגדכפת are usually not specially indicated in transliteration.
4. *Dāgēš forte* is indicated by doubling the consonant. Euphonic *dāgēš* and *dāgēš lene* are not indicated in transliteration.
5. *Maqqēp* is represented by a hyphen.

Greek

α	*a*	ξ	*x*
β	*b*	ο	*o*
γ	*g/n*	π	*p*
δ	*d*	ρ	*r*
ε	*e*	σ/ς	*s*
ζ	*z*	τ	*t*
η	*ē*	υ	*y/u*
θ	*th*	φ	*ph*
ι	*i*	χ	*ch*
κ	*k*	ψ	*ps*
λ	*l*	ω	*ō*
μ	*m*	ʽ	*h*
ν	*n*		

Notes on the Transliteration of Greek

1. Accents, lenis (smooth breathing), and *iota* subscript are not shown in transliteration.
2. The transliteration of asper (rough breathing) precedes a vowel or diphthong (e.g., ἁ = *ha*; αἱ = *hai*) and follows ρ (i.e., ῥ = *rh*).
3. *Gamma* is transliterated *n* only when it precedes γ, κ, ξ, or χ.
4. *Upsilon* is transliterated *u* only when it is part of a diphthong (i.e., αυ, ευ, ου, υι).

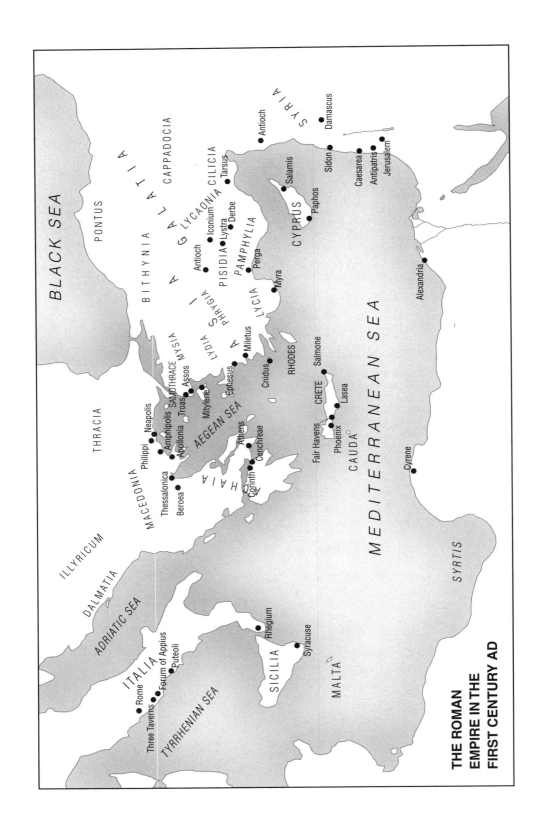

THE ROMAN
EMPIRE IN THE
FIRST CENTURY AD

Introduction to Galatians

Author

The author of the Letter to the Galatians identifies himself as "Paul the Apostle" (1:1), and the letter is full of corroborating personal references. Paul defends his independent apostleship by narrating his conversion/call and his early relationships with the Jerusalem apostles (1:11–2:10). He describes a difficult confrontation in Antioch with Peter (and Barnabas; 2:11–14). Paul reminds his readers of his earlier ministry with them (4:12–20). He cites his own attitudes and decisions as matters for the Galatians to emulate (2:18–21; 5:11; 6:14; perhaps 1:13–16). And he seeks to move his readers to embrace again the gospel he first preached to them by means of personal and even emotional appeals (1:6–10; 3:1; 4:11; 5:2–3; 6:17). Only 2 Corinthians and the Pastoral Epistles rival Galatians in degree of personal reference.

From the earliest days of the church, Paul's authorship of Galatians has been acknowledged and never seriously challenged. Only the more mechanical aspect of authorship is debated. In 6:11, Paul says, "See what large letters I use as I write to you with my own hand!" This claim probably applies only to 6:11 and following and not to the entire letter (on this issue and the reason why Paul might say this, see the commentary). A natural, though not inevitable, corollary is that someone else has "written down" the rest of the letter on Paul's behalf. We know, both from general ancient testimony and from Paul himself (Rom. 16:22), that he often—indeed, perhaps always—used what was called in the ancient world an "amanuensis" to perform the work of physically writing out his letters (R. Longenecker 1983; Richards 1991). Amanuenses were given varying degrees of freedom as far as their own involvement in the composition was concerned. An amanuensis who was a trusted confidant might be responsible for much of the actual wording of a letter based on a more or less detailed outline of content provided by the true "author" (many interpreters think that such a situation could explain the differences in vocabulary and style among the Letters of Paul; see, e.g., Carson and Moo 2005: 334–35). If Paul used an amanuensis in writing the bulk of Galatians (which is probable), the strongly personal nature of the letter argues for a situation closer to word-for-word dictation.

The Occasion for the Letter

The basic situation Paul addresses in Galatians is clear enough from the opening of the letter body. Omitting any thanksgiving for the Galatians,

Paul immediately decries their flirtation with "another gospel" (1:6–10). This counterfeit gospel is being propagated by false teachers who are "confusing" the Gentile Galatians (1:7; 5:10) by insisting that their faith in Christ be supplemented by submission to circumcision and other elements of the Mosaic law (esp. 5:2–4). Paul responds to this challenge in three stages. First, he uses his own experience to illustrate the relationship between "the truth of the gospel" (2:5, 14) and the law of Moses (1:11–2:21), with a particular focus on his relationship to the Jerusalem apostles (1:17–2:14). Second, he uses the Galatians' own experience and especially Scripture to argue that the justification that accompanies belonging to the "seed" of Abraham is by faith, apart from torah observance (3:1–5:12). Third, he shows that conduct pleasing to God is secured by that same faith and the work of God's Spirit apart from torah (5:13–6:18).

The Destination and Date of the Letter

The general circumstances that gave rise to Paul's Letter to the Galatians are not a matter of debate. But the specifics are much less clear. Who were the people "agitating" the Galatians by proclaiming a different gospel? And who were the Galatians? We will take up this second question first.

The destination of Galatians is one of the best-known and most intractable problems in NT introduction. To be sure, it is not the question of destination per se that is so important but the related question of the date of the letter. This latter issue bears on a range of significant issues, from the meaning of some specific verses in Galatians to the development and shape of Paul's theology, the historicity of the book of Acts, and the course of early Christian history.[1] Why is there so much disagreement over this issue? Very simply, it is because the location of the Christians that Paul addresses in the letter is unclear, and no other NT text settles the matter.

Paul addresses this letter to "the churches of Galatia" (ταῖς ἐκκλησίαις τῆς Γαλατίας, *tais ekklēsiais tēs Galatias*; 1:2); and note 3:1, "you foolish Galatians" (ὦ ἀνόητοι Γαλάται, *ō anoētoi Galatai*). This is the only letter that Paul addressed explicitly to a number of churches in a particular area (although his references in several other letters to believers in general could imply more than one congregation [probably in Rom. 1:7; perhaps in Eph. 1:1; less probably in Phil. 1:1 and Col. 1:2]). The name Γαλάται originally referred to a group of Celtic people from Gaul who migrated into Anatolia in central Asia Minor in the third century BC. (In addition to Γαλάται, these people were called Κέλτοι or Κέλται; in Latin, *Celtae, Galli,* or *Galatae*; see, e.g., Josephus *Ant.* 17.344; *J.W.* 4.547, 634; 7.88.) The predominance of this ethnic group in the

---

1. Hays's claim (2000: 191) that the question of destination/date is "almost entirely irrelevant for interpreting Paul's letter" (see also Brown 1997: 474) is true only for the very broad thrust of the letter as a whole. The specific sense of many verses is affected by the issue; and it has very important implications for our understanding of the course of Paul's life and ministry and for the development of his theology (see Silva 2001: 138–39).

region led the Romans to name a province in central and southern Asia Minor "Galatia" in the first century BC. In Paul's day, then, "Galatia" had both an ethnic/geographical and a political/geographical referent.[2]

Options

Paul could not have written this letter any earlier than the date at which he would have been able to visit the cities in question at least once. If, as we will assume, the book of Acts provides reliable (though not, of course, exhaustive) information about Paul's missionary travels, we can use specific references in Galatians to locate Paul within this narrative.

First, the earliest that we find Paul in *provincial* Galatia is during the first missionary journey of Acts 13–14. The Roman province of Asia covered a wide swath of central Asia Minor, extending from almost the Mediterranean Sea in the south to almost as far as the Black Sea in the north. Included within the province were the cities where Paul planted churches on this first missionary journey (Pisidian Antioch, Lystra, Iconium, Derbe; see Acts 13–14). A destination to provincial Galatia allows, then, a date as early as immediately after this first missionary journey. This is true even if Gal. 4:13 implies that Paul had made two visits to the Galatian churches before writing the letter. The meaning of this verse is debated (see the commentary) because Paul refers to his earlier visit(s) with a word (πρότερον, *proteron*) that could mean either "first" (of three or more) or "former" (of two). In other words, it is unclear whether this verse implies that Paul had made two visits to the Galatians before writing this letter or only one. Most scholars assume or argue that he is implying two previous visits, although we think it more likely that only one is in view. However, our point here is that our decision on this matter does not seriously affect the issue of destination and date. Even if we posit two visits to Galatia before the writing of the letter, a date immediately following the first missionary journey is still possible. For Luke tells us that Paul and his companions, after their initial evangelistic journey through South Galatia, retraced their steps to strengthen these new converts (Acts 14:22–25).

On this general reading of the data, then, Galatians could have been written before the meeting of the Jerusalem Council, perhaps around AD 48. Because the churches of the first missionary journey are located in the southern part of provincial Galatia, this view of the destination and date of Galatians has become known as the "South Galatian" theory. This understanding of the destination and date of Galatians was vigorously defended by William Ramsay and popularized by F. F. Bruce.[3] It should be stressed, however, that a South Galatian *destination* does not lock us into an early *date* of the letter:

---

2. The history of Galatia is treated in considerable detail in Mitchell 1993; cf. also K. Strobel, *New Pauly* 5:648–51; R. K. Sherk and S. Mitchell, *ANRW* 7/2:954–1081.

3. W. Ramsay, 1893: 97–111, passim; 1900: 1–164; Bruce 1982b: 3–18, 43–56; see also George 1994: 38–50; Witherington 1998: 2–20; Fung 1988: 1–3, 9–28; R. Longenecker 1990: lxi–lxxxviii; Schreiner 2010: 22–29 (weakly); Bauckham 1979; Hemer 1989: 247–51; Guthrie 1990: 465–72; McDonald and Porter 2000: 411–13; Breytenbach 1996: 99–176; Mitchell 1993: 2:3–10; Barnett

Paul could have written to these churches anytime after his initial visit. A fair number of scholars, then, while convinced of a South Galatian destination, argue for a date after the Jerusalem Council.[4]

If, on the other hand, we think that Paul wrote to ethnic Galatia, a somewhat later date is required. This is because it appears unlikely that Paul could have entered the region of ethnic Galatia, in north-central Asia Minor, before the beginning of the second missionary journey. Indeed, Luke tells us that, after revisiting the cities of the first missionary journey (Acts 16:1–4), "Paul and his companions traveled throughout the region of Phrygia and Galatia" (Acts 16:6). Thus if Paul wrote to ethnic Galatia, the earliest date for the letter would be sometime after this visit—around AD 50 or so. And if 4:13 is taken to refer to two visits to Galatia, an even later date would be necessary. This second visit would plausibly be identified with Luke's claim in Acts 18:23 that, at the beginning of the third missionary journey, "Paul . . . traveled from place to place throughout the region of Galatia and Phrygia, strengthening all the disciples." Hence the classic "North Galatian" theory holds that Paul wrote to ethnic Galatia, with its key cities Ancyra, Pessinus, and Tavium, sometime during the third missionary journey (perhaps around AD 55–56). This North Galatian view was defended by Lightfoot in his classic commentary and is still widely held, especially by German scholars.[5]

Although related, the questions of destination and date are independent. We will first look at the question of destination and then consider the matter of date.

Destination

The two options for the destination of the letter are more properly termed the "tribal" or "regional" (German *Landschaft*) view and the "provincial" view (see, e.g., Esler 1998: 32). In practice, however, since advocates of the "provincial" view identify the destination of the letter with the cities of the first missionary journey, the traditional "North" versus "South" nomenclature is the most useful. Dozens of arguments for and against these views are found

---

2000: 113–14; Carson and Moo 2005: 458–61; R. Schäfer 2004: 290–319; Burge, Cohick, and Green 2009: 268–69.

4. Dunn 1993a: 5–8; 2009: 720–25; Matera 1992: 19–26; G. Hansen 1994: 16–22; Silva 2001: 129–32; Elmer 2009; Fee 2007a: 3–5 (although he expresses some uncertainty about the destination).

5. See, e.g., Lightfoot 1881: 1–56; Rohde 1989: 5–13; Schlier 1989: 15–17; Oepke 1973: 23–27; Mussner 1988: 3–11; Betz 1979: 3–5; Borse 1972; Brown 1997: 474–77; Achtemeier, Green, and Thompson 2001: 372–75; Kümmel 1975: 296–304; Esler 1998: 32–36; Refoulé 1988; Murphy-O'Connor 1996: 159–62, 180–82. De Boer (2011: 3–5) argues for a North Galatian destination but thinks "Galatia" in 1:2 refers to the province. Breytenbach (1996: 101–3) notes a tendency for German scholars to favor (sometimes without argument) the North Galatian view, while British and American scholars are more divided. Which of these views is the "majority" view among scholars is obviously a judgment call. Compare Guthrie's (1990: 472) report that "most modern scholars lean to the South Galatian theory" with Brown's (1997: 476) report that the North Galatian view is "still the majority theory."

in the literature. Many of them are inconclusive or too subjective to be of much use.[6] And in any case, we need not evaluate or even list these many arguments, which are covered very adequately by NT introductions and other commentaries (see esp. Guthrie 1990: 465–83; R. Longenecker 1990: lxi–lxxxviii). We instead will focus on two issues that, we think, are the most significant in deciding this question: (1) the meaning of "Galatia/Galatians"; and (2) the route of Paul's travels. The first issue is usually cited in favor of the North Galatian view, the second in favor of the South Galatian view.

1. The meaning of "Galatia/Galatians." As we noted above, Γαλατία (*Galatia*, Galatia) in Paul's day referred both to a region in north-central Asia Minor and to a Roman province. Nothing in Galatians makes clear to which of these Paul refers in the address of the letter (1:2). The referents in Paul's other two uses of the word are also unclear: in 1 Cor. 16:1, he encourages the Corinthians to follow the example of "the churches of Galatia" (NRSV) in their generous giving to the collection; and in 2 Tim. 4:10 he mentions that "Crescens has gone to Galatia." The only other occurrence of Γαλατία in the NT comes in the address of 1 Peter: "the elect exiles of the dispersion in Pontus, Galatia, Cappadocia, Asia, and Bithynia" (1:1 ESV). It is almost certain that these names refer to Roman provinces (as most scholars agree; and note NIV and NLT). The word Γαλάται (*Galatai*, Galatians) occurs only in Gal. 3:1 (see also 1 Macc. 8:2; 2 Macc. 8:20). The referent of the adjective Γαλατικῆς (*Galatikēs*, Galatian), which occurs twice in Acts (16:6; 18:23), is also debated (see below on point 2).

Advocates of the North Galatian hypothesis argue that "Galatians" would naturally refer to people who were Galatian by ethnicity (see the data in BDAG 186–87). Indeed, to refer to other ethnic groups who were "Galatian" only because the conquering power, Rome, had imposed the name on them would have been both impolitic and unlikely (see, e.g., Lightfoot 1881: 19). On the other hand, C. Hemer (1989: 299–305) has shown that "Galatians" was, in fact, used to refer to people of various ethnic origins who lived in the southern part of the Roman province. And it is difficult to know what other word Paul could have used if he wanted to refer to all the Christians living in the cities of the first missionary journey (e.g., Burton 1921: xxix). Advocates of the South Galatian hypothesis note further that Paul generally uses provincial rather than ethnic names (Ramsay 1900: 147–64, 314–21). But this is not entirely clear (Kümmel 1975: 297; Rohde 1989: 7–8). The argument about the terms "Galatia" and "Galatians" is therefore inconclusive: they could refer either to the Roman province and people living in that province or to an ethnic region and to the people living in that region.

2. What might we learn from Paul's travels about the likely destination of the letter? No one doubts that Paul evangelized cities in the southern part of

---

6. Lightfoot (1881: 14–16), e.g., thought that the reputation of the ethnic Galatians for fickleness fit very well with the threatened theological defection that Paul deals with in the letter. R. Longenecker (1990: lxix) lists a series of arguments that he considers "ambiguous, inconclusive, or faulty."

the Roman province of Galatia: the South Galatian hypothesis has no problem on this score. The real question is whether Paul evangelized in the cities inhabited by ethnic Galatians in the north-central part of Asia Minor. Evidence from within the Pauline Letters is inconclusive. Of course, Paul rarely refers to his actual itineraries, and when he does, he does so in such passing fashion that little can be concluded about his routes. As we have seen, he refers twice to Galatia outside the Letter to the Galatians (1 Cor. 16:1; 2 Tim. 4:10), but neither reference enables us to locate the area. He refers to the South Galatian cities of (Pisidian) Antioch, Iconium, and Lystra in 2 Tim. 3:11 and never to any cities in north-central Galatia.

Evidence from Acts appears, at first sight, to be more helpful. Luke, of course, provides considerable detail about Paul's initial evangelistic work in the cities of South Galatia (chaps. 13–14). But he also refers twice to Paul's travels in the "Galatian" region. The former comes in Luke's description of the beginning of Paul's second missionary journey. Paul began this journey in the provinces of Syria and Cilicia (15:41), moved on to the cities of Derbe and Lystra (16:1), and then "traveled throughout the region of Phrygia and Galatia [διῆλθον δὲ τὴν Φρυγίαν καὶ Γαλατικὴν χώραν, *diēlthon de tēn Phrygian kai Galatikēn chōran*], having been kept by the Holy Spirit from preaching the word in the province of Asia" (Acts 16:6). The second reference occurs in Luke's narrative about the beginning of the third journey. "After spending some time in Antioch, Paul set out from there and traveled from place to place throughout the region of Galatia and Phrygia [διερχόμενος καθεξῆς τὴν Γαλατικὴν χώραν καὶ Φρυγίαν, *dierchomenos kathexēs tēn Galatikēn chōran kai Phrygian*], strengthening all the disciples" (18:23). Paul then took the road "through the interior," arriving ultimately in Ephesus (19:1).

Advocates of the North Galatian hypothesis typically cite these verses to substantiate a ministry of Paul in the ethnic region of Galatia, usually arguing that these two texts refer to the two visits that Gal. 4:13 is thought to indicate. Yet it is unclear here again whether "Galatia" in these texts refers to the ethnic region in the north or to the southern part of the province. In favor of the former is the sequence of movements suggested by Acts 16:1–6. Verse 1 depicts Paul's ministry in Derbe and Lystra, towns in the southern part of the province. We would then expect that the resumption of the travel narrative in verse 6 would refer to ministry in some other territory. Moreover, the aorist participle in verse 6b (κωλυθέντες, *kōlythentes*, being prevented) could suggest that the Spirit's intervention to keep Paul, Silas, and Timothy from preaching in the province of Asia took place earlier and indeed may have been the reason why they "traveled throughout Phrygia and Galatia" (so most English versions; and see, e.g., Barrett 1998: 768–69; Haenchen 1971: 483–84; Peterson 2009: 454). A glance at a map of first-century Asia Minor shows that this sequence of movements makes better sense if "Galatia" refers to the northern region; southern Galatia would be too far behind Paul and his companions to make it a likely place to go after being kept out of Asia. Moreover, the reference to "preaching the word" in the second part of the verse could suggest that Paul and his companions traveled throughout

Phrygia and Galatia for the purpose of evangelism—an assumption that appears to find confirmation in 18:23, which says that Paul and his companions were "strengthening all the disciples" when they next traveled through "the region of Galatia and Phrygia" (Brown 1997: 476). But southern Galatia was, of course, already evangelized. If Acts 16:6 is interpreted as a reference to northern Galatia, then, it is likely that the similar combination of "Galatia" and "Phrygia" in 18:23 would have the same meaning. This interpretation of "Galatia" in Acts receives some support from Luke's tendency to refer to traditional regions rather than to more recent Roman political entities. As Brown (1997: 475) notes, Luke uses these traditional regional names—*not* "Galatia"—when he locates the cities of the first missionary journey (Acts 13:14; 14:6).[7]

These considerations make it quite possible that Luke refers briefly to evangelistic work by Paul in northern Galatia. Yet this is not the only interpretation of these passages. Ramsay, in his classic defense of the South Galatian view, argued that the phrase τὴν Φρυγίαν καὶ Γαλατικὴν χώραν referred to "the Phrygian territory incorporated in the province of Galatia" (Acts 16:6; as Bruce [1988: 306] puts it [a shift from his earlier view in 1952: 309–10, 350]; see Ramsay 1893: 74–89; and also, e.g., Riesner 1998: 285; see esp. the discussion in Schnabel 2004: 1132–34). On this view, both geographical names are adjectives,[8] and the single article associates the two together as coordinate descriptions of one "region" (χώραν).[9] The problem of the sequence of movements is erased if the participle in verse 6b is taken to describe actions simultaneous to, or even future to, the action of the main verb in verse 6a (see HCSB; Ramsay 1893: 89).[10] The differently worded phrase in 18:23 is then taken to refer to two regions, "the Galatian country" of the first missionary journey and "Phrygia" (distinguished in this case from "Galatia" because the reference is to the part of Phrygia that lay in the province of Asia [Riesner 1998: 285–86; Schnabel 2004: 1199]).

A decision between these two interpretations of "Galatia" in Acts is difficult. We slightly prefer the South Galatian reading; but the evidence is too

7. Another argument in favor of the North Galatia hypothesis is the presence of Jews in the first missionary cities (Acts 13–14) while Galatians does not clearly indicate that Jews were among the audience (Brown 1997: 475).

8. K. Lake (1933) had argued that Φρυγίαν (*Phrygian*) could not be an adjective; but Hemer (1976; see also 1989: 280–99) has found a number of ancient inscriptions that prove the contrary (and cf. also *NewDocs* 4.174).

9. The argument from the single article is not, of course, conclusive. A. T. Robertson (1934: 787–88) draws attention to Acts 15:23, where a single article precedes the names of a city and two provinces (τὴν Ἀντιόχειαν καὶ Συρίαν καὶ Κιλικίαν, *tēn Antiocheian kai Syrian kai Kilikian*, [to the Gentile believers in] Antioch and Syria and Cilicia). Yet this may not be a true parallel, since the phrase lacks the substantive found in 16:6 (χώραν, *chōran*, region). The closest parallel is Luke 3:1, τῆς Ἰτουραίας καὶ Τραχωνίτιδος χώρας (*tēs Itouraias kai Trachōnitidos chōras*, the region of Iturea and Traconitis), where the two place names must refer to separate localities.

10. In NT Greek there is a tendency for aorist participles that precede the verb they modify to denote action antecedent to that of the main verb, while aorist participles that follow the main verb often do not (see G. Lee 1970). But the tendency is only that, and complicating factors (e.g., the more significant aspectual relationships) make it difficult to derive temporal indications from the sequence.

finely balanced to justify any great degree of probability. However, three other general considerations bear on the question of a Pauline ministry in northern Galatia: First, Paul generally focused his evangelistic work on cities with a strong Roman culture and used Roman roads to make his way from city to city. But North Galatia was not very Romanized in the first century (Ramsay 1893: 99), and major Roman roads were not constructed in north-central Galatia until the 70s and 80s of the first century (S. Mitchell, *ABD* 2:870). Second, it has been argued that the agitators were seeking to integrate the Gentile Christians of Galatia into existing synagogues; yet we have no firm evidence of Jewish influence in North Galatia until the third century (Breytenbach 1996: 140–48). This argument is not, however, compelling because (1) our knowledge of first-century North Galatia is fragmentary; and (2) it is not clear that the agitators' program required any local Jewish residents (see Schnabel 2004: 1134). Third, evidence for a Pauline mission in northern Galatia in the book of Acts is, as we have seen, uncertain. Yet in other cases Luke seems to have included explicit information about Paul's evangelistic work in churches to which he wrote letters (Guthrie 1990: 468–69). It appears, then, that evidence for a Pauline mission in South Galatia is explicit and unquestioned; evidence for such a mission in North Galatia is uncertain. Mitchell goes so far as to claim, "There is no evidence in Acts or any non-testamentary source that Paul ever evangelized the cities of N Galatia by any means" (*ABD* 2:871). As an expert in this part of the ancient world, Mitchell must be heard, but it appears that this claim may be exaggerated. Yet it is a salutary balance to the tendency among some scholars to assume a Pauline mission in North Galatia virtually without argument.

While, then, arguments about the meaning of "Galatia/Galatians" are inconclusive, the probable movements of Paul and his companions slightly favor a South Galatian destination of the letter.[11] But we cannot say any more on this matter until the related question of date is dealt with.

Date

Our decision about the destination of Galatians inevitably will affect our decision about its date. But the opposite is, of course, true as well, so that we cannot simply assume a view of destination as we look at the matter of date. Some discussions of Galatians, however, operate with an overly simplistic assumption about the relationship of these two issues—as, for instance, when it is assumed that a South Galatian destination means an early date for the

11. In addition to the arguments above, several less decisive considerations are said to point to a South Galatian destination, such as these: the significance of Antioch in Paul's argument (2:11–14) is easier to explain if the Galatian churches are close to Antioch (Dunn 1993a: 17); the references to Barnabas in Galatians make best sense if they know him; and though Barnabas was with Paul when he evangelized the South Galatian cities, he was apparently not with Paul on the alleged visits to North Galatia (Bauckham 1979; Dunn 1993a: 17). De Boer (2011: 4–5), on the other hand, argues that Paul would have mentioned Barnabas in 4:12–20 if he had been with Paul when the churches were founded. And Koch (1999: 94–98) claims that Paul writes as if he alone has founded the churches in Galatia.

letter, or a North Galatian destination means a late date. In point of fact, as we noted above, a South Galatian destination requires only that the letter be dated sometime after Paul's initial visit to the churches. Thus Paul could have written Galatians any time after the end of the first missionary journey (AD 48 or later). This remains the case even if one interprets Gal. 4:13 as a reference to two visits: Paul and his companions visited the churches of South Galatia a second time as they retraced their steps (Acts 14:21–23). A North Galatian destination, however, shifts the possible date of the letter forward only a year or two. Paul's initial visit to the churches would have taken place early on the second missionary journey (Acts 16:6), and he could have written the letter any time after that (AD 50 or later). If, however, 4:13 is thought to require two visits before the letter, then the date is shifted forward several years, because it is unlikely that Paul would have returned to North Galatia before the beginning of the third missionary journey (Acts 18:23). In this case, the letter could have been written no earlier than about AD 54. And this is the option that almost all defenders of the North Galatian hypothesis choose.

Combining destination and date, then, the main options that receive some significant support among scholars are the following:

1. Paul wrote to churches in the southern part of provincial Galatia
   a. just before the Jerusalem Council (AD 48);[12]
   b. early on the second missionary journey (AD 50–51);[13]
   c. during the third missionary journey (AD 54–57).[14]
2. Paul wrote to churches in ethnic (North) Galatia
   a. during the first missionary journey (AD 50–51);[15]
   b. early on the third missionary journey (AD 54–55);[16]
   c. late on the third missionary journey (AD 57).[17]

A decision among these options depends on two major issues and several minor ones.

1. The first major issue is the way in which Paul's autobiographical remarks in Gal. 1–2 fit with the narrative of Acts. In apparent response to the claims

12. Ramsay (1920: preface) first argued for a date on the second missionary journey, but later revised his view to place Galatians before the Jerusalem Council. See also Bruce 1982b: 3–18, 43–56; R. Longenecker 1990: lxi–lxxxviii; Fung 1988: 1–3, 9–28; Witherington 1998: 2–20; George 1994: 38–50; Schreiner 2010: 22–29 (hesitantly); Bauckham 1979; Hemer 1989: 260–71; Carson and Moo 2005: 461–65.

13. Dunn 1993b: 12–17; Elmer 2009: 117–31.

14. Burton 1921: xlvii–xlix (hesitantly); R. Schäfer 2004: 209–319; Fee 2007a: 4; Matera 1992: 19–26.

15. Martyn 1997: 19–20; de Boer 2011: 5–11. Betz (1979: 11–12) is open to a date anywhere between 50 and 55.

16. Brown 1997: 474–77; Kümmel 1975: 296–304; Murphy-O'Connor 1996: 159–62, 180–82; Hyldahl 2000: 426–28; Oepke 1973: 23–27.

17. Lightfoot 1881: 48–49; Borse 1972; Refoulé 1988; Buck 1951; Rohde 1989: 10; Mussner 1988: 9–10.

of the agitators, Paul emphasizes in 1:11–2:14 his independence from the apostles in Jerusalem. To establish this point, he goes into some detail about the course of his ministry experience from the time of his conversion to the time at which he wrote Galatians. As we often do in trying to pin down some of the circumstances in which Paul wrote his letters, we can take the information that Paul supplies in Galatians and try to match it with what Luke tells us about Paul's life and ministry in Acts. In this case, unfortunately, the correlation is not obvious, in particular with reference to the visits of Paul to Jerusalem. A chart of the respective sequences of events will provide a foundation for our discussion. (Events mentioned in both the Galatians and Acts columns in bold type are ones that most scholars agree in identifying; those highlighted in bold italics are the events whose identification is debated and critical to the issue.)

GALATIANS	ACTS
Persecution of the church (1:13–14)	**Persecution of the church (9:1–2)**
Conversion (1:15–16a) Trip to Arabia (1:17a) Return to Damascus (1:17b)	**Conversion (9:3–19a)** Ministry in Damascus (9:19b–25)
"After three years": **A visit to Jerusalem during which Paul "got to know" Cephas and met only Cephas and James among the apostles (1:18–20)** Ministry in Syria and Cilicia (1:21–24)	**Visit to Jerusalem (9:26–29)**
	Return to Tarsus (9:30; cf. 11:25) Ministry in Antioch (11:26) *Visit to Jerusalem to convey famine aid (11:27–30)* First missionary journey (12:25–14:25) (Paul, Barnabas [and John Mark])
"After fourteen years": *A visit to Jerusalem to consult with the "pillar" apostles over the nature of the gospel and spheres of ministry (2:1–10)*	
	Cyprus Pisidian Antioch Iconium Lystra Derbe Stay in Antioch (14:26–28)
Conflict in Antioch (2:11–14)	*Visit to Jerusalem for consultation about whether Gentile Christians need to be circumcised and to obey the law of Moses (15:1–29)* Ministry in Antioch (15:35) Second missionary journey (15:36–18:21) (Paul, Silas, Timothy [and Luke]) Syria and Cilicia Derbe Lystra

GALATIANS	ACTS
	"The region of Phrygia and Galatia" (16:6)
	Troas
	Philippi
	Thessalonica
	Berea
	Athens
	Corinth
	(Paul writes 1 and 2 Thessalonians)
	Ephesus
	Visit to Jerusalem (18:22)
	Ministry in Antioch (18:22b–23a)
	Third missionary journey (18:23b–21:16)
	(Paul [and Luke])
	"The region of Galatia and Phrygia" (18:23)
	Ephesus
	(Paul writes 1 Corinthians)
	Macedonia
	(Paul writes 2 Corinthians)
	Greece
	(Paul writes Romans)
	Troas
	Ephesus
	Tyre
	Ptolemais
	Caesarea
	Visit to Jerusalem (21:17–23:30)

Some of the events Paul narrates can rather easily be correlated with Acts, but others are not so easy to identify. Of course, many scholars avoid the challenge of correlating Galatians and Acts by dismissing the historical reliability of Luke's narrative. Their reconstruction of the Pauline chronology rests on the "primary" evidence of Paul's Letters alone, and the result is an outline of the life of Paul that bears little resemblance to the narrative of Acts (a notable example of this approach is Lüdemann 1984). We cannot enter into the question of Luke's accuracy here. But we will assume the historical accuracy of Acts in the following discussion, making reference as relevant to other options.

While there are a few dissenters among those who ignore Acts in reconstructing the chronology of Paul's life, most scholars agree that the visit to Jerusalem that Paul mentions in Gal. 1:18–19—the first after his conversion—is the same one that Luke describes in Acts 9:26–29. But there is no such agreement about the Jerusalem visit that Paul describes in some detail in 2:1–10. Is Paul describing the same meeting that Luke depicts in Acts 15, often called the "Apostolic Council" (see esp. Mussner 1988: 127–32; Silva 2001: 129–39)? Or is Paul describing an earlier Jerusalem meeting, perhaps one that took place during the so-called famine relief visit to Jerusalem that Luke narrates in Acts 11:27–30 (see esp. R. Longenecker 1990: lxxiii–lxxxiii; Schnabel 2004: 2.987–92)? The latter identification would be required if Paul writes before the Apostolic Council met; but the former identification is possible (though not, of course, required) if Paul writes anytime after the Council. Since the relationship between Gal. 2:1–10 and Acts 15 is crucial to dating Galatians and has significant implications for our interpretation of Galatians, we need to devote some space to this matter. Three particular pieces of evidence need to be assessed: (a) the chronology of Paul's early life and ministry; (b) the parallels between Gal. 2:1–10 on the one hand and Acts 11:27–30 and 15:1–29 on the other; and (c) the relationship between Paul's argument in Galatians and the "decree" issued at the Apostolic Council.

a. *Chronological considerations.* Paul claims that his first visit to Jerusalem came "three years after" his conversion (1:18) and that the visit of 2:1–10 came "after fourteen years." One would think that these specific chronological notices would enable us to decide whether 2:1–10 describes a meeting during the famine-relief visit to Jerusalem around AD 46 or the Jerusalem Council around AD 48–49. In fact, however, these notices do not help much because of three significant variables. First, we cannot date the key events—Paul's conversion, the famine-relief visit, the Jerusalem Council—with any degree of precision. Second, we cannot be sure whether the "fourteen years" of 2:1 are to be counted from Paul's conversion or from his first Jerusalem visit. And third, we cannot know whether "three years" and "fourteen years" are to be counted inclusively (so that, for instance, AD 33–45 would count as fourteen years, with both beginning and ending year counted) or exclusively (as we normally do; AD 33–47 would be "fourteen years"). Taking account of these three variables, the following range of dates is possible:

Paul's Conversion	Gal. 1:15–16	Acts 9:1–19	AD 33–35
First Jerusalem Visit	Gal. 1:18–19	Acts 9:26–29	"after three years"; AD 35–38
Second Jerusalem Visit	Gal. 2:1–10	Acts 11:27–30 *or* Acts 15:1–29	"after fourteen years"; AD 45–49 or 47–52

The famine-relief visit cannot be dated more precisely than 45–47; the Jerusalem Council is probably to be dated in 48 or 49. Therefore, as the chart shows, both the famine-relief visit of Acts 11 and the Jerusalem Council of Acts 15 could fit chronologically with either of the two schemes for counting the years in Gal. 1–2.[18]

b. *Parallels.* The key points in each narrative may be set out as follows:

18. For more detail on these issues of Pauline chronology as well as an attempt to assign absolute dates to the key events in Paul's life, see Carson and Moo 2005: 366–70. Constructing a chronology of Paul's life is fraught with difficulty, and scholars continue to debate the matter. So, for instance, Schnabel (2004: 1000) disagrees with the Carson and Moo dates, putting Paul's conversion in 31/32, his first Jerusalem visit in 33/34, the famine-relief visit in 44, and the Jerusalem Council in 48. Riesner (1998: 136) likewise insists that the latest possible date for the famine-relief visit is AD 45.

	Gal. 2:1–10	Acts 11:27–30	Acts 15:1–29
Location	Antioch and Jerusalem	Antioch and Jerusalem	Antioch and Jerusalem
Immediate Occasion	"by revelation"	prophecy	false teachers
Participants	Paul, Barnabas, Titus; James, Cephas, and John	Paul and Barnabas	Paul, Barnabas, and "some other believers"
		"Elders" are mentioned, but it is not clear how they are involved.	"apostles and elders"
	"private meeting"		Peter and James
Issue	circumcision of Gentile believers	famine relief	circumcision and obedience to law of Moses for Gentile believers
Format	Paul "sets forth" his gospel to the Gentiles.	no meeting mentioned	Paul reports on his Gentile mission; Peter confirms; James issues the decision.
Result	The "pillars" extend the "right hand of fellowship" to Paul and Barnabas; the "pillars" recognize different spheres of ministry.	nothing mentioned	James decides not to require Gentile believers to be circumcised or to obey the law of Moses; but he does insist that Gentile believers avoid certain practices especially offensive to Jews.
	Paul is asked to "remember the poor."	financial help for the poor in Jerusalem	

The agreements and disagreements among these three narratives have been discussed and debated for years, with no consensus about their relationship. None of the narratives purports to be anything like a complete or objective description of the meeting in question, and we would therefore expect differences even when the same event is being described. The brevity of the Acts 11 description of the famine-relief visit makes it especially difficult to make effective comparisons.

In general, those who identify the Gal. 2 meeting with Acts 15 emphasize the unlikelihood that two such similar meetings would have taken place in Jerusalem within a few years of one another. R. Longenecker (1990: lxxvii), although he does not identify Gal. 2 with Acts 15, summarizes the similarities very well: "Both speak of a meeting held in Jerusalem to deal with the question of Gentile Christians having to observe the Jewish law. In both, the discussion is prompted by Jewish Christian legalists. In both, the main participants are Paul and Barnabas, on the one hand, and Peter and James, on the other hand. And in both, the decision reached is in favor of a law-free mission to Gentiles." Lightfoot (1881: 124) therefore concludes: "A combination of circumstances so striking is not likely to have occurred twice within a few years"—a conclusion that Silva (2001: 135) labels a "major understatement." Of course, there are differences as well, and those who deny the identification focus on them. Some of these differences are easily explained.[19] Even the omission of the restrictions placed on Gentiles by the Jerusalem Council in Paul's narrative can be explained if the restrictions were intended for a limited time and/or specific area (as Paul's silence about the matter in 1 Corinthians might indicate). A more puzzling omission in Paul's narrative is the negative part of James's decision: that Gentile believers need not be circumcised or obey the law of Moses. Granted the issue in Galatia, one would have expected Paul to make this point the highlight of his report of the meeting. Instead, the issue of circumcision is mentioned early in Paul's narrative with respect to Titus (2:3–4) but receives no specific mention at the climax of his account. Ultimately, however, this kind of difference cannot bear much weight of argument, since one can always appeal to the selective nature of our accounts. What does have weight are contradictions. One such contradiction may be the difference between Paul's claim that he "met privately" with the pillars (2:2) and Luke's reference to "apostles and elders" (Acts 15:6, 22), "the whole assembly" (15:12), and "the whole church" (15:22; see also, e.g., Bauckham 2004: 135–39; Schnabel 2004: 987). However, while we think that Gal. 2:2 refers to a private meeting only, others interpret the text differently (see the commentary)—so the contradiction is not certain.

If we turn to compare Gal. 2:1–10 with Acts 11:27–30, we have much less to work with: Luke's account is very brief. As the chart above shows, the only real parallels are (1) the impetus for Paul's visit (if the "revelation" of Gal. 2:1 came via prophecy); (2) the location (movement from Antioch to Jerusalem); (3) the presence of Barnabas; and (4) concern with aid for the poor. None of these correspondences is so striking as to create a very strong presumption that the two narratives must refer to the same meeting. To be sure, there are few points of disagreement between the narratives, but the reason for this is simply that Luke provides so few details about this visit.

The argument from the parallels among these three accounts is, then, hardly decisive. The lack of detail in Acts 11:27–30 means that little can be said for or against the option of locating the meeting Paul describes in Gal. 2 during this visit. A comparison between the much more richly detailed narrative of Acts 15 with Gal. 2:1–10 reveals, as we have seen, both similarities and differences. On the one hand, the number of similarities, combined with the unlikelihood that two such similar meetings would have taken place in Jerusalem within the space of two or three years, is a strong argument for their identification. On the other hand, if the meeting of Gal. 2:1–10 was indeed a private one (see 2:2), then it is difficult, if not impossible, to identify them. Because we think that 2:2 is relatively clear about the private nature of the meeting, we incline

---

19. Silva (2001: 135) rightly notes that the differences between the accounts in Gal. 2:1–10 and Acts 15 are not as significant as the differences in many narratives of the same event among the Gospel writers.

very weakly to locate the meeting of Gal. 2:1–10 during the famine-relief visit of Paul to Jerusalem (Acts 11:27–30).

c. *Two arguments from silence.* Scholars who argue that Galatians was written before the Apostolic Council usually appeal to two arguments from silence as critical evidence in favor of this date (see esp. R. Longenecker 1990: lxxviii–lxxx).

First, why does Paul fail to mention one of his visits to Jerusalem in Gal. 1–2? If Gal. 2:1–10 = Acts 15 (and, as everyone agrees, Gal. 1:18 = Acts 9:26–29), Paul has failed to mention the visit recorded in Acts 11:27–30. Of course, this omission causes no problem for those scholars who do not think that Luke's reference to this visit is historically accurate.[20] But for those who view Luke's account as accurate, an explanation for this omission is necessary. Silva's explanation (2001: 136–39) may be taken as representative. According to him, the problem of the omission disappears once we understand the purpose and sequence of thought in Gal. 1–2. Paul is not concerned to detail every one of his contacts with Jerusalem between his conversion and the writing of this letter. Rather, his concern in Gal. 1 is to show that he did not learn his gospel from any human during his early years of ministry. The famine-relief visit occurred at a later period than covered in chapter 1; and in any case, Paul may not even have met any of the apostles on this occasion. Chapter 2, according to Silva, takes up a separate issue, as Paul treats two special situations that the Galatians need to know about.

Silva's argument is not, however, convincing. We think it unlikely that a transition of the sort that he suggests occurs between chapters 1 and 2. The ἔπειτα (*epeita*, then, 2:1) signals continuity from chapter 1 into chapter 2. In contrast to Silva, however (who acknowledges some degree of continuity), we think the continuity involves the very heart of Paul's argument (see also, e.g., R. Longenecker 1990: lxxix). The common denominator in Paul's narrative from 1:17 right through 2:14 is his relationship with the "pillars," the Jerusalem apostles. This note is sounded immediately after Paul's description of his conversion—"I did not go up to Jerusalem to see those who were apostles before I was" (1:17)—and is heard throughout the rest of Paul's narrative: "Then, after three years, I went up to Jerusalem to get acquainted with Cephas. . . . I saw none of the other apostles" (1:18–19); "I was personally unknown to the churches of Judea" (1:22); "after fourteen years, I went up again to Jerusalem" (2:1); "When Cephas came to Antioch" (2:11); "certain men came from James" (2:12). Even if Paul did not meet with any of the "pillars" during his famine-relief visit (an improbable supposition in itself), we would think that Paul would need to mention the visit, if only to claim he did not meet any of the pillars. The focus on the Jerusalem apostles that continues into Gal. 2 suggests that Paul wants to detail his contacts with these apostles

---

20. Scholars who doubt the accuracy of Luke's narrative usually argue either that (1) Luke has misplaced the event (it really happened on a later visit to Jerusalem [Acts 18 or Acts 21]; e.g., Lüdemann 1984: 13–14; Jewett 1979: 34); or (2) Luke has created two events on the basis of two reports of one event (the Apostolic Council; e.g., Lake 1933: 237–39). See Barrett 1998: 558–61 and R. Longenecker 1990: lxxiv–lxxv for discussion.

during all the time from his conversion to his writing of the letter. His claim in 1:22 to have been "unknown to the churches of Judea" seems designed to cover the entire period from his first visit (1:18–19) to the visit he narrates in 2:1–10. Barrett (1998), who identifies Gal. 2:1–10 with Acts 15, is typical of more critical scholars who conclude that the Acts 11 visit must be a Lukan fabrication precisely because Paul does not mention it in Galatians.[21]

A second argument from silence is Paul's failure to mention the Jerusalem decree anywhere in Galatians. In a letter that has at its heart an appeal to Gentile Christians not to undergo circumcision, we would expect Paul at least to mention the fact that the Jerusalem apostles themselves had agreed not to impose circumcision on Gentile converts. His silence about this decision only makes sense, it is argued, if that decision had not yet been reached. The force of this argument, however, is mitigated by two considerations: First, the intended scope and duration of the Jerusalem decision is unclear. The letter communicating the decision of the Council is addressed to "Antioch, Syria, and Cilicia," an area that does not include the churches of Galatia. Second, Paul's concern to distance himself from the Jerusalem apostles in his claims for "the truth of the gospel" might make him reluctant to appeal to those same apostles in his argument. Neither of these responses is entirely convincing. There is legitimate question about the scope of the Jerusalem decree; Paul's silence about it when he deals with an issue touched on in the decree (meat sacrificed to idols) in 1 Corinthians suggests that the scope was indeed limited. But, even if the restrictions imposed on Gentile believers were of limited applicability, the very important precedent established by the Council with respect to the circumcision of Gentile converts would surely have been of broader and more permanent significance. As to the other issue: the emphasis on agreement between Paul and the "pillars" in 2:1–10 shows that, while Paul wanted to show that his gospel was not derived from those leaders, he was quite happy to note when those leaders agreed with his understanding of it.

Arguments from silence are considered to be of minimal value—and often with good reason. But silence can sometimes be rather deafening; and we think there is considerable merit in these two particular arguments from silence. These two arguments, combined with the probability that the meeting of Gal. 2 was a private one, lead us to align Gal. 2:1–10 with Acts 11:27–30. Paul's failure to mention the Apostolic Council visit to Jerusalem can only be explained, then, if he wrote *before* the Council had met. On this scenario, the sequence of events would be as follows:

Planting (and follow-up visit) of the churches in South Galatia (Acts 13:1–14:25; cf. Gal. 4:12–20)

---

21. Barrett (1998: 559–60) says, "It is inconceivable that Paul should have been so foolish (not to say so untruthful) as to omit in the controversial epistle to the Galatians a visit of which his adversaries could have made good use." See also Burton (1921: 115–17): because he thinks it is overwhelmingly clear that Gal. 2:1–10 = Acts 15, he concludes that Acts 11 is "inaccurate."

Return to Antioch, where Paul stayed for "a long time" (Acts 14:26–28)

Arrival of agitators in the South Galatian churches during Paul's stay in Antioch (perhaps at the same time as the arrival of similar false teachers in Antioch: Acts 15:1)

Writing of Galatians

Jerusalem Council (Acts 15:1–29)

2. The second major factor in determining the date of Galatians is one internal to the Letters of Paul, and therefore often given decisive weight by scholars (esp. among those who doubt the historicity of Acts). The vocabulary and argument of Galatians find parallels in many of Paul's Letters, yet are especially close to the vocabulary and argument of Romans (Lightfoot 1881: 45–48 provides a full list):

a. Discussion of the Mosaic law is prominent in both letters. Of Paul's 121 uses of the word νόμος, seventy-four occur in Romans and thirty-two in Galatians. The phrase [τὰ] ἔργα [τοῦ] νόμου ([ta] erga [tou] nomou, the works of the law) occurs only in these letters, as does reference to Lev. 18:5 with respect to the law (Gal. 3:12; Rom. 10:5). In both letters (and only in these letters), Paul refers to "dying to" the law (Gal. 2:19; Rom. 7:4).

b. "Righteousness" language is prominent in both letters. The verb δικαιόω (dikaioō, justify) occurs eight times in Galatians and thirteen times in Romans (five occurrences elsewhere in Paul), the noun δικαιοσύνη (dikaiosynē, righteousness) four times in Galatians and thirty-three times in Romans (twenty elsewhere in Paul), and the adjective δίκαιος (dikaios, righteous) once in Galatians and seven times in Romans (and nine elsewhere in Paul). In both letters (and only in these letters) Paul uses two key OT texts to illuminate his teaching on righteousness: Gen. 15:6 and Hab. 2:4.

c. Both letters give pride of place to Abraham in their portrayal of salvation history, focusing on his faith, his inclusive significance, and the contrast between the promise God gave him and the Mosaic law (Gal. 3:6–9, 14, 15–18; Rom. 4:1–25). Both letters also single out the "true" children of Abraham from among all Abraham's biological descendants (Gal. 4:21–31; Rom. 9:7–13).

d. While Paul touches on the idea that Christians are "sons" (υἱοί, huioi) or "children" (τέκνα, tekna) of God in other letters (e.g., 2 Cor. 6:18; Eph. 5:1; Phil. 2:15), it is only in Galatians and Romans that Paul develops the concept, using the technical term υἱοθεσία (huiothesia, adoption), and linking Christian "sonship" to Christ as Son and to future inheritance (Gal. 4:4–7; Rom. 8:14–17).[22]

---

22. The gender-specific "sons/sonship" is used throughout the commentary in order to preserve the first-century concept of inheritance (almost always involving male offspring) and

e. In both letters (and only in these letters), Paul uses the imagery of being "crucified with" Christ to describe the transition from the old life to the new (Gal. 2:20; Rom. 6:6).

f. Only in Galatians and Romans does Paul claim that the law is "fulfilled" by the love command (Lev. 19:18; Gal. 5:13–14; Rom. 13:8–10).

g. Although Paul often refers to the Holy Spirit as basic to Christian existence, it is only in Galatians (5:16–26) and Romans (8:4–13) that he develops the nature of this relationship in some detail.

Other scholars have noticed similarities between Galatians and 2 Cor. 10–13 (see esp. Borse 1972: 84–119). The similarities between Romans (and to a lesser extent 2 Cor. 10–13) and Galatians strongly suggest, it is argued, that they were written at about the same time. Thus Galatians, like Romans, must have been written sometime on the third missionary journey.

The parallels between Romans and Galatians are clear, but it is not so clear how we are to interpret those parallels (see esp. the discussion in Bruce 1982b: 45–56). First, for all the overlap in themes, Romans and Galatians develop some of those themes in quite different ways; compare, for example, the treatment of Abraham and Gen. 15:6 in Gal. 3:7–29 and Rom. 4. And, as we argue below, Galatians and Romans focus on different aspects of justification. Thus Betz (1979: 12) argues that these differences suggest a distance in date between the two letters (cf. also Sampley 1985). Second, of more significance is the question about how to explain the similarities between Romans and Galatians. Paul's theology undoubtedly developed over the course of his ministry. But perspective is important. The conception of a Paul who suddenly had to begin working out his theology in his first letter and then developed his ideas dramatically over the course of his letter-writing career is belied by simple chronology: Paul spent almost as much time in ministry before he ever wrote a canonical letter (ca. AD 33–48) as he did during his letter-writing period (ca. AD 48–64; see Bruce 1982b: 46). In general the theological language and arguments used by Paul appear to have much more to do with the occasion for his writing than with any kind of trajectory in the development of his theology (which, in any case, is notoriously difficult to trace).[23] The similarities between Romans and Galatians, in other words, are not necessarily because Paul wrote them at the same time. The similarities could equally be explained as Paul's dealing with similar issues in the two letters.

Galatians, we conclude, was probably written in AD 48 just before the Apostolic Conference of Acts 15.[24] It is the earliest extant letter of Paul.

---

the relationship between the "sons" and the "Son" (4:5–6). The term refers, of course, to male and female believers equally.

23. This principle applies equally to other such arguments from theological development: e.g., Dunn (1993b: 17) thinks the failure to mention justification in the Thessalonian Letters suggests that they were written before Galatians.

24. A possible objection to this dating is the argument that Paul would have waited to write to the Galatians until the results of the Conference in Jerusalem were known. But (1) Paul may

Occasion and Purpose

The general circumstances in which Paul writes to the Galatian churches are quite clear from the letter itself. Eschewing his usual thanksgiving for his readers, Paul launches immediately into a strongly worded denunciation of "some people" who are "confusing" (ταράσσοντες, *tarassontes*) the Galatians and "trying to pervert the gospel of Christ" (1:7; cf. 1:6–10). Paul mentions these people again briefly in 4:17, where he accuses them of self-oriented zeal. But, in a kind of bookend around the main argument of the letter, 5:7–12 focuses again on these people, where he once more claims that they are "confusing" (ταράσσων, *tarassōn*) the Galatians and trying to keep them from "obeying the truth" (5:7). Paul does not indicate how these people are perverting the gospel, but several other passages make this clear enough. In 3:1–5 Paul alludes to the general problem: though the Galatians have entered into their Christian experience through faith and the Spirit, they are in danger of trying to "finish by means of the flesh" (3:3). A related rebuke passage (4:8–11) goes into a little more detail: the Galatians are being tempted to return to their slavery under "the weak and miserable elements [of the world; cf. 4:3]" by "observing special days and months and seasons and years" (4:9–10). With this last phrase Paul hints at the larger agenda of the "agitators" (as we will call the people who have brought false teaching to the Galatians). For this phrase almost certainly describes the festivals of the Jewish liturgical calendar. But Paul is explicit and direct about this agenda for the first time in the rhetorical climax of the letter, 5:1–6. Here he warns the Galatians about seeking to be "justified by the law" (v. 4) by undergoing circumcision (vv. 2–3). Paul directly describes the agitators one final time, in the letter's conclusion, where he mentions that they are arguing for circumcision, accuses them of behaving as they do in order to avoid persecution "for the cross of Christ," and claims that they themselves do not keep the law (6:12–13; see esp. de Boer 2011: 50–61 for a good survey and evaluation of the evidence).

These direct claims reveal that Paul writes Galatians to combat people who are pressuring the Galatians to undergo circumcision and submit to the law of Moses as a means of completing their Christian experience.[25] To these direct claims we may add indirect evidence. Here we enter into the tricky activity of "mirror-reading," using the text of Galatians as a mirror in which we catch reflections of the people and their agenda that Paul is writing about. Salutary warnings about the inevitably subjective nature of such mirror-reading have been sounded (see esp. Barclay 1987), but two aspects of these agitators are clearly reflected in the letter. First, they have stressed a certain kind of continuity in salvation history by arguing that the OT requires anyone who wants to belong to the "seed" or to be "children" of Abraham to be circumcised and

---

not have been aware of the Conference when he wrote; and (2) he may have thought the situation in Galatia to be so urgent that he could not delay his response to it.

25. Kwon (2004: 204) unconvincingly claims that law observance was not part of the agitators' program.

to commit themselves to a lifestyle set forth by the law of Moses. Only this kind of argument on the part of the agitators makes sense of the way Paul crafts his response in 3:7–4:7 (Barclay 1988: 65–66; G. Hansen 1989: 158–60; Hong 1993: 165–66).

Most interpreters are convinced of this general scenario, which is well summarized by Dunn (1993a: 11): "The letter makes clearest and fullest sense if we see it as a response to a challenge from *Christian-Jewish missionaries* who had come to Galatia to improve or correct Paul's gospel and to 'complete' his converts by integrating them fully into the heirs of Abraham through circumcision and by thus bringing them 'under the law.'" Yet five aspects of this summary require further comment.

First, by speaking of a single group of agitators, Dunn's summary implicitly dismisses the view that Paul fights a two-front war in Galatia: against legalism on the one hand (1:1–5:12) and "antinomians" on the other (5:13–6:10). The two-front view had some currency in the past (see esp. Lütgert 1919; Ropes 1929) and is picked up in modified form by R. Longenecker (1990: 236). But this interpretation of the situation Paul addresses introduces an unnecessary complication that is not required by the argument of the letter. The relationship of the so-called ethical part of the letter (5:13–6:10) to its "theological" part (1:1–5:12) is adequately explained on the hypothesis of a single Christian-Jewish opposition (see, e.g., Hong 1993: 100–101).

Second, by using the word "complete," Dunn (1993a: 16–17) hints at a point that he develops at greater length elsewhere: that the agitators' efforts were focused on what he calls the "second phase" of Christian experience; or, to put it in the language made so familiar by E. P. Sanders (1977), the agitators' focus was not on how one "gets in" but on how one "stays in." We think this general reading of the letter is very much on target (see also, e.g., Gundry 1985: 8–12; Barclay 1988: 73–74; Fee 1994: 384; Watson 2007: 113).[26] We would, however, suggest that the focus was not only, or perhaps even mainly, on "staying in" but on ultimate vindication in the judgment (see further "The Importance of Justification in Galatians" below).

Third, Paul's claim that the agitators were acting in order to avoid being persecuted for the cross of Christ (6:12) may best be explained if they were concerned to avoid giving offense to fellow Jews. As Jewett points out in an influential article (1970–71), the time in which Galatians was written was characterized by the increasing influence of the Zealot movement, a movement dedicated to maintaining the purity and independence of Judaism. Allowing Gentile converts to claim identification with blessings promised to Abraham and to his seed would have been deeply offensive to many Jews, and we can well understand some Jewish-Christians seeking to minimize this offense by

---

26. Even the demand for circumcision could fit this general scenario. Circumcision was sometimes viewed as not so much an entrance requirement, but "rather as a duty of obedience to God which those who have been converted must fulfill" (Bauckham 2004: 118; see also McKnight 1991: 79–82; Borgen 2000: 260–61).

insisting on circumcision and adherence to the law for Gentile converts. The same motivation may lie behind the "men from James" who stirred up so much trouble at Antioch (2:11–14).

Fourth, Dunn's summary speaks vaguely of missionaries who had "come to" Galatia. We can probably be more specific. It is likely that the agitators had, or claimed, some relationship to Jerusalem. Paul's focus on his own relationships with Jerusalem and the "apostles who were before him" in 1:13–2:10 arguably points in this direction. But it is in the "allegory" about Sarah and Hagar that the point becomes relatively explicit. Here Paul contrasts the free children of Abraham, descendants of Sarah through Isaac, with those who are descendants of Hagar, "the present city of Jerusalem," "in slavery with her children" (4:25; for this Jerusalem connection, see esp. Elmer 2009). Not only, then, did the agitators claim to represent Jerusalem; their perspective is also one that Paul identifies with Judaism in general. Thus the "Christian-Jewish" nature of the agitators was not such as to effectively erase the genuinely "Jewish" side of their viewpoint, contra, for example, Martyn (1997: 457–66), who views what he calls the "teachers" as rival Christian missionaries. Christian they clearly were; but Paul's argument makes clear that he views their position as fundamentally Jewish in orientation (see, e.g., Schreiner 1985: 254–55).

Fifth, at the opposite end of the spectrum is the view of Mark Nanos (2002: 110–99), who thinks the "influencers" (his term) had not come from outside the community but were Jews who were charged with admitting new members into Jewish communities. These "influencers" naturally insist that Jewish proselyte conversion requires more than Paul has told them: they must place themselves under the law. According to Nanos, then, the argument in Galatians remains an inner-Jewish argument, true to the period when distinctions between "Jews" and "Christians" were not yet being made. Nanos's view suffers from several problems, but fatal to it is his unconvincing explanation of 1:6–9. Paul's assertion in this passage that the agitators were preaching "another gospel" (1:6–9) only makes sense if they were claiming to be Christians; and his condemnation of them shows that their view has to do with far more than an inter-Jewish discussion of Gentiles and the law (see the commentary and, e.g., Dunn 2009: 721–22; Barclay 2010: 37).[27]

The Logic of Paul's Response

The "other gospel" being proclaimed by the agitators was obviously very attractive to the Galatians. There may have been social and personal reasons for this,[28] but clearly it was the persuasiveness of the agitators' argument

27. Note S. Chester's comment on Nanos and similar views: "It is striking that in each of the revisionist accounts, a legitimate, indeed essential, awareness of the potential for Paul's argument to be misused in an anti-Jewish or antinomian manner slips over into disregard for historical plausibility. The traditional reconstruction that Paul criticizes Jewish-Christian advocates of circumcision simply makes better sense of the available evidence" (2011: 65).

28. For instance, the identification with existing social institutions (the Jewish community), exemplified by tangible external markers (circumcision, the observance of Sabbath, avoidance

from Scripture that had the greatest influence. Paul's response in chapters 3–4 makes clear that they were arguing from a standard Jewish reading of the OT, according to which the people of God, who can hope for vindication on the day of judgment, are those who are Abraham's descendants. These descendents of Abraham, of course, were usually identified with his biological offspring through Isaac and Jacob, the people of Israel. Jews affirmed their identity as the people of Abraham by circumcision and adherence to the law of Moses. The agitators were Christians (as is apparent from their proclamation of a "gospel"; 1:6–9) who introduced into this typical Jewish scenario a belief that Messiah had come and that faith in this Messiah, the Lord Jesus, was now necessary for identification with Abraham's people. They were also apparently willing to allow Gentiles to become members of this people. But they also insisted that Gentiles who wanted to join Abraham's people in order to experience eschatological salvation needed to add to their faith in Christ those traditional requirements imposed on Gentiles who wanted to convert to Judaism: circumcision and adherence to the law of Moses. In arguing this case, the agitators could—and undoubtedly did—appeal to what they might claim to be the plain sense of the OT. Abraham believed (Gen. 15:6), but he was then required to be circumcised and to have all his male descendants circumcised (Gen. 17:1–14)—a pattern, they probably argued, for all converts (like Abraham) to follow.[29] And of course God eventually gave Abraham's descendants the law of Moses, obedience to which was required for all who claimed to be Abraham's offspring.

Paul's response to the agitators' argument assumes continuity while at the same time, in order to meet the challenge of the agitators' interpretation, highlighting discontinuity. In his reading of the OT, the key for Paul is the epochal significance of the crucified and resurrected Christ (1:4; 2:19–20; 3:1, 13–14; 4:4–5; 6:12–14). This event has inaugurated the eschatological "new creation" (6:15), and it is this new state of affairs, and the centrality of faith and the Spirit (5:5–6), that now marks the "Israel of God" (6:16), the true people of God and thus Abraham's descendants. By tying Christian identity in the new epoch to Abraham (3:7–9, 14, 29; 4:28–31) and by speaking of the law's fulfillment (rather than, for instance, its replacement or abolition; cf. 5:14), Paul reveals the underlying continuity that he finds in the story of God's redemptive plan. But this single plan has at its heart, and as its interpretive key, the Christ event. Contrasting evaluations of the significance of this event was the fundamental

---

of certain foods), might have been very enticing to people who had left their pagan associations and who had not yet found in the Christian community the kind of social cohesion and/or external structures that would provide them with a sense of security (see Esler 1998: 39–57). Coming under specific regulations such as found in the Mosaic law would have been attractive for a similar reason (Barclay 1988: 70–72). Arnold (2005) notes that some of the Jewish practices being advocated by the agitators would have found a resonance with practices that may have marked the Galatians' pagan past.

29. As Dunn (1993a: 15–16) notes, once the full inclusion of the Gentiles in Abraham's family became the issue, the requirement of circumcision would naturally follow.

factor in the different readings of salvation history espoused by Paul vis-à-vis the agitators. Central to Paul's discontinuous reading is the insistence that the Mosaic covenant, with its focus on the law, is a temporary phase in salvation history, subordinate to and intended to accomplish something different than the Abrahamic covenant (3:15–25). The law, with the works it calls for, entered into salvation history 430 years after Abraham (3:17) and was intended to be in effect only until Messiah came (3:19, 24–25). Recognizing the importance of this salvation-historical argument, many interpreters suggest that Paul's response to the agitators can be boiled down to the question "What time is it?" (e.g., Martyn 1985a: 418).

The contrast between eras in salvation history is indeed basic to the argument of Galatians. But a key issue in assessing the theological significance of Galatians is whether Paul's argument against torah observance in Galatians is limited to this salvation-historical argument. To deal with this issue, we need to move "behind" the argument to inquire about the fundamental logic of the argument.

The long and complex argument of Gal. 2:16–5:12 revolves around the polarity of doing the torah or "works of torah," on the one hand, and "Christ faith," on the other.[30] Paul begins with this polarity: "[We] know that a person is not justified by the works of the law, but by faith in Jesus Christ. So we, too, have put our faith in Christ Jesus that we may be justified by faith in Christ and not by the works of the law, because by the works of the law no one will be justified" (2:16). And he concludes on this same note: "You who are trying to be justified by the law have been alienated from Christ; you have fallen away from grace. For through the Spirit we eagerly await by faith the righteousness for which we hope" (5:4–5). This last text reveals just how serious the choice between these two options is. But our question at this point is this: Why does Paul erect so strong an antithesis? Why are observing torah and commitment to Christ absolutely opposed?

For centuries, interpreters of Galatians understood the antithesis between doing torah and Christ faith to reflect a more fundamental and general contrast that had relevance to all humans: the contrast between human believing and human doing as means of salvation. To be sure, isolated voices over the years questioned this way of explaining the logic of Galatians.[31] But it was only in the wake of the "Sanders revolution" that these voices swelled into a chorus. Sanders's insistence (1977) that Jewish soteriology was rooted in God's covenant grace and that torah observance therefore simply maintained covenant status ("covenantal nomism") made it difficult any longer to think that Paul and

---

30. We use the word "torah" here to accent appropriately Paul's concern in Galatians with a particular law, the law of Moses, the Jewish law. And we use the phrase "Christ faith" to keep open, for now, the options in explaining the relationship between these words.

31. For example, George Howard (1979: 82) anticipated the later New Perspective emphasis in his claim that "the key to Paul's thought in Galatians is his doctrine of the inclusion of uncircumcised Gentiles." Though published in 1979, Howard's monograph was written before Sanders's 1977 *Paul and Palestinian Judaism* had become widely known.

Jewish-Christian opponents could have taken the kind of contrasting views of faith and works that was required to make sense of the traditional view. And so new ways of explaining the logic of Galatians arose. The most prominent among these new readings was the so-called New Perspective, represented in this case especially well by James Dunn in his many writings on Galatians.[32] According to Dunn, Paul sets faith in Christ and doing the torah against one another because only the former opens the way for full inclusion of Gentiles in the people of God and because the era in which torah observance was required of the people of God ended with the coming of the Messiah. In seeking to impose torah on Gentile converts, the agitators were perpetuating a restricted and exclusivistic view of God's grace and were turning the clock back to an earlier time in salvation history. Loyalty to Christ and loyalty to torah are, then, incompatible because a new era that drops any ethnic focus in the people of God has dawned.[33] On this reading, the logic of Galatians is explained not in terms of general theological or philosophical principles but in terms of specific historical realities. The payoff of this logic for the contemporary church lies especially in the importance of maintaining Paul's resolute opposition to any kind of ethnic or national restriction in the scope of the gospel.

Nevertheless, in his more recent writings (which stand in some tension with the rhetoric of his earlier work), Dunn stresses that his New Perspective concentration on the problem of ethnic restrictiveness is by no means intended to deny the "Lutheran" concern about the danger of attributing salvation to human achievement. Both are present in Paul's argument, though exactly how they are related and which texts support the latter remain somewhat unclear.[34]

32. This is not the place to engage in further description or serious engagement with the New Perspective (for which see, e.g., Moo 1996: 211–17; 2004). But three quick points may be made. First, New Perspective advocates—and we have in mind especially the two key figures in the movement, James Dunn and N. T. Wright—are to be commended for pursuing an interpretation of Paul that tries to makes sense of Paul in his first-century Jewish environment. Second, however, the nature of this Jewish environment is itself a matter of controversy. Most interpreters of Judaism think that Sanders's "covenant nomism" is generally accurate. But it has also been shown that the Judaism of Paul's day was by no means monolithic. Jewish soteriology took a variety of forms, some of them tending toward the "legalistic" (see esp. Carson, O'Brien, and Seifrid 2001). Third, even Sanders's "covenant nomism" assumes that doing the law was necessary for salvation. While not required to "get in," adherence to torah was necessary to "stay in" and, more importantly, to be "declared in" at the time of the judgment. This last point, so fundamental to the argument of Galatians, is not given the attention it deserves by Sanders and many of his followers (see esp. Gathercole 2002b: 13–23, passim). When these last two points are recognized, the impetus for revisionist readings of Paul is greatly weakened.

33. Dunn appears to want to say that insisting on works of the law to mark out the people of God is wrong because (1) it misses the true intent of the law, and (2) it perpetuates a function of the law that has ended with Christ. For this latter emphasis, see esp. Dunn 2008e: 451–55, 464. As Das (2010: 104) has pointed out, Dunn's focus on both salvation history and Jewish misunderstanding sits uncomfortably together. If it is the coming of Christ that has first opened the way to the inclusion of Gentiles, then Jews have not misunderstood the OT or the covenant of the law.

34. "This, then, is what Paul meant by justification by faith, by faith alone. It was a profound conception of the relation between God and humankind—a relation of utter dependence, of unconditional trust. Human dependence on divine grace had to be unqualified or else it was not

It is this "both/and," this having one's historical cake and eating it theologically, to which John Barclay (2010: 43–47) objects. He contends that the nature of the Christ-torah antithesis in Galatians resists any extrapolation to broader theological principles. Barclay criticizes Luther's "universalizing" interpretation as an inappropriate "move towards abstraction," toward "an *abstract theory of practice*" that has no clear basis in the actual issues in Galatia, which are "specific practices within a particular framework of cultural allegiance" (40–41). Torah observance is ruled out by Paul because it fails to recognize that "the whole of life" must be "aligned to the world-changing Christ-event" (42). At this point in the article, Barclay sounds as if he is endorsing Sanders's widely criticized "dogmatic" interpretation of Paul's rejection of Judaism and the law—as Sanders (1977: 522) put it in the conclusion of *Paul and Palestinian Judaism*, "In short, *this is what Paul finds wrong with Judaism: it is not Christianity*" (with original emphasis). Yet Barclay goes on to suggest that it is not the mere fact of the Christ-event but Paul's interpretation of that event as "unconditioned gift" that rules out torah observance. Gift giving and receiving in the ancient world often operated within a system of recognizing worth. But Paul insists that the gift of Christ operates without regard for worth. It is for this reason that Paul argues against torah observance: it would "reinstate a standard of value or worth which denied the truth of the Christ-gift as unconditioned gift" (2010: 52). Barclay concludes, then, that grace is indeed

---

Abraham's faith, the faith through which God could work his own work. That was why Paul was so fiercely hostile to the qualification which he saw confronting him all the time in any attempt to insist on works of the law as a necessary accompaniment of or addition to faith. God would not justify, could not sustain in relationship with him, those who did not rely wholly on him. Justification was by faith, by faith alone" (Dunn 1998: 379). Luther could not have expressed "justification by faith alone" more clearly! Yet Dunn is ultimately not clear about how Paul's polemic against works of the law might feed into the broader "by faith alone" conclusion. In the quotation above they are linked (note the "That was why" transitional phrase). In a more recent publication, Dunn (2008d: 41–58) continues to recognize that Paul does indeed hold to "justification by faith alone," yet he decouples this point from Paul's polemic against works of the law, arguing that the broader theological point is grounded rather in a separate line of reasoning ("justification by grace and not human achievement" versus "justification by faith and not by becoming a proselyte" [57]). It is also fair to say that Dunn's actual exegesis of many of the key texts does not so clearly support the broad theological conclusions that he insists on in the opening quotation. N. T. Wright, apparently backing off from his rhetoric in the past, has recently been making some of these same points. See, e.g., his summary of his discussion of Galatians in his 2009 book on justification: "We . . . have shown the deep coherence there [in Galatians] of a theology of justification which includes all that the old perspective was really trying to say within a larger framework which, while owing quite a bit to aspects of the new perspective, goes considerably beyond it" (2009: 140). Such a "both/and" comparison of "old" and "new" perspectives appears to stand in some tension with claims in his earlier books. See, e.g., in his 2005 book on Paul: "His [Paul's] view of salvation history itself, and with it justification and all the rest, is not an ahistorical scheme about how individuals come into a right relationship with God, but rather tells how the God of Abraham has fulfilled his promises at last through the apocalyptic death and resurrection of his own beloved Son" (2005: 10). What Wright in this latter statement denies appears to be an important aspect of what the old perspective was "really trying to say."

central to the logic of Galatians, but not in the way the Reformers thought. Paul is not arguing from "a general principle that rules out 'law' or 'work' as elements of soteriology," but from a recognition that "the unconditioned Christ-gift . . . subverts and reconstitutes what counts as worth" (56).

Barclay's understanding of the logic of Galatians has much in common with the approach of Francis Watson in the revised edition of his book *Paul, Judaism, and the Gentiles* (2007: revised edition is subtitled *Beyond the New Perspective*). He also insists that the antithesis between Christ and torah is rooted in specific and unrepeatable historical circumstances: the Pauline antithesis has an "irreducible concreteness" (125, 128–29). "Works of the law," the key phrase that Paul uses six times in the letter, refers to "the distinctive way of life of the Jewish people . . . and nothing else"; "faith" is always "Christ faith." In a wide-ranging appendix devoted to larger issues of theological reasoning, Watson contrasts his "literal" reading of Paul with a "symbolic" reading that seeks general principles "behind" the historical realities of the text. He explores the implications of his own historical reading, suggesting, as Barclay has done, that Paul operates with a conception of grace that distances him from his Jewish contemporaries. Specifically, following up on a central theme of his 2004 work, *Paul and the Hermeneutics of Faith*, Watson (2007: 359) argues that Paul's emphasis on faith prioritizes divine action vis-à-vis human action in a way foreign to Judaism. And, while criticizing Luther for an ahistorical reading of Paul, Watson nevertheless concedes that "the symbolic interpretation has a genuine exegetical basis to which to appeal" (352; this acknowledgment stands in apparent tension with the strength of the denials on this point on 121–25).

Forcefully and clearly, Watson and Barclay raise not only the issue of the "logic" of Galatians but also a long-standing and fundamental issue in biblical interpretation: how can the particularities of biblical texts become the basis for timeless principles of Christian theology? In our view, both authors sometimes formulate the issue with an inappropriate bias against a long tradition of theological interpretation of the biblical text. Thus Barclay (2010: 40–41) suggests, without sufficient basis, that "abstraction" has no place in rigorously historical interpretation; and Watson (2007: 358) poses the problem in terms of an alternative between focusing on historical particularity and finding theological relevance in spite of it. Perhaps the Reformers may be criticized for moving too quickly and without what we in the modern era would consider sufficient argument from the historical particularities of first-century Galatia to the conflicts and issues of their own day. But the move to find abstract principles within the particularities of specific texts surely cannot be ruled out in principle (and, parenthetically, one might ask Barclay why the notion of "unconditioned gift" he associates with the Christ-event is not just such an abstraction). One may want to criticize the Reformers for deriving this or that theological principle from the text of Galatians, but their fault is not that they in principle seek to use Galatians to establish broad theological conclusions; their fault—if indeed they are to be faulted—would be that they misunderstand the text and its implications.

And so we return to the logic of Galatians, raising again the critical question: why does Paul so resolutely oppose "Christ faith" to torah observance? Dunn argues that there is something in torah observance as such that is problematic; Barclay and Watson, on the other hand, put all the weight on the nature of the Christ event. We contend that Dunn is right on this point, but that his critique of torah observance does not go far enough (or perhaps does not find adequate exegetical grounding). Specifically, we argue for the traditional but currently unfashionable view that underlying Paul's polemic against doing the torah in Galatians is his concern about human "doing" in general. The problem with human doing is that it is always and necessarily inadequate: sinful humans are incapable of rendering to God the obedience that God deserves. "Works of the law," like any other human "work," always fall short of what God expects of his creatures, leaving incorporation into Christ by faith as the only means of achieving righteousness. This way of reading the logic of Galatians follows a long line of interpreters—a line, it should be emphasized, that extends beyond the Reformers to at least as far back as Chrysostom, who regularly introduces this point about human inability into his homilies on Galatians.

At first glance Galatians does not seem to provide much basis for such theological abstraction. The letter contrasts faith with "works of the law" six times (2:16 [3x]; 3:2, 5, 10), and Paul never abbreviates this phrase by referring simply to "works"; he always abbreviates with "law" (see esp. 2:21; 3:11, 18; 5:4). This makes clear what nobody contests: that the issue in Galatians has to do with *torah* observance. The agitators were not arguing that people get right with God by doing good works but that people can have their right standing with God vindicated only by faithful observance of God's covenant stipulations. The disagreement is over the reason(s) that Paul opposes the program of the agitators. Does the apostle fault them only because they were insisting on *torah* observance? Or does he also fault them because they are proposing to make salvation contingent on *works*, on human "doing"?[35] Three elements in Paul's argument show that it is, indeed, valid to move from the particular phrase "works of the law" to the universal issue of "works."

First, at critical points in his argument, Paul introduces the verb "doing" (ποιέω, *poieō*) into his argument (3:10, 12; 5:3). To be sure, it is always a matter of "doing" torah, but Paul's use of this verb shows that we cannot ignore the word "works" in the phrase "works of the law." It is not just torah but *doing*

---

35. This is the critical issue in assessing the ultimate theological significance of the argument in Galatians. This point is recognized by, among others, Matlock and Das. Matlock (1996: 436) says, "The question it [the New Perspective] brings, particularly to Paul's Epistles to the Galatians and Romans, concerns Paul's overall argumentative context: is there, in Paul, a principled contrast between 'doing' (the law) and 'believing' (the gospel), or is the contrast between an 'exclusive' (a Jewish law) and 'inclusive' (a universally accessible faith) approach to God's saving prerogatives?" And Das (2009: 796) claims, "The perceived overemphasis on the boundary-marking 'works of the Law' has become the most prominent defining feature of this 'new perspective' on Paul. The pivotal question, then, is whether Paul's critique of the 'works of the Law' is limited to their boundary-marking function or whether his critique is articulated also in terms of human accomplishment."

the torah that is the problem.[36] What enables us to move beyond "doing the torah" to a more generalized "doing" are two other arguments that Paul uses to argue against torah observance. These arguments are more implicit than explicit and consequently, of course, quite debated. But we think that both arguments are indeed present in Galatians.

The first argument is implied in one text of Galatians and hinted at in another. According to 3:10, those who rely on "works of the law" fall under the curse pronounced by Deut. 27:26 on those who do not "uphold the words of this law by carrying them out." This verse makes sense only if Paul is assuming that people cannot "uphold the words of this law by carrying them out" (see esp. Schreiner 1984: 151–60; Kim 2002: 128–43; Westerholm 2004: 375). The logic of the verse can be expressed in a syllogism:

Only those who do everything written in the law will escape the curse (Gal. 3:10b).

No one can do everything written in the law (assumed).

Therefore, no one who depends on doing the law will escape the curse (v. 10a).

Paul's choice of a text that emphasizes both "doing" and "all" (as in the LXX that Paul quotes) suggests that he wants his readers to assume this second stage in his argument (see the commentary for detailed argument). In 5:3, similarly, Paul warns the man who is contemplating circumcision that he is "obliged to do the whole law"; while less clear, we should assume that the same point about inability to do the law also lies behind this claim.

This way of reading the logic of 3:10 (and 5:3) has a long history, extending, it should be pointed out, beyond the Reformation to at least as far back as Ambrosiaster and Chrysostom.[37] But Dunn, Barclay, and Watson, along with many other scholars, deny that any such assumption can be made. They observe that Paul never expresses this point in Galatians and that Paul would be unlikely to assume such an idea or his readers to infer it. But this objection is not cogent. If the Galatian Christians had even a cursory acquaintance with the OT, they would readily have assumed this point. The failure of the Israelites to "confirm" the covenant God made with them by obeying the law is clearly predicted within Deuteronomy itself (31:14–29) and becomes the leitmotiv of Israel's history. God sends his people into exile because "all Israel has transgressed your law and turned away, refusing to obey you" (Dan. 9:11). This history reveals, then, innate human failure to remain consistently

---

36. "The realm of human deeds is constitutive for Paul's argument (cf. the use of ποιέω [*poieō*, do] in Gal. 3:10–12) for it is only this realm that makes possible sin's assault" (Schnelle 2009: 300).

37. Ambrosiaster comments on 3:10, "The commandments are so great that it is impossible to keep them" (cf. Bray 2009: 16). Chrysostom (*Comm. Gal.* on 3:10 [NPNF[1] 13:26]) is explicit about this in his comments on 3:10: "Here again he establishes his point by a text which concisely states both points: that no man has fulfilled the Law (wherefore they are under the curse), and, that Faith justifies." See also Chrysostom's comments on 2:17, 19; 3:2, 12; 5:2.

oriented toward God and his law, a situation to be remedied only by God's own new work in the human heart, replacing the "heart of stone" with a "heart of flesh" and sending his Spirit to enable his people to produce the obedience that he expects (Ezek. 36:24–28). It is precisely this innate human inability to do God's law that Paul himself elaborates in Rom. 7:14–25: the Jew is in despair because of being unable to "do" the good law of God that God gave Israel. The law cannot bring the life it promises (7:10) because it "was weakened by the flesh" (8:3; for this reading of Rom. 7, see Moo 1996: 442–51). Thus in view of the massive OT witness to the problem of human inability to do the law, a viewpoint that Paul explicitly takes over in his other letters, it is hardly an arbitrary "reading into" this passage in Galatians to think that Paul assumes it here.

A related objection to our claim that Paul assumes inability to do the law is that such a view was unknown in Judaism and cannot therefore legitimately be inferred in this passage. But clarification about the Jewish view and the assumption required to make the logic work in this verse is needed. Indeed, there is considerable confusion in the literature about this point. Sanders's (1983: 28) summary of the Jewish viewpoint may be taken as representative: "The law is not too difficult to be satisfactorily fulfilled; nevertheless more or less everybody sins at some time or other . . . ; but God has appointed means of atonement which are available to all." As these statements make clear, the Jewish view was *not* that human beings could perfectly "do" the law, in the sense of successfully obeying all its commandments. Jewish claims that the law could be "done" mean, in effect, that a Jew can be viewed as being free of condemnation for inevitable transgressions by taking advantage of the provision for forgiveness via sacrifice included in that same law (and it is possible that this is what Paul means when he claims that, as a Jew, he was "faultless" with respect to the "righteousness based on the law"; Phil. 3:6).

Granted this view, then, there are two ways to understand Paul's language about the need to do all the law. First, he might mean that the requirement to undertake the whole law involves not only obedience to the commandments in general but also reliance on the law's provisions for atonement via sacrifice. The general reference to "doing all the law" in 5:3 could have this sense, but the language of "remaining in all the law to do it" in Gal. 3:10, especially granted the context in Deuteronomy from which Paul draws this language, is less amenable to such a meaning. And, of course, it is well known that Paul generally ignores, for whatever reason, provisions for sacrifice and worship in his discussion of the law. Thus more likely is the second interpretation: Paul assumes in his argument that the sacrifice of Christ has rendered the OT provisions for atonement null and void (see 1:4; 3:1, 13). The fact that Paul never touches on this matter in Galatians strongly suggests that the definitive nature of Christ's atoning sacrifice was common ground with his opponents. In the time after Christ, then, one is faced with two, and only two, options: find justification in Christ by faith; or find justification through the law, a justification that can now, apart from the provision of sacrifice, be secured only by doing "all" the law (see esp. Das 2001: 215–22; Laato 2004: 343–46).

A second argument suggesting that Paul's polemic against "works of the law" may rightly be viewed also as a polemic against works in general is the way he introduces the language of "grace" into his argument. While the word appears only seven times in the letter (1:3, 6, 15; 2:9, 21; 5:4; 6:18), "grace" is nevertheless a fundamental issue (Bryant 2001: 195–223). The positive assertion that the Galatians have been "called to live in the grace of Christ" (1:6) matches, as Silva (2003: 17) notes, the twofold warning in the rhetorical climax of the letter: "You who are trying to be justified by the law have been alienated from Christ; you have fallen away from grace" (5:4). One could almost say that "the grace of Christ" summarizes the argument of the letter. God has decisively manifested himself in Christ, thus sidelining the law, and his saving work in Christ is completely a matter of grace, to which humans can respond only with faith, not with works of any kind.

As we have noted, Barclay recognizes the importance of this word "grace" in the argument of Galatians, arguing that Paul uses it to characterize "the Christ-event, and especially the self-gift of Christ" (2010: 36–37n1; see also 47). But the referent is sometimes broader than Barclay recognizes, including not only, or mainly, the nature of Christ's giving of himself but also the manner in which human beings appropriate the benefits of that giving. Galatians 5:4 may certainly use "grace" in this sense, and it is also a better explanation of 2:21, where Paul's insistence that he does not nullify the grace of God is implicitly contrasted with "righteousness through the law." These texts suggest that Paul is using "grace" in the way he does more explicitly in his later Letter to the Romans. In Rom. 4:4–5, Paul appeals to grace as the reason why God justifies the ungodly: because a godly person, by virtue of works, is able to make a claim on God. But Paul's deep-seated conviction that God is the kind of God who can only ever deal with his sinful creatures through his own free and unconstrained purpose rules out any such relationship of obligation (Rom. 11:6 makes a similar point).

At this point we may be accused of reading Romans into Galatians, a charge that might seem to have good ground in light of my earlier work on Romans (Moo 1996). But while we must, of course, refrain from reading the logic or language of one particular letter into another, we are surely justified in looking to an author's longer and more explicit treatments of a given topic in order to shed light on shorter and more allusive references. The key point is whether one can find some basis in Galatians to think that grace here functions as it does in Romans. There is such basis, and Paul's appeal to grace in these two passages (Gal. 2:21; 5:4) suggests that he rules out justification by works of the law not only because the torah is involved but also because works—human doing—are involved. Galatians is not a polemic against semi-Pelagianism (N. T. Wright [e.g., 2002: 654] is right about this); but Paul's argument suggests that behind the agitators' views he finds a reliance on human achievement that indeed has fundamental resemblances to semi-Pelagianism.

These two arguments suggest that Paul's polemic against the law in Galatians rests, to some extent, on a pessimistic anthropology. Stephen Westerholm (2004: 381) puts the point well: "The fundamental question addressed by Galatians thus is not 'What is wrong with Judaism (or the Sinaitic law)?' but 'What is wrong with humanity that Judaism (and the Sinaitic law) cannot remedy?'" (See also, esp. Silva 2004; Gundry 1985; Kim 2002: 61–75.) A distinction between human doing and human believing, while not the focus in the letter, does underlie the argument of Galatians.

Theological Themes

Our discussion of the logic of the letter has touched on several of the theological issues that are important in Galatians. In what follows we isolate the key theological themes for further discussion, concluding with rather lengthy treatments of three issues that are especially crucial for understanding the letter.

Salvation History and Apocalyptic

Paul frames his letter with language that touches on one of the key points he makes against the agitators: the Galatians live in the time when God's glorious plan to redeem his entire creation is reaching its fulfillment: they have been "rescued from the present evil age" (1:4), and they participate in the "new creation" (6:15). Paul sounds this same note frequently within the letter. God sent his Son for us "when the time had fully come" (4:4). Paul's gospel was revealed to him in an "apocalypse" of Jesus Christ (1:12). The time of the law has ended because the "seed" that the promise to Abraham had especially in view, the Messiah, has come (3:15–18, 19, 25). The sharp divide between an "old age" of sin and a "new age" of righteousness is typical of Jewish apocalyptic. There can be little doubt, then, that the argument of Galatians employs these apocalyptic categories. This point has been made especially strongly by Martyn, who argues that "apocalyptic antinomies are at the heart of the letter."[38] Further, according to Martyn, this apocalyptic-oriented emphasis on the world-changing significance of the Christ event must not be compromised with any idea of a continuous salvation history. Christ cannot simply be inserted into the OT/Jewish "story" of redemption. The "apocalypse of Christ" breaks all the categories, undercutting any idea of a continuity in salvation history (see, e.g., 1997: 161–79).

Martyn's emphasis on the epochal significance of the Christ event is certainly justified: Paul's quarrel with the agitators can be boiled down to a difference of opinion over just how disruptive the Christ event is for the history of salvation. But for all the appropriate attention that Martyn gives to this "apocalyptic"

---

38. Martyn 1997: esp. 161–79. It should be noted, however, that Martyn gives his own peculiar spin to the notion of apocalyptic and how it functions in the letter.

focus, his denial of any real salvation history in Galatians goes too far.[39] The law remains God's law, has been given to serve certain specific purposes, and finds its ultimate goal in Christ (see our interpretation of 3:24–25). The OT is not just a negative foil for the gospel, but also prepares for it in certain central ways. Moreover, the OT sets many of the categories in which Paul now proclaims the gospel inaugurated by the Christ event. Salvation history, understood in the sense of a single plan of God to redeem his people and set the world to rights, is very much fundamental to Galatians and provides the framework within which the disruptive and world-changing apocalypse of Christ is to be understood (see Dunn 2009: 738; Childs 2008: 210–12; Starling 2011: 209; note also the interchange among B. Longenecker 2012; Maston 2012; and de Boer 2012). Salvation history and apocalyptic, in other words, need not be set in opposition: Christ (that is, "Messiah," a title connoting OT and Jewish expectation) can only be fully understood as the climax (apocalyptic) of an unfolding story (salvation history).

The Gospel

The language of "gospel" occurs (with two exceptions; see 3:8 and 4:13) only in chapters 1–2: the noun εὐαγγέλιον (*euangelion*, gospel / good news) in 1:6, 7, 11; 2:2, 5, 7, 14; the verb εὐαγγελίζομαι (*euangelizomai*, preach the good news) in 1:8, 9, 11, 16, 23. Paul's almost total abandonment of gospel language in chapters 3–6 might suggest that the gospel is important only for the first two chapters. However, a good case can be made for identifying the gospel as the best single unifying theme of the letter. The language is prominent in the critical opening section of the letter, where the issue that dominates the entire argument is introduced (1:6–10). The two incidents in 2:1–14 reveal Paul's battle for "the truth of the gospel" (2:2, 14). The importance of this phrase in 1:11–2:14 suggests that Paul's assertion of justification by faith in 2:15–21, a statement that introduces the key vocabulary and central argument to follow, might appropriately be viewed as his summary of "the truth of the gospel." Dunn (2009: 725) has appropriately characterized Galatians as "a restatement of Paul's gospel" (see also G. Hansen 1989: 83–84; Vouga 1998: 65; Bryant 2001: 235). The good news about the "apocalypse" of Jesus Christ (1:12; cf. 4:4–6), his death on behalf of sinners (1:4; 3:13), the inauguration of a new creation (6:15; see 3:28), and above all, justification by grace and by faith alone (2:15–21)—this gospel is the bedrock on which Paul builds his argument in Galatians and the critical truth that he uses to counteract the teaching of the agitators.[40] As Smiles (1998: 214) puts it, "The Galatian crisis was the

39. Another issue, which we will not take up here, is the appropriateness of the language of "apocalyptic" to describe what Martyn is talking about. For a critical analysis of the way the language of "apocalyptic" is used by NT scholars, see Matlock 1996.

40. N. T. Wright (1994: 229–32) suggests a definition of "gospel" in Galatians that has a different focus than this summary above. Noting the polemical nature of Paul's "gospel" claim vis-à-vis the Roman claims for the emperor, Wright identifies four key components of the gospel in Galatians: (1) the God of Israel is the one true God; (2) Jesus is Lord and King; (3) the exile

cauldron in which Paul's arguments were formed, but the guiding principle in these arguments is the supreme authority of the gospel."

Christ

The Letter to the Galatians offers no formal christological teaching of the sort that we find (e.g.) in Phil. 2:5–11 or Col. 1:15–20. But as we have noted above, Christology, understood in the sense of the epochal significance of the Christ event, is at the heart of Paul's argument in the letter (Gaventa 1991). Within that "Christ event," it is the death of Christ that draws Paul's particular attention in Galatians. Paul once speaks generally of God's sending his Son (4:4), and he mentions Christ's resurrection once in passing ("God the Father, who raised him from the dead"; 1:1), but he draws repeated attention to the significance of Christ's death (Matera 1993; cf. Russell 1997: 122–23; Weima 1993). Paul focuses especially on the cosmic significance of Christ's death. The christological bookends of the letter make this point: Christ "gave himself for our sins to rescue us from the present evil age" (1:4); "May I never boast except in the cross of our Lord Jesus Christ, through which the world has been crucified to me, and I to the world" (6:14; and see the reference to "new creation" in 6:15). In this latter text, Paul presents his own experience of "world-crucifixion" as paradigmatic for believers, a pattern found also in 2:19–20: "I have been crucified with Christ, and I no longer live, but Christ lives in me. The life I now live in the body, I live by faith in the Son of God, who loved me and gave himself for me." It is the vivid proclamation of the cross that should have made crystal clear the error of the agitators' teaching: "You foolish Galatians! Who has bewitched you? Before your very eyes Jesus Christ was clearly portrayed as crucified" (3:1). The agitators' teaching stands in fundamental contrast to the "cross of Christ" (5:11; 6:12). It was by "hanging on a pole" in crucifixion that Christ "redeemed us from the curse of the law" (3:13).

Especially important in the argument of the letter is the idea of incorporation into Christ. God promised to bless the nations "in" Abraham (3:8), and that blessing is now given to all who belong to Christ (3:14) because he is the (singular!) "seed" of Abraham (3:16). So, Paul concludes in the climax of his theological argument, "in Christ Jesus you are all children of God through faith" (3:26). Incorporation into Christ is a fundamental theological concept in the letter (as it is in Paul's theology generally). It is the theological center from which the various lines of Paul's theological reasoning radiate. Those who are "in Christ" enjoy the "blessing of Abraham," in the context of justification (3:14); and "those who belong to Christ Jesus have crucified the flesh with its passions and desires" (5:24). Thus both justification and sanctification are

---

of Israel is ended; and (4) the rule of pagan idols is broken. While each of these points can be inferred from Paul's argument in Galatians, none is a major emphasis. They do not fairly summarize the points that Paul actually makes in the letter and do not, therefore, provide an adequate description of the gospel in Galatians.

given believers via their union with Christ—the "double gift" that Calvin is especially concerned to emphasize.[41]

The Spirit

Cosgrove (1988), drawing attention especially to 3:1–5, argues that the Spirit is the central, integrating theme of the letter (see also Hafemann 1997: 350; and, on 3:1–4:7, de Boer 2011: 166–67). This is an exaggeration. But the Spirit is more significant in Galatians than has often been recognized. As he often does, Paul uses the Spirit to bridge the "already" and "not yet" of Christian experience. The Spirit makes a first appearance in the letter in the rhetorically important 3:1–6. Reception of the Spirit, Paul implies, marks the inauguration of Christian experience (3:2, 5; see also 4:6). But the Spirit, Paul insists, marks not only entrance into the life of Christ; the Spirit must also become the means by which believers continue and complete their Christian experience: "After beginning by means of the Spirit, are you now trying to finish by means of the flesh?" (3:3). This same point emerges in 5:5: "For through the Spirit we eagerly await by faith the righteousness for which we hope." These two texts provide the rhetorical bookends to Paul's theological argument and appeal to the Galatians. The Galatians are being tempted to allow some human-oriented program or teaching ("the flesh") to take the place of the Spirit as they seek to complete their Christian pilgrimage.

But most of the references to the Spirit in Galatians are in 5:13–6:10, where Paul argues that the powerful influence of the Spirit is more than able to guide and empower the life that meets God's approval. Christians, who receive the Spirit at conversion, are people who are from that point forward "led" by the Spirit (5:18), who produces "fruit" pleasing to God (5:22–23a). But Christians must also respond to the leading of the Spirit: they must "walk by the Spirit" (5:16) and "keep in step with" the Spirit (5:25). Paul underlines the importance of allowing the Spirit to control and direct Christians by reminding us that it is only by this means that we will be able to secure eternal life and so escape eschatological destruction (6:8). Paul's reference to the "promise of the Spirit" in 3:14 is an often-overlooked transitional point in his teaching about the Spirit. When believers receive the Spirit at conversion (3:2, 5), they experience the fulfillment of the OT prophecies about the coming of the Spirit (e.g., Joel 2:28–32; Ezek 36:22–32; Isa. 44:3). These prophecies often focus on the way the Spirit in the age of fulfillment will ensure the conformity to God's will that the law in itself was unable to provide ("I will put my Spirit in you and move you to follow my decrees and be careful to keep my laws" [Ezek. 36:27]). The "promise of the Spirit" in 3:14, then, both circles back to the theme of the initial reception of the Spirit in 3:1–5 as well as hinting at

---

41. On this theme in Paul generally, see C. Campbell 2012. Several recent works have explored the importance of union with Christ in Calvin (e.g., Billings 2007; Garcia 2008). And see S. Chester 2009 on the theme in Luther (taken to an extreme in the so-called "Finnish" school) and, on the Reformed tradition generally, Gaffin 2006; W. Evans 2008; and Letham 2011. See also Vanhoozer 2011 on the potential promise of the doctrine (union with Christ) for unifying Paul's theology.

Paul's argument about the Spirit's work in sanctification in 5:13–6:10 (see C. Lee 2009: 299–301).

The Law

The situation in Galatia forces Paul to focus considerable attention on the law of Moses. The word νόμος (*nomos*, law) occurs thirty-two times in Galatians and, with one clear and one possible exception, it always refers to the law of Moses, or torah (the clear exception is the second occurrence in 4:21, which refers to the Pentateuch; the possible exception is 6:2 ["the law of Christ"]). The agitators are insisting that the Gentile believers in Galatia begin to observe the torah in order to secure their place within the people of God and provide for their ultimate salvation in the judgment of God. Paul's emphasis in 5:3 on the obligation to obey "the whole law" might suggest that the agitators were insisting on obedience only to part of the law or had not made clear to the Galatians the extent of what was being required of them. But Paul's use of the general phrase "under the law" for what the Galatians were being tempted to do (4:21) suggests, rather, that the agitators were insisting on full obedience to the law.

Paul argues passionately against this step. We have discussed above his reasons for making this argument (see "The Logic of Paul's Response"). The movement of salvation history is clearly a key point: the law that came 430 years after God's promise to Abraham cannot annul that earlier faith-based covenant; and all along the law was intended to be in effect only until the "seed" of Abraham should come (3:19, 24). The law, then, was given for a limited time and for a specific purpose: by its nature it could not "give life" (3:21), nor was it ever intended to do so. Rather, it "supervised" the people of God during the stage of their childhood, or minority (3:24–25; 4:1–2), and functioned, by revealing the real nature of sin (3:19) and thus "imprisoning" Israel under sin (3:22), to anticipate and point toward Christ. The law, and the covenant within which it has its place, was thus an arrangement subordinate to the overarching covenant that God instituted with Abraham (3:15–18; see also 4:24).[42] But as we argue above, Paul's argument against the law is not confined to salvation history. As it did in the experience of Israel, the law in itself brings people under a curse—for human beings, locked up under sin, are unable to obey God's law and thus find themselves condemned by it (3:10; see also 5:3). By its nature the law is a matter of "doing" (not of "believing"; see 3:12); and human doing, or "works," can never be the basis for entering into or sustaining a relationship with God. This certainly does not mean that

---

42. Paul's view of the law in Gal. 3 is developed in terms of Israel and the Jews' experience with the law. This makes clear, as does the "we" in 2:15–16, that Paul relegates the law to an earlier stage of salvation history for all believers, not just Gentiles (contra Gaston 1987; Nanos 2010). For a good overview of the approach that tries to confine Paul's law criticism to the Gentile issue, see Nanos 2010. He argues that Paul's only problem with the law is the attempt to impose it on Gentiles; it remains fully in force for Jewish-Christians. Nor does Paul criticize Judaism; his problem is with Jews and Jewish-Christians who deny that Gentiles can be admitted to the end-time people of God apart from the law.

Paul dismisses the importance of "doing" for Christians; indeed, he suggests rather clearly in 6:8–9 that no one can find eternal life without obedience to the will of the Lord. But (1) what Christians obey as their fundamental authority is the "law of Christ," and not the law of Moses (6:2; see below); and (2) obedience is not the *basis* for eternal life but the necessary means by which our new life, based on Christ and faith and mediated by the Spirit, will be confirmed and sealed on the last day.

Paul's concern to deter the Galatians from becoming torah observant leads him to portray the law in quite a negative light. In chapter 4, for instance, he argues that the Galatians' submission to the law would be tantamount to their returning to their pagan existence under "the elements of the world" (4:3, 9). And in 3:19b–20, Paul claims that "the law was given through angels." Some interpreters think that this clause is better translated "given *by* the angels," with the implication that it was *not* given by God (see esp. Hübner 1984: 24–36; and also Martyn 1997: 364–70; Kuula 1999). However, this is not the most likely meaning of this text (see the commentary). And the analogy between the law and pagan religions that Paul hints at in chapter 4 must not be expanded beyond its intended point: the Galatians' submission to the law would be a return to an earlier stage of religious experience. Nothing in Galatians suggests that Paul seeks to disassociate God from the law. Indeed, his salvation-historical argument in 3:15–25 assumes throughout that God has been using the law to accomplish particular purposes. Moreover, we think that 3:24 claims not just that the law finds its "end" in Christ but also that it points to Christ as the climax of salvation history (see Rom. 10:4).

The consistently negative portrayal of the law in Galatians is, then, a direct result of the polemical situation that Paul faces in the letter. He must put all his weight on the negative side in order to right the balances that the agitators had tilted too far in the other direction. The overall teaching about the law in Galatians is more negative than in Romans. However, the difference between the two letters on this point is not that Paul retracts or fails to mention the negative points found in Galatians: all of them are there again in the later letter. The difference, rather, is that Paul adds positive assessments of the law in Romans, where the lack of a polemical context means he can be more balanced in his teaching. So, while Romans provides fuller teaching on the law, it does not contradict or "correct" what Paul says in Galatians.

A key but debated point Paul makes in Galatians is that believers are no longer "under the law." The phrase occurs four times in Galatians (and see also Rom. 6:14, 15; 1 Cor. 9:20):

Before the coming of this faith, we were held in custody under the law, locked up until the faith that was to come would be revealed. (3:23)

But when the set time had fully come, God sent his Son, born of a woman, born under the law, [5]to redeem those under the law, that we might receive adoption to sonship. (4:4–5)

Tell me, you who want to be under the law, are you not aware of what the law says? (4:21)

But if you are led by the Spirit, you are not under the law. (5:18)

Some interpreters argue that the phrase has the connotation "under the curse of the law" (Thielman 1989: 77–78; Hong 2002: 360–62; Wilson 2007: 30–44; Baumert and Meissner 2010: 101–10). This interpretation could work in 4:4–5, where Paul claims that Christ himself was "born under the law" (for Christ suffered the penalty for our sins), but it is harder to square with 4:21—in what sense would the Galatians *want* to be "under the curse of the law"? The phrase more likely has the general sense "under the authority of the law" (see esp. Belleville 1986), in parallel with comparable expressions such as "under sin" (3:22), "under a *paidagōgos*" (3:24–25), and "under guardians and trustees" (4:2). The claim this phrase makes is the natural corollary to the salvation-historical argument of 3:15–25: since the time of the law is at an end, believers are no longer subject to its authority. Of course, this claim must be carefully nuanced so as not to detract from the continuing general "authority" of the OT in the lives of believers and in order to do justice to NT texts suggesting that the OT law has some kind of continuing ethical import for believers (see esp. James 1:21–25; 2:8–13). The OT law has no direct authority over the believer but continues to be an indirect source (under the authority of NT teaching) for the moral life (see Moo 1993).

It is against this background that the related texts about "fulfilling the law" (5:14) and "the law of Christ" (6:2) must be viewed. Many interpret these texts to mean that the OT law is fulfilled when it is interpreted and applied to believers in light of Christ's work and teaching. "The law of Christ" means, then, "the OT law as fulfilled in Christ." However, we think a more natural reading of the phrase and one that better fits the things that Paul has said about the law earlier in the letter is to view it as contrasting "the law of Moses" with "the law of Christ." The phrase is a succinct way of summarizing the ethical guidance given to new covenant believers, found in Christ's teaching and the teaching of his accredited apostles (see also 1 Cor. 9:20–22). The OT law is "fulfilled" in the sense that the love command, taught by Christ, provides for all that the OT law itself was intended to accomplish.

The Christian Life

In 5:13 a decisive turn in the argument of the letter takes place. Having argued for four chapters toward the conclusion that we find in 5:1—"It is for freedom that Christ has set us free"—Paul now warns against the abuse of freedom in the form of a lifestyle that follows the dictates of the flesh. This section focuses not so much on the specifics of the Christian life as on its basic parameters. Some interpreters think that Paul, having contested legalists, now focuses on a different group of people with a libertine outlook. Others imply (without usually stating the point) that Paul adds ethical guidelines here at the end of his letter that have little to do with the argument of the letter as a whole. But recent interpreters have rightly argued that 5:13–6:10 is an integral part of the argument of Galatians (see esp. Barclay 1988). Issues of behavior were probably important in the Galatian situation. Putting themselves under the law of Moses was probably attractive to the Galatians partly because they would then find the security of a concrete series of ethical guidelines. Paul counters by stressing that the Spirit, introduced into the Galatians' lives by their faith in Christ, provides all the guidance and power necessary to fulfill God's law (5:18, 23). In this section Paul's argument is also designed to guard against any notion that Christians do not need to be concerned about behavior. The faith that Paul has been highlighting is a "faith that works through love" (5:6). By joining us with Christ and, in Christ, filling us with the Spirit, faith leads seamlessly to a life of obedience, centered on love for the neighbor (5:14; cf. 6:2). Yet this work of the Spirit must find a response from the believer—the one who now "lives by the Spirit" must "keep in step with the Spirit" (5:25) and is obliged to "sow to please the Spirit" in order to "reap eternal life" (6:8).

We turn now to two topics that, because of their importance in the letter and the debates about them, deserve more extended treatment.

"The Faith of Christ"

Faith is a dominant theme in Galatians. The verb πιστεύω (*pisteuō*, believe) occurs four times (2:7, 16; 3:6 [= Gen. 15:6], 22) while the noun πίστις (*pistis*, faith) is found twenty-two times (1:23; 2:16 [2x], 20; 3:2, 5, 7, 8, 9, 11, 12, 14, 22, 23 [2x], 24, 25, 26; 5:5, 6, 22; 6:10). Most of these occurrences of "faith" language have usually been interpreted as referring to human believing (exceptions are 1:23, which probably refers to the Christian "faith," and 5:22, which likely refers to "faithfulness"). But many contemporary interpreters think that some (or many) of these texts refer not to human believing but to Christ's own "faith" or "faithfulness." This view rests on a certain interpretation of the phrase πίστις ('Ιησοῦ) Χριστοῦ (*pistis [Iēsou] Christou*, faith of [Jesus] Christ). This phrase, or close variations of it (that is, the noun πίστις followed by the name of Christ [or some combination of Christ's names] in the genitive), occurs four times in Galatians (2:16 [2x]; 2:20; 3:22), twice in Romans (3:22, 26), once in Ephesians (3:12), and once in Philippians (3:9).[43] Elsewhere

---

43. A few interpreters think that 1 Thess. 1:3 might be another instance: μνημονεύοντες ὑμῶν τοῦ ἔργου τῆς πίστεως καὶ τοῦ κόπου τῆς ἀγάπης καὶ τῆς ὑπομονῆς τῆς ἐλπίδος τοῦ κυρίου ἡμῶν Ἰησοῦ Χριστοῦ ἔμπροσθεν τοῦ θεοῦ καὶ πατρὸς ἡμῶν (*mnēmoneuontes hymōn tou ergou tēs pisteōs kai tou kopou tēs agapēs kai tēs hypomonēs tēs elpidos tou kyriou hēmōn Iēsou Christou emprosthen tou theou kai patros hēmōn*, Before our God and Father, we remember your work produced by faith, your labor prompted by love, and your endurance inspired by hope in our Lord Jesus Christ [NIV with changed word order]; if one construes τοῦ κυρίου ἡμῶν Ἰησοῦ Χριστοῦ with τῆς πίστεως and τῆς ἀγάπης as well as with τῆς ἐλπίδος [see, e.g., Ulrichs 2007: 71–93]). See also Eph. 4:13: τὴν ἑνότητα τῆς πίστεως καὶ τῆς ἐπιγνώσεως τοῦ υἱοῦ τοῦ θεοῦ (*tēn henotēta tēs pisteōs kai tēs epignōseōs tou huiou tou theou*, unity in the faith and in the knowledge of the Son of God [NIV]; if one takes τοῦ υἱοῦ τοῦ θεοῦ with τῆς πίστεως as well as with τῆς ἐπιγνώσεως).

in the NT, such phrases occur in James 2:1; Rev. 2:13; 14:12. Similar are Acts 3:16, where πίστις is followed by τοῦ ὀνόματος αὐτοῦ (*tou onomatos autou*, the "name" of him [Jesus]; cf. Acts 3:13), and Rom. 3:3 and Mark 11:22, the two NT examples of πίστις followed by θεός (*theos*, God) in the genitive. It will be helpful to set out the actual texts (in Greek plus NIV, with the crucial phrases given alternate English readings):

PAULINE EXAMPLES: GAL. 2:15–16

Ἡμεῖς . . . εἰδότες [δὲ] ὅτι οὐ δικαιοῦται ἄνθρωπος ἐξ ἔργων νόμου ἐὰν μὴ **διὰ πίστεως Ἰησοῦ Χριστοῦ**, καὶ ἡμεῖς εἰς Χριστὸν Ἰησοῦν ἐπιστεύσαμεν, ἵνα δικαιωθῶμεν **ἐκ πίστεως Χριστοῦ** καὶ οὐκ ἐξ ἔργων νόμου, ὅτι ἐξ ἔργων νόμου οὐ δικαιωθήσεται πᾶσα σάρξ.

*Hēmeis . . . eidotes [de] hoti ou dikaioutai anthrōpos ex ergōn nomou ean mē **dia pisteōs Iēsou Christou**, kai hēmeis eis Christon Iēsoun episteusamen, hina dikaiōthōmen **ek pisteōs Christou** kai ouk ex ergōn nomou, hoti ex ergōn nomou ou dikaiōthēsetai pasa sarx.*

"We . . . know that a person is not justified by the works of the law, but **by faith in / the faithfulness of Jesus Christ**. So we, too, have put our faith in Christ Jesus that we may be justified **by faith in / the faithfulness of Christ** and not by the works of the law, because by the works of the law no one will be justified."

GAL. 2:19B–20

Χριστῷ συνεσταύρωμαι· ζῶ δὲ οὐκέτι ἐγώ, ζῇ δὲ ἐν ἐμοὶ Χριστός· ὃ δὲ νῦν ζῶ ἐν σαρκί, **ἐν πίστει** ζῶ τῇ **τοῦ υἱοῦ τοῦ θεοῦ** τοῦ ἀγαπήσαντός με καὶ παραδόντος ἑαυτὸν ὑπὲρ ἐμοῦ.

*Christō synestaurōmai; zō de ouketi egō, zē de en emoi Christos; ho de nyn zō en sarki, **en pistei** zō tē **tou huiou tou theou** tou agapēsantos me kai paradontos heauton hyper emou.*

"I have been crucified with Christ and I no longer live, but Christ lives in me. The life I now live in the body, I live **by faith in / the faithfulness of the Son of God**, who loved me and gave himself for me."

GAL. 3:22

ἀλλὰ συνέκλεισεν ἡ γραφὴ τὰ πάντα ὑπὸ ἁμαρτίαν, ἵνα ἡ ἐπαγγελία **ἐκ πίστεως Ἰησοῦ Χριστοῦ** δοθῇ τοῖς πιστεύουσιν.

*Alla synekleisen hē graphē ta panta hypo hamartian, hina hē epangelia **ek pisteōs Iēsou Christou** dothē tois pisteuousin.*

But Scripture has locked up everything under the control of sin, so that what was promised, being given **through faith in / the faithfulness of Jesus Christ**, might be given to those who believe.

ROM. 3:22

δικαιοσύνη δὲ θεοῦ **διὰ πίστεως Ἰησοῦ Χριστοῦ** εἰς πάντας τοὺς πιστεύοντας. οὐ γάρ ἐστιν διαστολή,

*Dikaiosynē de theou **dia pisteōs Iēsou Christou** eis pantas tous pisteuontas. ou gar estin diastolē,*

This righteousness is given **through faith in / the faithfulness of Jesus Christ** to all who believe. There is no difference. . . .

Rom. 3:26

ἐν τῇ ἀνοχῇ τοῦ θεοῦ, πρὸς τὴν ἔνδειξιν τῆς δικαιοσύνης αὐτοῦ ἐν τῷ νῦν καιρῷ, εἰς τὸ εἶναι αὐτὸν δίκαιον καὶ δικαιοῦντα τὸν **ἐκ πίστεως** Ἰησοῦ.

*En tē anochē tou theou, pros tēn endeixin tēs dikaiosynēs autou en tō nyn kairō, eis to einai auton dikaion kai dikaiounta ton **ek pisteōs Iēsou.***

He did it to demonstrate his justice at the present time, so as to be just and the one who justifies those who have **faith in / the faithfulness of Jesus.**

Eph. 3:12

ἐν ᾧ ἔχομεν τὴν παρρησίαν καὶ προσαγωγὴν ἐν πεποιθήσει **διὰ τῆς πίστεως αὐτοῦ.**

*En hō echomen tēn parrēsian kai prosagōgēn en pepoithēsei **dia tēs pisteōs autou.***

In him and **through faith in / the faithfulness of him** [Christ Jesus our Lord, v. 11] we may approach God with freedom and confidence.

Phil. 3:9

καὶ εὑρεθῶ ἐν αὐτῷ, μὴ ἔχων ἐμὴν δικαιοσύνην τὴν ἐκ νόμου ἀλλὰ τὴν **διὰ πίστεως Χριστοῦ,** τὴν ἐκ θεοῦ δικαιοσύνην ἐπὶ τῇ πίστει,

*Kai heurethō en autō, mē echōn emēn dikaiosynēn tēn ek nomou alla tēn **dia pisteōs Christou,** tēn ek theou dikaiosynēn epi tē pistei,*

. . . and be found in him, not having a righteousness of my own that comes from the law, but that which is **through faith in / the faithfulness of Christ**—the righteousness that comes from God on the basis of faith.

Other NT Examples: Acts 3:16

καὶ **ἐπὶ τῇ πίστει τοῦ ὀνόματος αὐτοῦ** τοῦτον ὃν θεωρεῖτε καὶ οἴδατε, ἐστερέωσεν τὸ ὄνομα αὐτοῦ, καὶ ἡ πίστις ἡ δι' αὐτοῦ ἔδωκεν αὐτῷ τὴν ὁλοκληρίαν ταύτην ἀπέναντι πάντων ὑμῶν.

*Kai **epi tē pistei tou onomatos autou** touton hon theōreite kai oidate, estereōsen to onoma autou, kai hē pistis hē di autou edōken autō tēn holoklērian tautēn apenanti pantōn hymōn.*

By faith in / the faithfulness of the name of Jesus, this man whom you see and know was made strong. It is Jesus' name and the faith that comes through him that has completely healed him, as you can all see.

James 2:1

Ἀδελφοί μου, μὴ ἐν προσωπολημψίαις ἔχετε **τὴν πίστιν τοῦ κυρίου ἡμῶν Ἰησοῦ Χριστοῦ** τῆς δόξης.

*Adelphoi mou, mē en prosōpolēmpsiais echete **tēn pistin tou kyriou hēmōn Iēsou Christou** tēs doxēs.*

My brothers and sisters, you who have **faith in / the faithfulness of our** glorious **Lord Jesus Christ** must not show favoritism. (NIV adapted)

Rev. 2:13

οἶδα ποῦ κατοικεῖς, ὅπου ὁ θρόνος τοῦ σατανᾶ, καὶ κρατεῖς τὸ ὄνομά μου καὶ οὐκ ἠρνήσω **τὴν πίστιν μου** καὶ ἐν ταῖς ἡμέραις Ἀντιπᾶς ὁ μάρτυς μου ὁ πιστός μου, ὃς ἀπεκτάνθη παρ' ὑμῖν, ὅπου ὁ σατανᾶς κατοικεῖ.

Oida pou katoikeis, hopou ho thronos tou satana, kai krateis to onoma mou kai ouk ērnēsō tēn pistin mou kai en tais hēmerais Antipas ho martys mou ho pistos mou, hos apektanthē par' hymin, hopou ho satanas katoikei.

I know where you live—where Satan has his throne. Yet you remain true to my name. You did not renounce **your faith in / the faithfulness of me** [the one who has "the sharp, double-edged sword," v. 12 = "someone like a son of man," 1:13], not even in the days of Antipas, my faithful witness, who was put to death in your city—where Satan lives.

Rev. 14:12

Ὧδε ἡ ὑπομονὴ τῶν ἁγίων ἐστίν, οἱ τηροῦντες τὰς ἐντολὰς τοῦ θεοῦ καὶ **τὴν πίστιν Ἰησοῦ.**

*Hōde hē hypomonē tōn hagiōn estin, hoi tērountes tas entolas tou theou kai **tēn pistin Iēsou.***

This calls for patient endurance on the part of the people of God who keep his commands and **the faith/faithfulness of Jesus.** (NIV adapted)

Similar Constructions with Θεου: Rom. 3:3

τί γάρ; εἰ ἠπίστησάν τινες, μὴ ἡ ἀπιστία αὐτῶν **τὴν πίστιν τοῦ θεοῦ** καταργήσει;

*Ti gar? ei ēpistēsan tines, mē hē apistia autōn **tēn pistin tou theou** katargēsei?*

What if some were unfaithful? Will their unfaithfulness nullify **God's faith/faithfulness?**

Mark 11:22

καὶ ἀποκριθεὶς ὁ Ἰησοῦς λέγει αὐτοῖς· ἔχετε **πίστιν θεοῦ.**

*Kai apokritheis ho Iēsous legei autois: exete **pistin theou.***

Jesus answered, "Have **faith in / the faithfulness of God.**"

The grammatical issue is obvious: how should we construe the genitive following the noun πίστις (*pistis*, faith) in each of these texts? Traditionally, the genitive has been interpreted as objective; hence the usual translation, found in most English versions, "faith in [Jesus] Christ." In past years a small number of scholars had argued for a subjective genitive interpretation, usually with πίστις understood to mean "faithfulness" (e.g., Torrance 1956–57; Howard 1973–74; D. Robinson 1970). But the subjective genitive interpretation has grown exponentially in the last thirty years, and it is now held by a significant number of Pauline interpreters (though found in the text of only two major English Bibles, the NET and CEB; see the survey of recent discussion in Hunn 2009). The reasons for the increasing popularity of this interpretation are not so much grammatical (although grammatical arguments are certainly used) but theological. Especially since Richard Hays's influential monograph on Galatians, *The Faith of Jesus Christ* (original ed. 1983), it has become common to discern in Paul's epistolary arguments a "narrative substructure" (the subtitle of Hays's book is *An Investigation of the Narrative Substructure of Galatians 3:1–4:11*) that features Jesus Christ as its central character. Paul's argument in Gal. 3–4, according to Hays, focuses on the believer's participation in Christ, whose "story" undergirds this section of the letter. Within this narrative and participatory framework, "faith" is not so much believing "in" Christ as it is believing "with" Christ: sharing with Christ the kind of faith in God that Abraham also exhibited. "Faith of [Jesus] Christ" then most naturally refers to Christ's own faith. The participatory focus in Hays's work has been picked up and extended to Paul's theology in general by many others in recent years, and it is this larger theological perspective that has given the greatest impetus to the "faith of Christ" interpretation. While focused initially on the specific "faith of Christ" phrases, this interpretation has been extended, quite naturally, to most of the other Pauline phrases that use πίστις absolutely (see D. Campbell 2009: 833–95; Choi 2005). The result of this general tendency is that Paul's teaching about the role of "faith" in justification is significantly refocused, from human believing to Christ's own faith or faithfulness.

Serious engagement with the larger theological issues informing this debate is beyond the scope of this introduction. Suffice it to say that we do not find the literary and theological reasons for adopting the faith-of-Christ interpretation to be convincing. We evaluate Hays's narrative focus in the introduction to 3:1–4:11 and conclude that the evidence for a controlling christological narrative is less than compelling. Also unconvincing are those who insist that the faith-of-Christ interpretation is necessary in order to rescue Paul's theology from anthropocentrism. A concern with human believing need not contradict Paul's obvious emphasis on God's sovereignty in salvation—particularly since Paul traces human believing in some fashion to God's initiative.[44] Indeed, some kind of balance between divine initiative and human response seems necessary to preserve the typical biblical tension between the two.[45] Nor is the faith-of-Christ interpretation necessary to give adequate space to Paul's participatory categories. Participation, or union, with Christ, is indeed fundamental to Paul's theology and to the argument of Galatians. But it is reductionistic to insist that this category must undergird all of Paul's language and theology. A focus on human believing, as the means by which that union is initiated and sustained, is quite complementary to this focus.

Evaluation of the faith-of-Christ interpretation must therefore focus on linguistic and contextual arguments. Unfortunately, as we suggest above, grammatical arguments fall far short of being conclusive. The genitive case in Greek is notoriously difficult to pin down. The genitive simply restricts the meaning of the head noun through specification; for example, the "faith" involved is a faith that, in some sense, has to do with Christ (see Porter and Pitts 2009: 38–48; Silva 2001: 64–65; Matlock 2000: 17). What exact relationship these two nouns have will depend on the expectations that listeners and readers

44. Indeed, Seifrid (2009) argues that the genitive ['Ιησοῦ] Χριστοῦ designates Christ as the author of our faith.

45. See, e.g., Riches 2008: 133: "Insofar as the argument [he refers specifically to Martyn's 1997 commentary] turns on the perception that Paul wishes above all to emphasize God's initiative in justification, and therefore to have Paul assert that even human believing is God's (not human) work, such a view seems to be in danger of voiding the human reception of such salvific action of any substance at all."

bring to the text.[46] Will their previous understanding lead them to think of Christ as the doer or as the receiver of the action implied in the word "faith"? Indeed, some interpreters argue that it is restrictive and misleading to interpret the genitives in question as either objective or subjective; Paul may intend a broader and less-defined idea (see esp. Ulrichs 2007: 11–23, passim; Schliesser 2007: 257–80; Sprinkle 2009). Nor has appeal to the presence or absence of the article proved useful in deciding the issue.[47] The grammar of the genitive construction is often decided by the meaning of the words within the construction. Here again, however, we face uncertainty. The "ruling" noun, πίστις, can mean either "faith" or "faithfulness," and either meaning can make sense with the two main options for the genitive (e.g., "Christ's faith" or "faith in Christ"; "Christ's faithfulness" or "faithfulness directed toward Christ").[48]

As many interpreters recognize, the meaning of the πίστις Χριστοῦ construction in Paul will have to be determined by broader contextual considerations. These may be divided into two basic categories: the general use of πίστις with genitives and parallel constructions, and the specific literary contexts in which the key phrases appear. We begin with the former.

Extrabiblical instances of πίστις followed by a personal name in the genitive and uninfluenced by biblical teaching are rare. Moreover, they shed little light on NT usage because πίστις typically has the meaning of either "evidence," or "proof" (with the genitive denoting that which is being "proved"),[49] or "confidence" (with the genitive denoting the thing or person in which one has confidence).[50] The LXX has five relevant instances: in each case πίστις means "faithfulness," and the genitive is subjective/possessive (e.g., 1 Macc. 14:35: καὶ εἶδεν ὁ λαὸς τὴν πίστιν τοῦ Σίμωνος, *kai eiden ho laos tēn pistin tou Simōnos*,

46. An example from English might help. One day I was conversing with a student about a photograph in my office and noted that it reminded me of the famous "Ansel Adams photograph." As I thought about what I had just said, I realized that the student would naturally interpret that phrase to mean "a photograph taken by Ansel Adams." For he would have brought to that phrase his understanding that Adams was a well-known photographer. However, in this particular case, I was referring to a photograph of me taking a photograph; and the "Ansel Adams photograph" that I mentioned is one taken by someone else of Adams standing on top of his station wagon with his large view camera on a tripod. My student, for good reasons, interpreted my phrase as a "subjective" genitive; I intended it as an objective genitive." But the point is that the successful interpretation of the phrase depends on information that an interpreter brings to the task.

47. Some interpreters (e.g., Hultgren 1980; Dunn 1997b: 64–66) argue that the NT follows a pattern of using subjective genitives after the articular πίστις (*pistis*, faith; e.g., "*the* faith that [you have]," quoting Fee 2007b: 224). Since, however, πίστις is anarthrous in each of the "faith of Christ" phrases, the genitive in these constructions may be objective. But the rule is not absolute (see Rom. 4:16), and in any case it could not prove anarthrous constructions were objective (see D. Campbell 2009: 643–47; Wallace 1996: 115–16).

48. The early Greek interpreters of Paul interpreted the genitive as objective (see esp. M. Elliott 2009: 277–82; Silva 2004: 228–30).

49. See, e.g., Philo, *Creation* 84: πίστις δὲ τῆς ἀρχῆς (*pistis de tēs archēs*, the proof of [human] rule [AT]).

50. E.g., Plutarch, *Pericles* 15.5: πίστις τοῦ ἀνδρός (*pistis tou andros*, confidence in him [AT]); Philo, *Moses* 2.288: πίστις τῶν μελλόντων (*pistis tōn mellontōn*, confidence in future things [AT]).

"The people saw the faithfulness of Simon").[51] Reflecting a significant new focus on the importance of "faith" (Matlock 2000: 19–20), phrases in which πίστις is followed by a genitive noun or pronoun referring to a person occur forty times in the NT. In almost all of these, the genitive is subjective, or more often, perhaps, simply possessive. Matthew 9:22 is representative: ὁ δὲ Ἰησοῦς στραφεὶς καὶ ἰδὼν αὐτὴν εἶπεν· θάρσει, θύγατερ· ἡ πίστις σου σέσωκέν σε. καὶ ἐσώθη ἡ γυνὴ ἀπὸ τῆς ὥρας ἐκείνης (ho de Iēsous strapheis kai idōn autēn eipen: tharsei, thygater: hē pistis sou sesōken se. kai esōthē hē gynē apo tēs hōras ekeinēs); "Jesus turned and saw her. 'Take heart, daughter,' he said, 'your faith has healed you.' And the woman was healed at that moment."[52] This usage is very common in Paul (Rom. 1:8, 12; 4:5, 11, 12, 16; 1 Cor. 2:5; 15:14, 17; 2 Cor. 10:15; Phil. 2:17; Col. 1:4; 1 Thess. 1:8; 3:2, 5, 6, 7, 10; 2 Thess. 1:3, 4; 2 Tim. 2:18; Titus 1:1; Philem. 5, 6).

In only six passages outside the disputed Pauline texts does a divine name in the genitive follow πίστις. One of these is unambiguously subjective: Rom. 3:3 ("the faithfulness of God"). Two are unambiguously objective: Mark 11:22 ("faith in God"); Acts 3:16 ("faith in his name"). And the other three are probably objective: James 2:1 ("faith in our glorious Lord Jesus");[53] Rev. 2:13 ("faith in me [Christ]"); 14:12 ("faith in Jesus"). Clearly, then, the evidence from πίστις plus personal nouns in the genitive is mixed: most are subjective or possessive; but in the only clear example of a divine name with a subjective genitive, πίστις means "faithfulness" and is therefore only possibly relevant to the (proposed) faith-of-Christ phrases. Moreover, the other five instances of πίστις with a genitive of a divine name are (probably) objective.

Stronger paradigmatic support for the objective genitive view of πίστις Χριστοῦ comes from alternative constructions. First are places where, in place of the genitive, we find a prepositional construction. Twelve (omitting some that are clearly not relevant and also Rom. 3:25 and Gal. 3:26)[54] are found in the NT, and in none of them is the object of the preposition the one who exercises faith. In four texts εἰς (eis, in/into) indicates the object of faith (Acts 20:21; 24:24; 26:18; Col. 2:5) while πρός (pros, toward) is used once in this

51. See also 1 Sam. 26:23; 2 Kings 12:15 (12:16 LXX); Sir. 46:15; Pss. Sol. 8.28.
52. Almost certainly possessive are also Matt. 9:2, 29; 15:28; Mark 2:5; 5:34; 10:52; Luke 5:20; 7:50; 8:25, 48; 17:19; 18:42; 22:32; Rom. 1:8, 12; 4:12, 16; 1 Cor. 2:5; 15:14; 2 Cor. 1:24; 10:15; Phil. 2:17; Col. 1:4; 2:5; 1 Thess. 1:8; 3:2, 5, 6, 7, 10; 2 Thess. 1:3, 4(?); 2 Tim. 2:18; Titus 1:1; Philem. 6; James 1:3; 1 Pet. 1:7; 2 Pet. 1:5; 1 John 5:4; Rev. 13:10.
53. Contra, e.g., Lowe 2009, who argues on the basis of a rhetorical pattern for a subjective genitive. Lowe fails to deal with the fact that every other instance of πίστις in James refers unambiguously to the faith of Christians (and in the immediate context: 2:5, 14–26; cf. McCartney 2009: 135–36).
54. In Rom. 3:25, it is perhaps more likely that ἐν τῷ αὐτοῦ αἵματι (en tō autou haimati, in his blood) modifies ἱλαστήριον (hilastērion, "a sacrifice of atonement [presented] in his blood" [AT]) than πίστεως (pisteōs, faith; Moo 1996: 236–37). Similarly, ἐν Χριστῷ Ἰησοῦ (en Christō Iēsou, in Christ Jesus) in Gal. 3:26 probably modifies the whole clause rather than just πίστεως (see NIV: "So in Christ Jesus you are all children of God through faith"; and our comments on the verse).

sense (Philem. 5). In five texts Paul modifies πίστις with the phrase ἐν [τῷ] Χριστῷ [κυρίου] Ἰησοῦ (*en [tō] Christō [kyriou] Iēsou*, in [the] Christ [Lord] Jesus), the phrase perhaps indicating object (faith in) or perhaps sphere (faith exercised in the sphere of Christ; Eph. 1:15; 1 Tim. 1:14; 3:13; 2 Tim. 1:13; 3:15). And two others, finally, indicate the source of (human) faith, one using διά (*dia*, by; Acts 3:16) and the other ἀπό (*apo*, from; Eph. 6:23). When, therefore, NT authors take the opportunity to make explicit the connection between πίστις and Christ by means of a preposition, they never suggest that the πίστις in question is exercised *by* Christ. This makes it unlikely that the simple genitive has the sense "exercised by."[55]

The second important line of paradigmatic evidence comes from verbal constructions. As their names suggest, the "subjective" and "objective" genitives concretize in nominal form essentially verbal ideas. Hence πίστις Χριστοῦ, if an objective genitive construction, would be verbalized as "one believes in/ toward Christ"; if a subjective genitive construction, "Christ believes/has faith/ is faithful." Yet only once in the NT (John 2:24) is Christ the subject of the verb πιστεύω (*pisteuō*), and the verb there means not "believe" but "entrust" (as the reflexive αὐτόν indicates): αὐτὸς δὲ Ἰησοῦς οὐκ ἐπίστευεν αὐτὸν αὐτοῖς διὰ τὸ αὐτὸν γινώσκειν πάντας (*autos de Iēsous ouk episteuen auton autois dia to auton ginōskein pantas*; "But Jesus would not entrust himself to them, for he knew all people").[56] In comparison, humans are the subject of the verb πιστεύω almost two hundred times in the NT, fifty of which are in Paul. This almost universal pattern—in which humans are the subject of πιστεύω and, when an object of some kind is indicated, it is invariably God or Christ or the gospel or the Word of God (using the dative or a variety of prepositions or, in the case of propositions, ὅτι, *hoti*, that)—provides a very strong argument for taking the disputed genitives in a general "objective" sense.

We turn now, finally, to what most interpreters rightly consider to be the single most important factor in deciding the meaning of the (proposed) faith-of-Christ phrases: the literary context in which the phrase appears. Our focus will naturally be on Galatians (for the contextual arguments in Romans, see Moo 1996, at the relevant verses). A considerable number of contextual arguments are advanced for the subjective-genitive interpretation, four of which we will mention here. The most important is the claim (noted above) that underlying Gal. 3–4 is a narrative about the life of Christ. If this were true, it would not prove that "faith of Christ" refers to Christ's own faith/faithfulness; but it

---

55. Of course, this pattern also raises the question of why Paul in these texts would choose to use the genitive rather than a prepositional phrase. Perhaps he wants to match the phrase with its opposite ἔργων νόμου (*ergōn nomou*, works of the law), which occurs in direct rhetorical opposition to "faith of Christ" in the first occurrence of the latter (Gal. 2:16) and is found in the near context of other occurrences (Rom. 3:22, 26; cf. Rom. 3:20, 28).

56. Douglas Campbell (2009: 914–24) has recently argued that the quotation of Ps. 116:10 in 2 Cor. 4:13 might be a second such instance; that Paul may intend to attribute the words ἐπίστευσα, διὸ ἐλάλησα (*episteusa, dio elalēsa*, I believed; therefore I have spoken) to Christ. See also Kibbe 2012 on "the obedience of Christ" in 2 Cor. 10:5.

would provide a context in which such references would make perfect sense. As indicated above, sufficient evidence to justify this underlying narrative is lacking (see the additional note on 3:7–4:11). A second argument for the faith-of-Christ interpretation is that reference to human faith "in" Christ in two of the key texts in Galatians (2:16 and 3:22) would be redundant since Paul explicitly refers to human believing in Christ in a verbal clause within each of the verses. The argument about redundancy has been significant in the debate, since the same issue arises in Rom. 3:22. While no consensus has emerged, there is a growing recognition on both sides of the issue that this argument is not compelling. What one interpreter labels "redundancy" or "tautology," another sees as repetition for emphasis. Third, Douglas Campbell (2009: 610–21) has argued that "faith of Jesus Christ" is ultimately rooted in Hab. 2:4, and that this verse is interpreted by Paul as a reference to the faith/faithfulness of Messiah. Campbell may be right to argue that Hab. 2:4 has influenced Paul's locution ἐκ πίστεως (ek pisteōs, by faith): the phrase is comparatively rare, and it is concentrated in just those books (Galatians and Romans) in which Paul quotes Hab. 2:4. But Campbell's claim that Paul identifies "the righteous one" of Hab. 2:4 with Christ cannot be sustained (see, e.g., Watson 2009: 149, 159–62 and my comments on Gal. 3:11).

The fourth argument is the single most important "surface" contextual argument in favor of the faith-of-Christ interpretation. Galatians 3:22–25, it is claimed, virtually requires that "faith of Christ" refer to Christ's own faith:

ἀλλὰ συνέκλεισεν ἡ γραφὴ τὰ πάντα ὑπὸ ἁμαρτίαν, ἵνα ἡ ἐπαγγελία ἐκ πίστεως Ἰησοῦ Χριστοῦ δοθῇ τοῖς πιστεύουσιν. ²³Πρὸ τοῦ δὲ ἐλθεῖν τὴν πίστιν ὑπὸ νόμον ἐφρουρούμεθα συγκλειόμενοι εἰς τὴν μέλλουσαν πίστιν ἀποκαλυφθῆναι, ²⁴ὥστε ὁ νόμος παιδαγωγὸς ἡμῶν γέγονεν εἰς Χριστόν, ἵνα ἐκ πίστεως δικαιωθῶμεν· ²⁵ἐλθούσης δὲ τῆς πίστεως οὐκέτι ὑπὸ παιδαγωγόν ἐσμεν.

Alla synekleisen hē graphē ta panta hypo hamartian, hina hē epangelia ek pisteōs Iēsou Christou dothē tois pisteuousin. ²³Pro tou de elthein tēn pistin hypo nomon ephrouroumetha synkleiomenoi eis tēn mellousan pistin apokalyphthēnai, ²⁴hōste ho nomos paidagōgos hēmōn gegonen eis Christon, hina ek pisteōs dikaiōthōmen: ²⁵elthousēs de tēs pisteōs ouketi hypo paidagōgon esmen.

But Scripture has locked up everything under the control of sin, so that what was promised, being given through faith in Jesus Christ, might be given to those who believe. ²³Before the coming of this faith, we were held in custody under the law, locked up until the faith that was to come would be revealed. ²⁴So the law was put in charge of us until Christ came that we might be justified by faith. ²⁵Now that this faith has come, we are no longer under the supervision of the law. (NIV adapted)

The "faith" mentioned in verses 23 and 25, it is argued, must be the same as the πίστις Ἰησοῦ Χριστοῦ in verse 22 (the article on πίστιν in verse 23 being anaphoric). Yet this faith, Paul says, "came," it was "revealed," and it ended the custodianship of the law. Human believing, as Paul makes clear with reference to Abraham, has always existed (3:6–9). The faith that enters salvation history, ending the era of the law's dominion, must thus be some other kind of faith. Moreover, it must be a singular event, since it created such a shift in salvation history. And since Paul in this context identifies the coming of Christ as the event that caused this shift, it makes good sense to identify πίστιν in verse 22 as Christ's own faith/faithfulness that led to and culminated in his giving of himself on the cross (see 2:20). (See Caneday 2009 for a good summary of the theological appropriateness of the subjective interpretation in Galatians.)

This last argument is strong, and it is understandable why so many interpreters have, for this reason and others, adopted the faith-of-Christ interpretation. Yet there are also strong contextual arguments for the traditional faith-in-Christ interpretation, arguments that we think ultimately carry more weight. First, negatively, the "faith" that "comes" in 3:23 and 25 might refer back to the participle τοῖς πιστεύουσιν at the end of verse 22 rather than to πίστεως Ἰησοῦ Χριστοῦ earlier in the verse (see our comments on this verse). Second, positively and more importantly, the reference to "faith" in 3:22 must be read in continuity with the theme of faith that is central to Paul's argument from 2:16 onward. And central to this whole argument is the faith of Abraham (3:6–9). The discussion of Abraham's faith in this paragraph is a Janus, pointing both backward and forward. As the καθώς in 3:6 shows, the "hearing of faith" (ἀκοὴ πίστεως) of 3:2 and 5 is compared to the faith of Abraham. And the reference to being blessed along with "Abraham who believed" (τῷ πιστῷ Ἀβραάμ, *tō pistō Abraam*) in verse 9 connects with the claim in verse 14 that the "blessing of Abraham," related in some way to the "promised Spirit," is given through faith. "Faith," then, in this crucial middle part of Paul's argument, is unarguably human faith.[57] This, however, makes it unlikely that "faith" has any other significance in those references that extend further in either direction: back to 2:16 and 20 (the references to πίστις immediately prior to 3:2) or forward to 3:22 (the next reference to πίστις after 3:14; see esp. Dunn 2008a: 361–65; Ulrichs 2007: 140–48; Hunn 2006: 30–33). We should also note that "faith" first appears in Galatians (apart from 1:23, where the word is used with a different sense) in contrast to "works of the law" (2:16; and see again 3:2, 5). Here we are in danger of arguing in a circle; but if, as we think very likely, "works of the law" refers to human doing of the law of Moses, the contrast with this phrase is more likely to be a reference to human believing than to Christ's believing, or faithfulness (Watson 2009: 150–52).

We conclude, then, that the traditional interpretation of the phrase πίστις Χριστοῦ as a reference to human believing "in" Christ is well grounded.[58] This understanding of the genitive is strongly suggested by parallel constructions and fits the context of Galatians better than the alternative. God has taken

---

57. It is significant that de Boer, who interprets πίστις (*pistis*) as the faith/faithfulness of Christ throughout the letter, must cavalierly dismiss the significance of Gen. 15:6 in Paul's argument (2011: 191).

58. After surveying early Christian interpreters, M. Elliott (2009: 289) concludes: "Any 'reintroduction' of 'the faith of Jesus Christ' will occur, it seems, *despite* the evidence of the witness of the tradition of Christian theology" (see also Wallis 1995; Harrisville 1994).

the initiative in salvation, sending his Son "in the fullness of time" to identify with humans for their redemption (4:4–5). Christ has willingly undertaken the mission, loving humans and giving himself up on their behalf (2:19). This divine initiative in salvation is what Paul calls "grace" (e.g., 2:21), and Paul assumes it throughout his argument in Galatians. But the particular issue he confronts in this letter requires him to focus attention on the human reception of this gift of God in Christ. "Faith" is the corollary, from the human side, of God's grace. The indispensability of and exclusivity of faith—not only "by faith," but also "by faith alone"—is the key theological argument of the letter.

Justification/Righteousness

The language of justification and righteousness is woven into the fabric of Galatians. The verb δικαιόω (dikaioō, justify) occurs eight times (2:16 [3x], 17; 3:8, 11, 24; 5:4), proportionately more often than in any of Paul's other letters (it occurs fifteen times in the 7,111 verses of Romans, compared with the eight occurrences in 2,230 verses of Galatians; it is found only four other times in the rest of Paul's Letters). The noun δικαιοσύνη (diakaiosynē, righteousness) occurs much less frequently: only four occurrences in Galatians (2:21; 3:6 [= Gen. 15:6], 21; 5:5), in comparison with thirty-three in Romans (and twenty elsewhere in Paul). The only other δικ- word in Galatians is δίκαιος (dikaios, righteous), which occurs once, in 3:11 (seven times in Romans, ten times elsewhere). Justification has long been thought to be a key (and for many *the* key) concept in Galatians. The subject is important enough, and the evidence complex and debated enough, to warrant a rather extensive discussion of the language and theology of justification in the letter.

I. RIGHTEOUSNESS LANGUAGE IN THE OT AND JUDAISM

The word δικαιόω and its cognates were used in secular Greek (survey in G. Schrenk, *TDNT* 2:178–225; Seifrid 2004), but the widespread and theologically significant use of the terminology in the LXX, along with Paul's frequent appeal to the OT in discussing the words, shows that the OT/Jewish background is decisive. Words from the δικ- root consistently (though not universally) translate words from the צדק (ṣdq) root: δικαιοσύνη normally translates צֶדֶק (ṣedeq) and צְדָקָה (ṣĕdāqâ; both probably have the same meaning);[59] δικαιόω usually translates צָדַק (ṣādaq), and δίκαιος renders צַדִּיק (ṣaddîq; for full survey of the OT data, see Ziesler 1972: 22–67; Seifrid 2001). By the same token, words from the צדק root are translated by Greek words from the δικ- root in the large majority of cases. This considerable linguistic overlap suggests that the meaning of δικ- words for Greek-speaking Jews like Paul would have been decisively influenced by the meaning of צדק words. The denotation of these words has been a matter of long-standing controversy. Older scholarship

---

59. Snaith 1946: 90; J. J. Scullion, *ABD* 5:725–26. Contra, e.g., Crüsemann 1976; Seifrid 2001: 428. On the recent discussion of this matter, see Schliesser 2007.

debated whether the root idea of צדק language was conformity to a norm[60] or "mutual fulfillment of claims arising from a particular relationship."[61] More recently, scholars have debated how closely righteousness language in the OT is tied to the covenant, some arguing that צדק words almost always assume the covenantal structure (see esp. N. Wright 2009: 55–78), while others think the language is set in a wider context. But we are not faced here with an either/or proposition. Many instances of צדק language reveal that the norm or relationship that lies behind צדק is God's own character or his commitment to do "right" to his creation. Indeed, the idea of "right order" or "rightness," stemming from the way that God has created the world we live in, seems to be a very common nuance in the language (see esp. Seifrid 2001; Westerholm 2004: 267–78). At the same time, then, God's decision to bind himself and Israel in a covenant relationship means that many instances of the צדק root assume that this "rightness" is defined (though certainly not exhausted) in terms of this covenantal structure.[62]

While heeding Seifrid's warning about not imposing on the rich vocabulary of righteousness in the OT a single *Grundbegriff* (basic idea; 2001: 418), we suggest that these words often, and perhaps even basically, allude to the notion of doing, or being, "right," the "rightness" being determined by the particular situation in which one is placed. A weight is "right" (צֶדֶק [ṣedeq], LXX δίκαιον [dikaion]) when it conforms to agreed-upon standards of measurement (Lev. 19:36); Noah is "right" (צַדִּיק [ṣaddîq], LXX δίκαιος) when he conforms to God's will for him (Gen. 6:9); a person, whether in covenant relationship or not, is "right" when conforming to the standards built into this world by God (צַדִּיק [δίκαιος] very often in Proverbs); an Israelite is "right" (צַדִּיק, LXX δίκαιος) when conforming to the expectations of the covenant relationship (e.g., Ezek. 18:9); God's decrees are "right" (צַדִּיקִים [ṣaddîqîm], LXX δίκαια) when (and because) they conform to his own person and will (e.g., Deut. 4:8; Ps. 119:7 and passim); God is "right" (צַדִּיק, δίκαιος) when he punishes his people (Neh. 9:33), because this judgment is in conformity with God's warning about punishment for covenant unfaithfulness; and at the same time, God is "right" (צְדָקָה, LXX δικαιοσύνη) when he acts to vindicate his people (e.g., Isa. 51:4–8) because this, too, is in conformity with his gracious promise to redeem his people after judgment. Of course, as we have noted, the "norm"

---

60. This view is associated esp. with Kautzsch 1881. Modern scholarship has tended to move away from this derivation; though see Snaith 1946: 90–97; Hill 1967: 83; and Kuyper 1977: 233–34 (however, the latter two understand the "norm" involved to be the terms of the covenant). For a concise survey, see Piper 1983: 82–83; Seifrid 2001: 419–22.

61. See esp. Cremer 1899, whose proposal has been followed by a large number of modern OT scholars. Seifrid (2001: 421) helpfully suggests that the fulfilling of the obligations of a relationship should be seen as a concretizing of the more general "conformity to a norm" idea. See also Schmid 1968.

62. For a balanced view that recognizes the significance of covenant for the OT righteousness language while at the same time rooting it in a larger and more basic context, see esp. Bird 2006: 116–18; Dumbrell 1992: 91–92. As Seifrid (2001: 424) puts it, "All 'covenant-keeping' is righteous behavior, but not all righteous behavior is 'covenant-keeping.'"

by which "rightness" is measured will often be a particular relationship (e.g., the covenant), but it is perhaps not common for the language to denote that relationship as such. On the other hand, "righteousness" language will, by a simple extension, often connote the status of a person who has conformed to the expected norm.

A. Δικαιόω. The verb δικαιόω occurs forty-four times in the LXX, and in all but six occurrences where there is a Hebrew original, it translates a form of צדק. In the Qal stem this verb means "to be righteous," in the Piel "to be demonstrated as righteous," and in the Hiphil "to declare righteous" (see Ziesler 1972: 18–22). The nine times δικαιόω translates the Hiphil of צדק are particularly significant for Paul's usage. This form of the verb almost always has a judicial or forensic flavor. Sometimes the "judge" who "pronounces righteous," or acquits, is human (Deut. 25:1; Isa. 5:23), and at other times divine (Exod. 23:7; 1 Kings 8:32; 2 Chron. 6:23; Ps. 82:3; Isa. 50:8). Even when the term is not used with explicit reference to the lawcourt, the forensic connotations remain (cf. Gen. 38:26; 44:16; Jer. 3:11; Ezek. 16:51–52). This legal justification is a recognition of the reality that the person being "justified" is, in fact, "just": Israelite judges are to "justify the just and condemn the ungodly [LXX: δικαιώσωσιν τὸν δίκαιον καὶ καταγνῶσιν τοῦ ἀσεβοῦς, *dikaiōsōsin ton dikaion kai katagnōsin tou asebous*]" (Deut. 25:1 AT; cf. 1 Kings 8:32; 2 Chron. 6:23). A key symptom of injustice is the "justifying" of the guilty (Isa. 5:23), in contrast to the strict and accurate judicial assessment of the Lord, who "will not justify the guilty" (Exod. 23:7 AT). Thus OT "justification" takes the form of a legal recognition of an already-existing "righteousness" (see, e.g., Westerholm 2004: 263–64).

B. Δικαιοσύνη. The noun δικαιοσύνη, which occurs more than three hundred times in the LXX, is applied both to God and to human beings. The forensic connotation in the use of the Hiphil of the verb is much less obvious in the case of human δικαιοσύνη. The word becomes a general way of describing what is "well pleasing" to God. When the psalmist asks God to deal with him "according to my righteousness," the word is set in parallel to "the cleanness of my hands" (Ps. 18:20; cf. also v. 24) and denotes the moral integrity of the psalmist. It is therefore frequently said that "righteousness" is an ethical idea in the OT.[63] This is not wrong, but it is somewhat inadequate. For "righteousness" is also more broadly a description of the "rightness" that is incumbent upon human beings by virtue of the divinely created world in which they live. "Righteousness" in this sense can describe the state of persons who have fulfilled the expectations placed upon them by their divinely created status and/or their covenant relation—including behavior but also penetrating to the heart attitude. In Isa. 46:12–13, for instance, the Lord says to Israel, "Listen to me, you stubborn-hearted, you who are now far from my righteousness. I am bringing my righteousness near, it is not far away; and my salvation will

---

63. E.g., Ziesler 1972: 24–27. Seifrid (2001: 422) criticizes Ziesler for using the overly generalized categories of "ethical" and "forensic."

not be delayed. I will grant salvation to Zion, my splendor to Israel." Motyer comments: "They *are far from righteousness*, from conformity to the will, character, and purposes of the Lord, and he will implement his *righteousness*, all that accords with his will, character and purposes, everything that is 'right' with God" (1993: 370).[64] In this sense, "righteousness" often serves as a summary term, describing the "state of rightness before God." See, for example, Ezek. 33:12–13:

> Therefore, son of man, say to your people, "If someone who is righteous disobeys, that person's former righteousness will count for nothing. And if someone who is wicked repents, that person's former wickedness will not bring condemnation. The righteous person who sins will not be allowed to live even though they were formerly righteous." [13]If I tell a righteous person that they will surely live, but then they trust in their righteousness and do evil, none of the righteous things that person has done will be remembered; they will die for the evil they have done.

The "righteousness" (צְדָקָה) to which Ezekiel refers appears to be the general state of "rightness" in which people may be tempted to put their trust, even as they do evil. As Seifrid notes, "An absolute distinction between 'status' and 'behavior' is illegitimate" (2001: 422). As the many places where people are said to be characterized by "righteousness" reveal (e.g., 1 Kings 3:6; 8:32; Pss. 7:8; 18:20), this is not a matter of sinless perfection, but of a person's fundamental spiritual direction and values.

This is also quite possibly the sense of Deut. 6:25 ("And if we are careful to obey all this law before the LORD our God, as he has commanded us, that will be our righteousness [צְדָקָה, *ṣĕdāqâ*; LXX ἐλεημοσύνη, *eleēmosynē*]") and of the well-known Gen. 15:6 ("Abram believed the LORD, and he credited it to him as righteousness [צְדָקָה, LXX δικαιοσύνη]"). "Righteousness" in these latter two texts is often said to mean "right relationship," an interpretation stemming from the popular belief that OT צדק language often has a relational sense. However, as we argue above, the connotation of "conformity to a norm" seems to be very common in the use of "righteousness" language, and so it might be the case in these texts that "righteousness" refers to this "rightness."

The noun δικαιοσύνη also occurs almost a hundred times in the OT (LXX) with reference to God. In secular Greek, God's δικαιοσύνη is usually a divine attribute, but most of the biblical occurrences possess a more active or relational meaning. For instance, in Ps. 51:14 David prays, "Deliver me from the guilt of bloodshed, O God, you who are God my Savior, and my tongue will sing of your righteousness [τὴν δικαιοσύνην σου, *tēn dikaiosynēn sou*]" (50:16 LXX). In such passages, "righteousness" becomes the norm by which God himself acts.[65] There is considerable debate, as we note above, over whether

---

64. See also, e.g., Davidson 1996: 109–10; Morris 1984: 234, who speaks broadly of conformity to God's standards.

65. See Exod. 15:13; Pss. 35:24; 36:6, 10; 71:2; 89:16; 103:17; 111:3; 119:40; 143:1, 11; 145:7 (LXX: 34:24; 35:7, 11; 70:2; 88:17; 102:17; 110:3; 118:40; 142:1, 11; 144:7); Isa. 38:19; 63:7. In these

this norm is an absolute (residing in God or as an aspect of God's person) or whether the norm is relational (existing because of the covenant to which God has bound himself). In the second sense, God's "righteousness" can sometimes come to refer to the norms of the covenant. Many contemporary scholars therefore think "God's righteousness" in Paul is basically God's "covenant faithfulness" (Hill 1967: 156; esp. N. Wright 2009: 55–78). In some contexts this is undoubtedly the case, but it would be wrong to establish this as the all-embracing *meaning* of God's righteousness. First, righteousness language and covenant language are rarely found together (Seifrid 2001: 423–24; although, in fairness, if covenant is a basic-enough category, this is not altogether surprising). And, as we noted above, there are many contexts in which the "standard" by which God is judged to do "right" goes beyond (and behind) the terms of the covenant. God's righteousness, then, while finding particular historical expression in his faithfulness in maintaining the "right" of his covenant people, is finally rooted more deeply in his own character as God.[66] Second, reference to "covenant faithfulness" begs a crucial question: what "covenant" are we talking about?[67] N. T. Wright, one of the most important defenders of the "covenant-faithfulness" interpretation, refers repeatedly to God's fulfillment of his promises made to Abraham in this regard (e.g., 2009: 57). The "covenant" involved, then, is not the Sinai covenant narrowly construed, but the promises that God first made to Abraham and the patriarchs and which he renewed in the Sinai covenant (see esp. Deut. 27–30). What, then, is the status of this language in Paul, who importantly distinguishes the Abrahamic covenant from the Mosaic (e.g., Gal. 3:15–18)?

In other OT passages, God's "righteousness" refers to his activity in establishing "right." God promises through the prophet Isaiah: "I am bringing my righteousness near, it is not far away; and my salvation will not be delayed" (Isa. 46:13). As the parallel with "salvation" shows, "God's righteousness" in such passages denotes his "putting his people in the right," not in a moral sense but as an act of justice, or vindication. This language is especially prominent in Isa. 46–55, a passage that exerted considerable influence on Paul. In addition to several other occurrences of δικαιοσύνη with this sense in these chapters (48:18; 51:5, 6, 8; 54:14), the verb is also found: "He who vindicates [δικαιώσας,

---

texts, δικαιοσύνη (*dikaiosynē*, righteousness) translates Heb. חֶסֶד (*ḥesed*, loving-kindness) twice (Exod. 15:13; Isa. 63:7), אֱמֶת (*ʾemet*, truth) once (Isa. 38:19), and is paralleled by words such as ἀλήθεια (*alētheia*, truth: Pss. 36:6; 88:12; 98:2–3; 143:1 [35:6; 87:12; 97:2–3; 142:1]; Isa. 38:3, 19), ἔλεος (*eleos*, mercy: Pss. 31:1; 36:6–7, 10; 88:11–12; 98:2–3; 103:17; 143:11–12 [30:2; 35:6–7, 11; 87:12–13; 97:2–3; 102:17; 142:11–12]), and χρηστότης (*chrēstotēs*, goodness: Ps. 145:7 [144:7]). Note, e.g., Ps. 36:6–7a (35:6–7a LXX): "LORD, your mercy [ἔλεος] is in heaven, and your truth [ἀλήθεια] unto the clouds; your righteousness [δικαιοσύνη] is as the mountains of God" (AT).

66. Piper (1983: 100 and elsewhere) has argued that the reference is specifically to God's acting for his own glory. But the connections with this idea are not direct enough to justify this more restricted interpretation.

67. Horton (2007: 11–36) has drawn attention to the tendency of contemporary NT scholars (and especially those who defend some form of the "New Perspective") to assume a mono-covenantalism that distorts the biblical categories.

dikaiōsas] me is near. Who then will bring charges against me? Let us face each other! Who is my accuser? Let him confront me!" (Isa. 50:8, a text Paul alludes to in Rom. 8:33).[68] While most occurrences of "righteousness" language in this sense refer to God's activity of "establishing right" or "vindication," a few may suggest the notion of the status of "having been vindicated." See, for instance, Isa. 46:12–13: "Listen to me, you stubborn-hearted, you who are now far from my righteousness. I am bringing my righteousness near, it is not far away; and my salvation will not be delayed. I will grant salvation to Zion, my splendor to Israel" (and see also Pss. 4:1; 35:27–28; 37:6; Isa. 62:2).

C. Δίκαιος. The adjective δίκαιος (*dikaios*, righteous), the most common δικ- word in the LXX (almost 400 occurrences), is used of the person who is characterized by δικαιοσύνη. It is the standard way by which the godly, or pious, person is denoted (cf., e.g., Prov. 10–13). It occurs only once in Galatians, in Paul's quotation of Hab. 2:4 (Gal. 3:11).

II. The Meaning of Righteousness Language in Galatians

In what remains the most substantial lexical/theological study of the language of righteousness in Paul, John Ziesler (1972) argues that the verb δικαιόω has a narrow forensic sense but that the noun δικαιοσύνη (*dikaiosynē*, righteousness) refers to a combination of forensic and moral righteousness (cf. also R. Longenecker 1990: e.g., 95). This neat distinction has, however, drawn few followers. And rightly so.[69] In Galatians, certainly, the verb and the noun overlap significantly. Every occurrence of the noun comes in close proximity to the verb (cf. 2:21 [noun] and 2:16 [verb]; cf. 3:6 and 3:8; cf. 3:21 and 3:24; cf. 5:5 and 5:4), and in each case the context strongly suggests that the verb and the noun occupy the same basic semantic space (for elaboration, see the commentary on the relevant texts).

Both δικαιόω (*dikaioō*, justify) and δικαιοσύνη have to do with the conveying of (in the case of the verb), or possession of (the noun), right standing with God. In using the language in this way, Paul follows one significant strand of usage in the OT. As we have noted, both words are used in the OT to refer to the establishment of legal right, or vindication. And we also noticed that Isa. 46–55 provides several significant occurrences of this language. These chapters predict that Yahweh, by means of his Servant (49:1–7; 52:13–53:12), will establish and display the "rightness" of Israel; he will "vindicate" his people. This seems to be one of the wells from which Paul draws his distinctive language of "justification." To be sure, unlike Romans, where allusions to these texts are obvious, Galatians does not clearly ground the language in these Isaiah texts (though it may be no accident that Paul quotes from Isa. 54:1 in Gal. 4:27). We may, however, surmise that this use of "righteousness" language was common

---

68. See also, with the noun δικιαοσύνη, Pss. 22:31; 35:28; 40:10; 69:27; 71:15, 16, 19, 24; 88:12; 98:2; 119:123 [LXX: 21:32; 34:28; 39:10; 68:28; 70:15, 16, 18, 24; 87:13; 97:2; 118:123]; Mic. 6:5; 7:9.

69. For brief critiques of Ziesler (1972) on this point, see Seifrid 2001: 442; Reumann 1982: 56–59.

ground among Paul, the agitators, and the Galatians. In his first use of the language, Paul's claim that he and his fellow Jews "know" about the manner of justification (2:15–16) certainly suggests that the language was common currency in the early church (or at least the Pauline-influenced early church) before Paul wrote Galatians. Another source for Paul's use of this language is, of course, Gen. 15:6, where God considers Abraham's faith to be equivalent to his discharge of all the obligations incumbent upon him (for this meaning of Gen. 15:6, see the additional note on 3:6).

If one might describe the material in the last paragraph as a matter of general scholarly consensus, the same cannot be said of another matter: the degree to which, in Galatians, Paul "redefines" justification language to mean "to be declared to be members of God's people." N. T. Wright (2009: 116), while acknowledging that justification language functions in the metaphorical sphere of the lawcourt, insists that Paul reflects the strongly covenantal context of the language in the OT, and in light of the immediate context (where the issue is "Who can eat at the same table together?"; 2:11–14), uses δικαιόω in its first programmatic occurrence in Galatians to mean "to be reckoned by God to be a true member of his family, and hence with the right to share table fellowship," thereby putting particular emphasis on the inclusion of Gentiles (2:15–16). This initial usage sets the tone for the letter as a whole, with δικαιοσύνη thus meaning, in turn, "membership in God's true family" (2009: 121). In typical Wrightian fashion, however, these apparently "either/ or" propositions—forensic verdict of acquittal *or* membership in God's family—are later (in his latest book on the matter) relativized with "both/and" language—forensic acquittal *and* membership in God's family (see esp. 2009: 133–34). So the real question is not whether, as Wright himself (too strongly) puts it, "The lawcourt metaphor behind the language of justification, and of the status 'righteous' which someone has when the court has found in their favor, has *given way to* [emphasis added] the clear sense of 'membership in God's people'" (2009: 121); the question is, rather, whether the notion of membership in the people of God should be *added to* the notion of forensic acquittal, and indeed added to such extent that the latter becomes the dominant idea in the letter.

N. T. Wright (and others who follow a similar interpretation) is correct, of course, that Paul's first announcement of "justification by faith" comes in a dual context, both contexts being dominated by the issue of Gentile inclusion: the dispute at Antioch (2:11–14) and the crisis in Galatia. However, more precisely, the issue in both situations was not the inclusion of Gentiles in the new messianic community per se (which, as far as we can tell, no one was disputing) but the terms on which they should be included. More important, Wright's claim that δικαιόω in 2:16 sheds some of its forensic connotation because "Paul is not in a lawcourt, he is at a dinner table" (2009: 116) illegitimately privileges context over semantics. Only a few pages later, Wright claims that lawcourt imagery is "always there by implication in the language of 'justification'" (128), and he should observe this sound semantic observation in his interpretation of 2:16. In this text, and the paragraph of which it is a part, Paul is using the Antioch incident as a jumping-off place to address the central theological issue that lies behind that incident and the situation in Galatia as well. And in both situations, this issue is the terms on which people can expect to find right standing with God. The focus is on Gentile inclusion; but Paul stresses that Jews also "know" that this right standing comes by christologically oriented faith and not by "works of the law" (2:16); if right standing with God could come by means of the torah, Christ need not have died at all (v. 21). This fundamental theological fact—"the truth of the gospel" for which Paul fought in Jerusalem (2:5) and which Peter has called into question by his conduct at Antioch (2:14)—makes clear that it is wrong for Peter, by his withdrawal from table fellowship in Antioch, to force Gentiles to "Judaize" (2:14)—and equally wrong for the agitators to insist that the Gentile Galatians succumb to circumcision and a torah lifestyle (3:1–5; 5:2–6). There is no good contextual reason to insist that "justify" in 2:16 must be redefined to mean, or to include, the notion of membership in God's people. There is no need to collapse the two concepts into one. As Simon Gathercole (2004a: 156) insists, "The *content* of the doctrine of justification by faith should be distinguished from its *scope*." The flow of the text makes perfect sense if Paul in 2:16 is using the δικαιόω language in its well-attested sense "declare righteous."

Membership in God's people and justification are closely related, but they are not identical. One entails the other, but they are not the same. Paul argues both points in Galatians: people by their faith in Christ are established as "righteous" in God's sight; and by that faith they are brought into the people of God. But in Galatians, as in Paul's Letters in general, justification does not in itself refer to belonging to God's people; still less does justification include how one *knows* a person belongs to God's people.[70]

One other definitional issue pertaining to justification in Galatians requires brief mention. Some recent interpreters (echoing, to be sure, a minor strand in the Reformation theological heritage), out of an express concern to counteract the ethical indifference that they think tends to follow from a strictly forensic view of justification, want to expand the scope of justification to include a transformative element.[71] Paul can certainly use the word

---

70. In N. T. Wright's earlier writing on justification, he separated justification from conversion, arguing that justification is a declaration of a relationship that has been previously established via conversion (2002: 268; see also 1997: 113–33; 2005: 111–13). This way of describing justification has considerable resonance with the Reformation tradition, which often conceptualizes the matter in just this way. But in contrast to Wright, the tradition rightly notes that justification is closely tied to conversion itself; if not the actual point of "transfer"—Sanders's "getting in"—it is clearly bound up with it (see, e.g., Rom. 5:1, 9; 1 Cor. 6:11; see on this point, e.g., Piper 2007: 39–44; Gathercole 2006: 228–31). This insistence on separating justification from conversion is not as evident in Wright's latest book on the subject (2009). For a broader criticism of Wright's view on justification, see esp. Gathercole 2006; Bird 2006: esp. 115–16; Bird 2007: 113–54; R. S. Smith 2001: 89–92; P. O'Brien 2004a: esp. 286–95; Piper 2007.

71. The transformative power of justification is an important part of Käsemann's famous definition of "God's righteousness" in terms of both gift and power (see, e.g., 1969). The

δικαιοσύνη, in continuation with the OT and other NT authors, to refer to appropriate ethical behavior (e.g., Rom. 6:13, 16, 18, 19, 20; Eph. 5:9; 1 Tim. 6:11; cf. Matt. 5:20; Luke 1:75; Acts 10:35; James 1:20). But these occurrences should not be incorporated into the concept of Pauline "justification." Here we face a fundamental methodological issue: which occurrences of δικ- language in Paul should be the building blocks in our construction of the *concept* of justification in Paul? Paul operates with two semantic categories of δικ- (*dik-*) *language*—for the sake of brevity, the "moral" and the "forensic"—which can be distinguished on the basis of sound syntagmatic considerations. Most of Paul's uses of δικαιοσύνη echo the basic semantic force of the verb, referring to the status of righteousness that the action, or verdict, of "justify" confers.[72] It is a mistake to merge these categories. Every occurrence of δικ- language in Galatians (with the possible exception of δίκαιος in 3:11) relates to the doctrine of justification; and in Galatians, justification is forensic. The issue in the letter is all about status before God.

Paul is certainly concerned about the transformation of character in Galatians, as the section 5:13–6:10 reveals most clearly. But to argue that this concern must be *part of* justification assumes that transformation can become part of what it means to be a Christian only if it is folded into justification. Following the lead of Calvin and many others in the Reformed tradition, we think it does much better justice to Paul if we connect forensic justification with transformation by viewing both as inevitable and necessary products of our being "in Christ." While certainly not explicitly taught in Galatians, the idea that our union with Christ produces these two inseparable but distinguishable benefits is clearly hinted at. Being "in Christ" is foundational, as the important summarizing paragraph 3:26–29 makes clear. Paul explicitly relates justification to participation in Christ in 2:17—"seeking to be justified *in Christ*"—and union with Christ appears at key points elsewhere in the letter (1:22; 2:4; 2:19–20; 5:6, 24; 6:14). Since Christ is *the* "seed of Abraham" (3:16), it can be only in and through Christ that a person can receive the promised "blessing of Abraham" and "the promise of the Spirit" (3:14). This verse reveals as clearly as any the underlying "theologic" of the letter. The "blessing of Abraham" is, in context, justification (C. Lee 2009: 48–57). "The promise of the Spirit" looks back to 3:2, 5; but just as important yet often not recognized, this language also anticipates Paul's argument in 5:13–6:10. Paul's association of the blessing of Abraham and the promise of the Spirit depends on the prophetic anticipation of the fulfillment of God's promise to Abraham being accompanied by the transforming work of God's Spirit (C.

---

transformative nature of justification was hinted at in the work of A. Schlatter (e.g., 1998: 248–50) and has also been a hallmark of Stuhlmacher's approach to righteousness (1966; 2001: 62–67; 2005: 332–34). See also Jüngel 2001: 208–11; Garlington 1994: 155–61; and most recently, Gorman 2009; D. Campbell 2009. (See Moo 2010b for a critical review of D. Campbell 2009.)

72. Westerholm (2004: 276–77) perceptively notes that Paul's use of δικαιοσύνη is derived from his use of the verb δικαιόω (*dikaioō*, justify) and that it is the verb that stands in continuity with the OT.

Lee 2009: esp. 312–13). It is this transforming work of the Spirit, creating the conformity to God's will that the law was unable to accomplish, that is the theme of 5:13–6:10. In 3:13–14, then, Paul traces back to our association with Christ in his death—taking our curse on himself—the twin blessings of justification and transformation. Union with Christ, not justification, lies at the heart of Paul's theology.[73] But forensic justification is one of the primary and critical benefits that people who belong to Christ by faith receive. And in Galatians this forensic issue comes to the surface because the letter focuses resolutely on key questions: Who will experience God's vindicating judgment in their favor? And by what means?

III. The Importance of Justification in Galatians

The trend in recent Galatians scholarship has been away from the traditional (and therefore, in some quarters, automatically suspect) focus on justification and toward various other emphases, such as the Spirit or, particularly, inclusion in the people of God, expressed in the language of being Abraham's sons/children/seed (3:7 [9], 29; 4:28–31) or God's sons/children (3:26; 4:5–7). The Spirit is an important motif in the letter, one that has undoubtedly been neglected.[74] Yet the Spirit appears to function more as an ancillary motif. Both justification and inclusion within the people of God are important and, we would argue, overlapping if not referentially equivalent concepts. But justification language, in comparison with "people of God" language, is more frequent and occurs at critical rhetorical points in the letter: it introduces the main argument (2:16) and climaxes Paul's appeal to the Galatians (5:5–6). Membership in God's people is basic to Paul's argument in

---

73. This does not mean, however, that "justification" is a mere "subsidiary crater" or a "battle doctrine," as was famously alleged by A. Schweitzer (1931) and W. Wrede (1908). Many contemporary scholars agree with Schweitzer and Wrede: E. P. Sanders (1977: 501–8) also privileged the participationist category over the judicial; see also Esler 1998: 153–59; Gorman 2009; and in more polemical form, D. Campbell 2009. These critics have a point. Many of Paul's Letters hardly refer to justification per se, and the texts in which the language is used (Galatians, Romans, Phil. 3) involve dialogue with Jewish viewpoints and disputes over torah. But Paul's teaching on justification is more than an occasional strategy to deal with Jewish opponents. The concept of "righteousness," and the juridical category to which it belongs, are important in the OT, and Paul's explanation of the Christ event in these terms is therefore rooted in a central biblical concern. U. Schnelle (2005: 471) accuses Schweitzer and Wrede of confusing the origin of Paul's view with its importance. Justification is not central in Paul's thought, but it is a critical and important means of explicating his gospel. Nor is there any need to set Paul's "juridical" and "participationist" categories in opposition to one another. The latter may be more fundamental for Paul, but it is also a very general category, including within it various other ways of thinking about the Christ event, including the juridical (see esp. Gaffin 2006: 35–41). The problem of positing a union with Christ that precedes the erasure of our legal condemnation before God (e.g., making justification the product of union with Christ; see, e.g., Horton 2007: 147) can be answered if we posit, within the single work of God, two stages of "justification" (using the term here very broadly): one involving Christ's payment of our legal debt, the basis for our regeneration; and the second our actual justification, stemming from our union with Christ (Blocher 2004: 497–98).

74. The centrality of the Spirit in Paul's argument is the basic thesis of Cosgrove 1988.

3:6–4:7, where being "sons of Abraham/God" brackets the argument (3:7 and 4:7).[75] We might conclude that the "seed of Abraham" argument is defensive, Paul responding to the agitators' own theological agenda, whereby his use of justification language is offensive, his own preferred way of putting the matter at issue. But what is truly theological bedrock for Paul is the idea of the believer's incorporation into Christ. Both membership in God's people and justification occur as a result of that fundamental union (see this emphasis in, e.g., Vanhoozer 2011).

The Means of Justification

In the OT, after the inauguration of the Mosaic covenant, the "righteousness" that God looks for in his people is defined in terms of conformity to the law. Characteristic of Paul's discussion of justification in Galatians is his claim that being justified is associated with faith and not with the law or the works of the law. As we have noticed, δικαιοσύνη (*dikaiosynē*, righteousness) occurs four times in the letter. Twice Paul denies that δικαιοσύνη can come via the law (2:21; 3:21); twice he affirms its connection with faith (3:6; 5:5). In the same way, the verb δικαιόω (*dikaioō*, justify), which occurs eight times, is associated with the law twice (3:11; 5:4) and with works of the law once (2:16c), while it is associated with faith in two texts (3:8, 24; see also 3:11b, where δίκαιος may be connected with faith). A full contrast, which denies that being "justified" is a product of doing works of the law and attributes it to faith, comes in the first two occurrences of the verb (2:16a–b). In every occurrence of δικ- language in Galatians, then, with the exception of the verb in 2:17 (which comes hard on the heels of the full contrast in 2:16), a faith-versus-law (or works of the law) contrast is found. Clearly this is the critical heart of Paul's teaching about justification in Galatians.

The nature and significance of the contrast between faith and "works of the law" or "law" is deeply contested in Pauline scholarship today—with quite significant consequences for one's overall soteriology. The Reformers understood the contrast that Paul draws in these texts to signal a fundamental distinction between human believing, on the one hand, and human "working" or "doing," on the other. This polarity is widely questioned today, with scholars proposing significant revisions to both ends of the spectrum. On the one end, "works of the law" are confined to "torah works" or "torah adherence."[76] And

75. See, e.g., Fee (1994: 379), who sees 3:7, "Those who have faith are the sons of Abraham," as the thesis statement, along with the double conclusion in 3:29, "You are the seed of Abraham," and in 4:7, "You are sons of God."

76. While distancing himself in several crucial ways from the New Perspective, F. Watson (2007: 25, plus argument on 121–31) has recently made this point quite vigorously: "The critique of Luther's essentially allegorical interpretation of Paul's critique of works is presented here with all the emphasis I can muster." See also, for this general point of view, Barclay 1988: 235–41; 2010; Matera 1992: 242–43; Dunn 1998: 354–66. New Perspective advocates are not always clear about whether Paul's polemic against "works of the law" has broader theological implications. For instance, in his commentary on Romans, N. T. Wright (2002: 459–61) insists quite strongly in the "Commentary" section that "works of the law" are signs that one belongs

on the other, "faith" is interpreted, at least in many of its occurrences, not as a human being's faith "in" Christ, but as Christ's own faith or faithfulness. We explore these proposals in detail in two other excursuses and in the commentary, where we conclude that "works of the law" refers to human doing of torah and that "faith" refers to human believing.[77] Here we want briefly to comment on the larger argument of the letter.

Paul's argument in Galatians is characterized by a strongly salvation-historical framework that focuses on the extension of God's blessing to Gentiles in the new covenant era. But there are strong indications that Paul also argues—at least implicitly—on another level in Galatians. And this is to be expected. For in itself, the salvation-historical argument does not explain *why* doing the torah cannot secure the promised Abrahamic blessing. Why couldn't the blessing of Abraham simply have been extended to Gentiles, as they were brought under the supervision of torah—as the agitators apparently argued? As we observe in the third additional note on 2:16 and in the discussion of "The Logic of Paul's Response" above, Gal. 2:16 and 3:10–12 suggest that human inability is an important part of Paul's answer to this question in Galatians. Stephen Westerholm puts the point well: "The fundamental question addressed by Galatians thus is not 'What is wrong with Judaism (or the Sinaitic law)?' but 'What is wrong with humanity that Judaism (and the Sinaitic law) cannot remedy?'"[78]

Another indication along these same lines comes in the verse that best captures the essence of the issue in Galatia. In 3:3, when Paul accuses the Galatians of trying to "finish" their spiritual journey "by means of the flesh" (σαρκί), the issue is not just salvation-historical (the "era of the flesh" vs. "the era of the Spirit") but also anthropological; thus NIV 1984: "After beginning with the Spirit, are you now trying to attain your goal *by human effort?*"

---

to Israel and that any notions of legalism or "proto-Pelagianism" are simply not present. But in the "Reflections" section he acknowledges other "overtones" in Paul's teaching, including some that are compatible with traditional Reformation teaching (2002: 464). Wright (2009) is even clearer about these "old perspective" elements in Paul's teaching in his latest book. Note also Dunn's remarks in his latest essay on the matter (2008d: 27–28).

77. In addition to attributing faith to Christ, interpreters sometimes lessen or remove a "doing" versus "believing" antithesis by defining faith to include good works. The equivalent Hebrew word includes the ideas of trust and faithfulness; and πίστις (*pistis*) in Paul clearly has this sense at times. But any attempt to collapse works into faith in Paul founders on the same evidence that we have noted above: the polarity between faith on the one hand and "works of the law" or "works" on the other includes a basic opposition between "believing" and "doing." Even in those texts where Paul appears to identify faith and obedience, he does not expand faith to include obedience; instead, he narrows down obedience to the one central requirement of faith. Believing in Paul is certainly more than an intellectual exercise: it involves the will and includes the disposition to trust and follow God. On this point Paul and James are in total agreement. True faith and works cannot be separated; but they also must be distinguished from one another. Faith is the disposition of the will necessary for works to be done in a way pleasing to God; but faith does not include those works in itself.

78. Westerholm 2004: 381, with his whole argument on 371–84; also see esp. Silva 2004; Gundry 1985; Kim 2002: 61–75; Bird 2007:123; B. Longenecker 1998: 76–77; Hofius 2006: 299–301.

(emphasis added).[79] Works are a problem in Galatians not simply because they involve an outmoded torah; they are also a problem, and more fundamentally, because human inability renders them incapable of delivering people from sin. And on the other side of the polarity, as Paul suggests, faith is the appropriate means of justification because it is the natural extension of God's grace into the human sphere. We noted earlier how Paul introduces the language of "grace"—somewhat unexpectedly—into his argument at several key points. Granted the significance of grace in Paul as a characteristic new covenant reality (see, e.g., Rom. 5:1–2), it is unlikely that Paul uses this language simply for defensive purposes. It is more likely that he wants to tie the agitators' demand for torah obedience to the broader issue of human "achievement" as a contrast to the utterly gracious character of God's justifying work in Christ. Again, the point is that this logic appears to move beyond (or behind!) salvation history to more fundamental theological issues, with anthropological and soteriological implications.

The Time of Justification

Perhaps the most interesting aspect of justification in Galatians is its time. Many traditional interpretations of the letter assume, or argue, that when Paul insists that people are "justified by faith," he is referring to entrance into Christian experience; to put it bluntly, "how you get saved." But in this commentary I argue that most of Paul's references to justification are either "timeless" and undetermined, on the one hand, or future, on the other (timeless/undetermined in 2:16, 21; 3:8, 11, 24; future in 2:17; 5:4–5; present [by implication] in 3:6). Overall, then, justification language in Galatians has a timeless and, if anything, future-oriented focus; as de Boer (2011: 316) puts it, "The point at issue in Galatians is not the 'when' of justification but its basis."[80] This focus makes good sense in light of the rhetorical situation of the letter. This situation is clearly revealed in 3:1–5, where Paul argues *from* the good start that the Galatians have made *onward to* the need for continuing as they began. It is therefore not surprising that righteousness language in Galatians has a general, gnomic quality. A definitive act of justification at the beginning of the Christian life is presumed, as the parallel that Paul draws between Abraham's experience and the Galatians makes clear. And Romans, written in a different (and arguably less polemical) situation, unmistakably affirms such a definitive initial justification (Rom. 5:1, 9; cf. 8:30). But the situation in Galatia requires that Paul emphasize how the Galatians are to *maintain* their status of righteousness and, especially, how they can expect to be found to be in the "right" in the judgment.[81] This last point

---

79. See also Sprinkle (2008: 150–63), who thinks that the basic dichotomy reflected in Paul's use of Lev. 18:5 in Gal. 3:12 is divine versus human action.

80. See also Gaffin 2006: 98; Das 1995: 173–86; Barrett 1985; Brinsmead 1982: 201. Kwon (2004: 51–76), indeed, argues that justification is exclusively future in Galatians.

81. The contrast between Galatians and Romans on this point relates to their situations. In Galatians, the agitators make it necessary for Paul to focus on continuing in righteousness now

deserves particular attention. Without denying that first-century Judaism viewed God's election as the ultimate basis for their place in the covenant, I think it is also the case that, in practice, many Jews operated with "a semi-tacit consciousness of having been born there, of always having been there," as Henri Blocher puts it (2004: 488–89; see also Watson 2004: 8–11). In this scenario, the question becomes not simply how one "gets in" initially or how one "stays in" but how one can hope to "get into" the eternal kingdom on the day of judgment.[82]

This seems to be exactly the issue that Galatians is addressing.[83] The resulting perspective on justification is therefore somewhat dialectical, participating in the "already/not yet" tension that typifies so many NT doctrines. Ridderbos (1975: 166) puts the issue well: On the one hand, "the future righteousness is not another than that which has already been revealed," and thus "nothing is . . . detracted from its character of fulfillment and from the assurance of salvation given in it." But, on the other hand, "What is true of all that has been given in Christ thus applies to justification, that we are not dealing here with a matter that has been concluded, which has been settled, and which we should thus be able to leave 'behind us.'"

Galatians is therefore not (mainly) about "sanctification," or "how to live" (as, e.g., argued by Wakefield 2003; Das 1995: 173; Esler 1998: 143), or even about "justification" in its usual sense of initial acceptance, but about

and looking for ultimate vindication in the event that is "not yet." In Romans, he focuses on the assurance promised to those who have been justified, the "already" event. The "already" and "not yet" aspects of justification overlap significantly with the tension between "justified by faith" and "judged according to works." See Ortlund (2009) for a useful survey of options, most of which apply also to the justification debate.

82. Simon Gathercole (2002b: 113–19) has drawn attention to the importance of this future "getting in" in Jewish literature and its comparative neglect in the debate. On Galatians, see also Stanton 1996: 99–116, esp. 103–4.

83. A reference to future justification in Galatians is at least consonant with two other phenomena. First, a good case can be made that Paul uses justification language to refer to a future time elsewhere. In contrast to the trend of recent interpretation (see esp. Schreiner 1993a; Gathercole 2002a; Bird 2007: 155–78; Garlington 1994: 56–71; N. Wright 2002: 440–42), I don't think Rom. 2:13 is one of these (see Moo 1996: 139–42, 147–48). But Rom. 5:19 and 8:33 are at least possible references to a future aspect of justification. Dunn (2008b: 401–2) thinks that other texts may also refer to a future element in justification: Rom. 3:20, 30; Gal. 3:8, 11, 24. I doubt that Rom. 3:20, 30 or Gal. 3:8 have a future focus; Gal. 3:11 and 24 might. Some others who advocate a future focus in justification are Stuhlmacher 1986a: 72 ("justification designates in Paul both the sharing in God's grace that has already been given by faith and acquittal before God in the last judgment"); Cosgrove 1987: 653–54; P. O'Brien 1992: 90; Rainbow 2005: 155–74. See also Gathercole (2006: 230), who argues that "salvation should be viewed as a unity, with justification referring to the whole while highlighting a certain aspect." Contesting any future element to justification in Paul are, e.g., Fung 1988: 232–35; VanLandingham 2006: 317–18. The second phenomenon is the fact that justification language often has an eschatological significance in Judaism and elsewhere in the NT (e.g., Matt. 12:37; James 2:21–25; see Moo 2000: 37–43, 139–41). Of course, we must recognize that linguistic parallels do not necessarily translate into conceptual parallels. But I think that many of these texts are indeed conceptually parallel to Paul's justification teaching.

ultimate justification. In response to false teachers who claim that this vindication, since it is promised only to Israel, can only be experienced by those who identify with Israel by doing torah, Paul reads salvation history in light of the epochal significance of the cross and insists that faith and faith alone (accompanied, to be sure, by the transforming power of the Spirit) maintains one's relationship to Christ, in whose person the people of God are now constituted. By seeking to "supplement" their faith in Christ with torah observance, the Galatian Christians are in danger of forfeiting their (apparent) standing in Christ and therefore failing to achieve that final vindication. In Galatians, then, righteousness tends to have the idea of vindication, in continuity with the usage of this language that we noted earlier in Isa. 46–55. In contrast to that Isaiah passage, of course—and this is the nub of the issue in Galatia—the people of God who can expect to be vindicated are now defined not by their biological connection with Abraham and/or by torah observance but by their connection with Messiah Jesus, a connection maintained by faith alone.

Genre and Rhetorical Stance

Galatians is obviously a letter, and further classification in terms of genre is not possible. The distinction between an "epistle" (a formal document intended for wide distribution) and a "letter" (informal, private) that A. Deissmann (1901) had proposed is no longer deemed helpful: there are too many mixed or transitional types to justify so neat a distinction. (For a recent survey of the "formal" issues in Paul's Letters, see Porter and Adams 2011.) Paul's Letters fall at various points on the spectrum from personal (e.g., Philemon) to public (e.g., Romans and Ephesians), but most, like Galatians, are intended for a wide audience. All of Paul's Letters carry the imprint of apostolic authority, with the letter functioning to some extent as a means of bringing Paul, though physically distant, into the midst of the pastoral situations he addresses (see, e.g., 1 Cor. 5:3). Paul makes clear that he would like to communicate his concerns to the Galatians in person (4:20), but for some reason he is unable to visit. His letter will have to suffice.

While we cannot know who carried the letter to the Galatian churches, we can be sure that this person (or a local leader) would have read the letter in the various churches to which it was addressed. Any assessment of the nature of Galatians must, then, reckon with the matter of its oral delivery. This situation, combined with the obvious argumentative intent of Galatians, raises the question of the rhetorical forms that Paul uses to convince his audience. Rhetoric, the art of persuasion, was very important in the Greco-Roman world of Paul's day, and we can assume that Paul, educated in that world and seeking to persuade people accustomed to rhetorical practices, would have naturally employed those practices in his letters. Galatians, focused as it is from start to finish on arguing a single basic point, offers a particularly attractive opportunity for rhetorical analysis. Scholars have accordingly spent a lot of time analyzing the rhetoric of Galatians.

Ancient writers classified the various forms of rhetoric, three in particular being usually identified: "forensic" (rhetoric that seeks to persuade people about a past event), "deliberative" (rhetoric that seeks to persuade people to take action), and "epideictic" (rhetoric that seeks to persuade people to reaffirm a particular view in the present).[84] Each of these has been identified in the argument of Galatians. H. D. Betz, in a 1975 article and then massively in his 1979 commentary, sparked the contemporary debate by arguing that Galatians is an "apologetic letter," utilizing forensic rhetoric. George Kennedy (1984: 141–52; see also Hall 1987; Witherington 1998: 25–36), who has specialized in these issues, disagrees, classifying Galatians as deliberative rhetoric. G. Hansen (1989: 57–67) and R. Longenecker (1990: c–cxix) cut between these proposals, arguing that Paul uses forensic rhetoric in the first part of the letter and deliberative rhetoric in the second part. However, the variety of conclusions raises questions about categorizing Galatians as a whole (or in its major parts) as one kind of rhetoric rather than another. Galatians does not appear to fit neatly into any of the major rhetorical categories (see esp. Kern 1998; and also Bryant 2001: 1–54). Indeed, the early interpreters' lack of interest in the rhetorical form of Galatians suggests that Paul is simply not casting his argument within the overall pattern of ancient rhetoric (Kern 1998: 167–203; Riches 2008: 67). Of course, this is not to deny that Paul may use certain rhetorical conventions in his argument. But we judge that the attempt to analyze and interpret Galatians in the terms of ancient rhetoric has only limited value (see Tolmie 2005: 1–30; de Boer 2011: 66–71).

Outline

    I. Introduction: The cross and the new age (1:1–10)
       A. Prescript (1:1–5)
       B. Rebuke: The occasion of the letter (1:6–10)
    II. The truth of the gospel (1:11–2:21)
       A. How Paul received and defended the gospel: Paul and the "pillars" (1:11–2:14)
          1. Thesis: Paul's gospel came through a revelation of Jesus Christ (1:11–12)
          2. Elaboration and proof: Paul's gospel and the "pillars" (1:13–2:14)
             a. Conversion and early travels (1:13–17)
             b. First Jerusalem visit and further travels (1:18–24)
             c. Second Jerusalem visit: The "pillars" confirm Paul's gospel (2:1–10)
             d. An incident at Antioch: Paul defends the gospel (2:11–14)
       B. The truth of the gospel defined (2:15–21)

---

84. See, e.g., Kennedy 1984: 19. As Kennedy points out, these three categories were first put forth by Aristotle (*Rhet.* 3.1.1358a) and elaborated especially by Quintilian in his *Education of the Orator* (*Institutio oratoria*).

III. The defense of the gospel (3:1–5:12)
    A. Rebuke and reminder: Faith, Spirit, and righteousness (3:1–6)
    B. Argument: Abraham's children through incorporation into Christ by faith (3:7–4:7)
        1. The blessing of Abraham (3:7–14)
        2. The law in salvation history (3:15–25)
        3. Sons of God in Christ (3:26–29)
        4. From slaves to sons of God (4:1–7)
    C. Appeal (4:8–31)
        1. Looking at the past: The Galatians' slavery (4:8–11)
        2. Looking at the past: Paul and the Galatians (4:12–20)
        3. Looking at the present: Children of the promise (4:21–31)
    D. Exhortation and warning: Faith, Spirit, and righteousness (5:1–12)
        1. Justified by faith and not by the law (5:1–6)
        2. Resisting the agitators (5:7–12)
IV. The life of the gospel (5:13–6:10)
    A. The basic pattern of the new life: Serving one another in love (5:13–15)
    B. Implementing the new life: Walking by the Spirit (5:16–24)
    C. Some specific parameters of the new life (5:25–6:6)
    D. The urgency of living the new life (6:7–10)
 V. Closing: Cross and new creation (6:11–18)

I. Introduction: The Cross and the New Age (1:1–10)

Following the general pattern of letters in the Greco-Roman world, Galatians has three basic parts: opening, body, closing. Galatians 1:1–10 is the letter opening. It falls into two parts: the typical epistolary salutation (vv. 1–5) and an identification of the letter's occasion (vv. 6–10). Paul's letter openings typically include four formal elements: an identification of the sender(s), an identification of the recipient(s), a "grace and peace" wish, and a thanksgiving. The first three are readily identifiable in verses 1–3. But the fourth is absent. In the place where we would usually find the thanksgiving, we have instead a doxology (v. 5), after which Paul somewhat abruptly turns to the situation in the Galatian churches. He expresses consternation that the new believers are paying serious attention to false teachers (v. 6) and condemns the false teachers in very strong terms (vv. 7–9). This departure from Paul's usual style (Titus is the only other Pauline letter that lacks a thanksgiving) reflects the situation he is addressing.[1] He has neither the time nor the inclination to thank God for the Galatians when their very identity as Christians hangs in the balance; as Chrysostom puts it, the letter "breathes an indignant spirit" (*Comm. Gal.* on 1:1 [*NPNF*[1] 13:1]).

---

1. If Galatians is the first canonical letter that Paul wrote, we cannot claim that Galatians is a departure from a clearly established pattern. But the consistency of Paul's Letters at this point suggests an established formal pattern. Voorst (2010) has also argued that thanksgiving "periods" were not common in ancient letters, so that the Galatians would not have been surprised at not finding one. But the departure from Paul's usual pattern is still significant.

A. Prescript (1:1–5)

The first five verses of Galatians form the prescript of the letter—the somewhat formalized introductory elements. The standard form of this introduction in ancient letters is quite simple, usually taking the form of "X to Y, greetings" (see Acts 15:23). Most of Paul's Letters follow this pattern with minimal adaptation and elaboration. In Galatians, however, as in some of his other letters (e.g., Romans and Titus), Paul adds quite a lot of material to this simple opening formula. These elaborations in Galatians, like the omission of the thanksgiving, probably reflect the situation in focus. Thus his typical identification of himself as an apostle is followed immediately by a defense of the divine authority of his office (v. 1)—an initial hint of an important argument in the letter (1:11–2:10). Another signal about the course of the argument comes in verse 4, where Paul describes Christ as the one who "gave himself for our sins in order that he might rescue us from the present evil age" (v. 4). The cross, and especially the epochal significance of the cross, is the fulcrum of Paul's strategy for persuading the Galatians to reject the overtures of the false teachers (see esp. 2:19–20; 3:1, 13; 6:14). More surprising is the brief reference at the end of verse 1 to the resurrection of Christ. Only in Romans, among the other Letters of Paul, is there any reference to the resurrection (1:4), and there is no further reference to the resurrection in Galatians. Paul may be reminding the Galatians of the "gospel" that he preached among them (cf. 1 Cor. 15:1–3). But the allusion probably also serves to underline the fundamental break in salvation history that the coming of Christ has created, for resurrection, against the background of the OT and Jewish theology, also signals the arrival of the new age.

Exegesis and Exposition

[1]Paul—an apostle chosen not by human beings nor by a human being but by Jesus Christ and God the Father, who raised him from the dead—[2]and all the brothers and sisters who are here with me to the churches of Galatia: [3]Grace to you and peace from ⌜God our Father and the Lord⌝ Jesus Christ, [4]who has given himself ⌜for⌝ our sins in order that he might rescue us from the present evil age, according to the will of our God and Father—[5]to whom be glory forever and ever. Amen.

1:1   Paul begins his Letter to the Galatians by identifying himself, as he does in all his letters, with his hellenized "Roman" name, Paul (Παῦλος, *Paulos*). Paul's "Hebrew" name, Σαῦλος (*Saulos*, Saul), used in the early narratives about Paul in Acts, is never used by Paul himself in his letters. It has been theorized that

Paul first took his Greek name in honor of his high-ranking convert, Sergius Paulus (Acts 13:6–12; Luke first uses "Paul" in 13:13). But it is much more likely that "Paul" was the apostle's Latin *cognomen* (see, e.g., Bruce 1974: 38). Paul also typically designates himself an "apostle" in his letter openings (although the title is absent in Philippians, 1 and 2 Thessalonians, and Philemon). The word "apostle" (ἀπόστολος, *apostolos*) means "one who is sent," an envoy; as Origen puts it, "Everyone who is sent by someone is an apostle of the one who sent him" (Origen, *Comm. Jo.* 32.17; quoted by H. D. Betz, *ABD* 1:309). Paul can use the word in a simple nontechnical sense (e.g., Phil. 2:25; 2 Cor. 8:23) and to denote Christians who have been sent as accredited missionaries (e.g., Rom. 16:7). But when describing himself, he uses *apostolos* to claim equal status with the original twelve apostles (e.g., Luke 6:13; see esp. 1 Cor. 9:1–5 and Gal. 1:17, 19). When he claims apostolic status in his letter openings, Paul will often also trace that status to the call of God, but only here in Galatians does Paul set that divine calling in contrast to any possible human derivation.[2]

Paul has been chosen to be an apostle (the idea "chosen" ["sent" in NRSV and NIV; "appointed" in NLT] is implied in the word "apostle") "by Jesus Christ and God the Father," and not "by human beings" (ἀπ' ἀνθρώπων, *ap' anthrōpōn*) nor "by a human being" (δι' ἀνθρώπου, *di' anthrōpou*). The denial of any human involvement in Paul's apostolic status is echoed in his later claim that his gospel was not of human origin (1:11–12). The most likely reason for this concern is that the agitators were attempting to undermine Paul's authority with the Galatians by arguing that his status and teaching depended on the Jerusalem apostles, whose views (as represented by the agitators) should therefore trump Paul's.[3] Paul not only highlights this denial by placing it before his reference to his divine commissioning; he also repeats the point for emphasis.

This repetition has sparked discussion because of the way Paul shifts the wording. He moves from the preposition *apo* to *dia* and from the plural *anthrōpōn* to the singular *anthrōpou*. The latter change may signal a move from general to particular: Paul does not owe his apostolic status to "human beings" in general; nor does he owe it to any particular human being—perhaps someone such as James or Peter (e.g., Martyn 1997: 84). Such a distinction is possible, but it is perhaps more likely that the shift from plural to singular is simply stylistic. The change from *apo* to *dia* might also be stylistic, since the two prepositions have a semantic overlap in the idea of "ultimate origin" (on

2. Note a similar contrast in Philo's (*Virtues* 63) representation of Moses: "I, indeed, myself, did neither undertake the charge of caring for and providing for the common prosperity of my own accord, nor because I was appointed to the office by any human being; but I undertook to govern this people because God manifestly declared his will by visible oracles and distinct commandments, and commanded me to rule them."

3. The polemical thrust of this denial has been dismissed by some who read Paul's argument in Gal. 1–2 very differently (e.g., on 1:1–5, J. Vos 1993: 14–15). See the introduction to 1:13–2:14. Voorst (2010: 167) has noted how unusual it is to have this extended description of the origins of Paul's apostolate in a letter opening.

both prepositions, see BDAG 105–7, 223–26). However, *dia* more often refers to an intermediate agent: "through" rather than "from" or "by" (see the careful distinction in 1 Cor. 8:6: "For us there is but one God, the Father, from [ἐξ, *ex*] whom all things came and for whom we live; and there is but one Lord, Jesus Christ, through [διά, *dia*] whom all things came . . .").

Paul therefore is probably making two slightly different points in these phrases: the ultimate source of his apostleship was not human; nor did he receive it from, or through, any human being ("source" vs. "agency" [A. Robertson 1934: 567]; "fountain-head" versus "channel" [Lightfoot 1881: 71]; see also R. Longenecker 1990: 4; Silva 2003: 6). This interpretation fits Paul's general use of the two prepositions (see the additional note on 1:1) and satisfactorily explains why he uses both phrases. Of course, Paul does not intend to deny all human involvement in his calling and ministry, such as Ananias's laying hands on Paul when he was converted (Acts 9:10–19) or the church at Antioch's commissioning him and Barnabas for their first missionary journey (Acts 13:1–3). Paul's point, rather, is that his apostolic status and authority do not depend on human beings in any essential way.[4]

An assertion of the divine origin of his apostleship is typical in Paul's letter openings, but the particular way he puts it here is again unique. Usually Paul attributes his apostleship simply to God: "called to be an apostle . . . by the will of God" (1 Cor. 1:1; cf. Rom. 1:1, "called to be an apostle"); "by the will of God" (2 Cor. 1:1; Eph. 1:1; Col. 1:1; 2 Tim. 1:1). Here, however, he attributes his calling to both "Jesus Christ" and "God the Father." Paul does this also in 1 Tim. 1:1 ("by the command of God our Savior and of Christ Jesus our hope"), but putting Christ before God still makes Galatians distinct. Paul reverses the usual order so that he can add to God's name a reference to his raising Christ. It is probably because Christ's name comes first that Paul uses the preposition διά (rather than, e.g., ἀπό, *apo*, from/by) before both divine names.

To be sure, as we have seen above, this preposition can refer to ultimate agency, and a number of scholars think this must be its meaning here (Bruce 1982b: 73). But it is more likely that the preposition retains its usual instrumental meaning and that Paul is already thinking of the revelation of Jesus Christ to him as the point of his apostolic calling: he was chosen as an apostle "through" Jesus Christ as he was manifested to him on the road to Damascus (see 1:15–16; e.g., Dunn 1993a: 27–28; C. Campbell 2012: 244–45). The difficulty then is to understand what this preposition means when it governs "God the Father"—for God is the originator rather than the mediator of Paul's apostleship.

One option is to think that the meaning of the preposition shifts from instrumental agent to ultimate agent.[5] But it is more likely that the preposition

---

4. It is unlikely (contrary to de Boer 2011: 22–23) that Paul contrasts two different kinds of apostles here.

5. R. Longenecker (1990: 5) suggests that we should assume the preposition ἀπό (*apo*, from) before "God the Father," producing a neat chiasm in the verse: Paul's apostleship is not "from" human beings or "through" a human being, but "through" Jesus Christ and "from" God the

has the same instrumental sense in relation to both Christ and God the Father. Without denying that the Father is the ultimate agent of his apostleship, the Father is, along with the Son, the instrumental agent as well (Lightfoot 1881: 72; Dunn 1993a: 27). Moreover, we should refrain from insisting on too much precision in Paul's language. Note, for instance, that in verse 3 Paul can use the preposition ἀπό to govern both the Father and the Son (Lagrange 1918: 3). The introduction of a second and different preposition in either verse would detract from Paul's obvious concern to associate the Father and the Son as closely as possible. In such verses we find the building blocks of an incipient trinitarian theology.

The distinctive nature of Paul's apostolic identification is seen again at the end of verse 1. Only in Galatians does Paul attribute his apostolic status to "God the Father"; and only here does he mention the resurrection with that status. (Paul does allude to the resurrection in the prescript of Romans [1:4], but it is not connected to Paul's apostleship.) Some scholars think that the reference to God the Father here and twice again in the letter's salutation (vv. 3 and 4) reflects an emphasis in the letter as a whole on God as the Father who adopts children to be his own (see 4:1–7; Betz 1979: 39; Martyn 1997: 84). Yet the fatherhood of God does not play that great a role in Galatians; it is, for instance, far more prominent in Ephesians. Perhaps, then, calling God "Father" reminds the readers of the ultimate authority from which Paul derives his apostleship (Dunn 1993a: 27). The reference to God as "the one who raised him [Jesus Christ] from the dead" might serve a similar purpose (e.g., Martyn 1997: 85).[6]

But there is a further and perhaps more important reason for mentioning the resurrection at the outset of this letter. Most Jews (esp. in the "apocalyptic" movement) believed that the ultimate establishment of God's kingdom would be marked by the resurrection of people from the dead (e.g., 2 Bar. 50.2: "the earth will surely give back the dead at that time"). Paul therefore alludes here to what will become the key theological argument of the letter: in Christ, God has inaugurated a new age in salvation history, a situation that "changes everything"—including especially the evaluation and application of the law (see, e.g., Cook 1992: 514–15).

Along with himself, Paul includes as senders of Galatians "all the brothers and sisters who are with me" (οἱ σὺν ἐμοὶ πάντες ἀδελφοί, *hoi syn emoi pantes adelphoi*).[7] It is not unusual for Paul to include others in his letter openings:

1:2

Father. However, as Bligh (1969: 61) points out, if Paul had intended this, he undoubtedly would have used the preposition (contra Longenecker, then, Bligh in fact dismisses the chiastic interpretation).

6. As is typical in the NT, Christ's resurrection is described as a resurrection "from among dead persons" (ἐκ νεκρῶν, *ek nekrōn*; see John 2:22; 21:14; Acts 3:15; 4:10; 13:30; Rom. 4:24; 6:4, 9; 7:4; 8:11; 10:9; 1 Cor. 15:12, 20; Eph. 1:20; Col. 2:12; 1 Thess. 1:10; 2 Tim. 2:8; Heb. 11:19; 1 Pet. 1:21; cf. ἀπὸ νεκρῶν, *apo nekrōn*, in Matt. 27:64; 28:7).

7. The inclusive "brothers and sisters" (see NIV, NLT, CEB; NRSV, "all the members of God's family") appropriately brings out the intended breadth of the Greek ἀδελφοί, (*adelphoi*,

Sosthenes in 1 Cor. 1:1; Timothy in 2 Cor. 1:1; Phil. 1:1; Col. 1:1; Philem. 1; Silas and Timothy in 1 Thess. 1:1; 2 Thess. 1:1. But Galatians is again unique in Paul's inclusion of such a large and undefined group. The personal and even emotional tone of the letter reveals that Paul is the sole author. He undoubtedly includes this wider group to lend strength to his appeal: the views he is teaching in the letter are not his alone but are widely shared.

On the basis of the apparent distinction in Phil. 4:21–22 between οἱ σὺν ἐμοὶ ἀδελφοί, and πάντες οἱ ἅγιοι (*pantes hoi hagioi*, all the saints), "all the brothers and sisters" here are often identified with Paul's ministry associates (see, e.g., Lightfoot 1881: 72; Burton 1921: 8; Bruce 1982b: 73–74; Betz 1979: 40).[8] Assuming an early date and a South Galatian destination (see the introduction), these associates may be specifically located in Syrian Antioch. But a reference to a general group of fellow Christians may accord better with Paul's usual use of ἀδελφοί (e.g., Dunn 1993a: 30; Mell 2006: 354–55). In the ancient world this word was widely used by various associations to stress the intimacy of relationship within these associations; members called one another ἀδελφός as a way of indicating that the association was a "second home" (see esp. Harland 2005; Aasgard 2004). Because this language is so common in the NT, we can easily overlook its significance. It is a reminder that believers are members of the same family and should adopt the attitudes and actions necessary to maintain familial unity (see esp. Horrell 2005: 110–15).

Paul's identification of the recipients of the letter is, compared with his other letters, quite brief: ταῖς ἐκκλησίαις τῆς Γαλατίας (*tais ekklēsiais tēs Galatias*, the churches of Galatia). Missing is any further description of his readers, such as ἅγιοι (*hagioi*, saints, or God's people). The abruptness of the address probably signals Paul's displeasure with the Galatians (Lightfoot 1881: 73), though caution on this point is called for: the description of the recipients of 1 and 2 Thessalonians, two other letters from Paul's earliest period, is also quite brief ("the church of the Thessalonians in God the Father and the Lord Jesus Christ"). As we argue in "The Destination and Date of the Letter," in the introduction, "Galatia" probably refers to the Roman province of that name, and the churches are likely those that Paul established in the southern part of the province on his first missionary journey (e.g., Pisidian Antioch, Lystra, Iconium, Derbe; see Acts 13–14).

1:3 In contrast to other elements in the prescript, the "grace and peace" wish of verse 3 follows the usual Pauline pattern. He prays that his readers might experience "grace" (χάρις, *charis*) and "peace" (εἰρήνη, *eirēnē*) from "God our Father" (θεοῦ πατρὸς ἡμῶν, *theou patros hēmōn*) and "the Lord Jesus Christ"

---

traditionally, "brothers"). See LN 125.11.23: "a close associate of a group of persons having a well-defined membership (in the NT ἀδελφός [*adelphos*] refers specifically to fellow believers in Christ)."

8. Bauckham (1979: 65) suggests that Paul's vague reference may be due to his embarrassment at not being able to include Barnabas (who worked with Paul in these churches) as a wholehearted endorser of the theology of the letter (see Gal. 2:11–14).

(κυρίου Ἰησοῦ Χριστοῦ, *kyriou Iēsou Christou*).[9] "Grace" is a fundamental aspect of NT revelation and of the gospel that Paul defends in Galatians (see also 1:6, 15; 2:9, 21; 5:4; 6:18); indeed, Paul can use "grace" to sum up the Christian message (e.g., Rom. 5:2). In addition to its importance for the Christian message, Paul may also refer to grace in the prescripts of his letters because of its similarity to the usual Hellenistic letter greeting, χαίρειν (*chairein*, greetings). The other key word, εἰρήνη, has its roots in OT and Jewish soil. The OT prophets looked forward to the day when God would put his creation in the right again, when he would institute *shālōm*, "well-being." Paul's wish that his readers experience "peace," then, is not a wish that they enjoy a quiet, happy life or that their souls may find rest but that they might experience the full measure of God's eschatological *shālōm*. At the end of the letter, Paul pronounces εἰρήνη and ἔλεος (*eleos*, mercy) on the "Israel of God" (Gal. 6:16). The grace and peace wish of 1:3 and this pronouncement of blessing form an inclusio in the letter as a whole (Garlington 2003: 28). The letter will explain to the Galatians how they can remain "the Israel of God" and so continue to experience the grace, peace, and mercy that God showers on his people. The grace and peace wish, then, while standard epistolary practice for Paul, also taps into important themes in the letter (Voorst 2010: 169). Paul again conjoins God the Father and the Lord Jesus Christ closely together in the provision of this grace and peace.[10]

In yet another departure from his typical letter opening, Paul now describes **1:4** the "Lord Jesus Christ" (v. 3) as the one who, through his sacrifice on the cross, "rescued" believers from "the present evil age." And we can see, yet again, how this addition anticipates the argument of the letter. By portraying the work of Christ as an "apocaplyptic rescue operation" (Hays 2000: 202), Paul "strikes the keynote of the epistle" (Lightfoot 1881: 73; see also B. Longenecker 1998: 36–46; Smiles 1998: 68–69).[11] Central to Paul's attempt to woo the Galatians back to the true gospel is his insistence throughout the letter that the cross of Christ is the decisive and uniquely sufficient means to rescue sinners from death. Embracing Christ's cross through faith is all that is needed to effect this rescue and to bring believers into the "new creation" (6:15). The law program advocated by the agitators effectively underplays the decisive turning point in all of human history.

The adjectival clause τοῦ δόντος ἑαυτὸν ὑπὲρ τῶν ἁμαρτιῶν ἡμῶν (*tou dontos heauton hyper tōn hamartiōn hēmōn*, "who gave himself on behalf of our sins") resembles language used elsewhere in the NT to characterize the death of Christ ("giving [with a form of δίδωμι] himself" in Mark 10:45//Matt.

---

9. The only exceptions are Col. 1:2, which omits reference to Christ, and 1 Thess. 1:1, where God the Father and Jesus Christ are mentioned in the previous clause.

10. The preposition ἀπό (*apo*, from) governs both names, accentuating their close relation (Harris, *NIDNTT* 3:1178; Bruce 1982b: 74).

11. Matera (1993: 286) notes that only here in his letter openings does Paul refer to the death of Christ and that Christ's death will figure prominently in the letter.

20:28; 1 Tim. 2:6; Titus 2:14; "on behalf of sins" in 1 Cor. 15:3; 2 Cor. 5:21; in a slightly different sense, Heb. 5:1; 7:27; 10:12). These similarities, coupled with the facts that Paul never elsewhere uses the verb ἐξαιρέω (exaireō, rescue) and only rarely refers to "sins" (plural; he mostly uses the singular),[12] have led many scholars to identify part or all of verse 4 as the fragment of an early Christian hymn or confession (e.g., Martyn 1997: 95–97; R. Longenecker 1990: 7; Vouga 1998: 19; Bryant 2001: 120–23). This is possible, but it is perhaps more likely that Paul is simply reflecting language that was being widely used in the church of his day to refer to Christ's death. And this language itself is rooted in the application of the Isaiah "servant" prophecies to Christ and his death. Isaiah 53 (esp. in the LXX) resembles Gal. 1:4 in portraying the Servant as "giving himself" for sins at the will of the Lord.[13] It was Jesus himself who pointed the early Christians to this background by applying the language of Isa. 53 to his own death (see esp. Mark 10:45//Matt. 20:28). While the preposition ὑπέρ (hyper) means, generally, "on behalf of," it sometimes also takes on the nuance of substitution, and this is probably the case here (Harris 2012: 214; Wallace 1996: 383–89 [though he does not explicitly include Gal. 1:4]; Garlington 2003: 36). As we noted above, however, what is particularly distinctive and therefore striking about Paul's portrayal of Christ's work in this verse is the focus on "rescue" "from the present evil age" (ἐκ τοῦ αἰῶνος τοῦ ἐνεστῶτος πονηροῦ, ek tou aiōnos tou enestōtos ponērou). The verb ἐξαιρέω, while used only here in the Pauline Letters, occurs several times in the book of Acts and frequently in the LXX to denote "rescue" or "deliver," usually from danger or from an enemy (typical are Nebuchadnezzar's words to Shadrach, Meshach, and Abednego in Dan. 3:15: "But if you do not worship it, you will be thrown immediately into a blazing furnace. Then what god will be able to rescue [ἐξελεῖται, exeleitai] you from my hand?" See also Acts 7:10, 34; 12:11; 23:27; 26:17).

New Testament scholars generally recognize that the NT language of a "present age" (Mark 10:30) versus "the age to come" (Matt. 12:32) reflects

12. Many scholars exaggerate the rarity of Paul's use of the plural "sins" because they dismiss as Pauline several letters that, in our estimation, should be considered to be Paul's. Apart from Gal. 1:4, Paul uses the plural of ἁμαρτία (hamartia, sin) nine times (apart from OT quotations): Rom. 7:5; 1 Cor. 15:3, 17; Eph. 2:1; Col. 1:14; 1 Thess. 2:16; 1 Tim. 5:22, 24; 2 Tim. 3:6.

13. See esp. Isa. 53:6 LXX: κύριος παρέδωκεν αὐτὸν ταῖς ἁμαρτίαις ἡμῶν (kyrios paredōken auton tais hamartiais hēmōn, the Lord gave him over to [for?] our sins [NETS]), on which see esp. Ciampa 1998: 51–60. Also, Isa. 53:10: καὶ κύριος βούλεται καθαρίσαι αὐτὸν τῆς πληγῆς· ἐὰν δῶτε περὶ ἁμαρτίας ἡ ψυχὴ ὑμῶν (kai kyrios bouletai katharisai auton tēs plēgēs; ean dōte peri hamartias hē psychē hymōn, and the Lord desires to cleanse him from his blow; if you offer for sin, your soul [NETS]), on which see Garlington 2003: 34; Harmon 2010: 56–66. And Isa. 53:12: παρεδόθη εἰς θάνατον ἡ ψυχὴ αὐτοῦ, καὶ ἐν τοῖς ἀνόμοις ἐλογίσθη· καὶ αὐτὸς ἁμαρτίας πολλῶν ἀνήνεγκεν καὶ διὰ τὰς ἁμαρτίας αὐτῶν παρεδόθη (paredothē eis thanaton hē psychē autou, kai en tois anomois elogisthē; kai autos hamartias pollōn anēnenken kai dia tas hamartias autōn paredothē, his soul was given over to death, and he was reckoned among the lawless, and he bore the sins of many, and because of their sins he was given over [NETS]), on which see Hays 2000: 203.

apocalyptic Judaism, which divided history sharply into two phases and looked for a decisive intervention of God to end the present age and usher in the new age of salvation.[14] In keeping with the typical NT perspective of inaugurated eschatology, Paul claims that, though this present evil age continues in force, believers are rescued from this present age of evil, sin, and death and find their true identity in the new age that has broken into history through Christ's epochal death and resurrection. This fundamental NT perspective on the "times" in which we live bookends Galatians. "This evil age" in 1:4 corresponds to the "world" of 6:14; both of which stand in contrast to the "new creation" (6:15). And Paul's point is that believers, with their sins forgiven through Christ's self-giving and identified with Christ in his triumphal resurrection (v. 1), belong to a whole new state of affairs.

In keeping with the portrayal of the mission of the servant in Isa. 53, Paul adds that Christ's giving of himself to effect their rescue was "according to the will of our God and Father" (κατὰ τὸ θέλημα τοῦ θεοῦ καὶ πατρὸς ἡμῶν, *kata to thelēma tou theou kai patros hēmōn*). This addition, as well as reflecting Isa. 53, may act as an implicit response to the agitators: God's "judgment" on the present evil age, a central element in the preaching of Paul, was willed by God himself (Silva 2003: 11). God has invaded human existence in Christ in order to rescue people from this evil world. He acts "on behalf of" sinful people, hinting perhaps at the idea of "grace" that plays a pivotal role in the argument of the letter (see esp. 2:21; 5:4; and the exposition of 1:3; cf. Engberg-Pedersen 2000: 142).

Paul occasionally uses a doxology to end a section of a letter (Rom. 11:36; Eph. 3:21; 1 Tim. 1:17) or a letter as a whole (Rom. 16:27; Phil. 4:20; 2 Tim. 4:18), but only here does he conclude a prescript with a doxology. The unprecedented placement of this doxology leads some to think that it was part of the confession that Paul is quoting (e.g., Witherington 1998: 77; R. Longenecker 1990: 9 [hesitantly]), but as we have seen, it is unlikely that Paul is actually using preexisting material. Others suggest that the doxology may be Paul's substitute for the missing thanksgiving, but the rebuke of 1:6–10 is better seen as the formal equivalent of the thanksgiving (Silva 2003: 11). The doxology is best seen, then, as a natural addition to the christological/soteriological assertion of verse 4. It is quite natural to ascribe glory to God for planning and putting into effect the rescue of sinners from this present evil age (e.g., Lightfoot 1881: 74; Bruce 1982b: 77).

1:5

Additional Notes

1:1. The alternation of prepositions in Paul's description of his apostleship—not ἀπό "human beings" or διά "a human being" but διά "Jesus Christ and God the Father"—is interesting and debated.

14. The NT references to "this age/the present age": Matt. 13:22, 39, 40, 49; 24:3; 28:20; Mark 4:19; Luke 16:8; 20:34, 35; Rom. 12:2; 1 Cor. 1:20; 2:6, 8; 3:18; 2 Cor. 4:4; Eph. 2:2; 1 Tim. 6:17; 2 Tim. 4:10; Titus 2:12; to the coming age: Mark 10:30; Luke 18:30; Heb. 6:5; and to both: Matt. 12:32; Eph. 1:21. See esp. de Boer 2011: 31–35 for the significance of "apocalyptic eschatology" in Galatians.

The prepositions are attached to the verbal notion implicit in the word ἀπόστολος: "send out," "commission." It would be typical to follow such a verbal idea with the idea of agency, an idea ordinarily indicated in the NT with the preposition ὑπό. However, most grammars note that both ἀπό and διά can sometimes have the idea of agency: "That *apo* occasionally stands for *hypo* seems incontestable" (Harris 2012: 222; and on διά, see Harris 2012: 62; Turner 1963: 267; BDF §223.2; and note BDR §223.2, where Gal. 1:1 is specifically mentioned). Wallace (1996: 432–33) does not list "ultimate agent" in his discussion of διά but does mention in a note that "διά is rarely used for ultimate agent." Paul may thus be making basically the same point in each of these phrases. However, in over 185 occurrences of διά in Paul, only two have a strong claim to indicate ultimate agency (1 Cor. 1:9; Gal. 4:7), while a reference to ultimate agency is possible in three other cases (Rom. 11:36; 1 Cor. 12:8; Philem. 7). It is therefore more likely that ἀπό, "the most common substitute" for ὑπό (A. Robertson 1934: 636), has the sense of ultimate agency but that διά, in both its occurrences, retains its more usual sense of mediation.

1:3. The textual tradition is rather evenly split over the placement of the pronoun ἡμῶν. Some MSS (among them ℵ and A) place it after θεοῦ πατρός ("from God *our* Father and the Lord Jesus Christ"; see NIV, ESV, NRSV, NASB, NAB). Others (as in 𝔓[46, 51vid] and B along with 𝔐) put it after κυρίου ("from God the Father and *our* Lord Jesus Christ"; see KJV, NJKV, RSV, NET, HCSB, NJB). A few MSS also omit the pronoun altogether (see CEB). The relatively even split among the translations for these two options shows how difficult the decision between them is. The former is the typical Pauline word order and is preferred by most scholars (see, e.g., Metzger 1994: 520; Burton 1921: 11). However, the second reading, precisely because it is unusual, could be argued to be the original that a scribe has conformed to Pauline practice via the first reading (Silva 2003: 13). Yet when Paul adds ἡμῶν to κύριος, he always uses the article (Lagrange 1918: 3); so perhaps the former word order should be preferred.

1:4. Many MSS, some of them important ones (𝔓[46] ℵ A D F G Ψ 1739 1881 and 𝔐), read περί in place of ὑπέρ. But the latter, also with solid support (𝔓[51] ℵ[1] B H 0278 and several minuscules), should probably be preferred (note the parallel texts 1 Tim. 2:6; Titus 2:14).

1:5. The English versions are almost unanimous in inferring an optative verb (εἴη, *eiē*)—"Let there be glory to God" (although not, perhaps, the NLT: "All glory to God forever and ever!"). But the commentators (at least those who comment on the issue) tend to favor the indicative (ἐστίν)—"There is glory to God" (cf., e.g., Lightfoot 1881: 75; Mussner 1988: 52; Fung 1988: 42; Garlington 2003: 34). The difference between the two in this context is not great, and it is very difficult to know which Paul would have intended. Indeed, it is tempting to think that he would have had both in mind: God certainly is glorious, and the readers should acknowledge it.

B. Rebuke: The Occasion of the Letter (1:6–10)

This paragraph forms the second part of the letter opening (de Boer 2011: 36–37). Based on Paul's other letters, at this point we would expect to find a thanksgiving (and usually prayer) for the readers. Such a thanksgiving, with a form of the verb εὐχαριστέω (*eucharisteō*, give thanks), occurs in seven of Paul's Letters (Rom. 1:8; 1 Cor. 1:4; Phil. 1:3; Col. 1:3; 1 Thess. 1:2; 2 Thess. 1:3; Philem. 4). Three others have generally comparable language (with χάρις [*charis*, thanks] in 2 Tim. 1:3; and with a "blessing" of God for his work among the readers in 2 Cor. 1:3 and Eph. 1:3; only 1 Timothy and Titus lack this feature entirely). The absence of any thanksgiving section here in Galatians is thus surprising.

But even more startling is what Paul puts in its place: instead of a thanksgiving for the readers' faith, we find Paul severely rebuking them for a potential defection from the faith (Silva 2003: 16). While we must exercise caution in inferring too much from unusual formal features (esp. if Galatians is the first letter Paul wrote), it seems justified to conclude, with most commentators, that Paul is signaling his extreme distress at the situation of the Galatian Christians. He cannot thank God for them when their spiritual status is so uncertain. Why is it so uncertain? Because "some people" have confused the Galatians about the meaning of the true gospel of Christ.

Paul says nothing here about the specific way in which these people are "perverting" the gospel. But specific references elsewhere in the letter (see esp. 5:2–4) as well as the general argument reveal that these false teachers were insisting that the Galatian Gentiles be circumcised and submit to the law of Moses in order to be counted among the true people of God and to achieve the righteous standing that they would need to go free in the judgment (see "Occasion and Purpose" in the introduction for more on the false teaching). At this point Paul's concern is not to describe or engage in detailed criticism of the false teaching. Rather, his purpose, encapsulating the central rhetorical thrust of the letter, is to warn the Galatians not to succumb to this teaching. He accomplishes this by using the strongest language he can muster to paint the false teachers as people who have perverted the gospel of Christ and who are thereby destined for eternal condemnation (vv. 8–9). In the beginning of the letter, the threat of divine judgment for following false teaching stands in antithetical contrast to the blessing promised for those who continue to follow the apostolic "rule" at the end of the letter (6:16; Betz 1979: 50–51; Wilson 2007: 26–27). Paul concludes the paragraph by contrasting himself, as a true servant of

Christ, with these false teachers (see our comments on v. 10 for a discussion of the place of this verse in Paul's argument).

Exegesis and Exposition

[6]I am ⌜amazed⌝ that you are so quickly turning away from the one who called you ⌜to live in⌝ the grace ⌜of Christ⌝ to another gospel, [7]which is really not another gospel—it is just that there are some people who are troubling you and trying to pervert the gospel of Christ. [8]But even if we or an angel from heaven should ⌜proclaim to you a gospel⌝ other than the one that we proclaimed, let that person fall under God's curse! [9]As I said before, so now I say again: if anyone should proclaim to you a gospel other than the one you received, let that person fall under God's curse.

[10]For am I now trying to persuade human beings or God? Or am I trying to please human beings? If I were yet trying to please human beings, I would not be a servant of Christ.

1:6   Paul begins by expressing his amazement at the sudden turn of events in Galatia. Some interpreters have downplayed the significance of θαυμάζω (*thaumazō*, I am astonished), suggesting that it functions as a literary marker (see the first additional note on 1:6; Paul uses the word elsewhere only in 2 Thess. 1:10). But there is no good basis for ignoring the force of the word; as Dunn (1993a: 39) puts it, it expresses "more passion than artifice." Paul is genuinely surprised and chagrined that his converts in Galatia are so quickly being tempted to exchange the true gospel that he preached to them for a substitute and false gospel. It is unclear, however, just what Paul means by saying that the Galatians have turned "so quickly" from the true gospel: so quickly after the arrival of the false teachers (Bligh 1969: 83; Hyldahl 2000: 428)? or so quickly after their conversion (Betz 1979: 47–48)? Or is Paul focusing on the rashness of their decision (BDAG 992; Lightfoot 1881: 75)? Paul can use ταχέως (*tacheōs*, quickly) in this latter sense (see esp. 1 Tim. 5:22, where Paul warns Timothy "Do not be hasty [ταχέως] in the laying on of hands"; and also 2 Thess. 2:2). But this meaning is rare in Paul and in the NT, and a temporal focus is probably intended.

If so, it probably makes better sense to think that Paul is referring to the brief interval between their acceptance of the true gospel that he preached and their dalliance with the false teachers. On our reading of the circumstances of the letter, Paul is writing within a year or so of his initial evangelizing trip through South Galatia. But the "so quickly" language might have another function also: to convey an OT allusion. Perhaps the most famous apostasy in the OT is the decision of the Israelites to fashion and worship a golden-calf image—an apostasy all the worse since it occurred "so quickly" after they had heard God's word at Sinai. Note Exod. 32:8—"They have been quick [ταχύ, cognate to the adverb ταχέως] to turn away from what I commanded them and have made themselves an idol cast in the shape of a calf. They have bowed down to it and sacrificed to it and have said, 'These are your gods, Israel, who brought you up out of Egypt'"—and Deut. 9:16—"When I looked, I saw that you had sinned against the LORD your God; you had made for yourselves an idol cast in the shape of a calf. You had turned aside quickly [nothing equivalent in LXX] from the way that the LORD had commanded you" (e.g., R. Longenecker 1990: 14; Ciampa 1998: 71–77).

Nevertheless, if Paul had intended to allude to this incident, we might have expected him to use the verb used in the LXX of these texts for "turn aside" (παραβαίνω, parabainō) rather than the verb that he does use (μετατίθημι, metatithēmi). This verb, which was occasionally used to refer to a change of philosophical or political belief (see Betz 1979: 47; Martyn 1997: 108), was also used to describe Jews who apostatized from the faith at the time of the Maccabean rebellion (see esp. 2 Macc. 7:24: "The youngest brother being still alive, Antiochus not only appealed to him in words, but promised with oaths that he would make him rich and enviable if he would turn from [μεταθέμενον] the ways of his ancestors"; see Dunn 1993a: 39–40). Paul uses the present tense of this verb to indicate that the apostasy is still being contemplated (R. Longenecker 1990: 14).

Paul's description of what the Galatians are being tempted to apostatize from is significant for the direction of his argument in the letter: "the one who called you to live in the grace of Christ." "The one who called" (τοῦ καλέσαντος, tou kalesantos) is God the Father (always the subject of the verb καλέω [kaleō, call] when used in a theological sense in Paul). But particularly significant is Paul's addition: that God has called them "to live in the grace of Christ" (on the question of whether "Christ" should be included, see the third additional note on 1:6). Our translation "to live in" represents the Greek preposition ἐν (en, in). This preposition is usually taken to indicate means ("by"; see NASB, NAB, HCSB, NET, NLT, CEB; R. Longenecker 1990: 15) or "sphere" ("in"; see RSV, NRSV, ESV, NKJV, NJB; Betz 1979: 48; Fee 2007b: 228). But a comparison with similar constructions in Paul favors our translation (see NIV and the second additional note on 1:6); and it fits the argument of the letter very well. Of course God has called the Galatians "in" and "through" the grace of Christ. But Paul's point here is to remind the Galatians that God has called them to *continue to live* and to *remain* in the grace associated with the decisive, epoch-changing Christ event (see also Ridderbos 1953: 47; Fung 1988: 44; Schütz 2007: 117).

The word χάρις (charis, grace) appears only seven times in the letter (1:3, 6, 15; 2:9, 21; 5:4; 6:18) but nevertheless touches on a key issue in Paul's argument. God has decisively manifested himself in Christ, thus sidelining the law, and his saving work in Christ is completely a matter of grace, to which humans can only respond with faith, not works of any kind. The positive assertion that the Galatians have been "called to live in the grace of Christ" matches, as Silva (2003: 17) notes, the twofold warning in the rhetorical climax of the letter: "You who are trying to be justified by the law have been alienated from Christ; you have fallen away from grace" (5:4). "The grace of Christ" is the touchstone of Paul's argument against the agitators.

Paul introduces another key word in the argument of Galatians at the end of this verse: εὐαγγέλιον (*euangelion*, gospel). Paul uses this word seven times in the opening section of Galatians (see also 1:7, 11; 2:2, 5, 7, 14) and the cognate verb also seven times in the letter (1:8 [2x], 9, 11, 16, 23; 4:13). It is "the truth of the gospel" (2:5, 14) for which Paul is contending in Galatians (on the importance of this theme in Galatians, see, e.g., Bryant 2001: 140–41; G. Hansen 1989: 83–84). The language of "gospel," or "good news," is rooted in the OT, especially in Isaiah, who foretells a day when God would proclaim "good news" to his people (40:9; 52:7; 60:6; 61:1; cf. also Joel 3:5 LXX; Nah. 1:15 [2:1 LXX]). This "good news" involves the establishment of God's reign—"Your God reigns!" is the good news in Isa. 52:7. Some recent interpreters mention this point and then also note that the idea of "good news" was common in the Roman world of Paul's day, where the reign of the emperor was sometimes said to be "good news" for the world. They therefore conclude that Paul's message of "good news" is basically the announcement of the reign of the Lord Jesus (in contrast to the reign of "Lord Caesar"; see esp. N. Wright 1994: 223–32; Hays 2000: 205). This focus on the reign of Christ is an attempt to correct an impression sometimes given that the "good news" involves simply "getting saved," with little regard for the lordship of Christ.

But Wright and Hays have overreacted. Both in the OT and in the Roman world of Paul's day, the news proclaimed by heralds was "good" because it meant the establishment of a beneficent reign. So Paul uses the language to focus not so much on the fact of God's reign or Jesus's lordship but on the wonderful benefits that the coming of Christ as Lord brings to his people. In Galatians, at least, this is certainly the case. The "truth of the gospel" that Paul contends for over against the agitators (1:7–9) and which he defends before the Jerusalem authorities (2:2, 5, 7) is not the lordship of Christ, over which there is apparently no disagreement. What is at stake, rather, is how the blessings of that lordship over individuals will be established and maintained. The "good news" that Paul has proclaimed in Galatia and over which there has arisen so much controversy is the message that God has in Christ made a way for sinners to be accepted before him and that this way, being an act of God's grace, is to be entered into and lived out by faith alone (see esp. P. O'Brien 2004a: 293–94; Piper 2007: 81–91; Kim 2008: 3–71; de Boer 2011: 44).

1:7   Paul immediately "corrects" himself. The "other" (ἕτερος, *heteros*) gospel (1:6) that the Galatians are attracted to is not really a gospel at all, for there is no "other" (ἄλλος, *allos*) gospel—except in the sense that the agitators are trying to present their message as one. A striking and much discussed feature of this passage is the shift from ἕτερος to ἄλλος to express the idea of "another." Many interpreters argue that, at least in this context, the two words have distinct nuances of meaning. Usually this distinction is said to be between "other" in the sense of "different in kind" (ἕτερος) and "other" in the sense of "another of a similar kind" (ἄλλος): the gospel to which the Galatians are attracted is a gospel of an entirely different kind than Paul's (v. 6b), yet that gospel is not another gospel that is anything like Paul's (v. 7a; "He admits ἕτερον, but refuses ἄλλο" [A. Robertson 1934: 747]; see also, e.g., Trench 1989: 357; Lightfoot 1881: 76; Burton 1921: 23–24, 420–22; R. Longenecker 1990: 15).[1]

Other scholars, however, cite instances in which the two words appear to have no difference in meaning in the NT and conclude that we would be forcing matters to insist on a difference in this text (BDF §306.4; Turner 1963: 197; Dunn 1993a: 38; Bruce 1982b: 81; Martyn 1997: 110). These scholars are probably right: there is good reason to see the two as semantically equivalent here. However, there may be a stylistic reason for Paul to shift words. The word ἕτερος often has a basic "dual" sense, comparing one thing with one other. Paul probably uses this word in verse 6b because he is thinking of the "false" gospel in contrast to the "true" gospel that he has proclaimed. In verse 7a, however, he shifts to the more general "enumerative" word, ἄλλος, because he is now denying that this false gospel has any claim to be a gospel (however many gospels one might want to consider;[2] see the additional note on 1:6–7 for more detail).

As we suggest above in our translation, the second part of verse 7 qualifies Paul's claim that the gospel to which the Galatians are attracted is not, in fact, "another gospel." The other gospel to which the Galatians are tempted to transfer their allegiance is a gospel only in the sense that some "agitators" (οἱ ταράσσοντες, hoi tarassontes) are claiming it to be a gospel. Rather than being adversative, then (BDAG 277–79; BDF §448.8; Betz 1979: 49), εἰ μή (ei mē, but/except) probably retains its normal "exceptive" significance (Lightfoot 1881: 76; Burton 1898: 274). Paul calls the false teachers in Galatia those who "agitate," "confuse," or "trouble" others (all within the semantic range of ταράσσω; cf. BDAG 990–91) both here and in 5:10 (with a generic singular), and the language has been widely adopted by recent scholars as a way of describing the false teachers (note also that the verb is applied to Jewish Christians who insist that Gentiles be circumcised and observe the law of Moses in Acts 15:24). Paul adds a second coordinate participle to his description, which probably explicates the former one: those who are "agitating" the Galatians are doing so by "trying" (θέλοντες, thelontes) to "pervert" or "distort" (μεταστρέψαι, metastrepsai) "the gospel of Christ" (τὸ εὐαγγέλιον τοῦ Χριστοῦ, to euangelion tou Christou).[3]

Paul puts both participles in the present tense, an obvious indication that the false teachers' work is ongoing as well as that they have not yet succeeded

1. Interestingly, however, William Ramsay (1900: 260–66) argues that the distinction worked exactly the opposite way.

2. Silva (2001: 54–56) suggests a different stylistic reason for the shift, noting that ἄλλος might be a more natural word than ἕτερος to use before the exceptive εἰ μή (ei mē, except/but) clause. But there is little evidence for this tendency (εἰ μή is preceded by ἄλλος once elsewhere in the NT [John 6:22] and by ἕτερος once elsewhere [Gal. 1:19]).

3. Both ταράσσοντες and θέλοντες are substantival participles, governed by οἱ (hoi, the) and standing in attributive relationship to τινές (tines, some): "There are some who are agitating . . . and troubling" (cf. BDF §412.4).

in winning the Galatians over to their view. The genitive qualifier τοῦ Χριστοῦ after τὸ εὐαγγέλιον has attracted the usual debate: is it "objective," meaning "the gospel about Christ," or "the gospel that proclaims Christ" (cf. NLT, "the truth about Christ"; Ridderbos 1953: 49)—or is it "subjective," meaning "the gospel that Christ preached" (Zahn 1907: 47–48)? Some interpreters suggest that it is both (e.g., Mussner 1988: 58; R. Longenecker 1990: 16), but it is better to view it as a "general" genitive: Paul identifies the only true gospel as the gospel that is connected with, or defined by, Christ (Schlier 1989: 39; Rohde 1989: 42; Silva 2003: 33–34).

1:8 The mention of the agitators in verse 7 leads Paul to turn away from direct address to the Galatians in order to pronounce judgment on people like those agitators who pervert the gospel. Of course, Paul still has the Galatians very much in mind: his purpose is to awaken them to the seriousness of the situation. What the agitators are teaching is not an interesting and inconsequential option to, or addition to, Paul's gospel: they are teaching something that will, literally, lead themselves to hell (and by implication, perhaps, the Galatians also if they embrace this teaching). This is the significance of the language that, in a rhetorically emphatic position, concludes both verse 8 and 9: ἀνάθεμα ἔστω (anathema estō, let that person be anathema).

The Greek word ἀνάθεμα has come over into English in transliterated form, where it means much what the Greek original means: to be under a curse. The Greek word, in turn, reflects the Hebrew חֵרֶם (ḥērem), "something dedicated," often "dedicated to destruction" (e.g., Num. 21:3; Deut. 7:26; Josh. 6:17; 7:12; Zech. 14:11). (All the NT occurrences have this sense: Rom. 9:3; 1 Cor. 12:3; 16:22; Acts 23:14 in a different sense ["We have bound ourselves to suffer a curse if . . . ," AT; cf. BDAG 63]). More than removal from the community (e.g., excommunication) is meant (contra, e.g., Betz 1979: 54); what is involved is nothing less than suffering the judicial wrath of God (e.g., Lightfoot 1881: 78; R. Longenecker 1990: 17).

The wrath of God, says Paul, will fall on anyone who preaches a gospel different from the gospel that the Galatians have first heard: whether that "other gospel" be proclaimed by Paul or by "an angel from heaven." Paul may use the first-person plural (εὐηγγελισάμεθα, euēngelisametha, we proclaimed good news) because he includes with him "the brothers and sisters" who accompanied Paul (v. 2) and/or missionaries such as Barnabas, who was with Paul when he first preached in Galatia (cf. Lightfoot 1881: 77; Dunn 1993a: 44). But it might be better to take the plural as "editorial," the plural being a stylistic device that refers to Paul exclusively (Wallace 1996: 396; Martyn 1997: 113).

More significant, and more difficult to understand, is why Paul refers to an "angel from heaven" here. Some surmise that the false teachers themselves may have been appealing to angelic messages to bolster their message (Martyn 1997: 113). Others note the importance of angelic messengers in Jewish apocalyptic (Betz 1979: 53). And since angelic messengers were sometimes associated with the giving of the law (a point made explicitly in Gal. 3:19), Paul might have in view specifically the angelic mediation of the law (Dunn 1990: 45). However, we have no evidence elsewhere that the false teachers were appealing to angelic revelation; and it seems to be a stretch to read angelic involvement with the law specifically into this allusion. It is better, then, simply to view the reference as hyperbolic (Bligh 1969: 88–89; Hays 2000: 206). Whether it be he himself or the most significant and spectacular messenger he could name that preaches a false gospel—they will suffer God's curse for their error.

The verb εὐαγγελίζηται (*euangelizētai*) is a "general precept with gnomic implications" (Wallace 1996: 525): whenever a gospel contrary to Paul's is proclaimed, or whoever proclaims it, God's curse will fall. Indeed, it is possible that Paul means to say, more specifically, that the gospel that brings God's curse is one that goes "beyond" the gospel that Paul has preached. This is a possible meaning for the preposition that Paul uses here (παρά, *para*) and could make sense in the situation, since the agitators are apparently claiming to "add" to the gospel that Paul has proclaimed (Lightfoot 1881: 77; Porter 1992: 167). But the strength of the language in these verses makes it more likely that Paul is anathematizing any gospel that stands in "contrast to" or "against" his gospel (another meaning for παρά; for this interpretation, see BDF §236.3; Moule 1959: 51; Burton 1921: 17–18; Schütz 2007: 121; it is reflected in all the major English versions).[4]

1:9

Paul repeats his "anathema," perhaps to make clear that what he says in verse 8 is not a momentary, irrational outburst but a carefully considered warning that needs to be taken with the greatest seriousness. Indeed, Paul claims that the Galatians have heard this warning before: ὡς προειρήκαμεν καὶ ἄρτι πάλιν λέγω (*hōs proeirēkamen kai arti palin legō*, as we said before and now again I say). Two matters, somewhat related, call for comment in this clause. First is the shift in verb number. As in the case of the verb εὐηγγελισάμεθα in verse 8, προειρήκαμεν may be a "true" plural, referring to Paul and others who preached the gospel in Galatia. In this case—to turn to the second issue—Paul would be comparing the warnings he and his missionary cohorts issued when they were in Galatia with his own present renewal of this same warning: "now *I* say again" (e.g., Lightfoot 1881: 78). However, as we argued in verse 8, the first-person plural form is better taken as "editorial," referring to Paul alone (note the similarly abrupt shift in person in 2 Cor. 10:2–3; 11:21; see e.g., Martyn 1997: 114). Paul may change the person of the verb to lend emphasis to his renewal of the "anathema" (see Gal. 5:2).

We are still left with the question whether Paul in the first case is referring to an earlier visit or to an earlier section of the letter. Paul can certainly use language broadly similar to what he uses here in the latter sense (e.g., 2 Cor. 7:3; and for this view, see, e.g., Bruce 1982b: 84; Bachmann 2003:

4. Of Paul's twelve uses of παρά with the accusative (outside Galatians), five have the sense "against," "contrary to" (Rom. 1:25, 26; 4:18; 11:24; 16:17), while three mean "beyond" (Rom. 12:3; 1 Cor. 3:11; 2 Cor. 8:3); four have other meanings or are hard to classify (Rom. 14:5; 1 Cor. 12:15, 16; 2 Cor. 11:24).

112–15), but the temporal focus here is stronger than in those cases—ἄρτι πάλιν (*arti palin*, now again)—and this makes it likely that he is repeating a warning given when he was ministering with the Galatians (R. Longenecker 1990: 17).[5]

Three other differences between the anathema in verse 8 and this one in verse 9 are also noteworthy. First, in place of "we" or "an angel from heaven," Paul names as the proclaimer of the false gospel "someone" (τις, *tis*). This is a thinly disguised way of referring to the agitators (v. 7; cf. 5:7). The singular form does not mean that Paul has a particular false teacher in mind; it is a rhetorical device intended to force the Galatians to make the identification: if it should be that "someone" is preaching a gospel contrary to ours (as for instance, these agitators). A second shift is from the so-called third-class conditional form—ἐάν (*ean*, if) with the subjunctive—to the "first class" (εἰ [*ei*, if] with indicative). It is now generally recognized that the difference between these two forms is not between a "hypothetical" situation and a "real" one. In fact, differences between these two forms of sentence are often very difficult to discern. Nevertheless, it is probably the case that the second type invites the reader or hearer to envisage the reality of the situation a bit more clearly. Silva (2003: 24) helpfully illustrates with two English examples: "If John comes, we'll go to the park" versus "If John is here, let us go to the park."[6] In our context, then, the difference might be between a general warning (v. 8) and a specific one (v. 9).

The third difference between verse 8 and verse 9 is the addition of the "receptive" side of gospel preaching. In contrast to verse 8, where the point is absent, Paul identifies the "true" gospel as the one that the Galatians have "received" (παρελάβετε, *parelabete*, you received). Paul uses this same language in verse 12, where he denies that he "received" the gospel from any human being; and the same verb occurs in the famous passage in 1 Cor. 15:1–6 about the transmission of the Christian message. What is interesting in this case is the way that Paul here begins appealing to the Galatians' own experience (thereby anticipating the longer and clearer 3:1–5). Implicitly, Paul is suggesting that the Galatians have had a true experience with God's grace (v. 6) and thus should evaluate any "new" revelation in the light of that experience. There is one gospel, revealed in Christ, to be "received" by those who hear it (Schütz 2007: 123).

5. Silva (2003: 26) argues that this interpretation favors a date for the letter following the Apostolic Council of Acts 15 because only after the Council would the need for such a warning have arisen. But this is not clear. Paul refers quite broadly here to any "gospel" that contradicts his, not to the specific false teaching that has arisen in Galatia. And it is not at all unlikely that Paul would have routinely warned his new converts about the dangers of "false gospels" in the extraordinarily diverse cultures in the first-century eastern Mediterranean.

6. See also the discussion of conditional sentences in Wallace 1996: 679–712 (he labels the first-class condition "assumption of truth for the sake of argument" versus the third-class condition "uncertain of fulfillment, but still likely"); Porter 1992: 254–67 (first-class condition, "an assertion for the sake of argument"; third-class condition, in distinction from the first class, "more tentative and simply projects some action or event for hypothetical consideration").

This verse is difficult: its interpretation and thus its contribution to Paul's argument at this point in the letter are both very unclear. The Greek text and most English translations (e.g., NRSV, ESV, NLT, NIV) reveal the uncertainty about sequence by putting the verse in its own paragraph. The NA[28] text formats the paragraph in such a way that it goes more with what follows than with what precedes it (and see also, e.g., Mussner 1988: 62; Vouga 1998: 25). But the UBS[4] text, as well as most of the English translations, aligns the verse with what precedes. This is probably the right decision (see also, e.g., Burton 1921: 33). Of course, the verse could be transitional, creating a bridge from the rebuke of 1:6–9 to Paul's defense of the gospel he preaches (1:11–2:21; e.g., Martyn 1997: 136–37; B. Dodd 1996: 92–94). But γνωρίζω . . . ὑμῖν (*gnōrizō . . . hymin*, "I want you to know," 1:11) probably marks the introduction of a new phase of the argument. Moreover, since verse 11 picks up the focus on the gospel and its proclamation from verse 9, it is likely that verse 10 is something of a parenthesis and thus to be taken with what has come before it. We cannot explain the precise way in which this verse functions in its context until we better understand its meaning.

The initial question is puzzling: ἀνθρώπους πείθω ἢ τὸν θεόν; (*anthrōpous peithō ē ton theon?* Am I trying to persuade people or God?). (Context makes clear that the present tense πείθω is conative [i.e., an action attempted but not accomplished], as most of the modern English translations recognize.) This question can mean two very different things, depending on the force that we give to the particle ἤ: (1) "Am I trying to persuade *either* people or God?" (2) "Who am I trying to persuade: people or God?" (cf. NLT: "I'm not trying to win the approval of people, but of God"). In the first case, Paul expects a negative answer to his question; it is tantamount to his claiming that he is not trying to "persuade" people *or* God.[7] In the second case, the answer could be "people," in the sense that Paul's gospel proclamation is, indeed, designed to "persuade" people about the truth of the gospel (Bruce 1982b: 84–85, who notes 2 Cor. 5:11: ἀνθρώπους πείθομεν, *anthrōpous peithomen*, we persuade people [AT]). But it is likely that the second question in the verse, "Am I seeking to please people?" is parallel to the first question. Moreover, a contrast between humans and God with respect to the gospel is important in the context (see vv. 11–12). If this is so, then Paul would be viewing both "seeking to persuade people" and "pleasing people" negatively; and the answer to his first question would have to be "God."

The problem with both views is obvious: what would it mean to "persuade God"? (The unusual nature of this language is revealed in the fact that nowhere else in the LXX or the NT does πείθω in the active voice take "God" as an object.) If Paul is denying any intent to "persuade God," then it can be

---

7. To be sure, Witherington (1998: 85) thinks that the answer is "yes" to both: Paul seeks to persuade people about the truth of his gospel and to "persuade God," in the sense of exhorting him to carry out his curse (see also Sandnes 1991: 54–55). However, as Silva (2003: 28) points out, there is no reason to think that God has to be "persuaded" to inflict his curse.

presumed that this is just what his opponents were criticizing him for doing. In this case, it is possible that πείθω implies a Greco-Roman tradition whereby untrustworthy soothsayers would try to "persuade the gods" (Betz 1979: 54–55; Lüdemann 1984: 51–52). But this accusation does not seem to make much sense in the Galatian situation. Probably, then, "persuade God" is Paul's own way of saying in other words what he says in the second part of the verse and elsewhere in his letters: in his ministry, he seeks not to curry favor with people but to find approval from God himself (see esp. 1 Thess. 2:4–6; and see, for this view, Lightfoot 1881: 79; and esp. Martyn 1997: 138–40).

The heart of Paul's concern, as the rest of the verse makes clear, is to deny accusations that he is seeking to "please people."[8] He makes this point with a second rhetorical question—ἢ ζητῶ ἀνθρώποις ἀρέσκειν; (ē zētō anthrōpois areskein? or am I seeking to please people?)—and with a conditional contrary-to-fact sentence: εἰ ἔτι ἀνθρώποις ἤρεσκον, Χριστοῦ δοῦλος οὐκ ἂν ἤμην (ei eti anthrōpois ēreskon, Christou doulos ouk an ēmēn, if I were yet trying to please people, I would not be a slave of Christ). (The imperfect ἤρεσκον, like πείθω earlier, is conative.) Rhetorically, this type of conditional sentence denies the premise by showing the untenable conclusion that would follow if it were true (if A, then B; not B, therefore not A). Paul clearly believes himself to be a "slave of Christ," language that both connotes (personally) his total dependence upon and dedication to the Lord Jesus (see esp. Harris 1999) as well as his "official" status (Moses [e.g., 2 Kings 18:12; 21:8] and esp. often David [e.g., 2 Kings 19:34; 20:6] are called "slaves" of God in the OT).

Since Paul's total focus is on pleasing his new master, it is clearly the case that he no longer is seeking to please people. The "no longer" represents the clear temporal focus that Paul introduces into his discussion of "pleasing people": ἄρτι at the beginning of the verse and ἔτι here in this last sentence. Lightfoot (1881: 79) thinks that these words imply no clear comparison with an earlier time ("at this late date"). But this is not the most natural reading of these words. More important, perhaps, is the parallel language in 5:11: "Brothers and sisters, if I am still [ἔτι] preaching circumcision, why am I still being persecuted?" Together these texts (and there are many other parallels in the respective contexts) suggest that Paul was being accused of continuing to do what he admits he used to do, or what he was accused of doing: proclaim the importance of circumcision and "please people." The reference in both cases could be to his pre-Christian insistence on circumcision and the law. He would not then, of course, have admitted that he was seeking to "please people." But in light of his conversion, he now can characterize his Jewish ministry in just these terms (see, e.g., Fung 1988: 50).[9]

---

8. B. Dodd (1996: 96–110; 1999: 143–55) argues that this "people-pleasing" motif has an implicit paradigmatic function: Paul is setting forth his own attitude as one for the Galatians to imitate. We will say more about this way of reading Gal. 1–2 below; but here we might just say that, if this note is present, it does not remove the rather clear apologetic focus on the larger passage.

9. Another option is to think that Paul refers back to his earlier preaching in Galatia (as interpreted by the false teachers): I am no longer doing what I have been accused of doing, that

But a better option is to think that Paul is alluding to his earlier preaching in Galatia—or more accurately, to how his opponents were portraying that preaching. According to them, Paul was a hypocrite: circumcising people when it suited him (5:11 may refer to incidents such as Paul's circumcision of Timothy [Acts 16:1–3]) while not insisting on circumcision on other occasions. Paul's opponents insist that such behavior reveals his desire to curry favor with people (Dunn 1990: 48). It is this (false) interpretation of Paul's motives that he denies here.

And this brings us back—finally!—to the question of the verse's function in the argument of Gal. 1. We have already suggested that the verse is something of a parenthesis; and it is best to see the γάρ (gar), as often in the NT, depending on an assumed line of thought. Paul's strong language about the "anathema" reminds him, somewhat ironically, of accusations to the effect that he seeks to "please people" in his preaching. In pronouncing damnation on false teachers, Paul implies, he can certainly not be accused of currying favor with people.

Additional Notes

1:6. Nanos (2002: 32–61, 296–309) argues that θαυμάζω introduces an "ironic rebuke," a standard literary device that signals to the reader that the document to follow is pervaded by irony. Paul, claims Nanos, writes in the role of a parent "disappointed" with the behavior of his children. This claim is basic to Nanos's approach to Galatians, enabling him to claim that much of the strong language that Paul uses about the "influencers" (his word) is not intended to be taken at face value. Thus, for instance, Paul's claim that the "influencers" are proclaiming a "different gospel" is Paul's ironic comment on the way the Galatians are, in effect, elevating the message of the influencers to an inappropriate rank. In the view of Nanos, the "influencers" are not Christians at all, nor do they claim to be preaching the gospel; they are Jewish leaders who insist that, if the Galatians want to identify with the Jewish community, they very properly must put themselves under the law of Moses. Nanos's overall reading of Galatians is fraught with problems (e.g., his definition of "gospel"); here we simply note that he is giving θαυμάζω a rhetorical significance far greater than it can bear. To be sure, the word is sometimes used to express irony (as Nanos shows from extrabiblical examples), but not consistently. There is certainly not enough evidence to justify the conclusion that the word in itself signals an "ironic rebuke."

1:6. Paul uses ἐν (en, in) with καλέω (kaleō, call [verb]) seven times, and at least three of these seem to have this "pregnant" sense of "living in": note especially the alternation in 1 Thess. 4:7 between ἐπί (epi, to) and ἐν (en, to [live]), both apparently in the sense of "destination": οὐ γὰρ ἐκάλεσεν ἡμᾶς ὁ θεὸς ἐπὶ ἀκαθαρσίᾳ ἀλλ᾽ ἐν ἁγιασμῷ (ou gar ekalesen hēmas ho theos epi akatharsia all' en hagiasmō, for God has not called us to live in uncleanness but to live in holiness [AT for all in this note]); and also 1 Cor. 7:15: ἐν δὲ εἰρήνῃ κέκληκεν ὑμᾶς ὁ θεός (en de eirēnē keklēken hymas ho theos, God has called you to live in peace); Eph. 4:4: ἐκλήθητε ἐν μιᾷ ἐλπίδι τῆς κλήσεως ὑμῶν (eklēthēte en mia elpidi tēs klēseōs hymōn, you have been called into one hope when you were called); and possibly Col. 3:15: εἰς ἣν καὶ ἐκλήθητε ἐν ἑνὶ σώματι (eis hēn kai eklēthēte en heni sōmati, to which [peace] you were called as/in/to become one body). Three other occurrences clearly indicate

---

is, watering down the gospel by ignoring the need for circumcision and other difficult covenant requirements (Dunn 1990: 48).

"sphere": Rom. 9:7 ("in Isaac"); 1 Cor. 7:18 ("in an uncircumcised state"); 7:24 ("in which state"). Paul can, of course, use other prepositions to indicate the ideas of agency or destination, as in Gal. 1:15: καλέσας διὰ τῆς χάριτος αὐτοῦ (kalesas dia tēs charitos autou, called [me] through his grace); 1 Cor. 1:9: δι' οὗ ἐκλήθητε εἰς κοινωνίαν τοῦ υἱοῦ αὐτοῦ Ἰησοῦ Χριστοῦ τοῦ κυρίου ἡμῶν (di' hou eklēthēte eis koinōnian tou huiou autou Iēsou Christou tou kyriou hēmōn, through whom you were called into fellowship with his Son, Jesus Christ our Lord); Gal 5:13: ἐπ' ἐλευθερίᾳ ἐκλήθητε (ep' eleutheria eklēthēte, you were called to be free); 1 Thess. 2:12: τοῦ θεοῦ τοῦ καλοῦντος ὑμᾶς εἰς τὴν ἑαυτοῦ βασιλείαν καὶ δόξαν (tou theou tou kalountos hymas eis tēn heautou basileian kai doxan, the God who has called you into his own kingdom and glory); 2 Thess. 2:14: εἰς ὃ [καὶ] ἐκάλεσεν ὑμᾶς διὰ τοῦ εὐαγγελίου ἡμῶν (eis ho [kai] ekalesen hymas dia tou euangeliou hēmōn, for which purpose he called you through our gospel); 1 Tim. 6:12: εἰς ἣν ἐκλήθης (eis hēn eklēthēs, into which you were called).

1:6. In his summary of the deliberations of the UBS committee, Metzger (1994: 520–21) notes that the decision about whether to include Χριστοῦ after χάριτι depended on whether to give greater weight to the external evidence or to transcriptional probabilities. The latter favor the omission of Χριστοῦ, since it is more likely that scribes would have added Χριστοῦ than omitted it and because the MSS contain several different options here (Χριστοῦ, Ἰησοῦ Χριστοῦ, Χριστοῦ Ἰησοῦ, or θεοῦ). On the other hand, the reading that includes no divine name here is found in only a part of the Western textual tradition (F and G), giving it rather weak external support. The UBS Committee, impressed by the argument from transcriptional probability yet worried about the slim external evidence, finally decided to put Χριστοῦ in the text, but in brackets.

But two further arguments bolster the case for including Χριστοῦ. First, in the nine other texts where Paul qualifies χάρις with a reference to Christ in the genitive, he always refers to the "Lord Jesus Christ" or to "the Lord Jesus" (1 Cor. 16:23; 2 Cor. 8:9; 13:13; Gal. 6:18; Phil. 4:23; 1 Thess. 5:28; 2 Thess. 3:18; 1 Tim. 1:14; Philem. 25; cf. also 2 Tim. 2:1, ἐν τῇ χάριτι τῇ ἐν Χριστῷ Ἰησοῦ). Referring simply to "the grace of Christ" is unprecedented in Paul and may therefore have led scribes to omit Χριστοῦ or to substitute other language (de Boer 2011: 38). A second reason to prefer Χριστοῦ is, as we note above in the commentary on 1:6, its very good fit with the argument of Galatians. We therefore have less hesitation than the UBS Committee in treating Χριστοῦ as original.

1:6–7. The argument for a semantic difference between ἕτερος and ἄλλος rests partly on the general usage of the two words (they were more frequently distinguished in earlier stages of Greek [see LSJ 70, 702] and continued to be distinguished to some extent in Koine Greek as well [see examples in MM 257]) and partly on texts in the LXX and the NT where a semantic distinction can at least be argued for. The argument for semantic equivalence notes, first, that there was a general tendency to blur the meanings of words originally distinct in meaning in the Koine period and, second, that there is evidence in the specific case of these two words for a blurring in meaning: ἕτερος was falling out of use in the NT period (it is absent entirely from Mark [though cf. 16:12], 1 and 2 Peter, and Revelation, and occurs only once in the Johannine writings; it has disappeared in Modern Greek) just because it was increasingly overlapping in meaning with ἄλλος. Most important, however, is the actual usage of the words, particularly when they occur together. The two are used together in ten passages (excluding Gal. 1:6–7), and in no case is a distinction between them in meaning very obvious: Matt. 16:14 (the parallels in Mark [8:28] and Luke [9:19] have ἄλλος in both); Luke 22:58–59; Acts 2:12–13; 4:12; 1 Cor. 10:29; 12:8–10; 14:17, 19; 15:39–41; 2 Cor. 11:4; Heb. 11:35–36. Two passages make this especially evident:

> To one there is given through the Spirit a message of wisdom, to another [ἄλλῳ] a message of knowledge by means of the same Spirit, [9]to another [ἑτέρῳ] faith by the same Spirit, to another [ἄλλῳ] gifts of healing by that one Spirit, [10]to another [ἄλλῳ] miraculous powers, to another [ἄλλῳ] prophecy,

to another [ἄλλῳ] distinguishing between spirits, to another [ἑτέρῳ] speaking in different kinds of tongues, and to still another [ἄλλῳ] the interpretation of tongues. (1 Cor. 12:8–10)

For if someone comes to you and preaches a Jesus other [ἄλλον] than the Jesus we preached, or if you receive a different [ἕτερον] spirit from the Spirit you received, or a different [ἕτερον] gospel from the one you accepted, you put up with it easily enough. (2 Cor. 11:4)

On the other hand, however, there is evidence from Paul's use that he continues to use ἕτερος when he contrasts one thing or person with another. In Rom. 13:8, for instance, he cites the "love command" in the form ὁ γὰρ ἀγαπῶν τὸν ἕτερον—not just some other person, but "that other person" (AT) before whom we stand (for other occurrences of this usage, see Rom. 2:1; 1 Cor. 6:1; 10:24, 29; 14:17; Gal. 6:4). Similar are places where Paul contrasts *the* law of God with "*the other* law [of sin]" (Rom. 7:23 AT), or contrasts Paul himself with "*the other* apostle" (that is, the other apostle discussed in the context, e.g., Apollos; 1 Cor. 4:6; cf. also 3:4). To be sure, Paul often uses ἕτερος with no difference in meaning from ἄλλος (as the evidence cited above reveals), but he does not seem to use ἄλλος with the distinctive "dual" force of ἕτερος. Revealing tendency in meaning is the fact that ἕτερος occurs absolutely with the article nine times, ἄλλος only once. Pauline usage thus suggests that he *sometimes* uses ἕτερος to contrast two persons or things, and this makes good sense in our text. However, this contrast does not justify the connotation of "different in kind," suggested by many commentators and most translations. The difference in vv. 6 and 7 is not "different in kind" versus "another of the same kind," but "a gospel in contrast to the true gospel" or "a competing gospel" versus simply "another."

1:8. The MSS offer several options to the text read in USB[4] and NA[28]: εὐαγγελίζηται [ὑμῖν]. In place of the present subjunctive verb, some MSS have the aorist subjunctive (εὐαγγελίσηται—ℵ[2] A and a few minuscules; ℵ* omits the following ὑμῖν). Others have the present indicative (εὐαγγελίζεται—K P [0278] and a few minuscules). The external support for the present subjunctive is stronger than for the aorist subjunctive and much stronger than for the present indicative (though the latter, being unexpected after the particle ἐάν, is the more difficult reading). In any case, the difference in these verbs has little impact on the meaning of the text. (Only if one overemphasizes the "punctiliar" force of the aorist [as, e.g., in Burton 1921: 26] does any real difference emerge.) More significant is whether we read ὑμῖν or omit it (and the MSS differ in placement, some putting it before the verb and some after). The UBS committee, as the brackets they place around the word indicate, were very uncertain about whether it belongs in the text or not. With its omission, the statement has a more general force; including ὑμῖν makes it refer more directly to the Galatians. On internal grounds, one might prefer the omission of the pronoun, since this would provide a nice progression from v. 8 to v. 9: general warning, introduced with ἐάν in 1:8, followed by application to the Galatians in 1:9 (with εἰ; and the pronoun ὑμᾶς is textually secure in 1:9). On the other hand, early copyists might have been tempted to remove the pronoun in order to generalize the verse (see, e.g., Metzger 1994: 521).

II. The Truth of the Gospel (1:11–2:21)

A "disclosure formula"—γνωρίζω γάρ ὑμῖν (gnōrizō gar hymin, for I want you to know)—marks the transition to a new section in the letter. From a formal literary standpoint, this next section incorporates the entire "body" of the letter, which runs from 1:11 to 6:10. But such a large and formally delimited section provides little help to the interpreter who is trying to understand the stages of Paul's argument in the letter. Accordingly, we break up the body of the letter into its rhetorical stages.[1] Interpreters generally agree that a new stage in the argument begins at 1:11, but they disagree about where the section ends. Most think the next major transition comes at 3:1 (e.g., Cosgrove 1988: 23–31; Martyn 1997: 152–53; Hays 2000: 199), while some put the transition point between 2:14 and 15 (e.g., Bruce 1982b: 87–88). Ultimately, it seems best to view 2:15–21 as a transitional paragraph, bringing to a conclusion Paul's defense of the truth of the gospel while simultaneously introducing some of the key theological categories that will dominate the rest of the letter. Locating it in either the first or the second major part of the letter body is therefore arbitrary: we have placed it in the first part simply on literary grounds (for more detailed discussion, see the comments on 2:15–21). Paul has used the language of the gospel to set up the basic issue of the letter in 1:6–10. The long section that begins in 1:11 has five more references to the gospel (1:11; 2:2, 5, 7, 14). In this section Paul clearly focuses on his own apostleship, but that apostleship in turn is focused on, and to some extent determined by, the gospel that he preaches (Schütz 2007: 115–58).

---

1. We use "rhetorical" loosely, to refer generally to the character of Paul's argument and without any intention of suggesting that the letter falls into the categories used by ancient rhetoricians (see "Genre and Rhetorical Stance" in the introduction). Those who do use such categories generally classify 1:11–2:14 as the *narratio*, where the circumstances of the situation being addressed are set forth (e.g., Betz 1979: 58–59; R. Longenecker 1990: vii–viii).

II. The Truth of the Gospel (1:11–2:21)
➤ A. How Paul Received and Defended the Gospel: Paul and the "Pillars" (1:11–2:14)
   B. The Truth of the Gospel Defined (2:15–21)

A. How Paul Received and Defended the Gospel: Paul and the "Pillars" (1:11–2:14)

Paul's argument in this section falls into two basic parts: a thesis statement in 1:11–12; elaboration and justification for that statement in 1:13–2:14. The second section divides further into four units. Paul structures a narrative of his conversion and ministry by reference to his relationship to Jerusalem and the apostles resident there—those he calls the "pillars" (2:9). In 1:13–17 he highlights God's initiative in turning him from persecutor of the church to evangelist of the Gentiles, laying particular stress on the fact that he did not, immediately after his conversion, "go up to Jerusalem to those who were apostles before me" (v. 17a). Next 1:18–24 describes his subsequent ministry, but with a focus again on his contacts with Jerusalem: "Then, after three years, I went up to Jerusalem . . ." (v. 18); "I was unknown personally to the churches in Judea" (v. 22). The "apostolic conference" in 2:1–10 is introduced with a formula similar to the one in 1:18: "Then, after fourteen years, I went up again to Jerusalem." In the subsequent narrative of the conference (vv. 2–10), however, the focus turns from the negative—"I did not have much contact with the Jerusalem apostles"—to the positive—"the Jerusalem apostles agreed with me about the nature of the gospel" (Silva 2001: 99–100). Paul's description of the "Incident at Antioch" (2:11–14) departs from the explicitly chronological narrative of 1:18–2:10 and abandons the Jerusalem focus. But the general theme of Paul's relationship with the "pillars" continues, and the Antioch incident thus becomes an add-on to the narrative. We may then paraphrase Paul's argument in this section as follows:

    I. Thesis: The gospel I preach (1) is not a human gospel but (2) came through a revelation of Jesus Christ (1:11–12)
   II. Elaboration and proof (1:13–2:14)
      A. To begin with the second, positive point of my thesis (1:12b): the unexpected and dramatic turnaround in my life took place solely by God's gracious initiative in revealing his Son to me (1:13–16a). And now turning to my first and negative point (1:11–12a), I did not rush to consult with the apostles in Jerusalem about the gospel I received by revelation (1:13–17).[1]

---

1. As we explain more fully below, the relationship between 1:11–12 and 1:13–17 is chiastic. Indeed, Jeremias (1958: 152–53) thinks that the rest of the letter builds chiastically on 1:11–12; thus 1:13–2:21 elaborates "not from a human being" in 1:12a; then 3:1–6:10 builds on "not in human terms" in 1:11 (see also BDF §477.1; Mussner 1988: 77). But this scheme is unlikely (R. Longenecker 1990: 21).

    B. I did go to Jerusalem after three years, but it was only to get to know Peter and not to receive instruction in the gospel. I had so little contact with Jerusalem that I was personally unknown to most of the Christians in the area (1:18–24).

    C. I was in Jerusalem again for a conference with the apostles; but far from their teaching me the gospel, they agreed with me about the basic elements of the gospel (2:1–10).

    D. True, as you may have heard, at Antioch Peter took a different view of the matter, but I did not concede his point; instead I opposed him to his face (2:11–14).

Paul's overall purpose in 1:13–2:14 is to assure the Galatians that they have indeed "received" (see 1:9) the true gospel. "Gospel" language is, of course, central in the rebuke passage of verses 6–9; but it is also central in verses 11–12, which set forth the thesis that Paul argues in 1:13–2:14, and it crops up repeatedly in the subsequent argument (1:16, 23; 2:2, 5, 7, 14). "The truth of the gospel" (2:5, 14) is Paul's focus in this section. But the Galatians received this gospel from Paul; and so, to have confidence in the gospel, they must also have confidence in the messenger who proclaimed that gospel to them. The truth of the gospel and Paul's credentials as an authoritative messenger of that gospel are therefore woven together in this part of the letter. But three aspects of Paul's narrative are notable: its focus on Jerusalem, its focus on contact with the Jerusalem apostles, and (in 1:16b–24) its negative character ("a negative travelogue" [Martyn 1997: 178]):

"I did not consult with flesh and blood" (1:16b)

"I did not go up to Jerusalem" (1:17)

"After three years I went up to Jerusalem to get to know Cephas, . . . but I stayed there only fifteen days, and I did not see any other apostle except James" (1:18–19a)

"I was unknown to the churches in Judea" (1:22)

"After fourteen years I went up again to Jerusalem" (2:1)

"the [pillars]" (2:2); "those who seemed to be something" (2:6); "Peter" (2:7, 8); "James and Cephas and John, those esteemed to be pillars" (2:9)

"I opposed Cephas to his face" (2:11)

The usual explanation for these emphases has been that Paul is in defensive mode, countering the agitators' claims about him. Judging from Paul's response, it appears that the agitators have been asserting that Paul is under the authority of the Jerusalem apostles and that therefore they, the (self-claimed) representatives of those apostles, should be listened to rather than Paul. As Dunn (1993a: 72) puts it, the distinctive character of this argument makes sense only if "what was at issue in the controversy was the independence of Paul's apostleship and gospel."

This traditional understanding of the opening part of the letter body has been challenged by scholars who argue that it does not integrate the section sufficiently with the overall argument of the letter (see esp. Lyons 1985: 123–76; Gaventa 1986: 311–19; Garlington 2003: 47; Cummins 2001: 98–101, 114–37; Verseput 1993; Matera 1992: 53–55; Vouga 1998: 29–30). They claim that Paul's purpose here is not negative, to defend himself against false accusations, but positive, either to highlight the divine origin of the gospel or to present himself as a model for the Galatians to imitate. Of course, the former point is clear in the text whether Paul asserts it for apologetic reasons or not. In this text the latter view has less explicitly to commend it, but Paul does make clear elsewhere in the letter that he presents himself as a paradigm for the Galatians: "Become like me, for I became like you" (4:12). In effect, then, Paul would be saying in 1:13–2:14: "Become like me, in my renunciation of my Judaism in response to the grace of God in revealing his Son to me."

Those who argue for this view have a point: it makes good sense to think that Paul has one eye on the Galatians as he talks about his own dramatic conversion. But the distinctive features of the passage that we have listed above simply are not adequately explained by this "paradigmatic" interpretation of the passage (Dunn 2010: 29–34). Nor does a simple positive assertion of the gospel's power and divine origin suffice to explain these features. Paul's main purpose is to establish his independent authority as an apostle, in response to the false claims of the agitators, so that the gospel he has preached to the Galatians might retain its truth and authority (see, e.g., Tolmie 2005: 32–47; Silva 2003: 38–39; Sandnes 1991:49–51; Eckert 1971: 163–228).

1. Thesis: Paul's Gospel Came through a Revelation of Jesus Christ (1:11–12)

In verses 11–12, Paul combines and elaborates two important claims that he has made in verses 1–10: (1) that his apostleship, and thus his authority, is not of "human origin" but came "through Jesus Christ" (v. 1); and (2) that "the gospel of Christ" the Galatians have received should not be exchanged for any other "gospel," no matter what the claims about its origin might be (vv. 6–9).

Exegesis and Exposition

[11]⸢Now⸣ I want you to know, brothers and sisters, that the gospel that I preach is not a human gospel. [12]For I did not receive it from a human being, ⸢neither⸣ was I taught it. Rather, it came through a revelation of Jesus Christ.

1:11   Paul connects this next stage of his argument to the preceding context with a γάρ (*gar*, now; see the additional note on the textual issue). This conjunction, of course, often introduces a reason for, or explanation of, what has come before (hence the common English rendering "for"; and cf. here RSV, NRSV, ESV, NASB). If γάρ has this sense here, the connection is probably with an implication of what Paul has said in 1:8: "if we . . . should preach to you a gospel contrary to the one we preached to you"—(implying that) we did preach the true gospel to you—*for* let me now explain how I received that gospel. However, γάρ often loses its causal/explanatory sense, functioning as "a narrative marker to express continuation or connection" (BDAG 189.2). It is best rendered in English as "now" (NAB, NET, NJB) or not translated at all (NIV, NLT, CEB). The "disclosure formula" γνωρίζω . . . ὑμῖν (*gnōrizō hymin*, I want you to know) is used by Paul elsewhere to call attention to what he is about to say (1 Cor. 12:3; 15:1; 2 Cor. 8:1; see esp. Runge 2010: 111). Paul's address of the Galatians as "brothers and sisters" (ἀδελφοί, *adelphoi*; see the note in the commentary on 1:2) signals a change in tone from the rather harsh warning of verses 6–9. "The gospel that I preach" (τὸ εὐαγγέλιον τὸ εὐαγγελισθέν ὑπ᾽ ἐμοῦ, *to euangelion to euangelisthen hyp᾽ emou*, lit., the gospel that is preached by me) brings us back to the language of verses 6–9, after the parenthetical verse 10.[1] Defining the gospel in terms

---

1. It is an all-too-common kind of overinterpretation of the aorist to think that the form εὐαγγελισθέν (an aorist passive participle) refers to Paul's initial preaching in Galatia (Burton 1921: 37; Fung 1988: 54). The participle probably refers simply to Paul's previous preaching in general (Dunn 1993a: 52).

of the one that Paul preaches is not intended to suggest that he preaches a "private" gospel, distinct from other forms of the gospel—for this would make nonsense of verses 6–9. Paul puts it this way because he was the one who first evangelized the Galatians, but also because he is highlighting the distinctive focus in his proclamation of the gospel: its law-free application to Gentiles (Bruce 1982b: 88).

This gospel, Paul claims, is not κατὰ ἄνθρωπον (*kata anthrōpon*, according to a human being). Interpreting this phrase to mean "not of human origin" (NIV, NRSV, NET, NAB) probably reads too much of verse 12 into this phrase. Paul uses the phrase five other times, and in each case it means a general sense of "human," with the emphasis ranging from a relatively neutral idea (Rom. 3:5; 1 Cor. 9:8; 15:32; Gal. 3:15) to a distinctly negative one (1 Cor. 3:3). Thus Paul is simply denying here that his gospel is a "human" gospel: "it was no human message" (NJB; see, e.g., H. Meyer 1873: 32).

Verse 12 explains the last part of verse 11: my gospel is not a human gospel because I did not receive it from a human being but through a revelation of Jesus Christ. The γάρ (*gar*) in this case, therefore, has its usual causal force. Paul makes his negative point with two correlated clauses: οὐδὲ . . . ἐγὼ παρὰ ἀνθρώπου παρέλαβεν αὐτό (*oude . . . egō para anthrōpou parelaben auto*, I did not receive it from a human being) and οὔτε ἐδιδάχθην (*oute edidachthēn*, neither was I taught it).[2] Why Paul includes both these clauses is not clear (this is the only place in the NT that these two verbs occur together). He may not intend any difference in meaning, the repetition being simply for emphasis (Bruce 1982b: 89). Or the second may prove the first: the fact that I was not "taught" it shows that I did not "receive" it (Bonnard 1972: 28). But it is most likely that the second verb is more specific: Paul is saying that he did not receive the gospel in any way from a human being; specifically, he did not sit under a teacher (such as one of the Jerusalem apostles) to learn it (for similar suggestions, see Schlier 1989: 46–47; Silva 2003: 43–44). Paul's use of the personal pronoun ἐγώ (*egō*, I) may put emphasis on himself in contrast to other missionaries (Dunn 1993a: 53), but is more likely simply a stylistic carryover from the pronoun in verse 11 (ἐμοῦ, *emou*, me). Paul's claim that he did not "receive" his gospel from any human being raises questions about what he might then mean when he says in 1 Cor. 15:1–3:

1:12

> Now, brothers and sisters, I want to remind you of the gospel I preached to you, which you received and on which you have taken your stand. ²By this gospel you are saved, if you hold firmly to the word I preached to you. Otherwise, you have

2. The normal correlative combination in Greek is οὐδὲ . . . οὐδέ (and some MSS read just this; see the additional note on 1:12), but οὐδὲ . . . οὔτε also occurs (BDAG 740; BDF §445.2). It is possible that παρὰ ἀνθρώπου goes with both verbs (see NET: "I did not receive it or learn it from any human source"; and Fung 1988: 52), but it is more likely that ἐδιδάχθην is used absolutely. The verb διδάσκω (*didaskō*, teach) occurs only four other times in the NT in the passive, and only once does it have an explicit agent, which is indicated with διά (*dia*, by/through) not παρά (*para*, by; 2 Thess. 2:15; the other occurrences are in Matt. 28:15; Eph. 4:21; Col. 2:7).

believed in vain. [3]For what I received [παρέλαβον, *parelabon*] I passed on to you as of first importance: that Christ died for our sins according to the Scriptures. . . .

How can Paul say that he "received" the gospel (1 Cor. 15:3) and yet claim that he did *not* "receive" it from any human being? Of course, since "receive" in 1 Cor. 15:3 is not qualified, it could be claimed that Paul there is referring to his receiving it from the Lord, or through revelation. But Paul's use of this same verb to describe the Corinthians' "receiving" of the gospel from Paul (1 Cor. 15:1) strongly suggests that the verb in verse 3 also has the sense "receive from another human." Paul uses the verb elsewhere with this sense, in imitation of the Jewish use of the verb קִבֵּל (*qābal*, receive; often paired with מָסַר, *māsar*, hand down; see παρέδωκα [*paredōka*, I passed on] in 1 Cor. 15:3); see esp. 2 Thess. 3:6: τὴν παράδοσιν ἣν παρελάβοσαν παρ' ἡμῶν (*tēn paradosin hēn parelabosan par' hēmōn*, the tradition that you received from us [NIV note]) and also 1 Cor. 11:23; Phil. 4:9; 1 Thess. 2:13. Nevertheless, these two texts can be reconciled if we pay close attention to their respective contexts. Here in Gal. 1:12 Paul needs to stress that the essential "truth of the gospel"—the fact of Christ's death and resurrection and its implications for Gentiles and the law[3]—was revealed to him by God and not taught to him by any human being. In 1 Cor. 15:1–3, on the other hand, he wants to remind the Corinthians that Christ's death for sins and especially his resurrection are the common teaching of the early church. And so he points out that he has handed on to them the common teaching that he also received. The point is that there is no conflict in Paul claiming that he received information about the gospel from both sources. The indisputable reality of the gospel that Paul received through revelation (and for which no human is responsible) was also confirmed to him by those who were "in the faith" before him. We have here no necessary "either/or" but a "both/and."

Paul imitates the sequence of 1:1 by following up a pair of denials with a positive assertion:

1:1: ἀπόστολος (*apostolos*, apostle)

οὐκ ἀπ' ἀνθρώπων (*ouk ap' anthrōpōn*, not from human beings)

οὐδὲ δι' ἀνθρώπου (*oude di' anthrōpou*, neither through a human being)

ἀλλὰ διὰ Ἰησοῦ Χριστοῦ καὶ θεοῦ πατρός (*alla dia Iēsou Christou kai theou patros*, but through Jesus Christ and God the Father)

1:12: οὐδὲ γὰρ ἐγὼ παρὰ ἀνθρώπου παρέλαβον αὐτό (*oude gar egō para anthrōpou parelabon auto*, for I did not receive it from a human being)

οὔτε ἐδιδάχθην (*oute edidachthēn*, neither was I taught [it])

3. Howard's view (1979: 34), however, that it was only "the particular form of the gospel preached by him" (e.g., the "non-circumcision gospel to the Gentiles") that was revealed to Paul is too narrow.

ἀλλὰ δι᾽ ἀποκαλύψεως Ἰησοῦ Χριστοῦ (*alla di᾽ apokalypseōs Iēsou Christou*, but through a revelation of Jesus Christ)[4]

This positive clause is elliptical, with a verb to be supplied. Many naturally suppose that "received" should be carried over from the first part of the verse (Lightfoot 1881: 80; and so most English versions). But the language of "revelation," or "apocalypse," suggests a stronger antithesis with the beginning of the verse. What had been planned by God, yet hidden from human perception, now comes onto the scene of human history, revealing by the very fact of the event the purposes of God. The word also has eschatological connotations, as Dunn (1993a: 53) indicates: "To describe this event as an 'apocalypse' not only underlined its heavenly authority but also implied that it had eschatological significance, that is, as the key which unlocked the mystery of God's purpose for his creation, the keystone of the whole arch of human history" (for similar uses of ἀποκάλυψις in Paul, see Rom. 2:5; 8:19; 16:25; 1 Cor. 1:7; 2 Cor. 12:1; Eph. 3:3; 2 Thess. 1:7). Any verb that implies a normal human means of disclosure should thus be avoided, in favor of the simple "came": the gospel "came through a revelation of Jesus Christ" (RSV; see, e.g., Fung 1988: 53; Hays 2000: 211). While a few scholars deny it (e.g., Bonnard 1972: 30), it seems relatively clear that the "revelation" Paul has in view is particularly the "revealing" (ἀποκαλύψαι [*apokalypsai*]) of Jesus Christ to Paul at the time of his conversion (see v. 16). This being the case, it would seem likely that we should construe the genitive Ἰησοῦ Χριστοῦ as an objective genitive: the truth of the gospel came to Paul when God revealed Jesus Christ to him (e.g., Burton 1921: 41–43; Bruce 1982b: 89; Martyn 1997: 144; Hays 2000: 211). But the immediate context of the phrase, with its emphasis on the source of knowledge, could instead suggest a source or subjective genitive: the truth of the gospel came to Paul when Jesus Christ revealed it to him (Légasse 2000: 80; R. Longenecker 1990: 24; Bonnard 1972: 28; Fee 2007b: 229; hence the "from" in many English versions [NIV, HCSB, NLT]). The meaning we have given "revelation" certainly favors the objective genitive over the subjective; but this is one of those texts where it might be best to refrain from locking the meaning into either option: perhaps Paul simply means that the "revelation" he received is bound up with, and has to do with, Jesus Christ (see Silva 2003: 45; Newman 1992: 200–201).

Additional Notes

1:11. The transitional particle that Paul uses to connect v. 11 (or vv. 11–12) to its context is difficult to identify. The MS tradition is divided rather evenly between δέ (𝔓⁴⁶ ℵ*,2 A and some other MSS) and γάρ (ℵ¹ B and others). Paul uses the disclosure formula with γνωρίζω three other times, once

---

4. Indeed, R. Longenecker (1990: 23) suggests that παρὰ ἀνθρώπου παρέλαβον matches ἀπ᾽ ἀνθρώπων in v. 1, while ἐδιδάχθην matches δι᾽ ἀνθρώπου. However, while the verses share a parallel structure, it is unlikely that the clauses can be matched up in this way.

with διό (1 Cor. 12:3) and twice with δέ (1 Cor. 15:1; 2 Cor. 8:1). On this basis, one could argue that δέ should be read here, as conforming more closely to typical Pauline style (e.g., R. Longenecker 1990: 22; the argument gains some force from the fact that 1 Cor. 15:1 is a close parallel to Gal. 1:11). On the other hand, one could argue, for this same reason, that scribes may have been more likely to change an original γάρ to δέ (e.g., Burton 1921: 36; Metzger 1994: 521). In each case the argument depends on a rather narrow data base (two other instances of γνωρίζω δέ). Perhaps more significant is the slight tendency of scribes generally to change from a more definite to a more general particle (Silva 2001: 43–49). On this basis, γάρ has a slight preference.

1:12. A significant number of MSS read οὐδέ before ἐδιδάχθην in place of the οὔτε of the NA[28] and UBS[4] texts. Despite the rather strong support for οὐδέ, it is suspect because of possible assimilation to the first οὐδέ in v. 12 and because the combination οὐδὲ . . . οὐδέ is more typical (see, e.g., Burton 1921: 40–41).

2. Elaboration and Proof: Paul's Gospel and the "Pillars" (1:13–2:14)

As many interpreters have pointed out (e.g., Vouga 1998: 29), the narrative of Paul's conversion and early travels is structured by temporal indicators: ποτε (*pote*, at one time; 1:13); ὅτε (*hote*, when; 1:15); ἔπειτα (*epeita*, then; 1:18); ἔπειτα (1:21); ἔπειτα (2:1). As we noted above (see the introduction to 1:11–2:14), this section focuses on Paul's relationships with Jerusalem, almost certainly for apologetic reasons. That is, the way he writes this narrative of his conversion and travels is best explained if he is defending himself against charges that the agitators have made about him. Throughout the account Paul focuses on the Jerusalem apostles, those he calls "the pillars" in 2:9. He insists that his understanding of the gospel did not depend on the pillars (1:13–24), that the pillars themselves agreed with his version of the gospel (2:1–10), and that he defended the gospel when it came under attack from one of those pillars (2:11–14). We can therefore surmise that the agitators were accusing Paul of having learned his gospel from the Jerusalem authorities—"the apostles before me" (1:17)—but then departing from it (or deducting from it) in his preaching to the Galatians.[1] There is good evidence that these agitators claimed to be teaching the "authentic, original Jerusalem gospel" and accused Paul of departing from it (see the "people from James" in Antioch [2:12] and the polemic against the "present Jerusalem" in 4:25). It is for this reason that Paul details the circumstances of his conversion and minimal contacts with Jerusalem in 1:13–24, demonstrates the "ratification" of his own gospel in Jerusalem (2:1–10), and gives his version of the Antioch incident (2:11–14).

---

1. This reading of 1:13–2:10 is often accused of being an invalid mirror-reading—looking at the text of Galatians as at a mirror to see what it might "reflect" about the underlying situation. To be sure, some forms of mirror-reading of NT books make the mistake of constructing rather elaborate structures on very slim evidence. But this does not invalidate mirror-reading in general. As we have argued above, the distinctive way in which Paul writes about his early ministry in Gal. 1–2 demands an explanation. And when he explicitly highlights the entry of agitators with "another gospel," it is hardly a stretch to think that these distinctive features are designed to counter the claims of these agitators.

a. Conversion and Early Travels (1:13–17)

Paul sets the stage for the narration of his contacts with Jerusalem by reminding his readers of his own radical conversion from persecutor to apostle. Particularly striking in his narrative is Paul's emphasis on the divine initiative in the whole matter. Far from being "prepared" for his conversion by a time of soul-searching, Paul testifies that he was a convinced and indeed "zealous" Jew until God called him "through his grace" (v. 15) and revealed his Son to him (v. 16). These emphases suggest that, while the revisionist interpreters are wrong to deny the overall apologetic character of 1:13–2:10, they are right to see in this narrative, and particularly in this paragraph, a concern on Paul's part to present himself as one to emulate (e.g., Verseput 1993). Like Paul, the Galatians have been "called" "to live in grace" (1:6), and like Paul, they should stay firmly rooted in this gracious gospel and not exchange it for any "other" gospel. At the same time, the very syntax of the paragraph points to the overarching apologetic focus. For, remarkably, Paul narrates his conversion in the subordinate clause of a sentence whose main clause is about his contact with other humans: "when God was pleased . . . to reveal his Son in me, . . . I did not immediately consult with any human being, nor did I go up to Jerusalem" (vv. 16–17a). As we suggested above, these two basic parts of the paragraph develop chiastically the thesis of verses 11–12:

> A my gospel is not from any human source (vv. 11–12a), rather
> B it came by revelation (v. 12b);
> B′ when God revealed his Son to me (vv. 13–16a),
> A′ I did not consult with any human being (vv. 16b–17).

We have referred above to Paul's "conversion." Some recent interpreters doubt the appropriateness of this language, arguing that what Paul describes in this paragraph is a "call," not a conversion. Alluding to the prophetic calls from the OT (v. 15), Paul claims that the revelation of God's Son to him was for the purpose of preaching Christ among the Gentiles. "Conversion," suggesting a move from one religion to another, is not an accurate description of Paul's metamorphosis since, according to him, he never left his Jewish faith.[1] There is, of course, some truth to these points.

---

1. See, esp. Dunn 1993a: 63–65 (though Dunn is a bit more nuanced in a more recent work [2005a: 351–58], where he speaks of Paul's "conversion" from Judaism, understood in terms of a cultural emphasis on Gentile distinctiveness); see also Hays 2000: 214–15; Eisenbaum 2009: 132–49; Nanos 2010.

2. Elaboration and Proof: Paul's Gospel and the "Pillars"
    a. Conversion and Early Travels
Galatians 1:13–17

Paul always claimed his new "religion" was nothing less than the authentic expression of OT faith in a new era. And he certainly highlights his call to preach among Gentiles in his Damascus Road narratives. But in this very text Paul suggests that the revelation of God's Son to him led him to contrast his new faith with his earlier "Judaism" (vv. 13–14). To label Paul's experience simply a "call" drastically underplays Paul's own claim about the dramatic change that his conversion involved (e.g., Donaldson 1997: 249–60; Kim 2002: 1–19). The "Judaism," as it was then practiced and in which Paul was raised, was clearly something that he left behind when Christ was revealed to him. The word "conversion" is appropriately applied to this thoroughgoing change, and only a difference of fundamental importance can explain why Paul would have persecuted the early Christians and then gone to suffer persecution himself after embracing Christianity. When God revealed his Son to Paul, he was both converted *and* called: "conversion and commission came together" (Bruce 1982b: 93; and see esp. S. Chester 2003: 3–42, 153–72; P. O'Brien 2004b).[2]

Exegesis and Exposition

[13]For you have heard about my former way of life in Judaism: that I intensely persecuted the church of God and tried to destroy it, [14]and that I was advancing in Judaism beyond many of those my own age among my people, being exceedingly zealous for the traditions of my fathers. [15]But when ⌜God⌝, who set me apart from the womb of my mother and called me through his grace, was pleased [16]to reveal his Son in me—in order that I might preach the good news about him among the Gentiles—I did not immediately consult with human beings, [17]neither did I go up to Jerusalem, to those who were apostles before me, but I went away into Arabia and then again returned to Damascus.

The γάρ (*gar*, for) at the beginning of this verse probably introduces all of **1:13** 1:13–2:14 (similarly R. Longenecker 1990: 27; Martyn 1997: 153). In these verses Paul explains and justifies his claim that his gospel is not a human gospel and that it came to him by revelation. Perhaps Paul also intends a more immediate connection, introducing verses 13–16a as an explanation of how he received the gospel "through a revelation of Jesus Christ" (v. 12; cf. Betz 1979: 66). The Galatians have "heard" (ἠκούσατε, *ēkousate*, you have heard) about Paul's past life in Judaism (vv. 13–14) and perhaps also about his conversion (v. 16a). Paul, of course, may have told them about these matters when he was with them (Lightfoot 1881: 81); but it is also possible that they have heard about Paul's former life from other sources, including the agitators, who may have stressed Paul's Jewishness for their own purposes (Bruce 1982b: 90; Martyn 1997: 153). As he does elsewhere,

---

2. See also R. Longenecker 1997: 27–29; Barnett 2008: 54–75. Corley (1997) notes that "conversion" is the language that has been applied to Paul's experience throughout church history.

Paul stresses the strength of his devotion to his Jewish faith. The temporal notes in the phrase τὴν ἐμὴν ἀναστροφήν ποτε ἐν τῷ Ἰουδαϊσμῷ (*tēn emēn anastrophēn pote en tō Ioudaismō*, my former way of life in Judaism)[3] suggest that he has left this way of life behind (ἀναστροφή; elsewhere in Paul in Eph. 4:22; 1 Tim. 4:12; see esp. 1 Pet. 1:18: ἀναστροφῆς πατροπαραδότου [*anastrophēs patroparadotou*, way of life handed down to you from your ancestors]). Dunn (1993a: 56–57; cf. also Haacker 1986: 96–97; Miller 2011: 48–49) minimizes the significance of this claim by arguing that Ἰουδαϊσμός refers not to "Judaism" in general but to the distinctive nationalist Jewish movement that arose at the time of the Maccabees. He notes, rightly, that the word is first attested in sources from this time (2 Macc. 2:21; 8:1; 14:38 [2x]; 4 Macc. 4:26; cf. Ciampa 1998: 106–7). However, while the word first occurs here, these texts do not suggest the sort of restrictive focus that he argues for (BDAG 479 defines Ἰουδαϊσμός as "the Judean way of belief and life"; and note Ign. *Magn.*10.3, where "Judaism" is contrasted with "Christianity"). Nor does Paul's usage of the word here and in verse 14 (its only NT occurrences) suggest any such restriction; indeed, in both verses, "in Judaism" appears to refer broadly to the Jewish faith as a whole, within which Paul distinguished himself for his devotion and zeal.

With a ὅτι (*hoti*, that), Paul elaborates on the specifics of that "former way of life in Judaism." First, he was "intensely persecuting the church of God and trying to destroy it" (καθ᾽ ὑπερβολὴν ἐδίωκον τὴν ἐκκλησίαν τοῦ θεοῦ καὶ ἐπόρθουν αὐτήν, *kath' hyperbolēn ediōkon tēn ekklēsian tou theou kai eporthoun autēn*). Both verbs are in the imperfect tense, the former because it is a durative idea—"I was persecuting"—and the second because it is conative—"I tried to destroy" (Wallace 1996: 551). The prepositional phrase καθ᾽ ὑπερβολήν (lit., "according to excess") is adverbial, stressing the extremity or intensity of his persecuting efforts (the phrase is used only by Paul in the NT; see also Rom. 7:13; 1 Cor. 12:31; 2 Cor. 1:8; 4:17). Paul's persecution of early Christians is narrated in Acts (8:3; 9:1–2), and is a staple of his autobiography (Acts 22:4–5; 26:9–11; 1 Cor. 15:9; Phil. 3:6).[4] "The church of God" that Paul was persecuting may refer to a local church, such as the one in Jerusalem (e.g., Bruce 1982b: 90; de Boer 2011: 87). But Paul's usage of the phrase elsewhere (1 Cor. 1:2; 10:32; 11:22; 15:9; 2 Cor. 1:1; 1 Tim. 3:5, 15) along with the parallel in 1 Cor. 15:9 (ἐδίωξα τὴν ἐκκλησίαν τοῦ θεοῦ [*ediōxa tēn ekklēsian tou theou*, I persecuted the church of God]) suggests rather that Paul is referring to the "universal church" (e.g., R. Longenecker 1990: 28). The phrase is probably a deliberate echo of the OT "assembly [קָהָל, *qāhāl*] of Israel" (e.g., Deut. 31:30; 1 Kings 8:14); cf. "assembly of the LORD" (e.g., Deut. 23:2, 3; 1 Chron. 28:8)

---

3. The ποτε modifies ἀναστροφήν, an article before ποτε not being required in these kind of constructions (BDF §169.1). The possessive adjective ἐμήν (in contrast to the genitive of the personal pronoun, μοῦ [*mou*, me]) is probably not emphatic here (BDF §285.1).

4. Schnabel (2004: 927) suggests, following Niebuhr (1992: 60–61), that "trying to destroy the church" means that he was trying to deny the right of Christ-followers to maintain their place in the synagogue.

or "assembly of God" (Neh. 13:1; Martyn 1997: 154). God's people are now to be found in those "assembled" around the risen Lord Jesus.

A second facet of Paul's "way of life in Judaism" is that he "was advancing in Judaism beyond many of those my own age among my people" (προέκοπτον ἐν τῷ Ἰουδαϊσμῷ ὑπὲρ πολλοὺς συνηλικιώτας ἐν τῷ γένει μου, *proekopton en tō Ioudaismō hyper pollous synēlikiōtas en tō genei mou*; this phrase is also dependent on ὅτι in v. 13). The verb προέκοπτον is again in the imperfect because it covers the course of Paul's early life; the verb is used the same way in Luke 2:52: "And as Jesus grew up, he increased [προέκοπτεν] in wisdom and in favor with God and people" (TNIV). Paul was very serious about his Jewish faith and so surpassed many of those his own age (συνηλικιώτας—the only occurrence of this word in the NT) who were "within my people," or who "belonged to my nation" (ἐν τῷ γένει μου; see also Phil. 3:5 and 2 Cor. 11:26 for other Pauline uses of γένος in this sense). The broad scope of γένος sheds light on Ἰουδαϊσμός earlier in the verse, which seems to be in parallel with it: Paul has in view not a sect within Judaism but Judaism per se.

1:14

The last part of verse 14 consists in a participial clause that is loosely tied to his claim in the earlier part of the verse: περισσοτέρως ζηλωτὴς ὑπάρχων τῶν πατρικῶν μου παραδόσεων (*perissoterōs zēlōtēs hyparchōn tōn patrikōn mou paradoseōn*, being extremely zealous for the traditions of my fathers). Rather than being causal—"I advanced in Judaism . . . because I was extremely zealous . . ." (HCSB; see also NRSV, NAB; Burton 1921: 46–47)—the clause probably "specifies in what way the προέκοπτον . . . γένει μου found active expression" (H. Meyer 1873: 36; see, e.g., RSV: "I advanced in Judaism, . . . so extremely zealous was I . . ."). As the RSV translation suggests, περισσοτέρως, while comparative in form, is probably an elative superlative (Betz 1979: 68; contra Lightfoot 1881: 81). Paul's claim to be a "zealot" (ζηλωτής) does not mean that he belonged to the actual Zealot party, or sect (contra Lightfoot 1881: 81–82) but that he had a deep passion for his Jewish faith (see also Acts 22:3; cf. Phil. 3:6).

The great OT example of such zeal was Phinehas: when confronted with a blatant violation of God's law, he killed the Israelite sinner and his pagan lover (Num. 25:6–15). Phinehas was commended by the Lord himself because he was "jealous [or "zealous"] with my jealousy" (Num. 25:11, 13 NASB; see also Ps. 106:30; 1 Macc. 2:54; 4 Macc. 18:12). Phinehas's "zeal" was directed toward God and his honor and name (as was Jesus's zeal; cf. John 2:17). But in a natural development, Jews during the Maccabean Revolt viewed zeal for the laws and regulations that they were certain God had given Israel as an appropriate expression of zeal for God. Indeed, this zeal for God's laws and for the Jewish culture they fostered became, for many, an all-consuming passion in the face of the danger of assimilation to Gentile culture (see the analysis in Dunn 1993a: 60–62). However, while often exhibiting itself in a concern for Israel's special role, zeal was ultimately focused on the God who had given Israel the law and special privileges. When Paul, then, claims that he was excessively "zealous," he refers to his basic orientation to God and to the demands that God made of him (see Ortlund 2012: esp. 137–49). Paul numbers himself among those who were caught up with this kind of zeal, a zeal that he ultimately sees to be, in his case, as for so many of his compatriots, "not according to knowledge" (Rom. 10:2 KJV).

Paul's zeal, he says, was directed toward τῶν πατρικῶν μου παραδόσεων (πατρικός, used only here in the NT, connotes "that which pertains to my father," or "the father's house" [BDAG 788]). This phrase may refer to the OT law per se (e.g., Martyn 1997: 155), or to the "oral law," what Jesus called "the tradition of the elders" (Matt. 15:2; Mark 7:3, 5; see also Josephus, *Ant.* 13.297; and Lightfoot 1881: 82; Bruce 1982b: 91; Dunn 1993a: 60; Silva 2003: 56). But it is likely that these were not separated in the mind of Paul and other "zealous" Jews like him: they understood the written OT law to have received crucial and definitive interpretation in the oral law (Betz 1979: 68)—just as today, passionate advocates of a certain theological position will decline to distinguish between Scripture and its (for that person) definitive elaboration in a system of belief.[5]

1:15 Verses 15–17 comprise one sentence, with a long subordinate clause describing Paul's conversion—ὅτε δὲ εὐδόκησεν . . . ἀποκαλύψαι τὸν υἱὸν αὐτοῦ ἐν ἐμοί (*hote de eudokēsen . . . apokalypsai ton huion autou en emoi*, but when [God] was pleased . . . to reveal his Son in me)—and a compound main clause indicating what Paul did (or did not do) after his conversion—εὐθέως οὐ προσανεθέμην σαρκὶ καὶ αἵματι οὐδὲ ἀνῆλθον εἰς Ἱεροσόλυμα . . . ἀλλὰ ἀπῆλθον εἰς Ἀραβίαν καὶ πάλιν ὑπέστρεψα εἰς Δαμασκόν (*eutheōs ou prosanethemēn sarki kai haimati oude anēlthon eis Hierosolyma . . . alla apēlthon eis Arabian kai palin hypestrepsa eis Damaskon*, immediately I did not consult with flesh and blood, neither did I go up to Jerusalem, . . . but I went away into Arabia and again returned to Damascus). As we noted earlier, the structure of this sentence reflects Paul's concern, for apologetic reasons, to establish his apostolic independence, and especially his independence from Jerusalem. Whether we include ὁ θεός (*ho theos*, God) in the text or not (see the additional note), the subject of the verb εὐδόκησεν is clearly God. This verb, which means basically "to take pleasure in," "be pleased with," often has an additional nuance: "take pleasure in and so decide to do." See, for example, Ps. 68:16 (67:17 LXX), "the mountain on which God *has chosen* to dwell" (τὸ ὄρος ὃ εὐδόκησεν ὁ θεὸς κατοικεῖν ἐν αὐτῷ, *to oros ho eudokēsen ho theos katoikein en autō*) and 1 Thess. 2:8 (NRSV), "We *determined* to share with you not only the gospel of God but also our own souls" (εὐδοκοῦμεν μεταδοῦναι ὑμῖν οὐ μόνον τὸ εὐαγγέλιον τοῦ θεοῦ ἀλλὰ καὶ τὰς ἑαυτῶν ψυχάς, *eudokoumen metadounai hymin ou monon to euangelion tou theou alla kai tas heautōn*

5. A few interpreters have argued that Paul's zeal had to do not with the law but with the political position of Jews in their Gentile-dominated communities—the proclamation of a crucified Messiah being a danger to the standing of the Jewish communities (Fredriksen 1991; N. Elliott 1994: 148).

psychas). This is clearly its sense here (see also, in Paul, with God as subject, 1 Cor. 1:21; Col. 1:19).

Paul completes his main sentence with an infinitive at the beginning of verse 16 (ἀποκαλύψαι). But before he does this, he adds a compound participial description of God: ὁ ἀφορίσας με ἐκ κοιλίας μητρός μου καὶ καλέσας διὰ τῆς χάριτος αὐτοῦ (*ho aphorisas me ek koilias mētros mou kai kalesas dia tēs charitos autou*, the one who set me apart from the womb of my mother and called [me] through his grace).[6] The verb ἀφορίζω (*aphorizō*) means "to separate" (Matt. 13:49; 25:32 [2x]; Luke 6:22; 2 Cor. 6:17; Gal. 2:12) and comes to be used in the sense of "set apart, appoint" (BDAG 158.2; cf. Acts 13:2; Rom. 1:1).[7]

Paul's claim that he was "set apart" ἐκ κοιλίας μητρός μου can be variously interpreted. The ἐκ in this phrase can denote "separation" (Job 38:8; cf. also Ps. 71:6 [70:6 LXX]), giving rise to the KJV rendering, "separated me from my mother's womb." But ἐκ usually has a temporal meaning in this phrase (Lightfoot 1881: 82). The question is then whether the meaning is "set me apart *from the time of* my birth" or "set me apart *before* birth." Most occurrences of the phrase in the LXX and NT have the former meaning, as in Acts 3:2, where Luke introduces "a man who was lame from birth" (see also Judg. 16:17; Ps. 22:10; Matt. 19:12; Acts 14:8). But the phrase probably has the latter meaning in Luke 1:15 (so most English translations), and in Isa. 49:1, where the Servant says, "from the womb the LORD called me; from the belly of my mother he mentioned my name" (AT; LXX is slightly different: "the Lord called my name from the womb of my mother" [κύριος ἐκ κοιλίας μητρός μου ἐκάλεσεν τὸ ὄνομά μου, *kyrios ek koilias mētros mou ekalesen to onoma mou*]). The parallelism strongly suggests that "from the womb" here refers to the Lord's call of the Servant before he was born. This text is important because Paul clearly depends on this text and on the prophetic call of Jeremiah in Jer. 1:5 as he describes his own apostolic call (see esp. the careful analysis of Ciampa 1998: 111–18; Harmon 2010: 76–85; Wilk 1998: 292–93, although he contests any reference to Jeremiah).[8] Jeremiah 1:5 does not have the same complete phrase that we have here in Galatians, but it is very close in both wording and concept: "Before I formed you in the womb [ἐν κοιλίᾳ, *en koilia*] I knew you, before you were born [πρὸ τοῦ σε ἐξελθεῖν ἐκ μήτρας, *pro tou se exelthein ek mētras*] I set you apart; I appointed you

---

6. The article governs both participles as a valid example of "Sharp's Rule" (Wallace 1996: 275).

7. It has been argued that Paul's use of ἀφορίζω, "separate," is a play on the word for "Pharisee," the "separated one": Paul truly became a "separated one" when God set him apart for the gospel (Dunn 1993a: 63). But the allusion is unlikely: Paul has not actually used the word "Pharisee," whose etymology is, in any case, debated (Betz 1979: 70; Schlier 1989: 53).

8. S. Kim (2002: 101–6) argues that Paul also has the initial "call" of the Servant, in Isa. 42:1–9, in view in this text. He notes that some LXX MSS use the verb εὐδοκέω (*eudokeō*, be pleased) in v. 1; that the LXX reference to the Servant as ὁ ἐκλεκτός (*ho eklektos*, chosen) may have influenced Paul's claim to have been "set apart" (ἀφορίσας); and that Isa. 42:6 refers to the Servant as a "light for the Gentiles."

as a prophet to the nations." Paul's dependence on these texts makes it very likely that he is claiming to have been "set apart" "before he was born" (e.g., Lightfoot 1881: 82; Bruce 1982b: 92).

Neither of these two prophetic texts on which Paul probably depends uses the verb ἀφορίζω (in Isa. 49:1 ἐκ κοιλίας μητρός [ek koilias mētros, from my mother's womb] is attached to καλέω [kaleō, call]), so they provide no help in determining how Paul relates his being "set apart" to his "calling." He might view them as two ways of describing the same thing (Martyn 1997: 156–57, who notes that Paul reverses the sequence of the two ideas in Rom. 1:1 [κλητός . . . ἀφωρισμένος, klētos . . . aphōrismenos, called . . . set apart]). But it is also possible that he views them as two separate stages: being "set apart" before birth and "called" when God revealed his Son to him (Betz 1979: 70; P. O'Brien 2004b: 364–65). Perhaps the parallel Paul suggests between his own experience and that of the Galatians (1:6) favors the latter. It is, in each case, God's grace that is the dominating force.

1:16 Paul now completes the verbal idea begun with εὐδόκησεν in verse 15: ἀπο-καλύψαι τὸν υἱὸν αὐτοῦ ἐν ἐμοί (apokalypsai ton huion autou en emoi, to reveal his Son to me). The reference is to the appearance of the risen Christ to Paul as he was traveling to Damascus to persecute the Christians there (Acts 9:1–9). But Paul's way of describing the experience is noteworthy. Only here (and indirectly in 1:12) does Paul use "revelation" language to depict his Damascus Road encounter with the risen Christ. Not only that: his claim that the Son was revealed "in" him is also surprising; we would have expected Paul to say that God revealed his Son "to" him. To be sure, some interpreters think that the ἐν could have this meaning here (BDF §220.1; Martyn 1997: 158). But this is doubtful. Paul elsewhere uses the dative (Eph. 3:5) or εἰς (Rom. 8:18) after ἀποκαλύπτω (apokalyptō, reveal) to designate the recipients of revelation. His choice to use ἐν here is likely intended to denote that the revelation of God's Son had a transformative power "in" his very being: "the revelation had enlightened his whole soul, and . . . he had Christ speaking within him" (Chrysostom, *Comm. Gal.* on 1:16 [*NPNF*[1] 13:11]; see esp. Dunn 1993a: 64; B. Longenecker 1998: 149–50; also, e.g., Burton 1921: 49–51; Betz 1979: 71; Bruce 1982b: 93).[9] God broke into Paul's life as a Jew and indeed persecutor of the risen Christ and his people, through an "apocalyptic" transformative event (Boers 2006: 31–32). We should also take note of the object of the revelation: "God's Son." Sonship plays a critical and indeed central role in Galatians: Paul tries to convince the Galatians that they become and remain "the sons [or children] of Abraham," and thus "sons of God" through faith in Christ alone (3:7, 26; 4:4–7; cf. 4:22, 30 and 2:20). Note particularly 4:4–5, where Paul connects the sending into the world of God's Son with Christians' attainment of "sonship." Paul's choice to identify the one who was revealed in him as the Son of God therefore implies

---

9. Two other options for ἐν ἐμοί are (1) that the phrase is instrumental, denoting the revealing of God's Son through Paul in his ministry (Lightfoot 1881: 82–83); or (2) that the phrase refers to God's revelation "in my former manner of life" (de Boer 2011: 92).

that his experience has been, in a certain basic sense, similar to the Galatians: in both cases, God worked in grace through his Son to make them his sons.

Distinct from the Galatians' experience, however, is the purpose for which God revealed his Son in Paul: ἵνα εὐαγγελίζωμαι αὐτὸν ἐν τοῖς ἔθνεσιν (hina euangelizōmai auton en tois ethnesin, in order that I might proclaim him among the Gentiles).[10] This clause does not mean that Paul views his Damascus Road experience as a call and *not* as a conversion: it is a logical error to think that because Paul speaks of his calling as a purpose of the experience that it is the *only* purpose of that experience (contra Dunn 1993a: 65). Indeed, the transformative revelation of God's Son in itself suggests the idea of conversion. Of course, Paul typically associates his encounter with the risen Christ with his distinctive call to preach the gospel to Gentiles (Acts 9:15; 22:15; 26:17–18). But here he does so because his focus, from this point forward in his autobiography, is on his mission and its relationship to the Jerusalem apostles. Perhaps Paul wants to make clear that his calling ultimately rests on God's revelation, not with, for example, a human "commissioning," either at Antioch (cf. Acts 13:1–3) or, as the agitators may have alleged, at Jerusalem (Mussner 1988: 87).

After a long and relatively complex subordinate clause (vv. 15–16a), Paul finally arrives at his main clause, which, as we noted earlier, is made up of two negative clauses, "I did not consult with flesh and blood" and "neither did I go up to Jerusalem," and one positive clause, "I went away to Arabia." After his conversion/commissioning, Paul felt no need to consult with other people about the meaning of his experience, and still less any need to find legitimation from the Jerusalem apostles. "Flesh and blood" is a typical idiom for "human beings," and it is typically used, as here (versus "revelation"), to set up a contrast with something divine (Matt. 16:17; 1 Cor. 15:50; Eph. 6:12; Heb. 2:14; cf. Mussner 1988: 89–90). The verb he uses—προσανατίθημι (prosanatithēmi, only here and at Gal. 2:6 in NT, lacking in LXX)—has the sense "consult with."[11] There is considerable debate about which clause the adverb εὐθέως (eutheōs, immediately) modifies. Is Paul saying "I did not immediately consult with people or go up to Jerusalem" (NIV, ESV, NLT; R. Longenecker 1990: 33); or "I immediately went away to Arabia" (NRSV; Lightfoot 1881: 83; Burton 1921: 53–54; Bruce 1982b: 94)? Since Paul's emphasis in this passage is on the former point, we should probably conclude that he is claiming he did not "immediately" consult with any human being.[12]

---

10. Hultgren (2006: 22–25, 29–32) suggests that, partly because of the OT prophetic background, ἔθνεσιν here means "nations." But, as Schnabel (2004: 935) notes, parallel passages (esp. Rom. 1:13) suggest that "Gentiles" is the best reading (the ἐν means "among" [A. Robertson 1934: 587]).

11. Dunn (1993a: 67), citing Diodorus Siculus, *Library of History* 17.116.4, argues that the verb has a more technical sense: "consult in order to be given a skilled and authoritative interpretation." But the verb does not have this particular sense often enough to assume that Paul has this distinct idea in mind (Silva 2001: 58–61).

12. Bruce (1982b: 94) suggests the latter is more likely because, if Paul had intended εὐθέως to qualify the verbs in the negative clauses, it would have followed the negative οὐ (as in Luke 14:5;

1:17 Together, the two assertions—positively, that God "revealed his Son in me" and negatively, that he did not immediately consult human beings—substantiate his claim that he received his gospel, not from a human source, but from a "revelation of Jesus Christ" (vv. 11–12). The second negative clause that opens this verse moves the argument into the specifics that were apparently in question in the Galatian crisis. As we noted above, the consistent focus on the Jerusalem apostles from this point forward in Paul's narrative is best explained if the agitators were arguing that Paul was an unlearned or perhaps disobedient disciple of the Jerusalem apostles. Paul counters this accusation head-on by elaborating "flesh and blood" in terms of "the apostles who were before me" (τοὺς πρὸ ἐμοῦ ἀποστόλους, *tous pro emou apostolous*). These apostles, as Paul will make clear subsequently, are especially Cephas (or Peter), James (the brother of the Lord), and John (1:18–19; 2:7–9). To see them, he would have had to "go up" (ἀνῆλθον, *anēlthon*) to Jerusalem. (Jerusalem was situated on an elevated area; hence the traditional language of "going up" to Jerusalem; cf., e.g., 2 Sam. 19:34; 1 Kings 12:27; Ezra 1:3; Zech. 14:17; Acts 15:2; 21:12; 25:9.)[13]

"Instead" (ἀλλά, *alla*) of "going up" to Jerusalem, Paul "went away into Arabia." In none of his other autobiographical comments does Paul mention such a trip to Arabia, and the reference here is so brief that we can only speculate about it. "Arabia" (Ἀραβία, *Arabia*) in Paul's day would have referred to any part of a fairly large area to the northeast, east, and south of Israel, including portions of Transjordania, south Syria, the Negev, and the northwest Arabian Peninsula. But "Arabia" was more likely to be a political designation, referring to the Nabatean Kingdom, a Romanized nation whose capital was in Petra and whose influence extended as far as Damascus to the north and the Sinai Peninsula to the south (R. H. Smith, *ABD* 1:325).

What Paul was doing there has almost evenly divided interpreters for centuries. Some think that he got away from Israel in order to meditate on the significance of the revelation that he had received (e.g., Burton 1921: 55–57, who notes that this would make a good contrast with his decision not to consult with people; cf. also, e.g., Riesner 1998: 258–60). A particular twist on this suggestion that has gained currency recently is that Paul went, specifically, to Mount Sinai (which Paul explicitly locates in Arabia in 4:25), where he reflected on the relationship between the law given by God at that spot and the revelation of Jesus Christ that he had just experienced (Lightfoot 1881: 87–90; N. Wright 1996; Ciampa 1998: 121; Hays 2000: 216; Garlington 2003: 62).

This thesis is difficult to prove or disprove, but the fact that Paul was persecuted by the Nabatean King Aretas (2 Cor. 11:32) might suggest rather that

---

21:9). But the compound negative in Gal. 1:16–17, οὐ . . . οὐδέ (*ou . . . oude*, not . . . neither), seems to warrant putting the adverb before the first negative.

13. Paul uses the more Hellenized form of the name for Jerusalem here, Ἱεροσόλυμα (*Hierosolyma*), as opposed to Ἱερουσαλήμ (*Ierousalēm*), which he more often uses (Rom. 15:19, 25, 26, 31; 1 Cor. 16:3; Gal. 4:25, 26; he uses Ἱεροσόλυμα elsewhere only in 1:18 and 2:1). Adams (2000: 222) suggests that Paul may intend to "de-sacralize" the city; but this is probably too speculative.

Paul went to Arabia to preach the gospel that had been revealed to him (e.g., Betz 1979: 74; Bruce 1982b: 96; Murphy-O'Connor 1993: 733). Of course, Paul could have done both: Hengel and Schwemer (1997: 109–19) argue that Paul might have begun preaching in Nabatea because it was closest (both geographically and ethnically) to Israel but that Paul might also have journeyed to Mount Sinai for reflection. We simply cannot know for sure, but we think it slightly more likely that Paul mentions Arabia in his travelogue here because he began his preaching ministry there.[14]

After his stay in Arabia, Paul says, "I returned again" (πάλιν ὑπέστρεψα) to Damascus. The language implies, of course, that Paul had already been in Damascus, a fact that is clear from other texts and that his readers may perhaps have known from Paul's teaching (Mussner 1988: 92–93). The information Paul provides in this text reveals that the Damascus stay recorded by Luke in Acts 9:8–25 was interrupted by a perhaps extended stay in Arabia (on the relationship between Paul's narrative here and Acts, see Schnabel 2004: 997–1006; Barnett 1999: 249–86).

Additional Note

1:15. A large and diverse group of MSS read ὁ θεός after the verb εὐδόκησεν while an equally diverse group omit it. It could be argued that the text virtually demands the noun, since Paul only mentions God earlier in a subordinate phrase in v. 13 (τὴν ἐκκλησίαν τοῦ θεοῦ), and the only earlier place where God is the subject of a verb is all the way back in v. 1 (τοῦ ἐγείραντος; cf. also v. 5). The UBS committee, on the basis of strong external testimony, decided to include it (Metzger 1994: 521). Of course, this is just the reason why there might have been an overwhelming pressure on scribes to add the noun. On the whole, it seems best to omit the word (in agreement with the [rare] explicit dissent of Metzger and Wikgren in Metzger 1994: 521–22; see also Fee 2007b: 221).

---

14. S. Kim (2002: 103–4; cf. also 2011: 13–14) suggests that Paul might have had a "biblical" reason for going to Arabia. He thinks that Paul may well have read the geographical references in Isa. 42:11 (which immediately follows the passage about the commissioning of the Servant to which Paul may make allusion in v. 15), "Kedar" (קֵדָר, qēdār) and "Sela" (סֶלַע, selaʿ), as references to "Arabia" (סֶלַע, selaʿ, "crag" or "cliff," is similar to the name of the Nabatean capital, Petra [= "rock"]; and the Targum paraphrases both here as "the wilderness of Arabia").

b. First Jerusalem Visit and Further Travels (1:18–24)

The chronological indicators in 1:18 and 1:21 mark out the next stages in Paul's travelogue. Two specific movements are noted, each introduced with ἔπειτα (*epeita*, then): a visit to Jerusalem (1:18) and a move to "the regions of Syria and Cilicia" (1:21). Paul spends no time describing his ministry during these years (the events he narrates in this paragraph may have covered as many as ten years). He concentrates, rather, on the negative point that he introduced in verse 17a: his minimal contact with Jerusalem and the apostles resident there.

Exegesis and Exposition

¹⁸Then, after three years, I went up to Jerusalem to get acquainted with ⌜Cephas⌝; and I spent fifteen days with him. ¹⁹I saw no other apostles except James, the brother of the Lord. ²⁰But concerning the things I am writing about, I testify before God that I am not lying. ²¹Then I went into the regions of ⌜Syria and Cilicia.⌝ ²²I was personally unknown to the churches in Judea that are in Christ. ²³The only thing they were hearing was "The one who at one time persecuted us is preaching the faith that he once tried to destroy." ²⁴And they were glorifying God because of me.

1:18 "Then, after three years" almost certainly should be connected not with Paul's stay in Arabia or Damascus (v. 17b; as, e.g., Mussner 1988: 93; Lüdemann 1984: 60) but with his conversion (v. 15a; e.g., R. Longenecker 1990: 37; Martyn 1997: 181). For it is not Paul's ministry per se that is the focus of this narrative but his contacts with the Jerusalem apostles. Thus, as we have seen, the main clause in the long sentence that runs from verse 15 through verse 17 features the negative claims "I did not consult with flesh and blood" and "I did not go up to Jerusalem to those who were apostles before me" (vv. 16b–17a). The chronological marker in verse 18, then, picks up the "immediately" that modifies both these clauses: "after my conversion, I did not immediately consult with humans, including the Jerusalem apostles; it was only 'then, after three years' that I went to Jerusalem." In modern English, "after three years" would mean that three years intervened between his conversion and this visit to Jerusalem. In the ancient world, however, the comparable Greek phrase—μετὰ ἔτη τρία, *meta etē tria*—could mean a period anywhere from two to three years. For even in expressions using μετά, ancient writers would sometimes count "inclusively." In effect, the phrase would then mean "in the third year." This visit to Jerusalem, which is the same as the one recorded by Luke in Acts

9:26–30, thus probably took place in AD 36–37 (dating Paul's conversion in 33–34). In fact, however, the precise chronological significance of this phrase has little bearing on the meaning of the passage: for our purposes what is important is that some time intervened between Paul's conversion and his "consultation" with the Jerusalem apostles, thereby proving his point that his gospel was not derived from human beings (1:12).

Paul's purpose in "going up" (ἀνῆλθον, anēlthon; see v. 17) was to "get acquainted with" Peter. The verb Paul uses here, ἱστορέω (historeō), is properly translated "get acquainted with," "visit"; it does not signify that Paul went to Jerusalem to receive instruction about the basic meaning or implications of the gospel (which would contradict his whole point in this passage; see the first additional note on 1:18). Of course, it is inconceivable, as C. H. Dodd (1937: 16) has put it, that Paul and Cephas spent fifteen days discussing the weather. They would certainly have talked about their respective Christian experiences; and it would not be counter to Paul's argument to think that Paul would have eagerly sought information from Peter about Jesus's life and teaching and the history of the early Christian movement. As we noted in commenting on verses 11–12, Paul has no intention of denying that he received much useful information about Jesus and the gospel from others. What he is keen to deny is the agitators' charge that his understanding of the gospel *depends* on anyone else, especially the Jerusalem apostles.[1]

Paul typically refers to the apostle Peter by his Aramaic name (כֵּיפָא, kêpā'), as transliterated into Greek (κηφᾶς, kēphas; Gal. 2:9, 11, 14; 1 Cor. 1:12; 3:22; 9:5; 15:5; only in Gal. 2:7, 8 does he use his Greek name, πέτρος [petros]). Scholars have suggested various reasons for this habit, but none is convincing.[2] The chronological exactitude (rare in the NT) that we have seen at the beginning of the verse—"after three years"—continues at the end of the verse: ἐπέμεινα πρὸς αὐτὸν ἡμέρας δεκαπέντε (epemeina pros auton hēmeras dekapente, I remained with him for fifteen days).[3] Recognizing that his every word will be scrutinized by opponents, Paul is being as precise as he can be.

1. Howard (1979: 36) argues that the point is not whether Peter gave Paul information, but just the reverse: On this occasion Paul did not inform Peter about his law-free gospel. But this interpretation ignores the way vv. 11–12, with their focus on Paul's receiving knowledge of the gospel, dominate this section.

2. For example, Perkins (2003: 45) thinks that Paul's use of Peter's Aramaic name, while using a Roman name for himself, suggests a separation of ministry spheres, while Dunn (1993a: 74) thinks that the Aramaic form of Peter's name may suggest his status with the Jewish churches. But neither explanation appears to make good sense in 1 Corinthians, where Paul also uses (exclusively) Peter's Aramaic name.

3. Paul's choice of the compound form ἐπιμένω instead of the simple μένω (menō, remain) probably has no semantic significance (see his other uses of the compound verb in Rom. 6:1; 11:22, 23; 1 Cor. 16:7, 8; Phil. 1:24; Col. 1:23; 1 Tim. 4:16; it is difficult, for instance, to detect any difference in meaning between ἐπιμένω in Phil. 1:24 and μένω in v. 25). The preposition πρός (pros) with the accusative, similarly, here simply means "with"; any particular nuance (distinct, for instance, from μετά [meta, with] with the genitive or σύν [syn, with] with the dative) is difficult to detect (contra, e.g., Martyn [1997: 173], who suggests Paul here means he was Peter's houseguest). The only other time Paul uses μένω or ἐμιμένω to denote a "stay"

1:19 Continuing his careful rehearsal of events, Paul notes that he did not see any other apostle—εἰ μὴ Ἰάκωβον τὸν ἀδελφὸν τοῦ κυρίου (*ei mē Iakōbon ton adelphon tou kyriou*, except James, the brother of the Lord). Four men with the name Ἰάκωβος figure in the NT: (1) James the son of Zebedee, brother of John, one of the Twelve (very frequently in the Gospels; he suffered an early martyrdom [Acts 12:2]); (2) James, the son of Alphaeus, also one of the Twelve (see Mark 3:18; he may be the same as "James the younger" [Mark 15:40]); (3) James the father of Judas (Luke 6:16; Acts 1:13); (4) James, a leader in the early church (see Acts 12:17; 15:13; 21:18), and (almost certainly) the writer of the Letter of James (1:1) and brother of Jude (Jude 1). The James that Paul mentions here cannot be the son of Zebedee (he died before the likely date of this Jerusalem visit) and almost certainly is not the son of Alphaeus or the father of Judas, who play no significant role in the NT or in early Christian literature. James, the leader of the Jerusalem church, on the other hand, has just the role that explains his prominence in Gal. 1–2 (see also 2:9, 12).

The real debate in this passage is not over the identity of James but whether Paul explicitly includes him among the apostles. Note these two different English translations:

> I saw none of the other apostles—only James, the Lord's brother. (NIV)
> The only other apostle I met at that time was James, the Lord's brother. (NLT)

The difference in these two translations is the way the phrase introduced by εἰ μή is understood. This combination of words normally indicates an "exception" to the previous statement, but it is not clear in this case whether the exception relates specifically to the apostles or more generally to "people in authority." That is, we could paraphrase (as the dash in the NIV seems to imply): "I saw none of the other apostles; but I did see another important person, that is, James, the brother of the Lord"; or, as the NLT rendering suggests: "I saw none of the other apostles, with the exception of James, the brother of the Lord." The latter is arguably the more natural reading of the syntax and should probably be accepted (see the first additional note on 1:19). Of the apostles, Paul "saw" (εἶδον, *eidon*) Peter and James on this trip to Jerusalem (see the second additional note on 1:19). His purpose is, again, to minimize the extent of his contact with the Jerusalem apostles. Paul spent some time with Peter, "getting acquainted" with him and—certainly—learning more about the life and teaching of Jesus. James he only "saw," suggesting perhaps a briefer meeting.

1:20 Paul adds a solemn oath to underscore the truthfulness of what he is saying: ἃ δὲ γράφω ὑμῖν, ἰδοὺ ἐνώπιον τοῦ θεοῦ ὅτι οὐ ψεύδομαι (*ha de graphō hymin, idou enōpion tou theou hoti ou pseudomai*, in the things that I am writing about, I testify before God that I am not lying). The ὅτι depends on a verb that

---

with someone, he also uses πρός with the accusative (1 Cor. 16:7; though note Phil. 1:25: μενῶ καὶ παραμενῶ πᾶσιν ὑμῖν [*menō kai paramenō pasin hymin*, I will remain and I will continue with all of you]; here the dative probably depends more on παραμέμω).

must be supplied with the phrase ἐνώπιον τοῦ θεοῦ. Based on similar asseverations in Paul, the verb we should most likely supply is μαρτυρέω (*martyreō*, testify; see Rom. 10:2; 2 Cor. 8:3; Gal. 4:15; Col. 4:13) or the compound form, διαμαρτυρέω (*diamartyreō*; 1 Tim. 5:21; 2 Tim. 4:1—Paul never uses the verb ὀμνύω [*omnyō*], take an oath). The use of ἰδού (*idou*, traditionally "behold," in modern English, "see," or "note well") is also significant. Unlike some biblical authors, Paul rarely uses the word (only five other times outside OT quotations: 1 Cor. 15:51; 2 Cor. 5:17; 6:9; 7:11; 12:14), so its presence here brings clear emphasis (perhaps carried over into modern English best with an exclamation mark at the end of the sentence; see RSV, NRSV, ESV, NET). As Sampley (1977) notes, the Romans viewed an oath as the "final word" in a trial. Paul is trying to make it as clear as he can that "the things he writes" (ἃ γράφω) here should have decisive significance in the "trial" between himself and his opponents. But what in particular are "the things he writes"? The plural suggests that more than verse 19 is in view (contra Schlier 1989: 62); most think that Paul has all of verses 13–19 in mind (e.g., Burton 1921: 61; Betz 1979: 79; R. Longenecker 1990: 39–40). It is also possible, however, that Paul intends this oath to apply to all of verses 13–24 and even into Gal. 2 (Martyn 1997: 174).

A second ἔπειτα (*epeita*, then; see v. 18) marks the next stage of Paul's selective autobiography. His purpose remains clear: to show how little contact he had with the Jerusalem apostles so that no one can accuse him of having learned his gospel from them (v. 12). According to Luke, Paul's first postconversion Jerusalem visit ended when his attempts to evangelize Hellenistic Jews stirred up persecution against him. To save his life, the Jerusalem believers "took him down to Caesarea and sent him off to Tarsus" (Acts 9:30). It was after some time—probably around eight years—that Barnabas brought Paul from Tarsus to Antioch to join him in ministry in that key city (Acts 11:25–26). Tarsus was one of the major cities in the Roman province of Cilicia. So Paul's claim here in Galatians that ἦλθον εἰς τὰ κλίματα τῆς Συρίας καὶ τῆς Κιλικίας (*ēlthon eis ta klimata tēs Syrias kai Kilikias*, I went into the regions of Syria and Cilicia) must describe his move to Tarsus. However, since Paul follows up this notice of movement with a description of activity during that period, the combination ἦλθον εἰς probably has the sense "Then I came into" (cf. KJV). Paul's use of the two provinical names, Syria and Cilicia, shows that Paul has in mind the entire period of time from his move to Tarsus until his next journey to Jerusalem for the council described in Gal. 2:1–10. Assuming, as we argue, that this council took place during the visit to Jerusalem described in Acts 11:27–30, this period of time includes ministry in Tarsus for around eight years and ministry in Antioch for at least a year: see Acts 11:26: "So for a whole year Barnabas and Saul met with the church [in Antioch] and taught great numbers of people. The disciples were called Christians first at Antioch."

Paul denotes the region of this activity quite generally: "the regions of Syria and Cilicia." "Regions" (κλίματα) probably refers to geographical areas within

1:21

the provinces of Syria and Cilicia (Paul's two other uses of κλίμα also seem to have a geographic, rather than political, focus: Rom. 15:23; 2 Cor. 11:10; cf. LN 15.1.79; R. Longenecker 1990: 40). The separate mention of Syria and Cilicia does not conform to the official Roman usage at that time (Syria-Cilicia was a single Roman province until AD 72 [Riesner 1998: 266]), but it undoubtedly reflects common local practice. The letter from the Apostolic Council is addressed to believers in τὴν Ἀντιόχειαν καὶ Συρίαν καὶ Κιλικίαν (*tēn Antiocheian kai Syrian kai Kilikian*, Antioch and Syria and Cilicia; Acts 15:23); and Paul, with Silas, is described as "strengthening the churches" in τὴν Συρίαν καὶ [τὴν] Κιλικίαν (*tēn Syrian kai [tēn] Kilikian*, Syria and Cilicia) after the Council (Acts 15:41). Moreover, Syria and Cilicia are often separated in Acts: for Syria see 18:18; 20:3; 21:3; for Cilicia see 21:39; 22:3; 23:34. We might have expected Paul to have mentioned the provincial regions in reverse order, since Acts shows that he ministered in Cilicia (Tarsus) first, and then moved to Syria (Antioch). Probably Paul mentions the more important area first (Lightfoot 1881: 85). We should also note a region of significant Pauline ministry that is *not* mentioned here: Cyprus and the "Galatian" region of the first missionary journey (Acts 13–14). While arguments from silence are always precarious, it does seem unusual, if the journey had taken place before the Council described in Gal. 2, that Paul makes no reference to those regions here (Martyn 1997: 183–86).[4]

1:22 The remaining verses of chapter 1 reveal again Paul's very specific purpose in the narration of his conversion and early ministry. In these verses we read nothing about the many years of ministry in Tarsus (a period of time Pauline students would love to have information about!) or the significant work in the mixed Jewish-Gentile church in Antioch. Rather, Paul concentrates on his relationship (or lack thereof) with the distant churches in Judea. The point is clear enough: during all these years, Paul felt no need to stay in Jerusalem and learn about the gospel. He pursued a ministry in other regions for which, in fact, Christians in Judea gave glory to God (v. 24). Here we find, Paul is suggesting, further evidence that "I did not receive [the gospel] from any human source" (v. 12).

In verses 22–24, Paul, having narrated his movement into "the regions of Syria and Cilicia" with an aorist verb (ἦλθον), now characterizes the period of time he spent there with three imperfect verbal forms: ἤμην . . . ἀγνοούμενος (*ēmēn . . . agnooumenos*, I was unknown); ἀκούοντες ἦσαν (*akouontes ēsan*, they were hearing); ἐδόξαζον (*edoxazon*, they were glorifying). The imperfect periphrastic form that Paul uses in verse 22 probably emphasizes the duration of the period of time: during all those years that Paul was in Syria and Cilicia,

---

4. Dunn (1993a: 80), indeed, thinks these regions may be included in vv. 21–24, but there is nothing in Paul's narrative to suggest it. An even stronger "argument from silence" is Lüdemann's (1984: 59–61) contention, in support of his wildly revisionist chronology, that Paul includes in these verses his ministry in Macedonia and Achaia. This is quite unlikely (R. Longenecker 1990: 40).

he "remained unknown" to the churches in Judea.[5] Or more specifically, he "remained personally unknown": the dative τῷ προσώπῳ (tō prosōpō; probably a dative of manner [A. Robertson 1934: 530]) qualifies the verb by indicating that Paul was unknown to the churches of Judea "in terms of his face," the "face" in biblical languages representing personal presence (BDAG 887–88; see, e.g., Acts 20:25: "Now I know that none of you among whom I have gone about preaching the kingdom will ever see me [τὸ πρόσωπόν μου, to prosōpon mou] again"). As Paul will make clear in Gal. 1:23–24, the believers in these churches, while not knowing Paul personally, did know *of* him.

Paul's reference to "the churches in Judea" is interesting in light of the focus on Jerusalem in this narrative elsewhere (1:17, 18; 2:1). There are three main options to explain this reference: (1) Paul refers to the larger territory of "Judea," including Samaria and Galilee, with possible reference to believers who left Jerusalem because of persecution (Bruce 1982b: 103); (2) Paul refers to Judea in the narrow sense (excluding Samaria and Galilee), including Jerusalem (BDAG 477–78; Burton 1921: 63; R. Longenecker 1990: 41); (3) Paul refers to Judea in the narrow sense, but excluding Jerusalem (Betz 1979: 80). The last option seems to be the least likely, since it would run counter to Paul's general polemic for him to omit reference to the crucial site, Jerusalem (and Paul's reference to "Judea" in Rom. 15:31 and 2 Cor. 1:16 certainly includes Jerusalem). The choice between the other two is almost impossible to make; the closest parallel, 1 Thess. 2:14 (τῶν ἐκκλησιῶν τοῦ θεοῦ τῶν οὐσῶν ἐν τῇ Ἰουδαίᾳ ἐν Χριστῷ Ἰησοῦ, tōn ekklēsiōn tou theou tōn ousōn en tē Ioudaia en Christō Iēsou, the churches of God that are in Judea in Christ Jesus [AT]), has the same ambiguity. In either case, Paul's claim stands in some tension with Luke's claims about Paul's persecuting activity in these regions (Acts 8:1, 3; 9:1; Martyn [1997: 175] claims they are "incompatible"). But the tension is resolved once one understands the narrative structure of verses 22–24. Paul's claim that he "was personally unknown" to the churches is not a general, undefined assertion but a description of the state of affairs *after* he had "come into Syria and Cilicia," some years after his conversion (Fung 1988: 82). We should not overlook one other thing that Paul says about these churches: they were ἐν Χριστῷ. As Martyn (1997: 176) puts it, "While the churches are geographically located in Judea, they are more importantly located in Christ."

Paul balances the negative point he makes in verse 22 with two positive points in verses 23–24. Although not personally acquainted with Paul, the believers in Judea had heard about Paul's dramatic turnaround and glorified God for him. The transition is accomplished by means of the adverb μόνον (monon):

1:23

---

5. R. Longenecker 1990: 41; see also, e.g., BDF §353.1. The imperfect periphrastic form is more common in the NT than in other Greek, probably due to Semitic influence (A. Robertson 1934: 888). Partly for this reason, the periphrastic imperfect does not always (or even, perhaps, usually) have a greater durative force than the simple imperfect (see, e.g., Wallace 1996: 657). Burton (1898: §429) takes ἀγνοούμενος as a predicative adjective rather than as part of a periphrastic construction. Moulton (1908: 227), citing classical precedents, thinks the construction might be emphatic; he paraphrases "I was *entirely* unknown—only they had been *hearing*."

"[it was] only [that] they were hearing. . . ." Paul again employs a periphrastic imperfect form (ἀκούοντες ἦσαν, *akouontes ēsan*) to denote continuous action: "they kept hearing" (NASB, NAB, HCSB).[6] The quotation that follows (introduced by ὅτι [*hoti*, that]) may be Paul's direct quotation of what the Judean believers were saying but is perhaps more likely Paul's own summary (R. Longenecker 1990: 42). It is interesting that Paul chooses to mention this particular point, revealing again how significant he viewed his transformation from persecutor to preacher. He has highlighted his career as persecutor earlier, mentioning it as the first element in his "manner of life in Judaism" (v. 13). In fact, Paul here returns to the same verb he used in that earlier passage to describe his attempts to "destroy" (the verb is πορθέω [*portheō*]) the church. The point is similar to what Luke reports about the reaction of the Damascus Christians to Paul's turnaround:

> At once he began to preach in the synagogues that Jesus is the Son of God. [21]All those who heard him were astonished and asked, "Isn't he the man who raised havoc [πορθέω, the only other NT occurrence of the verb] in Jerusalem among those who call on this name? And hasn't he come here to take them as prisoners to the chief priests?" (Acts 9:20–21)

As we noted earlier, this focus on Paul's previous career as persecutor highlights the power of God's transforming grace.

In Gal. 1:13 Paul speaks of attempting to "destroy the church"; here he refers to attempting to destroy (ἐπόρθει, as in v. 13 a conative imperfect) "the faith" (τὴν πίστιν, *tēn pistin*). "Faith" in Paul normally refers to the act of believing, and some interpreters think it has this sense here also (Fung 1988: 83). However, in a natural transfer, what was so basic for the Christian church, "faith" in Christ, came to be a way of referring, objectively, to the movement itself: "π[ίστιν] can be understood as *the Gospel* in terms of the commitment it evokes" (BDAG 820.2.d.α). This meaning may also be found, with more or less degree of certainty, in Rom. 12:6; 1 Cor. 16:13; 2 Cor. 13:5; Gal. 1:23; 3:23–25; 6:10; Eph. 4:13; Phil. 1:27; Col. 1:23; 2:7; 1 Tim. 1:2, 19; 3:9; 4:1, 6; 5:8; 6:10, 21; 2 Tim. 3:8; 4:7; Titus 1:4, 13; 3:15; Philem. 6. The clearest example is outside Paul, in Jude 3: "Dear friends, although I was very eager to write to you about the salvation we share, I felt compelled to write and urge you to contend for the faith that the Lord has once for all entrusted to us, his people" (TNIV). It is very likely that this is what Paul means in this verse (e.g., Bruce 1982b: 105; Dunn 1993a: 84–85).[7]

6. The "they," representing a masculine plural form (ἀκούοντες), has as its implicit antecedent the believers in the "churches of Judea" (the use of a masculine participle to follow up a feminine word (ἐκκλησίαις, *ekklēsiais*, churches) is a typical "construction according to the sense" (BDF §134.2).

7. Exemplifying a trend in recent interpretation to view almost all references to "faith" in Galatians as meaning "the faith of [exhibited by] Christ," de Boer (2011: 103) argues that this is the meaning here.

The καί (*kai*) connecting verse 24 to verse 23 could be coordinating ("and"; so all the English versions), but it could also have a slight consecutive sense: "the Judean believers recognized my transformation from persecutor to preacher *and so* praised God in me" (see BDAG 495.1.b.ζ). The implicit reminder of God's grace as the transformative power in Paul's turnaround makes it reasonable to add, as the result, that the Judean believers ἐδόξαζον ἐν ἐμοὶ τὸν θεόν (*edoxazon en emoi ton theon*, were glorifying God in me). In these kinds of contexts the verb δοξάζω (*doxazō*) means "praise, honor, extol" (BDAG 258.1; cf. LEH); the Scriptures regularly picture God's people "extolling" him for all manner of things and in all manner of circumstances. In such texts and others outside the Scriptures, the verb δοξάζω is sometimes followed by ἐν (*en*, in), which is then used to indicate the time (Sir. 10:26; 1 Pet. 2:12), the means (Isa. 43:23; Rom. 15:6; 1 Cor. 6:20), or the manner (Sir. 3:10; 7:27; 10:28; 35:7) of the praise. Of these, the only one that might work in this verse is means, or instrument: "they praised God through me" (Lightfoot 1881: 83). But especially pertinent to Gal. 1:24 are the places where ἐν introduces the reason for God being extolled. Often in these instances, the verb is in the passive, as in John 13:31b: νῦν ἐδοξάσθη ὁ υἱὸς τοῦ ἀνθρώπου, καὶ ὁ θεὸς ἐδοξάσθη ἐν αὐτῷ (*nyn edoxasthē ho huios tou anthrōpou, kai ho theos edoxasthē en autō*, "Now is the Son of Man glorified, and God is glorified in him" [TNIV]). Yet occasionally the verb, as here in verse 24, is in the active voice: οὕτως ἐν μυριάσιν ἐδόξασαν αὐτὸν (*houtōs en myriasin edoxasan auton*, "so they glorified him for the tens of thousands [he conquered]" [Sir. 47:6]). Thus, most of the English versions here translate "they glorified [or praised] God *because of* me." However, although this rendering is on the right track, it is easily susceptible of a misinterpretation, as if the people were praising God for something inherent in Paul himself. The sense, rather, is that people were praising God "in Paul's case" (BDAG 329.8), or that "they found in me an occasion" for praise (Burton 1921: 65; cf. Mussner 1988: 99, who sees the construction as equivalent to an accusative of reference). As Lagrange (1918: 21) puts it, they were praising God "because of that which happened in me and was done by me." Perhaps the NJB, "They gave glory to God for me," best captures the idea.

The combination of δοξάζω + ἐν + personal pronoun occurs several times in the Greek Bible, but it is comparatively rare. This circumstance makes it likely that Paul deliberately alludes to what is said in Isa. 49:3 (LXX) about the "Servant": καὶ εἶπέν μοι δοῦλός μου εἶ σύ Ισραηλ καὶ ἐν σοὶ δοξασθήσομαι (*kai eipen moi doulos mou ei sy Israēl kai en soi doxasthēsomai*, "and he said to me, 'You are my servant Israel, and in you I will be glorified'"). Paul has alluded to this same Servant passage earlier in describing his "conversion/call" (Isa. 49:1 in v. 15). These allusions suggest that Paul generally views his mission to the Gentiles in terms of the prophecies about the Servant in Isaiah. It is a text from this same passage (49:6) that Paul and Barnabas quote to justify their turn to the Gentiles: "For this is what the Lord has commanded us: 'I have made you a light for the Gentiles, that you may bring salvation to the ends of the earth'" (Acts 13:47). (For the influence of the Servant passages of Isaiah on Paul here, see esp. Ciampa 1998: 124–25; Harmon 2010: 88–89; Wilk 1998: 296.) Allusion to the mission of the Servant enhances the very positive view of Paul and his ministry that he describes in verses 23–24. Indeed, here we see the beginning of a shift in Paul's argument from the negative ("I did not learn my gospel from Jerusalem") to the positive: "believers [vv. 23–24] and apostles [2:1–10] in Jerusalem have recognized God's work in my ministry."

Additional Notes

1:18. Paul's purpose in going up to Jerusalem, "to visit with Cephas" (ἱστορῆσαι Κηφᾶν), has been variously interpreted. The verb ἱστορέω occurs only here in the NT, and its three occurrences in the LXX clearly move in a different direction: they all occur in the passive, in the sense "to be recorded" (see LEH; 1 Esd. 1:31 [2x]; 1:40; this meaning is frequent in Josephus [e.g., *Ant.* 1.160; 12.112]). In Greek outside the NT and LXX, the verb often has the sense "to learn by inquiry," "to get information" (LSJ 842); but the meaning "visit" is also found (*NewDocs* 4:135). A few interpreters have argued that the verb has this meaning here (see esp. Kilpatrick 1959; Dunn 1990: 110–13; and see NET: "to visit Cephas and get information from him"). But in the Koine period, the verb came to have a meaning close to the verb ὁράω, with an emphasis on the significance of what one had seen. See, e.g., Josephus, *Ant.* 1.203: "But Lot's wife continually turning back to view the city as she went from it, and being too nicely inquisitive what would become of it, although God had forbidden her so to do, was changed into a pillar of salt; for I have seen [ἱστόρησα] it, and it remains at this day" (see Silva 2003: 66). Thus the verb probably means here simply "get acquainted with" (NIV; most English versions have something like this; see esp. Hofius 1984: 76–77; Bruce 1982b: 98; Martyn 1997: 171–72; Dunn 1993a: 73–74 [who changed his view]).

1:18. Some MSS (including 𝔐) have here the Greek name Πέτρον. However, the Aramaic form Κηφᾶν should surely be read (as in 𝔓⁴⁶,⁵¹ ℵ* A B 33 and some other minuscules): it is more likely that Greek-speaking scribes would have changed the Aramaic into the Greek form (in conformity also with 2:7, 8) than that scribes would have changed the Greek into the Aramaic (in conformity with 2:9 and Paul's usage elsewhere).

1:19. The combination εἰ μή is very common in the NT (see the brief survey in BDF §376). In most cases, it straightforwardly introduces an exception to something said previously, usually without an expressed verb but sometimes with one: for examples, see 1 Cor. 1:14 (οὐδένα ὑμῶν ἐβάπτισα εἰ μὴ Κρίσπον καὶ Γάϊον) for the former and Mark 6:5 (καὶ οὐκ ἐδύνατο ἐκεῖ ποιῆσαι οὐδεμίαν δύναμιν, εἰ μὴ ὀλίγοις ἀρρώστοις ἐπιθεὶς τὰς χεῖρας ἐθεράπευσεν) for the latter. The problem in understanding the precise force of εἰ μή in Gal. 1:19 is that the clause in which the particle combination occurs often assumes information that the reader needs to supply (A. Robertson 1934: 1025). Matthew 12:4, a text often cited in the discussion of εἰ μή, is a good example: πῶς εἰσῆλθεν εἰς τὸν οἶκον τοῦ θεοῦ καὶ τοὺς ἄρτους τῆς προθέσεως ἔφαγον, ὃ οὐκ ἐξὸν ἦν αὐτῷ φαγεῖν οὐδὲ τοῖς μετ᾽ αὐτοῦ εἰ μὴ τοῖς ἱερεῦσιν μόνοις; Translators often render εἰ μή here as an adversative, as in NIV: "He entered the house of God, and he and his companions ate the consecrated bread—which was not lawful for them to do, *but only* for the priests" (emphasis added; and Zerwick [1963: §470] argues that εἰ μή sometimes = ἀλλά). However, the εἰ μή probably retains its exceptive force here, stating an exception to an implied general rule: "which was not lawful for anyone to eat, not even the followers of David—the exception to this general rule being the priests" (that we are to infer this general principle is strongly implied by the otherwise difficult-to-explain οὐδέ). In the case of Gal. 1:19, then, we could similarly infer a general principle to which the εἰ μή introduces an exception: "I saw no other apostle nor anyone else in authority except James the brother of the Lord" (so, e.g., Betz 1979: 78; Mussner 1988: 95–96; Martyn 1997: 173–74). However, in this case it is reasonable to ask whether we have sufficient ground to introduce this general principle: Paul does not appeal to any authority but an apostle in Gal. 1–2. Thus we think it more likely that εἰ μή introduces an exception to the explicit claim that Paul had seen "no other apostle"—he did, he adds as an afterthought (presumably because he did not spend significant time with him), see James (so, e.g., Lightfoot 1881: 84–85; Burton 1921: 60; R. Longenecker 1990: 38). Appeal is sometimes made to 1 Cor. 9:5 to claim that Paul does not view "the brothers of the Lord" as apostles: μὴ οὐκ ἔχομεν ἐξουσίαν ἀδελφὴν γυναῖκα περιάγειν ὡς καὶ οἱ λοιποὶ ἀπόστολοι καὶ οἱ ἀδελφοὶ τοῦ κυρίου καὶ Κηφᾶς; (e.g., Betz 1979: 78). However, as Bauckham (1990: 57–59) points out, this verse could prove just the opposite, since Paul obviously includes "Cephas" among the apostles.

1:19. Paul's claim that, of the apostles, he saw only Peter and James during his first postconversion visit to Jerusalem stands in some tension with Acts 9:27, which describes this same visit: Βαρναβᾶς δὲ ἐπιλαβόμενος αὐτὸν ἤγαγεν πρὸς τοὺς ἀποστόλους. Luke seems to imply that Barnabas introduced Paul to "the apostles" as a group. Paul's careful statement does not appear to allow any exception; so it is perhaps best to think that "apostles" in Acts 9:27 includes only Peter and James. Bruce (1982b: 103–4) speculates that most of the apostles may have been away from Jerusalem because of the persecution that had broken out, but Acts 8:1 suggests that the apostles were not forced to leave Jerusalem.

1:21. It is not clear whether the article before Κιλικίας should be included or not. The repetition of the article tends to distinguish the two territories, and the lack of article tends to view them together (note the article before Συρίας). (Yet a strict reading of "Sharp's Rule" does not really apply here because the nouns are proper [Wallace 1996: 271–74].) This verse (1:21) has a related textual issue, with the bulk of the MS tradition having articles before both Συρίας and Κιλικίας, while a few MSS (e.g., ℵ*) omit the second article. Omitting the article before Κιλικίας would have the effect of bringing Paul's designation into closer conformity to the actual political boundaries of the time: the idea in both texts may be "the Syria-Cilicia province" (see, e.g., Bruce 1982b: 103; Riesner 1998: 266).

1:23. Many argue that the "church" that Paul was trying to "destroy" was specifically the Greek-speaking Jewish Christian church that began to play fast and loose with the torah (e.g., Hengel and Schwemer 1997: 36–37; Pate 2000: 154–57).

c. Second Jerusalem Visit: The "Pillars" Confirm Paul's Gospel (2:1–10)

With this text Paul's sketch of his relationship with the Jerusalem authorities shifts direction. In the previous chapter Paul was concerned to show that he received his gospel through a dramatic revelation of Jesus Christ and not from any human being (1:12–16a). The rest of the chapter elaborates this negative point, especially with respect to the Jerusalem authorities. As we have seen, this very selective autobiography has in view the agitators' attempt to portray Paul as a poor (or perhaps rebellious) pupil of the apostles in Jerusalem. Paul's account of his meeting with the "pillar" apostles in Jerusalem in 2:1–10 has in common with the previous narrative a focus on Jerusalem. And it is bound to that narrative also by an explicit temporal connection: "Then, after fourteen years" (v. 1; see "then after three years" in 1:18; "then" in 1:21). But if Paul in Gal. 1 shows that he did not *learn* his gospel *from* the Jerusalem apostles, he now demonstrates that those apostles did not *add anything* to his gospel (2:6; see, e.g., Silva 2000: 55; Tolmie 2005: 71–73). In fact, there was unanimity on the matter at issue both in this Jerusalem meeting and in the churches of Galatia—the inclusion of Gentiles in the people of God without the law. Paul's independence was not the independence of a maverick or a cultist. His sphere of ministry might have differed from that of the Jerusalem apostles, but there was no fundamental difference among Paul and the others over the essence of that gospel.

In this passage Paul's description of the meeting in Jerusalem brings us face-to-face with the historical and chronological issue that has long bedeviled Galatians interpreters. Is the meeting he here describes the same "council" that Luke narrates in Acts 15? Or does he describe a meeting that took place during the famine-relief expedition to Jerusalem (Acts 11:27–30)? While the arguments for each of these two options are very finely balanced—far more finely balanced than most interpreters acknowledge—we prefer the latter option. While many points must be considered, we think an especially important argument is the match between Paul's chronology and Luke's narrative in Acts. If 2:1–10 describes the Jerusalem Council of Acts 15, then either (1) Paul does not include all his visits to Jerusalem here in Galatians, or (2) Luke is wrong about the famine-relief visit. We see no good reason to doubt Luke's accuracy about this visit; nor do we think it likely that Paul would have failed to mention one of his Jerusalem visits in this highly charged polemical atmosphere (for greater detail and other issues, see "The Destination and Date of the Letter" in the introduction; and see esp. D. Wenham 1993: 226–43; Schnabel 2004: 989–991).

Assuming this identification, the meeting that Paul describes in this passage was probably a private consultation between Paul and some of the Jerusalem apostles, a consultation that was stimulated by the startling degree of assimilation between Jewish and Gentile believers that was beginning to characterize the church in Antioch (Acts 11:20–26).[1] On a likely chronology of Paul's early ministry, this meeting would have taken place in AD 45–47. It would thus have preceded Paul's initial church-planting ministry in Galatia (Acts 13–14) and indeed provided assurance to Paul that the gospel he presented to the Gentiles on this mission trip would be widely recognized. Only after that trip did there arise a further dispute on these matters in Antioch (Gal. 2:11–14; cf. Acts 15:1–2), an incident that probably provided ammunition to the agitators in Galatia (on this chronology, see esp. Bauckham 1995: 468–70).

Paul's description of his meeting with the apostles in Jerusalem features some of the most convoluted language that is to be found in his letters. The passage is filled with parentheses, sentence fragments, and ellipses.[2] He begins straightforwardly, in verse 1 describing his journey to Jerusalem and his companions; in verse 2 identifying the reason for going ("by revelation"), the general issue to be discussed ("the gospel I preach among the Gentiles"), and his concern ("lest I am running or have run in vain"). But then he suddenly mentions that Titus was not compelled to be circumcised (v. 3) and more seriously interrupts the flow of the passage with an extended parenthesis about "false brothers" who infiltrated the church (vv. 4–5). Verse 6, which returns to the main lines of the narrative, begins a long sentence that extends to the end of the paragraph (v. 10). Here Paul insists that the Jerusalem apostles, negatively, "added nothing" to his gospel (v. 6); and positively, recognized that they and Paul were all animated in their ministries by the same grace of God and were preaching the same gospel (vv. 8–9a). At the same time, there was a recognition of different spheres of ministry: Paul going to the Gentiles, the "uncircumcised"; and Peter, James, and John going to "the circumcised" (vv. 7, 9b). Paul also gladly acceded to the Jerusalem apostles' request that he continue to "remember the poor" (v. 10).

The cause of these syntactical and logical difficulties is the tightrope that Paul walks in this paragraph. On the one hand, he acknowledges the legitimate authority and significance of the Jerusalem apostles and recognizes that their agreement with his understanding of the law-free gospel is important (for this latter point, see esp. v. 2b). Indeed, granted an allusion to the motif of an eschatological temple in the reference to the Jerusalem apostles as "pillars" (v. 9), we can understand Paul's purpose as wanting "to have his divine commission to preach the [law-free] gospel affirmed in

---

1. Some interpreters, on the other hand (usually identifying this meeting with the Council of Acts 15), think that Paul here describes basically a conference between delegates from two churches: Antioch and Jerusalem (e.g., Schütz 2007: 138–39; Martyn 1997: 196).

2. Schütz (2007) solves these problems by reorganizing the text, but does so without any textual basis.

the center of the eschatological community of the Messiah, in the 'eschatological temple' in Jerusalem" (Schnabel 2004: 991). But on the other hand, he also wants to reduce the overly slavish regard for these "pillars" among the agitators and especially to deny that his law-free gospel depends for its truthfulness on their attestation. Paul's use of the verb δοκέω (dokeō) to characterize the apostles is symptomatic of this ambivalence. In verse 2, where it is used absolutely, it is neutral or even positive: "those who appear to be important." But in verses 6 and 9 the word is used in constructions that have a somewhat ironic note: "those who seem to be something," "those who seem to be pillars."

Among the many points that need to be teased out of this narrative is the basic question of what the specific matter of debate actually was. The general issue clearly had to do with "the gospel that I preach among the Gentiles" (v. 2). And the decisive point is that the Jerusalem apostles "added nothing" to this gospel (v. 6), with the result that "the truth of the gospel" might be upheld. But despite Paul's lack of clarity, the specific issue is clear enough. His abrupt mention of the issue of Titus's circumcision (and calling attention to his Gentile status) in verse 3, along with the contrast between "the circumcised" and "the uncircumcised" in verses 7–9, reveals that the circumcision of Gentile believers was the point of specific debate. And for first-century Jews, circumcision carried with it the larger obligation to submit to the law of Moses. It is, then, the law-free gospel for the Gentiles that is the key issue in this meeting in Jerusalem. And it is the Jerusalem apostles' agreement with this gospel that is the key rhetorical point of the story. Paul makes this clear in verse 5b, where he indicates, as the result of his refusal to submit to the "false brothers," that "the truth of the gospel might remain *for you*." The Jerusalem apostles' agreement with Paul's law-free gospel for the Gentiles shows how wrong the Galatians would be to succumb to the agitators' perversion of the gospel into a gospel-plus-law message.

Exegesis and Exposition

[1]Then, after fourteen years, ⌐I went up again⌐ to Jerusalem. I went with Barnabas and also took along Titus. [2]I went up in response to a revelation. And I set before them the gospel that I preach among the Gentiles—but privately, to those who appeared to be important. I did this so that I would not be running or had run in vain.

[3]But not even Titus, who was with me, and a Greek, was compelled to be circumcised. [4]Now this matter arose because of the false brothers who had sneaked in. They slipped in to spy on the freedom that we have in Christ Jesus. They wanted to enslave us. [5]We did ⌐not submit to them for even⌐ a moment, in order that the truth of the gospel might remain with you.

[6]But as for those who appeared to be something—what kind of people they were does not matter to me; God is not partial—these men who seemed to be something added nothing to me. [7]On the contrary, they recognized that I had been entrusted with

2. Elaboration and Proof: Paul's Gospel and the "Pillars"
c. Second Jerusalem Visit: The "Pillars" Confirm Paul's Gospel

Galatians 2:1–10

the gospel for the uncircumcision even as Peter [had been entrusted with the gospel] for the circumcision. [8]For the one who was at work in Peter to make him apostle for the circumcised was working also in me on behalf of the Gentiles. [9]And, recognizing the grace that had been given to me, ⌜James and Cephas⌝ and John—those who appeared to be pillars—gave me and Barnabas the right hand of fellowship, in order that we might go to the Gentiles and they to the circumcision. [10]They requested only one thing: that we remember the poor—which very thing I was eager to do.

The ἔπειτα (epeita, then) at the beginning of this paragraph creates a narrative connection with 1:18, "then [ἔπειτα] after three years I went up to Jerusalem," and with 1:21, "then [ἔπειτα] I went into the regions of Syria and Cilicia." Paul describes a sequence of events with Jerusalem as the focal point: conversion; first Jerusalem visit; ministry in Syria and Cilicia, during which he was personally unknown "to the churches in Judea" (including Jerusalem); second Jerusalem visit. The ἔπειτα links these key points in Paul's story. The more precise temporal indication, διὰ δεκατεσσάρων ἐτῶν (dia dekatessarōn etōn), creates more difficulties. Interpreters agree that the διά in this context conveys the idea "after the lapse of" (BDAG 224.2.c; BDF §223.1; Moule 1959: 56; Lightfoot 1881: 102; cf. Mark 2:1; Acts 24:17; the διά here would then be simply a stylistic variant of μετά [meta, after] in 1:18 [Bruce 1982b: 106]). Two other matters are not so clear.

First, δεκατέσσαρες ἔτη could denote a period of as few as twelve years (counting "inclusively"; see the comments on 1:18) and a few months or as long as fourteen years. Second, whatever the length of time, the starting point of the numbering could be (1) Paul's conversion (1:15–16a; e.g., R. Longenecker 1990: 45; Martyn 1997: 181–82); (2) Paul's first Jerusalem visit (1:18; e.g., Lightfoot 1881: 102; Burton 1921: 68; Schlier 1989: 64–65; Vouga 1998: 42); or (3) Paul's move to Syria and Cilicia (1:21; Silva 2003: 73; R. Schäfer 2004: 162–63).

The combination of these uncertainties creates a wide range of chronological possibilities. Paul could be locating this Jerusalem visit anywhere from a little over twelve years to as many as seventeen years or more after his conversion. This uncertainty makes it possible, on any reasonable outline of a chronology of Paul's life, to identify the Jerusalem meeting in 2:1–10 with either the famine-relief visit (Acts 11:27–30) or with the Jerusalem Council (Acts 15; they were probably no more than two–three years apart). In fact, whether they admit it or not, most interpreters probably end up deciding the meaning of 2:1 on the basis of their larger decision about the relationship between this narrative and the book of Acts. And so uncertain is the meaning of 2:1 that this is not a bad procedure. Since on other grounds we think there are good reasons to believe that the Jerusalem meeting in this passage took place during the famine-relief visit of Acts 11 (see above and "The Destination and Date of the Letter" in the introduction), we conclude that Paul is probably here counting from his conversion (to be dated perhaps in AD 34–35) and that δεκατέσσαρες ἔτη probably indicates a time of a little over twelve years.

For the first time in his travelogue, Paul mentions coworkers who accompanied him. Barnabas was an important associate of Paul's during his early ministry. A trusted "apostle" before Paul (Acts 4:36), Barnabas was instrumental in getting the newly converted Saul accepted by the Jerusalem Christians (9:27) and later invited Paul to join the ministry in Antioch (11:22–26). Barnabas and Paul then traveled together to Jerusalem to bring aid from the Antioch church to the believers in Jerusalem (11:27–30). And, of course, Barnabas joined Paul (or more accurately, initially, Saul joined Barnabas) on the first missionary journey (Acts 13–14). The two were sent again from Antioch to Jerusalem to debate the question of circumcising of Gentile believers (15:1–35). When, however, Paul decided to return to the churches of the first missionary journey, he and Barnabas could not agree over whether John Mark should be allowed to go with them; so they separated (15:36–39). Paul's commendation of Barnabas in Col. 4:10 suggests, however, that the two were eventually reconciled.

Paul mentions Barnabas (and see also v. 9) not only because he was well known to the Galatians (he accompanied Paul on his initial preaching mission there; Acts 13–14) but also, perhaps, because of his later "defection" at Antioch under pressure from the people from James (2:13). The agitators may have played up Barnabas's actions at Antioch, since he was known to the Galatians. Paul therefore wants to make clear that Barnabas was present when a fundamental decision in favor of the law-free gospel was reached. Because Paul mentions Titus in a separate construction, συμπαραλαβὼν καὶ Τίτον (*symparalabōn kai Titon*, taking along also Titus), Titus is given special prominence here (Mussner 1988:101). We do not know when Paul first encountered Titus (not mentioned in Acts), but in Titus 1:4 Paul's calling him "my true son in our common faith" may imply that Paul was instrumental in his conversion. Titus had an especially important role with the Corinthian church on Paul's third missionary journey (2 Cor. 2:13; 7:6, 13–14; 8:6, 16, 23; 12:18), but he may also have been known to the Galatians (R. Longenecker 1990: 47). Paul's reason for highlighting his presence at this meeting becomes clear as the narrative progresses: he was a Greek, and the fact that he was not compelled to be circumcised is powerful evidence that Paul's law-free gospel was acknowledged to be correct (v. 3). In fact, it is possible that Paul brought Titus along to Jerusalem precisely for the purpose of forcing the issue (e.g., Hays 2000: 222; Garlington 2003: 71).

2:2 The δέ (*de*) at the beginning of the verse introduces a further explanation: ἀνέβην κατὰ ἀποκάλυψιν (*anebēn kata apokalypsin*, I went up in response to a revelation).[3] Paul again follows the convention of describing travel to Jerusalem as "going up" (because Jerusalem is located in the hills; see 1:17 and 18), although he uses a different verb (ἀναβαίνω [*anabainō*] here, as opposed

---

3. Runge (2010: 31), focusing on discourse function, usefully defines δέ as "a coordinating conjunction like καί [*kai*, and], but it includes the added constraint of signaling new development." The kind of development between vv. 1 and 2 requires no explicit conjunction in English; hence the modern English versions have none here. On this use of δέ, see also Zerwick 1963: §467.

to ἀνέρχομαι [*anerchomai*] earlier). In using the word ἀποκάλυψις Paul clearly wants to claim that he went to Jerusalem by divine invitation. How this invitation came to Paul is unclear and probably unimportant—although it is natural if, as we think, Paul is describing the famine-relief journey, to identify the revelation with the prophecy of Agabus (Acts 11:28; e.g., R. Longenecker 1990: 47).[4] What is important for Paul's purpose is that he went to Jerusalem by divine direction and not because he was summoned to the city by the apostles—as the agitators may have been claiming (R. Longenecker 1990: 47; Silva 2003: 73).

On our understanding of the sequence of events, then, Paul and Barnabas traveled to Jerusalem because Agabus had predicted a famine and the church at Antioch wanted to provide help for the believers there. While he was at Jerusalem, and perhaps in response to some concerns about the way Jews and Gentiles were mixing in the church in Antioch, Paul "laid before" (ἀνεθέμην [*anethemēn*]; cf. also Acts 25:14) the apostles the "gospel that I preach among the Gentiles." This, at least, is one reading of the situation. In fact, however, Paul first uses the simple personal pronoun αὐτοῖς (*autois*, them) to describe those before whom he set forth his gospel; only later in the verse does he add that he communicated it "privately before those who appeared to be important" (κατ᾽ ἰδίαν δὲ τοῖς δοκοῦσιν, *kat' idian de tois dokousin*). Most interpreters think that Paul is describing two meetings: a public one, with a large number of Jerusalem Christians (αὐτοῖς would then have as its antecedent "Jerusalem" in a *constructio ad sensum*, a construction based on sense rather than strict grammar); and a private one, with the apostles (e.g., Lightfoot 1881: 103; Burton 1921: 71; Mussner 1988: 104; Martyn 1997: 191; Vouga 1998: 43; Silva 2003: 74–75). However, following almost all the English translations, there is good reason to think that Paul describes only one meeting here, with the second clause specifying the meaning of the initial vague αὐτοῖς (Fung 1988: 87–89; Witherington 1998: 132–33). If Paul had intended to describe two meetings, we would have expected him to repeat the verb in the second instance or in some other way to make the two expressions parallel—by contrasting "privately" with "publicly" or by using a καί (*kai*, also) in the second reference.[5]

4. Paul uses the phrase κατὰ ἀποκάλυψιν twice elsewhere (Rom. 16:25; Eph. 3:3), and at least in the second instance the reference is to Paul's vision of Christ on the Damascus Road. Paul has used the verbal form of this word to describe the Damascus Road vision earlier in Galatians (1:16). For these reasons, a few scholars (e.g., Howard 1979: 38–39; Cummins 2001: 129–30) think that this is Paul's reference here also. But the construction κατά plus accusative (which means here "as a result of," "on the basis of" [BDAG 513.B.5.a.δ]) would be a very unusual way to express this idea. Paul uses ἀποκάλυψις in 1 Cor. 14:6, 26 in association with the gift of prophecy. An equally unlikely meaning of κατά is suggested by de Boer (2011: 108–9), who thinks it denotes the purpose of the vision: Paul went up to Jerusalem in order to "reveal" his gospel to the apostles.

5. Burton (1921: 71) indeed argues just the reverse: that, based on the parallel in vv. 1–2—ἀνέβην εἰς Ἱεροσόλυμα [*anebēn eis Hierosolyma*, I went up to Jerusalem] . . . ἀνέβην δὲ κατὰ ἀποκάλυψιν—we would have expected Paul to repeat the verb if he had intended the second phrase to qualify the first clause. But the two examples are not parallel, since "Jerusalem" in

As the text stands, it is more natural to take κατ' ἰδίαν δὲ τοῖς δοκοῦσιν as a qualification of ἀνεθέμην αὐτοῖς. Greek pronouns can receive specification from what follows; and as we have seen, throughout this passage Paul writes with a certain lack of precision. Note, for instance, how Paul refers to "those who appeared to be important" in verse 2 and again with similar language in verse 6 before actually identifying them in verses 7–9. Probably because the meeting has already been brought up by the agitators for their own purposes, Paul assumes that the Galatians know quite a lot about it.

What Paul set forth for consideration was "the gospel I preach among the Gentiles." Despite the reference to Barnabas in verse 1, Paul uses the first-person singular here—perhaps because of Barnabas's later defection (2:13–15), but more likely in conscious imitation of 1:16, where Paul claims that God revealed his Son in him "so that I might proclaim him among the Gentiles" (Dunn 1993a: 92). Paul also uses the present tense of the verb to stress that the gospel he is now preaching—to the Galatians—is the same one that he presented to the authorities in Jerusalem.

Paul refers to these authorities as τοῖς δοκοῦσιν, literally, "those who appear" or "those who seem." The phrase was used in Greek to denote people of influence or people who had significant standing in a community (BDAG 255.2.β): hence our translation "those who appeared to be important." The term itself need not have any negative nuance (Lightfoot 1881: 103). Still, this way of describing authorities is unusual (only here in the NT or the LXX) and suggests at the least that Paul is portraying them from the standpoint of the way they are viewed rather than necessarily from the standpoint of who they inherently are. As de Boer (2011: 107) puts it, the word has "an ironic flavor." This distancing quality in the language will become more evident in verse 6, where he uses a fuller expression (see also v. 9).

The last clause of verse 2 is introduced with μή πως (*mē pōs*). This phrase could depend on an understood idea of "fearing" (cf. 4:11; and Burton 1921: 73–74), but it is better seen as a negative purpose clause dependent on ἀνεθέμην: "I set my gospel before the Jerusalem leaders (hoping for their approval) with the purpose that I not be running or had run in vain."[6] Paul elsewhere uses the image of running to depict the Christian life (Gal. 5:7) or his own ministry (1 Cor. 9:26; Phil. 2:16). Paul uses the verb τρέχω in both the present (τρέχω, *trechō*, run—which could be either indicative or [more probably] subjunctive) and the aorist (ἔδραμον, *edramon*) tenses.[7] The second verb is a

---

v. 1 has nothing corresponding to it in v. 2 (unlike the situation in v. 2, where τοῖς δοκοῦσιν corresponds [at least syntactically] to αὐτοῖς).

6. Lagrange (1918: 27; cf. also Bligh 1969: 154) suggests that the phrase could be an indirect question: "Could it be that I am running or have run in vain?" This interpretation neatly solves the interpretive issue, but it is unlikely that μή πως would be used to introduce such a question.

7. The subjunctive is normal after μή πως. But the indicative is found in both general and NT Greek "when the object of apprehension is conceived of as already present or past, *i.e.* as a thing already decided, although the issue is at the time of speaking unknown" (Burton 1898: 227; cf. also A. Robertson 1934: 988).

bit of an afterthought, Paul adding it to make reference directly to his original preaching ministry among the Galatians. This whole clause confronts us with an interpretive difficulty. Paul uses the phrase "in vain" (εἰς κένον, *eis kenon*) elsewhere to express concern that, despite his apostolic labor, his readers may not attain final salvation (2 Cor. 6:1; Phil. 2:16; 1 Thess. 3:5). But how, after Paul has insisted so strongly that his gospel comes from God and is not dependent on any human being in Gal. 1, can he here suggest that the verdict of the Jerusalem apostles might prevent his readers from experiencing the gospel promise of salvation? As most interpreters insist, then, Paul must use the phrase here in a nuanced way (e.g., Smiles 1998: 40–43; Lightfoot 1881: 103–4; Bruce 1982b: 111).[8] His fear is not that his gospel will be voided of its power if the decision in Jerusalem should go against him; what he fears, rather, is that a negative verdict will create a fissure in the church between its Jewish and Gentile wings. And the seriousness of such an eventuality explains the strength of the language Paul uses here. The good news has power only as it fulfills the single plan of the biblical God, who made promises to his people in the OT (cf. Rom. 1:2–3; chaps. 9–11). Cutting Gentiles off from the spiritual root that nourishes them (Rom. 11:17–24) would endanger their continuing experience of God's blessing and favor. And a split between Jewish and Gentile Christians could lead, Paul fears, to just such a situation (see esp. Dunn 1993a: 93–94; see also Martyn 1997: 192–93; Schütz 2007: 139–40).

After Paul summarizes the setting (v. 1) and the purpose (v. 2) of his visit to Jerusalem, we expect him to continue with a description of the discussion between him and "those who appeared to be important" or at least the decision that was reached among them. In a sense Paul does announce the verdict in verse 3, but allusively; and in verses 4–5 he backs up to provide further background information. Verses 3–5 therefore interrupt the flow of verses 1–2, which is only resumed in verse 6: "I set before the people who appeared to be important [τοῖς δοκοῦσιν] my gospel [v. 2], . . . and these people who seemed to be something [οἱ δοκοῦντες] added nothing to it" (v. 6).

2:3

To understand the connection between verses 2 and 3, we must appreciate the meaning and significance of the verse's claim that Titus was not "compelled" (ἠναγκάσθη, *ēnankasthē*) to be circumcised. A few interpreters have suggested that Titus was, in fact, circumcised, the point of the verse being that he was not forced to be circumcised by the Jerusalem apostles. This reading of the verse is possible but seems to put too much weight on the verb "compel." Along with the majority of interpreters, then, we think it is more likely that Paul intends to deny that Titus was circumcised at all. Paul may be hinting that the Jerusalem apostles at first wanted to circumcise Titus but were dissuaded by Paul's arguments (Lightfoot 1881: 105–6; Howard 1979: 28; Dunn 1993a: 96); but this is not clear. In any case, what is significant about this decision, as Paul points out, is that Titus was a "Greek" (Ἕλλην, *Hellēn*). Semantically

---

8. Chrysostom (*Comm. Gal.* on 2:1–2 [*NPNF*[1] 13:14]) thinks that Paul's concern is to convince his accusers that he has not been running in vain.

this word has the same sense as Paul's usual ἔθνη (*ethnē*, Gentiles), "non-Jews" (Paul usually explicitly contrasts Ἕλλην with Ἰουδαῖος [*Ioudaios*, Jew]: Rom. 1:16; 2:9, 10; 3:9; 10:12; 1 Cor. 1:22, 24; 10:32; 12:13; Gal. 3:28; Col. 3:11; in Rom. 1:14 the word is contrasted with "barbarian"). He uses Ἕλλην here for stylistic reasons: Paul never uses the singular of ἔθνη to mean "Gentile" (his only use of the singular of ἔθνος means "nation" and comes in an OT quotation [Rom. 10:19]). With most of the English versions, we should probably construe the clause Ἕλλην ὤν (*Hellēn ōn*, being a Greek) as concessive: Titus was not compelled to be circumcised even though he was a Greek (see, e.g., Burton 1921: 75–76; Fung 1988: 91).

The decision not to circumcise Titus, then, has great symbolic significance: it signals the fact that the Jerusalem apostles essentially endorsed Paul's version of the law-free gospel for the Gentiles (e.g., Mussner 1988: 106–7). Indeed, his choice of the verb "compel" ties this decision very closely to the wider problem that Paul is fighting in Galatia; note the other two uses of the verb in the letter: "When I saw that they were not acting in line with the truth of the gospel, I said to Cephas in front of them all, 'You are a Jew, yet you live like a Gentile and not like a Jew. How is it, then, that you force [ἀναγκάζεις, *anankazeis*] Gentiles to follow Jewish customs?'" (2:14); "Those who want to impress others by means of the flesh are trying to compel [ἀναγκάζουσιν, *anankazousin*] you to be circumcised. The only reason they do this is to avoid being persecuted for the cross of Christ" (6:12; see, e.g., Martyn 1997: 194).[9] Instead of stating in so many words the decision of the authorities (as he does in v. 6), Paul rushes ahead to cite what was for him the deeply significant practical outcome of the meeting in Jerusalem.

With the meaning and significance of verse 3 before us, we are now in a position to understand the connection between verse 3 and its context. The adversative at the beginning of the verse (ἀλλ᾽, *all'*, but) is most naturally taken with the end of verse 2: Paul feared that his ministry among the Gentiles might have been in vain, *but*, in fact, his law-free gospel for the Gentiles was vindicated, as evidenced in the critical decision not to compel Titus to be circumcised (Burton 1921: 75; Silva 2003: 78). Why Paul adds οὐδέ (*oude*, not even) is not clear. Some think that lying behind the issue of Titus's circumcision is the decision of Paul to circumcise Timothy (Acts 16:1–3; e.g., Lightfoot 1881: 104–5). In light of the reason why Paul circumcised Timothy, then, he might be saying, in effect, "True, I circumcised Timothy to advance his work among Jews, but I did that because he was, in fact, Jewish. But not even for the sake of his ministry among Jews would I agree to let Titus be circumcised, because he was a Gentile." However, on our reading of the sequence of events, the incident Paul here describes took place several years before Timothy's circumcision. A better option is to explain the "not even" by reference to the phrase ὁ σὺν ἐμοί (*ho syn emoi*, the one with me), which, in light of verse 1, is

---

9. In this reference to circumcision, Boers (1994: 59–65) finds an indication of the basic issue of the letter.

hardly necessary: not only did the Jerusalem authorities not impose circumcision on distant Gentiles, but "not even" Titus, who was right there before them, was forced to be circumcised (similarly, Silva 2003: 78). And the fact that Paul mentions Titus already in verse 1 indicates that he intended all along to mention the issue of his circumcision. Verse 3 may be a syntactical detour, but it is integral to the point that Paul wants to make in this passage (contra, e.g., BDF §448.6, suggesting that the verse is an "afterthought").

In this verse, Paul begins a sentence that he does not finish. The opening prepositional phrase, διὰ δὲ τοὺς παρεισάκτους ψευδαδέλφους (*dia de tous pareisaktous pseudadelphous*, but because of the false brothers who had slipped in), is never completed with a main clause.[10] Instead we find in verses 4b–5 two relative clauses that describe these false brothers (οἵτινες . . . [*hoitines . . . , who . . .*]; οἷς . . . [*hois . . . , to whom . . .*]). The memory of these false teachers and the threat they posed to the gospel is so vivid to Paul that he digresses into a description of them and his reaction to them, finally abandoning the sentence he began in verse 4a altogether (this syntactical inconsistency is called "anacolouthon" and is relatively common in Paul; cf. BDF §467). But what would Paul's main clause have been? Several of the English translations supply something such as we have in the NIV: "This matter arose because . . ." (see also NLT, HCSB, NET). Most of the commentaries agree in understanding "this matter" as referring to the pressure to have Titus circumcised (v. 3; see, e.g., Burton 1921: 79–82; Betz 1979: 89; Bruce 1982b: 116; R. Longenecker 1990: 50; Coppins 2009: 96).[11] Verses 4–5 therefore interrupt the narrative flow to provide some important background information.

Paul never identifies these "false brothers." The pejorative language he uses of them—"sneaked in," "slipped in," "spying on"—makes it impossible to think that they are the Jerusalem apostles, whom Paul describes in (at worst) mildly ironic language (vv. 2, 6, 9). The context suggests that they were insisting that Gentile Christians be circumcised and (almost certainly) submit to the law of Moses. By calling them "false brothers," Paul leaves us in no doubt about his evaluation of them; in Lightfoot's vivid language, "Pharisees at heart, these traitors assume the name and garb of believers" (1881: 106; and see 2 Cor. 11:26).[12] "Sneaked in" translates the Greek adjective παρείσακτος (*pareisaktos*), which appears only here in the Greek Bible, though the cognate verb occurs

2:4

10. A few interpreters have sought to "rescue" Paul's syntax by attaching v. 4 to another clause in the context; e.g., Blommerde (1975) thinks that both the ἀπό phrase in v. 4 and the one in v. 6 depend on ἠναγκάσθη περιτμηθῆναι (*ēnankasthē peritmēthēnai*, compelled to be circumcised; see also Zerwick 1963: §467). But this only works by effectively ignoring the negative particle that governs the phrase.

11. In two articles, Orchard (1973; 1976) has objected to this reading of the clause, arguing that there is a break between vv. 3 and 4 and that the implied main clause refers back to the general situation that Paul is addressing: "But the whole upset, your backsliding, my own distress, is because of . . ."

12. Paul would not use the language of "brothers" if these people were not at least claiming a relationship to Christ (contra Nanos 2002: 150–52; 2005: 63–68).

in 2 Pet. 2:1 with reference to false teaching. The form of the word is passive, and some have suggested that these false brothers were "secretly brought in" by James or one of the other apostles (cf. 2:12; and see, e.g., Witherington 1998: 136; Garlington 2003: 78). But the passive element in the word probably has a middle sense (Burton 1921: 78; R. Longenecker 1990: 51): Paul simply claims that they "slipped in" and gives no suggestion of a further agent in the process.[13] Jude uses a related word with a similar reference: "For certain individuals whose condemnation was written about long ago have secretly slipped in [παρεισέδυσαν, *pareisedysan*] among you" (v. 4).

Where and when the false brothers "slipped in" is not clear. One attractive option is to identify this event with the one that Luke narrates in Acts 15:1: "Certain individuals came down from Judea to Antioch and were teaching the believers: 'Unless you are circumcised, according to the custom taught by Moses, you cannot be saved'" (TNIV). If the Jerusalem meeting Paul describes in 2:1–3 and 6–10 is the same as the Jerusalem Council of Acts 15, then this infiltration of the false brothers would have taken place in Antioch just before the Council meeting (e.g., Martyn 1997: 196; Munck 1959: 97–98; Mussner 1988: 109; Watson 2007: 103–5). On the other hand, if the Jerusalem meeting of 2:1–3, 6–10 took place *before* the council of Acts 15, then Paul would be glancing ahead to an incident in Antioch that took place sometime after the Jerusalem meeting he describes in Gal. 2 (see esp. Bruce 1982b: 115–17; Schnabel 2004: 997). The problem with both these views is that they locate the infiltration of the false brothers in Antioch. To be sure verses 4–5 interrupt the narrative of the Jerusalem meeting, and it is possible that the scene shifts. But these verses can be more successfully integrated with the overall narrative if the incident described here took place in Jerusalem. Paul has gone out of his way to draw attention to the fact that Titus accompanied him to Jerusalem. This narrative element is most naturally explained if it was in Jerusalem that the pressure to circumcise Titus was successfully resisted (v. 3)—and therefore in Jerusalem also that the pressure first arose (e.g., Dunn 1993a: 97). The similarity between this incident and the one that Luke mentions in Acts 15:1 is not hard to understand. What the false brothers in Jerusalem were apparently advocating was the mainstream Jewish view: that Gentiles who converted to the God of Israel needed to be circumcised and obey the law of Moses. We would expect this issue to have emerged as soon as Gentiles began associating with Jews within a single "Messianic" community. Exactly such a community was established sometime in the 40s in Antioch, where a new name, "Christians," had to be coined to denote this mixed group (Acts 11:19–26). Paul and Barnabas were deeply involved in this community. These developments probably led some "false brothers" to take the opportunity of Paul and Barnabas's presence in Jerusalem to bring up the issue with the "pillars." The view advocated by these false brothers has, then, a basic generic similarity

---

13. Dunn (1993a: 98, 99) suggests that παρείσακτος might refer not to "slipping into" a meeting but to these false teachers' "slipping into" the Christian movement.

2. Elaboration and Proof: Paul's Gospel and the "Pillars"
    c. Second Jerusalem Visit: The "Pillars" Confirm Paul's Gospel

Galatians 2:1–10

to what the "people from Judea" were teaching later in Antioch (Acts 15:1), what "some from the party of the Pharisees" were arguing at the Jerusalem Council (15:5), and what the agitators were teaching in Galatia.[14]

Paul piles up words to characterize the false brothers in as negative a light as possible. Not only did they "sneak in," but, as he goes on to say in the next clause, "They slipped in to spy on the freedom that we have in Christ Jesus." "Slip in" translates the verb παρεισέρχομαι (pareiserchomai), which basically means "come in beside." It has the connotation, as BDAG (774) puts it, of "come in as a side issue" (Paul uses it in this sense in its only other biblical occurrence, referring to the law in Rom. 5:20). But it can also take on the more pejorative idea "slip in with unworthy motives" (again, as BDAG 774 puts it; see the list of examples). The context suggests that the word has this connotation here. "Freedom" (ἐλευθερία, eleutheria), while not used often in Galatians, is an important summary of the view for which Paul is fighting in the letter (see esp. 5:1, 13; the adjective occurs in 3:28 and five times in 4:21–31). "The freedom that we have in Christ Jesus" is, in context, the freedom from the law and similar "powers" (see 4:3) that Gentiles (and by extension, Jews also) who are in union with Jesus the Messiah enjoy (the ἐν [en, in] has a local sense, with a slight causal flavor: "by virtue of our union with" Christ [Burton 1921: 83]).[15] The false brothers, Paul claims, insinuated themselves into the meeting in Jerusalem not to engage in honest debate about the Gentiles and the law but to "spy on" (κατασκοπῆσαι, kataskopēsai) this freedom. The flavor of the verb can be seen from its only other occurrences in the Greek Bible: Ammonite commanders warn their master that David has sent envoys with hidden motives, to "spy out" the land (2 Sam. 10:3; 1 Chron. 19:3). As a natural contrast to the freedom that believers enjoy in Christ, the purpose of the false brothers, Paul asserts, is to "enslave us" (ἡμᾶς καταδουλώσουσιν, hēmas katadoulōsousin)—that is, to bring believers generally (which is what the ἡμᾶς here must cover) under the authority of the Mosaic law (see also the only other use of this verb in the NT, in 2 Cor. 11:20: "In fact, you even put up with any who enslave [καταδουλοῖ, katadouloi] you or exploit you or take advantage of you or push themselves forward or slap you in the face" [TNIV]).[16]

In this verse Paul continues his parenthetical description of the false brothers **2:5** with a second relative clause (οἷς, hois, to whom; cf. οἵτινες, hoitines, who [in v. 4]). The relative pronoun therefore refers to the false brothers. They were

14. There is no need, then, to think that the false brothers Paul refers to in this verse were advocating a new or novel position (contra Fredriksen 1991). And while there is a general similarity between the view advocated here by the "false brothers" and the view advocated at the Jerusalem Council (contra, e.g., Dunn 1993a: 98): on our view, not only are these different occasions, but Luke significantly and explicitly labels those advocating this view at the Council "believers" (Acts 15:5). They can hardly be the same as the "false brothers."

15. Coppins (2009: 93–103), following Jones (1987), thinks that the freedom here is comprehensive, including, e.g., freedom "from the present evil age" (1:4).

16. We would normally expect a subjunctive verb after ἵνα (hina, in order that), but an indicative (in this case καταδουλώσουσιν) is not uncommon (BDF §369.2).

insisting, as verse 4 implies, that Titus be circumcised. But, Paul claims, he did not yield to their wish even for an instant: οὐδὲ πρὸς ὥραν εἴξαμεν τῇ ὑτοταγῇ (*oude pros hōran eixamen tē hypotagē*, not even for an hour did we yield in submission). An "hour" was the shortest demarcation of time in Paul's day, so the phrase οὐδὲ πρὸς ὥραν, in this context, means "not even for a moment" (e.g., NIV, ESV; cf. Matt. 8:13; 9:22; 15:28; 17:18; Luke 2:38; John 4:53; Acts 16:18; 22:13; Rev. 11:13).[17] The verb εἴκω (used only here in the NT; it is in the aorist; on the unaugmented form, see BDF §67.1) would have been sufficient by itself for Paul to make his point; but he adds the dative τῇ ὑποταγῇ to accentuate the idea (the dative may be epexegetic [Burton 1921: 84]; or it could be adverbial: "yield submissively" [Moule 1959: 45]). The article with ὑποταγῇ may suggest a definite "act of submission": the "submission that the authorities were demanding of me" (e.g., Lightfoot 1881: 107).

The end of the verse indicates the purpose for which Paul refused to yield to the false brothers: ἵνα ἡ ἀλήθεια τοῦ εὐαγγελίου διαμείνῃ πρὸς ὑμᾶς (*hina hē alētheia tou euangeliou diameinē pros hymas*, in order that the truth of the gospel might remain with you). Paul succinctly summarizes what, for him, was at stake in this Jerusalem meeting: "the truth of the gospel." The genitive in the underlying Greek phrase is one of those that defies simple classification. Perhaps it is loosely possessive: the truth that belongs to, that is part of, the gospel. As Silva (2000: 54) has argued, both words in this phrase, which is unique to Gal. 2 in Paul's writings (see also v. 14), are important: truth is upheld only by the gospel; and the gospel is truly the gospel only if it corresponds to the truth. The particular aspect of the "truth of the gospel" in view here is its power both to bring Gentiles into relationship with God and to maintain them in that relationship right up through the judgment day. Titus, the test case before the council, is a Gentile who has believed the gospel, and he need not add circumcision (or by derivation, obedience to the law of Moses) to that step of faith. By extension, then, the "truth of the gospel" refers to the inherent power of the gospel, by God's grace, to justify and vindicate at the last judgment any human being. Grace is the critical matter (cf. v. 7; 2:21; and Lightfoot 1881: 107; Betz 1979: 92).

This view of the gospel, Paul suggests, is what he has been preaching and what the Galatians have themselves accepted; thus he wants it to "remain with you."[18] "You" must certainly include the readers of the letter, the Galatian Gentile Christians, but probably also includes all Gentile believers (R. Longenecker 1990: 53; Dunn 1993a: 101). Paul again suggests that the decisions reached at this meeting in Jerusalem will have a wide impact on the status of the Gentiles in the early church (see v. 2b).

---

17. We stress "in this context" because the three other NT uses of this phrase denote a short but not "momentary" period of time (John 5:35; 2 Cor. 7:8; Philem. 15).

18. In translating πρός as "with," we follow most commentators and versions (see, e.g., Silva 2003: 94). But the word could also mean "for" (Martyn 1997: 198–99). The problem with this interpretation is that the word does not fit well with διαμείνῃ.

2. Elaboration and Proof: Paul's Gospel and the "Pillars"
  c. Second Jerusalem Visit: The "Pillars" Confirm Paul's Gospel

Galatians 2:1–10

As we noted in our comments on verse 3, Paul in this verse resumes the main line of thought that he began in verses 1–2: He went to Jerusalem to consult with "those who appeared to be important" about the gospel he was preaching among the Gentiles; and the result of that consultation was that these people who "appeared to be important" did not call into question Paul's gospel by trying to add anything to it. Verses 6–10, in fact, constitute a single sentence in Greek, with several main components:

2:6

v. 6b ἐμοὶ ... οἱ δοκοῦντες οὐδὲν προσανέθεντο (*emoi ... hoi dokountes ouden prosanethento*, to me those who appeared to be important added nothing)

v. 7 ἀλλὰ (*alla*, but)

  ἰδόντες ... (*idontes*, seeing)

v. 9 καὶ γνόντες ... (*kai gnontes*, and knowing)

  δεξιὰς ἔδωκαν ἐμοὶ καὶ Βαρναβᾷ κοινωνίας (*dexias edōkan emoi kai Barnaba koinōnias*, they gave to me and Barnabas the right hand of fellowship)

The main point of verse 6 is therefore expressed at the end of the verse, and Paul again takes a roundabout way of getting to it. The verse opens with a prepositional phrase—ἀπὸ δὲ τῶν δοκούντων εἶναί τι (*apo de tōn dokountōn einai ti*, but as for those who appear to be something)—that we would expect Paul to complete with something like "My gospel received no additions." Instead, Paul again changes syntactical gears, interrupting his main clause with two related parenthetical clauses:

ὁποῖοί ποτε ἦσαν οὐδέν μοι διαφέρει (*hopoioi pote ēsan ouden moi diapherei*, what kind of people they were does not matter to me)

πρόσωπον [ὁ] θεὸς ἀνθρώπου οὐ λαμβάνει (*prosōpon [ho] theos anthrōpou ou lambanei*, God is not partial)

By the time his readers (or listeners) have negotiated these clauses, Paul is afraid that they will have forgotten where this sentence began. So he mentions again the people he is concerned about, this time making them the subject of the clause—ἐμοὶ γὰρ οἱ δοκοῦντες οὐδὲν προσανέθεντο (*emoi gar hoi dokountes ouden prosanethento*, for the ones who seem important added nothing to me). (On the syntax of the verse, see BDF §467; Wallace 1996: 54; Lightfoot 1881: 108.)

Paul uses the same verb that he used in verse 2 to denote the Jerusalem leaders: δοκέω. However, while in verse 2 and again at the end of this verse he uses it absolutely, here he adds an object, τι: "those who appeared to be *something*." It is doubtful if this addition changes the basic neutral sense of the word δοκέω. Paul again chooses language that focuses on the reputation of the Jerusalem leaders without clearly agreeing or disagreeing with that evaluation. Some interpreters suggest that the present tense of the participle δοκούντων shows that Paul focuses on the current reputation of the Jerusalem apostles, with particular reference to how the agitators in Galatia are viewing them (e.g., Lightfoot 1881: 107; Klein 1960: 290). But this point cannot be pressed, because the present tense in participles of this kind often has little or no independent temporal significance (see, e.g., A. Robertson 1934: 1115 with examples; the decision of most English translations to put this verb in a past tense to match the narrative flow therefore is justified). Paul himself realizes that his use of this language requires some further explanation, and so he detours from his main clause to add a parenthetical explanation—or rather a parenthesis within a parenthesis. The first, "main," parenthesis stresses Paul's unconcern about the status of the Jerusalem apostles: ὁποῖοί ποτε ἦσαν οὐδέν μοι διαφέρει (*hopoioi pote ēsan ouden moi diapherei*, what kind of people they were does not matter to me). The second parenthesis then justifies Paul's attitude: πρόσωπον [ὁ] θεὸς ἀνθρώπου οὐ λαμβάνει (*prosōpon [ho] theos anthrōpou ou lambanei*, God is not partial). The point is clear enough: Paul distances himself from the high repute accorded the Jerusalem leaders because he himself does not care what their reputation has been; and this attitude is justified because God himself shows no partiality. An unexpected feature in this claim, however, is the imperfect tense of ἦσαν in the first clause. Why does Paul refer to what the Jerusalem leaders "were" rather than what they "are"?[19]

Interpreters have put forth three main explanations for this temporal force: the apostles have died (Heussi 1955: 1–5; contra, see Aland 1956: 267–75); Paul no longer holds the apostles in the same regard that he did at the time of the consultation (Betz 1979: 93–95; cf. Dunn 1993a: 102); Paul does not care about their past, whether negative (their vacillating during Jesus's trial and crucifixion; Munck 1959: 99) or positive (their physical relationship to Jesus and priority in apostolic office; Calvin 1854: 54; Bruce 1982b: 117–18; Gathercole 2005: 316–17). Perhaps the last of these options makes the best sense in light of Paul's implicit claim to equality with the Twelve. Like them, he also had seen the risen Lord (1 Cor. 15:3–11), and so he refuses to concede to them any higher repute or authority than he himself enjoys.

Paul justifies his own attitude toward the Jerusalem apostles by appealing to a well-known biblical claim about God: he shows no partiality. The Greek πρόσωπον ... λαμβάνει brings over into Greek a Hebrew idiom that connotes partiality: נָשָׂא פָּנִים, *nāśā' pānîm*, "receive," or "have regard for" "faces."[20] It is a staple of both the OT and Judaism that God does not judge

---

19. This temporal focus is underscored by ποτε (*pote*, once). To be sure, it could modify ὁποῖοι (*hopoioi*, what[ever] kind of people) and therefore lack any temporal nuance. Note, e.g., the NIV "whatever"; and see Turner 1963: 196; Mussner 1988: 113; BDAG 856.3, with examples of similar constructions. However, in all its other NT occurrences ποτε has a temporal force (in Paul: Rom. 1:10; 7:9; 11:30; 1 Cor. 9:7; Gal. 1:13, 23 [2x]; Eph. 2:2, 3, 11, 13; 5:8, 29; Phil. 4:10; Col. 1:21; 3:7; 1 Thess. 2:5; Titus 3:3; Philem. 11; see esp. Betz 1979: 93–94).

20. The same construction is found in Luke 20:21. Three compound words, built on the verb λαμβάνω + πρόσωπον, are found also: the noun προσωπολημψία (*prosōpolēmpsia*, favoritism;

by appearances or by external qualities: "For the LORD your God is God of gods and Lord of lords, the great God, mighty and awesome, who shows no partiality and accepts no bribes" (Deut. 10:17; see also 2 Chron. 19:7; Job 34:19; Sir. 35:15–16 [35:12–13 LXX]; Jub. 5.16; Pss. Sol. 2.18). Paul probably places the subject, θεός, after πρόσωπον to accentuate the contrast with the immediately following ἀνθρώπου (see Lightfoot 1881: 108; the present tense of the verb is gnomic).

The γάρ introducing the final clause of the verse may suggest that Paul sees a loose relationship between the parenthesis and this resumption of the main point of the verse: those who appear to be important mean nothing to me, "for" to me they "added nothing." Or it may function here like a resumptive δέ, as Paul returns to his main sentence (Lightfoot 1881: 108; Silva 2003: 82). The emphatic position of ἐμοί may further support this relationship. In any case, Paul now states the key point of the whole paragraph: the Jerusalem apostles "added" (the verb is προσανατίθημι, which clearly has a different meaning than it did in 1:16 ["consult"]; see, e.g., Fung 1988: 96) no essential requirement to Paul's preaching of the gospel to the Gentiles. In wording the matter this way, we bring out what Paul clearly intends, in context, by his simple "added to me." He has made clear that the issue at this consultation was the "truth of the gospel" (v. 5), especially here, its essentially gracious nature. The Jerusalem apostles did nothing to interfere with that understanding of the gospel. Their request that Paul "remember the poor" (v. 10) or, later in time, their request that Gentile Christians refrain from certain practices to facilitate fellowship with Jewish believers (Acts 15:20–29) does not contradict this decision (contra, e.g., Martyn 1997: 200; Hays 2000: 225–26).

Having stated the very important negative result of the Jerusalem conclave in verse 6, Paul now, by contrast (ἀλλὰ τοὐναντίον, *alla tounantion*, but instead),[21] states the positive result: the Jerusalem apostles expressed their endorsement of the gospel preached by Paul and Barnabas among the Gentiles by extending to them the right hand of fellowship. This main point of the second part of Paul's compound sentence is delayed until verse 9. Paul leads up to it by noting two facts that the apostles recognized about Paul and his ministry: (1) that Paul had been entrusted with the gospel for the uncircumcision (v. 7) and (2) that Paul's ministry was the result of God's grace working in and through him (v. 9). Each of these points is introduced with an adverbial participle: ἰδόντες (*idontes*, seeing) in verse 7; γνόντες (*gnontes*, knowing) in verse 9. Both verbs connote mental perception in this context (R. Longenecker 1990: 55), and the aorist form

2:7

Rom. 2:11; Eph. 6:9; Col. 3:25; James 2:1); the verb προσωπολημπτέω (*prosōpolēmpteō*, show favoritism; James 2:9), and the adjective προσωπολήμπτης (*prosōpolēmtēs*, showing favoritism; Acts 10:34).

21. Only here in the NT is the adverb τοὐναντίον (a combination of the article with ἐναντίον, which means "on the other hand" [BDAG 330.2]) used with ἀλλά (τοὐναντίον also occurs in 2 Cor. 2:7 and 1 Pet. 3:9).

of both participles may suggest an inceptive idea: the Jerusalem leaders "came to recognize" these key facts about Paul's ministry (Martyn 1997: 201, 203).

What the Jerusalem apostles recognized was that "I had been entrusted with the gospel for the uncircumcision even as Peter [had been entrusted with the gospel] for the circumcision." "Entrust" translates πεπίστευμαι (*pepisteumai*), the perfect tense stressing the ongoing state of "being entrusted with" the gospel (on the "stative" force of the perfect, see esp. Porter 1989: 251–59).[22] What Paul has been entrusted with, the Jerusalem leaders recognize, is "the gospel for the uncircumcision" (τὸ εὐαγγέλιον τῆς ἀκροβυστίας, *to euangelion tēs akrobystias*; ἀκροβυστίας is an objective genitive [BDF §163; Turner 1963: 211])—even as Peter [has been entrusted with the gospel for] "the circumcision" (τῆς περιτομῆς, *tēs peritomēs*; the words in brackets are supplied from the first clause). The noun ἀκροβυστία means "foreskin" and is thus the opposite of περιτομή. Paul, following precedents elsewhere, uses the two nouns to describe the people who are characterized by one or the other; hence ἀκροβυτία = Gentiles (note the shift to ἔθνη [*ethnē*, Gentiles] in v. 8; see also Rom. 2:25–27; 3:30; 4:9; 1 Cor. 7:18–19; Eph. 2:11; Col. 3:11) and περιτομή = Jews (so also in vv. 8 and 9; and cf. also Rom. 3:30; 4:9; 15:8; Col. 3:11). In light of Paul's strong insistence on the one true gospel in 1:8–9, he cannot mean that he and Peter preach two different gospels (as suggested by Schnelle 2005: 126–28; and Elmer 2009: 99). But nor is this simply a "difference of sphere" (Lightfoot 1881: 109). What he intends, perhaps, is best captured in our modern idea of "contextualization." Proclaiming the same gospel to different audiences means inevitably that different emphases will rise to the surface (Dunn 1993a: 106). In this case, then, Paul's preaching to Gentiles would require that he make clear to them that the gracious nature of the gospel means that they should not be circumcised or put themselves under the law of Moses. Peter, on the other hand, while also making clear to a Jewish audience the gracious character of the gospel, would not necessarily bring up circumcision or the law in the same manner.

2:8   The legitimacy of Paul's ministry is grounded (γάρ, *gar*, for) in the fact that the one who was "at work" (ἐνεργήσας, *energēsas*) through Peter was also "working" (ἐνήργησεν, *enērgēsen*) through Paul. Although the name does not appear here, it is clear enough from biblical usage that "the one who worked" through Peter is God. The verb ἐνεργέω (*energeō*, work) is typically Pauline (eighteen of the twenty-one NT occurrences are in his letters), and he most often uses the verb, as here, to refer to the powerful working of God in and for his people (1 Cor. 12:6; Gal. 3:5; Eph. 1:11; 3:20; Phil. 2:13 [2x]; Col. 1:29; 1 Thess. 2:13 [with reference to the Word of God]). We cannot be certain how it was that the Jerusalem apostles recognized this working of God through Paul. But comparable situations in the book of Acts suggest that it would have been the tangible evidence of God's power in converting Gentiles and giving them his Spirit (see esp. Acts 11:1–18; 15:6–12; and in our letter, Gal. 3:1–5).

22. Using an accusative such as εὐαγγέλιον after a passive verb is quite common (BDF §159.1).

As Paul puts it elsewhere, "My message and my preaching were not with wise and persuasive words, but with a demonstration of the Spirit's power" (1 Cor. 2:4; see Calvin 1854: 58–59). The precise sense of the datives that Paul uses in the verse (Πετρῷ [Petrō]; ἐμοί [emoi, me]) is debated. They may be local: "in Peter," "in me" (cf. KJV, NKJV, NIV); or datives of advantage: "for Peter," "for me" (BDAG 335.1.a; Burton 1921: 94; Lightfoot 1881: 109; Lagrange 1918: 37); or instrumental: "through Peter," "through me" (RSV, NRSV, ESV, NLT). While the point is far from decisive, Paul's penchant to use ἐν (en, in) after this verb (energeō) when he intends a local sense may suggest that the simple dative has a different sense. The decision between a dative of advantage and instrumental dative is hard to make and, ultimately, of little significance. But perhaps the instrumental should be preferred; as Wallace (1996: 163) puts it, Paul portrays Peter and himself as "instruments in the hands of God." Paul writes this verse from his own perspective, as the ἐμοί reveals. He thus disrupts the syntax of the sentence, which is cast in the third-person plural: "those who seemed to be important added nothing to me, but seeing . . . and recognizing . . . gave to me and Barnabas the right hand of fellowship." The verse is therefore somewhat parenthetical, as Paul reflects on what led the Jerusalem apostles to make the decision that they did.

Since the point of this verse is to put Paul's ministry and Peter's ministry on equal footings, with a view to confirming the legitimacy of the former, it is striking that the two ministries are not presented in precisely parallel terms. In Peter's case, God was working εἰς ἀποστολὴν τῆς περιτομῆς (eis apostolēn tēs peritomēs, for apostleship of the circumcision; for ἀποστολή see also Acts 1:25; Rom. 1:5; 1 Cor. 9:2). In Paul's case, on the other hand, God was working simply εἰς τὰ ἔθνη (eis ta ethnē, for the Gentiles). It is possible that this difference is simply syntactical and that Paul intends us to insert ἀποστολήν in this second phrase on the basis of its earlier occurrence (e.g., as "brachylogy," a condensed expression; e.g., Mussner 1988: 116–17; and note NIV, ESV, NLT, NET, CEB). There is a rough parallel in verse 7, where the word εὐαγγέλιον is clearly to be inferred at the end of the verse on the basis of its previous mention in a parallel phrase. The supposition of a brachylogy is preferable to the other interpretations: that the council may have refused to recognize Paul's apostleship (Dunn 1993a: 107) or that Paul does not want to claim the title here because he did not want to suggest that his apostleship had anything to do with Jerusalem (Betz 1979: 98–99).

2:9

In this verse Paul adds a second reason for the Jerusalem apostles' decision—"recognizing the grace that had been given to me"—and finally states that decision itself, the main point of the long sentence extending from verse 6 through verse 10: the Jerusalem apostles, the "pillars" James, Peter, and John, extended to Paul and Barnabas "the right hand of fellowship." (The καί [kai, and] therefore links γνόντες [gnontes, knowing] with ἰδόντες [idontes, seeing/recognizing] in v. 7.) The aorist participle γνόντες, like the parallel ἰδόντες in verse 7, probably has an inceptive force: "coming to know," or "recognize."

Burton (1921: 95) rightly claims that "it is an overrefinement to attempt to discover a marked difference between ἰδόντες and γνόντες." Both verbs convey the idea of "perceive," "recognize." It is "the grace that has been given to me" (τὴν χάριν τὴν δοθεῖσάν μοι, *tēn charin tēn dotheisan moi*) that the apostles have come to recognize. Paul uses similar language elsewhere to refer to his ministry (Rom. 12:3; 15:15; 1 Cor. 3:10; Eph. 3:2, 7; cf. Rom. 1:5, χάριν καὶ ἀποστολήν [*charin kai apostolēn*], perhaps "the grace that is my apostleship" [AT]), but he also uses this expression to refer to grace given to believers in a more general sense (in Rom. 12:6 and 1 Cor. 1:4, the expression refers to grace distributed in gifts to the whole community; in 2 Cor. 8:1, to the grace of giving; in 2 Tim. 1:9, to the saving grace given to all Christians). While it is certain, then, that the main reference here is to Paul's special apostolic ministry, there may also be some allusion to that grace in a general sense that is so central to the debate with the agitators (cf. 2:21; 5:4; Martyn 1997: 203–4).

For the first time in this paragraph, Paul names the Jerusalem leaders with whom he was consulting: Ἰάκωβος καὶ Κηφᾶς καὶ Ἰωάννης (*Iakōbos kai Kēphas kai Iōannēs*, James and Cephas and John). The James here is clearly James, "the brother of the Lord" (1:19), the sobriquet being dropped here simply because there is no need to repeat it.[23] James's name probably comes first because, while Peter was prominent as the "apostle-missionary" to the Jewish world (v. 8), James held a key position within the Jerusalem church (cf. 2:12; Acts 15; cf. Lightfoot 1881: 109). Moreover, on our reading of the narrative, Peter had left the city a few years earlier because of persecution (Acts 12:17), and it may well have been that James took his place of leadership during that time (Barnett 1999: 243). John, on the other hand, was prominent in the early days of the Jerusalem church (Acts 3:1, 3, 4, 11; 4:13, 19; 8:14) but fell out of view after that: he is not mentioned later in Acts or anywhere else in the NT Letters. Paul again uses the verb δοκέω (*dokeō*) to describe these leaders (see vv. 2 and 6) but changes the construction in which it occurs. In verse 2, he used the word absolutely: τοῖς δοκοῦσιν (*tois dokousin*), "those who appear [to be important]"; in verse 6 he completed it with τι (*ti*), "those who appear to be something"; and now he completes it with στῦλοι εἶναι (*styloi einai*), "those who appear to be pillars." Paul again combines respect and reserve in referring to the Jerusalem apostles. Paul's language does not necessarily question the right of James, Peter, and John to be called "pillars," but it also makes clear that Paul will not unequivocally use this language about them—probably because the agitators were putting too much stock in their authority (R. Longenecker 1990: 57–58). The word στῦλος occurs four times in the NT, in each case with metaphorical reference (see also 1 Tim. 3:15; Rev. 3:12; 10:1). But it occurs very often in the OT, sometimes metaphorically (e.g., the "pillar of cloud" and "pillar of fire" [Exod. 13:21–22; et al.]), but usually literally and with particularly frequent reference to the pillars of the tabernacle or the

---

23. Contra, e.g., Lightfoot 1881: 109, who thinks that there is no need for the addition because the "other" James, the son of Zebedee, had in the meantime died (cf. Acts 12:2).

2. Elaboration and Proof: Paul's Gospel and the "Pillars"
c. Second Jerusalem Visit: The "Pillars" Confirm Paul's Gospel

Galatians 2:1–10

temple. This LXX usage helps explain why the word is applied to James, Peter, and John: they are being pictured as the key supports in God's new temple, the people of God (see, e.g., Bruce 1982b: 122–23; Dunn 1993a: 109–10).[24] Also informing the usage here may be the Jewish tradition that characterized the three patriarchs as "pillars": "As God once 'established the world,' the covenant community, on the basis of the three patriarchs, so in the messianic period . . . God was thought of by Jewish Christians as having 'established the world' anew, the new covenant community" (Aus 1979: 256–57; and see also esp. Bauckham 1995: 442–46).

These pillars of the early Jewish-Christian church recognized the ministry of Paul and Barnabas by extending to them "the right hand of fellowship." As often in Greek, the "right hand" is denoted simply by the adjective δεξιός (see, e.g., Rom. 8:34; Heb. 1:3), the plural being used either because it was common in directional terms (BDF §141.2) or because the picture is of the clasping of two hands. "Giving the right hand" as a symbol of friendship and/or agreement is well known in the ancient world (W. Grundmann, TDNT 2:38; cf., e.g., 1 Macc. 6:58: νῦν οὖν δῶμεν δεξιὰς τοῖς ἀνθρώποις τούτοις, *nyn oun dōmen dexias tois anthrōpois toutois*, "now then let us come to terms with these people"). The addition of κοινωνίας (*koinōnias*, fellowship) solidifies the idea.

The ἵνα (*hina*, in order that) introducing the last clause of the verse could indicate that what follows is the content of the agreement (e.g., Burton 1898: §217), but this would unduly restrict the scope of the agreement specified in this verse in light of 2:6. Thus the clause likely indicates one particular and specific aspect of that agreement. Bruce (1982b: 124) suggests that ἵνα has the sense "on condition that" (see also A. Robertson 1934: 1000). This agreement involves a division of labor: Paul and Barnabas would be "for" (εἰς, *eis*) the Gentiles, while the "pillars" would be "for" (εἰς) the Jews (περιτομή, *peritomē*, circumcision; see the additional note on 2:7–8). What verb to supply is not clear. Most English translations use "go" (for a defense, see Burton 1921: 97–98), but "minister" might be a better choice in light of the language of verses 7–8 (Silva 2003: 86; Dunn [1993a: 111] suggests simply "be," in the sense of "being responsible for"). In any case, we should not read this agreement too rigidly, as if the agreement was to put a concrete barrier between ministry to Jews and Gentiles, whether geographically or ethnically. Certainly the NT makes clear that neither Paul (in the book of Acts) nor Peter (judging from the likely audience of 1 Peter) followed this stricture. What was agreed to, rather, was probably a simple difference in focus.[25] James, Peter, and John recognized that they had been entrusted especially with "the gospel for the circumcision,"

---

24. On the theme of the temple in biblical theology, see esp. Beale 2004 (though, oddly, with no reference to Gal. 2:9).

25. Kinzer's claim (2005: 263)—that the Jerusalem agreement involved not two missionary missions, but "also two distinct networks of communities resulting from those missions and two distinct leadership structures overseeing those missions and communities"—therefore reads too much into this verse.

while they recognized at the same time that Paul had been called by God to preach the gospel among the Gentiles.

2:10 The μόνον (*monon*, only) that introduces this verse marks it as a qualification to the agreement that Paul has just described (see the parallel constructions in 1:23; 5:13; 6:12). The consultation in Jerusalem resulted in a victory for Paul and, more importantly, for "the truth of the gospel." The "pillars" of the early church recognized the validity of Paul's law-free preaching to the Gentiles. But they did add one request: that he "remember the poor."[26] There is no reason to think, as do some interpreters, that this request took the form of an authoritative requirement revealing Paul's subordinate status. To be sure, as we have seen, Paul walks a very fine line throughout his description of this consultation. He says nothing that would negate his claim to have an authority that comes directly from Christ and that therefore must stand over against any human authority (see Gal. 1). But on the other hand, he does go to Jerusalem, he does present his gospel for evaluation by the leaders there, and he does express concern about their verdict (v. 2). There is a certain sense, then, in which he voluntarily puts himself under their authority for the sake of the gospel. But as Paul makes clear, the request that the pillars made of him in this verse was no onerous imposition on him. It was, rather, "the very thing" (αὐτὸ τοῦτο, *auto touto*) that he himself "had been eager to do." As Silva (2003: 89) suggests, the aorist verb ἐσπούδασα (*espoudasa*, I was eager) is best taken as a reference to indefinite past time, including the time *before* this consultation (see also R. Longenecker 1990: 60–61; Schnabel 2004: 988; B. Longenecker 2010: 190–95). The pillars ask him, in effect, to continue to do something that he had already been doing.[27]

But what is it that he had been doing and that he was asked to continue? In the OT, the "poor" (πτωχοί, *ptōchoi*; Heb. עֲנָוִים, *'ănāwîm*), because of their lack of worldly resources, depend wholly on the Lord for their needs. They are often pictured as the righteous, in contrast to the rich and powerful (e.g., Isa. 29:19: "Once more the humble will rejoice in the LORD; the needy [πτωχοί; עֲנָוִים] will rejoice in the Holy One of Israel"). This usage of the language continues in the NT (e.g., Luke 6:20, 24; James 5:1–6). Particularly important for Gal. 2:9 is Paul's reference in Rom. 15:26 to τοὺς πτωχοὺς τῶν

---

26. The ἵνα may be imperatival (e.g., Turner 1963: 95; Bruce 1982b: 126): "only: remember the poor!" But it is better seen as dependent on an elided verb: "they asked that . . ." B. Longenecker (2010: 189–90), on the other hand, thinks that the μόνον qualifies the main clause in v. 6—"those who seemed to be something added nothing."

27. The shift from the plural μνημονεύωμεν (*mnēmoneuōmen*, that we remember) to the singular ἐσπούδασα (*espoudasa*, I was eager) is striking. Why Paul excludes Barnabas from his commitment to this enterprise is not clear. Some (e.g., Lightfoot 1881: 111; Betz 1979: 102) think that, in the interval between the consultation and the writing of the letter, the split between Paul and Barnabas had occurred (Acts 15:36–41). This reading, of course, assumes a date for the letter after the Acts 15 Council, which we have found reason to doubt. A more likely explanation is that Paul wants to focus here on his own personal commitment—a commitment that he cannot necessarily make for Barnabas.

ἁγίων τῶν ἐν Ἰερουσαλήμ (*tous ptōchous tōn hagiōn tōn en Ierousalēm*, the poor of the saints in Jerusalem [AT]). It is unlikely that Paul is simply identifying the "poor" with the "saints" (as if the genitive τῶν ἁγίων were epexegetic; see Moo 1996: 903–4); indeed, nowhere in the Scriptures does "poor" have a purely spiritual sense. But Paul does speak of poor Christians in Jerusalem, and in a context where the relationship between Gentiles and Jews in the early church is the underlying theological issue. Most interpreters therefore think that Paul has the same group in view here: the "pillars" are asking Paul to continue to aid Jewish Christians in Jerusalem (Bruce 1982b: 126; Martyn 1997: 207; de Boer 2011: 127). This would probably not be a reference to the famous "collection" for the saints in Jerusalem that Romans has in view (as, e.g., Mussner 1988: 124–26 and Vouga 1998: 49–50 think); on our dating, this collection lies sometime in the future. It is also possible, however, that "poor" in this verse has a wider and general reference (see esp. B. Longenecker 2010: 157–206). Jews viewed almsgiving as one of the key aspects of a truly pious attitude toward God (Dunn 1993a: 112), and perhaps the Jerusalem pillars are asking that Paul's Gentile mission continue to make financial support of the poor a priority. This request would make especially good sense if, as we think, Paul is being asked to do this as he visits Jerusalem to bring aid to Jerusalem Christians (Acts 11:27–30; see esp. Downs 2008: 34–37).

Additional Notes

2:1. Most MSS have the sequence πάλιν ἀνέβην, while a few (mainly Western) witnesses reverse the order. Other MSS omit πάλιν while a few others substitute for ἀνέβην the synonymous ἀνῆλθον (which is used in 1:17 and 18).

2:5. The opening of the verse is marked by several variants, some of which significantly affect the sense of the verse. The original hand of the uncial D (06) along with some old Italian and Latin MSS (according to Victorinus of Rome) omit οἷς οὐδέ, while other Greek and Latin MSS (according to Ambrosiaster and Victorinus, respectively) omit οὐδέ. If this reading should be adopted, Paul would be saying that he did, in fact, yield in submission for the sake of the truth of the gospel. Still other MSS (the corrector of D and some Greek and Latin MSS, according to Jerome) omit only the οἷς, which would have the effect of suggesting that it was to those who appear to be important rather than to the false brothers that Paul refused to submit. Neither of the variants, however, has strong enough support to think that they represent Paul's original words here (see esp. Bruce 1982b: 113–15 for the patristic evidence; and also Coppins 2009: 93–95).

2:7–8. The way in which v. 7 could be taken to refer to the un-Pauline idea of "two gospels," along with some other unusual features in vv. 7–8 (such as the use of the Greek name Πέτρος, which occurs only here in the Letters of Paul), has led some scholars to think that Paul quotes language from the "concordat" reached at the consultation (Barnikol 1931; Dinkler 1967: 278–82; O. Cullmann, *TDNT* 6:100), and has led others to suggest that he is at least incorporating language from that agreement into his wording (e.g., Betz 1979: 96–97; R. Longenecker 1990: 55–56; Martyn 1997: 211–12). (Most improbable is the thesis of Lüdemann [1984: 69–71] that Paul cites a tradition that predates the conference of Gal. 2.) This possibility cannot be ruled out, but the evidence for it is far from compelling. References to "the gospel for the uncircumcision" and "the gospel for the circumcision" are not far removed from "the gospel I preach among the Gentiles" (Gal. 2:2) or the way Paul will sometimes refer to "his gospel" (e.g., Rom. 2:16; 16:25; 1 Thess. 1:5; 2 Thess. 2:14; 2 Tim. 2:8). And, as we noted above, these phrases are susceptible of an interpretation that is thoroughly Pauline. Why Paul would switch to the Greek name Πέτρος when he uses the Aramaic Κηφᾶς elsewhere (in Galatians, see 1:18; 2:9, 11, 14) is difficult to know. The attempt to solve the discrepancy on textual grounds fails: the reading Πέτρος in Gal. 1:18; 2:9, 11, 14 in some mainly Western MSS is clearly secondary; and the suggestion that Κηφᾶς may have originally been in vv. 7–8 (e.g., Holl 1928: 45) has no textual basis at all. Nor are there any grounds for thinking that "Peter" is the apostle's "personal" name, in contrast to the official "Cephas" (Gaechter 1958: 385), that Πέτρος was a title for the apostle's position vis-à-vis Israel (Stuhlmacher 1968: 94), or that Πέτρος is a different individual than "Cephas" (contra Ehrman 1990; cf. Allison 1992). In this case we must be content simply to admit that we do not know why Paul would have changed names.

2:9. The names of the three "pillars" vary in the MS tradition. One uncial (A) drops the name Κηφᾶς, while many others replace the Aramaic Κηφᾶς with the Greek Πέτρος. Of these, 𝔓⁴⁶ puts Πέτρος in second position, while the others (e.g., D F G) put the name in first position. All these variants appear to be secondary assimilations to the context (cf. Πέτρος in vv. 7 and 8) or to the usual order of the three names (albeit, with reference to a different James; e.g., Matt. 17:1; Mark 9:2; 13:3; 14:33; Luke 8:51; 9:28).

d. An Incident at Antioch: Paul Defends the Gospel (2:11–14)

This narrative concludes the section of the letter written in first-person narrative style. Since 1:11, Paul's focus has been on his own history: his background in Judaism, his conversion, his relationship (or lack thereof) with the Jerusalem apostles, and his consultation with those apostles. Yet Paul's interest is not in himself per se, but in his role as apostle to the Gentiles and therefore especially in the gospel that he preaches among the Gentiles. The same interest is manifest again in the present paragraph: what Paul is fighting for in Antioch is "the truth of the gospel" (2:14). This phrase binds together the two narratives in 2:1–14 (de Boer 2011: 104). In Jerusalem, Paul wins agreement from the Jerusalem apostles for his version of the law-free gospel: and so "the truth of the gospel" is maintained for Gentile Christians (v. 5). In Antioch, by contrast, Paul fights for the truth of the gospel against at least one of those same Jerusalem apostles (Peter); and the outcome of that fight is not at all clear.

In fact, there is a lot that is unclear about this narrative, and we need at least to touch on some of the major issues before moving into detailed exposition (for a history of interpretation, see Mussner 1988: 146–67).

1. Did this incident take place before or after the consultation in 2:1–10? In contrast to the specific chronological markers in 1:18–2:10—"then after three years" (1:18); "then" (1:21); "then after fourteen years" (2:1)—this narrative is connected to its context with the vague ὅτε δέ (*hote de*, but when). Both because of this different transitional marker and because it is easier to explain Peter's actions if the Antioch incident precedes the Jerusalem consultation, some interpreters think that 2:11–14 is chronologically displaced, with the confrontation in Antioch taking place sometime before the Jerusalem meeting (e.g., Calvin 1854: 40; Lüdemann 1984: 75–77; Munck 1959: 100–103). But, in fact, the strength of the language Paul uses to criticize Peter—"condemned" (v. 11), acting in "hypocrisy" (v. 13), "not acting in line with the truth of the gospel" (v. 14)—makes better sense if the kind of agreement described in 2:1–10 was already in place (e.g., Murphy-O'Connor 1996: 132). Moreover, ὅτε δέ, while not as explicit as Paul's earlier transitions, still suggests that this narrative follows the one before it chronologically. If, then, as we suspect, the Jerusalem consultation narrated in 2:1–10 took place during the famine-relief visit of Paul to Jerusalem (Acts 11:27–30), then this incident in Antioch must have occurred sometime between that visit and the writing of Galatians, just before the Jerusalem Council of Acts 15. It must also have occurred during a time when Peter and Barnabas were

in Antioch for a period and while Paul was absent ("when I saw" in v. 14 suggests that Paul was confronted with a new state of affairs in Antioch after an absence from the city). Taking all these factors into consideration, it seems best to think that this incident took place shortly after Paul and Barnabas returned from their first missionary journey. Indeed, it is quite possible that Acts 15:1 is Luke's summary of this same incident: "Certain people came down from Judea to Antioch and were teaching the believers: 'Unless you are circumcised, according to the custom taught by Moses, you cannot be saved.'"[1]

2. What was the basic problem? This is the linchpin issue, and it has attracted a great deal of attention—partly because it involves uncertain and controversial evidence about underlying Jewish attitudes toward eating meals with Gentiles and partly because it carries implications for broader issues such as theological tensions within the early church and the nature of the relationship between Jewish and Gentile Christianity. What is clear is that Paul is deeply upset with the decision of Peter (and Barnabas also) to stop eating meals with Gentiles (almost certainly regular meals rather than the Eucharist specifically [contra Esler 1995: 286–311; Schlier 1989: 83–84]). There were apparently diverse views among first-century Jews over how much contact with Gentiles was allowable (see esp. Bauckham 2004; Dunn 1983; Sanders 1990). But we have good reason to think that the viewpoint reflected in the Antioch incident was what we may call rigorous, urging pious Jews to avoid as much contact with Gentiles as possible. Some texts suggest such a viewpoint:

> Letter of Aristeas 142: "To prevent our being perverted by contact with others or by mixing with bad influences, [Moses] hedged us in on all sides with strict observances connected with meat and drink and touch and hearing and sight, after the manner of the Law."

> Jubilees 22.16: "Eat not with them . . . for their works are unclean."

> Acts 10:28 (RSV): "You yourselves know how unlawful it is for a Jew to associate with or to visit any one of another nation."

Following Bauckham (2004), then, we think it likely that Peter, and perhaps the emissaries from James also, feared contact with Gentiles, and especially the intimate contact of eating together, out of fear that they might be contaminated by their immorality. The concern was not with how

---

1. See, e.g., D. Wenham 1993: 241; Barnett 1999: 285; Bauckham 2004: 136; Bruce 1982b: 128–29. Some scholars might object to this identification because of the supposition that "the incident at Antioch did not concern the question of the circumcision of Gentile Christians" (Schnabel 2004: 1004; cf. also Dunn 2009: 447–48). However, though circumcision was clearly not the "presenting" issue, the fundamental concern about "Judaizing" (Gal. 2:14) would certainly at some point involve circumcision.

the meal was prepared or even what was eaten during the meal (neither of which is mentioned in our narrative), but the mere fact of intimate contact with Gentiles (see also Mussner 1988: 140–41; de Boer 2011: 134–36). The church at Antioch was a laboratory for Jewish-Gentile relationships in the early church. Here, indeed, a "new race" of people, neither Jews nor Gentiles, was being created, requiring the coining of a new name for them: "Christians" (Acts 11:19–26). Our text makes clear that the Christians in Antioch, recognizing the removing of barriers between Jew and Gentile in Christ, were accustomed to eat meals together. Peter, apparently during an extended stay in Antioch, followed suit. But under pressure from some emissaries claiming to represent James in Jerusalem, he withdrew from this intimate fellowship. Peter probably viewed this action as a tactically wise accommodation to the concerns of stricter Jewish Christians. Paul, however, sees the matter very differently. For him, Peter's act sends the signal that Gentiles in Christ are not truly and fully cleansed from sin in Christ; that they remain morally stained and must be avoided; and that they can finally remove that stain only by themselves taking on Jewish customs ("to Judaize," v. 14—as Silva [2003: 103] notes, this issue is the crux of the Antioch incident). And all this is a flat contradiction to "the truth of the gospel."

3. How does the incident in Antioch relate to the decision reached in 2:1–10? If the Antioch incident took place after the Jerusalem consultation, how could Peter act as he did? What is important to recognize is the inherently ambiguous nature of the kind of agreement we have in 2:1–10. The focus of that agreement is the recognition that the kind of law-free gospel that Paul is preaching to the Gentiles is legitimate. The Jerusalem consultation focused on what should be required of Gentile converts. In Antioch, on the other hand, the issue had to do with how Jewish converts should relate to Gentile converts. On this matter, apparently, Peter and Paul drew different conclusions from the Jerusalem decision. Peter perhaps thought that the Jerusalem agreement simply did not cover the kind of situation he encountered in Antioch. For Paul, on the other hand—and perhaps this is why he gives particular prominence to it (2:1, 4)—the situation of Titus is telling. He is a Gentile who accompanies Paul and Barnabas and who probably participates with them and the Jewish-Christian leaders in the consultation—perhaps even eating meals together with them (Gathercole 2005: 315; though see Dunn 2009: 478–79). The fact that he is not required to be circumcised, then, is for Paul of utmost significance. As Bauckham (2004: 122) puts it, "Paul at least must have thought—and this is why he includes the detail about Titus—that the Jerusalem agreement ensured full and equal membership by Gentiles of the one messianic people of God, such that close association between such Gentiles and Jewish Christians was entailed." The point, then, is that Paul could legitimately appeal to the Jerusalem decision in his strong criticism of Peter in 2:11–14. While the latter may have pled that nothing explicit was said at the consultation about eating with Gentiles, Paul is justified in claiming that a decision about this

matter was implicit in the circumstances surrounding that consultation. Peter was not simply following the kind of "accommodation" principles Paul lays out for his own gospel ministry in 1 Cor. 9:19–23, for Paul would never recognize as valid an accommodation that negated an essential truth of the gospel (see esp. Carson 1986; contra Richardson 1980).

4. Why does Paul include this story here in Galatians? We do not know how the Antioch incident ended. But Paul's failure to say anything about a change of mind on the part of Peter may suggest that, at least at the time of writing, Peter (and perhaps Barnabas also) were unrepentant. Thus the incident could be seen as a defeat for Paul and his view of the gospel, making it all the more interesting that he chooses to end his autobiographical section on such a low note (see esp. Dunn 1983: 39; 1993a: 130–31; and also Elmer 2009: 110–16). But there are two good reasons for Paul to include the story here. First, since Antioch was not far away from the cities of South Galatia to which Paul is writing, the Christians in Galatia may have heard rumors about this incident; and it is also possible that the agitators were citing their own version of the story for their propaganda purposes. The prominence of Peter in Paul's version of this story is striking. Even though people "from James" instigated the problem, and Barnabas and all the Jewish Christians in Antioch were complicit (v. 13), it is Peter on whom Paul focuses. Perhaps, then, it was especially Peter's actions at Antioch to which the agitators were appealing. Thus Paul may have needed to clear the air about the matter. Second, however, the Antioch incident provides a natural entrée into the argument of Galatians. The central issue in that incident, as Paul makes clear at the end of the story, is whether Gentile Christians should be forced to take on the Jewish law in order to attain full status within the Messianic community. And this is just the issue that Paul's letter is designed to tackle. As Dunn (1993b: 73) puts it, "Galatians is what he should have said to Peter at Antioch had time and sufficient reflection allowed it" (cf. also Heiligenthal 1984: 42).

Exegesis and Exposition

¹¹But when ⌜Cephas⌝ came to Antioch, I resisted him to his face, for he stood condemned. ¹²For before some men from James arrived, he was eating with the Gentiles. But when ⌜they⌝ came, he withdrew and separated himself, because he feared the people of the circumcision. ¹³And the rest of the Jews joined him in this hypocrisy, so that even Barnabas was led astray by their hypocrisy. ¹⁴But when I saw that they were not walking a straight line with respect to the truth of the gospel, I said to Cephas before all of them: "If you, being a Jew, are living like a Gentile and not like a Jew, how will you compel the Gentiles to live like Jews?"

2:11   The story of Paul's rebuke of Peter at Antioch is connected to its context by a temporally vague ὅτε δέ (*hote de*, but when). The δέ suggests a mild contrast with the previous paragraph, with Paul in effect declaring: "At Jerusalem, Peter and I agreed about the essence of the gospel, *but* at Antioch . . ." (In contrast, Burton 1921: 102 and Mussner 1988: 136 argue that the δέ is continuative, introducing another illustration of the fact that Paul's gospel is not a human gospel.) The ὅτε suggests that this incident takes place after the Jerusalem consultation of 2:1–10.[2] We do not know when it was that "Cephas came to Antioch" (ἦλθεν Κηφᾶς εἰς Ἀντιόχειαν, *ēlthen Kēphas eis Antiocheian*). Peter (i.e., Cephas; as is his custom, here Paul again uses the Aramaic name) is located in Jerusalem during the early years of the Christian movement but is forced to leave the city at the time of Herod Agrippa I's persecution (AD 43–44): Luke tells us in a famously ambiguous text that "he went to another place" (Acts 12:17 RSV). But most scholars theorize that he would have stayed relatively near Jerusalem (e.g., Barnett 1999: 242–43) since he is back in Jerusalem at the time of the consultation Paul has just described (probably ca. AD 45–47) and again at the Apostolic Council (Acts 15, AD 48). We have suggested that Peter may have made this trip to Antioch just after Paul's first missionary journey. It may have been an "inspection" trip in which one of the Jerusalem apostles checks out the nature of the Christian movement in cities of the near Diaspora (see Acts 8:14; 9:32).

Without any preliminaries about issues of the dispute or how it arose, Paul cuts right to the conflict between himself and Peter. He minces no words about his response to Peter or his opinion about who was in the right: "I opposed him to his face" (κατὰ πρόσωπον αὐτῷ ἀνέστην, *kata prosōpon autō anestēn*), "for he was condemned" (ὅτι κατεγνωσμένος ἦν, *hoti kategnōsmenos ēn*). Paul stresses his bold and vigorous response to Peter: he did not talk about him behind his back but confronted him κατὰ πρόσωπον (the κατά in the phrase is distributive: "face-to-face" [BDAG 888.1.b.β.ꓶ]; cf. 2 Cor. 10:1, where most English versions translate κατὰ πρόσωπον "face-to-face"). Why did he act so boldly toward this great "pillar" of the church? Because Peter "stood condemned." This rendering of the perfect periphrastic participial phrase κατεγνωσμένος ἦν, adopted by most of the English versions, is well justified. The perfect tense, as we have noted, usually has a stative force, and this force is very clear in this periphrastic perfect participial phrase. Peter is "in the state of having been condemned" (the verb καταγινώσκω means "condemn" in five of its other six LXX and NT occurrences [Deut. 25:1; Sir. 14:2; 19:5; Gal. 2:11; 1 John 3:20, 21; cf. also Prov. 28:11]). But condemned by whom? Some think it refers to Peter's condemning of himself (by his actions; cf. Lightfoot 1881: 111); others to other people's condemnation of Peter (Chrysostom, *Comm. Gal.* on 2:11–12 [NPNF[1] 13:19]). But the only way this phrase makes sense in its context (e.g., as the basis for Paul's strong resistance to Peter) is if we assume that Paul means "condemned by God" (R. Longenecker 1990: 72).

---

2. Every other occurrence of the phrase ὅτε δέ in the NT introduces something that follows what comes before it: Matt. 9:25; 13:26; 21:34; Luke 15:30; Acts 8:12, 39; 11:2; 12:6; 21:5, 35; 27:39; 28:16; Gal. 1:15; 2:12; 4:4; Titus 3:4. It is unlikely, however, that Paul uses ὅτε δέ here as a conscious pickup of the same phrase in 1:15 (contra Ramsay 1900: 304).

Through the centuries interpreters have struggled with this frank acknowledgment of serious differences between two of the great apostles of the church. Some in the early church went so far as to suggest that the conflict was contrived for the sake of the Antioch Christians (e.g., Chrysostom, *Comm. Gal.* on 2:11–12 [*NPNF*[1] 13:19]). In more recent times, this text was seen as one important indicator of a fundamental theological split between Paul and Peter, a split that cleaved the early church into two parts, a split that certain NT writers (e.g., Luke) have tried in vain to paper over. This interpretation, associated especially with the so-called Tübingen School in the nineteenth century, has left a lasting impression on scholars and laypeople alike. In fact, however, little good evidence for any such fundamental theological difference between the two apostles exists (see esp. the recent work of Schnabel 2004). The disagreement in this text between the two in the matter of association between Jewish and Gentile believers should not be minimized: Paul does think that the truth of the gospel is at stake. Yet the difference is not fundamentally over theology but over the implications for a specific form of conduct that arises from theology. And Paul's inclusion of Peter with himself in expressing that theology in 2:15–18 demonstrates the fundamental agreement between the two at that level.

2:12 Paul of course realizes that he has jumped ahead in his narrative of this incident, and so he now backs up to explain (hence the γάρ, *gar*, for) what led to the need for him to resist Peter to his face. Peter, who had apparently been staying in Antioch for some time, had been in the habit of "eating with" his Gentile brothers and sisters (the verb συνήσθιεν [*synēsthien*] is in the imperfect tense, signaling continuous or repeated action). It is difficult to know just what this language implies. Dunn has argued that Peter would probably have continued to keep Jewish food laws, and that believers in Antioch were accommodating Jewish dietary restrictions via various well-known means to provide for Jewish-Gentile interaction in the Diaspora (see, e.g., Dunn 1983; 1993a: 121–22; and also Hays 2000: 232; Sanders 1990). But Paul's claim that Peter is "living like a Gentile" in verse 14 appears to suggest that Peter had gone farther and had begun to give up Jewish scruples about food in general (Martyn 1997: 232; Witherington 1998: 153). Peter would have been acting on the basis of the vision he had received in Acts 10, where God showed him that there were no truly "impure" foods. There is no reason to think that this practice was restricted to or particularly focused on the Lord's Supper (Hays 2000: 233–34; contra, e.g., Esler 1995: 286–311; Schlier 1989: 83–84).

But Peter's practice of eating with the Gentiles changed when "some men from James arrived." He then "withdrew and separated himself" (ὑπέστελλεν καὶ ἀφώριζεν ἑαυτόν, *hypestellen kai aphōrizen heauton*). The verb ὑπέστελλεν could be intransitive, "he drew back" (Bruce 1982b: 130–31)—or it could have as its object ἑαυτόν, meaning "he withdrew himself" (Lightfoot 1881: 112; R. Longenecker 1990: 75; see BDAG 1041 for these options). It is also possible that it has an inceptive force here: Peter "began to draw back" (cf. NIV, NAB, NASB, NET, CEB).[3]

Peter changed his habits in Antioch when "some men from James arrived" (ἐλθεῖν τινας ἀπὸ Ἰακώβου, *elthein tinas apo Iakōbou*) and "because he feared the people of the circumcision" (φοβούμενος τοὺς ἐκ περιτομῆς, *phoboumenos tous ek peritomēs*; the participle is causal). Three major questions arise with respect to these clauses. What was the relationship between James himself and the envoys from James? What is the relationship between these two groups of people? And what was it specifically about these groups or their message that led Peter to change his behavior? We take these questions in order.

It is unclear whether ἀπὸ Ἰακώβου modifies τινας—"some men belonging to, or representing, James came"; or modifies the verb ἐλθεῖν—"some men came from James" (so most of the translations). In any case, this unclarity makes little difference to the meaning (see discussion in Burton 1921: 107). In either case, the text indicates some kind of relationship between these people who arrived in Antioch and James, one of the "pillars" of the Jerusalem church (v. 9). Interpreters have often tended toward opposite poles in assessing this relationship. Some think the envoys accurately conveyed James's own message (e.g., R. Longenecker 1990: 73; Martyn 1997: 233; Bockmuehl 2000: 71–73; Schnabel 2004: 1003–4; Elmer 2009: 104–5). Others, however, insist that the envoys only claimed to be representing the apostle and were in reality seeking authority for their message by a bogus appeal to James (e.g., Lightfoot 1881: 112; Barnett 1999: 285–86). Our text does not allow us to make a clear decision between these options (Silva 2003: 101). But what we can be sure of is that on the two occasions when James is called on to make a decision about the inclusion of Gentiles *as Gentiles* within the Messianic community, he sides with those who insist that Gentiles should not be required to "Judaize" (Acts 11:1–18 [James is not mentioned, but we can assume that he was involved] and Acts 15). Nevertheless, as we have seen, the issue in our text is different. It is not *explicitly* a question of the basis on which Gentiles should be allowed to join the church but a question of how Jewish believers should relate to those believing Gentiles. And on this question, James (along with Peter, Barnabas, and the "rest of the Jewish believers" in Antioch [v. 13]) could very well have taken a "conservative" position.

If it is possible, then, that the people who came from James really were representing his own view, were these the same as "those from the circumcision" whom Peter feared? The designation of people as ἐκ [τῆς] περιτομῆς occurs five other times in the NT: Acts 10:45; 11:2; Rom. 4:12; Col. 4:11; Titus 1:10. In this last text, the reference seems to be to people from "a circumcision party," that

---

3. Hays (2000: 233) calls this a "tactical retreat," but his interpretation appears to be based on the false assumption that the word would reflect the military reference that the term sometimes has (see Betz 1979: 108, to which Hays refers). But despite claims that this is a "military or political term" (Witherington 1998: 154), actual usage in the LXX and NT simply does not support this sweeping claim (Exod. 23:21; Deut. 1:17; Job 13:8; Wis. 6:7; Hab. 2:4; Hag. 1:10; Acts 20:20, 27; Heb. 10:38). Nor does the usage of the verb in Philo or Josephus tend in this direction.

is, as the NLT puts it, "those who insist on circumcision for salvation." This could be the meaning in our text also (e.g., R. Longenecker 1990: 73; Martyn 1997: 236–40). But this is the only other text where the phrase has this meaning. In the other texts, the context makes clear that the author is referring to Jewish Christians, and it is not, therefore, surprising that many interpreters think that is the reference here also (e.g., Lightfoot 1881: 112; Bauckham 2004: 116–17; de Boer 2011: 133). However, in each of these contexts (except, perhaps, Acts 11:2), reference to Jewish *Christians* comes not from the phrase ἐκ περιτομῆς but from other contextual factors. The phrase in itself seems to mean simply "belonging to the group of people who are circumcised" (see Turner 1963: 260 on the use of ἐκ in Paul to mean "belonging to"). Moreover, the simple word περιτομή in Paul consistently means "the act of circumcision" and thus "people who are circumcised," such as Jews (vv. 7, 8, and 9). This is likely the meaning here also (Burton 1921: 108; Bruce 1982b: 131; Witherington 1998: 154–55; Watson 2007: 106–7). In this case, "those from James" are not identical to "those of the circumcision" (see, e.g., Schütz 2007: 153; R. Longenecker 1990: 74–75; contra, e.g., Smiles 1998: 89–91; Mussner 1988: 141).

With these identifications in place, we can now answer our third question and suggest that each group is important in understanding why Peter withdrew from the Gentiles. Although we cannot be certain, the following scenario makes good sense of the text and what we know of the larger and more specific background. The envoys from James were probably sent to investigate and convey concern about the degree to which Jewish believers were associating with Gentiles. From James's perspective, nothing in the agreement hammered out between the "pillars" and Paul suggested that Jewish believers would be free to put aside the traditional, torah-based barriers to fellowship (and potential moral contamination) with Gentiles. And fueling his concern was the larger social-political situation. Persecution (esp. at the time of the Maccabees) and exile (the Diaspora) led many Jews to erect or insist on careful barriers between themselves and the Gentiles as means of preserving their religious identity. These factors produced a situation in which, as Dunn (1983: 10) puts it, "wherever this new Jewish sect's belief or practice was perceived to be a threat to Jewish institutions and traditions its members would almost certainly come under pressure from their fellow Jews to remain loyal to their unique Jewish heritage." And this pressure was increasing as the radical Zealot movement, which insisted on strict separation from Gentiles, grew stronger during these years in Palestine (see esp. Jewett 1970–71; and also, e.g., Hays 2000: 232–33; Witherington 1998: 155–56). This background explains why Peter—and James—would be fearful of "the circumcision." Outright persecution was perhaps part of the issue, but perhaps even more important was concern about how Jews in Jerusalem would perceive this new messianic movement (this is explicitly a concern that James expresses on a later occasion [Acts 21:20–24]). The envoys from James would, on this reading of the situation, have urged Peter and other Jewish Christians in Antioch to refrain from close contact with Gentiles, out of fear that their behavior would bring disrepute to Christians in Jerusalem and elsewhere. For James and Peter, then, separating from the Gentile believers would have been perceived as an accommodation to facilitate Jewish evangelism. But Paul rightly sees that such an accommodation cannot be allowed because of what it would say about the Gentiles' status within the community.

The focus of Paul's narrative is on Peter; but now he indicates that Peter was not the only one to succumb to the pressure brought to bear by the emissaries of James: "the rest of the Jews [i.e., the other Jewish Christians in Antioch] joined him in this hypocrisy." The verb Paul uses (συνυπεκρίθησαν, *synypekrithēsan*) is rare, occurring only here in the NT and the LXX (Josephus uses it twice). It can mean simply "play a part," as when Josephus refers to some Jews, during the rebellion against Rome, who pretended to surrender along with one of their leaders (*J.W.* 5.321). But in this case, the part that Peter is playing is one that he knows, at some level, to be in contradiction to his own convictions (vv. 14, 15–17)—and "hypocrisy" is therefore an appropriate translation in English. Paul again suggests that Peter was the leader in this situation: the other Jews joined "with him" (αὐτῷ, *autō*: the dative pronoun, dependent on the σύν prefixed to the verb, denotes the person "with whom" they joined in hypocrisy [BDAG 976–77]). Indeed, so influential was Peter's action that "even [καί, *kai*] Barnabas was led astray by their hypocrisy."[4] The verb Paul uses (συναπήχθη, *synapēchthē*, from συναπάγω, "lead away") occurs with a similar sense in 2 Pet. 3:17: "Be on your guard so that you may not be carried away [συναπαχθέντες] by the error of the lawless." As in the 2 Peter text, it is possible that the dative following the verb in our text (τῇ ὑποκρίσει, *tē hypokrisei*) is instrumental: "by the hypocrisy [just mentioned]" (so most English translations; and cf. A. Robertson 1934: 533; Burton 1921: 109; the σύν in the verb would therefore have "them" as its understood object). But the dative could also indicate the element "with which" they were carried away (Lightfoot 1881: 113); or even perhaps the object to which they were led (see NLT: "even Barnabas was influenced to join them in their hypocrisy").

In this verse Paul circles back to where this brief paragraph began: his public rebuke of Peter in Antioch (v. 11). The ἀλλά (*alla*, but) contrasts Paul's response with the situation that he has described in verses 12–13. The implication of the phrase ὅτε εἶδον (*hote eidon*, when I saw) is that Paul was away from Antioch when the delegation from James arrived and instigated the change in behavior among the Jewish Christians (e.g., Burton 1921: 109–10; R. Longenecker 1990: 77). On his return, he was presented with a fait accompli. In verse 13, Paul accused Peter, Barnabas, and the other Jewish Christians of failing to live out their own convictions ("hypocrisy"); now he accuses them, more seriously, of failing to act in accordance with the gospel. Paul couches this accusation in a

2:13

2:14

---

4. This clause is introduced by ὥστε (*hōste*, so that); since it is followed by an indicative verb in a dependent clause (only here and John 3:16 in the NT), it indicates an "actual result" (e.g., Wallace 1996: 593).

metaphor: "they were not walking uprightly with respect to the truth of the gospel" (ὀρθοποδοῦσιν πρὸς τὴν ἀλήθειαν τοῦ εὐαγγελίου, *orthopodousin pros tēn alētheian tou euangeliou*). The verb ὀρθοποδέω (*orthopodeō*), which occurs only here in the NT or LXX, means "to walk uprightly," "to walk straight" (our word "orthopedics" comes from this Greek root), and πρός probably indicates that "with reference to which" the walking occurs ("to pursue a straight course in relation to the truth of the gospel" [Burton 1921: 110]; cf. ESV: "their conduct was not in step with the truth of the gospel").[5]

"The truth of the gospel" is a key concept in this chapter and indeed, as we have suggested, in this entire first major section in the letter. As its other explicit occurrence in verse 5 reveals, it has particular reference to the issue at stake in Jerusalem (2:1–10), Antioch (2:11–14), and in the Galatian crisis: the entirely gracious character of the gospel, which renders any attempt to impose other obligations beyond faith in Christ a de facto turn to "another gospel, which is no gospel at all" (1:6–7). Because Paul is convinced of the seriousness of the matter, he takes the bold step of rebuking Peter "in front of everyone" (ἔμπροσθεν πάντων, *emprosthen pantōn*). The reference is probably to a public meeting of the Christians in Antioch, perhaps called at Paul's request to hash out this issue in particular.[6]

At the end of verse 14 Paul begins to record what he said to Peter during this public dispute: "If you, being a Jew, are living like a Gentile and not like a Jew, how can you compel the Gentiles to live like Jews?" What Paul meant by this rebuke is debated. It is cast in the form of a conditional sentence: the word introducing the apodosis, πῶς (*pōs*), has the sense "with what right?" or "how dare you?" (BDAG 901.1.a.γ). The key contrast in the verse is between living Ἰουδαϊκῶς (*Ioudaikōs*, in a Jewish way) and ἐθνικῶς (*ethnikōs*, in a Gentile way). Peter, Paul claims, had given up a "Jewish" way of life and adopted a "Gentile" way of life. But by reverting again to a Jewish way of life, he was, in effect, forcing the Gentile believers also to adopt a Jewish way of life. The rarity of these words (they occur only here in the NT and LXX and never in Philo or Josephus) makes it difficult to identify the specific behavior that would be included in these terms. Had Peter given up all of the Jewish law? Was he no longer eating kosher or observing the Sabbath? Dunn (1993a: 128), among others, claims that it is very unlikely that he had gone this far; he thinks that "living in a Gentile manner" reflects internal Jewish debates about how much was required of "true" Jews (cf. also Sanders 1990: 186–87; Kinzer 2005: 84, thinks the language is ironic). However, in contrast to ἐθνικῶς, this

5. Another option is to take the verb to refer more to the direction of movement rather than the kind of movement and then to interpret πρός as directional: "they were not on the right road toward the truth of the gospel" (Kilpatrick 1954; Bruce 1982b: 132). Wisdom (2001: 137) thinks that Paul might allude to teaching in Deuteronomy about Israel's need to walk faithfully with God and not turn aside to other gods (5:32; 17:20; 28:14).

6. It is possible that Peter and the delegation from James had come to Antioch for the purpose of a conference on this matter (e.g., Farmer 1999: 146–49; Bauckham 2004: 138), although this is not clear.

term would be expected to have a general sense. Moreover, Paul seems to argue in this context (v. 18) that Paul (and by implication in the context, Peter and other Jewish Christians) had "torn down" the law.

Equally unclear is the scope of the verb at the end of the verse. Some claim that Ἰουδαΐζειν (*Ioudaizein*) means "to become a Jew," "to embrace the Jewish faith" (e.g., R. Longenecker 1990: 78). However, while some occurrences of this verb could have this meaning (e.g., Esther 8:17; cf. W. Gutbrod, *TDNT* 3:383), others seem more naturally to mean, generally, "adopt a Jewish way of life" (e.g., Josephus, *J.W.* 2.454, 463; Plutarch, *Cic.* 7.5, 864C; Ign. *Magn.* 10.3; cf. esp. Dunn 1993a: 129). Nevertheless, in this context a good case can be made for the stronger sense of the word. The logic of the situation would seem to require that circumcision (and therefore full "conversion") be intended here. As Bauckham (2004: 126) puts it, "If it is because the Gentile Christians are *Gentiles* that the men from James have persuaded Peter not to eat with them, then eating with them would only be possible if they became Jews." Probably, then, we are to view the contrast between Ἰουδαϊκῶς and ἐθνικῶς as a quite fundamental one (see, e.g., Boers 2006: 26). But how was it that Peter's return to "living like a Jew" was "compelling" Gentile believers to live like Jews also? The situation in Jerusalem, where Paul claims that Titus was not "compelled" (ἠναγκάσθη, *ēnankasthē*) to be circumcised (v. 3), could suggest that Peter was using his authority as an apostle to order that the Gentile believers live like Jews. But this is unlikely in this context.[7] More likely, it was the behavior of Peter and the other Jewish Christians itself that was exerting pressure on the Gentile believers.[8] In what sense? To explain this rebuke, we must assume that Paul viewed the sharing of meals between Jewish and Gentile believers as a critical indication of the status of the Gentiles within the people of God. For this reason, celebration of the Lord's Supper was probably one aspect of the sharing of meals that was involved in the Antioch dispute, although there is no evidence it was the primary focus. By withdrawing from fellowship with Gentile believers on the basis of the Jewish law, the Jewish believers are, in effect, demanding that the Gentile believers meet them on their Jewish terms: they must, in effect, take up the law themselves if they want to reestablish fellowship with the Jews. For Paul, however, as he will explain in more detail in verses 15–21 (and indeed in the rest of the letter), to require this of the Gentiles is to abandon the grace of God that is a fundamental hallmark of the gospel.

As the climax of Paul's speech to Peter reveals, then, the critical issue in the Antioch incident, for Paul—and the reason he includes the story here—is

---

7. Yet Bauckham (2004: 128–30) does suggest that passages speaking of Jews as compelling Gentiles to be circumcised (e.g., Josephus, *Ant.* 13.257–58; 13.318; 1 Macc. 2:46) may "color" Paul's use of the word. See also de Boer 2011: 138.

8. The verb ἠναγκάσθη is then probably not conative—"attempting to compel" (e.g., A. Robertson 1934: 880; R. Longenecker 1990: 78; Dunn 1993a: 129)—but "factual": Peter's conduct was actually compelling the Gentiles to adopt a Jewish way of life (Mussner 1988: 145).

the question of what should be required of Gentiles who have come to faith in Jesus Christ.

Additional Notes

2:11. As in other texts where the name appears in Galatians, the Aramaic Κηφᾶς is replaced by the Greek Πέτρος in a few, mainly Western MSS and in 𝔐. The Greek name is undoubtedly secondary.

2:11–14. In the wake of the thorough reassessment of first-century Judaism that has marked NT scholarship over the last several decades, renewed attention has been given to the nature of Jewish-Gentile contact, particularly in Diaspora cities such as Antioch. Many scholars now doubt what Bockmuehl (2000: 57–61) calls the "all or nothing" interpretation of this interaction—that is, that it was standard Jewish practice to abstain from virtually all contact with Gentiles. He and others (see esp. Sanders 1990; Dunn 1983) argue that it is far more likely that Jews took a variety of positions on this matter, from a hard-line no-contact policy to softer positions that allowed for certain kinds of contact between Jews and Gentiles—even at mealtime. In an interesting twist on this argument, Bauckham (2004), while agreeing that Jews did not always consider Gentiles ritually impure, claims that Jews did view them as morally impure (esp. because of idolatry). He suggests that this may have been the fundamental problem in Antioch: that Jews who shared meals with Gentiles would have been in danger of contracting the moral impurity of Gentiles. Furthermore, there is some evidence that Jews in Palestine would have taken a harder line on this matter than Jews in the Diaspora. Thus we can understand why "those from James" (in Jerusalem) might have objected to a practice that had been accepted in Antioch. Certainly, as we note above, the issue as Paul presents it has to do not with the niceties of Jewish ritual law, but with the fact of contact between Jewish and Gentile Christians. And the background that Bauckham sketches explains this situation as well as other similar situations (e.g., Acts 10 and 15).

2:12. Some early and reliable witnesses read the singular ἦλθεν in place of the plural ἦλθον; and one early MS (𝔓⁴⁶ᵛⁱᵈ) also reads a singular pronoun τινα instead of the plural τινας (𝔓⁴⁶ᵛⁱᵈ then consistently reads a singular: "before a person from James came, . . . when he came"). It is probably the shift of the verb number that led to the shift in pronoun number; and the singular verb is probably an assimilation to the context (ἦλθεν in v. 11; and the singular verbs in v. 12; cf. Metzger 1994: 523–24; R. Longenecker 1990: 63).

B. The Truth of the Gospel Defined (2:15–21)

The gospel, as Paul understands it and as he has been preaching it, is central to the first major section of the letter body. Throughout this part of the letter, Paul focuses on what we might call the authority of that gospel. His basic argument, enunciated in 1:11–12, is that the gospel he preaches has not come to him from any human source but from Jesus Christ himself. Twice, in 2:5 and 14, Paul refers to "the truth of the gospel" without explaining just what that "truth" is. In both texts his concern is rather on the negative: to circumcise Titus and for Cephas and other Jewish Christians to withdraw from their fellowship with Gentile Christians would violate the truth of the gospel. This negative focus prepares the way for and anticipates the central rhetorical point of the letter, as Paul seeks to convince the Galatians that the agitators who have appeared in their midst are teaching a message that also violates the truth of the gospel. We may then view the paragraph 2:15–21 as a positive assertion of this truth of the gospel. The key point that Paul wants to make comes in verse 16, where he asserts that justification before God comes through faith in Jesus Christ and not through "works of the law." Contextually, this assertion of a key element of the truth of the gospel applies first of all to the situation at Antioch that Paul has just described (vv. 11–14). The connection with the Antioch episode is made clear by the way in which Paul introduces this assertion in verse 15: "We who are Jews by birth." This becomes the subject of the verbs in verse 16—"knowing," "we have believed," "that we might be justified"—and connects what Paul says here to his speech at Antioch. But the first-person plural is continued in verse 17, "we are found," and verses 18–21 are logically tightly bound to verse 17. This makes it likely that Paul continues to "quote" his speech at Antioch right up through the end of verse 21 (so NIV, NKJV, NASB; other versions [NAB, RSV, NRSV, ESV, HCSB, NET, CEB] end the quotation at the end of v. 14 [NLT at the end of v. 16]).

However, if this key paragraph looks backward to the Antioch incident, it also looks ahead to the argument that Paul will be making to the Galatians. Key words that are central to that argument are first introduced here in 2:15–21 (cf. Matera 1992: 98):

νόμος (nomos, law)—6 times here; 27 times in the rest of the letter (none in 1:1–2:14)

ἔργα νόμου (erga nomou, works of the law)—3 times; 3 times in the rest of the letter (none in 1:1–2:14)

δικαιόω (dikaioō, justify)—4 times here; 4 times in the rest of the letter (none in 1:1–2:14)

δικαιοσύνη (*dikaiosynē*, righteousness)—1 time; 3 times in the rest
of the letter (none in 1:1–2:14)

πίστις (*pistis*, faith)—3 times; 18 times in the rest of the letter (once
in 1:1–2:14 [1:23], but in a different sense)

πιστεύω (*pisteuō*, believe)—1 time; 2 times in the rest of the letter
(once in 1:1–2:14 [2:7], but in a different sense)

ζάω (*zaō*, live)—5 times here; 3 times in the rest of the letter (once in
1:1–2:14 [2:14])

This makes clear that in verses 15–21 Paul introduces some of the key
theological themes that will dominate the rest of the letter (Allaz 1987:
34–35; Eckstein 1996: 79). It is for this reason that some scholars (e.g.,
Bruce 1982b: 135) view this paragraph as the opening part of the central
section of the letter. Most scholars, however, noting the formal connection
with 2:11–14 that we outline above, put 2:15–21 in their outlines as the
concluding paragraph of the first part of the letter body (1:11–2:21). The
problem is the nature of our outlines, which tend to force us to put a set of
verses in one section or another. In reality, as most scholars also recognize,
2:15–21 is a transitional paragraph. We cannot be sure how accurately Paul
quotes the actual "speech" that he made before everyone in Antioch. But it
is clear that Paul wants to apply the content of that speech to the Galatian
situation; as Betz (1979: 114) puts it, "Paul addresses Cephas formally, and
the Galatians materially" (see also esp. Smiles 1998: 103–4; Schlier 1989:
87–88).[1] Or, as I. Scott (2006: 180) puts it, Paul wants "to lay the situation
in Antioch alongside the situation in Galatia, to see the crises as parallel
and the true solution as the same in both cases."

The paragraph divides into three basic parts. As we have noted, verses
15–16 state the essential theological point of the paragraph: Jews like Paul
and Peter understand that they have been justified by faith in Christ and
not by "works of the law." In place of the agitators' synthesis of faith in
Christ *and* the law, Paul insists on an antithesis: it is Christ and therefore *not*
the law. The rest of the paragraph elaborates on this negative claim about
justification and the law. Verses 17–20 spell out how finding justification "in
Christ" has implications for the law; and verse 21 shows why righteousness
(e.g., the status granted by justification) cannot come via the law. While
its meaning is debated, verse 17 makes the best sense if we posit a shift in
the meaning of "sin" between its beginning and its end. Jewish-Christians
object that discarding the law means that they will be considered just like
"Gentile sinners" (see v. 15) and that Christ will therefore, in effect, be
promoting sin. Paul strenuously rejects any such notion (v. 17b), arguing

---

1. Betz, following his general rhetorical approach to the letter, views this paragraph as the
propositio, which has the function of summing up the argument to this point and creating a
transition into the main argument (1979: 113–14; see also Witherington 1998: 169–73; R. Longenecker 1990: 80–81).

that it is only if the law is reestablished as a standard of right conduct (as Peter implicitly did at Antioch) that Jewish-Christians who no longer follow it could be truly considered sinners (v. 18). What Jewish-Christians need to do is imitate Paul, who, in order truly to live for God, has replaced his attachment to the law with an attachment to Christ (vv. 19–20). In verse 21, then, continuing his first-person narrative, Paul puts forth his own attitude and practice for his readers to emulate. He will not reject God's grace. That grace is decisively revealed in the death of Christ; and to seek righteousness by the law is actually to deny the effect of that death—in the epochal significance with which Paul views it. So unexpected and so amazing is the death of God's own Son—especially in its character as a pure gift of grace—that it must be seen as relativizing every other means of righteousness/justification.

The juxtaposition in this passage of two great overarching Pauline themes, justification (v. 16 esp.) and union with Christ (vv. 19–20), has thrust this passage into the role of contested territory in the old and ongoing debate about the relationship between participatory and forensic categories in Paul's theology. Certain strands of Reformation teaching (though by no means all of them) held up forensic justification as the real heart of Paul's teaching. In response, others have insisted that participation with Christ is the center of Paul's theology, with forensic justification a "subsidiary crater" (to use the language of A. Schweitzer 1931: 225). A particular twist on this latter view has recently had some prominence, according to which justification is subsumed within the participationist perspective. The swift move from justification to union with Christ in 2:16–21, it is argued, gives reason to think that justification must not be confined to forensic status but that it must have broad transformational significance (see esp. Gorman 2009: 63–72; D. Campbell 2009: 851–52). In contrast, we think there is good reason to understand justification/righteousness in Galatians in forensic terms. But it is also true that union with Christ is a key (perhaps *the* key) idea in the letter (for both these points, see "Justification/Righteousness," in the introduction). But there is no need to merge these two concepts in order to do justice to their prominence in Galatians, or in 2:16–21 specifically. Justification indeed takes place "in Christ" (v. 17); and union with Christ, as Paul develops it in 2:19–20, clearly involves a total transformation of the human being. But neither in this paragraph nor elsewhere does Paul connect the two in such a way that justification must include this transformational element. The person who is joined to Christ enjoys both forensic justification (vv. 16, 21) and transformation (vv. 19–20). They are inseparable but distinct effects of our union with Christ.

Current scholarship on Galatians emphasizes that Galatians is about salvation history, and there is considerable truth in this claim. But it should not be missed that the central argument of the letter is framed by principial statements about justification by faith—applied to both Jews and Gentiles (2:16; 5:4–5).

Exegesis and Exposition

[15]"We are Jews by birth and not sinners from among the Gentiles; [16]┌yet┐ we know that a person is not justified by works of the law, but by faith in Jesus Christ. So we, too, have put our faith in Christ Jesus in order that we might be justified by faith in Christ and not by works of the law, because by works of the law no one will be justified. [17]But if, in seeking to be justified in Christ, we also find ourselves to be sinners, doesn't that mean that Christ is a servant of sin? Absolutely not! [18]For if I rebuild what I destroyed, then I would be a transgressor. [19]For through the law I died to the law so that I might live for God; I have been crucified with Christ. [20]I no longer live, but Christ lives in me; and the life I now live in the flesh, I live by faith in ┌the Son of God┐, who loved me and gave himself for me. [21]I do not set aside the grace of God; for if righteousness could be gained through the law, Christ died for nothing!"

2:15 The emphatic reference to "we . . . Jews by birth," along with the first-person plural form of this verse (ἡμεῖς, *hēmeis*, we) and the next one (ἡμεῖς . . . ἐπιστεύσαμεν, *hēmeis . . . episteusamen*, we believed), suggests that Paul continues to relate the contents of the speech he addressed to Peter in Antioch (2:14b; contra Bring 1961: 86). However we construe the syntactical relationship between the two verses (for which see the second additional note on 2:16), verse 15 introduces the subject of the verbs in verse 16. It is likely that verse 15 has a mildly concessive function in relation to verse 16 (Burton 1921: 119; Mussner 1988: 167—signaled by the "yet" in v. 16 in RSV, NRSV, ESV, NLT, NET). In effect, Paul would be saying, "Although we Jews, in contrast to the Gentiles, would seem to have an inherent right to justification, even we have turned our backs on the law of Moses and have embraced faith in Christ as the means to justification." To be Jews "by birth" (φύσει, *physei*; perhaps a dative of respect [BDF §197]) means that their status is a "condition or circumstance as determined by birth, . . . esp. as inherited fr[om] one's ancestors" (BDAG 1069.1; see also Rom. 2:27; 11:21, 24). The contrast to this birth privilege is to be "sinners from among the Gentiles" (ἐξ ἐθνῶν ἁμαρτωλοί, *ex ethnōn hamartōloi*; the ἐξ denotes origin [BDAG 296.3.b]). Paul is almost certainly using ἁμαρτωλοί from the typical Jewish perspective that viewed Gentiles as by definition "excluded from citizenship in Israel and foreigners to the covenants of the promise, without hope and without God in the world" (Eph. 2:12). See, for example, Matt. 26:45: "Then he returned to the disciples and said to them, 'Are you still sleeping and resting? Look, the hour has come, and the Son of Man is delivered into the hands of sinners'" (and also Luke 6:32–33; Isa. 14:5; Jub. 23.23–24; Pss. Sol. 1.1; 2.1; see esp. Dunn 1993a: 133).[2] Paul uses the language in this traditional sense only to debunk it; as Martyn (1997: 249) puts it, "Verse 15 proves, then, to be the baiting of the trap, so to speak, which will be sprung in verse 16" (cf. also Smiles 1998: 107). The gospel reveals that all people are "sinners" and therefore equally in need of finding justification in Christ.

2. However, as Bauckham (2004: 125–26) reminds us, granted the reality of God's law and its demands, the Gentiles are not simply "ritual" sinners but also real sinners.

This verse is one of the most important and debated in the Letters of Paul. It is his first explicit reference to justification (using the δικ- root), and its contrast between ἔργα νόμου (*erga nomou*, works of the law) and πίστις Ἰησοῦ Χριστοῦ (*pistis Iēsou Christou*, faith of Jesus Christ, or "Christ faith") touches on a point vital to Paul's theology. Much of the rest of Galatians is devoted to elaborating this fundamental contrast (Stanton 1996: 101). The central claim of the verse comes in its middle (indicative) clause: "So we, too, have put our faith in Christ Jesus in order that we might be justified by faith in Christ and not by works of the law." As the connection with verse 15 makes clear, "we" refers to Paul and Peter and, by extension, to other Jewish believers. Surrounding this assertion about the attitude of Jewish Christians are two statements of general theological principle, subordinated (at least grammatically) to the central assertion: "yet we know [translating the participle εἰδότες, *eidotes*] that a person is not justified by works of the law" and "because by works of the law no one will be justified." As the thrice-repeated "not by works of the law" reveals, Paul's concern in this verse is especially with the negative point that Christian Jews like Paul and Peter have come to understand: they cannot be justified in terms of the law and its demands. None of the key parties—Paul, Peter, the agitators, the Galatians—were questioning the need for Christ faith for justification. What was in dispute was whether "works of the law" needed to be *added* to Christ faith for justification. Paul's insistence on Christ faith and *not* works of the law is typical of his antithetical argument in Galatians. What should not be overlooked, however, is the real force of Paul's argument in this verse (and indeed, in this paragraph). He is not arguing that Gentiles should be included, with Jews, in the people of God; he is arguing, rather, that Jews should be included, with Gentiles, in the mass of ordinary humanity. Jews are "sinners" just like the Gentiles, with the radical implication that follows: their obedience to the covenant stipulations cannot put them right with God; only a total reliance on Christ, by faith, can do so. As Westerholm (2004: 374) puts it, "Nowhere has Paul suggested that the Christian gospel was needed if Gentiles were to enjoy blessings already experienced by Jews under their law (or covenant); it was needed, Paul indicates, not so Gentiles might become like Jews, but because in essential respects Jews under the law did not differ from Gentiles."

The participial clause that opens the verse is causal: "because we know" (εἰδότες) that people in general (ἄνθρωπος, *anthrōpos*, a person)[3] are not justified (δικαιοῦται [*dikaioutai*], a gnomic present) by works of the law (ἐξ ἔργων νόμου, *ex ergōn nomou*) but by "Jesus Christ faith" (διὰ πίστεως Ἰησοῦ Χριστοῦ, *dia pisteōs Iēsou Christou*), "we Jews have believed in Christ Jesus. . . ." In this clause the contrast between ἔργα νόμου (*erga nomou*, works of the law) and πίστις Ἰησοῦ Χριστοῦ, repeated later in the verse, gets at the heart of current debates about Paul's understanding and critique of Judaism. We

---

3. The view that ἄνθρωπος refers to Gentiles and not Jews (argued, e.g., by Gaston 1987: 66; Gager 1983: 233; cf. 2000: 58) lacks lexical support.

therefore need to spend some time looking at each of these phrases before returning to exposition of the verse.

Traditionally, especially among interpreters in the Reformation tradition, the contrast between these phrases focused on the words ἔργα and πίστις. Paul was seen to be enunciating a critical distinction between human doing and human believing when it came to justification (Luther 1963: 136–39; Calvin 1854: 69–70). This anthropologically focused contrast is, however, widely contested today, with particular focus given to the phrase ἔργα νόμου, "works of the law."

This phrase occurs six times in Galatians (2:16 [3x]; 3:2, 5, 10) and twice in Romans (3:20, 28), always with reference to the attaining of justification or a similar concept. The phrase does not appear in the LXX or, indeed, anywhere in pre-Christian Greek. And there are few equivalents to the phrase in Jewish Hebrew or Aramaic (for more detail, see the third additional note on 2:16). The genitive in the phrase could be subjective, "works prescribed by the law"; but it perhaps more likely is objective, "works done in obedience to the law." Thus the phrase semantically matches phrases such as "doing the law" (Rom. 2:14, 25, 27; Gal. 3:10; 5:3; 6:13; cf. Rom. 10:5 and Gal. 3:12 [Lev. 18:5]) or "doers of the law" (Rom. 2:13 ESV). In any case, there is general agreement that the phrase *means* "doing what the law requires" (with some exceptions; see the third additional note on 2:16). James Dunn (2009: 475), who has written more on this phrase than any other person, and whose views about the meaning of the phrase have sometimes been misunderstood (and/or confusingly stated), says explicitly in one of his latest contributions to the subject, "The phrase 'works of the law' simply denotes doing what the law requires."

The real debate is over the significance of the phrase or, more particularly, *why* this doing of the law cannot justify. The Reformers thought that "works of the law" could not justify because they were "works" and therefore suffered from the problem of all human works: sinful humans could not perform enough works well enough to be justified. However, many contemporary interpreters insist that the problem is not with "works" but with "law." Specifically, they argue that "works of the law" must be seen in the context of Jewish views of the law and its significance in the first century. Following the lead of E. P. Sanders (1977) in his well-known interpretation of first-century Judaism as "covenantal nomism," they argue that Paul has in mind the typical Jewish insistence that adherence to torah was necessary to maintain the Jews' place within the covenant graciously given to the Jewish people—and only to the Jewish people. "Works of the law" functioned in that context to mark out Jews as God's true people, in distinction from the Gentiles. And it was because they had this function that those elements of the law that most obviously distinguished Jews from Gentiles received the greatest emphasis: circumcision, food laws, the observance of Jewish festivals. Galatians, of course, highlights just these issues. Why, then, can't "works of the law" justify? Because they are *torah* works: insisting on them is effectively to turn back the clock in salvation history, to a time before Messiah came and when Gentiles were excluded from the kingdom (for this line of argument, see esp. Dunn 1993a: 134–41; 2005b: 412–21; Garlington 2003: 102–12; 2009; N. Wright 2002: 458–64; Barclay 1988: 235–41).

Anyone familiar with Galatians will recognize much in this revisionist reading of Gal. 2:16—often called the "New Perspective"—that fits the argument of the letter. The people to whom Paul was responding were not "legalists" in the sense of people insisting on doing works to become saved; they were "nomists," insisting that faith in Christ had to be combined with law obedience in order to secure ultimate salvation (Gorman [2004: 190] calls them "*messianic* covenantal nomists"). In this regard it is significant that, when Paul "abbreviates" the phrase elsewhere in the letter, it is always as "law," never as "works" (the absolute ἔργον/ἔργα [*ergon/erga*, work/works] occurs only once in Galatians [6:4], but with a different sense).

In order to meet the challenge of the agitators, Paul does indeed focus on salvation history. However, we do not think that the classic New Perspective reading accounts adequately for all the details of Paul's argument.[4] Salvation history surely is crucial to Paul's argument in Galatians: it is partly because the era of the law is over that its "works" cannot justify. Yet implicit in Paul's argument in Galatians and rising to the surface at several points is a more fundamental critique of "works" in terms of human-oriented accomplishment. Perhaps the clearest evidence of this argument comes in 3:10–12 (see the commentary on these verses and "The Logic of Paul's Response," in the introduction). But it is also hinted at in the present context. The somewhat abrupt appeal to the bedrock principle of grace in verse 21 suggests that it has been an underlying factor throughout this paragraph. And the end of verse 16 hints in the same direction. It is widely recognized that in this final clause Paul alludes to Ps. 143:2: "Do not bring your servant into judgment, for no one living is righteous before you." "One living" translates חַי (*ḥāy*), rendered as ζῶν (*zōn*, one living) in the matching 142:2 LXX. Paul's decision to use σάρξ (*sarx*, flesh) in place of ζῶν may simply be an unconscious assimilation to a more common LXX word (Silva 2007: 790–91), but is more likely to be a deliberate change to emphasize the nature of human beings as frail and weak (see esp. Thielman 1989: 62–65).[5] It is the human being as "flesh" who is not justified by works of the law: thus Paul suggests that it is partly *because* human beings are flesh that they cannot fulfill the law and so be justified. (For further discussion of this point, see "The Logic of Paul's Response," in the introduction.)

---

4. At this point, one of the difficulties we face in our analysis is the clear demarcation of what is meant by *the* "New Perspective." The movement has always embraced quite a bit of diversity among its proponents. And especially important for our present argument is the explicit insistence on the part of the two leading New Perspective advocates, James Dunn and N. T. Wright, that Paul dismisses "works of the law" *both* because of salvation history *and* because of human inability and the grace of God (Dunn 2009: 488; N. Wright 2009: 118).

5. Dunn (1993a: 140), on the other hand, thinks Paul's change to σάρξ is to draw attention to the Jewish focus on "external" markers such as circumcision.

The word "law" in the phrase "works of the law" should not, then, be so stressed that it diminishes the significance of the word "works." The Reformers may have moved too quickly from this phrase to general theological conclusions about "works." But many contemporary interpreters go too far in the other direction when they insist that the phrase is "irreducibly concrete," referring *only* to the torah, the law of Moses (Watson 2007: 121–31; cf. also Mundle 1977: 99–103). To argue so is to miss the indicators of a deeper, anthropological argument in the letter (see esp. Westerholm 2004: 366–84; Kim 2002: 61–66). The traditional Reformation emphasis on justification *sola fide*, "by faith alone," is a legitimate theological derivation from the antitheses of Gal. 2:16.

Over the last thirty years, the phrase πίστις (᾽Ιησοῦ) Χριστοῦ has received almost as much attention as the phrase ἔργα νόμου. The genitive in this phrase establishes a general relationship between "faith" and "[Jesus] Christ," which can be rather neutrally expressed with the English "Christ faith." If we seek to unpack this relationship in more specific terms, two options arise. On the one hand, the genitive could be objective, leading to the translation found in most English versions "faith *in* Jesus Christ"; that is, faith "directed toward" Jesus Christ. On the other hand, the genitive could be subjective, leading to the translation "faith *of* Christ," or "faithfulness *of* Christ"; that is, the faith or faithfulness exhibited by Christ. The former has been the traditional interpretation, but a significant and growing number of scholars have argued strongly for the latter interpretation (this view has found its way into two recent translations: NET and CEB: "the faithfulness of Jesus Christ"; it is also mentioned as an alternative translation in NIV and NRSV).[6] Coupled with revisionist interpretations of "works of the law" (see above), this interpretation has the effect of shifting the contrast in verse 16 from the anthropological ("doing" versus "believing") to the salvation-historical: the torah and the era it represents versus Christ and the new age (see esp. Martyn 1997; D. Campbell 2009: 833–95).

The arguments for interpreting the phrase (and the other Pauline occurrences of the construction: Gal. 2:20; 3:22; Rom. 3:22, 26; Eph. 3:12; Phil. 3:9) in this way range from the narrowly grammatical to the broadly theological. We list and interact with these reasons in the introduction (see "The Faith of Christ" in the section on theology), where we also present our case for adopting the usual objective-genitive interpretation. Briefly, we think this interpretation is preferable because (1) it matches Paul's invariable custom of using the cognate verb to refer to human believing (and never to Christ's "believing"); (2) it fits with the two critical OT passages that he cites to buttress his emphasis on πίστις (Gen. 15:6 and Hab. 2:4); and (3) it better fits in

6. The bibliography is lengthy, and we cite some of the more important studies in the introduction. See esp. Hays 2002, which includes a response to Hays from J. D. G. Dunn and Hays's rejoinder; and the very helpful series of essays from various perspectives in Bird and Sprinkle 2009 (who provide the best entrance point into the debate). A few interpreters have argued for a genitive of authorship, or source: "the faith that is generated by Christ (in and by his death)" (e.g., Martyn 1997: 270).

the respective contexts where the phrase occurs. In the case of Gal. 2:16, it is important to see that the key and even programmatic link between πίστις and justification is taken up again in Gal. 3, where Paul cites Abraham's "believing for righteousness" (v. 6). Moreover, in the context of 2:16, the explicit reference to human believing in the middle clause, far from being a problem for the objective-genitive interpretation (allegedly because the phrases would then simply repeat the emphasis on human believing), actually supports this interpretation. For these clauses, as we have seen, provide the basis for the central claim in the middle of the verse. And to do so, εἰς Χριστὸν Ἰησοῦν ἐπιστεύσαμεν (eis Christon Iēsoun episteusamen, we believed in Christ Jesus) must be roughly equivalent to πίστις Ἰησοῦ Χριστοῦ (see Matlock 2007: 195–99 for a similar argument). We think that there are good reasons, therefore, to interpret "faith of Christ" here, and its other occurrences in Galatians, as "faith in, or directed toward, Christ."[7]

One other significant term requires attention before we turn back to our exposition of the verse: δικαιόω (dikaioō, justify). This word occurs as the central element in each of the three parts of this verse and is picked up again at critical points of the following argument (2:17; 3:8, 11, 24; 5:4). The complexity and significance of the debate over this word and the theology it represents make the battles over the meanings of "works of the law" and "faith of Christ" seem like minor skirmishes. Once again, we treat some of the larger issues briefly in the introduction (see "Justification/Righteousness" there). As is almost universally recognized, Paul's use of this verb reflects the use of the Hebrew verb צדק in the OT, which, in its Hiphil form, refers to a forensic, or judicial, declaration that a person is "just." There is very good reason to think that Paul consistently uses the verb in this sense. To be sure, N. T. Wright (see esp. 2009: 116–19) has argued that the context of Gal. 2, along with the covenant associations of the word, suggests that Paul has particularly in view here the notion of membership in the people of God. For is this not the issue in Jerusalem (2:1–10), Antioch (2:11–14), and Galatia? Paul is certainly concerned to show that his gospel provides entry for the Gentiles into the people of God, so that they can, for instance, eat with Jews. But Paul's point in 2:16, while deeply significant for each of these situations, is slightly different and more basic. Here he wants to establish the bedrock principle that all people—with the focus in this verse, as we have seen, on Jewish Christians—can be pronounced "just" before God through faith in Christ alone and not on the basis of "works of the law." And because this is so, it is wrong for the Jerusalem authorities to impose circumcision on Gentile believers, it is wrong for Peter to refuse to eat with Gentiles, and it is wrong for the agitators to insist that the Galatian Christians submit to the law. Justification, one's legal standing before God,

---

7. The usual terms of the debate—"subjective" versus "objective" genitive—may oversimplify the issue. For instance, while dismissing the subjective genitive interpretation, Ulrichs (2007: 11–23, passim) does not clearly defend an "objective" genitive, arguing rather for a looser connection between πίστις (pistis, faith) and Χριστοῦ (Christou, in/of Christ; "a faith defined in terms of Christ"; see also, e.g., Matlock 2000: 17).

is fully secured by faith in Christ. Nothing should be added; nothing can be added; nothing must be added (Smiles 1998: 123–28).

The three occurrences of δικαιόω in this verse come in three different tenses: present indicative (δικαιοῦται in 16a), aorist subjunctive (δικαιωθῶμεν, *dikaiōthōmen*, we might be justified), and future indicative (δικαιωθήσεται, *dikaiōthēsetai*, will be justified). The first is probably gnomic and therefore suggests nothing about the "time" of justification. The second, expressing purpose after ἵνα (*hina*, in order that), shows only that the justification takes place after believing. The future tense, unlike the present and the aorist, often more directly suggests the time of the action. But in the present case, it is uncertain whether the future should be viewed from the standpoint of the OT text to which Paul is alluding (e.g., Martyn 1997: 253) or from the standpoint of the Galatians (e.g., Silva 2001: 173–74; Witherington 1998: 183). However, the language of justification elsewhere in the letter, as well as the situation Paul is addressing, point to the latter (the Galatians' standpoint). Indeed, Paul's teaching about justification in Galatians is (deliberately) vague with reference to time. His focus is on the general principial point: justification, or the status of righteousness, is tied to faith—and faith alone. But the rhetorical situation of Galatians provides good reason to think that Paul implies some kind of future aspect to justification. The agitators probably adopted the usual Jewish view that justification was tied to the last judgment, and in that judgment God's positive verdict would take into account the degree to which one had done "the works of the law" (e.g., de Boer 2005: 205–9). Paul responds that justification is always, whatever its time, a matter of faith and *not* works of the law—or of works of any kind.

Having analyzed the structure and discussed the key terminology, we can now turn to other matters in the verse. Four times in 2:16 Paul uses the preposition ἐκ (*ek*) to connect the verb δικαιόω with ἔργα νόμου or πίστις. The use of ἐκ after this verb is rare outside Paul (Cosgrove 1987: 656–58). Some interpreters think he may have been influenced in his usage by Hab. 2:4, ὁ δὲ δίκαιος ἐκ πίστεώς μου ζήσεται (*ho de dikaios ek pisteōs mou zēsetai*, but the righteous one will live by my faith), a verse he twice quotes with reference to his teaching on justification (Gal. 3:11; Rom. 1:17; Mussner 1988: 174; Watson 2007: 239–44; D. Campbell 2009: 377). The preposition probably has an instrumental force: works of the law cannot be, while faith in Christ is, the means by which human beings can become justified.[8] In this first clause, after denying that a person can be justified "by works of the law," Paul adds: ἐὰν μὴ διὰ πίστεως Ἰησοῦ Χριστοῦ. The ἐὰν μή (*ean mē*) is usually understood to establish an antithetical relationship between "works of the law" and faith (hence the translation "but" in most English versions). Dunn (1993a: 137),

---

8. See, e.g., Cosgrove 1987: 656–60. Garlington (2003: 111; 2008), however, argues that the ἐκ denotes origin; when used, then, with "works of the law," it signifies that "justification does not originate from or find its location within the parameters of the ancient covenant people." Martyn (1997: 251) also thinks that ἐκ in these constructions may move from instrument to cause.

however, argues that the phrase normally denotes an exception, not a contrast; he thinks the translation should be "a person is not justified by works of the law except when those works are accompanied by faith." The context, however, creates problems for this view, and Dunn himself is forced to admit that Paul withdraws this "both/and" possibility later in the verse. In fact an adversative interpretation of ἐὰν μή is possible, since its parallel εἰ μή does sometimes function this way in the NT (see Matt. 5:13; 12:4; Rom. 14:14; Bruce 1982b: 138; Martyn 1997: 251, 264; Bergmeier 2010: 21–22). Another possibility is that the exception stated in the ἐὰν μή clause is to be attached only to "a person is not justified": that is, "a person is not justified by works of the law, except a person can be justified by faith in Christ" (Lightfoot 1881: 115; Burton 1921: 121; R. Longenecker 1990: 84; Walker 1997).

The main clause of verse 16 is introduced with καί, which serves to highlight the following ἡμεῖς: "We who are Jews by birth [v. 15] . . . , *even we* have believed in Christ Jesus in order to be justified by faith in Christ and not by works of the law." Here Paul utilizes another rare construction: the combination of the verb πιστεύω with the preposition εἰς is virtually unknown before the NT.[9] This sequence, however, is quite common in the NT, and especially in the writings of John, where it occurs thirty-seven times, almost always with Christ as the object (it also occurs in Matt. 18:6 and Acts 10:43; Paul uses it only once elsewhere [Phil. 1:29]). The distinctive language connotes a distinctive view of faith, typical of the NT (Harris 2012: 236–37). The phrase could indicate a general connection between believing and Christ—"believing with respect to Christ" (e.g., D. Campbell 2009: 840)—or perhaps in analogy to the notion of "baptism into [εἰς] Christ" (Gal. 3:27; Rom. 6:3; cf. 1 Cor. 12:13), that one believes and so enters into union with Christ (Bassler 2007: 31). However, apparently parallel expressions in Paul (πιστεύω + ἐπί [Rom. 4:5, 24; 9:33; 10:11; 1 Tim. 1:16]; πίστις + πρός [1 Thess. 1:8; Philem. 5]) as well as the Johannine evidence strongly point to a "directional" idea: the faith Paul has in view is faith that is directed toward Christ (Ridderbos 1975: 239). This faith has a cognitive element—a "believing *that*" certain things are true—but the language of believing "into Christ" shows that it is much more, involving both trust and commitment. "*Pisteuo* (or *pistis*) *eis Christon* depicts the committal of one's self to the person of Christ, something more than an intellectual acceptance of the message of the gospel or a recognition of the truth about Christ" (Harris 2012: 236–37).

This verse consists of a conditional sentence followed by Paul's typical strong negation:

2:17

Protasis: εἰ δὲ ζητοῦντες δικαιωθῆναι ἐν Χριστῷ εὑρέθημεν καὶ αὐτοὶ ἁμαρτωλοί (*ei de zētountes dikaiōthēnai en Christō heurethēmen kai*

---

9. There are only two possibly relevant pre-Christian examples: Xenophon, *Ages.* 3.4.2–3; and Dionysius of Halicarnassus, *Is.* 14.26. The former is probably not a true example, however, since the εἰς probably does not go with πιστεύω.

autoi hamartōloi, but if, in seeking to be justified in Christ, we also find ourselves to be sinners)

Apodosis: ἆρα Χριστὸς ἁμαρτίας διάκονος; (*ara Christos hamartias diakonos?* doesn't that mean that Christ is a servant of sin?)

Rejection: μὴ γένοιτο (*mē genoito*, absolutely not!)

The meaning of this verse and the next one (which are closely related) and their contribution to the argument of this paragraph are unclear. Two main options confront us, determined according to whether "find ourselves to be sinners" takes place at conversion or after conversion and, correspondingly, what "sinners" refers to.

1. One interpretation holds that Paul is reflecting on the experience that he, Peter, and other Christian Jews had when they first came to Christ to be justified. At that moment, they found themselves to be sinners—that is, they understood that they were truly as sinful as the Gentiles they had scorned, and accordingly they needed to depend on Christ alone for justification. But this discovery did not make Christ a servant of sin, for their sin existed all along. Verse 18 explains: it is when people (whether Jewish Christians or Gentile Christians, such as the Galatians) try to go back to the law (again) that they become "transgressors," either in the sense that they become guilty of their sin again or in the sense that they break the fundamental "law of the gospel." (For this general interpretation, see, e.g., Lightfoot 1881: 116–17; Ridderbos 1953: 101–3; Smiles 1998: 147–59; Lambrecht 1978; 1987; 1996; Hunn 2010).

2. Other interpreters think that Paul has in view a postconversion situation. Peter, Paul, and other Jewish Christians are seeking to find ultimate justification in their union with Christ and, in doing so, have recognized the implications that Paul states in verse 16: they have abandoned the law as a means of finding that justification. They therefore "find themselves" to be in the same category as the Gentiles (v. 15): "sinners" who do not live by God's law. But this does not make Christ the servant of sin (in the ultimate sense of that word). This would be the case only if Jewish Christians would "rebuild" the law as a fundamental authority; they would then truly be "transgressors." (So, in general, Burton 1921: 124–30; Betz 1979: 119–21; Dunn 1993a: 141–42; Martyn 1997: 254–56; Kruse 1996: 69–71; Winger 1992: 142–45.)

Neither interpretation is without its problems (and hence the division of opinion among scholars), but the second reading has fewer problems. The following exposition of these verses will seek to demonstrate this.

The opening participial clause is temporal and takes its specific time orientation from the verb it modifies, εὑρέθημεν. This verb, in the passive, has the sense "be found, appear, prove, be shown (to be)" (BDAG 411–12) and in this context is best translated "find ourselves" (NIV; for similar usages, see esp. Rom. 7:10; 1 Cor. 15:15; 2 Cor. 5:3; 12:20; Phil. 2:7; 3:9). The aorist form of the verb may point to a past experience: the discovery would have taken place either when Paul and Peter first found justification in Christ or, more likely, when fellow Jews (and Jewish Christians, such as the "men from James" [2:12]) recognized the degree to which Paul and Peter had abandoned the law. On the other hand, it might be wrong to find any temporal force in the aorist when it occurs in a protasis such as this (Porter 1989: 298). In any case, we think that Paul is probably referring to the experience of Jewish Christians who, taking the principle of verse 16 seriously, have recognized that justification "in Christ" means treating obedience to the law as optional. The protasis, then, states a "real" condition (Schlier 1989: 95; contra, e.g., Mussner 1988: 176–77). The "moment" of justification will once again be future (as in v. 16c; e.g., Martyn 1997: 254; Seifrid 2003: 218). Paul's claim that this justification takes place "in Christ" introduces a critical theological point into the argument. The preposition, ἐν, is almost certainly local (though a few think it might also have instrumental force [R. Longenecker 1990: 89; C. Campbell 2012: 114–15]) and therefore expresses Paul's fundamental and characteristic theology of "union with Christ." Justification takes place as believers are incorporated into Christ, and by sounding this note here, Paul reveals that the explicit teaching about this union with Christ in verses 19–20 is by no means a shift to a different, or competing, perspective on the work of God in Christ.

By seeking to be justified in Christ, Peter and Paul appear to be placing themselves in the same position as the Gentiles (v. 15): they themselves (αὐτοί) have also (καί) become "sinners" (ἁμαρτωλοί), that is, people who, like the Gentiles, show no allegiance to the torah by which God's people were to be defined. Paul's use of the word ἁμαρτωλοί in this verse is the strongest point in favor of the second interpretational option that we are defending—for it very likely reflects Paul's use of this same word in verse 15, where it focuses on the way the torah has excluded Gentiles from participation in the people of God. Paul then goes on to ask: does this mean that Christ is a "servant of sin?"[10] It is likely that this question reflects an actual accusation flung at Jewish Christians such as Paul and Peter (perhaps by the "men from James"? e.g., Betz 1979: 120; Dunn 1993a: 141–42; Martyn 1997: 255). "Sin" (ἁμαρτία) will have, then, its usual "absolute" sense. Paul asks if Christ, in, as it were, requiring Jewish Christians to abandon their allegiance to torah as the authoritative revelation of their conduct, is "serving" or "leading others to commit" sin.[11]

Paul rejects this implication with his typically strong negative, μὴ γένοιτο—"absolutely not!" (KJV: "God forbid").[12]

10. Since μὴ γένοιτο always follows a question in Paul, it is likely that we should accent ἀρα (ara) as an interrogative (ἆρα, ara [interrogative particle expecting negative response]) instead of as an inferential conjunction (ἄρα, ara, therefore); see, e.g., BDF §440.2.

11. It is also possible that the question "Is Christ a servant of sin?" has in view the conduct of Jesus during his earthly ministry, a conduct notorious for his consorting with "tax collectors and sinners" (Dunn 1993a: 141–42).

12. The formula, which uses the optative of "wish" (e.g., "may it never be") is found mainly in Paul (Rom. 3:4, 6, 31; 6:2, 15; 7:7, 13; 9:14; 11:1, 11; 1 Cor. 6:15; Gal. 3:21; cf. Luke 20:16) in the NT and may reflect diatribe style (see Malherbe 1980).

2:18 Verse 18 is closely tied to verse 17, providing the reason (γάρ, *gar*, for) for Paul's strong rejection of the logic of verse 17. The connection between the verses makes best sense if we supply an implied ellipsis: "by no means, in fact, the case stands just the opposite" (Barclay 1988: 80). Jewish Christians are not sinful if, in order to be justified in Christ, they abandon the authority of the law; "rather" (NLT), they would be considered "transgressors" only if they rebuild what they have already torn down. This sequence of thought seems to be disrupted, however, by a shift from the first-person plural, used in verses 15–17, to the first-person singular in verse 18. Nevertheless, it is unlikely that this shift signals a break in the argument (as Lambrecht 1978: 491–93 argues). The "I" in this verse concretizes the "we" of verses 15–17, focusing now on a "representative type" (A. Robertson 1934: 402; Mussner 1988: 177–78). And since the "we" of verses 15–17 refers to Jewish Christians, the "I" in this verse will refer to a representative Jewish Christian—perhaps with particular reference to Peter, in light of his conduct at Antioch. However, the shift to the singular may also suggest that Paul is moving further away from the situation at Antioch and beginning to focus more specifically on the situation of the Galatians (Hays 2000: 242). The "I" makes it easier for the Galatians to identify with what Paul is saying here and to take warning from it (Wallace 1996: 391–92).

The contrast between "destroy" (καταλύω, *katalyō*) and "rebuild" (πάλιν οἰκοδομέω, *palin oikodomeō*) refers most naturally to the law: if Peter, as a Jewish Christian, should try to reinstitute the law as an absolute authority for conduct (as his actions at Antioch suggested he was doing), then he would, in effect, be rebuilding that which, in coming to Christ alone for justification, he had earlier torn down (καταλύω is used with reference to the law in the well-known Matt. 5:17; cf. Betz 1979: 121, for the "legal sense" of the word). The plurals ἅ (*ha*, which things) and ταῦτα (*tauta*, these things) refer to provisions of the law, probably especially the provisions that tended to segregate Jews from Gentiles (if, as is likely, the scenario of 2:11–14 is still to some extent in view). While using different imagery and directed to a slightly different (but related) issue, the language of Eph. 2:14–15 moves in a similar direction: "For he himself is our peace, who has made the two groups one and has destroyed the barrier, the dividing wall of hostility, by setting aside in his flesh the law with its commands and regulations."[13] When "I" as a Jewish Christian "rebuild" the law as my authority, I "prove myself to be a transgressor" (ESV; παραβάτην ἐμαυτὸν συνιστάνω, *parabatēn emauton synistanō*). The verb συνίστημι (*synistēmi*) has the sense "to cause something to be known by action" (to use the language of LN [341.28.49] for this category; the closest parallels in Paul are Rom. 5:8 and 2 Cor. 6:4). In Peter's case, his action of withdrawing from meals with Gentiles would be to brand himself, in relationship to his previous eating with them

---

13. The verbs καταλύω and οἰκοδομέω are directly contrasted elsewhere in Scripture only in the Synoptic passages about "tearing down" and "rebuilding" the temple (Matt. 26:61//Mark 14:58; Matt. 27:40//Mark 15:29).

and in many other infringements of torah or its contemporary application, a "transgressor" of that law. The lesson would not be lost on the Galatian Gentiles: if they, after coming to Christ for justification, should erect the law as their authority, they, too, would be branded as transgressors.

The meaning of this word "transgressor" is another key turning point in the interpretation of these verses. If Paul in Gal. 2:17–18 is referring to the conversion experience of Jewish Christians (view 1 in the comments on 2:17), then the word probably refers to a violation of the ultimate intention of the law. The law finds its *telos* in Christ (Rom. 10:4; cf. Gal. 3:24–25), and those who put themselves under the law are in effect denying that truth (e.g., in different senses, R. Longenecker 1990: 91; Lambrecht 1978: 494; 1991: 230–36; Bachmann 1992: 73–77; Garlington 1997: 90; Hays 2000: 242). There is good reason to think that παραβάτης refers to violation of the law; in the NT this word, along with its cognate παράβασις (*parabasis*, transgression), refers to violation of the law (usually the Mosaic law; παραβάτης: Rom. 2:25, 27; James 2:9, 11; παράβασις: Rom. 2:23; 4:15; 5:14; Gal. 3:19; 1 Tim. 2:14; Heb. 2:2; 9:15). But to extend the idea to a violation of the *ultimate intent* of the law is quite a stretch, for which there is no good precedent in Paul's use of these words. It is more likely, then, that παραβάτης refers simply to one who is in violation of the law. The transgressions that Paul has in view would be the disobedience of those parts of the law that in various ways segregated Jews from Gentiles. If Jewish Christians tacitly reestablish (e.g., through behavior such as Peter's at Antioch) those parts of the law, their earlier flouting of those very provisions would mean that they would be turning themselves into "transgressors" of those provisions. It would not be Christ who is leading them to sin (v. 17b); they themselves would be the ones responsible for turning themselves into transgressors. (For this general approach, see esp. Bruce 1982b: 142; G. Hansen 1994: 104–6; Matera 1992: 95, 102; Watson 2007: 127.)

In verses 19–20, Paul justifies his implicit claim in verses 17–18 that what constitutes sin is not rejecting the law but rebuilding the law (R. Longenecker 1990: 91; Schlier 1989: 98; Tannehill 1967: 57). "I" would be a transgressor if "I" rebuilt the authority of the law because (γάρ, *gar*) "I" am in a totally new relationship to the law. "I" have experienced a reorientation of values so radical that it can only be compared to death and new life: "I have died to the law," and "I live for God." This extraordinary transformation comes through identification with Christ's own death: "I have been crucified with Christ." The language of these verses is very well known and often quoted as a vivid description of the radically new nature of the Christian believer. But whether it is appropriate to apply the language so broadly depends on how we interpret the first-person singular form of these verses. The strength of Paul's language strongly suggests that he reflects his own experience in coming to Christ (e.g., Dunn 1993a: 143). But does he speak narrowly as a "typical" Jewish Christian (e.g., McKnight 1995: 117–18; 2000)? Or is he voicing the experience ultimately of every Christian (BDF §281; Betz 1979: 121; Smiles

2:19

1998: 164)? The continuing focus on the law might suggest the former, for in this verse Paul clearly has in view the Mosaic law, and that law was given to Israel.[14] But, while never rising to the level of an explicit claim, what Paul says about the law in many contexts clearly presupposes that he thinks the Mosaic law and Israel's experience with it are paradigmatic of the experience of all people. We think it likely, then, that the experience Paul refers to in verses 19–20 is broadly applicable (though perhaps in somewhat different ways) to all believers.

In terms of the argument of this paragraph, the most important claim in verses 19–20 is the first one: "through the law I died to the law" (ἐγὼ . . . διὰ νόμου νόμῳ ἀπέθανον, *egō . . . dia nomou nomō apethanon*). The juxtaposition of "through the law" and "to the law" (esp. in the Greek, where νόμου and νόμῳ are right next to each other) is deliberately paradoxical—even provocative. In abbreviated fashion the phrases refer to broad theological conceptions that Paul enunciates elsewhere. The meaning of "to the law" is clear enough from other contexts that use the same language. A central claim of Rom. 6:1–14, for instance, is that believers have "died to sin" (6:2, 10; cf. v. 11). In the next chapter Paul provocatively uses this same basic language to refer to the believer's relationship to the law: "You have been put to death with respect to the law" (7:4 AT); we believers have died "to what [the law] once bound us" (7:6). In each of these texts a word referring to death is followed by a dative noun (probably a dative of respect [Thüsing 1965: 79–81]; perhaps a dative of disadvantage [A. Robertson 1934: 539; BDF §188.2]). In each case Paul denotes a decisive release from the authority, or power, of a particular entity (sin, law).[15] The metaphor combines two key ideas. (1) The language of death, particularly since Paul usually follows it with reference to life, makes clear how radical the break is: it is like dying and being reborn. (2) As the following reference in this text to being "crucified with Christ" shows (and note the prominence of "with" language in Rom. 6), the Christian's death (and new life) takes place in conjunction with Christ's own death (and rising to new life). See especially in this regard, Gal. 6:14: "May I never boast except in the cross of our Lord Jesus Christ, through which the world has been crucified to me, and I to the world [δι' οὗ ἐμοὶ κόσμος ἐσταύρωται κἀγὼ κόσμῳ, *di' hou emoi kosmos estaurōtai kagō kosmō*]."

When Paul therefore claims that he has "died to the law," he means that he has been released from the binding authority of the law of Moses. How

14. A few interpreters think that Paul may refer to a legalistic perversion of the law (e.g., Burton 1921: 132; Fuller 1980: 114); but such an interpretation unduly minimizes the force of Paul's antithesis between the law and Christ.

15. Note also the comparable phrases in Rom. 14:7–8a: οὐδεὶς γὰρ ἡμῶν ἑαυτῷ ζῇ καὶ οὐδεὶς ἑαυτῷ ἀποθνῄσκει· ἐάν τε γὰρ ζῶμεν, τῷ κυρίῳ ζῶμεν, ἐάν τε ἀποθνῄσκωμεν, τῷ κυρίῳ ἀποθνῄσκομεν (*oudeis gar hēmōn heautō zē kai oudeis heautō apothnēskei; ean te gar zōmen, tō kyriō zōmen, ean te apothnēskōmen, tō kyriō apothnēskomen*, for no one of us lives to oneself and no one dies to oneself; for if we live, we live to the Lord, and if we die, we die to the Lord [AT]).

foolish, then, for Peter, or any other Jewish Christian, to "rebuild" that authority again (v. 18)! "The question of transgressing the law does not arise for one who has died in relation to the law" (Bruce 1982b: 142). And how wrong for Jewish Christians, and by extension Gentile Christians such as the Galatians, to try to be justified in terms of the law (v. 16). Parallel texts, then, enable us to decide what "I died *to* the law" means. Unfortunately, in the case of the phrase "*through* the law," we have no such parallels, and the meaning is disputed. One option is that Paul has in view his frustration and ultimate failure in trying to live by the law. Paul would be saying, in effect, "Through my recognition that I could not fulfill the law, I came to understand that I must die to it" (e.g., Lightfoot 1881: 118; Burton 1921: 133–34; Mussner 1988: 179–80). Support for this view is sometimes found in Gal. 3:24, interpreted, as the KJV renders, "the law was our schoolmaster to bring us unto Christ." But this is almost certainly not what this text means (see the comments on 3:24). However, Paul does give some grounds elsewhere for thinking that his struggle with the law was a factor in his recognition that he needed to die to the law so that he could come to Christ (Rom. 7:14–25, which comes in the same context where Paul's other "death to the law" language appears). This view must take the διά in less than a straightforward "instrumental" way, but the radically abbreviated nature of the phrase might explain this.

The second major interpretation, and the one most popular with modern interpreters, is that Paul is hinting at the idea spelled out in Gal. 3:13: "Christ redeemed us from the curse of the law by becoming a curse for us, for it is written: 'Cursed is everyone who is hung on a pole.'" Paul died to the law through his identification with Christ, whom the law itself cursed (see, e.g., Martyn 1997: 257; Tannehill 1967: 57–58; Smiles 1998: 170–77).[16] This view can also appeal to the Romans parallel, since in Rom. 7:4 Paul claims that Christians are put to death "to the law *through the body of Christ*" (emphasis added); thus in Rom. 7:4 also the means of death to the law is participation in the death of Christ (his body given on the cross). Still, it is not clear how sharing in Christ's experience of being cursed by the law could become the means by which believers experience a decisive separation from the law (Hays 2000: 243). The choice between these options is difficult (one that Silva [2001: 175] chooses not to make, claiming that both may be intended). But the former, in our view, makes slightly better sense of the passage and might find a parallel idea in Gal. 3:10 if, as we think, this verse refers to a curse that comes upon all people because of their failure to keep the demands of the law (Thielman 1989: 130). See the NLT: "For when I tried to keep the law, it condemned me. So I died to the law" (2:19).

As in the parallels to this passage elsewhere in Paul, death is followed by life; see Rom. 7:4: "You also died to the law through the body of Christ, that

---

16. Another option, less likely than these two, is that Paul refers to his career as a persecutor of the church (cf. Gal. 1:13–14). It was "through" his misguided passion for the law that he came to see his need to die to the law (Bruce 1982b: 143; Dunn 1993a: 143).

you might belong to another." Dying to the law was not an end in itself (Gal. 2:19): it had the purpose (ἵνα, *hina*, in order that) of enabling Paul to live for God (θεῷ ζήσω, *theō zēsō*). The dative in this phrase is usually taken to be a dative of advantage (e.g., Mussner 1988: 182; the English versions render with "to" or "for"). Yet here again the more general relationship suggested by a dative of reference might be preferable. For the concept here appears to be broad, encompassing, as Betz suggests, "soteriology as well as ethics" (1979: 122; contra, e.g., Burton 1921: 135, who takes it in the second sense only). It thus may signify both that the believer now finds salvific life "in relationship to God" and that the believer enters a new life that has God as its focus. Before leaving this verse, we should not overlook how shocking is the claim—particularly for first-century Jewish ears—that Paul makes here: he could only truly live "for God" by dying to the law that God himself gave to his people! But this claim is part and parcel of the radical antinomies that Paul works with throughout Galatians, as he tries to persuade the Galatians to understand the epochal shift of focus that the cross of Christ has introduced into salvation history (see esp. Martyn 1997: 237—although, typically, he overplays the contrast).

Like many English versions, the NIV follows the versification of the KJV and puts the clause "I have been crucified with Christ" in verse 20 (see also RSV, ESV, NASB, NLT, NET). Other versions, however, follow the Greek texts (both NA[28] and UBS[4]) and place the clause in verse 19. Of course, not being original, the verse division is not the important consideration here. What is important is the punctuation, which signals the connection that this brief but important claim has to its context. The NIV puts a major stop at the end of verse 19 and no punctuation after it, thereby suggesting that it is basically connected with what follows: "I have been crucified with Christ and I no longer live" (similar are NET, putting a comma after the clause; and RSV, NRSV, NASB, and NAB, which use a semicolon). These versions follow the lead of the Greek texts, which put a major stop before the clause and a minor stop after it. There is good reason to read the sequence in this way, for it provides a neat parallelism in two successive sentences of a movement from death to life: "I died to the law so that I might live for God"; "I have been crucified with Christ and I no longer live, but Christ lives in me." However, the connection between "I have been crucified with Christ" and what precedes it should not be overlooked: it is through Paul's identification with Christ in his death that he has "died to the law" and is now able to live for God.

The perfect form of συνεσταύρωμαι (*synestaurōmai*) emphasizes the continuing state of the subject of the verb: "I am in the state of being crucified with Christ."[17] This verb occurs prosaically in the narratives of the crucifixion (Matt. 27:44; Mark 15:32; John 19:32), but its only other theological use comes in Rom. 6:6: "For we know that our old self was crucified with him [συνεσταυρώθη,

17. Here we follow the view of the perfect aspect of the Greek verb taken by Porter (1989: 245–59; 1992: 39–40).

synestaurōthē] so that the body ruled by sin might be done away with, that we should no longer be slaves to sin." Paul's use of the verb is a reflection of one of his core theological convictions: that the spiritual state of believers is the product of their real identification with Christ in the redemptive events of his crucifixion, burial, and resurrection. To be "crucified with Christ," then, does not mean that believers undergo a metaphorical "crucifixion" similar to Christ's actual crucifixion but that believers are regarded by God as having hung on the cross with Christ (see esp. Tannehill 1967; Ridderbos 1975: 57–62; on Paul's "with Christ" language, see Moo 1996: 391–95; Schweizer 1967–68; Siber 1971; Smedes 1970). The imagery is intended to highlight a decisive and total transfer from one state to another.

In this verse, Paul describes the nature of this new state, using the verb ζάω **2:20** (*zaō*, live) in the present tense four times. Its first two clauses antithetically and hyperbolically depict the nature of the new existence that Paul (and other believers) enters as a result of crucifixion with Christ: "and I no longer live, but Christ lives in me" (ζῶ δὲ οὐκέτι ἐγώ, ζῇ δὲ ἐν ἐμοὶ Χριστός, *zō de ouketi egō, zē de en emoi Christos*; the first δέ is continuative, and the second is adversative). "I no longer live" means that the "old I," the "I" enslaved to sin and the law, has been done away with, to be replaced by a new "I" whose existence is determined by the indwelling Christ. Paul speaks both of believers as living "in Christ" and, less commonly, of Christ as living "in" believers (see also Rom. 8:10; 2 Cor. 13:5; Eph. 3:17; Col. 1:27; cf. Gal. 1:16; 4:19), but the basic conception is the same: a vital union that dominates the believer's life in all its aspects. The last part of the verse unpacks this idea.

"The life I now live in the flesh, I live by faith in the Son of God, who loved me and gave himself for me." "The life," found in most English versions, translates the relative pronoun ὅ (*ho*), which functions as an adverbial accusative (A. Robertson 1934: 479), in effect meaning "what I am now living." The word σάρξ (*sarx*, flesh) in the phrase ἐν σαρκί (*en sarki*, in flesh) refers to simple physical life on earth; hence NIV's "in the body." "Faith in the Son of God" is again, as with the similar construction in verse 16, an interpretation of a genitive construction in an "objective" sense (ἐν πίστει . . . τῇ τοῦ υἱοῦ τοῦ θεοῦ, *en pistei . . . tē tou huiou tou theou*). The grammatical, contextual, and theological issues are basically the same as in verse 16, so we need not repeat the reasons why the objective interpretation is to be preferred (on this verse, see Ulrichs 2007: 132–40). Two matters particular to this context call for brief comment. First, with "in faith" put first in the clause (perhaps for emphasis), before the verb, Paul feels it necessary to use an article (τῇ, *tē*, the) in order to make clear that the following genitive phrase goes with the noun πίστει. But the presence of the article does nothing to change the basic semantic situation (contra D. Campbell 2009: 644–46). Second, Paul describes "the Son of God" with two parallel participial clauses: τοῦ ἀγαπήσαντος με καὶ παραδόντος ἑαυτὸν ὑπέρ ἐμοῦ (*tou agapēsantos me kai paradontos heauton hyper emou*): "who loved me and gave himself for me" (the article goes with both participles). Rhetorically, these descriptions help explain why Paul now lives a life so totally dedicated to the Son of God. But the fact that they undeniably focus on Christ's own activity provides no reason to think that πίστει must also describe an activity of Christ (contra D. Campbell 2009: 847–49). Paul only rarely refers to Christ's love for us (Rom. 8:37); he more often speaks of Christ as "giving himself over" (with a form of παραδίδωμι, *paradidōmi*) on our behalf (Rom. 4:25; 8:32). The preposition ὑπέρ after παραδόντος basically means "on behalf of." But to do something on behalf of someone can take the form of doing it in their place; and some interpreters, based on texts such as Gal. 3:13 and 2 Cor. 5:14, think that the preposition could have that significance here (e.g., Ridderbos 1975: 190). But this is not clear. Particularly interesting are two other passages where Paul brings together Christ's love and his giving himself for us: "Christ loved us and gave himself up for us as a fragrant offering and sacrifice to God" (Eph. 5:2); "Christ loved the church and gave himself up for her" (5:25). The two ideas are naturally closely related, so there is no reason to think that Paul is quoting a piece of traditional language (contra Schauf 2006).

Some recent interpreters (Schauf 2006: 96–101; de Boer 2005; Gorman 2009: 63–69) argue that in this paragraph the connections between justification (vv. 16–17) and cocrucifixion, or union with Christ (vv. 19–20), reveal that, to quote Gorman (2009: 67), "co-crucifixion is what Paul means by justification." But this argument confuses proximity with identity. As we have seen, verses 19–20, with their central claim about "dying to the law," directly support the importance of not "rebuilding" the law again (v. 18) and, more distantly, Paul's claim that justification takes place apart from the law (v. 16). There is no reason to suppose that they are describing justification. Nor does the reintroduction of "righteousness" in verse 21 suggest any kind of equation. Contra to (e.g.) Schauf (2006: 96), verse 21 is not closely tied to verses 19–20. In fact, with its references to righteousness and the law, it appears to pick up the main line of Paul's teaching from verse 16.

2:21 On any view, however, verse 21 appears somewhat abruptly in this context. It has no explicit connection with its context (e.g., it is asyndetic, with no particle or conjunction to tie it to the preceding context). And it unexpectedly introduces "grace" (χάρις, *charis*), a word that has not occurred in the letter since 2:9. Many interpreters think that the negative formulation "I do not set aside" (οὐκ ἀθετῶ, *ouk athetō*) suggests that Paul is responding to an accusation, perhaps to the effect that his rejection of the law means a rejection of grace, which the agitators connected to the law (e.g., Burton 1921: 140; Bruce 1982b: 146; R. Longenecker 1990: 94; Martyn 1997: 259). But this assumes quite a bit that perhaps would not be clear to the Galatian audience. It is more likely that Paul offers this statement on his own as a final argument for the truth of what he has been saying in this paragraph (Schauf 2006: 95–96). The personal form in which it is couched (continuing the first-person singular of vv. 18–20) could suggest that Paul is referring to the particular instantiation of grace in his own ministry (as in the last reference to grace in 2:9; Dunn 1993a: 147–48;

Silva 2007: 788–89). But a reference to the grace of Paul's ministry does not fit well with the second part of the verse, which explains (γάρ, *gar*, for) the first part. This second clause, which basically sets righteousness by the law in antithesis to the death of Christ, suggests that grace refers broadly to the free-gift nature of the new era inaugurated by Christ; indeed, that era can be called, simply, "grace" (Rom. 5:2). Paul often juxtaposes grace in this sense with righteousness or justification by the law (Rom. 4:4, 16); see especially Gal. 5:4: "You who are trying to be justified by the law have been alienated from Christ; you have fallen away from grace." The self-giving of Christ (2:20), a manifestation of God's own free and unconstrained giving, is at root a matter of grace. The attempt, however, to connect "righteousness" (δικαιοσύνη, *dikaiosynē*, the status of being justified)[18] with the law (διὰ νόμου, *dia nomou*, through the law) is to introduce the qualification of human obedience into the securing of righteousness. This, Paul claims, would be to make Christ's death—a gracious act through and through—of "no effect" (δωρεάν, *dōrean*; cf. BDAG 266.3; for this view of the verse, see esp. Kim 2002: 45–51). As Calvin (1854: 76) comments, "For, if we do not renounce all other hopes, and embrace Christ alone, we reject the grace of God."

Additional Notes

2:16. Several witnesses, among them some early and good ones, omit the δέ at the beginning of this verse. Some interpreters think the omission represents the original text (e.g., Burton 1921: 119), while most are inclined to include it (Lightfoot 1881: 114; R. Longenecker 1990: 82; Betz 1979: 115). If δέ is read, it is probably mildly adversative: "Although we are Jews by birth . . . *yet*, because we know that . . . even we have believed in Christ Jesus. . . ."

2:16. There are basically three ways that v. 15 may be related to v. 16. First, v. 15 may be an assertion about the status of Peter and Paul that stands independent of v. 16. In this case, we assume a copulative verb in v. 15 that we must supply in English; hence (e.g.) ESV: "We ourselves *are* Jews by birth and not Gentile sinners" (emphasis added; see, e.g., Lightfoot 1881: 114). Second, ἡμεῖς . . . Ἰουδαῖοι in v. 15 could be the subject of the main verb in v. 16, with the pronoun repeated in v. 16 because of the distance between subject and verb: "We Jews . . . , knowing that a person is not justified by works of the law but by faith in Jesus Christ, have believed . . ." (I. Scott 2006: 186–88). Third, ἡμεῖς could be the subject of the verbs in v. 16, with the rest of v. 15 and the first part of v. 16 functioning as parallel descriptions of ἡμεῖς: "We who are Jews . . . and who know . . . have believed . . ." (R. Longenecker 1990: 81). If δέ is included in the text, then the second option is unlikely (see the previous note). There is little to choose between the other two options, but perhaps the first one best explains the apparent emphasis conveyed by καὶ ἡμεῖς: "We are Jews by birth . . . yet even we have believed in Christ Jesus. . . ."

2:16. The phrase ἔργα νόμου (both terms are always anarthrous) has played a role in recent debates about Paul's theology far out of proportion to its length or frequency of occurrence. One's understanding of the nature of Paul's opposition to "works of the law" is a key test case in the debate over just what Paul found to be wrong with the law of Moses and, by extension, Judaism in general.

18. "Righteousness" (δικαιοσύνη) refers to the status of forensic righteousness, in correspondence with δικαιόω (*dikaioō*, justify) in vv. 16–17 (contra, e.g., Ziesler [1972: 174] and R. Longenecker [1990: 95], who take it to refer to both status and lifestyle).

Any serious study of this phrase and its contexts has, accordingly, the potential to lead us into an exegetical, historical, and theological labyrinth. A general overview of the issue will have to suffice (for more detailed treatment, see Moo 1983; 1996: 211–17).

In all eight places where Paul uses ἔργα νόμου, he contrasts the phrase with πίστις as a means of securing a justified status before God or similar concept. (In Gal. 3:2 and 5 Paul refers to the experience of the Spirit rather than justification; but the two are, at least, overlapping concepts. In Gal. 3:10 reference to justification comes in the context [3:11], while in both Gal. 3:10 and Rom. 3:20 reference to πίστις also comes via the context [Gal. 3:11 and Rom. 3:22, respectively].) Traditionally, especially among Reformation interpreters and their heirs, "works of the law" has been understood to refer generally to anything a person might do in obedience to the law of Moses and by extension to anything that a person "does."[19] These texts were then used to buttress a theological point that is at the heart of traditional Protestantism: that no one can be justified before God by what they do and that justification comes, accordingly, by "faith alone." Interpreters have occasionally questioned this interpretation, arguing that "works of the law" has a restricted sense; the Reformers, for instance, engaged in debate with earlier theologians who confined "works of the law" to the ceremonies alone.[20] But in recent years, this general line of interpretation has become quite widespread due to the influence of the New Perspective. As we have noted in the commentary on 2:16, this approach sees the issue of "works of the law" in terms of their social function, to mark out God's people by means of the law and thereby exclude Gentiles from full participation in the new-covenant people of God. Some scholars who adopt this line of interpretation, notably James Dunn, think that Paul's polemic against "works of the law" can be extended to include works of any kind.[21] Other interpreters resist any such move to draw wider theological consequences from Paul's polemic.[22]

This interpretation of "works of the law" and its significance for Paul's theology must be assessed on several levels. The first and most obvious is the linguistic level. At the level of syntax, the force of the genitive νόμου must be considered. In itself, the genitive construction tells us only that the "works" belong to the category "law"; the specific relationship between the words can be determined only

---

19. In contrast to the claims of some interpreters, the Reformers did not miss the original historical referent in the phrase. In the preface to his commentary on Galatians, for instance, Calvin notes that the phrase refers to "the ceremonies," but, he argues, more than ceremonies are involved. He claims, "The question could not be settled without assuming the general principle, that we are justified by the free grace of God; and this principle sets aside not only ceremonies, but every other kind of works." Similarly, in his comments on 2:16, he notes that Origen and Jerome take "works of the law" to refer to ceremonies. He agrees but then argues that Paul extends the significance of the phrase to the larger and more consequent issue. Paul deals with works "of the law," then, partly because they are demanded by God; they are the highest form of works.

20. For example, the observance of the ritual or ceremonial law (see, e.g., Wiles 1967: 67–69) or a legalistic approach to the law (Fuller 1975–76: 31–33). S. Chester (2008) discusses the Reformers' polemic against any restriction in the scope of "works of the law," a debate that in some way mirrors the current discussion.

21. While arguing that "works of the law" in Gal. 2:16 has particular reference to "the Jewish way of life," Dunn (2009: 475–88) also argues for a broader significance: "In other words, here again Paul drives through the confusing ambiguity of Peter's attitude and conduct, as indeed the confusing ambiguity of covenantal nomism, to the core principle, the fundamental axiom on which all else rested: that acceptance by God and God's final verdict on a life does not depend on particular requirements of the law being observed" (486). Similarly, N. T. Wright (2009: 118; see also 212) argues that Paul denies that works of the law can justify *both* because they separate Jew and Gentile and "because what the law does is to reveal sin. Nobody can keep it perfectly."

22. Watson 2007: 128–29; cf. also Barclay 2010: 41–42. And see the discussion under "The Logic of Paul's Response" in the introduction.

by context (Winger 1992: 138).[23] Some interpreters argue that the genitive is subjective and that the phrase focuses on the law and what it "produces" (e.g., Owen 2007; Bachmann 2005: 72–102).[24] But a subjective-genitive interpretation could also have the sense "[the doing of] the works that the law requires," in which case the focus would still be on human works (cf. Cranfield 1991: 100; Schreiner 1993b: 235; NRSV has "deeds prescribed by the law" in Rom. 3:20). It is, however, a bit more likely that the genitive is objective, with "works of the law" therefore being the substantive equivalent to "doing the law," in the sense of "works done in obedience to the law."[25] What is clear is that the significance of the genitive provides no real help in settling the meaning of the phrase.

Of more potential, one might think, is the use of this phrase elsewhere in Paul's environment. Unfortunately, the data are few and debated. The only possible linguistic equivalents to Paul's ἔργα νόμου occur in the Dead Sea Scrolls, and only one text is universally agreed to offer a true parallel to Paul's phrase: 4QMMT (4Q398 frgs. 14–17, col. 2, line 3).[26] The occurrence of the phrase מעשי התורה is particularly interesting because it comes in a context that refers to a "reckoning" of "justice," or "righteousness" (צדקה) to those who do "what is upright and good before [God]" (line 7). Dunn has argued that this occurrence of the phrase supports his own New Perspective interpretation since it is used in a context in which the issue has to do with the "boundary markers" of the Qumran community (Dunn 1997b; see also N. Wright 2002: 460–61). But this is not clear (see esp. C. Evans 2005; also, e.g., Fitzmyer 2006: 89–90; Das 2010: 105–6; de Boer 2005: 197–201). Rough parallels to Paul's "works of the law" may also be found in 2 Bar. 57.2 ("the works of the commandments") and possibly also in the common rabbinic reference to "works" in general (Str-B 3:160–61).

On the whole, then, the Jewish precedents for Paul's "works of the law" do not provide evidence that the phrase in itself functioned to signal the "boundary markers" connotation that Dunn and others have seen in the phrase. The (few) parallels suggest that "works of the law" connotes, simply, "things done in obedience to the law." Any further nuance in the phrase would need to be the product of the way the phrase functions in its larger context. Dunn and others claim that first-century Judaism, being preoccupied with "boundary" issues, provides that context. However, while obedience to the law was indeed stressed as a means of erecting a boundary between Judaism and the Gentiles, it also had great "intrinsic" significance, as the means by which covenant membership, or "righteousness," was to be maintained and secured on the day of judgment. "Works of the law," then, could function in this latter context as well as the former. The key question is this: how do they function in Paul? The

23. The interpretation that construes ἔργων (ergōn, works) as dependent on νόμου (nomou, of law; e.g., "a law of works"; cf. Baumert and Meissner 2010: 28–53) is syntactically and semantically unlikely.

24. Bachmann (1998; 2005: 72–102) has argued at some length that the phrase in the Dead Sea Scrolls and in Paul refers to the rules or commandments of the torah itself rather than human response to the torah. But the elimination of all reference to human response from the phrase fits neither the language nor the contexts where the phrase occurs (see esp. Dunn 2005b: 412–19; Roo 2007: 84–94; Brawley 2005).

25. This marks a change from our earlier preference for the subjective genitive (Moo 1983: 90–96; 1996: 209).

26. There are other possible parallels in the scrolls, but all of them are debated. In 4QFlor (4Q174 frg. 1, col. 1, 21, 2, line 7) it is not clear whether we should read מעשי תורה (ma'ăśê tôrâ, works of the law) or מעשי תודה (ma'ăśê tôdâ, works of thanksgiving; cf. García Martínez and Tigchelaar 1997–98: 352–53; Kuhn 1994: 173–75). The closest parallel to Paul's language elsewhere in the scrolls is the phrase מעשי בתורה (ma'ăśê batôrâ, his works in the law) in 1QS 5.21 and 6.18. Roo (2007: 74–75) argues that this phrase is no true parallel (she translates "his works vis-à-vis the law"), but we think it probably is roughly similar (see also Hofius 2006: 309). Note also the frequent reference to "observing the law" (עושי התורה, 'ôśê hatôrâ) in 1QpHab (e.g., 7.11; 8.1; Watson 2009: 150).

interchange between "works of the law" and "works" in Romans suggests that the former is a subset of the latter (cf. Rom. 3:28 with 4:1–8; and see also Rom. 9:11–12, 30–32; 11:6). To be sure, Dunn argues that "works" is an abbreviation of the full phrase, so that, in effect, the issue throughout these texts is "works of the law." But this interpretation runs into difficulties. In Gal. 3 Paul argues that the law had not been given in Abraham's day, so it is difficult to think that Paul would have assumed that Abraham could have done "works of the law." The same is true in Paul's references to Jacob and Esau in Rom. 9. In Romans, therefore, a good case can be made that Paul is just as concerned with "works" as he is with the "law." The problem with "works of the law" is not just that they are bound to a law that kept Gentiles out or that they belong to an age now outmoded in Christ, but also that they are works.

This case is much more difficult to make in Galatians, which is more focused than Romans on salvation history and the extension of God's grace to Gentiles. But at several points the nature of Paul's argument shows that his concern about "works of the law" goes further than their ethno-exclusiveness (see "The Logic of Paul's Response" in the introduction). As far as 2:16 itself goes, it is clear that Paul is dealing with the behavior of Jewish believers at Antioch, who have indirectly put pressure on the Gentiles to "Judaize." The assertion that people are justified by faith in Christ rather than by works of the law is certainly addressed to this situation. But there is no suggestion that "works of the law" are to be abandoned because they keep Gentiles out. Rather, Paul sets forth a basic assertion, explicitly directed to Jewish believers, about how a "person" is justified. How would Gentile adoption of "works of the law" function to maintain Israel's "set-apartness"? As the contexts of later passages in the letter (3:10–12; 5:2–6) make clear, the issue is not the (social) matter of Israel's special position vis-à-vis Gentiles, but the issue of what will be necessary to complete salvation and avoid the curse. The agitators, in a word, were insisting on works of the law not to maintain Israel's special status (although this was undoubtedly an assumption of their approach) but to enable Gentile converts to "stay in" the realm of God's grace and therefore experience salvation on the last day.

"Works of the law," therefore, is a phrase that refers simply to things that people do in obedience to the law. The "law" in view is, of course, the law of Moses. And while it is clear from Galatians that Paul sees the law as outmoded, we need to penetrate behind this simple temporal claim to ask why the law needed to become outmoded. Some indeed think that Paul announced the end of the law simply because Christ had come. But most interpreters have rightly recognized the need to go beyond this dogmatic claim to inquire about Paul's reason for ruling out the law. The New Perspective approach in general argues that this reason was the law's exclusion of Gentiles. However, the OT itself grounds the need for a new covenant on human incapacity (see esp. Ezek. 36:22–32), and I believe that there are solid grounds within Paul's letter to think that the ultimate and more important reason for his polemic against the law had to do also with human captivity to sin (see, among others, Silva 2004; Kim 2002: 61–75; Hofius 2006: 306–10; Gathercole 2006: 238–39; and see "The Logic of Paul's Response" in the introduction). This being the case, the Reformers, we think, were entirely justified in viewing Paul's phrase "the works of the law" as a synecdoche for the more general category "works."

2:20. Several good witnesses read θεοῦ καὶ Χριστοῦ in place of υἱοῦ τοῦ θεοῦ. Despite the fact that this is arguably the "harder" reading, most interpreters view it as secondary because of the fact that Paul never elsewhere "speaks of God as the object of a Christian's faith" (Metzger 1994: 524). However, as we have noted in our exposition, many interpreters are convinced that the genitives should be construed as subjective: and there is certainly precedent in Paul for the idea of "faithfulness shown by God" (Rom. 3:5). For other reasons, however, the reading should probably be dismissed. While a reference to the faithfulness of both God and Christ is possible, it is unprecedented in Paul and a somewhat odd combination.

III. The Defense of the Gospel (3:1–5:12)

Galatians 3:1–5:12 constitutes the central argument of the letter (e.g., Dunn 1993a: 150). The boundaries of this section are debated. Galatians 2:15–21 introduces many of the key words and issues of 3:1–5:12 (see the introduction to 2:15–21). But formally 2:15–21 belongs to 1:11–2:14. The first-person plurals and singulars indicate that Paul is to some extent relating the content of the speech he gave at Antioch (2:11–14). The direct address to the Galatians in 3:1 signals a shift. Second-person plurals, absent in 1:11–2:14 (with the exception of "disclosure formulas" [1:11, 13]), now emerge at critical places in Paul's argument (3:1–5, 26–29; 4:6–20, 21; 4:28–5:4; 5:7–10). There likewise is debate over where to place the boundary at the end of this section, but I think that a good case can be made for putting it between 5:12 and 13 (see my comments in the introduction to 5:1–12).

This second major part of the letter is framed by two passages of rebuke and exhortation (3:1–6; 5:1–12). A similar text of rebuke and exhortation, mixed with personal appeal, comes in 4:8–20. On this basis, the central section could be divided into two roughly parallel parts, each comprising an exegetical argument focused on Abraham (3:7–4:7; 4:21–31) and followed by an exhortation (4:8–20, 5:1–12; e.g., Martyn 1997: 24–27; Mussner 1988: 205; cf. Beker 1980: 47). However, while clearly somewhat of a mixed genre, Paul's "allegory" based on Sarah and Hagar in 4:21–31 is more exhortation than it is argument. Therefore we prefer to divide the central section into two parts: theological argument (3:7–4:7) and an appeal based on that argument (4:8–5:12).[1] Of course, the boundaries of the letter are, as always, more or less permeable, and we must avoid imposing our own neat outlines on what might be Paul's less architectonic structure.[2] We must likewise avoid any kind of facile contrast between "theology" and "practice." As always, Paul mixes the two in various degrees.

In 2:15–21, which is a key transitional passage between the opening section and this central section of the letter, Paul briefly delineates the gospel. This next part of the letter is a prolonged defense of that gospel. Especially important in this defense is the key distinction that Paul first introduces in 2:16: "works of the law" versus "Christ faith." This antithesis is a thread

---

1. While their overall structural proposal and its rhetorical underpinnings are not entirely convincing, G. Hansen (1989: 78–79) and R. Longenecker (1990: 97) also emphasize the hortatory character of all of Gal. 4:12–6:18.

2. See on this issue esp. Beker 1980: 64–69, who is speaking about Romans but whose warnings apply equally to the other Letters of Paul—especially those such as Galatians that engage in sustained theological argument.

that weaves together the disparate subjects of this part of the letter. In the opening passage, in which Paul sets the tone for the argument to follow, he confronts his readers with this fundamental issue: did they experience the Spirit by "the works of the law" or by "the hearing that accompanies faith" (3:2, 5)? This contrast, stated with several different combinations ("law," "doing" vs. "faith," "believing," "[Jesus] Christ faith"), repeatedly surfaces in the argument that follows. And this same antithesis is central to 5:1–6, the rhetorical climax of the letter. Some recent interpreters think that this is fundamentally a salvation-historical contrast between the law (the center of the old covenant) and Christ's "faith" or "faithfulness" (the animating force of the new covenant). However, while the importance of salvation history for Paul's argument cannot be denied, the contrast between "works of the law" (or "law") and "faith" is finally a contrast between two means of accessing God's grace in Christ, between "doing the law" (or "doing") and believing (in Christ). (See my comments on 2:16 and the sections in the introduction on "The Logic of Paul's Response" and "The Faith of Christ," as well as the third additional note on 2:16.)

In the rhetorically important exhortatory passages that frame the argument in this part of the letter, Paul pairs faith with the Spirit (see 3:3 and 5:5). The Spirit, the characteristic gift and mark of the new age of salvation (3:2, 5, 14), has an important, and often underappreciated, role in Paul's argument (see esp. Cosgrove 1988).

Paul, of course, emphasizes faith and the Spirit not for themselves only but as the means to an end. He expresses this end in two fundamental concepts: inclusion within the people of God and justification/righteousness. Paul never uses the phrase "people of God" in Galatians (λάος [laos, people] does not occur in the letter), but the language of being Abraham's sons/children/seed (3:7 [9], 29; 4:28–31) or God's sons/children (3:26; 4:5–7) refers to this concept. Paul's use of this language is almost certainly a reflection of the agitators' terms of argument: the Galatian Gentiles could become Abraham's "seed" or "heirs" only if they came under the torah. "Who are Abraham's children?" is the question that Paul and the agitators are debating, with the Galatians as their audience. Paul's basic argument is that one becomes Abraham's heir, with all its promised blessings, by faith and by the Spirit—indeed, by "faith alone," apart from works (of the law).

Justification/righteousness is the second goal of faith and the Spirit. The final verse of the opening exhortation concludes with a reference to "righteousness" (3:6), and Paul elaborates this issue (in connection with Abraham) in the initial scriptural argument in this section of the letter (3:7–9). Justification is again central in Paul's summing up of his argument in 5:1–6 (see vv. 4–5). Justification by faith is the goal toward which salvation history has been moving (3:24). And this justification language continues the theme first announced in Paul's summary of the gospel in 2:15–21, a passage that anticipates the central section of the letter. Particularly significant in tying the letter together is 3:8, which defines the "gospel preached ahead of time to Abraham" as the "justifying of the Gentiles." It is quite natural, granted the situation addressed in the letter, for Paul to highlight the purpose of God to include Gentiles in the scope of his justifying work. But it should be emphasized that Gentiles are included not because justification is directed only to their situation. Rather, justification includes Gentiles because it embraces all humans (see "all flesh" [i.e., "no one"; KJV: "no flesh"] in 2:16 and the first-plural verbs in 3:24; 5:5).

The prominence of both inclusion in God's people and justification in Paul's argument naturally raises the question of the relationship between them. N. T. Wright (2009: 116) has argued that the latter is another way of referring to the former: to be "justified" means to be recognized as one who belongs to God's people.[3] However, this does not do justice to the fundamental nature of justification in Galatians, which, as Paul makes clear, involves a divine verdict of ultimate importance. It thus is better to view justification as God's pronouncement of the righteous status that is granted to all who truly belong to the people of God. Inclusion in God's people leads to justification, the status of righteousness that is the ultimate goal of faith and the work of the Spirit. In Galatians justification thus refers not so much to the way one gets into relationship with God as to the vindication of a belonging-to-Christ that has already been attained. (See, further, "Justification/Righteousness" in the introduction.)

This last sentence touches on the fifth theological theme that is fundamental to Paul's argument in this part of the letter: union with Christ. Since Christ is himself *the* "seed" of Abraham (3:16), one becomes Abraham's child by becoming integrated with Christ (3:7, 29). In the period inaugurated by Christ's coming into the world, the "fullness of the time" (4:4 AT), God's people are defined in terms of Christ, and Christ alone (esp. see 3:26–29). We become "sons of God" in our relationship to *the* Son of God (4:1–7). And, as belonging to Christ is the only entry into God's people and the righteous verdict pronounced over God's people, so that entry into Christ is by faith alone. The great Reformation slogans of "Christ alone" (*Christus solus*) and "by faith alone" (*sola fide*) find solid scriptural basis in this central section of Galatians.

---

3. N. T. Wright is sometimes criticized at this point for putting ecclesiology in the place of soteriology. But, in fact, belonging to the people of God is, for Wright, a soteriological matter.

A. Rebuke and Reminder: Faith, Spirit, and Righteousness (3:1–6)

The rebuke and exhortation of these verses, coming as they do at a pivotal point in the letter, are especially significant in setting the rhetorical direction for the whole argument. With "You foolish Galatians," the first direct address of his readers since 1:11, Paul signals a new movement in his argument. The contrast between "You foolish Galatians" and that earlier address to "brothers and sisters" sets the tone for what follows. After a long narrative about Paul's experience with the gospel, which Paul uses both to stress his independent apostolic authority and to bring to the fore elements of "the truth of the gospel" that the Galatians need to be reminded of (1:11–2:21), Paul again, as in 1:6–10, rebukes the Galatians for their obtuseness. Martyn (1997: 282) thus labels this paragraph the "second rebuke" section, while Dahl (2002: 130) has drawn attention to the "ironic rebuke," a form characterized by "a mood of disappointment and a note of reproach" shared by Paul with other ancient letters. Paul issues his rebuke in the form of five rhetorical questions (vv. 1, 2, 3, 4a, 5). In this paragraph the key motif is the experience of the Galatians (v. 4). Christ was "placarded" among them (v. 1); they have received the Spirit (vv. 3 and 5) and experienced the Spirit's power (v. 5). But the key point in the paragraph, which Paul will develop in the theological argument that follows, is the means by which the Galatians have experienced these signs and blessings of the era of fulfillment: not by "works of the law" but by means of "a hearing accompanied by faith" (vv. 3, 5). The strong contrast between faith and torah that was introduced in 2:16 surfaces here with respect to the Galatians' experience (de Boer 2011: 166). Yet Paul's real concern is not how they began but how they are to continue: "hearing characterized by faith" is the means by which they will sustain their Christian experience (v. 3). Paul's confirmatory reference to Abraham's experience in verse 6, while obviously introducing what follows, should probably nevertheless be attached to this opening paragraph, as corroboration of the importance of faith in the Galatians' experience (so, e.g., ESV, NIV; and see Bruce 1982b: 152–53; Silva 2001: 253; Wakefield 2003: 136; contra, e.g., NRSV, NLT; Burton 1921: 153; R. Longenecker 1990: 112).

Exegesis and Exposition

[1]You foolish Galatians! Who has bewitched you ⌐ ⌐? Before your very eyes Jesus Christ was publicly portrayed ⌐ ⌐ as crucified. [2]This only do I want to learn from you: Did you receive the Spirit by works of the law, or by hearing accompanied by faith?

³Are you so foolish? After beginning with the Spirit, are you now trying to finish by the flesh? ⁴Have you experienced so much in vain—if it really was in vain? ⁵Does the one who gives you his Spirit and who works miracles among you—does he do this by works of the law, or by hearing accompanied by faith? ⁶Even as Abraham "believed God, and it was credited to him as righteousness."

Most modern versions substitute something like "You foolish Galatians" for the increasingly archaic "O foolish Galatians" (e.g., NIV, NRSV, NJB, HCSB, NASB, NET). The Greek ὦ (ō) functions to introduce a rebuke (BDF §146.2), and the nominative ἀνόητοι Γαλάται (anoētoi Galatai, foolish Galatians) is used, as so often in NT Greek, for the vocative (Wallace 1996: 56–57). The strength of this address is suggested by the fact that Paul only four times elsewhere in his letters directly names his audience (2 Cor. 6:11; Phil. 4:15; 1 Tim. 1:18; 6:20). "Foolish," used again in 3:3, refers to a failure of intellect, of understanding or comprehension (1 Tim. 6:9; Titus 3:3; cf. Luke 24:25). The Galatians, Paul suggests, are failing to draw the obvious inference from their experience as Christians.

3:1

What has caused them to be so foolish? Witchcraft, Paul implies. Someone has "bewitched" them. The verb Paul uses, βασκαίνω (baskainō), means "to exert an evil influence through the eye" (BDAG 171.1); we might say, "to bewitch with the 'evil eye'" (NLT: "Who has cast an evil spell on you?"). Some interpreters argue that we should take Paul's claim seriously: he thinks that the Galatians are under an evil spell (Neyrey 1988). Others think the word is purely rhetorical, meaning simply "pervert" or "confuse the mind" (e.g., R. Longenecker 1990: 100; Lemmer 1992: 372–73). The truth probably lies between these views. While it is unlikely that Paul means to say that the Galatians are under a spell cast by a sorcerer, his choice of this word does suggest that the Galatians' turnaround in their thinking can only be explained by recourse to an evil spiritual influence (see, e.g., Dunn 1993a: 151; Garlington 2003: 133; Mussner 1988: 206; B. Longenecker 1998: 150–55; see *NewDocs* 4:31).[1]

The second part of the verse justifies Paul's claim that the Galatians are being foolish: it was before their "very eyes" that "Jesus Christ was clearly portrayed as crucified." Several modern English versions turn this into a new sentence (NIV, NRSV, ESV, NET, CEB), but it is really a continuation of the question from the beginning of the verse (see NASB, RSV, HCSB). The combination κατ' ὀφθαλμούς (kat' ophthalmous, "before one's eyes" [BDAG 744.2]) and προεγράφη (proegraphē, portray publicly) makes clear that Paul is thinking of an open and evident declaration of the crucifixion (for this meaning of προγράφω, see BDAG 867.2; the verb occurs in the NT elsewhere with the

---

1. J. Elliott (1990) argues that reference to the evil eye might cohere with other references (implied or explicit) to the "eye" in Galatians (e.g., 4:15). And Eastman (2001: 69–72) notes a possible association between the evil eye and the curse in 3:10, 13–14. The word βασκαίνω can also mean "envy" (BDAG 171.2), and some interpreters think that there might be a secondary allusion to this meaning: the agitators, Paul might be hinting, were envious of the Galatians (Lightfoot 1881: 133; Dunn 1993a: 152).

meaning "write beforehand" [Rom. 15:4; Eph. 3:3; Jude 4]). The visual imagery may pick up on the allusion to the "evil eye" earlier in the verse: the agitators may be trying to persuade the Galatians by means of the demonic device of the "evil eye"; but the Galatians, who have seen Christ's cross with their own eyes, should know better. "This placard ought to have kept their eyes from wandering, and so to have acted as a charm" (Lightfoot 1881: 134). The reference is undoubtedly to Paul's preaching about Christ among the Galatians: by means of vivid word pictures, Paul presented to them the central salvific reality of the cross of Christ (esp. see 1 Cor. 2:1–5). What is meant, then, is a "vivid verbal description" (LN 410.33.191; for the nuance of vividness in this verb, see Martyn 1997: 283). As he has just done in 2:21, Paul again invests the fact of the crucifixion with considerable significance. When truly appreciated, the cross of Christ, *the* manifestation of God's wisdom, power, and grace, should rule out of court the kind of human-oriented law program that the agitators are perpetrating.

3:2 Paul asks another rhetorical question about the Galatians' initial experience of the gospel as a way of rebuking them for their openness to the message of the agitators. He prefaces the question with an introduction that signals its importance: "this only do I want to learn from you." By asking about how they "received the Spirit," Paul assumes something that is central to his theology: when a person comes to Christ and is justified, that person receives the Spirit of God (cf. esp. Rom. 8:9–10). The bestowal of the Spirit is a mark of the new age of salvation, predicted in the prophets (see esp. Joel 2:28–32, quoted in Acts 2:17–21; cf. Rom. 10:13; see esp. Fee 1994: 383–84). The Galatians know full well that they have, indeed, received the Spirit, not only because of the inner witness of that Spirit to their new spiritual identity (Gal. 4:6; Rom. 8:14–17) but also because of the miracles produced by the Spirit in their midst (v. 5; cf. Dunn 1993a: 153).

But the main issue Paul wants to raise in his rhetorical question is the means by which the Galatian Christians first came to experience God's Spirit: was it "by means of works of the law" (ἐξ ἔργων νόμου, *ex ergōn nomou*) or "by means of hearing accompanied by faith" (ἐξ ἀκοῆς πίστεως, *ex akoēs pisteōs*)? These phrases pick up the key contrast in Gal. 2:16 between "works of the law" and "the faith of Christ." "Works of the law" will again refer to human actions done in obedience to the torah, the law of Moses (see the commentary and the third additional note on 2:16). But the phrase ἀκοὴ πίστεως is much harder to interpret since the meaning of both nouns is disputed and their genitive relationship is ambiguous. We begin with the qualifying genitive πίστεως. Some interpreters downplay any focus on human response in the word, arguing that it can be reduced basically to "the proclamation of the gospel," "the faith message" (Hays 2002: 130–31; Martyn 1997: 284, 286–89), or even "the message about Christ's faithfulness" (Matera 1993: 290; D. Campbell 2009: 853–56; cf. de Boer 2011: 174–76). This interpretation is interwoven with the larger interpretive issue of the πίστις Χριστοῦ (*pistis Christou*, faith of/in

Christ) debate. We have found good reasons for maintaining the traditional understanding of this phrase as an objective genitive ("faith in Christ"; see the comments on 2:16 and "The Faith of Christ" in the introduction), making it likely that the reference here also is to human believing in Christ. And this interpretation receives confirmation from the connection that Paul makes between the Galatians' πίστις and Abraham's faith (v. 6; see esp. Hunn 2006).

If the genitive πίστεως, then, refers to human faith, it is possible to understand ἀκοή to refer to "what is heard," meaning "the message." This could make contextual sense, since there is implied reference to the preaching of the gospel in verse 1 (Boers 2006: 165–68). The genitive πίστεως could then be an objective genitive, yielding the interpretation "the message that evokes faith" (H. Johnson 1987: 185–88; Das 1995: 178; Mundle 1977: 15). But there is little in the context to suggest that the gospel creates faith. On this understanding of ἀκοή and πίστις, it is more likely that the genitive is loosely attributive, the idea amounting to "believing what you heard" (NIV, NRSV, NLT, NET, NJB, CEB; see, e.g., Bruce 1982b: 149; R. Longenecker 1990: 103). But the word ἀκοή can also mean the activity of hearing; so it is also possible that the phrase in this verse (and in v. 5) means "hearing accompanied by faith" (RSV, ESV, NASB, HCSB; e.g., Burton 1921: 147; Lightfoot 1881: 135; Dunn 1993a: 154; Hong 1994: 170–71; Vanhoye 1993: 98–101; Silva 2004: 236; Harmon 2010: 125–33). Paul brings together the word ἀκοή with faith in only one other text, Rom. 10:16b–17, which provides some evidence for each of these interpretations of ἀκοή: κύριε, τίς ἐπίστευσεν τῇ ἀκοῇ ἡμῶν; ἄρα ἡ πίστις ἐξ ἀκοῆς, ἡ δὲ ἀκοὴ διὰ ῥήματος Χριστοῦ (kyrie, tis episteusen tē akoē hēmōn? ara hē pistis ex akoēs, hē de akoē dia rhēmatos Christou, Lord, who has believed our report? Faith, then, comes from hearing, the hearing through the word of Christ [AT]). As our translation suggests, ἀκοή in verse 16b refers to "what is heard," but in verse 17 ἀκοή means "hearing" itself. This latter meaning is the one that ἀκοή usually has in Paul (1 Cor. 12:17; 1 Thess. 2:13 [likely]; 2 Tim. 4:3, 4), and probably what the word means also here in Gal. 3. "Hearing" conveys something of the connotation of the equivalent Hebrew word: faithful receptivity, an "attentiveness" to the word of God that includes both trust in its content and giver and the disposition to obey. See שָׁמַע (šāma', hear), for example, in Exod. 15:26; 19:5; 23:22; Deut. 11:13, 27; 15:5; 28:1, 2; 2 Sam. 22:45; Jer. 17:24; and 1 Sam. 15:22 LXX ("To hear [ἀκοή] is better than sacrifice" [AT]; cf. Garlington 2003: 134; O'Donovan 1994: 110). The genitive πίστεως, then, indicates that the "hearing" here is a "hearing" that "involves" faith, or that is "accompanied by faith" (attributive genitive), or even, "the 'hearing' that Christians call faith" (epexegetic genitive; cf. Williams 1989: 83–93; Hong 1993: 129–31). As Paul's argument proceeds, it becomes clear that faith is the key issue. But here Paul wants to associate faith with "hearing" in order to remind the Galatians of their initial response to the preaching of the gospel.

The οὕτως (houtōs) at the beginning of this verse could function as a connective with what precedes ("*thus* you are foolish") or what follows ("you are

3:3

being foolish *in this way:* . . ."). But, as the English translations recognize, the word is probably functioning as an adverb modifying ἀνόητοί ἐστε (*anoētoi este*, you are foolish): "can it be that you are *so* foolish?" (BDAG 742.3; LN 685.78.4). The accusation of foolishness thus frames verses 1b–2 and probably relates especially to what follows: can you be so foolish that, having begun your Christian journey by means of the Spirit, you are now trying to finish it by means of the flesh? The aorist participle ἐναρξάμενοι (*enarxamenoi*, having begun) refers to the inauguration of Christian experience (as in its only other NT occurrence, Phil. 1:6), which, with an allusion back to verse 2, Paul claims to have taken place πνεύματι (*pneumati*), "by means of the Spirit" (a dative of means; cf. Wallace 1996: 166). Despite this good beginning (see also Gal. 5:7), the Galatians are being tempted by the agitators to shift to another means of completing their Christian pilgrimage. The verb ἐπιτελεῖσθε (*epiteleisthe*) could be passive, in which case the idea would be "are you trying to be perfected?" (cf. NASB, ESV; the only other comparable form of this verb in the NT is passive, but with a different meaning [1 Pet. 5:9]). But it is more likely to be middle, with the sense "finish," "bring to completion."[2] Paul expresses the same basic idea with the same verbs in Phil. 1:6: "He who began [ἐναρξάμενος, *enarxamenos*] a good work in you will carry it on to completion [ἐπιτελέσει, *epitelesei*] until the day of Christ Jesus" (Kwon 2004: 46).

In contrast to πνεύματι stands σαρκί (*sarki*), "by means of the flesh" (another dative of means). In light of the significance of circumcision in the larger argument of Galatians, σάρξ (*sarx*, flesh) might have a simple physical reference: as Martyn paraphrases, "Are you . . . really so foolish as to think that . . . you can now move on to perfection by means of a severed piece of flesh?" (Martyn 1997: 294; see also de Boer 2011: 177). But it is likely that, without excluding this allusion, the word has a broader significance. Just what this broader significance might be is bound up with the interpretation of "works of the law." For, just as "by the Spirit" is associated with "the hearing of faith" in verse 2, so "by the flesh" is naturally to be associated with "works of the law." Since this latter phrase refers to the typically Jewish concern with obedience to the law of Moses, "flesh" might refer especially to Jewish ethnicity (see, e.g., Garlington 2003: 136). However, as we have seen, "works of the law" is a subset of the larger category of "works" of any kind (see the third additional note on 2:16). "Flesh," then, may have the typically Pauline sense of human existence, usually set in contrast to the spiritual realm. This meaning fits every occurrence of σάρξ in Galatians, whereas the meaning "Jewish ethnicity" is not clearly present anywhere (1:16; 2:16, 20; 4:13, 14, 23, 29; 5:13, 16, 17 [2x], 19, 24; 6:8 [2x], 12, 13). Especially significant are texts in which, as here, Paul contrasts σάρξ and πνεῦμα (Gal. 4:29; 5:16–24; 6:8; Rom. 1:3–4; 2:28–29; 7:5–6; 8:4–13; Phil. 3:3; Col. 2:5; 1 Tim. 3:16). Galatians 4:23 and 29 offer perhaps the closest parallels, where σάρξ takes on the sense "human effort"

---

2. Some interpreters suggest that the verb might mean "perfect" (Fung 1988: 134; Schlier 1989: 123–24), but there is little basis for this.

(NIV, NLT, NET; R. Longenecker 1990: 104; Hays 2000: 252). Paul's warning about "works of the law," then, is not based only on the fact that these works belong to an outmoded era or that they reflect Jewish ethnocentrism (though both may be involved). Rather, Paul's switch to "flesh" in this verse implies that his warning is ultimately about the broadly human issue of "doing." Of course, Paul is not denying the importance of "doing" in the outworking of the salvation bestowed initially by the Spirit. Faith certainly "works" (5:6), and a true work of God's Spirit will always issue in works of obedience (5:22–24). But the agitators were apparently insisting that becoming a "son" of Abraham and attaining ultimate righteousness with God were based on faith + torah observance. It is this synergism with respect to righteousness that Paul denies.

The concern that Paul expresses in this verse reaches to the rhetorical heart of Galatians. The Galatian Christians have started well; they have received the Spirit and have been justified by their faith in Christ, a gift of God's grace. But the agitators have come on the scene, arguing that people can go free in the judgment only if they add to their faith the "works of the law." Paul seeks to persuade the Galatians not to buy into this scheme: as they began, with the Spirit and with faith, so they must continue (see 5:5).

Paul continues his rebuke with a fourth rhetorical question: τοσαῦτα ἐπάθετε εἰκῇ; (tosauta epathete eikē? Have you experienced so many things in vain?). The word τοσαῦτα, a neuter-plural form of τοσοῦτος (tosoutos), can have a quantitative sense ("so many things") or a qualitative sense ("such great things"; BDAG 1012). Either meaning could fit here. While there is no clear plural antecedent for this demonstrative adjective to refer to in context, it is quite likely that the word refers to the experiences associated with the Galatians' receiving the Spirit: see the "miracles" (δυνάμεις, dynameis) in verse 5 (Mussner 1988: 209). Thus Paul may be referring to the great number of those experiences or to their great significance. These options assume, however, that the verb ἐπάθετε means "experience someth[ing] (pleasant)." This is certainly a possible meaning for the verb πάσχω (see BDAG 785.1; LSJ 1346–47; and also, e.g., Josephus, Ant. 3.312), and many interpreters think the context here suggests it (see esp. R. Longenecker 1990: 104; also Dunn 1993a: 156–57; Martyn 1997: 285; Fee 1994: 386–87; see NIV, RSV, NRSV, NLT, NAB, NJB, CEB). But this would be the only place in the NT where the verb has this meaning (out of 42 occurrences, 7 in Paul), and many other interpreters think the usual meaning "suffer" can also fit this context (W. Michaelis, TDNT 5:905–23; Lightfoot 1881: 135; Bruce 1982b: 150; Baasland 1984: 139–40; Eastman 2007: 109; Wilson 2007: 87–89; see ESV, NASB, NET, KJV, NKJV). They point to the fact that Paul explicitly refers to the Galatians' suffering persecution in 4:29. Moreover, Luke narrates the suffering of Paul and Barnabas during their evangelism of the churches to which Galatians is probably written (Acts 13:50; 14:5, 19), and Paul's warning to one of those churches that "we must go through many hardships to enter the kingdom of God" (14:22) suggests that this persecution may have extended to the new Christians as well. We

3:4

think it is better, then, to keep the normal NT sense of πάσχω in this verse. The suffering they have experienced in conjunction with their reception of the Spirit and his continuing ministry among them should teach them about the complete adequacy of the Spirit to bring them successfully to the final day of judgment. For them to turn their backs on the Spirit now would make their experiencing all the Spirit's works to be "in vain" (εἰκῇ, an adverb used only by Paul in the NT: Rom. 13:4; 1 Cor. 15:2; Gal. 4:11; Col. 2:18).

Paul adds to his question an almost offhand remark designed to bring home the significance of his question: εἴ γε καὶ εἰκῇ (*ei ge kai eikē*), "if indeed it has been in vain."[3] In contrast to most versions, which insert a past-tense verb, "if it really was in vain" (e.g., NIV), it is preferable to use the English perfect in order to show that Paul is now referring to the Galatians' *current* evaluation of these experiences (see RSV, NLT, NJB). It is also unclear whether the addition reinforces the warning: "unless all this, indeed, is in vain"; or whether it sounds a hopeful note: "if indeed [as I cannot believe] it has been in vain." The latter is more likely, since Paul generally uses εἴ γε to introduce a qualification to something he has just said (2 Cor. 5:3; Eph. 3:2; 4:21; Col. 1:23). Lightfoot is often quoted: "The Apostle hopes better things of his converts. Εἴ γε leaves a loophole of doubt, and καί widens this" (1881: 135; see also Thrall 1962: 86; Bruce 1982b: 150; Dunn 1993a: 157; Martyn 1997: 285).

3:5 Paul connects this verse to the preceding verses with οὖν (*oun*, therefore, then), left untranslated by many English versions. Its function is probably to introduce verse 5 as a summarizing recapitulation of verses 2–4 (brought out well by the NRSV "well, then"). The substance of this verse repeats what Paul has said in verse 2b—with two differences. First, the form of the rhetorical question in this verse is different than verse 2b. In place of a question about how the Galatians received the Spirit, Paul now asks about how God has supplied the Spirit to the Galatians. Paul uses two parallel substantival participles, characterizing God as "the one who gives you the Spirit" (ὁ ἐπιχορηγῶν ὑμῖν τὸ πνεῦμα, *ho epichorēgōn hymin to pneuma*) and "the one who works miracles among you" (ἐνεργῶν δυνάμεις ἐν ὑμῖν, *energōn dynameis en hymin*; the article with ἐπιχορηγῶν goes with ἐνεργῶν also). In a notable example of verb ellipsis (BDF §479.1), then, the corresponding finite forms of these verbs must be supplied in the second part of the verse, which simply consists of the two contrasting prepositional phrases: "by works of the law, or by hearing accompanied by faith" (ἐξ ἔργων νόμου ἢ ἐξ ἀκοῆς πίστεως, *ex ergōn nomou ē ex akoēs pisteōs*). This contrast is the same, verbally and substantively, as the one we have already seen in verse 2.

The second difference between verse 5 and verse 2b is that Paul mentions the Spirit's continuing manifestation among the Galatians and adds that to his reminder of their initial reception of the Spirit. This initial reception is

---

3. Interpreters and the versions disagree about whether this should be punctuated as a question (NIV, ESV, NASB, NLT, NJB, NKJV) or as an assertion (RSV, NRSV, NET), but since the question would be rhetorical, it makes little difference.

conveyed by a present participle (ἐπιχορηγῶν, from a verb that means "convey as a gift"), and this leads some interpreters to think that Paul may refer, in Dunn's (1993a: 158) words, to the "beginning of a continuing relationship with God sustained by him through the Spirit" (cf. Bruce 1982b: 151; Martyn 1997: 285). But, considering its similarity to verse 2b, it is more likely that the present tense signifies what Porter calls "timeless action" (1992: 33): the focus is entirely on the nature of the God who gives. Thus the reference could well be to the gift of the Spirit at conversion (R. Longenecker 1990: 105). It is the second participle that then conveys the ongoing experience of the Spirit among the Galatians. To be sure, Paul does not explicitly connect the Spirit with this second description of God's activity among the Galatians. But he often attributes miracles (δυνάμεις; cf. BDAG 262–63) to the Spirit (see esp. 1 Cor. 12:10, 28 [cf. 12:8]), and the prominence of the Spirit in this paragraph makes it likely that Paul thinks of the miracles that God is working among them as coming through the power of the Spirit (Burton 1921: 151; Bruce 1982b: 151; Dunn 1993a: 158). These miracles occur ἐν ὑμῖν (en hymin), which could mean "in each one of you" (e.g., Lightfoot 1881: 137), but more likely means "among you" (Schlier 1989: 126).

This verse is a Janus, connected to verses 1–5 by means of καθώς (kathōs, even as) and the theme of faith (vv. 2, 5), yet also connected to what follows with its focus on the experience of Abraham, to which Paul regularly alludes in the rest of Gal. 3 (vv. 7, 8, 9, 14, 16, 18, 29). It is difficult to decide whether to view the verse as the conclusion to verses 1–5 (NIV, ESV; Bruce 1982b: 152; Silva 2001: 253; Wakefield 2003: 136) or as the introduction to verses 7–9 (e.g., NRSV, NLT; Burton 1921: 153; R. Longenecker 1990: 112). The introductory καθώς finally inclines me to attach verse 6, from a literary standpoint, to verses 1–5.

3:6

This καθώς is sometimes taken as an abbreviation for Paul's familiar citation formula, καθὼς γέγραπται (kathōs gegraptai, even as it is written [e.g., Rom. 1:17]; cf., e.g., Hays 2002: 169–70; G. Hansen 1989: 112; Dunn 1993a: 160), in this case introducing the quotation of Gen. 15:6 that follows. But one must wonder why Paul does not simply use the usual phrase if this is what he means. R. Longenecker (1990: 112) suggests that the word may be "an *exemplum* reference," in the sense "Take Abraham as an example" (see NIV 1984: "Consider Abraham:"). But it is better to give the word its usual comparative force and view it as linked specifically with a thought assumed in the context. Paul clearly expects his rhetorical question in verse 5 to be answered with the response "not by works of the law, but by hearing accompanied by faith." The καθώς builds on this: "Surely it is by 'hearing accompanied by faith' [v. 5b], even as it was in the case of Abraham, who . . ." (Williams 1987: 92–95; Silva 2001: 253; Stanley 1992: 235; similarly, Howard 1979: 55; and cf. BDAG 493.1).

It is not clear whether Paul introduces this specific point in response to the agitators' interpretation of Gen. 15:6 (Barrett 1976: 6; Silva 2004: 223n17 [citing 4Q398 frgs. 14–17, col. 2, line 7 of 4QMMT]). The contours of Paul's argument certainly imply that the agitators were using the traditional Jewish nomenclature of "seed/children of Abraham" to argue that the Galatians could only find ultimate "righteousness" by attaching themselves to Abraham—through the accepted means of taking upon themselves obedience to the torah. First-century Judaism generally focused on Abraham's obedience, and especially the obedience he so memorably revealed when God "tested" him by calling on him to sacrifice his son Isaac (Gen. 22). On the basis of Gen. 26:5, Jewish interpreters also viewed Abraham's obedience as directed to the law itself (see the additional note on 3:6). The agitators were probably using this view of Abraham to argue that righteousness was tied to doing the law. The appeal to Gen. 15:6 may, then, be a reflection of Paul's own reading of the Abraham narrative (Martyn 1997: 297). The text brings together two of the words critical for his argument: πιστεύω/πίστις (*pisteuō*/*pistis*, believe/faith) and δικαιοσύνη/δικαιόω (*dikaiosynē*/*dikaioō*, righteousness/justify).

Watson (2004: 174–93) argues that Paul's focus on this text is in keeping with Genesis: Gen. 15:6, he claims, is the "hermeneutical key" to the Abraham story, underlining the centrality of promise and the divine initiative. Genesis 15:6 recounts Abraham's response to the Lord's promise that Abraham's "seed," coming from his own body, would be as numerous as the stars in the heaven (15:4): "Abram believed the LORD." In turn, the Lord responded to Abraham and "credited it to him as righteousness." The meaning of this passage is disputed, but it is best taken to mean that God graciously viewed Abraham's faith as having in itself fulfilled all that God expected of Abraham in order for him to be in the right before God. (This cannot be, it should be emphasized, *covenant* righteousness: no "covenant" existed yet [Yeung 2002: 264–71; Piper 2007: 40–42].) Paul's appeal to this verse for the connection between forensic righteousness and faith is, therefore, a fair application of the intention of Gen. 15:6 (see the additional note on 3:6).

Just as, then, it was Abraham's faith that led to his being considered "in the right" before God, so it was the faith of the Galatians that led them to be "declared right" (Gal. 2:16, 21; cf., e.g., Eckstein 1996: 98–99). The particular connection that Paul might have in mind with the previous paragraph is not clear. His implicit comparison between the Galatians' experience of the Spirit and Abraham's righteousness reveals that Paul views justification and the Spirit as closely related (e.g., Williams 1987: 95; Byrne 1979: 148). Yet this does not mean (contra, e.g., G. Hansen 1989: 115) that "righteousness" includes the transforming work of God's Spirit: the Spirit functions in verses 1–5 not as an agent of transformation but as the confirmation that the believers have indeed entered into relationship with God. Further, however, does Paul suggest that Abraham's attaining righteousness is to be compared to the Galatians' initial experience ("after beginning," v. 3) or to their continuing experience ("are you now trying to finish?")? Perhaps this is not a fair question. As often in Galatians, Paul appears to view "righteousness" as right standing without particular focus on its initiation. His concern is to make clear to the Galatians that, in contrast to the views of the agitators, righteousness is always and at every stage manifested through faith.

Additional Notes

3:1. Two textual variants in this verse deserve brief comment. Along with a few other MSS, 𝔐 adds, after ἐβάσκανεν, the words τῇ ἀληθείᾳ μὴ πείθεσθαι: hence NKJV's "Who has bewitched you, that you should not obey the truth?" The external attestation for this reading is not strong. 𝔐, along with representatives of the Western text, add the prepositional phrase ἐν ὑμῖν after προεγράφη, which could be taken with the preceding verb: "clearly portrayed among you as crucified" (NKJV)—or with what follows: "set forth, crucified among you" (KJV). Again, however, the external support is weak.

3:6. As is Paul's custom, the quotation of Gen. 15:6 generally follows the LXX. The sources are compared below:

Gal. 3:6: ['Αβραὰμ] ἐπίστευσεν τῷ θεῷ, καὶ ἐλογίσθη αὐτῷ εἰς δικαιοσύνην.
Gen. 15:6 LXX: καὶ ἐπίστευσεν Αβραμ τῷ θεῷ, καὶ ἐλογίσθη αὐτῷ εἰς δικαιοσύνην.
Gen. 15:6 MT: וְהֶאֱמִן בַּיהוָה וַיַּחְשְׁבֶהָ לּוֹ צְדָקָה

The only difference between the LXX and Paul's quotation is the sequence of the initial subject and verb; but, as our brackets suggest, Ἀβραάμ may be Paul's identification of the subject that follows rather than part of the quotation (Stanley 1992: 235; cf. NIV, NRSV, ESV). The LXX and Paul differ from the MT in shifting the active formulation, וַיַּחְשְׁבֶהָ, "he credited it"—to a passive, ἐλογίσθη, "it was reckoned," perhaps doing so to avoid the ambiguity of what the subject of the Hebrew active verb is. A few interpreters have resolved this ambiguity in favor of "Abraham," arguing that the subject of the first clause should be extended into the second clause; hence, perhaps, the verse would mean something like "he [Abraham] believed the Lord, and he [Abraham] reckoned it [the promise of seed] as justice before him [the Lord]" (Oeming 1983; cf. J. J. Scullion, ABD 5:727). But although this reading of the syntax is possible, it must give a strained interpretation to some of the key words (Schliesser 2007: 115–50).

The appropriateness of Paul's appeal to Gen. 15:6 for his teaching about "justification by faith" is debated. In his commentary on Genesis, for instance, John Walton (2001: 423, 432) claims that "Abram's belief has nothing to do with salvation and nothing to do with a faith system"; Gen. 15:6 is not "a reflection of soteriology proper" but "an *analogy* to salvation" (although, to be fair to Walton, he is working with a very narrow definition of "soteriology": "being saved from sin by the blood of Christ"). Yet Paul seems to say more than this: his appeal to Gen. 15:6 works only if there is significant overlap between the Galatians' (salvific) experience of the Spirit (vv. 1–5) and the "justification" of the Gentiles (v. 8), for which Abraham's "righteousness" serves as the analogy. Can Paul's application of this text to new covenant justification find any basis in the text? Three issues are important.

The first issue is Abraham's faith. The Hebrew verb is a converted perfect form of the verb אָמַן in the Hiphil, which means "to regard something as trustworthy," "to have trust in" or "believe in" (HALOT 64). Other places in the OT where this verb in the Hiphil is followed (as here) by בְּ + a divine name confirm that the idea is trust, reliance, or confidence in the Lord, especially in light of the revelation of his deeds and words (Exod. 14:31; Num. 14:11; 20:12; Deut. 1:32; 2 Kings 17:14; 2 Chron. 20:20; Ps. 78:22, 32; Jon. 3:5). Moreover, the "faith" in these texts often denotes people's fundamental stance vis-à-vis God, with consequences involving inclusion or exclusion from God's promises. So in the case of Gen. 15, while v. 6 follows directly on the renewal of God's promise to Abraham, it expresses a fundamental and characteristic feature of Abraham's response to God. This is not the first time that Abraham has trusted God: his response to God's call in Gen. 12 expresses faith in some sense (and indeed, some interpret וְהֶאֱמִן to mean "he went on believing" [GKC 112e; J. J. Scullion, ABD 5:727; see the discussion in Vickers 2006: 78n12]). But it is, significantly, the first time that this verb is used of Abraham—or anyone else. It is commonplace to claim that the OT idea of "faith" includes what, from the NT perspective, might be labeled a combination of "faith" and "faithfulness." Without quarreling with this claim, we stress that the key texts in which "faith" in God is expressed in the OT certainly include a disposition that would necessarily lead to a life of obedience; but that obedience, in itself, is not clearly included in the "faith" spoken of in these texts.

A second matter of importance in assessing the appropriateness of Paul's appeal to Gen. 15:6 is the nature of the "reckoning/crediting" that this verse refers to. The relevant Hebrew is (1) the verb חָשַׁב with (2) a suffix referring to an impersonal object, followed by (3) the preposition לְ plus (4) an object denoting a person, followed by (5) an adverbial accusative. Thus in Gen. 15:6: he (1) "reckoned" (2) it [e.g., faith] (3) to (4) him [Abraham] (5) [as] righteousness. No text in the MT exactly duplicates this sequence, but several come close.

One set of texts uses the לְ + חָשַׁב combination followed by a personal pronoun but without a concluding impersonal object (e.g., these texts include elements 1, 3, and 4). See, e.g., Lev. 7:18: לֹא יֵחָשֵׁב לוֹ—"it [the meat of the fellowship offering] will not be reckoned to him [i.e., his credit]" (AT); 2 Sam. 19:19 (19:20 MT): אַל־יַחֲשָׁב־לִי אֲדֹנִי—"Let not my lord reckon me as guilty [i.e., on the basis of my wrongdoing]" (AT). Probably to be put in this category is Ps. 32:2, which adds an impersonal object at the end (i.e., elements 1, 3, 4, and 5): אַשְׁרֵי אָדָם לֹא יַחְשֹׁב יְהוָה לוֹ עָוֹן—"Blessed is the man whose sin the Lord does not reckon against him" (AT).

A second set of texts includes an object after the verb plus an impersonal object (e.g., all five elements are found, although the verb is sometimes in the passive rather than the active). See (e.g.) Job 13:24: וַתַּחְשְׁבֵנִי לְאוֹיֵב לָךְ—"You reckon me to be in the category of your enemy," or "consider me your enemy" (NIV; also Job 33:10; cf. also Job 19:11 [with כְ in place of לְ on word for enemy]); Num. 18:30: וְנֶחְשַׁב לַלְוִיִּם כִּתְבוּאַת גֹּרֶן—"and it will be reckoned to the sons of Levi as the product of the threshing floor" (AT; see also Prov. 27:14; Lam. 4:2). Particularly significant, because it also uses חָשַׁב לְ with צדקה, is Ps. 106:31: וַתֵּחָשֶׁב לוֹ לִצְדָקָה—"And it [Phinehas's intervention to prevent Israelite unfaithfulness] was reckoned to him for righteousness" (AT).

In the first set of texts, the "reckoning" involves a creative act whereby something is "credited" in such a way as to produce something else: thus David blesses the man whose sin is not credited against him in such a way as to rescue him from judgment. In the second set of texts, on the other hand, the "reckoning" involves equivalence: something is considered equivalent to something else. If one focuses on the first set of passages, Gen. 15:6 might mean that Abraham's faith led God to consider him to be "righteous," that is, to have the status of righteousness or be in right relation with God (see esp. O. Robertson 1980; Brueggemann 1982: 144–46; Childs 1985: 219–20; Schliesser 2007; Hamilton 1990: 425–26; F. Hahn 1971; Vickers 2006: 83–89; and for the Hebrew construction, see von Rad 1951 [who has been criticized by Oeming 1983 and others]). On the other hand, the second set of texts suggests that Gen. 15:6 might mean that God considered Abraham's faith to be equivalent to "righteousness" (see, e.g., Waltke 2001: 242; Ziesler 1972: 43, 181–85). This latter option should probably be favored, since these texts are semantically closest to Gen. 15:6 (in the sense that one thing is "counted" as something else). This, then, leads to the third issue: what does צְדָקָה mean in Gen. 15:6?

Interpreters who see in Gen. 15:6 a creative act often suggest that צדקה refers to "relationship"; and this view, in turn, is often tied to the broader understanding of צדק terminology in the OT as having to do fundamentally with relationship. However, we have seen some reason to doubt this general approach to צדק language in the MT (see "Justification/Righteousness" in the introduction). "Righteousness" in the OT is oriented more to the idea of standard, to the "right order" that God has built into his creation. "Righteousness" in Gen. 15:6, then, could refer to faith as a particular manifestation of this "right order": Abraham's belief in God would be a "right" act, an instance of righteous behavior. But we have seen that "righteousness" in the OT frequently refers more broadly to the total "right" response to God that he demands of his people, a response that involves, as Keil and Delitzsch (1969a: 213) put it, "correspondence to the will of God both in character and conduct"; see again the introduction). We think this definition best explains Gen. 15:6. God considers Abraham's faith to be equivalent to his having met God's standard of "rightness." Our interpretation is thus similar to Sailhamer's (2009: 244), who argues that God counted Abraham's faith as "the keeping of the law" (see also G. Wenham 1987: 330).

If we are right about the meaning of Gen. 15:6, the text does not directly refer to what Paul would call "justification by faith." Justification, for Paul, is forensic status, and this is not what Gen. 15:6 is saying. On the other hand, if, as we think, Gen. 15:6 is referring to the full conformity to the "rightness" that God expects of his people, then Paul's use of the text is a quite legitimate application. It was Abraham's faith that God regarded as having met the "standard" that God expected of his people. And it is an obvious inference, justified by the close relationship in the OT between a person's "righteousness" and their acceptance before God, that Abraham, having by his faith met God's standard of "rightness," would be then presumed to be "in the right" with God. The "rightness" that God demands of his people, later encoded in the law, has been fully met by Abraham in his simple yet profound act of faith. Abraham's "works," while naturally and inevitably flowing from this faith (cf. James 2:22–23), were not what constituted Abraham's "rightness" in God's eyes. And so Paul uses this central OT statement about Abraham to say to the Galatians, in effect: just as Abraham's full and complete "rightness" before God came by virtue of his faith—and so he was accepted on that basis before God—so your full and complete "rightness" before God (in a distinctively forensic sense) comes by virtue of your faith—"alone."

B. Argument: Abraham's Children through Incorporation into Christ by Faith (3:7–4:7)

The significance of Abraham, and especially the promises made to him, is a recurring theme in this part of the letter ("Abraham" occurs in vv. 7, 8, 9, 14, 16, 18, 29; and reference to the promise[s] in vv. 8, 14, 16, 17, 18, 19, 21, 22, 29). Abraham, of course, plays a foundational role in the unfolding drama of redemption in the OT, so it is not unexpected for Paul to make significant reference to him in his attempt to persuade the Galatians to accept his view of redemptive history. However, most scholars rightly think that Paul's extended references to Abraham are also or mainly polemical, directed against the teaching of the agitators (e.g., Beker 1980: 48; contra Byrne 1979: 148–49). In Paul's day Jews traced their spiritual status to their biological relationship to Abraham, the "father of the nation." John the Baptist reflects this tradition when he warns those who came to him to be baptized, "And do not think you can say to yourselves, 'We have Abraham as our father.' I tell you that out of these stones God can raise up children for Abraham" (Matt. 3:9; see also Luke 3:8; John 8:39–40; Acts 7:2; Rom. 4:1; James 2:21). Paul reflects this tradition by introducing the language of "sons of Abraham" in verse 7—and at the same time strongly suggests that the issue was already a matter of contention in Galatia by introducing the concept without explanation. Jewish appropriation of the Abraham story also tended to highlight his own virtues as an explanation of his foundational role in salvation history, focusing especially on his obedience and even at times claiming that he obeyed the law before it had been given (see the additional note on 3:7–29). The agitators were probably citing the Abraham story in just these terms, arguing that the Galatian Christians could secure their righteous status before God by becoming "sons of Abraham" through the time-honored means of submission to the torah.

Paul responds to this argument in two ways in 3:7–4:7. First, as we have seen already in verse 6, he singles out Abraham's faith as the crucial element in his story. But for Paul it is not only that Abraham was characterized by faith (a point that first-century Jews and the agitators would not contest). What is particularly important for Paul is to show that (1) the "blessing" of faith for righteousness was always intended to include Gentiles (vv. 8, 14; cf. "you all" in v. 26); and (2) faith is in itself adequate to secure this righteous standing with God. The former point is important to establish, but it is not critical to Paul's argument—simply because we have no evidence that the agitators were disputing the *fact* that Gentiles could be included in Abraham's family. The issue, rather, was the *means* by which they could be included. And it therefore is the second aspect of the Abraham argument that is significantly developed. In verses 10–12, Paul is at pains to show that "works of the law"—and by extension, "works" of any kind—add nothing to the adequacy of faith as a means of righteousness (see de Boer 2011: 167). What gives rise to Paul's confidence in the ability of faith "alone" to justify is his insistence that faith brings people into union with Christ (vv. 14, 26–29). It therefore is Paul's conviction about the utter adequacy of *Christ* that engenders his insistence on the adequacy of *faith*.

This argument about theological principle is accompanied by a second argument, which also takes Abraham as its starting point but focuses on salvation history. "Works of the law" are problematic not only because they are "works" (implied in the argument of 3:10–14) but also because they are "of the law." But this law, the torah, came long after Abraham, with whom the fundamental nexus of promise and faith had been established (vv. 15–18). It had very specific purposes, and it was all along intended to be in force only until the Messiah came (vv. 19–25). The law of Moses cannot be a necessary part of Abraham's righteousness—or, by implication, the righteousness of the Galatians. For all its differences from the roughly parallel argument in Rom. 4, then, Gal. 3 follows a similar sequence of argument as does this later text, moving from principial arguments about faith versus works/law (Rom. 4:1–8; Gal. 3:7–14) to salvation history (Rom. 4:9–25; Gal. 3:15–25).

The topic of this section is identified in an inclusio involving the opening paragraph (vv. 7–9) and the climactic paragraph of the section (3:26–29): being "sons/seed" of Abraham (vv. 7, 29), inclusion of Gentiles (v. 8; "you all" in vv. 26, 28), and the importance of faith (vv. 7, 8, 9, 26). Being "sons of Abraham/God" brackets the argument in 3:7–4:7 (see, e.g., Fee 1994: 379). After expounding the positive side of the principle of 2:16 in 3:7–9 (justified by faith), Paul turns in 3:10–14 to the negative side (*not* justified by works of the law). Woven together in this paragraph, as in the preceding one, is the general principle that "faith" is the means of finding righteousness/blessing (vv. 7, 9, 11, 14) *and* that faith also enables the inclusion of Gentiles within the people of God (vv. 8, 14). As Starling (2011: 55) neatly summarizes, Paul here shows that "Israel's inheritance of the Abrahamic promises comes only in Christ, only together with the Gentiles, and only by faith."

In this part of the letter the argument unfolds via a series of linking words. "Faith" in 3:1–6 triggers Paul's focus on the faith of Abraham in 3:7–9. The "blessing" God promises to those who rely on faith (v. 9) becomes the climax of the next paragraph (v. 14) at the same time as that blessing brings up its opposite, the curse (vv. 10, 13). Mention of the "promise of the Spirit" at the end of verse 14 stimulates Paul's discussion of the contrast between promise and law in verses 15–18. Paul's depreciation of the law vis-à-vis the promise in salvation history leads him then to raise the obvious question: "What was the purpose of the law?" (v. 19). Paul insists on the compatibility of law and promise and sustains this consonance by sharply distinguishing the purposes of each: the law acts as the guardian of the people of Israel during their "minority" and locks everyone up under sin (v. 22); the promise (and response to that promise in faith) produces life and righteousness. After being absent for several verses, "faith" emerges again as a key point in verse 22 and is then presented in verses 23–25 as the goal of salvation history.

Verses 26–29 are the rhetorical and theological heart of 3:7–4:7. Paul circles back to the beginning of his argument in verses 7–9, even as he gathers up some of the key themes of verses 15–25. He alludes to the inclusion of Gentiles that was touched on in verse 8 (see also v. 14). Identifying these believers as "sons/children" (υἱοί, *huioi*) harks back to verse 7 ("sons/children of Abraham"). Key language from verses 15–25 is also integrated into this paragraph: "faith" (v. 26; see verses 6, 7, 8, 9, 11, 12, 14, 22, 23, 24, 25), "seed" (v. 29; see vv. 16, 19), "heir/inheritance" (v. 29; see v. 18), "promise" (v. 29; see vv. 8, 16, 17, 18, 19, 21, 22). Central to all these points is the believer's union with Christ, a fundamental building block of Paul's theology. This participationist focus is fully compatible with the traditional interpretation of the "faith" language in this section as having to do with human believing. For it is by believing in Christ that one is joined with him and thus receives all the benefits of that union (see further the additional note on 3:7–4:11).

1. The Blessing of Abraham (3:7–14)

Chapter 3:7–14 is characterized by a series of short theological claims based on quotations of the OT (Silva 2007: 792): Gen. 12:3 (cf. 18:18) in verse 8, Deut. 27:26 in verse 10, Hab. 2:4 in verse 11, Lev. 18:5 in verse 12, Deut. 21:23 in verse 13 (a survey of the texts with relevant Jewish interpretations is found in Oegema 1999: 59–117; see also Wakefield 2003: 66–96; I. Scott 2006: 203–16). Each of these quotations poses problems of interpretation, involving both the meaning Paul intends them to have and the relationship between Paul's application and their original meaning; indeed, perhaps nowhere else in the Letters of Paul do we more insistently confront the hermeneutical issues raised by his use of the OT.

Some interpreters (e.g., Wakefield 2003: 136; cf. also, less elaborately, Boers 2006: 237) discern a chiastic structure:

> Faith (vv. 6, 7–8)
>   Blessing (v. 9)
>   Curse (v. 10)
>   Life (v. 11)
>   Life (v. 12)
>   Curse (v. 13)
>   Blessing (v. 14a)
> Faith (v. 14b)

However, while one can see how this structure has some basis in the text, it is ultimately not satisfactory. Faith, for instance, is important throughout, not just at the beginning and end (see vv. 9, 11–12), while the center of the chiasm, "life," can hardly be identified as the key theme in the section (contra Wakefield 2003: 131–45). A more linear reading of the passage is therefore to be preferred. Though we have argued that verse 6 is more closely attached to verses 1–5 than to verses 7–9, obviously it also serves as the impetus for Paul's crucial claim in verse 7 that it is by faith that a person can be joined to the people of Abraham. Verse 8 carries on the emphasis on faith and introduces a new idea: that the initial promise to Abraham included, according to Gen. 12:3, the Gentiles in its scope. Verse 9 draws a conclusion: it is "those of faith" who receive the blessing of Abraham. These verses do not follow an obvious logical flow; they depend, rather, on a logic rooted in Paul's polemical posture and hint at theological ideas he develops elsewhere.

The juncture between verses 9 and 10 is the hinge in this passage, as the language of blessing (vv. 8–9) gives way, naturally, to its opposite: curse (vv.

10, 13). It is crucial to Paul's argument not only to make the positive point, that one becomes a son of Abraham through faith, but also the negative point, that it is by faith and *not* by the law or the works required by the law. To establish this point, Paul points out that "those who rely on the works of the law" (ὅσοι ... ἐξ ἔργων νόμου, *hosoi ... ex ergōn nomou* [v. 10]; contrasted with οἱ ἐκ πίστεως, *hoi ek pisteōs*, "those who are of faith" [vv. 7, 9]) fall under the curse that inevitably arises by virtue of the human failure to do the law (v. 10). The contrast echoes the basic antitheses that Paul has set up in 2:16, "works of the law" versus "faith in Jesus Christ"; and in 3:2 and 5, "works of the law" versus "hearing accompanied by faith." Verses 11–12 are somewhat of a parenthesis, as Paul pauses to establish the vital point that faith, which Scripture privileges as the means of righteousness, operates in a different sphere than the law. In verse 13 Paul returns to the curse language, proclaiming the good news that Christ redeems from that curse. Verse 14 is an important concluding statement, gathering up elements from verses 7–13 and, with the insistence that the blessing of Abraham is found "in Christ" and is related to the promise of the Spirit, touching on key themes from elsewhere in the letter.

Exegesis and Exposition

[7]Understand, therefore, that it is those who are of faith who are the sons of Abraham. [8]Moreover, the Scripture, foreseeing that God would justify the Gentiles out of faith, announced the gospel ahead of time to Abraham: "In you all the Gentiles will be blessed." [9]So that those who are of faith are blessed together with Abraham, the man of faith.

[10]For as many as are of the works of the law are under a curse; for it is written, "Cursed be anyone who does not remain in all that is written in the book of the law to do them." [11]And it is clear that no one will be justified before God by the law, for "the one who is righteous will live by faith." [12]And the law is not "of faith"; rather, "The one who does these things will live in them." [13]Christ redeemed us from the curse of the law—having become a curse on our behalf, as it is written, "Cursed be anyone who hangs on a tree"—[14]in order that the blessing of Abraham might be given to the Gentiles in Christ Jesus, in order that we might receive the ⌜promise⌝ of the Spirit through faith.

3:7 In this verse Paul connects two points vital to his argument against the agitators: faith as the way in which people are justified (2:16; esp. 3:6; cf. 3:2, 5) and the identity of the "sons of Abraham."[1] The verb at the beginning of the verse (γινώσκετε, *ginōskete*) may be indicative: "you understand that," "you see that" (NRSV; Lightfoot 1881: 137; R. Longenecker 1990: 114); but

---

1. As I explained in the introduction, the gender-specific "sons/sonship" is used here and elsewhere in the commentary in order to preserve the first-century concept of inheritance (almost always involving male offspring) and the relationship between the "sons" and the "Son" (4:5–6). The term refers, of course, to male and female believers equally.

it more likely is imperative: "understand that," "realize that" (most versions; cf. Bruce 1982b: 155; Mussner 1988: 213). I have rendered οἱ ἐκ πίστεως (*hoi ek pisteōs*) quite literally as "those who are of faith" in order to preserve in English some of the connections that Paul makes by using this particular language. The use of the preposition ἐκ in these kinds of expressions suggests that the people referred to are "marked by" or "characterized by" the concept denoted in the object of the preposition (Turner 1963: 260; and see my comments on 2:12). In this context, the idea may, further, have the sense "those who depend on." Here Paul would then be identifying people "whose identity is derived from faith" (Martyn 1997: 299; Hays 2000: 256); and further in this context, "those whose relationship to God is determined by faith" (Rohde 1989: 137).[2] Paul uses an emphatic construction to identify these people "of faith" with the "sons of Abraham": "the ones who are of faith, *these* [οὗτοι, *houtoi*] are the sons of Abraham." A few interpreters have argued that πίστις here refers to God's faithfulness (Howard 1979: 57–58) or Christ's faith, or faithfulness (de Boer 2011: 191–92; he sees a secondary reference to human believing). The latter interpretation would result in a meaning such as "those who are given life on the basis of [Christ's] faith" (Hays 2002: 170–73; he thinks human believing may be a subordinate idea). But this interpretation does not give enough weight to the connection between verses 6 and 7. While verse 7 is a conclusion drawn from several texts in the preceding context, verse 6 is certainly primary; and verse 6 refers unambiguously to the faith of Abraham.[3]

We have suggested that justification/righteousness language (2:16, 17, 21; 3:6) may be Paul's preferred way of referring to the status of Christians before God. Rather clearly, however, the agitators preferred the language "sons/seed" of Abraham because it more clearly tied Christian status to OT and Jewish tradition. "Sons of Abraham" is not an OT expression, where "seed" of Abraham is more common.[4] Some interpreters (e.g., Bruce 1982b: 155) suggest that υἱοί (*huioi*) with the genitive reflects the Semitic idiom "son of" to denote the quality of a person. But it is more likely that the expression denotes people who belong to Abraham and hence participate in his blessing. Paul may use "son" rather than "seed" here because he wants to develop his distinctive notion of "seed of Abraham" (3:16) before applying the language to Christians (as he does in 3:29).

2. As we noted in our comments on 2:16, several interpreters think that Paul might derive the somewhat unusual expression ἐκ πίστεως from Hab. 2:4, ὁ δίκαιος ἐκ πίστεως ζήσεται (*ho dikaios ek pisteōs zēsetai*, the one who is righteous will live by faith), which Paul quotes in 3:11; see esp. Hays 2002: 132; D. Campbell 2009: 859). However, there is reason to doubt this (H. Johnson 1987: 188–93).

3. Dunn (2009: 733) claims that Hays's separation of οἱ ἐκ πίστεως in v. 7 from ἐπίστευσεν (*episteusen*, believed) in v. 6 is "frankly incredible."

4. Note, however, the association of phrases in Ps. 105:6 (104:6 LXX): σπέρμα Αβρααμ δοῦλοι αὐτοῦ, υἱοὶ Ιακωβ ἐκλεκτοὶ αὐτοῦ (*sperma Abraam douloi autou, huioi Iakōb eklektoi autou*, O offspring [seed] of Abraam, his slaves, sons of Jakob, his chosen [*NETS*]).

Verse 7 is therefore transitional, connecting the focus on faith in 2:16–3:6 with the focus on the identity of the "sons of Abraham" in 3:7–29. Yet it is not immediately clear how Paul's "therefore" (ἄρα, *ara*) is justified: that is, how can Paul argue from the fact that Abraham's righteousness was based on faith (v. 6) to the fact that Abraham's *sons*, or descendants, are also those who believe? Abraham's "descendants" are mentioned frequently in Gen. 15, but the context could suggest that these descendants are Abraham's biological offspring; thus Gen. 15:4 promises that "a son who is your own flesh and blood [יֵצֵא מִמֵּעֶיךָ, *yēṣēʾ mimmēʿékā*, one who comes from your loins] will be your heir." Paul's conclusion probably rests on two assumptions, one articulated in the previous verses and one in Gal. 3:8. In verses 1–5 Paul has argued from the Galatians' experience, reminding them that they have been brought into the people of God by their faith. Clearly, then, what was true of Abraham, according to Gen. 15:6, must be true of all who belong to him. In verse 8, on the other hand, Paul argues that the blessing to come to the Gentiles would come "in Abraham," and for him this implies that, at least for the Gentile "sons of Abraham," it would be faith, as it was for Abraham, that secured their new status before God.

3:8   The δέ (*de*) probably marks verse 8 as a continuation or new stage in the argument (on this use of δέ, see Runge 2010: 28–36); compare NLT, "What's more. . . ." Faith as the means by which one enters the people of God is one obvious point of continuity: as οἱ ἐκ πίστεως are "sons of Abraham" (v. 7), so it is ἐκ πίστεως that God justifies Gentiles. The more important development from verse 7 to verse 8, however, is Paul's claim, on the basis of Scripture, that Gentiles are to be included among those who, by faith, make up "the sons of Abraham." This verse therefore combines two of Paul's key concerns in this part of the letter: to show that justification is by faith alone and to show that the gift of justification has been extended to Gentiles (Dunn 1993b: 82–83). Following his pattern of argumentation in verses 7–14, Paul bases his claim in this verse on Scripture. "The Scripture" (ἡ γραφή, *hē graphē*) might refer to a particular text of the OT (Gen. 12:3 later in the verse); Paul often uses γραφή this way (Rom. 4:3; 9:17; 10:11; 11:2; Gal. 4:30; cf. 1 Tim. 5:18; 2 Tim. 3:16; cf. R. Longenecker 1990: 115). However, it is more likely that Paul refers broadly to the teaching of the OT in general (see BDAG 206.2.b.β). The first clause thus makes the general claim that the OT looks ahead to the time when God will justify Gentiles by faith; the second claims that a particular text proclaimed the gospel beforehand to Abraham. The relationship between these clauses is not clear. The first is attached to the second by means of the participle προϊδοῦσα (*proidousa*, from προοράω, *proorao*, see ahead of time; elsewhere in the NT only in Acts 2:25, 31; 21:29). The participle could be causal (NJB; cf. Burton 1921: 160; Mussner 1988: 220) but is perhaps more likely to be a participle of identical action. On this view, the claim of the first clause is essentially repeated in different terms in the second. God's justification of the Gentiles, foreseen by Scripture, is the essential content of the gospel, a gospel that was "announced ahead of time" to Abraham in the promise that "all the nations would be blessed" in him.

The phrase ἐκ πίστεως in the first clause comes first, probably for emphasis: "it is *by faith* that God will justify the Gentiles." The verb "justify" is in the present tense (δικαιοῖ, *dikaioi*), but the tense indicates nothing about the "time" of justification, taking on a future reference from its dependence on the verb προϊδοῦσα. Paul's claim that the Scripture "announced the gospel ahead of time" (προευηγγελίσατο, *proeuēngelisato*; the verb occurs only here in Biblical Greek) is striking because he usually connects the gospel firmly to the new era of salvation history inaugurated by Christ's death and resurrection (e.g., Rom. 1:2–4; 1 Cor. 15:1–4). God's promises to Abraham, Paul affirms, are important announcements of the good news that is bound up with Christ. Among other things, this verse shows that "justification by faith," while not exhausting the meaning of "gospel," is certainly foundational to it.

The text that Paul cites is built mainly on Gen. 12:3. Genesis 12:1–3 is, Waltke (2001: 208) claims, "the thematic center of the Pentateuch." It contains God's call to Abraham to leave his home country and journey to a new land, along with promises that God would make him into a "great nation" and make his "name great," so that he would be a blessing (v. 2). God also promises to bless those who bless Abraham and curse those who curse him, and concludes with the promise that "all the peoples on earth will be blessed through you." Some OT scholars debate about whether this is the best translation of Gen. 12:3b (see the additional note on 3:8), but it is the interpretation explicitly assumed in the LXX, which Paul, as is his habit, quotes here. However, in place of the LXX's αἱ φυλαὶ τῆς γῆς (*hai phylai tēs gēs*), "the peoples [tribes] of the earth," Paul has πάντα τὰ ἔθνη (*panta ta ethnē*), "all the Gentiles." Paul may himself change the wording to suit his argument, since an explicit reference to Gentiles obviously provides better support for his point than the LXX rendering (which translates the Hebrew straightforwardly; Stanley 1992: 237). But it is perhaps more likely that he conflates Gen. 12:3 with other roughly parallel promises in Genesis that refer to "all the nations" (πάντα τὰ ἔθνη, *panta ta ethnē*), as in Gen. 18:18: "Abraham will surely become a great and powerful nation, and all nations on earth will be blessed through him"; Gen. 22:18: "and through your offspring all nations on earth will be blessed, because you have obeyed me"; or Gen. 26:4: "I will make your descendants as numerous as the stars in the sky and will give them all these lands, and through your offspring all nations on earth will be blessed."[5] With its reference specifically to Abraham, Gen. 18:18 may be the most likely source of the language, particularly since

---

5. As in Gen. 12:3, one other text in the book reiterates the promise by using φυλαί, in Gen. 28:14: καὶ ἐνευλογηθήσονται ἐν σοὶ πᾶσαι αἱ φυλαὶ τῆς γῆς καὶ ἐν τῷ σπέρματί σου (*kai eneulogēthēsontai en soi pasai hai phylai tēs gēs kai en tō spermati sou*, and all the tribes of the earth shall be blessed in you and in your offspring [seed] [NETS]). The Genesis promise is also quoted in Acts 3:25, but with the word πατριαί (not found in the Genesis promise texts): καὶ ἐν τῷ σπέρματί σου [ἐν]ευλογηθήσονται πᾶσαι αἱ πατριαὶ τῆς γῆς (*kai en tō spermati sou [en]eulogēthēsontai pasai hai patriai tēs gēs*, and through your offspring [seed] all peoples

the promise in both Gen. 22:18 and 26:4 is attached to Abraham's obedience (the marginal cross-reference in NA[28] cites Gen. 18:18 in italics, indicating that the editors viewed it as the source for Paul's language in Gal. 3:8; and see Koch 1986: 162–63; Silva 2007: 793).

However, the language of "offspring," or "seed" (σπέρμα, *sperma*) in the other two passages (22:18; 26:4) certainly anticipates a key move in Paul's interpretation of this promise (see Gal. 3:16; Watson 2004: 189–90), so it is quite possible that Paul has the general theme of these texts in view. The claim that Gentiles will be blessed "in" Abraham is unclear. The underlying Hebrew may have the sense of "accompaniment": the nations will be blessed via their association with Abraham. And verse 9 could suggest that this was Paul's understanding (Dunn 1993a: 166; Eckstein 1996: 116; H. Johnson 1987: 193–95). However, it is also possible that Paul is already hinting at the direction his argument will take later in the chapter, where Abraham's seed is identified with Christ, and our incorporation into Christ by faith creates our status as "seed of Abraham" (3:16, 26–29; cf. Martyn 1997: 302; Mussner 1988: 222; Heckel 2002: 123; Watson 2004: 187–90). If Paul is hinting at such an idea here, the verse would explain how Paul in verse 14 can claim that the "blessing of Abraham" is found "in Christ Jesus."

3:9 Paul now draws a conclusion (ὥστε, *hōste*, so): "those of faith are blessed together with Abraham, the man of faith." As Martyn (1997: 302) notes, this verse brings together the emphasis on faith from Gen. 15:6 with the promise of blessing from Gen. 12:3 (cf. also Dunn 1993a: 166). This conclusion also shows that, while Paul is obviously concerned to provide a basis in Scripture for the inclusion of Gentiles, his more fundamental concern (in keeping with 2:16; 3:2, 5; and what follows in 3:10–14) is to show that faith is the means by which Jews and Gentiles alike can access the blessing. And finally, this verse also reveals that Paul closely associates, if he does not identify, the "blessing" promised to Abraham and his descendants with justification.

As noted in our comments on verse 8, Paul here interprets the connection between Abraham and "those of faith" ("in you" in the quotation of Gen. 12:3) in terms of association (σύν, *syn*, with). Abraham, in this verse at least, is an example of how the promise of blessing is accessed. Yet Abraham's special role in salvation history means that he is not just any example; his response to God's promise is foundational to the fulfillment of God's purposes and becomes a determinative paradigm for those who follow. Paul's interpretation of the Genesis narrative about Abraham, focused on Gen. 15:6, makes clear that his description of Abraham as πιστός (*pistos*) must be taken to mean "believing" (Bruce 1982b: 157; R. Longenecker 1990: 116) rather than "faithful" (e.g., Hays 2000: 256): hence our translation of the adjective (following NIV) with the substantive expression "man of faith" (also ESV, NJB; "the believer" in NASB and NET; "who believed" in NRSV, CEB).

---

on earth will be blessed). Sanders (1983: 21) thinks that Paul quotes Gen. 18:18 exclusively; S. Hahn (2009: 246–47), on the other hand, thinks that Paul has mainly Gen. 22:16–18 in view.

As we stated in the introduction to verses 7–14, this verse opens a new stage
in Paul's argument. In a sense, this new argument extends through verse 25, as
Paul throughout this section focuses on the inability of the law to secure the
Abrahamic blessing: sonship (George 1994: 227). The contrast in this passage
between "by faith" (vv. 7–9) and "not by works of the law" or "the law" (vv.
10–25) carries forward this same contrast from 2:16 and 3:1–5. The immediate
connection with verses 7–9 is clear enough: reference to the "blessing" that
comes to "those who are of faith" naturally suggests its opposite: "cursing."
Verse 10, with its warning of curse, is paired with verse 13, which proclaims
that Christ has brought redemption from the curse. Between these texts lie
two verses that are also closely related via key vocabulary: ἐκ πίστεως and ζάω
(zaō, live). Verse 14 weaves together many of the key ideas from verses 1–14,
functioning therefore as the conclusion not only to verses 10–14 but also, to
some extent, verses 1–14.

The γάρ (gar, for) in 3:10 introduces the following verses as an explanation of an implied negative counterpart to verse 9: "those who are of faith"
inherit the Abrahamic blessing *and not "those who are of works of the law"*
because . . . . (Mussner 1988: 223). Specifically, Paul claims, first, that Ὅσοι
. . . ἐξ ἔργων νόμου εἰσίν, ὑπὸ κατάραν εἰσίν (hosoi . . . ex ergōn nomou eisin,
hypo kataran eisin): "as many as are out of the works of the law, are under
a curse." The word ὅσοι, in contrast to οἱ [ἐκ πίστεως] in verse 9, expresses
"an element of 'uncertainty' or 'potentiality' regarding the membership" of
this group (Stanley 1990: 498). In effect, Paul is warning the Galatians against
joining this group. Paul uses explicit "curse" language only here and in verse 13
(κατάρα occurs in Heb. 6:8; James 3:10; 2 Pet. 2:14; cf. also Gal. 1:8–9; Rom.
9:3; 1 Cor. 12:3; 16:22). To be "under a curse" is to be under God's judgment
for failure to live up to his covenant requirements. Reference to "curse," and
especially to the blessing/cursing contrast, equally naturally draws attention
to Deut. 27–30, where Moses sets before the people of Israel the alternatives
of blessing for covenant faithfulness and cursing for unfaithfulness (19 of
the 48 LXX references to ἐπικατάρατος [epikataratos, cursed] occur in these
chapters; and 6 of the 46 references to κατάρα [katara, curse]). It is no surprise,
then, that Paul quotes from these chapters in verse 10b. His base text is clearly
Deut. 27:26, the climax and summary of a series of curses for various sins.
Paul's version of the text differs slightly from both the LXX and the MT, but
the changes are insignificant and probably reflect the influence of several other
similar texts in Deut. 27–30 (28:58–61; 29:19–20; 29:28; 30:1, 10; and see the
additional note on 3:10). These texts summarize a key theological thrust of
the book: that continued enjoyment of God's blessing in the land of Israel
depends on the people's faithful obedience to the law of Moses: a failure to
do that law would result in curse and exclusion from the land. Paul connects
this quotation to his claim in the first part of the verse with a γάρ (gar, for),
showing that this quotation explains or grounds that claim.

How to understand the logical relationship between the two parts of 3:10
is quite controversial because the verse is a kind of linchpin in the argument of

Gal. 3. Its interpretation determines—and perhaps more often is determined by—the nature of the larger argument that Paul is making in these verses. At first glance it appears as if the quotation in the second part of the verse proves just the opposite of what Paul says in the first part of the verse (as, e.g., Luther [1963: 252] points out). The quotation from Deuteronomy encourages obedience to the law as a means of avoiding the curse; yet Paul claims that it is just those people who are bound up with law who suffer that curse. The initial response to this problem is to recognize that Paul refers not to people who are doing the law but to people who are ἐξ ἔργων νόμου. As the parallel with οἱ ἐκ πίστεως in verse 9 (and cf. vv. 7, 8, 11, 12) suggests, the phrase refers not to those who "do the law" but to those who are somehow identified with the law.[6] This identification with the law has usually been taken to refer to people who, as Thomas Aquinas puts it, "trust in the works of the Law and believe that they are made just by them" (cf. Riches 2008: 173). The ἐξ would then have the instrumental force that we have identified in this phrase in its earlier occurrences (2:16; 3:2, 5), and the ὅσοι would have the rhetorical effect of warning the Galatians against taking this step. On this reading of the initial clause, the quotation would then function as the statement of a principle that explains why the curse comes on such people: *everything* that is written in the law must be done if the curse is to be avoided.

But one more logical step is necessary if this principle is to ground Paul's claim: the assumption that no one can, in fact, do *everything* that is written in the law. Put in the form of a syllogism, the logic of verse 10 looks like this:

Only those who do everything written in the law will escape the curse (v. 10b).

No one can do everything written in the law (assumed, as in v. 11).

Therefore: No one who depends on doing the law will escape the curse (v. 10a).

This way of making Paul's argument work has been the traditional approach to this verse (e.g., Ambrosiaster [cf. Bray 2009: 16]; Chrysostom, *Comm. Gal.* on 3:10 [*NPNF*[1] 13:26–27]; Luther 1963: 253; Lightfoot 1881: 137; Burton 1921: 164) and continues to be held by a significant number of interpreters (e.g., Bruce 1982b: 159; Mussner 1988: 224–26; R. Longenecker 1990: 117–18; Hübner 1984: 18–19; B. Longenecker 1998: 134–42; Waters 2006: 93–100; Kim 2002: 139–52; and see esp. Schreiner 1984). But a rival interpretation has gained considerable support in recent years.[7] According to this view, "those who are

---

6. Contra Gordon 2009: 244–45, who contests the idea of "depend on" or "rely on" works of the law, as found in most translations (e.g., NIV, NRSV, ESV, NET, NAB, NASB, CEB).

7. Several alternative explanations have been put forward, but the two we examine above are the most popular and the most likely. But we should mention here the view of James Dunn (esp. 1993a: 171–73), which has its starting point in his interpretation of "works of the law" in terms of a law-doing distinctive to Judaism and thus inherently antagonistic to Gentiles. It is, then, those who insist on maintaining these Jewish boundary markers who are missing the true intent

out of the works of the law" refers to people "whose identity is derived from works of the Law" (Hays 2000: 258), and the ἐξ would function as it does in 2:12, where τοὺς ἐκ περιτομῆς (*tous ek peritomēs*) means "belonging to the group of people who are circumcised" (e.g., Gordon 2009). On this view, the phrase refers to the people of Israel in general; and the Galatians are being warned not to join themselves to Israel by their "works of the law." Paul then cites Deut. 27:26 not as a principle that functions in a larger argument but as a reminder of historical fact: Israel did, in fact, incur the curse (of exile) because of the people's failure to remain faithful to God's covenant. Paul's point, then, would be to warn his Galatian readers that, if they try to identify with Israel by taking on the distinctive "markers" of Judaism, "the works of the law," they will themselves fall under the curse that hangs over Israel (see esp. Stanley 1990; J. Scott 1993; N. Wright 1991: 141–48; cf. also Hays 2000: 258; Thielman 1989: 66–69; Braswell 1991: 74–76; Caneday 1989: 192–95; Dumbrell 2000: 23–25, 27–29; and in modified form, Starling 2011: 49–52). This interpretation fits neatly into the more "narratival" reading of Paul's argument in this part of Galatians that has gained support in recent years. Yet we think there are good reasons for preferring the "traditional" view—although modified a bit in terms of the more historical approach (for many of the points we make below, see esp. Schreiner 1984: 154–59; 1985: 257–66).

Particularly important, as we noted above, is the significance given to the phrase ὅσοι ἐξ ἔργων νόμου. The controversial and critical phrase "works of the law," as we have argued above (see the additional notes on 2:16), is a general way of referring to "doing" the law. It cannot be reduced to a way of denoting identification with Israel. Moreover, Paul emphasizes the "works," or "doing," part of the phrase: his quotation from Deuteronomy ends on this note: τοῦ ποιῆσαι αὐτά (*tou poiēsai auta*, to do them). He picks up this emphasis again in verse 12 (Silva 2001: 259–60; Das 2001: 151–53; Gundry 1985: 24–25) and in 5:3: "Now I testify again to every man who wants to be circumcised that he is obligated to do the whole law." Although the "law" is the law of Moses, and much of Paul's argument in Galatians rests on the contrast between the era of the law and the era of fulfillment in Christ,[8] this verse in its context suggests that Paul is also concerned with what is in many ways the more fundamental issue of "doing." The critical point in unpacking

---

and purpose of God's law to include Gentiles. They do not "remain in the law" as reconfigured in Paul's interpretation and thus fall under the curse (cf. also Dunn 1985: 533–34; 1993b: 84–86; Wisdom 2001). Quite inadequate is the view of Stanley (1990) that Paul cites this text simply because it is the only OT verse in which both "curse" and "law" are found (cf. also Sanders 1983: 20–27). Nor does Paul intend to suggest that doing the law is itself sinful (contra, e.g., Schlier 1989: 134–35). For a critique of several of these alternative explanations, see Matlock 2009a.

8. Dumbrell (2000: 23–25), therefore, suggests that the implied premise in Paul's argument is this: "since the era of the Mosaic covenant has now ended." Because the coming of Christ had ended the covenant and its associated provisions for atonement, identification with that covenant by means of "the works of the law" inevitably puts a person under the curse.

the logic of this verse, then, is that "works of the law" at the beginning of the verse and "doing" at the end refer to the same basic thing.

A simple claim that Christ has superseded the law may be adequate for Paul's purposes; but we might expect him to push farther and ask why it was necessary for Christ to supersede the law. In other words, though much of Paul's argument in this letter could be summarized as "doing is wrong because (and when) it is tied to an outmoded law," Paul here suggests that he has moved to a deeper and more universal issue: "the law provides no basis for the blessing because it involves 'doing': a 'doing' that humans find to be impossible." This argument, central to the Reformation soteriology, seems to be present in our text. Another reason to prefer the traditional interpretation is the text that Paul quotes. There are many OT texts, even some from Deut. 27–30 (e.g., 29:27), that refer more clearly and obviously to the curse that fell on Israel. Paul instead selects a text that focuses on individuals, πᾶς ὅς (*pas hos*, everyone who), and on their consistent obedience, ἐμμένει . . . ποιῆσαι (*emmenei . . . poiēsai*, remain [faithful] . . . to do).[9] The quotation serves perfectly as a way of reminding the Galatian Christians of a central principle in the law: that blessing and cursing depend on doing.[10]

But what of the objection that we must read into the text an assumption about the impossibility of fulfilling the law—an assumption that neither Paul's argument in Galatians nor his Jewish milieu can justify? We might first observe that both views require a central element in the argument to be assumed: the unfulfillability of the law on the traditional view, and identification with Israel on the revisionist view. Of course, revisionists would argue that the assumption they make is much more likely than what is required in the traditional view. For the idea that humans could not do the law perfectly was not, it is argued, a common teaching in the Judaism of Paul's day; nor does Paul clearly teach it anywhere else. How could he then assume that his readers would infer it? In response, the repeated mention of "all" in the Deuteronomy texts to which Paul refers provides clear warrant for Paul's inference that "perfect" or "complete" adherence to the law is necessary if the curse is to be avoided. And Paul makes clear that this is, in fact, his view in Gal. 5:3: "Again I declare to every man who lets himself be circumcised that he is obligated to obey the whole law" (Westerholm 2004: 375). Jews would respond that, though they certainly could not perfectly obey the law, the law itself provided the means of atonement for those failures. But arguing from this side of the cross, Paul assumes that Christ has provided the final and only means of atonement (a point that the agitators may also have accepted; and see esp. "The Logic of Paul's Response" in the introduction). This new "either-or" situation created by the climax of salvation history now forces

---

9. The infinitive ποιῆσαι might indicate result but should probably be combined more closely with ἐμμένει in a single verbal idea: "keep on doing" (NET); or better, "remain in by doing."

10. On the theology and significance of blessing and cursing in Deut. 27–30, see esp. Waters (2006: 29–77), who questions whether a single clear tradition can be read from these chapters.

obedience to the law to be perfect if it is to furnish a basis for the blessing (see esp. Das 2003: 36–42).

Paul's polemic against the law as a means of securing the Abrahamic blessing/ justification continues in verses 11–12, which function together to reinforce the point that Paul has made in verse 10. What the law *does* accomplish for those who depend on it for justification (the curse) is the burden of verse 10; what it *cannot* accomplish (justification/life) is the focus of vv. 11–12. The δέ (*de*) therefore is continuative ("now" [NRSV, ESV, NASB, NET] is a good English rendering; contra R. Longenecker [1990: 118], who sees an adversative relationship). The argument of verses 11–12 unfolds in three stages: (1) the law cannot justify (v. 11a) because (2) it is faith that justifies (v. 11b) and (3) the law is not a matter of faith (Stanley 1990: 503). This description of the logic assumes that the main point of Paul's argument comes in verse 11a. The English versions and most interpreters agree, putting verse 11a into a main clause and verse 11b into a supporting clause. The NIV 1984 is representative: "Clearly no one is justified before God by the law, because, 'The righteous will live by faith.'" This understanding of the verse takes the ὅτι (*hoti*, that) at the beginning of the verse as dependent on the δῆλον (*dēlon*, [it is] clear) that comes much later and the second ὅτι as causal: to render literally, "But that no one is justified before God in the law is clear, because . . ." However, it has been argued (esp. by Wakefield 2003: 207–14) that this way of understanding the verse runs afoul of the syntax. He has shown that, in Greek contemporaneous to Paul, the ὅτι that depends on δῆλον usually follows this word (as in the only other parallel text in Paul, 1 Cor. 15:27). He therefore wants to reverse the logical relationship of the two clauses: "But since no one is made righteous by the Law as far as God is concerned, it is clear that *the righteous one will live on the basis of faith*" (CEB; see also Hays 2000: 259; Thielman 1994: 127–28; B. Longenecker 1998: 164; de Boer 2011: 202). However, as Wakefield admits, there are plenty of examples of a ὅτι dependent on a following δῆλον (see, e.g., Josephus, *J.W.* 6.422; *Ag. Ap.* 2.13; and with the cognate verb in Luke 20:37 *v.l.*). And in this context there are compelling reasons to think that we should read the sequence of words in this way. Making the quotation in verse 11b the basis for Paul's assertion in 11a fits the pattern of Pauline assertions of scriptural grounding that we find in this context (vv. 8, 10, 12, 13). Moreover, the logic works better with the traditional arrangement of the clauses. The OT claim that people are justified by faith (11b) constitutes logical grounds for the negative claim that people are not justified in the law. If the relationship of the clauses is reversed, however, the logic is not airtight: the negative claim that people are not justified in the law does not provide clear reason to conclude that they are justified by faith.

As he tends to do in Galatians, where the issue is fundamental and principial (How is one justified?), Paul refers to justification with a timeless present (δικαιοῦται, *dikaioutai*, is being justified). Forensic acquittal, right relationship "before" (παρά, *para*) God, does not come ἐν νόμῳ (*en nomō*), which may

3:11

indicate sphere, "in" the law (Vouga 1998: 74), but more likely is instrumental, "by means of the law" (e.g., Mussner 1988: 228). As we noted above, this clause states negatively what Paul has argued in verse 10. Paul grounds this claim in an "implicit" quotation of Hab. 2:4: ὁ δίκαιος ἐκ πίστεως ζήσεται (ho dikaios ek pisteōs zēsetai, the one who is righteous by faith will live; there is no introductory formula, but it is clear Paul intends the words to be read as a quotation). This is another of the contested examples of Paul's appropriation of the OT that litter this passage. In its original context, Hab. 2:4b appears to be an implicit call on the faithful among the people of Israel to look beyond the confusing and depressing circumstances of their historical situation and to "live" on the basis of steadfast faithfulness in the Lord and his encouraging revelation (cf. vv. 2–3): "the righteous person will live by his faithfulness" (AT). Some interpreters think that Paul uses the text to urge the Christians in Galatia to live out their time on earth by faith/faithfulness (see esp. Wakefield 2003: 167–76).[11] But it is more likely that "live" has deeper theological significance, as in verse 12; and note also verse 21, where "making alive" (ζωοποιέω, zōopoieō) and "righteousness" are closely related (see our comments below and see Hays 2002: 133; Estelle 2009: 132–36).

Paul's omission of any pronoun in his quotation of the verse, in contrast to all known forms of the text, creates a possible ambiguity about whose πίστις (pistis, faith/faithfulness) he might have in mind (see the additional note on 3:11 for the textual situation). A few interpreters think that Paul might be referring to Christ's faith/faithfulness (Howard 1979: 63–64; Matera 1992: 119; de Boer 2011: 202–4) or to both Christ's faithfulness and human faith (Hays 2002: 138–41; Martyn 1997: 314; Roo 2007: 206–7). But πίστις (and the cognate πιστεύω [pisteuō, believe]) has referred to human faith thus far in Gal. 2–3 (see the comments on 2:16 and "The Faith of Christ" in the introduction); and Hab. 2:4b almost certainly also refers to human faith/faithfulness. The form of Paul's quotation also leaves open the question of how to integrate the prepositional phrase ἐκ πίστεως into the sentence (the same issue arises in Paul's quotation of the same half verse in Rom. 1:17b). Most of the English versions and interpreters attach the phrase to the verb: "the one who is righteous will live by faith" (see esp. Cavallin 1978; Yeung 2002: 208–10). But it is also possible that it should be construed with δίκαιος: "the one who is righteous by faith will live" (RSV, NAB; Bruce 1982b: 161; Morris 1996: 104; Eckstein 1996: 143–44; Smiles 1998: 204; Watson 2009: 159–62). Yet another option is that the phrase modifies both ζήσεται and δίκαιος (Dunn 1993a: 174; Martyn 1997: 314; de Boer 2011: 206). Paul's tendency in Galatians to attach ἐκ πίστεως to righteousness language is a strong argument for the second option (2:16; 3:8, 24; 5:5; the phrase never elsewhere modifies "life," although in 2:20 ἐν πίστει modifies ζῶ, zō, live). But it is slightly more likely that we should construe the phrase with ζήσεται. Of course, connecting "by faith" to "live"

---

11. The other occurrences of ζάω (zaō, live [verb]) in Galatians have this "nontheological" sense (Gal. 2:14, 19, 20 [4x]; 5:25).

maintains the connection found in the OT text. And this relationship is also suggested by the fact that ἐν νόμῳ, the functional equivalent to ἐκ πίστεως in verse 11a, modifies the verb (Hays 2002: 133) and that Paul again focuses on "life" in v. 12b (Silva 2007: 801–2).[12]

If we are right about the connection of the words and phrases in Paul's quotation, then his application of the Habakkuk text exhibits that "deepening" of the original sense that is a hallmark of the NT use of the OT (see Moo 1986). In both Habakkuk and Paul, "righteous" (δίκαιος) refers to the person who is in good standing with God, but in Paul the word takes on the specific sense of the forensic status of "being justified." Both Habakkuk and Paul single out πίστις/אֱמֻנָה (ʾĕmûnâ) as the quality that God's righteous people need as they look to the future. And, though many interpreters insist that Paul's "faith" is quite different from the "faithfulness" that Habakkuk calls for, the two words, if not synonymous, nevertheless occupy overlapping semantic ranges. The OT אֱמוּנָה has the basic sense of "firmness," "steadiness of conviction," but this firmness includes the root attitude toward God that Paul designates as faith. The biggest difference between Habakkuk and Paul seems to lie in the use of the verb, "live." Most interpreters of Habakkuk think that this word has the simple sense of "live one's life," while Paul, as we have argued, uses "live" in a soteriological sense. Nevertheless, at the risk of being accused of reading Paul into Habakkuk, there is some basis to think that Habakkuk himself uses the word with a more theological nuance: "experience God's blessing." (On these points, see the additional note on 3:11.) In general, then, Paul's application of Hab. 2:4 is just that: a legitimate reappropriation of a key prophetic witness to the priority of faith in relating to God. Paul is undoubtedly drawn to this passage because, along with Gen. 15:6, it is one of the few OT texts that connect "righteousness" language with faith.

As we noted above, verses 11 and 12 function together to argue for the assertion in verse 11a: "no one will be justified before God by the law." Verse 11b quotes Hab. 2:4 to show that it is "by faith" (ἐκ πίστεως) that a person finds life/justification; verse 12 completes the argument by showing that the law is not "of faith." The δέ (de, but) develops the argument by adding a contrasting point: "a person finds life by faith, *but* the law is not 'of faith.'" The clue to recognizing the logical function of verse 12a, then, is to understand rightly the syntactical significance of the phrase ἐκ πίστεως. Most of the English translations and many of the commentators understand this phrase as referring to the origin of the law: "the law is not based on faith" (NIV; cf. also NRSV, ESV, NET; R. Longenecker 1990: 120; Martyn 1997: 315). This interpretation

3:12

---

12. A few interpreters take an entirely different tack in their interpretation of this text, arguing that, perhaps in Habakkuk but certainly in Paul, δίκαιος refers to the Messiah. See esp. Hays 1989b; 2002: 134–41 (although Hays thinks there is allusion also to people who are righteous by the faith of the Messiah/their own faith); D. Campbell 2009: 683–84 (and 613–16 gives more detail on Rom. 1:17). The fullest treatment is Heliso (2007: focusing on Rom. 1:17), who does not conclude in favor of a messianic interpretation but does argue that scholars should be open to the option.

gives to the preposition ἐκ the meaning we would expect it to have in this kind of sentence. However, it fails to recognize that the phrase of which it is a part—ἐκ πίστεως—has become in this context virtually a technical expression, occurring in verses 7, 8, 9, 11, and 12.[13] Particularly significant is its occurrence in verse 11b, in the quotation of Hab. 2:4. (Indeed, as we have noted, some interpreters think that Paul may derive the phrase from this text.) Paul uses the phrase in verse 12a, then, as a way of contrasting clearly and directly what he is saying here about the law with what Hab. 2:4 says about gaining life: "the righteous person will find life 'through faith'; but the law is not a matter of 'through faith'" (BDAG [285.10] paraphrases "the law has nothing to do with faith"; cf. also Schlier 1989: 134; Dunn 1993a: 175; Hofius 2006: 306). The NLT captures the ultimate point quite well: "This way of faith is very different from the way of law."

As he does throughout this part of Gal. 3, Paul grounds this claim about the law in Scripture. The ἀλλ' (*all'*) is an abbreviation for ἀλλ' ὁ νόμος λέγει (*all' ho nomos legei*), "but the law says: . . ." (Burton 1921: 167). The words Paul quotes are from Lev. 18:5: "Keep my decrees and laws, for the person who obeys them will live by them. I am the Lᴏʀᴅ." Leviticus 18:6–23 comprises a series of specific commandments that have to do with sexual relationships. The series is introduced (vv. 1–5) and concluded (vv. 24–30) by general exhortations to obey the law of God, grounded in warnings about what would happen if the people failed to obey and in promises of what God would do if the people did obey. This context strongly suggests that Lev. 18:5 functions as one of the promises of blessing for obedience. Its crucial phrase וָחַי בָּהֶם (*wāḥay bāhem*; LXX ζήσεται ἐν αὐτοῖς, *zēsetai en autois*) will mean, then, not "live one's life in them" but "find life by [obeying] them" (cf. NAB, NJB, NLT).[14] In other words, the verse intends to motivate Israel to obey God's law by promising them life if they obey. The "life" in view here, as typically in the Pentateuch in these kinds of texts, is the blessing of God's covenant promises: health, fruitful crops, security in the land ("a happy life in which a man enjoys God's bounty of health, children, friends, and prosperity" [G. Wenham 1979: 253]). This verse is frequently quoted later in the OT and in Judaism with a similar purpose; in places it takes on a more spiritual interpretation of "life," even at times explicitly eternal life (see the additional note on 3:12). The widespread use of this verse in Judaism explains how Paul can quote it without introductory

---

13. Those who see in these earlier texts a reference to the faith of Christ find it here again (e.g., Matera 1992: 119; D. Campbell 2009: 863). Howard (1979: 63–64) thinks the reference is the faithfulness of God.

14. See, e.g., G. Wenham 1979: 253; Sprinkle 2008: 28–34. In Lev. 18:5, the בְּ (*bā*) prefixed to הֶם (*hem*, them; i.e., "the decrees and the laws") will therefore be instrumental, "by them"—not locative, "in them." Leviticus 18:29, which comes in a section that forms an inclusio with vv. 1–5, confirms this interpretation. "Being cut off" from the people of Israel is the opposite of the "life" that is promised in Lev. 18:5; clearly, then, that life must be "soteriological" in some sense. For the nonsoteriological view, taking the בְּ as locative, see esp. Kaiser 1994: 1125; and in more detail, Kaiser 1971; also Chibici-Revneanu 2008.

formula and in such abbreviated fashion. And we have every reason to think that he also views the text as a key statement of the conditions that the law sets for the life that it promises: that is, "doing" is the way to life.[15] In contrast, then, to Hab. 2:4, which claims that faith is the means to life, the law, in the words of Lev. 18:5, claims that "doing" (ὁ ποιήσας, *ho poiēsas*, the one who does) brings life. Indeed, these two texts are antithetically parallel:

ὁ δίκαιος ἐκ πίστεως ζήσεται· (*ho dikaios ek pisteōs zēsetai;* the one who is righteous will live by faith; Gal. 3:11, quoting Hab. 2:4).

ὁ ποιήσας αὐτὰ ζήσεται ἐν αὐτοῖς (*ho poiēsas auta zēsetai en autois,* the one who does these things will live in them; Gal. 3:12, quoting Lev. 18:5).

The αὐτοῖς has as its antecedent αὐτά, which in turn has its antecedent in "the decrees and the laws" from earlier in Lev. 18:5. "Doing the commandments" is therefore contrasted with "faith" as the means of life.[16] The implications of this juxtaposition are keenly debated: does Paul claim that the OT teaches two different ways of salvation?[17] Almost certainly not. Rather, he may view Lev. 18:5 as a summary of the particular "covenant life" promised to Israel, while Hab. 2:4 states the overall OT teaching about finding true life with God (e.g., Kline 2000: 321–26; Horton 2007: 80–101). Or he may think that Lev. 18:5 is a valid promise of true life with God, which because of human sin, however, can never come to pass (e.g., Ridderbos 1975: 134).

In any case, verse 12, while tied logically to verse 11, also has an important relationship to verse 10. In both verses Paul quotes texts that emphasize that the law makes promises and issues threats on the basis of "doing." Dependence on doing the law brings not "life," but a curse, because (1) principially, life comes by faith (v. 11), and (2) practically the law cannot be done (v. 10). This argument is deployed to convince the Galatians not to succumb to the agitators' insistence that they add law observance to their faith in Christ. Faith, Paul implies, is the only instrument by which justification/life can be attained: whether at the beginning of one's Christian experience or at its end. And, though in this context directed explicitly against doing the law, the torah, Paul's argument in these verses transcends the particular circumstances of his

15. See esp. Sprinkle 2008: 136–42; Gathercole 2004b; also Watson 2006: 101. Other interpreters think that Paul quotes Lev. 18:5 simply as a way of summing up the "torah way of life," that is, that torah regulates life in Israel (e.g., Dunn 1993a: 175; Avemarie 2005: 127–41; Willitts [2003] argues that Paul uses the text to describe the pre-Christian situation of Israel, in contrast to the new era of faith [Gal. 3:11; cf. also Garlington 1997: 103–8]). Still less likely is the view that Paul quotes this text as his opponents twist it in a legalistic direction (e.g., Burton 1921: 165–68; Fuller 1980: 98–99).

16. It is also possible, of course, if ἐκ πίστεως in v. 11 modifies δίκαιος, that Paul parallels "righteous" in v. 11 and "will live" in v. 12. As we noted in our comments on v. 11, the difference is not significant, since in this context Paul clearly views justification and life as closely related, if not identical (see, e.g., Bruce 1982b: 163).

17. For various approaches dealing with alleged "contradiction" between these texts, see J. Vos 1992; Martyn 1997: 328–34; Dahl 1977: 169–74; Gignac 1994.

situation. For his polemic is not only directed to the law but also to "doing"; indeed, one of the reasons (although not the only one) why Paul denies that the law can lead to justification is precisely because it is, by its nature, something to be "done." The Reformers, therefore, were entirely justified to find in Paul's argument here a fundamental and universally valid principle about the exclusive value of believing versus doing.

3:13 After the relatively self-contained argument against justification by the law in verses 11–12, verse 13 returns to the main line of Paul's argument from verse 10 (e.g., Waters 2006: 103–5). The return to the language of curse (v. 10) and blessing (v. 9) in the single sentence that comprises verses 13–14 makes this clear. The asyndeton (e.g., lack of an explicit connection) also suggests a break between verses 12 and 13, at the same time as it draws attention to this sentence (R. Longenecker 1990: 121).[18] And the reference to Christ, the first since verse 1, also suggests a certain emphasis. "The curse of the law" (τῆς κατάρας τοῦ νόμου, *tēs kataras tou nomou*) refers to the situation that Paul has warned about in verse 10: that people who depend on "the works of the law" for their justification will find themselves "under a curse" (ὑπὸ κατάραν, *hypo kataran*), the curse that is pronounced over those who fail to do all that the law demands.[19] The curse in Scripture refers to God's judgment, a judgment that takes the form of exclusion from God's land and God's people (Wisdom 2001: 43–62). From this curse, Paul says in verse 13, Christ "redeems us" (ἐξηγόρασεν ἡμᾶς, *exēgorasen hēmas*). The verb ἐξαγοράζω is a compound form of the verb ἀγοράζω (*agorazō*). The simple verb means "to buy" and, when compounded with ἐκ, has the sense "buy out of," or "redeem." The compound verb occurs only here and in the similar Gal. 4:5 in the NT in this sense (in Eph. 5:16 and Col. 4:5, it probably means "buy up" [Moo 2008: 327–28]). The word probably conjures the widespread ancient practice of manumission, whereby slaves could purchase their freedom (F. Büchsel, *TDNT* 1:125–27). So, Paul asserts, Christ has liberated "us" from our bondage to the curse pronounced by the law.

After this main clause, the sentence comprising verses 13–14 consists of four further subordinate clauses:

> Χριστὸς ἡμᾶς ἐξηγόρασεν ἐκ τῆς κατάρας τοῦ νόμου
> γενόμενος ὑπὲρ ἡμῶν κατάρα,
> ὅτι γέγραπται· ἐπικατάρατος πᾶς ὁ κρεμάμενος ἐπὶ ξύλου,
> ἵνα εἰς τὰ ἔθνη ἡ εὐλογία τοῦ Ἀβραὰμ γένηται ἐν Χριστῷ Ἰησοῦ,
> ἵνα τὴν ἐπαγγελίαν τοῦ πνεύματος λάβωμεν διὰ τῆς πίστεως.

18. As Runge (2010: 20–23) points out, asyndeton is the "unmarked" choice, used when an author sees no need to specify a relationship between clauses.

19. Dunn (1993a: 177–78) suggests that the "curse of the law" might refer to the curse of being outside the law, outside the covenant. However, although curse certainly suggests the notion of judgment by exclusion, the curse of the law in v. 13 must be correlated with the reason for the curse in v. 10: disobeying the law. Nor is the curse pronounced on "legalism" (contra Burton 1921: 168–70).

Christos hēmas exēgorasen ek tēs kataras tou nomou
genomenos hyper hēmōn katara,
  hoti gegraptai: epikataratos pas ho kremamenos epi xylou,
  hina eis ta ethnē hē eulogia tou Abraam genētai en Christō Iēsou,
  hina tēn epangelian tou pneumatos labōmen dia tēs pisteōs.

Christ redeemed us from the curse of the law
  by becoming a curse for us—
    for it is written: cursed be anyone who hangs on a tree—
  in order that the blessing of Abraham might come to the Gentiles
    in Christ Jesus,
  in order that we might receive the promise of the Spirit through
    faith.

One of the most controversial matters in these clauses is the series of three first-person plural pronouns or verbs: Christ redeemed "*us*" (ἡμᾶς), by becoming a curse for "*us*" (ἡμῶν), in order that the blessing of Abraham might come to the Gentiles, in order that "*we*" might receive (λάβωμεν) the promise of the Spirit. At first sight it might be hard to see why there would be any controversy: Paul consistently uses the first-person plural throughout the sentence, and as is usually the case in Paul, we should assume that he intends to include himself and his readers. On this view, the pronouns refer throughout to Christians in general (this is the majority view; see, e.g., Bruce 1982b: 166–67; Martyn 1997: 334–36; Dunn 1993a: 176–77; Kuula 1999: 46–57; Waters 2006: 100–103; Das 2001: 228; de Boer 2011: 209; F. Büchsel, *TDNT* 1:450–51). Yet there is some reason to think that Paul restricts the scope of the pronouns, referring at least in verse 13, to Jewish Christians (see, e.g., Lightfoot 1881: 139; Betz 1979: 148; Braswell 1991: 74–75; N. Wright 1991: 151–53; Donaldson 1986: 95–98; Kruse 1996: 86–89).[20] Several lines of evidence need to be considered.

First, the argument from the first-person form of these verses is double sided. On the one hand, Paul has explicitly used first-person plurals in Galatians to refer to Jewish Christians in distinction from Gentile Christians (Gal. 2:15–16). Indeed, some interpreters think that in Galatians Paul consistently uses the first-person plural to refer to Jews or Jewish Christians (e.g., R. Longenecker 1990: 229; Witherington 1998: 369; Garlington 2003: 221). Such a consistency in usage would be very helpful, providing an objective basis on which to decide to whom Paul is referring. Unfortunately, Paul's pronouns defy any such simple classification: either here in Galatians or elsewhere (see the first additional note on 3:13). Nevertheless, the first-person plural pronouns in verse 13 could certainly reflect the same referent as the last occurrence of first-person plural forms in 2:15–16. And this possibility is strengthened by the fact that the first-person plural forms

---

20. A few interpreters have suggested that the reference is exclusively to Gentiles (Gaston 1987: 82; Dalton 1990: 38; Eisenbaum 2009: 218). But this view depends on a very unlikely reading of Paul's teaching about the curse and the law of Moses.

in 3:23–25 may also refer to Jews. On the other side of the argument, however, 2:15–16 is quite a distance removed from 3:13: would the reader (or hearer) of Galatians have identified the "us" in the latter text with the Jewish Christians of 2:15–16? It could be argued that they would more naturally assume that Paul is referring to himself and his readers and, by implication, all Christians. This argument is strengthened by verse 14b: "that we might receive the promise of the Spirit." Receiving the Spirit here forms an inclusio with 3:1–5, where Paul refers to the Galatians' experience of the Spirit. The "we" in verse 14b, therefore, must include Gentile believers. Yet in turn this argument is blunted by the claim that Paul may deliberately move from the differentiation of "us" and the Gentiles to the inclusive "we" of all believers (e.g., Dumbrell 2000: 27).

A second line of evidence is the shift in the sentence from "us" in verse 13 to Gentiles in verse 14a: "Christ redeemed *us*, by becoming a curse for *us*, in order that the blessing of Abraham might come to *the Gentiles*." The "us" (ἡμᾶς) in verse 13a and "the Gentiles" (τὰ ἔθνη) in verse 14a are placed early in their respective clauses, probably for emphasis and perhaps to contrast them. The referents of the pronouns in verse 13 must then be a different group than the Gentiles of verse 14a. However, this argument is mitigated by the fact that, as we have seen, the "we" in 14b is difficult to restrict to Jewish Christians. To put it another way, the emphatic reference to Gentiles in 14a can be explained either because Paul wants to contrast them with Jewish Christians or because he wants to single out Gentiles from among Christians in general.

Third, the sequence of teaching in 3:13–14 must be compared with passages elsewhere in Galatians, and especially with 4:4–5:

Galatians 3:13–14	Galatians 4:4–5
	God sent his Son (4b)
1. Christ redeemed (ἐξηγόρασεν) *us* from the curse of the law	in order to redeem (ἐξαγοράσῃ) *those under the law* (5a)
2. by becoming (γενόμενος) a curse for *us*	born (γενόμενον) of a woman, born (γενόμενον) *under the law* (4c)
3. in order that the blessing of Abraham might come to *the Gentiles*	
4.	in order that *we* might receive sonship. (5b)
5. in order that *we* might receive the promise of the Spirit	And because *you* are sons, God has sent the Spirit of his Son into *our* hearts . . . (6a)

These passages are related by means of common vocabulary (the verb ἐξαγοράζω occurs only in these two texts in the NT with the sense "redeem"; the participle γενόμενος) and similar themes: Christ's identification with the plight of humans to rescue them, culminating in the gift of the Spirit (3:14b; 4:6; see esp. Hays 2002: 76–77, 108–11).[21] The "law" in 4:4–5 is the law of Moses,

21. Elsewhere in Paul we also find this pattern of identification of Christ with Jews for the sake of their salvation and, ultimately, for the blessing of Gentiles. Note Rom. 15:8–9a: "For I tell

and "those under the law" must therefore refer to Jews, the people who were given the law. Similarly, those who need to be rescued from "the curse of the law" would also be Jews. Yet while Paul certainly views the Mosaic law as given exclusively to Israel (see, e.g., the implications of Rom. 2:12–13; 1 Cor. 9:20–22), he also implies that Gentiles somehow share in the condition of Jews under the law (see the implications of Rom. 6:14, 15; 7:4; see, e.g., Donaldson 1986: 103–4; Smiles 2008: 4). It therefore is possible that "those under the law" in 4:5 and those suffering the "curse of the law" in 3:13 could include Gentile Christians. That this is possible is suggested also by the way Paul in both texts makes clear that Christians in general ("we" in 3:14b and 4:5b) experience the benefits of Christ's redemptive work (Westerholm 2004: 302–3).

The arguments are finely balanced. But the balance very slightly tilts toward the inclusive view. Since Paul views the extension of the blessing of Abraham to the Gentiles to be contingent on the redemption he describes in verse 13, a reference to the redemption of Jews, or Jewish Christians, almost requires that we read the sequence in these verses in a historical way: God redeems Israel from the curse of the law, manifested in exile, in order that he might extend his blessing to Gentiles. Of course, this way of reading verses 10–14, as well as significant other parts of Paul's Letters, is quite popular (see esp. N. Wright 1991: 137–56). Yet it does not fit this context especially well. In this particular context, as we have seen, Paul's purpose is to warn the Gentile Christians in Galatia about depending on their doing of the law for their justification (v. 10). It therefore makes slightly better sense to think that Paul assures them in verse 13 that they have themselves been definitively rescued (the aorist ἐξηγόρασεν) from the curse that stands over all human beings by virtue of their failure to meet the demands of God, expressed in its clearest form in the law of Moses. As he does elsewhere, then, Paul implicitly associates the Gentiles with the plight of Israel that has resulted from its failure to obey the law of Moses (Westerholm 2004: 415–17; Starling 2011: 203, 211). From that plight God has redeemed both Jew and Gentile by means of his Son's identification with that plight.

This identification is expressed in the first subordinate clause, introduced by the participle γενόμενος. The participle is instrumental, referring to the means by which God has redeemed his people: Christ became "a curse for [ὑπέρ, *hyper*] us." The preposition ὑπέρ means basically "on behalf of," but in certain contexts what is done "on behalf of" takes the form of doing something "in place of." This substitutionary idea is likely present here, since Christ is pictured as identifying with the plight of those he redeems (Harris 2012: 214; A. Robertson 1934: 631; Wallace 1996: 387). It is not that ὑπέρ here *means* "in place of"; it is rather that Christ's work "on our behalf" involves the specific mechanism of identification with us.

---

you that Christ has become a servant of the Jews on behalf of God's truth, so that the promises made to the patriarchs might be confirmed and, moreover, that the Gentiles might glorify God for his mercy" (for this reading of the syntax, see Moo 1996: 875–77). The similarity in language suggests to some that Paul might be quoting a tradition in Gal. 3:13–14 (R. Longenecker 1990: 121–22), but this is not clear.

Paul justifies (ὅτι, *hoti*, for/as) his claim that Christ became a curse for us by quoting yet another scriptural passage, introduced with his typical formula, "it stands written" (γέγραπται, *gegraptai*). He quotes a clause from Deut. 21:22–23, a passage that refers to the custom of exposing a criminal who has been put to death by hanging them on a pole. According to verse 23, "You must not leave the body hanging on the pole overnight. Be sure to bury it that same day, because anyone who is hung on a pole is under God's curse. You must not desecrate the land the LORD your God is giving you as an inheritance." In Deuteronomy, hanging on a pole is not the means of death, but the means of displaying the condemned person's body after death. However, there is evidence from the Jewish world of Paul's day that the text was being interpreted as a reference to execution itself and indeed execution by crucifixion (see the second additional note on 3:13). Paul appears to apply the verse in this sense, since the NT elsewhere uses the language of "hanging on a tree" (κρεμάννυμι + ξύλον, *kremannymi* + *xylon*) in this way (Acts 5:30; 10:39; "hang" is also used with reference to the crucifixion in Luke 23:39). The body that was hung on a pole was under a curse because of the manner in which the person had died: executed for a heinous sin against the law of God (Craigie 1976: 285). Paul likewise implies that Christ has suffered the curse in connection with being hung on a tree because of sin—but because of the sins of others, not his own. As he puts it in 2 Cor. 5:21: "God made him who had no sin to be sin for us, so that in him we might become the righteousness of God." Christ suffered exclusion from the people of God and, more terribly, separation from God the Father himself (Mark 15:34), so that those people who had been excluded because of their sin could be brought back in again.

3:14   Paul completes his sentence with two purpose clauses (ἵνα . . . ἵνα, *hina* . . . *hina*, in order that . . . in order that) that bring to a climax two of the key themes of 3:1–9: the extension of the blessing of Abraham to the Gentiles (vv. 7–9) and the gift of God's Spirit as evidence that the new age of redemption has arrived (vv. 1–6). At the same time, the verse again emphasizes that faith is the means by which these blessings are received and, anticipating a key idea to come, that all this takes place "in Christ."

We have labeled the two clauses "purpose" clauses; but this may be one of the many places where ἵνα combines the ideas of purpose and result (on this overlap, see, e.g., Moule 1959: 142–43). The relationship between these two clauses is not clear. The second may depend on the first, in which case Paul would be asserting that God has extended the Abrahamic blessing to the Gentiles with the purpose that, or the result that, Christians might experience the Spirit (Lightfoot 1881: 140; Caneday 1989: 205–6). Yet it is more likely that the two clauses are coordinate, each of them expressing a purpose/result of God's redemptive work in Christ (the majority view; see, e.g., R. Longenecker 1990: 123; de Boer 2011: 214).[22]

22. Other places where Paul uses two ἵνα clauses with no intervening main clause or conjunction cannot decide the issue here. In three texts, the second clause appears to build on the

The phrase ἡ εὐλογία τοῦ Ἀβραάμ (*hē eulogia tou Abraam*, the blessing of Abraham) is a general way of referring back to the blessing "associated with Abraham" that Paul discusses in verses 8 and 9; there is therefore no reason to think that Paul has a specific OT verse in mind (e.g., Gen. 28:4, where τὴν εὐλογίαν Αβρααμ occurs). This blessing, as verse 8 reveals, is specifically interpreted by Paul in this context in terms of justification. As we noted above, Paul emphasizes εἰς τὰ ἔθνη (*eis ta ethnē*, to the Gentiles) by putting it first in its clause (the preposition εἰς functions like a dative [BDF §207; Turner 1963: 253]). This emphasis matches Paul's concern in verses 7–9 to show that the Abrahamic promise of blessing included, from the first, the Gentiles. If Paul has all Christians in view in verse 13, then the focus on Gentiles in this verse is because of his concern to make clear (not least to the Galatians themselves) that God has included Gentiles within the scope of Abraham's blessing. More significant for Paul's argument, however, and too easily overlooked, is the qualification of the way in which this blessing is extended to the Gentiles: ἐν Χριστῷ Ἰησοῦ (*en Christō Iēsou*). This phrase is locative ("in Christ Jesus" [NRSV, ESV, NASB, NET]), not instrumental ("by/through Christ Jesus" [NIV, NLT, NAB, CEB]; C. Campbell 2012: 82). Gentiles experience the blessing of Abraham not by identification with Israel through the law but simply and definitively by their relationship to Christ Jesus.[23]

The phrase διὰ πίστεως (*dia pisteōs*, through faith) in the second clause corresponds, by virtue of both its placement in the clause and by its meaning, to ἐν Χριστῷ Ἰησοῦ in the first clause. If the blessing of Abraham comes to Gentiles "in Christ Jesus," then "the promise of the Spirit" is given "by faith." Paul's association of union with Christ and faith as the way in which all God's blessings are enjoyed (e.g., 3:26–29) makes clear how Paul ultimately insists that both the Abrahamic blessing and the Holy Spirit are experienced both "in Christ" and "by faith." "Faith" again refers to the Christian's faith and not the "faith of Christ" (contra, e.g., Matera 1992: 120–21; Hays 2000: 261 [though both see some reference to the faith of Christians also]). The prepositional phrases concluding each of these clauses are therefore fundamental to Paul's argument (Mussner 1988: 235) and echo a similar emphasis in 3:26: "*In Christ Jesus* you are all sons of God *through faith*."

What we receive by faith is "the promise of the Spirit." The "we" (signaled by the first-person plural form of the verb λάβωμεν [*labōmen*, we might receive]) refers to Christians generally (as most interpreters agree [e.g., Hays 2000: 262]; see, however, N. Wright 1991: 154) and particularly to the Galatian Christians, as Paul here returns to the theme of 3:1–5. The Galatians have experienced the Spirit by means of "hearing accompanied by faith" (3:2, 5);

---

former (Rom. 15:31–32; 1 Cor. 4:6; 2 Cor. 11:12); but in three others, the clauses appear to be parallel (2 Cor. 9:3; 12:7; Col. 4:3–4); cf. also Gal. 4:5, where the issue is the same as in 3:14.

23. Hodge (2007: 104) suggests that Paul may be paraphrasing Gen. 22:18 (addressed to Abraham): "and through your seed all nations on earth will be blessed, because you have obeyed me" (NIV margin). In place of "seed," Paul has put Christ, in anticipation of his claim in Gal. 3:16 that the seed of Abraham *is* Christ.

so they have "received" "the promise of the Spirit" by faith. Most interpreters think that the genitive τοῦ πνεύματος (*tou pneumatos*, of the Spirit) is epexegetic, an interpretation that appears to be reflected in several English translations that render "the promised Spirit" (e.g., ESV, NLT, NJB; the phrase is found in Moule 1959: 176; and cf. Eph. 1:13: ἐσφραγίσθητε τῷ πνεύματι τῆς ἐπαγγελίας τῷ ἁγίῳ [*esphragisthēte tō pneumati tēs epangelias tō hagiō*, you were sealed with the Holy Spirit of promise]). But the genitive might also be subjective: "the promise [perhaps, that is, the inheritance—cf. vv. 15–18] that is mediated to us by the Spirit" (Fee 1994: 394; Byrne 1979: 156). The association of "promise" with "Spirit" reflects the eschatological nature of the early Christian movement: the evident presence of God's Holy Spirit in power among the believers constitutes clear evidence that the "last days" have dawned (Acts 1:4; 2:33, 39). Most scholars think that the parallelism of the clauses suggests that "the promise of the Spirit" is identical to, or at least forms a part of, "the blessing of Abraham"; see, for example, Hays (2000: 261): "Paul regards the promise of Abraham as being fulfilled in the church's experience of the Holy Spirit." But it is probably better to view "the blessing of Abraham" (which, as we have seen, Paul appears to identify basically with justification) and "the promise of the Spirit" as related but separate gifts of the new covenant era (Kwon 2004: 107–17; see esp. C. Lee 2009: 302–10). The Spirit as the promised blessing of new covenant fulfillment is a significant prophetic theme (e.g., Joel 2:28–32; Ezek 36:22–32). Isaiah 44:3 might be especially important since it brings together the words "blessing" and "Spirit": "For I will pour water on the thirsty land, and streams on the dry ground; I will pour out my Spirit on your offspring, and my blessing on your descendants" (Hays 2000: 261; Waters 2006: 110–11; Harmon 2010: 146–50; Morales 2009; C. Lee 2009: 188–91, 197–98, 302–5). With the reference to the Spirit at the climax of this section of the letter, Paul also anticipates the important argument about the role of the Spirit in the life of new covenant believers (5:13–6:10; see again C. Lee 2009: 299–301).

Additional Notes

3:7–29. Abraham was naturally a focal point of Jewish interpretation. The traditions emphasize especially his true piety, as evidenced in his obedience and even in his conformity to the law. "Abraham was perfect in all his deeds with the Lord, and well-pleasing in righteousness all the days of his life" (Jub. 23.10); Abraham "did not sin against you" (Pr. Man. 8); "no one has been found like him in glory" (Sir. 44:19). Abraham's faithfulness amid his trials (preeminently his "sacrifice" of Isaac [Gen. 22]) was especially important: Jewish tradition tends to locate Abraham's "justification" after and in response to trials (Gathercole 2002b: 236–38). On the basis of Gen. 26:5—"Abraham obeyed me and did everything I required of him, keeping my commands, my decrees and my instructions"—it was sometimes taught that Abraham had obeyed the law before it was given (m. Qidd. 4.14; Sir. 44:19–21; 2 Bar. 57.2). For surveys of Abraham in Jewish literature, see Calvert-Koyzis 2004: 6–84; Harrisville 1992: 47–135; Yeung 2002: 232–64.

3:7–4:11. The undeniable importance and even centrality of incorporation into Christ in this section (esp. in vv. 26–29) is the starting point for Richard Hays's influential reading of this passage (first published in 1983 with a considerably reworked new edition in 2002). Following the general structural interpretation of narrative advanced by A. J. Greimas, Hays argues that an "actantial" style narrative, which focuses on the relationships among agents and objects in a story, provides the "logic" that undergirds this passage. This narrative logic surfaces most clearly in the roughly parallel 3:13–14 and 4:3–6, where Christ is put in the role of the "subject" of the story: the one who receives a mandate from the "sender" (God) to carry out a particular mission. This mission is carried out in the face of an "opponent" (the law) and by aid of a "helper" (faith). Specifically, Hays claims that "faith" "is the power or quality which enables [Christ] to carry out his mandate" (2002: 115). And when 3:21–22 is allowed to make its contribution to this narrative logic, it becomes clear that this "faith" is not something that humans do, but something that Christ, the "subject" of the narrative, does. The focus of the section, then, is not on how people must believe to attain the blessing of Abraham, but on the need for people to be incorporated into Christ's story of believing/faithfulness as the means of securing this blessing. Interpreting Paul's references to "faith" in this section, then, as having to do with "the faith of Christ" (vv. 8, 9, 11, 12, 14, 22, 23, 24, 25, 26) is to some extent the basis for and to some extent the result of this reading of the chapter.

This analysis of the role of faith in Gal. 3–4 faces an obvious stumbling block: At the beginning of this section, Paul highlights Abraham's "believing" (v. 6). Yet Hays actually argues that these opening verses buttress his argument. For the critical phrase οἱ ἐκ πίστεως (v. 7) must be interpreted not in light of v. 6 but in light of the quotation of Hab. 2:4 in v. 11 and the phrase ἀκοὴ πίστεως in 3:2 and 5. The latter means "the faith message," and Paul reads Hab. 2:4 as a reference to the faith of the Messiah. Here again, then, "faith" is (mainly) "the faith of Christ." In fact, Hays argues, only by reading vv. 6–9 with a focus on what Christ has done (rather than what we do) can it be reconciled with the obvious participationist focus of vv. 26–29. The whole passage needs to be read in terms of this focus on our participation in what Christ has done; and when it is, all its diverse elements fall into place.

Hays's reading of Gal. 3–4 as a story in which God initiates a mission carried out by Christ on behalf of his people is surely, in general, unobjectionable (yet for some critical assessment of the function of narrative in Paul, and esp. the narrative of Jesus's story, see Watson 2002; and also Matlock 2002: 47–50). But the conclusions that Hays draws from this analysis for the meaning of "faith" do not follow. First, the critical move from "faith" as a generalized "helper" to faith as specifically the "faith of Christ" is not sufficiently grounded. Without commenting on the usefulness of the Greimas analysis of narrative, one must surely allow for the "helper" role in stories to take a wide variety of forms, depending on the circumstances. There is no reason, even if we follow the basic Greimas scheme, that human belief in Christ could not function in this role. To be sure, Hays claims that Gal. 3:21–22 requires that this "helper" be Christ's faith. But this point is asserted rather than argued, and the text is not as straightforward as he suggests (see the commentary on these verses). Second, Hays's interpretation of 3:7–9 is particularly problematic. His claim that οἱ ἐκ πίστεως refers (mainly) to "those who share the faith of Christ" rests on the very debatable (and in our view, quite improbable) claim that ἀκοὴ πίστεως means "the faith message" (with a deemphasis on human believing) and that v. 11, with its quotation of Hab. 2:4, refers to faith of the Messiah. Yet one would have thought that πίστις in v. 7 naturally refers to the same thing as its cognate verb in v. 6: human (in this case Abraham's) "believing." Finally, third, the claim that an interpretation of these verses in terms of human believing stands in conflict with the participationist focus of vv. 26–29 ignores the many ways in which exegetes and theologians over the centuries have, in fact, integrated these two perspectives.

We therefore do not think that Hays has made a convincing case for his particular narrative reading of this part of Galatians. Of course, figuring out just what πίστις Χριστοῦ means involves many other considerations (see our treatment of "The Faith of Christ" in the introduction). But we do not think that an alleged narrative substructure can be used to support a "faith of Christ" reading.

3:8. Paul's quotation reflects a series of passages in Genesis, all of which express God's promise that he would "bless" other peoples/nations in or through Abraham:

Gal. 3:8b: ἐνευλογηθήσονται ἐν σοὶ πάντα τὰ ἔθνη
"All the Gentiles will be blessed in you." (AT)

Gen. 12:3: וְנִבְרְכוּ בְךָ כֹּל מִשְׁפְּחֹת הָאֲדָמָה (MT)
καὶ ἐνευλογηθήσονται ἐν σοὶ πᾶσαι αἱ φυλαὶ τῆς γῆς (LXX)
"All the peoples of the earth will be blessed in you." (AT)

Gen. 18:18: וְנִבְרְכוּ בוֹ כֹּל גּוֹיֵי הָאָרֶץ (MT)
καὶ ἐνευλογηθήσονται ἐν αὐτῷ πάντα τὰ ἔθνη τῆς γῆς (LXX)
"All the nations of the earth will be blessed in him." (AT)

Gen. 22:18: וְהִתְבָּרֲכוּ בְזַרְעֲךָ כֹּל גּוֹיֵי הָאָרֶץ (MT)
καὶ ἐνευλογηθήσονται ἐν τῷ σπέρματί σου πάντα τὰ ἔθνη τῆς γῆς (LXX)
"All the nations of the earth will be blessed in your seed." (AT)

Gen. 26:4: וְהִתְבָּרֲכוּ בְזַרְעֲךָ כֹּל גּוֹיֵי הָאָרֶץ (MT)
καὶ ἐνευλογηθήσονται ἐν τῷ σπέρματί σου πάντα τὰ ἔθνη τῆς γῆς (LXX)
"All the nations of the earth will be blessed in your seed." (AT)

Gen. 28:14: וְנִבְרְכוּ בְךָ כָּל־מִשְׁפְּחֹת הָאֲדָמָה וּבְזַרְעֶךָ (MT)
καὶ ἐνευλογηθήσονται ἐν σοὶ πᾶσαι αἱ φυλαὶ τῆς γῆς καὶ ἐν τῷ σπέρματί σου (LXX)
"All the peoples of the earth will be blessed in you and in your seed." (AT)

In all five texts the LXX is quite similar, with all five using the passive form of ἐνευλογέω. However, the underlying Hebrew shows more variety, with three of the texts using a Niphal form of the verb ברך (12:3; 18:18; 28:14) while the two others use a Hithpael (22:18; 26:4). This variation, and the meaning of the two forms, has been a topic of lively debate. Some interpreters argue that the Hithpael is clearly reflexive and that the Niphal forms should be interpreted in light of them (e.g., Westermann 1995: 151–52). Hence, each passage would mean something like "by you all the families [nations] of the earth shall bless themselves" (12:3 RSV). Others suggest that both Hithpael and Niphal have a middle sense, "find blessing" or "pronounce blessings on one another using his name" (G. Wenham 1987: 277–78; NAB, NET). Still others, however, argue in just the opposite way: the Niphals, they claim, are passive, and the Hithpaels should be viewed accordingly in each text (translating as passives in each passage are NIV, ESV, NLT, NASB). The fourth option is to treat the two sets of passages differently, understanding the Niphal texts as passive but the Hithpael texts as reflexive. For careful studies favoring a consistently passive rendering of the Niphal, see esp. Grüneberg 2003; C. Lee 2009: 85–97, 117–21; and also Waltke and O'Connor 1990: 395. The Hithpael forms, rather than being reflexive, may be "declarative": "the nations/peoples declare themselves blessed in Abraham" (see NRSV and its marginal note; C. Lee 2009: 118–22).

3:10. Paul's quotation of Deut. 27:26a follows the LXX text, with a few differences:

Deut. 27:26a MT: אָרוּר אֲשֶׁר לֹא־יָקִים אֶת־דִּבְרֵי הַתּוֹרָה־הַזֹּאת לַעֲשׂוֹת אוֹתָם
Deut. 27:26a LXX: ἐπικατάρατος πᾶς ἄνθρωπος ὃς οὐκ ἐμμενεῖ ἐν πᾶσιν τοῖς λόγοις τοῦ νόμου τούτου τοῦ ποιῆσαι αὐτούς
Gal. 3:10: ἐπικατάρατος πᾶς ὃς οὐκ ἐμμένει πᾶσιν τοῖς γεγραμμένοις ἐν τῷ βιβλίῳ τοῦ νόμου τοῦ ποιῆσαι αὐτά.

The differences between Paul's wording and the LXX are minor and probably reflect parallel passages in Deuteronomy (Heckel 2002: 129). He omits LXX ἄνθρωπος (which has no explicit Hebrew equivalent), drops the ἐν after ἐμμένει, and substitutes τοῖς γεγραμμένοις ἐν τῷ βιβλίῳ for τοῖς λόγοις. The latter language echoes several comparable passages in Deuteronomy (on this theme in Deuteronomy, see Noth 1966):

> Deut. 28:61: "The LORD will also bring on you every kind of sickness and disaster not recorded in this Book of the Law [μὴ γεγραμμένην ἐν τῷ βιβλίῳ τοῦ νόμου τούτου], until you are destroyed."
>
> Deut. 29:21 (29:20 MT, LXX): "The LORD will single them out from all the tribes of Israel for disaster, according to all the curses of the covenant written in this Book of the Law [κατὰ πάσας τὰς ἀρὰς τῆς διαθήκης τὰς γεγραμμένας ἐν τῷ βιβλίῳ τοῦ νόμου τούτου]."
>
> Deut. 29:27 (29:26 MT, LXX): "Therefore the LORD's anger burned against this land, so that he brought on it all the curses written in this book [κατὰ πάσας τὰς κατάρας τὰς γεγραμμένας ἐν τῷ βιβλίῳ τοῦ νόμου τούτου]."
>
> Deut. 30:10: "If you obey the LORD your God and keep his commands and decrees that are written in this Book of the Law [φυλάσσεσθαι καὶ ποιεῖν πάσας τὰς ἐντολὰς αὐτοῦ καὶ τὰ δικαιώματα αὐτοῦ καὶ τὰς κρίσεις αὐτοῦ τὰς γεγραμμένας ἐν τῷ βιβλίῳ τοῦ νόμου τούτου] and turn to the LORD your God with all your heart and with all your soul . . ."

The πᾶσιν in the quotation, which Paul takes over from the LXX, has no comparable Hebrew, but the Hebrew of similar passages in Deuteronomy often does have such a word (e.g., 6:24); and the Sam. Tg. of Deut. 6:24; Lev. Rab. 25; and *y. Soṭah* 21d include a comparable word in their quotation of this verse. All this being the case, it is unlikely that any of the differences between Paul's wording and the LXX have any interpretive significance (contra Koch 1986: 120, 164; Stanley 1992: 239; Hays 2000: 258); Paul has probably assimilated the wording of Deut. 27:26 to these other texts.

3:11. Paul's quotation of Hab. 2:4b follows neither the LXX nor the MT. The relevant forms of this verse are as follows (on which see esp. Fitzmyer 1981):

MT: וְצַדִּיק בֶּאֱמוּנָתוֹ יִחְיֶה
LXX (MSS S, B, Q, V and W*): ὁ δὲ δίκαιος ἐκ πίστεως μου ζήσεται
LXX (MSS A and C): ὁ δὲ δίκαιος μου ἐκ πίστεως ζήσεται
8HevXIIgr: [δίκ]αιος ἐν πίστει αὐτοῦ ζήσετ[αι]
Aquila: δίκαιος ἐν πίστει αὐτοῦ ζήσεται
Symmachus: δίκαιος τῇ ἑαυτοῦ πίστει ζήσεται

The pronoun μου in the LXX MSS may have arisen as a misreading of the final *waw* (= "his") on בֶּאֱמוּנָתוֹ as a *yod* (= "my"; Andersen 2001: 211). The author of Hebrews, in keeping with his usual practice, follows the LXX (MSS A and C) reading: ὁ δὲ δίκαιος μου ἐκ πίστεώς ζήσεται (Heb. 10:38; though he also rearranges the lines of Hab. 2:3–4 to suit his argument). As we have noted above, Paul, in both Gal. 3:11 and in Rom. 1:17, departs from all known forms of the text by omitting a pronoun entirely. He has probably dropped the pronoun to aid his application of the text (see, e.g., Ellis 1978: 174–77; Lindars 1961: 231; Koch 1985: 68–85). It is less clear that Paul has used this text because it had already become one of the early Christian "testimonies" to Christ in the OT (as C. H. Dodd [1952: 49–51] argues).

To understand how Paul is applying this verse, we must first set it in its context. Habakkuk 2:1 concludes the prophet's second complaint about the Lord's way with his people (1:12–2:1) with him taking his stand to await the Lord's answer. That answer comes in 2:2–4:

> Then the LORD replied: "Write down the revelation and make it plain on tablets so that a herald may run with it. ³For the revelation awaits an appointed time; it speaks of the end and will not prove false. Though it linger, wait for it; it will certainly come and will not delay. ⁴See, the enemy is puffed up; his desires are not upright—but the righteous will live by their faithfulness— (NIV adapted)

As the dashes around v. 4b in the NIV suggest, the reference to the "righteous person" interrupts a denunciation of the person whose soul is "puffed up" and "not upright" (v. 4a; the Heb. here is difficult). A few interpreters have suggested that "the righteous" might refer to the Messiah (e.g., Strobel 1961: 47–56; Hays 1989b), but the implied contrast with the "puffed-up" person along with Habakkuk's other uses of צַדִּיק/δίκαιος (1:4, 13) show that he is referring to the person within the covenant community who remains loyal to Yahweh. This kind of person, Habakkuk proclaims, "will live by his faith/faithfulness" (NIV; the plural adjustment of the NIV preserves the generic significance of the claim without succumbing to inappropriate gender specificity). It is usually thought that "live" here means "live out one's life." However, the use of חָיָה in the Book of the Twelve gives some reason to suspect that the word may have a more theological sense. The verb occurs sixteen times, and, apart from places where it refers simply to "living beings," most of the occurrences refer to "true life," "life before God," "blessing" (Hosea 6:2; 14:7; Amos 5:4, 6, 14; Zech. 10:9 KJV, NASB; the only other occurrence in Habakkuk refers to God's "reviving" his works [3:2]). The word בֶּאֱמוּנָתוֹ goes with this verb (following the Masoretic punctuation), but the identification of the antecedent of the pronominal suffix is unclear. The NIV, along with most English versions, assumes that the pronoun refers to "the righteous." But it could also refer to the Lord (this is the way the LXX reads it, whether as an inadvertent misreading or a deliberate interpretation) or to the "revelation" (Andersen 2001: 213–14; Watts 1999: 9–10). Probably, however, a reference to the stance of the righteous person is intended. The half verse was so interpreted in the Dead Sea Scrolls, as faithfulness or loyalty to the Teacher of Righteousness (1QpHab 8.1–3), and in later rabbinic texts that identified Hab. 2:4 as a summation of the entire Mosaic law (b. Mak. 24a). The key word אֱמוּנָה has the sense of "faithfulness" (NIV), "fidelity," or "steadfastness" (A. Jepsen, TDOT 1:154–55). In the OT this faithfulness to the Lord was manifested in obedience of his law. However, it is not the case that אֱמוּנָה itself refers to this obedience. Rather, the word refers to the underlying commitment to the Lord that takes the form of such obedience; especially in this context, where the word refers to "confident waiting on God to act" (Bruce 1993: 861; cf. also Patterson 1991: 178–81; Scobie 2003: 704–6). The meaning of the word is summed up in the concluding verses of the prophecy (Hab. 3:16–19; see A. Jepsen, TDOT 1:156):

> I heard and my heart pounded, my lips quivered at the sound; decay crept into my bones, and my legs trembled. Yet I will wait patiently for the day of calamity to come on the nation invading us. [17]Though the fig tree does not bud and there are no grapes on the vines, though the olive crop fails and the fields produce no food, though there are no sheep in the pen and no cattle in the stalls, [18]yet I will rejoice in the LORD, I will be joyful in God my Savior. [19]The Sovereign LORD is my strength; he makes my feet like the feet of a deer, he enables me to tread on the heights.

The sense of אֱמוּנָה here is not so distant from Paul's concept of "faith." Particularly is this so if the prophet is himself dependent on Gen. 15:6 for his emphasis on faith (see esp. Silva 2007: 802). As we noted above, Paul has "deepened" the sense of some of the key words in Habakkuk. But he remains essentially faithful to the prophet's emphasis: that the person who is loyal to God will look for and wait for vindication on the basis of a deep-seated trust in the Lord and his promises. As Watson (2004: 161) comments, "'Faithfulness' speaks more adequately of the way of life that corresponds to the vision, whereas 'faith' speaks of the fundamental orientation towards the vision presupposed in this way of life; but each clearly entails the other" (also see his larger discussion on this matter in Watson 2004: 157–63).

3:12. Paul's quotation of Lev. 18:5 is abbreviated:

Gal. 3:12: ὁ ποιήσας αὐτὰ ζήσεται ἐν αὐτοῖς.
Lev. 18:5 MT: וּשְׁמַרְתֶּם אֶת־חֻקֹּתַי וְאֶת־מִשְׁפָּטַי אֲשֶׁר יַעֲשֶׂה אֹתָם הָאָדָם וָחַי בָּהֶם אֲנִי יְהוָה׃

Lev. 18:5 LXX: καὶ φυλάξεσθε πάντα τὰ προστάγματά μου καὶ πάντα τὰ κρίματά μου καὶ ποιήσετε αὐτά, ἃ ποιήσας ἄνθρωπος ζήσεται ἐν αὐτοῖς· ἐγὼ κύριος ὁ θεὸς ὑμῶν.

Lev. 18:5 NIV: "Keep my decrees and laws, for the person who obeys them will live by them. I am the LORD."

(Rom. 10:5: ὁ ποιήσας αὐτὰ ἄνθρωπος ζήσεται ἐν αὐτοῖς.)

As can be seen, Paul's wording reproduces the substance of the third clause of the LXX which, in turn, translates the Hebrew quite directly. But Paul's abbreviation of the text leads to two minor changes: the LXX adverbial participle ποιήσας (translating the Heb. Qal imperfect יַעֲשֶׂה) becomes a substantival participle, and an article is added accordingly (e.g., "by doing" becomes "the one who does"). A more interesting change is Paul's omission of ἄνθρωπος, the equivalent of which is also found in the Hebrew (הָאָדָם). The omission in Galatians could also simply be a product of Paul's intent to abbreviate. But in Paul's other quotation of this same text, he includes the word (Rom. 10:5; see above). Some interpreters therefore speculate that the omission in Galatians might have a reason related to the circumstances of the letter. They note that the rabbis sometimes interpreted the word הָאָדָם ("man" or "human being") in this verse to mean that Gentiles were to be included among those who could do the law and live (b. Sanh. 59a; b. B. Qam. 38a; Midr. Teh. 1.18; Num. Rab. 13.15–16). The agitators may have been quoting the verse in this way, and Paul drops the word to give no basis for this application (R. Longenecker 1990: 120–21; Martyn 1997: 315–16 [as possible]). This whole chain of reasoning is, however, quite speculative.

As we note above, the language of Lev. 18:5, and especially the portion that Paul quotes, became almost proverbial in later Judaism. It is alluded to in Ezek. 20:11, 13, 21; Neh. 9:29; CD 3.14–16; 4Q266; Philo, *Prelim. Studies* 86–87; L.A.B. 23.10; Pss. Sol. 14.1–2; Luke 10:28. Gathercole (2004b) and Sprinkle (2008: 34–130) have shown that most of these texts (the only clear exception being the Philo passage) interpret the verse as a soteriological promise (and note rabbinic texts such as *t. Šabb.* 15.17: "The commands were given only that men should live through them, not that men should die through them" [cf. Urbach 1979: 1.424–26]). Both Targum Onqelos and Targum Pseudo-Jonathan paraphrase the Hebrew with the language of "eternal life."

3:13. As we noted above, the interpretation of vv. 13–14 (and of several other texts in Galatians) is closely bound up with the significance of the person of the pronouns and verbal forms that Paul has chosen to use. Some scholars insist that the significance of the pronouns is tied to 2:15, where Paul uses the first-person plural to refer to Jewish Christians: ἡμεῖς φύσει Ἰουδαῖοι. On this basis, they conclude that most, if not all, of Paul's first-person pronouns and verbs refer to Jews and/or Jewish Christians. But a systematic distinction between the first person = Jews/Jewish Christians, and the second person = Galatians/Gentiles, is actually difficult to maintain in Galatians.

First, we note passages in which Paul uses first-person plural forms, as he does regularly in his letters, to refer to Christians in general:

Grace and peace to you from God our Father and the Lord Jesus Christ, ⁴who gave himself for *our* sins to rescue *us* from the present evil age, according to the will of our God and Father, ⁵to whom be glory for ever and ever. Amen. (1:3–5)

It is for freedom that Christ has set *us* free. Stand firm, then, and do not let yourselves be burdened again by a yoke of slavery. (5:1)

But by faith *we* eagerly await through the Spirit the righteousness for which *we* hope. (5:5)

Since *we* live by the Spirit, let *us* keep in step with the Spirit. ²⁶Let *us* not become conceited, provoking and envying each other. (5:25–26)

> Let *us* not become weary in doing good, for at the proper time *we* will reap a harvest if *we* do not give up. [10]Therefore, as *we* have opportunity, let *us* do good to all people, especially to those who belong to the family of believers. (6:9–10)

Second, we note passages in which any change in referent with a shift in the person of the pronoun/pronominal form would create problems for the integrity of Paul's argument. See, in this regard, 5:1 above—"Christ has set *us* free . . . [you] stand firm, then . . ."—as well as the following:

> But the Jerusalem that is above is free, and she is *our* mother. [27]For it is written: "Be glad, barren woman, you who never bore a child; shout for joy and cry aloud, you who were never in labor; because more are the children of the desolate woman than of her who has a husband." [28]Now *you*, brothers and sisters, like Isaac, are children of promise. [29]At that time the son born by human effort persecuted the son born by the power of the Spirit. It is the same now. [30]But what does Scripture say? "Get rid of the slave woman and her son, for the slave woman's son will never share in the inheritance with the free woman's son." [31]Therefore, brothers and sisters, *we* are not children of the slave woman, but of the free woman. (4:26–31)

> What I am saying is that as long as heirs are underage they are no different from slaves, although they own the whole estate. [2]They are subject to guardians and trustees until the time set by their fathers. [3]So also, when *we* were underage, *we* were in slavery under the elemental spiritual forces of the world. [4]But when the set time had fully come, God sent his Son, born of a woman, born under the law, [5]to redeem those under the law, that *we* might receive adoption to sonship. [6]Because *you* are his sons, God sent the Spirit of his Son into *our* hearts, the Spirit who calls out, "Abba, Father." [7]So *you* are no longer slaves, but God's children; and since *you* are his children, he has made *you* also heirs. (4:1–7)

This last text is indeed difficult, and some interpreters think that a consistent difference in referent between first-person and second-person forms makes sense. But Paul's insistence that the Galatians are themselves enslaved under the στοιχεῖα (v. 9) almost requires that they be included in the first-person plural address of v. 3: "when we were underage, we were in slavery under the στοιχεῖα." And Paul's logic is very difficult to follow if the "you" in v. 6a, "You are his sons," refers to a different group than the "our" in v. 6b, "God sent the Spirit of his Son into our hearts."

Thus although specific contextual considerations can suggest a specific referent of Paul's pronouns, no systematic distinction between first-person plural and second-person plural in terms of referent can be made. His choice appears to be governed by rhetorical considerations: the "we" formulations have a confessional flavor in which Paul includes himself with the believers he is addressing (on this point [with particular respect to 3:23], see Hartman 1993: 142–43).

3:13. Paul's quotation from Deut. 21:23 is worded differently than both the MT and the LXX:

> Deut. 21:23 MT: קִלְלַת אֱלֹהִים תָּלוּי ("the one who is hung [Qal passive participle] is a curse of God" [some traditions—Symmachus, Tg. Onqelos, Tg. Pseudo-Jonathan—understand this in the sense of the one who is hung cursing God; cf. Wilcox 1977: 87; Caneday 1989: 196–97])
> Deut. 21:23 LXX: κεκατηραμένος ὑπὸ θεοῦ πᾶς κρεμάμενος ἐπὶ ξύλου ("cursed by God is everyone who is hung on a tree").
> Gal. 3:13: ἐπικατάρατος πᾶς ὁ κρεμάμενος ἐπὶ ξύλου.

Paul's wording is closer to the LXX, and he has probably taken his text from the Greek, as is his custom. If that is so, however, two differences call for comment. First, in place of the LXX κεκατηραμένος (a perfect passive participle from καταράομαι, curse), Paul uses ἐπικατάρατος (an adjective). Paul undoubtedly makes this change in order to match this text with its companion in v. 10, where ἐπικατάρατος occurs in the quotation of Deut. 27:26 (Stanley 1992: 245–46). Second, Paul's omission of the LXX ὑπὸ θεοῦ has been variously explained, from those who think that it is a purely incidental change (e.g., Silva 2007: 797), perhaps to avoid misunderstanding (Bruce 1982b: 165), to those who think that Paul wants carefully to separate the curse of God from the curse of the law (Koch 1986: 124–25; Burton 1921: 172; Smiles 1998: 198). The idea, however, that Paul would have distinguished between the curse of the law and the curse of God assumes a view of the law that is very unlikely for Paul to have held (see comments on 3:19–20). We should probably not view the omission of ὑπὸ θεοῦ in Paul as being substantivally significant. And we should also reckon with the possibility that Paul is not, in fact, quoting the old Greek but that he is translating a current form of the Hebrew text (Wilcox 1977).

The language of Deut. 21:22–23 played a significant role in later Judaism (see esp. Chapman 2008: 117–32; and also Wilcox 1977; Caneday 1989). Particularly interesting are two texts in the Qumran scrolls that use its language. One (11QTᵃ [11Q19] 64.7–12) commands the people what to do with a serious sinner: "You shall hang him on a tree and he will die" (64.8, 10–11). This text makes clear that hanging on a tree is being viewed as the means of execution. The same point is made in 4QpNah (4Q169) frgs. 3–4, col. 1, lines 5–8, which refers to "the Angry lion" who "hanged living men [from the tree, committing an atrocity that had not been committed] in Israel since ancient times, for it is [hor]rible for the one hanged alive from the tree." The reference is to the Jewish intertestamental ruler Alexander Jannaeus, and we know from Josephus (*Ant.* 13.380) that Jannaeus executed these men by crucifixion; Fitzmyer 1998: 131; Sänger 1994; Borgen 2000: 347–48). These texts make clear, then, that in the Judaism of Paul's day the "hanging on a tree" in Deut. 21:22–23 was connected with crucifixion (Fitzmyer 1998: 136–37). It is apparently this connection that Paul assumes in his application of the text. Still, it is clear that Paul cannot use Deut. 21:22–23 to "prove" that Christ was accursed. But we should not assume that this was Paul's purpose. He often cites Scripture more to illustrate than to prove a point; and this may be one of those places (see the discussion in Silva 2007: 799–800; and Lim [1997: 166–67] suggests that Paul may be quoting the content of Deut. 21:22–23 rather than a particular text).

Many interpreters have also argued that this text played a significant role in the early Jewish persecution of believers, since Jews understood Deut. 21:22–23 to "prove" that a person who had been crucified was under God's curse. Paul's use of this text, then, may be an attempt to counter such propaganda by turning the idea of the curse into a positive theological point (see, e.g., Schoeps 1959: 178–79; Beker 1980: 182–89; Stuhlmacher 1986b: 139–40; but for a demurral, see K. O'Brien 2006; Fredriksen 1991: 551–52).

3:14. Several witnesses read εὐλογίαν τοῦ πνεύματος in place of ἐπαγγελίαν τοῦ πνεύματος, an obvious case of assimilation to εὐλογία earlier in the verse (Metzger 1994: 525).

2. The Law in Salvation History (3:15–25)

In these verses, Paul continues to make his case that "those who depend on faith" are the "sons of Abraham" (v. 7). In contrast to the typical Jewish view, which insisted that doing the law was the necessary accompaniment of faith, Paul separates them. It is not his view that doing the law is necessarily a bad thing; in other letters, he is quite clear that Jewish believers can work out their new life in Christ while following the law (see, e.g., Rom. 14:1–15:13; 1 Cor. 9:20–22). But he is insistent that (1) obedience to the law is in no way a necessary requirement for justification, either in the present or in the future; and that (2) the law should not be required of Gentiles. These are the points that he must hammer home in Galatia in response to the agitators, who are insisting, in standard Jewish terms, that the new Gentile believers complete their faith by submitting to the law. And the agitators could certainly make a good case for their view. True, Abraham believed (3:6; Gen. 15:6). But it was just in that context that God also established a covenant with Abraham, a covenant whose sign was the circumcision of Abraham and all his male descendants (Gen. 17:9–14). God eventually added to his requirement of circumcision the obligation that Abraham's descendants obey the law of Moses that God gave to Israel. And was not Abraham himself said to have received God's promises "because [he] obeyed me and did everything I required of him, keeping my commands, my decrees and my instructions" (Gen. 26:5)?

The agitators, then, were undoubtedly building their version of the gospel on what they considered to be a straightforward reading of the OT. The Galatians, like Abraham, were proselytes, converts to the Jewish faith; and like Abraham, they needed to follow up their faith with circumcision and obedience to the law of Moses. Paul, however, insists on a different reading of redemptive history. While the agitators placed the law and God's promise to Abraham on the same level, viewing the law as an addition to the promise, Paul saw the law as operating on a different plane entirely. He insisted that the law could not alter the terms of the relationship that God had established with Abraham. "What the Galatians perceive as a necessary supplement to their faith Paul views as a radical break with faith" (Beker 1980: 53). The opening paragraph (vv. 15–18) of this next stage of Paul's argument establishes this fundamental redemptive-historical point. The key word in the paragraph, and to some extent in subsequent verses, is "promise" (vv. 16, 17, 18 [2x], 21, 22 [the corresponding verb occurs in v. 19]). The promise is God's promise to Abraham (v. 8), and Paul anticipates this new direction in his teaching at the end of verse 14, with his mention of "the promise of the Spirit."[1] In contrast to verses 7–14, in which Paul quoted specific texts of Scripture, there is only one quotation in verses 15–25 (v. 16). But the OT remains just as important as Paul shifts to general arguments from Scripture in this new section (George 1994: 243–44): "There is hardly a clause in this section . . . that does not allude to the OT in a fairly explicit manner" (Silva 2007: 804).

Paul's take on salvation history raises two key questions, which set the agenda for verses 19–25.[2] The broad, overarching question is obvious: if the law did not materially add anything to the promise, then why did God give the law to his people? After asking just this question in verse 19a, Paul devotes verses 19b–25 to answering it. He makes two basic points. First, the law and the promise serve distinct purposes: the law was given to exacerbate and reveal sin (vv. 19b, 22a) and was not intended to, or able to, give the life that only the promise and faith could achieve (v. 21). Second, all along the law was intended to last only until the promised Messiah came (vv. 19b, 23–25). This second point provides the answer to a second subsidiary question that Paul must deal with if his argument against the law is to make sense: why could not the Galatians continue to obey the law as long as it was understood as Paul has defined it? It is the movement of redemptive history that explains why the law is no longer necessary. What Paul says in these verses certainly shows that he holds to a single, continuous history of salvation.[3] But he also views the coming of Christ—"Christ crucified" (3:1; cf. also 2:19–20; 6:14)—as a climactic moment that introduces a significant shift in the history of salvation. At base, the disagreement between the agitators and Paul lies just here: how significant is the shift in salvation history that Christ's coming has inaugurated?

Exegesis and Exposition

[15]Brothers and sisters, I am speaking in human fashion. Even when a human testament is ratified, no one can reject it or add conditions to it. [16](Now the promises were made to Abraham "and to his seed." It does not say "to seeds," as if with reference to many, but it refers to one: "and to your seed"—who is Christ.) [17]So what we are saying is this: the law that came four hundred and thirty years afterward cannot nullify the covenant that was ratified beforehand by God and so invalidate the promise. [18]For

---

1. On the basis of the correlation of promise and Spirit in 3:14, de Boer (2011: 216) argues that "promise" in this passage always refers to the Spirit, making the Spirit the central concern of these verses. But Paul has identified other "promises" given to Abraham in this context, and it is the promise of many descendants through faith (3:8) that appears to be the more fundamental point for Paul.

2. A few interpreters (e.g., Mussner 1988: 212–13; Martyn 1997: 294–95) divide the passage at v. 19, where Paul shifts to a series of rhetorical questions; de Boer (2011: 216) divides it at v. 23.

3. We make this point chiefly in response to Martyn (1997: esp. 161–79), who argues that in Galatians Paul highlights antithetical contrasts to the point that any notion of a continuous salvation history is abandoned. But his position is too extreme (see the discussion in the introduction, in the section on "Salvation History and Apocalyptic").

if the inheritance came through the law, then it would no longer come through the promise. But God graciously gave it to Abraham through a promise.

[19]Why then the ⌜law? It was added because of transgressions⌝ until the seed came to whom it was promised; and it was put in place by angels through the hand of a mediator. [20]Now the mediator is not of one; but God is one. [21]Is the law, then, against the promises ⌜of God⌝? By no means. For if a law had been given that was able to make alive, then truly righteousness ⌜would have come through the law⌝. [22]But the Scripture confined all things under sin, in order that what was promised might be given through faith in Jesus Christ for those who believe.

[23]Now before faith came, we were guarded under the law, confined until the faith that was about to be revealed. [24]So the law became our guardian until Christ, in order that we might be justified by faith. [25]But since faith has come, we are no longer under a guardian.

3:15   The direct address ἀδελφοί (*adelphoi*, brothers and sisters) and the rhetorical question τί οὖν ὁ νόμος; (*ti oun ho nomos?* Why then the law?) in verse 19 establish literary boundaries, setting out verses 15–18 as a paragraph in its own right.[4] The key point comes in verse 17, where Paul claims that the promise God entered into with Abraham cannot be nullified by the subsequent law. He prepares for this point in verse 15 by citing the parallel of a human testament. Verse 16, though important to Paul's larger argument in this part of the letter, is parenthetical within the logical flow of this paragraph. Verse 18 provides an important further reason why the law cannot interfere with the promissory arrangement between God and Abraham.

By addressing the Galatians as ἀδελφοί, for the first time since 1:11 and in marked contrast to "You foolish Galatians!" (3:1), Paul expresses "both frustrated affection and gentle coercion" (Dunn 1993a: 181). He thereby draws attention to the importance of the argument in the following verses. Paul introduces this argument by citing a "human" situation: he explicitly warns us that he is speaking κατὰ ἄνθρωπον (*kata anthrōpon*, according to a human). Some interpreters think that Paul intends this to be heard as somewhat negative, as if he is signaling a shift from the scriptural (and implicitly divine) arguments of verses 7–14 (Witherington 1998: 241) or as if he is making it clear that the ideas he is about to cite are not his, but his opponents' (Matera 1992: 130; Cosgrove 1988: 543–46). Elsewhere in Paul the two clauses closest in language to the wording here have a negative nuance: κατὰ ἄνθρωπον λέγω (*kata anthrōpon legō*, I am using a human argument) in Rom. 3:5 and κατὰ ἄνθρωπον . . . λαλῶ (*kata anthrōpon . . . lalō*, I say . . . merely on human authority) in 1 Cor. 9:8. But Paul uses a very similar clause in Rom. 6:19 in a neutral way (ἀνθρώπινον λέγω, *anthrōpinon legō*, I speak in human fashion [AT]), and it is likely that he does so here in Gal.

4. Some interpreters treat 3:15–20 as a paragraph (Bonnard 1972: 70; Matera 1992: 129), while others connect vv. 15–18 with vv. 6–14 (Mussner 1988: 211–13; Martyn 1997: 295), but most agree that 3:15–18 is the key unit. At the same time, however, the continuity within vv. 15–25 should not be neglected (Hays 2000: 263).

3:15 also: thus R. Longenecker (1990: 127) paraphrases, "Let me take an example from everyday life."

The example that Paul cites is the status of a "human" (ἀνθρώπου, *anthrōpou*) διαθήκη (*diathēkē*, testament), which, once "ratified" (κεκυρωμένην, *kekyrōmenēn*—the perfect denotes the state of "having been ratified"), "no one can revoke or add to." The example is introduced with the conjunction ὅμως (*homōs*, even/nevertheless), which usually has an adversative force (as in John 12:42). It can only have such an adversative sense here, however, if it is taken with the main clause of the sentence, the resulting sense being "even though it is a human covenant being ratified, *nevertheless* [ὅμως] no one can revoke it or add to it" (see esp. Burton 1921: 178; Turner 1963: 337; Bruce 1982b: 169). The displacement of a conjunction or a particle in this way is not uncommon (it is called "hyperbaton"; see A. Robertson 1934: 423). However, since both Pauline occurrences of ὅμως occur in comparisons (see also 1 Cor. 14:7), it is more likely that the word has taken on the meaning of the similarly spelled ὅμοιος and means here "likewise," "also" (BDAG 710; BDF §450.2; R. Longenecker 1990: 127). It thus functions to introduce the comparison with a divine διαθήκη (v. 17); hence the NIV translation: "Just as no one can set aside or add to a human covenant that has been duly established, *so it is in this case.*"

The translation "covenant" in the NIV (also in ESV, KJV, NASB, NET, HCSB) reflects the usual meaning of διαθήκη in Biblical Greek, where it has become virtually a technical term for contracts entered into between God and his people. All eight of Paul's other uses of this word have this meaning (Rom. 9:4; 11:27; 1 Cor. 11:25; 2 Cor. 3:6, 14; Eph. 2:12), including the two other occurrences in Galatians (3:17; 4:24; for this meaning here, see Lightfoot 1881: 141; Burton 1921: 179; and esp. S. Hahn 2005: 80–88). However, the fact that Paul explicitly claims he is citing the example of a "human" arrangement makes it more likely that διαθήκη in verse 15 has its other, "secular" meaning: "will" or "testament" (see RSV, NRSV, NAB, NJB, CEB; see, e.g., Bruce 1982b: 169; Eckstein 1996: 172–76).[5] Whether we translate "covenant" or "will," the situation to which Paul refers when he claims that "no one can revoke or add to it" (οὐδεὶς ἀθετεῖ ἢ ἐπιδιατάσσεται, *oudeis athetei ē epidiatassetai*) is difficult to identify. When used in this kind of context, both verbs have a legal sense: the first (ἀθετέω, *atheteō*) refers to revocation or annulment (see, e.g., 2 Macc. 13:25: "The people of Ptolemais were indignant over the treaty; in fact they were so angry that they wanted to annul [ἀθετεῖν, *athetein*] its terms"); the second (ἐπιδιατάσσομαι, *epidiatassomai*) means "add a codicil to a will" (BDAG 370). The problem is that there are no clear examples of Greek or Roman "wills" or "testaments" that could not be revoked or modified after being put into effect. Various options have been suggested,[6] but the precise

5. A similar, though even more heated, debate focuses on the use of διαθήκη in Heb. 9:15–17. Here also, it is likely that there is a play on the word, with διαθήκη meaning "covenant" in v. 15 and "will" in vv. 16–17.

6. Several scholars (Betz 1979: 155; Mussner 1988: 237) have followed the suggestion of Bammel (1960) that Paul may have been thinking of a Jewish ritual called the *mattenat bari*, a legal

situation that Paul has in view is really not important for his purposes. What is important is the unchangeable nature of the agreement.

3:16   The comparison that Paul has introduced in verse 15 is completed in verse 17: just as in the case of a human will (διαθήκη), so it is in the case of the διαθήκη that God has initiated. Verse 16 is therefore somewhat parenthetical (Burton 1921: 182). Paul uses this aside to identify the "covenant" that he will be talking about in verse 17 with the "promises" that God gave to Abraham and to his seed. The word ἐπαγγελία (epangelia, promise) occurs only seven times in the LXX and never in the patriarchal narratives, but it describes very well the way in which God takes the initiative to hold out the prospect of blessings—of land, of numerous descendants, and of the extension of blessing to other nations—to Abraham (Gen. 12:1–3; 15:1–5; 17:1–8; 22:15–18) and to the other patriarchs (Gen. 26:1–5; 28:13–15; 35:11–12). "Promise" is especially associated with these patriarchal promises throughout the NT (Acts 13:23, 32; 26:6; Rom. 4:13, 14, 16, 20; 9:4, 8, 9; 15:8; Heb. 6:12, 15, 17; 7:6; 11:9, 13, 17). The plural ἐπαγγελίαι (epangeliai) here in verse 16 (and also in v. 21) may therefore connote the several provisions of the promise or the several reiterations of the promise; in any case, the plural does not function any differently for Paul than the singular.

These promises were "spoken" (ἐρρέθησαν, errethēsan, a "perfective present" [Wallace 1996: 533]) "to Abraham and to his seed" (τῷ Ἀβραάμ . . . καὶ τῷ σπέρματι αὐτοῦ, tō Abraam . . . kai tō spermati autou). In the rest of this verse, Paul's commentary shows that the phrase "[and] to his seed" is a quotation from Scripture. The phrase "and to your seed" occurs in Gen. 13:15; 17:8; and 24:7 (LXX), while the phrase "to your seed" is found in 12:7; 15:18; 22:18; and 24:7. It is difficult to know which of these texts Paul might have had in mind, although the focus on "testament/covenant" in verses 15 and 17 suggests either Gen. 15:18 or 17:8, since in the context of these two passages both "seed" and "covenant" are found.[7] The earlier passage (Gen. 15:18) comes at the climax of the narrative in which God solemnizes and reiterates his promise to Abraham: "On that day the LORD made a covenant with Abram and said, 'To your descendants [σπέρμα, sperma, seed] I give this land, from the Wadi of Egypt to the great river, the Euphrates.'" Genesis 17:8 focuses on Abraham's many descendants (see Gal. 3:7–8) and comes in a passage in which

---

agreement by which a person, before death, could transfer property to someone else and which, purportedly, could not be revoked. There are problems with this identification, however, and so it has been noted that there is some evidence in the papyri for a custom among the Greeks somewhat similar to this Jewish mattenat bari which could provide the background for Paul's reference (NewDocs 6:44–47). Lim (1997: 59–62), on the other hand, has cited such a document from Cave of Letters in Nahal Hever, just west of the Dead Sea (PYadin 19). In his lengthy discussion of the matter, R. Longenecker (1990: 128–30) concludes that we cannot identify the exact situation that Paul has in view.

7. S. Hahn (2009: 245–46, 256–59), on the other hand, thinks the reference is esp. to Gen. 22:16–18, a passage (because of its focus on Isaac as "the" seed) that facilitates Paul's claim about the singular focus of the promise to the "seed" in this verse.

σπέρμα and διαθήκη occur frequently. The text of Gen. 17 may thus be the one that Paul has especially in view (Mussner 1988: 238; Martyn 1997: 339):

> When Abram was ninety-nine years old, the LORD appeared to him and said, "I am God Almighty; walk before me faithfully and be blameless. ²Then I will make my covenant [διαθήκην] between me and you and will greatly increase your numbers." ³Abram fell facedown, and God said to him, ⁴"As for me, this is my covenant [διαθήκη] with you: You will be the father of many nations. ⁵No longer will you be called Abram; your name will be Abraham, for I have made you a father of many nations. ⁶I will make you very fruitful; I will make nations of you, and kings will come from you. ⁷I will establish my covenant [διαθήκην] as an everlasting covenant [διαθήκην] between me and you and your descendants [σπέρματος, *spermatos*] after you for the generations to come, to be your God and the God of your descendants [σπέρματος] after you. ⁸The whole land of Canaan, where you now reside as a foreigner, I will give as an everlasting possession to you and your descendants [σπέρματι] after you; and I will be their God."

This identification of the "covenant" of verse 15 with the "promise" to Abraham and to his seed serves Paul's purpose in this parenthesis. In the second half of verse 16, Paul's christological interpretation of the "seed" then is a parenthesis within a parenthesis. While tangential to Paul's focus in this paragraph, however, it is a very significant claim for his overall argument about the way the promise to Abraham becomes applicable to the Galatian believers. But what are we to make of Paul's claim about the significance of the singular form of the word σπέρμα in his Genesis citation: οὐ λέγει· καὶ τοῖς σπέρμασιν, ὡς ἐπὶ πολλῶν ἀλλ' ὡς ἐφ' ἑνός· καὶ τῷ σπέρματί σου, ὅς ἐστιν Χριστός[8] (*ou legei: kai tois spermasin, hōs epi pollōn all' hōs eph' henos; kai tō spermati sou, hos estin Christos*, it does not say: "and to seeds," as if it were referring to many,[9] but, as if referring to one; [it says] "and to your seed," who is Christ). This exegetical move seems to be an obvious example of forced interpretation in order to make a point: for σπέρμα, being a collective noun, while singular in form, is plural in meaning (like our term "people"). But four things need to be noted about what Paul is doing here. First, what may be forced or unconvincing to a modern reader would not necessarily have been perceived that way in Paul's context. In fact, what Paul does here is quite in line with certain kinds of rabbinic interpretation. Second, Paul makes clear in this very context that he understands the collective sense of σπέρμα; see verse 29: "If you [plural ὑμεῖς, *hymeis*] belong to Christ, then you are Abraham's seed [σπέρμα], heirs according to the promise." Third, there is good reason to think

---

8. The masculine ὅς after the neuter σπέρματι is an obvious case showing attraction of the relative pronoun's case to the real referent of the word (the predicate noun Χριστός; Wallace 1996: 338).

9. In the two phrases ὡς ἐπὶ πολλῶν and ὡς ἐφ' ἑνός, the ὡς marks an ellipse—"he speaks not as one would of a plurality/of one" (BDAG 1104.1.b.α)—while the preposition ἐπί means "about" (e.g., "speak about"; BDF §234.6).

that some of the promise texts in Genesis do, in fact, use σπέρμα as a semantic singular, referring to Isaac, Abraham's immediate "seed," or "descendant." Fourth, Paul's application of the "seed" language to Christ may also reflect the later traditions about a "seed" of David; for example, see 2 Sam. 7:12, where σπέρμα refers to David's immediate descendant, Solomon, but ultimately to the Messiah who would come from David's line: "When your days are over and you rest with your ancestors, I will raise up your offspring to succeed you, your own flesh and blood, and I will establish his kingdom" (Dunn 1993a: 184; Mussner 1988: 238–39; Hays 2000: 264). Genesis itself suggests that its "seed" language has ultimate reference to this "seed" of David (Alexander 1989: 19; cf. also Sailhamer 2009: 473–81, 535–36). These considerations suggest that, while Paul's claim resembles Jewish interpretation of his day at the level of his exegetical technique, he is, in fact, operating with certain hermeneutical axioms that provide warrant for his interpretation. Especially important is Paul's reading of salvation history as the story of how God's promises become concentrated in one person, Christ, *the* seed, through whom those promises become applicable to a worldwide people. The claim, therefore, that "Paul is using the Old Testament in a way that has nothing to do with how the Old Testament is to be understood in its original context" (Enns 2005: 137) assumes an understanding of "original context" that severs the text from its larger theological and salvation-historical context—a questionable Christian way of reading the Scriptures.

3:17   "Now what I am saying is this" (τοῦτο δὲ λέγω, *touto de legō*) looks ahead to the rest of verse 17. This verse applies the illustration of verse 15 (v. 16 being parenthetical; cf. Burton 1921: 182) and states the main point of this brief paragraph. The διαθήκη of God is like a human "testament" or "will" (διαθήκη in v. 15): it cannot be annulled or modified by any later document or agreement. Paul's argument requires that we identify the διαθήκη in this verse with the Abrahamic covenant. There is ample OT precedent for this identification (Gen. 15:8; 17:1–21), but the dominant OT and Jewish usage of διαθήκη ties it to Moses. Paul's implicit but clear distinction between "covenant" and law here is both unusual and quite deliberate (Martyn 1997: 344–46). Jewish theology generally viewed the Abrahamic covenant, with the requirement of circumcision, as the first stage of a covenant arrangement that was later expanded in the Mosaic covenant. The agitators were undoubtedly arguing from this traditional understanding, while Paul insists on severing the initial promise covenant that God made with Abraham from the later law covenant that God instituted through Moses. Paul's argument is based on temporal priority, which he indicates both in the verb προκυρόω (*prokyroō*, ratify beforehand—a biblical hapax), in the form of a perfect participle (connoting the state of ratification), and with the adjectival participial clause μετὰ τετρακόσια καὶ τριάκοντα ἔτη γεγονώς (*meta tetrakosia kai triakonta eti gegonōs*—another stative perfect): the law (νόμος, *nomos*) "came into the picture four hundred and thirty years after [the covenant]." This law, Paul notes, "does not annul" (οὐκ ἀκυροῖ, *ouk akyroi*) the covenant (the present tense expresses timeless action). Paul stresses this last point by adding an infinitive clause at the end of the verse: εἰς τὸ καταργῆσαι τὴν ἐπαγγελίαν (*eis to katargēsai tēn epangelian*). The infinitive probably expresses result (Burton 1898: §411; A. Robertson 1934: 1072): "so as to nullify the promise" (NRSV). The verb καταργέω is distinctively Pauline: twenty-five of the thirty-one occurrences in the LXX and NT are his. Paul uses the verb to connote a "release" from a power or obligation (Rom. 7:2, 6; Gal. 5:4), the destruction of something (e.g., 1 Cor. 6:13; 15:24, 26), or less strongly, "render inoperative" or "make powerless" (e.g., Rom. 3:3; 6:6; Gal. 5:4, 11; Eph. 2:15). This last meaning fits in the present context: the law, precisely because it "came into the picture" (Martyn's [1997: 341] appropriate rendering of γεγονώς) so long after God's promise to Abraham, could not cause that promise to lose its validity and power. Promise, in the case of both Abraham (3:6) and all who experience his blessing (3:8–9), is activated by faith, and—as Paul is especially at pains to argue in this context, versus the agitators—by "faith alone."

In a way typical of Paul's argument in this part of Galatians, the temporal, salvation-historical argument of verse 17 is matched by an argument from principle in verse 18. This verse provides a further explanation (γάρ, *gar*, for) for why the law cannot annul the promise: the law introduces an element that is antithetical to the nature of promise, which is a matter of grace. In this verse Paul introduces a concept that will be important in his subsequent argument: "inheritance" (κληρονομία, *klēronomia*; see κληρονόμος [*klēronomos*] in 3:29; 4:1, 7). Paul may have been influenced by the reference to a "will" in verse 15 to introduce this word into his argument at this point. God's promise covenant with Abraham, he suggests, also involves the promise of an inheritance. In the OT, the "inheritance" is usually identified with the land (e.g., Gen. 28:4; Deut. 1:39); for Paul (and for other NT authors), the "inheritance" is Christ himself and all the blessings Christ provides his people. The verb that Paul uses to describe God's "giving" of the inheritance is κεχάρισται (*kecharistai*, a perfect form that emphasizes the continuing effects of the "gracious giving"). The notion of *gracious* giving is warranted based on Paul's other uses of the verb χαρίζομαι (*charizomai*: Rom. 8:32; 1 Cor. 2:12; 2 Cor. 2:7, 10 [3x]; 12:13; Eph. 4:32 [2x]; Phil. 1:29; 2:9; Col. 2:13; 3:13 [2x]; Philem. 22). And it is just here that an important perspective on Paul's argument emerges. "Promise," by its nature, involves a free and unconstrained decision to commit oneself or specific objects to another. It is this nature of promise that Paul highlights in order to show why the inheritance cannot be based on the law. As Paul has explained in Gal. 3:12, "law" operates according to the principle of doing: it demands works.[10] And as Paul makes clear elsewhere, grace and works are

3:18

---

10. Dunn (1993a: 187–88) is representative of interpreters who illegitimately diminish the force of Paul's polemic against the law by arguing that his target is not the law per se, but "a mind-set too narrowly focused on the law" (see also, e.g., Fuller 1980: 199–204; Cranfield 1964; for rebuttals, see Moo 1983: 85–90; Das 2001: 161–63; Westerholm 2004: 330–35).

antithetical. In fact, Paul's logic in this verse is very similar to his logic in Rom. 4:4–5, where he argues that Abraham could not have been justified by works because, if he had, his status before God would not be based on grace. Explicit in his argument there and implicit here is the fact that God always operates with his sinful creatures on the basis of grace (see also Rom. 11:6: "And if by grace, then it cannot be based on works; if it were, grace would no longer be grace"). Paul argues against imposing the law on the Galatian Christians, then, not *only* because it belongs to an earlier phase of salvation history. It is also not a channel of blessing or inheritance, because its nature contradicts the fundamentally gracious manner in which God bestows his blessing on his people. As Dunn (1993a: 186) rightly says, "Paul stakes his case on the theological axiom that salvation is always, first to last, a matter of divine initiative and grace." And we will let Calvin (1854: 63) have the last word: "Let us carefully remember the reason why, in comparing the promise with the law, the establishment of the one overturns the other. The reason is, that the promise has respect to faith, and the law to works. Faith receives what is freely given, but to works a reward is paid. And he immediately adds, *God gave it to Abraham*, not by requiring some sort of compensation on his part, but by the free promise; for if you view it as conditional, the word *gave* (κεχάρισται) would be utterly inapplicable."

3:19   Paul has argued that the works of the law cannot justify (2:16; cf. 3:2, 5), that the law brings a curse (3:10) from which Christ has released us (3:13), and that it cannot confer the inheritance (3:18). No wonder, then, that Paul asks "Why then the law?" (τί οὖν ὁ νόμος; *ti oun ho nomos?* Wallace [1990: 231–32] defends the adverbial use of τί, as in meaning "why"). This question, repeated in a more specific form in verse 21, introduces a new stage in Paul's argument that extends through verse 25. Throughout these verses the focus is on the limited time and specific purpose of the law. Some interpreters, noting especially the similarities between these verses and 4:1–7, think that 3:19–4:7 should be kept together as a discrete stage in Paul's argument (R. Longenecker 1990: 135; Mussner 1988: 243; Eckstein 1996: 190). However, the inclusio created by the focus on Abrahamic descent in 3:6–9 and 3:29 is a more important marker of argumentative progression. Within this larger argument, verses 19–25 may be viewed as a kind of digression (Betz 1979: 162–63). But from another perspective this section is vital to Paul's argument (Dunn 1993a: 188). Paul is no Marcionite: for his interpretation of salvation history to be convincing, he must explain how God's law functions within that history. Therefore, although we find nothing in Galatians explicitly comparable to Paul's "the law is holy, and the commandment is holy, righteous and good" of Rom. 7:12, the assumption of the divine origin and therefore fundamental "goodness" of the law is implicitly present (contra, e.g., Martyn 1997: 353).

Paul's immediate answer to his question about the purpose of the law in 3:19b–c is indirect and unclear. The one point that is clear is Paul's intent to set specific temporal limits on the law. Paul's argument runs contrary to many Jewish traditions holding that the law is eternal (e.g., Josephus, *Ag. Ap.* 2.277: "our Law at least remains immortal"; Jub. 1.27; Wis. 18:4; 2 Esd. [4 Ezra] 9:37). Paul, on the other hand, insists that the law had a definite beginning: it was "added" (προσετέθη, *prosetethē*, from προστίθημι)—that is, in light of verse 17, it was introduced into salvation history "four hundred and thirty years" after the promise. The implied subject of the passive verb is God (Wallace 1990: 235), in contrast to those who argue that Paul in these verses seeks to disassociate the law from God (e.g., Hübner 1984: 26; de Boer 2011: 228–29). If the law has a definite beginning, it also—and this is more directly relevant to the Galatian situation—has a definite end: it was to be in force only "until the seed to whom it was promised came" (ἄχρις οὗ ἔλθῃ τὸ σπέρμα ᾧ ἐπήγγελται, *achris hou elthē to sperma hō epēngeltai*).[11] The "seed," of course, is Christ (v. 16), and Paul has already made clear that the promise God made to Abraham had Christ as its ultimate referent. The NIV captures the sense: "until the Seed to whom the promise referred had come."

It is much more difficult to determine what Paul means by claiming that the law was added τῶν παραβάσεων χάριν (*tōn parabaseōn charin*). The word χάριν is a preposition that usually occurs, as here, in the "postpositive" position, after its object (Luke 7:47; Eph. 3:1, 14; 1 Tim. 5:14; Titus 1:5, 11; Jude 16; in 1 John 3:12 it comes before its object). The preposition can indicate a goal ("for the sake of") or a reason ("because of"; BDAG 1078–79). Paul uses it with both meanings. In Titus 1:11, he refers to rebellious people who are "teaching things they ought not to teach—and that *for the sake of* dishonest gain [αἰσχροῦ κέρδους χάριν, *aischrou kerdous charin*]." But in Eph. 3:1—Τούτου χάριν ἐγὼ Παῦλος ὁ δέσμιος (*Toutou charin egō Paulos ho desmios*)—it means "because of": "For this reason I, Paul, the prisoner . . ."). Interpreters debate which meaning Paul intends here, and what specifically he might be saying about the law in its relationship to "transgressions." There are four main options:

First, χάριν may mean "because of," and the phrase could refer to the law's function in revealing sin, in giving people a realization of their sinfulness: "the law was added because of the need to reveal to people their sins" (Calvin 1854: 64; cf. NLT: "[The law] was given alongside the promise to show people their sins"). This may be what Paul has in view in Rom. 3:20b, where he claims that "through the law we become conscious of our sin." A second view, sometimes not distinguished from the first, also takes χάριν to mean "because of," but understands the relationship between the law and sins more generally: "The law was given because of the need to deal with sins" (R. Longenecker 1990: 138). This "dealing with" sins could have either a negative sense, providing the mechanism to punish sins (Thielman 1989: 74–75)—or a positive sense, providing a means of keeping those sins in check or even a remedy for them (in the sacrificial system; Dunn 1993a: 189–90; cf.

---

11. The prepositional phrase ἄχρις οὗ is a well-established abbreviation of ἄχρις ἐκείνου χρόνου ἐν ᾧ, "until that time in which" (Moule 1959: 82).

also B. Longenecker 1998: 122–28; Burchard 1998: 189–91; Garlington 2003: 161). Third, χάριν might mean "for the sake of," and the phrase could refer to the way the law provoked sin: "the law was added for the sake of causing sins" (Betz 1979: 164–65; Schreiner 1993b: 74; Räisänen 1983: 14–48). The phrase "sinful passions aroused by the law" in Rom. 7:5 could indicate this concept. Fourth and finally, χάριν might mean "for the sake of," and the phrase may refer to the law's function of exacerbating the seriousness of sin and thereby uncovering its ultimate nature: "the law was added for the sake of turning sin into transgressions" (Mussner 1988: 245–46; Schlier 1989: 152–53; Witherington 1998: 255–56; Ridderbos 1975: 150–51).[12] It is likely that this is what Paul means in Rom. 5:20a when he says that "The law was brought in so that the trespass might increase [ἵνα πλεονάσῃ τὸ παράπτωμα, *hina pleonasē to paraptōma*]" (Moo 1996: 347–48).

Each of these interpretations has some basis in this context and/or in Paul's teaching elsewhere. But we think a crucial factor is Paul's decision to use the word παράβασις (*parabasis*, transgression) rather than, for instance, ἁμαρτία (*hamartia*, sin). The former word has a very definite sense in Paul, referring to the violation of a known law (see also Rom. 2:23; 4:15; 5:14; 1 Tim. 2:14). Paul's decision to use this word therefore favors the translation "for the sake of." As Burton (1921: 188) nicely puts it, παράβασις shows that Paul must be speaking "not of that which is antecedent but of that which is subsequent to the coming of the law." The law was not added, then, because of existing sins; Paul must be thinking of ways in which the coming of the law led to "transgressions." But this same consideration suggests that Paul is thinking not about the way the law might have led to more sinning, but the way in which the law in a sense turned existing sin into "transgression." In addition to Rom. 5:20a, cited above, Rom. 4:15 also supports this idea: "the law brings wrath. And where there is no law there is no transgression."[13] This verse comes in a context similar to the one we are considering, as Paul argues that it is the promise and not the law that can make people "heirs" (Rom. 4:14). The point of Rom. 4:15 is that the law, far from securing the promise, actually leads to more wrath because the law creates the necessary context for "transgression" (παράβασις). "Sin" is worthy of punishment; but the particular form of sin known as "transgression" evokes greater punishment because it involves conscious violation of a known law of God.

12. Of course, some interpreters suggest an allusion to two or more of these ideas. Bruce (1982b: 175) and R. Longenecker (1990: 138–39), e.g., think Paul intends a reference both to the exacerbating of sin and to an increase in actual sinning. Wallace (1990: 236–38) declines to decide between them.

13. Some interpreters rule out any appeal to Romans on the grounds that we should not "read into" one letter the argument from another. However, while it is necessary to pay careful attention to the argument of each letter in its own right, it is also surely legitimate, when seeking to understand an elliptical and enigmatic passage from an author, to look for evidence (even, in this case, evidence later in time) in other writings from that same author that might reveal more fully the writer's thinking on the particular matter.

Although the last clause of verse 19 is grammatically tied to the preceding context (the participle διαταγείς [*diatageis*, ordained, commanded] modifies προσετέθη), semantically it introduces a new idea that is developed in verse 20 (hence NIV and NET begin a new sentence with this clause). The verb διατάσσω (*diatassō*), from which διαταγείς comes, is an unusual choice to describe the giving of the law. It means "arrange" (e.g., Acts 20:13) or "command" (1 Cor. 7:17; Titus 1:5) and is never used elsewhere in Biblical Greek to refer to the giving of the law. This unusual verb and Paul's reference to angels rather than to God have led some interpreters to argue that he is deliberately distancing the law from God (see esp. Hübner 1984: 26–29; and also Schoeps 1959: 182–83; Räisänen 1983: 129–31; Schlier 1989: 159–60; Vouga 1998: 83; Martyn 1997: 356–57; Kuula 1999: 104–17; G. Delling, *TDNT* 8:35). But these factors are not nearly strong enough to lead us to think that Paul is suggesting so extreme a view here (see Bring 1969: 81–86; Westerholm 2004: 412–14). The preposition διά (*dia*), while it can signify origin, much more commonly refers to instrumentality (e.g., Wallace 1996: 434). In other words, Paul is claiming not that "the law was put in place *by* angels" but that "the law was ordained *through* angels." The idea that angels were involved in the giving of the law is not taught anywhere in the OT (though see Deut. 33:2 LXX), but it is a common Jewish tradition (Jub. 1.27–2.1; Philo, *Somn.* 1.143; Josephus, *Ant.* 15.136) that has left its mark on the NT elsewhere (Acts 7:38, 53; Heb. 2:2). In none of these texts does the mention of angels suggest any question about its divine origin; on the contrary, the emphasis, if anything, is on the holiness and majesty of the law (Bring 1969: 81–83). Nevertheless, this kind of emphasis seems out of keeping with Paul's depreciation of the law's importance in this context, leaving open the question of why he adds this idea here. The best explanation is that he is setting up a contrast that he intends to draw in verse 20 (see comments on 3:20).

The final phrase of verse 19 also sounds a traditional note: the law was put in place "by the hand of a mediator" (ἐν χειρὶ μεσίτου, *en cheiri mesitou*). "By the hand of" is a standard Hebrew idiom signifying instrumentality; most English versions drop the idiom in favor simply of "through" or "by." A few interpreters have thought that the mediator might be Christ (e.g., Chrysostom, *Comm. Gal.* on 3:20 [*NPNF*[1] 13:28]; Calvin 1854: 65; cf. 1 Tim. 2:5; Heb. 8:6; 9:15; 12:24). But according to the OT, it is Moses who is the mediator of the law. While the word μεσίτης is never used of Moses or with reference to the law (it only occurs once in the OT [Job 9:33]), the phrase ἐν χειρὶ Μωυσῆ (*en cheiri Mōysē*, by the hand of Moses) occurs twenty-one times, usually with reference to Moses as the one through whom God gave his law to Israel. This common phrase makes it questionable whether Paul has a particular text in view (Exod. 34:29 [Callan 1980: 559–61] or Lev. 26:46 [Silva 2007: 805; Bruno 2010: 268–72]). In any case, there is no reason to doubt that it is Moses whom Paul has in mind.

Having introduced the "mediator" in verse 19c, Paul now adds an argument based on the concept of mediation. Unfortunately, what argument he intends to make is unclear and perhaps not even recoverable. A bewildering number of

3:20

interpretations exist (one interpreter, hyperbolically and with allusion to verse 17, claims 430 construals [Oepke 1973: 82]), and none has commanded even a significant plurality of support. In the second half of the verse, the basic challenge is to figure out how Paul's claim that "God is one" functions in relationship to the first half of the verse. The most natural reading is that Paul is contrasting the work of a mediator, which is *not* "of one" (ἑνός, *henos*), with God, who is "one" (εἷς, *heis*). But what does this contrast mean? And how does it contribute to Paul's overall argument in these verses about the law in relationship to the promises?

Answers to these questions tend to fall into three basic categories. First, some interpreters think that "the mediator is not of one" establishes a contrast with the many angels who, Paul has claimed in verse 19, were involved in the giving of the law (e.g., Schlier 1989: 161; Martyn 1997: 365–70; Kuula 1999: 104–17). Those who adopt this view usually identify the "mediator" in verse 20a as Moses (taking the article as anaphoric [A. Oepke, *TDNT* 4:618]). Moses's mediation on behalf of many (the angels) shows that he is not a mediator of "one." Yet God is "one," and so Moses's work of mediation could not have been on behalf of God. According to this interpretation, then, verse 20 puts a distance between God and the law.

A second direction of interpretation understands the contrast implied by the emphasis on "one" as referring to the two different parties involved in the notion of mediation (e.g., Lightfoot 1881: 146–47; Burton 1921: 190; R. Longenecker 1990: 142; Mussner 1988: 248–50; Ridderbos 1975: 216). Most who take this view then think that μεσίτης refers to a mediator in general (the article suggesting a generic reference). "A mediator" (so most English versions) by definition implies the existence of two parties. And it does, indeed, require the cooperation of two parties to make the law effective: the lawgiver as well as response from the people to whom the law is given (the "doing" of vv. 10, 12). The promise arrangement, on the other hand, involves "one" party, God, who initiates the arrangement (with faith itself being more of an acceptance of the arrangement than a true requirement for enactment).

A third option is less often found in the literature but deserves mention. Common to this approach is the suggestion that the focus on "one" in this verse might be illuminated by the significant mention of "one" only a few verses earlier: "The promises were spoken to Abraham and to his seed. Scripture does not say 'and to seeds,' meaning many people, but 'and to your seed,' meaning one person, who is Christ." N. T. Wright (1993: 157–74) thinks that the "one person" in verse 16 refers to the one people of God (see our comments on 3:16), and so, here, Paul is saying that Moses is not the mediator through which the one people of God can be created (the article with μεσίτης would again signal anaphora). Bruno (2010: 274–83), on the other hand, suggests that "one," in light of verse 16, might refer to the Abrahamic covenant: Moses is not the one who mediates the promise covenant, a covenant that ultimately envisages the inclusion of Gentiles.[14]

---

14. See also somewhat similar proposals by Calvin 1854: 66; Garlington 2003: 162; Bring 1969: 73–111; Brawley 2002: 103–5.

A decision among these options is not easy. One important matter is how the confession "but God is one" (ὁ δὲ θεὸς εἷς ἐστιν [*ho de theos heis estin*]) fits into the argument. Paul is alluding to the Shema, the classic Jewish confession rooted in Deut. 6:4: "Hear, O Israel: The LORD our God, the LORD is one" (LXX: κύριος ὁ θεὸς ἡμῶν κύριος εἷς ἐστιν [*kyrios ho theos hēmōn kyrios heis estin*]). On either of the first two interpretations, this assertion functions as a simple reminder that God is a single entity. But the assertion has more point with the first view because of the contrast with angels. Common to the third view is an allusion to Gentile inclusion; and this could make sense because the confession that "God is one" in Rom. 3:29–30 also functions to warrant the full membership of Gentiles within the people of God.[15] Another point in favor of the first interpretation is its ability to explain the otherwise somewhat puzzling mention of the angels in verse 19. Yet the idea that Paul might be trying to distance God from the giving of the law remains problematic. And the third view, while attractively drawing attention to the significance of "one" in this context, requires that we read too much into either verse 16 or verse 20. On the whole, then, the second general approach to this verse offers the fewest difficulties. The very existence of a mediator in the giving of the law implies an involvement on the human side that stands in contrast to the gift-character of the promise, suggested (albeit very remotely) by the confession that God is one.

Verse 21 opens with a rhetorical question: ὁ οὖν νόμος κατὰ τῶν ἐπαγγελιῶν (*ho oun nomos kata tōn epangeliōn*), "Is the law therefore against the promises?" The question puts more sharply the issue raised by the question "Why then the law?" in verse 19. This new question could arise from what Paul has said in the immediate context (vv. 19b–20; see Betz 1979: 173) or in the much wider context (vv. 1–20; see Hays 2000: 268), but it more likely reflects the argument about the relationship of law and promise from verse 15 onward (Burton 1921: 192; R. Longenecker 1990: 143). The question may embody just the kind of objection that Paul knows is being brought against him by the agitators (Martyn 1997: 358). But it might be better to see the question as Paul's means of introducing his own conclusion; as Calvin (1854: 67) paraphrases, "Who will then dare to imagine a disagreement between the law and the promises?" (This question and its answer are very hard to explain if Paul has just claimed that the law did not come from God.)

Paul rejects any such contradiction between the law and the promises with his characteristic vigorous μὴ γένοιτο (*mē genoito*): "Absolutely not!" (NIV; see 2:17). In the second part of the verse, he explains (hence the γάρ [*gar*], for) why the two are not in conflict: εἰ γὰρ ἐδόθη νόμος ὁ δυνάμενος ζῳοποιῆσαι, ὄντως ἐκ νόμου ἂν ἦν ἡ δικαιοσύνη (*ei gar edothē nomos ho dynamenos zōopoiēsai, ontōs ek nomou an ēn hē dikaiosynē*), "for if a law that could make

3:21

---

15. Bruno (2010) argues, specifically and convincingly, that this notion of Gentile inclusion comes via the allusion to the Shema (Deut. 6:4) in Zech. 14:9: "The LORD will be king over the whole earth. On that day there will be one LORD, and his name the only name."

alive had been given, then truly righteousness would have come by the law. The ἄν in the second clause marks this as a "contrary to fact" conditional sentence.[16] The logic of this kind of sentence is "if A then B; not B; therefore not A." What this means is clear: Paul is proving that a law able to make alive has not been given, and the fact that righteousness does not come by the law shows this. Paul has made this last point in, among other places, 2:21b–c, a sentence in the same form (without the ἄν) as the one in this verse and filling out the argument that Paul is making here:

Christ did not die in vain (2:21c).

Therefore righteousness does not come by the law (διὰ νόμου, *dia nomou*; 2:21b).

And since righteousness does not come by the law (ἐκ νόμου, *ek nomou*; 3:21d),
no law that can make alive has ever been given (3:21c).

Our paraphrase "no law" reflects the likelihood that the anarthous νόμος means "any God-given law" (R. Longenecker 1990: 143). And the logic of Paul's argument also reveals that "making alive" and "righteousness" are closely related. The verb ζωοποιέω (*zōopoieō*) is, as Betz (1979) notes, a "soteriological term in Paul." In some Pauline texts, it refers to ultimate life, resurrection life (Rom. 8:11; 1 Cor. 15:22, 36, 45; cf. also the way present justification is the cause of future life in Rom. 8:10–11). Some interpreters therefore think that here Paul argues from cause to effect: righteousness, given in Christ, provides infallibly for the resurrection life of the last day (e.g., Fung 1988: 163). Others, however, argue in just the opposite way: "'righteousness' describes the status before God of one who has been 'made alive' by his Spirit" (Dunn 1993a: 193; cf. Rom. 4:17 and 2 Cor. 3:6, where the verb refers generally to soteriological life). Effectively, however, the two terms ("making alive" and "righteousness) are virtually equivalent, the one focusing on process and the other on resultant status (Burton 1921: 195; Bruce 1982b: 180; D. Campbell 2009: 866–67).[17] The equivalence of the two terms is suggested also by 3:11–12, where "live" (ζάω) is a soteriological term. But the reference to 3:12 raises another issue: how are we to square Paul's reference to the typically Jewish view that "the one who does [the commandments of the law] will find life by them" with his claim here that no law can make alive? As we have suggested earlier (in comments on 3:10–12), we think the answer that Paul implies in Galatians and makes explicit in Romans (1:18–3:20) is that no person is able

16. This contrary-to-fact conditional sentence using ἄν is comparatively rare in Paul: cf. Rom. 9:29 [= Isa. 1:9]; 1 Cor. 2:8; 11:31; Gal. 1:10.

17. Contra D. Campbell, however, there is no reason to think that Paul presents this righteousness/life as providing the answer to the confinement under that law that Paul refers to in this context—an argument that Campbell uses to buttress his "forensic-liberative" notion of justification (see "The Importance of Justification in Galatians" in the introduction).

to meet the demands of the law. The life that the law promises, a common Jewish teaching that Paul endorses (Rom. 7:10; cf., e.g., Sir. 17:11: "the life-giving law" [AT]; *m. 'Abot* 2.8: "the more Torah, the more life"), is inevitably frustrated by the debilitating reality of human sinfulness. Thus there is no conflict between God's law and God's promises. Only through the promise arrangement that God entered into with Abraham and that requires faith in response can righteousness/eschatological life be found. The law has other purposes, which Paul delineates in this context. From a soteriological perspective, then, the law plays a subsidiary role, entering into salvation history to "administer" the promise covenant that God established with Abraham and his "seed" (see McComiskey 1985).

Paul introduces this verse with ἀλλά (*alla*, but), signifying that he intends to contrast what the law cannot do—make alive/secure righteousness (v. 21)— with what it does do: confine all things under sin. Yet Paul disrupts this contrast somewhat by shifting terms, from νόμος, which he uses in verse 21 (and in vv. 17–19) to ἡ γραφή (*hē graphē*, the Scripture). Paul may do so because he has in view a single verse from within the law, such as Deut. 27:26, which he has quoted in verse 10 (Lightfoot 1881: 147–48; Burton 1921: 195; R. Longenecker 1990: 144; Howard 1979: 59). As we noted in our comments on 3:8, Paul often singles out a particular text in this way when he refers to the singular γραφή. Yet we think it more likely that Paul here, as in 3:8, has in view the testimony of Scripture in general, with a focus perhaps on how the OT as a whole functions, via the law, to bring everything under sin's power (Mussner 1988: 253; cf. similarly Dunn 1993a: 194; Belleville 1986: 56). The demands of the law, because they are ultimately impossible for sinful humans to fulfill, serve to "confine" all things under sin. The verb Paul uses, συγκλείω (*synkleiō*), means to "enclose" (as fish are enclosed in a net; Luke 5:6) or "confine," "imprison" (see BDAG 952). Paul's three uses of the word all have this sense (see also v. 23; Rom. 11:32). Here the object of the imprisoning power of the law is "all things" (πάντα, *panta*). The neuter plural can have a limited reference, to humans only (BDF §138.1; R. Longenecker 1990: 144; note NASB, "everyone"), but in contrast to Rom. 11:32 (where in a similar clause Paul claims that God has "confined all persons [τοὺς πάντας, *tous pantas*] to disobedience"), Paul may deliberately here use the neuter form to indicate a broader reference to the whole cosmos, in keeping with the reversal that Paul proclaims with the language of "new creation" (6:15; Martyn 1997: 360; Witherington 1998: 260). Romans 8:18–22 shows that Paul views the entire cosmos as having been made subject to "bondage of decay" (8:21) because of sin.

"Under sin" (ὑπὸ ἁμαρτίαν, *hypo hamartian*) is the first of an important series of phrases that refer to humans (or in this case, all creation) being placed "under the power" of something ("under the law" [Gal. 3:23; 4:4, 5, 21; 5:18], "under a *paidagōgos* [παιδαγωγός, guardian]" [3:25], "under guardians" [4:2], "under the elements of the world" [4:3] [cf. "under a curse" in

3:22

3:10]). Paul pictures sin as a power that exerts its influence over the world, with particular focus in this context on the condemnation that results from sin's domination.[18]

The imprisoning of all things under sin has the purpose (ἵνα, *hina*, in order that) of ensuring that "what was promised might be given through faith in Jesus Christ for those who believe." This purpose clause shows that behind "the Scripture" in verse 22a stands God himself, who has worked through the imprisoning and condemning effect of Scripture to accomplish his ultimate purpose. "What was promised" translates ἡ ἐπαγγελία (*hē epangelia*, the promise), denoting not the act of promising but the content of what is promised (see RSV, NRSV, NIV). In context, this content is the righteousness to which Paul has referred in verse 21, the justification, extended to the Gentiles, that was originally promised to Abraham (v. 8) and sealed by the Spirit (v. 14). It is "those who believe" (τοῖς πιστεύουσιν, *tois pisteuousin*) who receive this promise, and it is given ἐκ πίστεως Ἰησοῦ Χριστοῦ (*ek pisteōs Iēsou Christou*). Here we confront another of the debated faith-of-Christ phrases, which many recent interpreters construe as a reference to the faithfulness of (shown by) Jesus Christ (taking the genitive as subjective; e.g., Martyn 1997: 361; Hays 2002: 112–16, 141–53; Wallace 1996: 115–16; D. Campbell 2005: 208–32). Advocates of this interpretation think that it makes particularly good sense in this verse since it avoids the apparent redundancy of referring to human belief twice in the same clause. However, as we argue in the section on "The Faith of Christ" in the introduction, there are good reasons for rejecting the subjective-genitive interpretation of this and related phrases. Paul's focus on Abraham's faith as the corollary to the Galatians' faith (3:5–6) sets the parameters for his understanding of faith in this context (Dunn 1993a: 195; Ulrichs 2007: 140–48; Matlock 2007: 187–93; 2009b: 81–83). The claim of redundancy can be refuted (if not entirely dismissed) by recognizing the different emphases in the two phrases. What God promised—righteousness—is given to people who *believe* (emphasis on the activity) by means of faith *in Christ Jesus* (emphasis on the object of faith).

Calvin (1854: 68) remarks about this verse:

> This sentence is full of the highest consolation. It tells us that, wherever we hear ourselves condemned in Scripture, there is help provided for us in Christ, if we betake ourselves to him. We are lost, though God were silent: why then does he so often pronounce that we are lost? It is that we may not perish by everlasting destruction, but, struck and confounded by such a dreadful sentence, may by faith seek Christ, through whom we "pass from death unto life."

3:23 Verses 23–25 form a unit, framed by references to the "coming" of faith (Mussner 1988: 254). In these verses, Paul provides more detail about the sequence of law/imprisonment and Christ/faith/righteousness that he has just described

---

18. This focus on sin as a power is particularly common in Romans, where ἁμαρτία occurs almost fifty times, usually in the singular. The word plays little role in Galatians, occurring only three times (in addition to 3:22 are 1:4 and 2:17).

(vv. 21–22) and that he has introduced in other terms in verses 15–18, with its contrast between law, on the one hand, and Christ, promise, and inheritance, on the other. Paul describes this contrast in personal terms, using the first-person plural: "We were guarded . . . our guardian . . . that we might be justified . . . We are no longer under the law." As we noted in our comments on 3:13, the people that Paul has in mind when he uses these first-person plural forms is unclear. Paul uses his pronouns so flexibly and with so many contextually related considerations that it is impossible to establish any general rule. The first-person plural form could naturally refer to Paul and the Galatians, and thus by extension to Christians generally, or even to all humans (van Dülmen 1968: 46; Bruce 1982b: 182; Hübner 1984: 33; Mussner 1988: 256; Martyn 1997: 362; de Boer 2011: 238; Dalton 1990: 39–40). But Paul's explicit reference to "we who are by nature Jews" in 2:15 also sets up the possibility that he has mainly or even exclusively Jews in view (Dunn 1993a: 198; R. Longenecker 1990: 145; Garlington 2003: 165; Matera 1992: 143–44; Witherington 1998: 267). This seems likely here because of the focus on historical experience with the law—which in Paul usually refers to the Mosaic law, the body of commandments that God handed down to Israel at Sinai. Probably, then, we should read verses 23–25 as a description of salvation history, and especially of the movement from the old era when the law had a central role in governing the relationship between God and his people to the new era, in which the law no longer continues to function in this way. Nevertheless, the sequence of Paul's argument, as he applies this salvation-historical sequence to the situation of the Galatians (see esp. 4:4–9), reveals that he somehow views this salvation-historical sequence as relating to and even in some sense including the Galatians (Räisänen 1983: 20–21).

Within this salvation-historical framework "the faith" (τὴν πίστιν, *tēn pistin*) that "has come" will refer to the faith in Jesus Christ that Paul has just mentioned in verse 22 (the article, therefore, has an anaphoric significance: hence NIV "*this* faith"; and see, e.g., Burton 1921: 198). Of course, if the genitive construction at the end of verse 22 is construed as subjective, then "the faith" in verse 23 will refer to the faith/faithfulness exercised *by* Jesus Christ. And to be sure, this opening clause in verse 23 constitutes perhaps the strongest single exegetical point in favor of this interpretation. Paul has made quite clear that Abraham, long before the coming of Christ, had faith: so, it is argued, the "faith" that had not yet arrived in the era of the law cannot refer to human faith (see, e.g., Hays 2000: 269–70). Despite this point, however, we think that the weight of the evidence favors a reference to human faith throughout this section of the letter. Paul may thus be referring to the "era characterized by the dominance of faith" (Bruce [1982b: 181] argues that this is part of the meaning), or perhaps more likely, to faith in its distinctly christological dimension. Faith has always been the means by which humans relate to God. The object of that faith has now been revealed as the God who has decisively revealed himself in the Son: and this, for Paul, is the key point to be made in response to the agitators.

In the era before faith in its christological shape arrived, the people of Israel were "guarded under the law" (ὑπὸ νόμον ἐφρουρούμεθα, *hypo nomon ephrouroumetha*), "confined" (συγκλειόμενοι, *synkleiomenoi*) until that faith was revealed. Paul continues to use the language of "imprisonment" that he introduced in verse 22: συγκλειόμενοι is from the same verb that Paul has used in verse 22, and φρουρέω (*phroureō*) has the sense of "guard," "confine" (see 1 Cor. 11:32). To be sure, φρουρέω can also have the relatively positive nuance of "keep under protection," as in Phil. 4:7 ("the peace of God . . . will *guard* your hearts") and 1 Pet. 1:5 ("*shielded* by God's power"). Dunn (1993a: 197) and Matera (1992: 136) argue that the verb may have this meaning here: the law exercised a protective and even benevolent watch over Israel (see also O. Michel, *TDNT* 7:746). We certainly need to avoid an overly negative view of the law's ministry in the life of Israel. Yet the parallel between "under the law" in this verse and "under sin" in verse 22, as well as the obvious point that Paul views being *not* "under the law" as a good thing, suggests that the idea here tends toward the negative rather than the positive. Israel was "in custody" under the law and, for all the undeniably positive aspects of this custodianship, it was nevertheless a custody that brought with it a servitude to sin from which the law was unable to provide a release. "The Law discloses the truth about our human condition: We are alienated from God and stand under God's righteous judgment" (Hays 2000: 268). To be "under the law," then, is to be subject to the law's power (see Belleville 1986; and the additional note on 3:23).

This subjection is related to, but not identical to, subjection to the domination of sin (v. 22) and the curse that sin brings with it (see 3:10, 13).[19] The law, God's good and holy law (Rom. 7:12), is in itself impotent to rescue fallen human beings from their sinful state and the wrath that sin brings in its wake. It is the coming of faith that ends this situation, as Paul notes again at the end of the verse: "until the faith that was about to be revealed" (εἰς τὴν μέλλουσαν πίστιν ἀποκαλυφθῆναι, *eis tēn mellousan pistin apokalyphthēnai*). As at the beginning of the verse, "the faith" refers to faith in Christ. Most of the English versions and commentators treat the εἰς as temporal: "*until* faith [in Christ] should be revealed." This interpretation of the preposition makes good sense in the context, which has explicit temporal indicators ("before faith came" [v. 23]; "when faith came" [v. 25]). However, a purely temporal meaning of εἰς is very rare in Paul.[20] It is preferable, then, to interpret εἰς as

---

19. Contra those who think that the phrase functions as shorthand for "under the curse of the law" (as do Thielman 1989: 77–78; Hong 2002: 360–62; Wilson 2007: 30–44). Marcus (2001: 72–80) suggests that Paul may have inherited the phrase from the agitators, but the idea that the agitators may have used the phrase in a threatening manner seems unlikely.

20. The most likely place in Paul where εἰς has a purely temporal meaning is 1 Thess. 4:15: ἡμεῖς οἱ ζῶντες οἱ περιλειπόμενοι εἰς τὴν παρουσίαν τοῦ κυρίου (*hēmeis hoi zōntes hoi perileipomenoi eis tēn parousian tou kyriou*, we who are still alive, who are left *until* the coming of the Lord). BDAG (289.2.a.α) also cites Phil. 1:10 and 2 Tim. 1:12, but the εἰς ἡμέραν (*eis hēmeran*) in both texts probably has at least a slight telic nuance: "looking to the day . . ." The same is probably true for the (debated) phrase εἰς [τὸ] τέλος (*eis [to] telos*, to the end, at last) in 2 Cor. 3:13; 1 Thess. 2:16.

having its very common combined temporal/telic sense, perfectly captured in the (unfortunately outdated) English "unto" (see KJV). Paul may have chosen this preposition (instead of, for instance, ἄχρι [achri, until] or ἕως [heōs, until]) to hint at his view of salvation history as a series of events that lead up to a point of climax or culmination (see esp. Rom. 10:4 and Moo 1996: 636–43). God imposed the custodianship of the law not simply "until" faith in Christ arrived but "with a view to" that eschatological climax.

The ὥστε (hōste, so that) at the beginning of the verse introduces verses 24–25   **3:24** as the summing up of Paul's explanation of the relationship between the time of the law and time of "faith in Christ" that began in verse 21b. The verses are structured chiastically: time of the law, coming of Christ—coming of faith, time of the law. Paul introduces a fresh metaphor to capture the nature of the relationship between the two eras of salvation history: the παιδαγωγός (paidagōgos, guardian). What Paul intends to convey with this word has been much debated. One view, given classic representation in the famous language of the KJV—"the law was our schoolmaster to bring us unto Christ"—is that the παιδαγωγός presents the law as a positive, educating force that brings people (perhaps by making them cognizant of their sin) to Christ. In addition to giving παιδαγωγός the meaning of "teacher" or "tutor" (NKJV, NASB), this view also assumes that the εἰς (eis, to/unto/until) that governs Χριστόν (Christon, Christ) has a telic sense. Both these decisions have good support in the older literature (e.g., Burton 1921: 200) but do not receive much support from contemporary scholars. Dunn (1993a: 198–99; 1995: 460–63) is something of an exception to this trend: he suggests that Paul views Israel as a child who needs the law to protect it from the evil influence of sin and idolatry (cf. also Braswell 1991: 84–85; for a critique of Dunn's view, see Riches 2008: 187, 203–4).

Nevertheless, the nature of the παιδαγωγός in the ancient world and the context combine to make clear that Paul's use of the imagery here is at least neutral, if not slightly negative. R. Longenecker (1990: 146–48) provides an excellent summary of the ancient descriptions of the παιδαγωγός (see also Witherington 1998: 262–67). This person (almost always a male, usually a slave) had the responsibility of caring for the young children, seeing that they did their chores, got back and forth to school safely, and so forth (see, e.g., Plato, *Lysis* 208c). They were not teachers and were sometimes noted for the harsh discipline that was considered indispensable for raising children well. The parallel images of "guardians and trustees" in 4:2 suggests, however, that these negative associations are not to the fore here (contra, e.g., Betz 1979: 177–78; Martyn 1997: 363; Hong 2002: 363–64; Pollmann 2012: 184–88). Rather, as B. Longenecker (1998: 127) concludes, the imagery would naturally convey the two ideas of supervisory role and temporal limits. The law was given by God to supervise Israel in its "childhood"—but only εἰς Χριστόν. Most of the modern translations and commentators (e.g., Bruce 1982b: 183; Fung 1988: 169; R. Longenecker 1990: 148–49) treat this phrase as temporal: "until the Messiah came." As we noted in our comments on verse 23, however, a purely temporal meaning of εἰς is unlikely. We are not therefore suggesting a reversion to the older idea of the law as that which "leads us" to Christ—a view that fits neither the imagery of the παιδαγωγός nor Paul's conception of the law. Rather, Paul will again be suggesting the dynamic and forward-looking quality of salvation history. The era when the law "kept watch" over Israel anticipated and looked toward the time when the Messiah would arrive—ending that function of the law. As Calvin (1854: 70) puts it, "The *law* was the grammar of theology, which, after carrying its scholar a short way, handed them over to *faith* to be completed." This emphasis on faith in the final clause of the verse—ἵνα ἐκ πίστεως δικαιωθῶμεν (*hina ek pisteōs dikaiōthōmen*, in order that we might be justified by faith)—is a reminder that throughout this text Paul is concerned not only with the coming of Christ and the inclusion of Gentiles but also with the establishment of faith (as opposed to "doing"; cf. vv. 10, 12) as the means of gaining righteousness (Starling 2011: 54).

3:25 Paul now repeats what he has said in verse 24, reversing the order of elements for rhetorical effect. He again uses "faith" to characterize the new era of salvation history, with the article before πίστεως (*pisteōs*, faith) again denoting the particular manifestation of faith in Christ that marks this new era. The first-person plural form, as in verses 23 and 24, probably refers to the people of Israel. However, particularly here, where Paul is bringing to a climax his argument about the salvation-historical shift that has taken place with the coming of Christ/faith, there may also be some indirect reference to the Galatians as well: "We Jews—and certainly, therefore, any of us, including you Galatians—are no longer under a guardian." It is hard to know whether the anarthrous παιδαγωγόν (*paidagōgon*, guardian) is qualitative (perhaps the TNIV's "under the supervision of the law" captures this nuance), indefinite (in most translations), or (most likely) definite (see Wallace 1996: 263–64, who notes that anarthrous nouns that precede the verb [as here] are usually qualitative or definite).

Additional Notes

3:16. The general similarity of Paul's exegesis of the "one seed" of Genesis to Jewish methods can be seen in Gen. Rab. 22.9, which cites Gen. 4:10—"your brother's blood [דְּמֵי, a plural construct] cries out to me from the ground"—and gives Rabbi Judah's explanation: "It is not written, 'your brother's blood,' but 'your brother's bloods'—his blood and the blood of his descendants" (Silva 2007: 807).

The evidence for a singular reference in the word σπέρμα in some of the Genesis promise texts has been marshaled by Collins (2003) and Alexander (1997), who argue that זֶרַע, "seed," has a singular reference when it is followed by a singular possessive. Thus, for instance, in Gen. 22:17–18, וְיִרַשׁ זַרְעֲךָ אֵת שַׁעַר אֹיְבָיו, the word זַרְעֲךָ may have a singular reference because of the singular possessive on אֹיְבָיו: "your seed shall take possession of the cities of *his* enemies." The "seed" in such texts would, of course, be Isaac, the immediate descendant of Abraham. Moreover, Paul may cite Gen. 22:18 in Gal. 3:8 (see also, for this general line of argument, S. Hahn 2005: 95–96; Watson 2004: 191; Garlington 2003: 159). Some Jewish texts also single out a single "descendant" of Abraham in commenting on these texts: see, e.g., Jub. 16.16b–18:

And through Isaac a name and seed would be named for him. And all of the seed of his sons would become nations. And they would be counted with the nations. But from the sons of Isaac one would become a holy seed and he would not be counted among the nations because he would become the portion of the Most High and all his seed would fall (by lot) into that which God will rule so that he might become a people (belonging) to the Lord, a (special) possession from all people, and so that he might become a kingdom of priests and a holy people. (O. S. Wintermute, *OTP* 2:88)

3:17. Paul's figure of "four hundred and thirty years" for the interval between God's promise to Abraham and the giving of the law to Moses seems to be taken from Exod. 12:40: "Now the length of time the Israelite people lived in Egypt was 430 years" (see also Josephus, *Ant.* 2.318: the Israelites "left Egypt in the month of Xanthicus, on the fifteenth by lunar reckoning, 430 years after the coming of our forefather Abraham to Canaan"). An interval of four hundred years, however, is given in Gen. 15:13: "Then the Lord said to him, 'Know for certain that for four hundred years your descendants will be strangers in a country not their own and that they will be enslaved and mistreated there'" (see also Acts 7:6). The rabbis commented quite a bit on this apparent discrepancy in numbers, most of them concluding that the four hundred and thirty years applied to the time from God's covenant with Abraham to the giving of the law, while the four hundred years referred to the time that Israel spent in Egypt (Str-B 2:670). Paul may therefore be relying on this Jewish tradition rather than on Exodus for his four hundred and thirty years (R. Longenecker 1990: 133).

3:19. In place of Τί οὖν ὁ νόμος; τῶν παραβάσεων χάριν προσετέθη, one uncial (D*), along with some ancient versions, reads Τί οὖν ὁ νόμος; τῶν παραδόσεων χάριν ἐτέθη (Why then the law? It was established because of traditioning); two other uncials (F and G, as well as several MSS of the old Latin) have Τί οὖν ὁ νόμος τῶν πράξεων; ἐτέθη ("Why then the law of deeds? It was established . . ."); and one early papyrus MS ($\mathfrak{P}^{46}$) reads simply Τί οὖν ὁ νόμος τῶν πράξεων ("Why then the law of deeds?"). None of these alternative readings has any claim to be original; they may be due to "inattentive copyists" (Metzger 1994: 525) or to the theological difficulty of the accepted text.

3:21. Most of the MSS include the words τοῦ θεοῦ after ἐπαγγελιῶν. But they are absent in two important MSS ($\mathfrak{P}^{46}$ and B). It is difficult to know if scribes have added the words from similar passages, such as Rom. 4:20, τὴν ἐπαγγελίαν τοῦ θεοῦ, and 2 Cor. 1:20, ἐπαγγελίαι θεοῦ, or if the words have been accidentally omitted. The UBS committee (cf. Metzger 1994: 525–26) slightly preferred this latter option, as do most commentators (e.g., Burton 1921: 193; R. Longenecker 1990: 143), and all the major English versions include the equivalent of these words.

3:21. The sequence and choice of words in the last part of the verse varies in the MSS:

> ἐκ νόμου ἂν ἦν (A C 81 1241 2464)
> ἂν ἐκ νόμου ἦν (D² 0176^vid 𝔐)
> ἐκ νόμου ἦν ἄν (א Ψ* 0278 33 104 365 630 1175 1739)
> ἐν νόμῳ ἦν ἄν ($\mathfrak{P}^{46}$)
> ἐν νόμῳ ἂν ἦν (B)
> ἐκ νόμου ἦν (D* 1881)
> ἐκ νόμου (F G)

The variations are probably due to scribal mistakes (writing ἄν or ἦν, and ἐκ or ἐν [Betz 1979: 174]). The only issues affecting interpretation are whether the ἄν should be included (the weight of the evidence suggests it should be) and whether the preposition should be ἐκ or ἐν (where, again, the MSS point strongly to ἐκ). For evaluation, favoring option 1 (which is the NA²⁸ and UBS⁴ reading), see Burton 1921: 194.

3:21. Reformed theologians, especially, have long debated the relationship between the Abrahamic and Mosaic covenants and, related to this issue, the relationship between the alleged covenant with Adam in the garden of Eden and the Mosaic covenant (for discussion, see, e.g., Schrenk 1923; Karlberg 2000). Our comments about the subordinate and, in a sense, nonsoteriological nature of the Mosaic covenant are focused on the way Paul presents the matter here in Galatians. It must always be remembered that the polemical nature of the letter leads Paul to stress certain aspects of the salvation-historical relationship while neglecting others. Paul does not give us a false picture of the matter in Galatians; but he does give us a partial and imbalanced one. Particularly important for Paul's theology in general is to recognize his fundamental and quite radical distinction between faith and works. He therefore presents the law, and by extension the Mosaic covenant, as a matter of works and not of faith (e.g., 3:11–12). He does not thereby deny that the Pentateuch and even, in one sense, the law itself call for faith (e.g., the "circumcision of the heart"). But for Paul it is a matter of definition that "law" involves "doing" in distinction from believing. From his standpoint at the "turn of the ages," Paul therefore speaks about the law "in itself" (what Calvin called the "bare law"; *Institutes* 2.7.2) and contrasts it with the Abrahamic covenant.

3:23. The meaning of the phrase "under the law" (ὑπὸ νόμον), which occurs both here and in some other key verses in Galatians, is debated. The phrase occurs five times in Galatians:

> Before the coming of this faith, we were held in custody *under the law*, locked up until the faith that was to come would be revealed. (3:23)

> But when the set time had fully come, God sent his Son, born of a woman, born *under the law*, ⁵to redeem those *under the law*, that we might receive adoption to sonship. (4:4–5)

> Tell me, you who want to be *under the law*, are you not aware of what the law says? (4:21)

> But if you are led by the Spirit, you are not *under the law*. (5:18)

It also occurs twice in Romans and four times in one verse in 1 Corinthians:

> For sin shall no longer be your master, because you are not *under the law*, but under grace. (Rom. 6:14)

> What then? Shall we sin because we are not *under the law* but under grace? By no means! (Rom. 6:15)

> To the Jews I became like a Jew, to win the Jews. To those *under the law* I became like one *under the law* (though I myself am not *under the law*), so as to win those *under the law*. (1 Cor. 9:20)

The parallel between being "under sin" in 3:22 and being "under the law" in 3:23, as well as the contrast between being "under the law" on the one hand, and being "led by the Spirit" (Gal. 5:18) and being "under grace" (Rom. 6:14–15) on the other, has led many interpreters to think that the phrase refers to the condemnation experienced by those who, governed by the law, are unable to fulfill its demands. In Galatians, then, "under the law" would be equivalent to being under "the curse of the law" (3:13). (For this line of interpretation, see Schreiner 1993b: 77–81; Hong 2002: 360–70; Wilson 2007: 35–36; Baumert and Meissner 2010: 101–10; on Romans, e.g., Murray 1957: 187–88; Cranfield 1975: 319–20.)[21] But there is some reason to think that this understanding of the phrase may go too far. If being "under the law" means simply being subject to the curse of the law, it is difficult to understand why the Galatian Christians would be seeking to be "under the law" (Gal. 4:21). Moreover, while the text is debated, 1 Cor. 9:20 appears to use the phrase to refer simply to being under the jurisdiction of the law. It seems better, then, to view the phrase "under the law" in Galatians as roughly parallel to the phrases "under a *paidagōgos*" (3:24, 25) and "under guardians and trustees" (4:2). It refers, in the first instance at least, to Jews who, by virtue of their membership in the people of the covenant, are

---

21. A few interpreters have suggested that the phrase might signal a legalistic abuse of the law (Moule 1967: 394–95; Hübner 1984: 134–35 [on Rom. 6:14–15]; Fuller 1980: 96, 203). For responses to the idea that Paul refers to legalism in such phrases, see Moo 1983; Westerholm 2004: 330–35.

subject to the law of that covenant (see esp. Belleville 1986). Being subject to the law in the era after Christ does, in fact, entail condemnation, because only in Christ is justification to be found; and one cannot be both "in Christ" and be bound to the law (see, e.g., Rom. 7:4–6). (Of course, this does not mean that Jewish Christians cannot continue to follow torah [cf., e.g., Rom. 14:1–15:13]. But it does mean that Jewish Christians cannot be "under the law" in the sense of a ruling power.)

3. Sons of God in Christ (3:26–29)

Paul brings to a climax the argument of 3:7–25 by circling back to his beginning point. In verse 7 he declared that "those who have faith are the children of Abraham." Now, at the conclusion of this paragraph, he proclaims that all those who belong to Christ are "the seed of Abraham" (v. 29)—that is, the true people of God. The beginning of the paragraph makes this same point, introducing for the first time in the letter the language of "sons of God" and bringing out what has been central to his argument throughout this section: that one becomes a "son of God" by faith—by implication, in light of the argument of verses 15–25, not through the law. But the keynote of this paragraph, which again echoes earlier texts (vv. 14, 16), is union with Christ. Each verse in the paragraph makes this point: "in Christ Jesus" all believers are sons of God (v. 26); those who have been baptized "into Christ" have "put on Christ" (v. 27); "in Christ Jesus" believers are one (v. 28); those who are "of Christ" are the seed of Abraham (v. 29). In contrast to the law and the works that it demands, faith is the way any person, Jew or Gentile, can join the people of God. But faith accomplishes what it does only because it is the means by which we are brought into union with Christ. This is the critical focus of Galatians, justifying the conclusion that verses 26–29 are the heart of Paul's argument in chapters 3–4 (Betz 1979:181; Heiligenthal 1984: 47–48) and perhaps of the letter as a whole. We should also note Paul's return here to the second-person plural form of address, suggesting that he is bringing home to the Galatians the argument of verses 7–25.

The language and ideas of verses 26–28 find parallels elsewhere in Paul: for verse 26, see Rom. 8:14–17; for verse 27, see Rom. 6:3–4; 13:14; for verse 28, see 1 Cor. 12:13; Col. 3:11. Particularly significant are texts that have the same combination of ideas that we find here. In Col. 3:10–11, for instance, Paul speaks of "putting on" Christ ("the new man") and of a oneness in Christ that transcends this world's dual oppositions (with verbal parallels to earlier references to baptism [2:12]):

> [since you have taken off your old self . . .] and have put on [ἐνδυσάμενοι, *en-dysamenoi*] the new self, which is being renewed in knowledge in the image of its Creator. [11]Here there is no *Gentile* or Jew, circumcised or uncircumcised, barbarian, Scythian, slave or free, but Christ is all, and is in all.

See also 1 Cor. 12:13, which refers to baptism and to the overcoming of traditional dualities in Christ:

For we were all baptized by one Spirit so as to form one body—whether Jews or Gentiles, slave or free—and we were all given the one Spirit to drink.

These similarities have led some scholars to think that Paul is quoting an early liturgical (perhaps baptismal) fragment (Betz 1979: 181–85; R. Longenecker 1990: 151; G. Hansen 1989: 136–37; Martyn 1997: 378–83; Bouttier 1976: 6–8). It is perhaps more likely, however, that the similarities are due to a basic pattern of thought that comes to expression in different ways and combinations in different contexts (Dunn 1993a: 201; Byrne 1979: 166–68).

Exegesis and Exposition

[26]For in Christ Jesus you are all sons of God through faith. [27]For as many of you as were baptized into Christ have put on Christ. [28]There is neither Jew nor Greek, there is neither slave nor free, there is neither male and female—for you are all one in Christ Jesus. [29]And if you belong to Christ, then you are the seed of Abraham, heirs according to the promise.

Paul again shifts person: from the first-person plural in verses 23–25, "*We* are no longer under a guardian" (v. 25)—to second-person plural in verses 26–29, "*You* all are sons of God" (v. 26). And once again, scholars differ on the significance of the shift. Some think that it is rather inconsequential, the reference throughout being to Christians generally (Mussner 1988: 260–61; Westerholm 2004: 416–17; Schreiner 2010: 256).[1] Others think the shift signifies a move from the particular situation of the Jews under the law to the status enjoyed by all believers (Bruce 1982b: 183; Burton 1921: 202 [as one option]) or by all Gentile believers (Betz 1979: 185; Dunn 1993a: 201; Byrne 1979: 172–73). As we have argued earlier (see the first additional note on 3:13), a mediating position on this argument best explains Paul's usage. In itself, the shift in person does not signal a change in audience: Paul's pronoun choice is governed by rhetorical concerns. And given the emphatic position of πάντες (*pantes*, all), he probably has all believers in view. But Paul also holds the traditional Jewish view of the law as the body of commands given uniquely to Israel. When he discusses the history of the law, then—as he does in verses 23–25—his focus is on the experience of Israel. But as his larger argument reveals (see esp. 4:1–7), this history is one in which Gentiles such as the Galatians also participate in some way. Paul thus uses the second-person form of address in verses 26–29 in order to bring his argument to bear on the Galatian Christians. How closely this argument is related to verses 23–25 depends on the meaning of the connecting conjunction γάρ (*gar*, for). If it has its most common causal meaning, Paul could be saying that Christians are no longer under the law as their παιδαγωγός (*paidagōgos*, guardian) because they are

3:26

---

1. Lightfoot (1881: 149) cites 1 Thess. 5:5: "You [ὑμεῖς, *hymeis*] are all children of the light and children of the day. We do not belong [ἐσμέν, *esmen*, we are/belong] to the night or to the darkness."

no longer children but full-grown sons (e.g., Mussner 1988: 265; Fung 1988: 170; Schreiner 2010: 255). However, it is unclear that the language "sons of God" per se could connote the contrast between the young child and the full-grown son that this reading of the conjunction requires. It is also uncertain that Paul would have viewed the Galatian Gentiles as having been "under the law" in the full sense of this language (Dunn 1993a: 201). Therefore it may be that this is one of those verses in which γάρ is more inferential than causal (BDAG 190.3, "marker of inference, *certainly, by all means, so, then*"; see NIV "so"). If so, the inference would be from the argument of 3:7–25 as a whole, and especially from 3:7–9.

Since Paul clearly intends verse 26 to apply to both male and female Christians, translating υἱοὶ θεοῦ (*huioi theou*) as "children of God" makes some sense (KJV, NIV, NRSV, NLT, NAB, NJB, CEB). However, although this translation accurately conveys the referent, it runs the risk of missing some of the connotation that Paul intends. "Sonship" in the Greco-Roman world symbolized a certain status and right of inheritance (an idea that Paul plays on in verse 29; cf. Fung 1988: 170). The language of "sons" also highlights the significant organic connection between Christ as "*the* son" and Christians (see 4:4–7; Humphrey 2009: 256). As applied to women, then, Paul's point would be that they can now enjoy, equally with men, the status of being "sons." Ultimately, however, Paul's choice of sons-of-God language probably owes more to the OT than to his Greco-Roman context (Ridderbos 1975: 197–99). The language of sonship is applied to Israel in the OT. God names Israel his "son" (e.g., Exod. 4:22; Jer. 31:9), and the people of Israel are "sons of God" (in LXX, NASB, e.g., Deut. 14:1–2; Hosea 1:10). This language was appropriated by Jews in Paul's day and often focused on the eschatological gathering of God's people (Jub. 1.24–25; Sir. 36:17; 3 Macc. 6:28; 2 Esd. [4 Ezra] 6:55–59; Pss. Sol. 17.26–27; cf. Byrne 1979: 62–63). To claim that all believers—and especially, of course, Gentile believers such as the Galatians—are "sons of God" is to claim that they enjoy the full status of God's people.

The Gentiles enjoy this status, Paul emphasizes, "through faith" (διὰ τῆς πίστεως, *dia tēs pisteōs*). The reference is again to the faith of the Galatians rather than to the faith, or faithfulness, of Christ (for this latter view, see, e.g., D. Campbell 2005: 100, 221; others suggest the reference is both to Christ's faith and to the Galatians' faith [Martyn 1997: 375; Engberg-Pedersen 2000: 150]). The following phrase, ἐν Χριστῷ Ἰησοῦ (*en Christō Iēsou*), could denote the object of that faith, "faith in Christ Jesus" (Morris 1996: 120; C. Campbell 2012: 118),[2] but is better taken absolutely, as most commentators recognize.[3]

---

2. Because they maintain the sequence of phrases found in the Greek, the following English versions suggest that the verse should be read in this way (e.g., "through faith in Christ Jesus"): KJV, NKJV, NLT, NASB, HCSB, CEB.

3. This interpretation is signaled in English by changing the position of the phrase "in Christ Jesus," as in NIV's "So in Christ Jesus you are all children of God through faith" (also RSV, NRSV, ESV, NET), or by separating the two phrases with a comma: "for all of you are the children of God, through faith, in Christ Jesus" (NJB).

Paul does not often use ἐν to introduce the object of faith (Eph. 1:15; Col. 1:4; 1 Tim. 3:13; probably in 2 Tim. 1:13; possibly, but not probably in Rom. 3:25). Taken independently, these two phrases summarize two key elements of Paul's teaching in Galatians and indeed of his theology as a whole: our relationship with God is established by our union with Christ Jesus, and that union is in turn secured by our faith.

In verse 27 Paul provides further explanation and rationale (γάρ, *gar*, for) for his claim in verse 26 that all the Galatian believers are sons of God in Christ Jesus. As the language of verse 27 reveals, Paul is especially concerned to emphasize (1) that this sonship is universal, including especially Gentiles such as the Galatians; and (2) that this sonship is grounded in one's relationship with Jesus Christ. The former point is evident from the ὅσοι (*hosoi*, as many as), which picks up πάντες from verse 26 (Mussner 1988: 262). The latter point forms, of course, the heart of the verse, in which Paul ties baptism εἰς Χριστόν (*eis Christon*, into Christ) to "putting on" Christ, another and more vivid way of claiming that believers are ἐν Χριστῷ Ἰησοῦ (v. 26; see Schlier 1989: 173). What is somewhat surprising is the shift from faith as the means of union with Christ in verse 26 to baptism in verse 27. As we observed in the introduction, many interpreters think that this is one reason to suppose that Paul is quoting an early Christian baptismal tradition or liturgy. The evidence may not justify the claim of an actual quotation. But Paul is clearly working with a motif that he uses elsewhere. In Rom. 6:3, for instance, arguing that believers are "dead to sin," Paul claims that "as many as" (ὅσοι) were baptized "into Christ Jesus" (εἰς Χριστὸν Ἰησοῦν) were baptized "into his death" (AT). A similar argument, tying Christian status with its benefits to union with Christ in conjunction with baptism, is found in Col. 2:12.

Paul appeals to baptism in these texts for two reasons. First, water baptism, which Paul almost certainly has in view here (contra Dunn 1993a: 203; Witherington 1998: 276–77), was the normal culminating event in a person's coming to Christ. It was not, in and of itself, a means of salvation or incorporation into Christ (contra, e.g., Schlier 1989: 172; cf. Betz 1979: 187–88). Faith, which Paul repeatedly highlights in this passage and in his other letters, is the only means of coming into relationship with Jesus Christ. However, baptism is more than simply a symbol of that new relationship; it is the capstone of the process by which one is converted and initiated into the church. As such, Paul can appeal to baptism as "shorthand" for the entire conversion experience.[4] A second reason to bring water baptism into the argument is the connection between baptism and incorporation into Christ. The phrase εἰς Χριστόν is sometimes interpreted as shorthand for "in the name of Christ" (e.g., Burton 1921: 203; Beasley-Murray 1962: 147),[5] a formula that occurs

---

4. For this view of water baptism in Paul, and in the NT, see esp. Dunn (1970), who argues that faith, repentance, the gift of the Spirit, and water baptism were viewed together in the NT as part of what he calls "conversion-initiation"; and Beasley-Murray (1962: 150–51) on Gal. 3:27.

5. Somewhat similar is the view that εἰς indicates reference (R. Longenecker 1990: 155).

several times in the NT (Matt. 28:19; Acts 8:16; 19:5; 1 Cor. 1:13, 15). But it is better to give εἰς a local sense and to view the phrase as indicating the (metaphorical) movement of the believer into union with Christ (Fung 1988: 172; Dunn 1993a: 203). Informing this phrase is Paul's theology of Christ as the "last Adam," a corporate figure with whom believers are joined by faith and whose acts and benefits can be transferred to them. "By their being baptized into Christ, and thus belonging to Christ, that which once took place in him is also valid for his own" (Ridderbos 1975: 207). In this case, as Paul will make more explicit in 4:5–7, believers enjoy "sonship" (v. 26) because, in baptism, they are incorporated into *the* Son.

Paul's claim that believers who have been baptized into Christ "have put on" (ἐνεδύσασθε, enedysasthe) Christ is probably part of the traditional complex of ideas that Paul is working with in our passage.[6] Colossians 3:10–11, quoted above in the introduction to this section, is the most important. Here Paul claims that believers have "put on the new man" (KJV), which is Christ (see also Eph. 4:24). What is a matter of fact in these texts becomes an exhortation in Rom. 13:14: "Clothe yourselves with the Lord Jesus Christ." In this latter text, the context makes clear that "putting on" Christ has ethical implications, and some interpreters find similar ideas here in Gal. 3:27 (e.g., Witherington 1998: 278; cf. R. Longenecker 1990: 156). But the context in Galatians suggests, rather, that simple identification is intended. At a relatively early date in church history those being baptized would be clothed with a new, white robe, to symbolize their new life in Christ; and it is possible that the word may reflect this literal act of "putting on" clothes. But the word was so widely used metaphorically that this connection is unclear. A more likely connection is with the use of this language in the OT to refer to being "clothed with" salvation (see esp. Isa. 61:10: "I delight greatly in the LORD; my soul rejoices in my God. For he has clothed [ἐνέδυσεν, enedysen] me with garments of salvation and arrayed me in a robe of his righteousness"; see, e.g., Bruce 1982b: 186; Garlington 2003: 167). But this connection also is uncertain.

3:28 This well-known saying about the way traditional religious, social, and gender barriers are transcended in Christ is not explicitly tied to its context: unusually for Greek, there is no particle or conjunction that introduces the verse (asyndeton). Our understanding of the role of the verse in Paul's argument will therefore depend on larger issues of interpretation. As was noted in the introduction to the section, the particular form and teaching of this verse have parallels elsewhere in Paul. In two other texts, we find a similar claim that common religious, social, or gender oppositions have been relativized in Christ, in whom a new unity is to be found. Comparison with these reveals

---

6. The form of the verb is middle, and it could, therefore, have a reflexive sense: "You clothed yourselves with Christ" (NIV, NRSV, NAB, NASB, NET; cf. Chrysostom, *Comm. Gal.* on 3:27 [NPNF[1] 13:30]; Witherington 1998: 278). But in a context that stresses faith and the status that faith confers, the simple "put on" (with no emphasis on personal initiative) is preferable (RSV). The middle form can also have a passive sense (1 Cor. 15:53–54; cf. BDAG 334.2.b).

the obvious similarities as well as the distinct nature of the way that Paul formulates that tradition in this context.

Galatians 3:28	1 Corinthians 12:13 (AT)	Colossians 3:11
	καὶ γὰρ ἐν ἑνὶ πνεύματι ἡμεῖς πάντες εἰς ἓν σῶμα ἐβαπτίσθημεν, (*kai gar en heni pneumati hēmeis pantes eis hen sōma ebaptisthēmen*, for also we all by one Spirit have been baptized into one body,)	
οὐκ ἔνι Ἰουδαῖος οὐδὲ Ἕλλην, (*ouk eni Ioudaios oude Hellēn*, there is neither Jew nor Greek,)	εἴτε Ἰουδαῖοι εἴτε Ἕλληνες (*eite Ioudaioi eite Hellēnes*, whether Jews or Greeks)	ὅπου οὐκ ἔνι Ἕλλην καὶ Ἰουδαῖος, (*hopou ouk eni Hellēn kai Ioudaios*, where there is no Greek and Jew,)
		περιτομὴ καὶ ἀκροβυστία, (*peritomē kai akrobystia*, circumcision and uncircumcision,)
		βάρβαρος, Σκύθης, (*barbaros, Skythēs*, barbarian, Scythian,)
οὐκ ἔνι δοῦλος οὐδὲ ἐλεύθερος, (*ouk eni doulos oude eleutheros*, there is neither slave nor free,)	εἴτε δοῦλοι εἴτε ἐλεύθεροι, (*eite douloi eite eleutheroi*, whether slaves or free,)	δοῦλος, ἐλεύθερος, (*doulos, eleutheros*, slave, free,)
οὐκ ἔνι ἄρσεν καὶ θῆλυ· (*ouk eni arsen kai thēly*, there is no male and female;)		
πάντες γὰρ ὑμεῖς εἷς ἐστε ἐν Χριστῷ Ἰησοῦ. (*pantes gar hymeis heis este en Christō Iēsou*, for you are all one in Christ Jesus.)	καὶ πάντες ἓν πνεῦμα ἐποτίσθημεν. (*kai pantes hen pneuma epotisthēmen*, and we all have drunk from one Spirit.)	ἀλλὰ [τὰ] πάντα καὶ ἐν πᾶσιν Χριστός. (*alla [ta] panta kai en pasin Christos*, but Christ is all things and in all things.)

A connection among these sayings is obvious: each of them features pairs of opposites, introduced in Galatians and Colossians with οὐκ ἔνι (and ἔνι, meaning "there is," is rare in the NT, occurring only in these two texts and 1 Cor. 6:5 and James 1:17) along with an assertion of "oneness" in Christ. While the form of the saying may borrow from some ancient models, Paul, as is typically the case, has so transformed whatever pattern he may have depended on that our interpretation of the saying should be constrained by the NT evidence (see the additional note).

The first two pairs that Paul mentions have parallels in both the other texts. "Neither Jew nor Greek" depicts the key distinction among humans from the Jewish perspective: between those who were chosen to be God's people and all others. "Greek" (Ἕλλην) is basically equivalent to "Gentile" in Paul's vocabulary (BDAG 318.2; cf. Rom. 1:16; 2:9–10; 3:9; 10:12; 1 Cor. 1:24; 10:32). The claim that distinctions between Jew and Greek had been erased in Christ is key to Paul's argument in Galatians, undercutting the agitators' insistence on law obedience, and is thus perfectly fitting in this context. Less clear is why Paul goes on to mention two other contrasting pairs. However, since "slave" and "free" are found in both other parallel texts, it could be that Paul includes the erasure of distinction within the two most important social classes in the Roman Empire simply because he is following the tradition. But dependence on a traditional formulation cannot explain the inclusion of the third pair, "male" and "female," for neither parallel text includes this pair. The choice of the distinctive gender words ἄρσεν and θῆλυ (in contrast to ἀνήρ [*anēr*, man/husband] and γυνή [*gynē*, woman/wife], which can connote marital roles) suggests an allusion to Gen. 1–2: the other places where these terms are contrasted in the NT are allusions to the creation account (Matt. 19:4; Mark 10:6; cf. Rom. 1:26–27). The influence of the creation account could also account for the change in construction between the first two pairs and the third: the conjunction καί is found also in Gen. 1:27 (LXX: ἄρσεν καὶ θῆλυ ἐποίησεν αὐτούς, *arsen kai thēly epoiēsen autous*, male and female he made them; see Fung 1988: 175; R. Longenecker 1990: 157). One reason, then, for Paul to include this third pair is to emphasize his concern in Galatians to recast the fundamental nature of the world in light of Christ: his coming means a "new creation," "in which neither circumcision nor uncircumcision means anything" (Gal. 6:15). And the mention of circumcision may be a subsidiary reason for the inclusion of this third pair: by putting so much stress on circumcision, Paul suggests, the agitators are effectively marginalizing women (Witherington 1998: 279–80; Martin 2003; Schreiner 2010: 258).[7]

In place of the dualities and even conflicts that mark human society in general, Paul asserts about the Galatians, and thus about Christians in general, "You are all one in Christ Jesus." We note the prominence again of the leitmotif of this paragraph: union with Christ as the basis for the new reality that Paul proclaims. And the masculine form of "one" (εἷς) may reinforce this christological focus, signifying perhaps "the one new man" (KJV; e.g., "new self" in Eph. 4:24; Col. 3:10; see B. Hansen 2010: 99–101): "members of the church are not one *thing*; they are one *person*, having been taken up into the corpus of the One New Man" (Martyn 1997: 377). But how far-reaching is this new reality? It is easy to quote the saying in this verse as a slogan that proclaims the erasure of any distinctions within the Christian community. But of course Paul recognizes the continuing reality of the male/female distinction among human beings; "androgyny," the creation of a new being neither male nor female, is far from Paul's idea. For all his insistence that Jews and Gentiles

---

7. Ciampa (2010: 164–65) suggests that male and female are included here because of the theme of freedom from oppression that he thinks is important in the letter.

are on equal footing before God in the new era of salvation, he also allows them to work out their relationship to Christ in terms distinctive to their particular backgrounds (e.g., Rom. 14:1–15:13). And while setting in place principles that undercut the institution of slavery, the continuing social reality of slaves is also recognized (e.g., 1 Cor. 7:17–24; Eph. 6:5–9; Col. 3:22–4:1; Titus 2:9–10). These continuing realities, then, lead many other scholars to suggest a rather severe delimitation in applying the principle that Paul announces here: only one's access to grace in Christ is in view (see, e.g., Hove 1999). But this would be to go too far in the other direction. Paul obviously applies the principle here to the basic matter of status within the people of God; but the principle itself, being a general claim about the new reality created by and in Christ, extends beyond this particular application. The saying in this verse is rightly prized as a far-reaching and fundamental claim about the way in which the distinctions that "matter" in the world we live in are to be left at the door of the church. But this "adiaphorizing" of difference within the Christian community does not entail an erasure of difference (to use Gundry-Volf's [1997: 456] language) and cannot be used arbitrarily to rule out any distinctions in roles that Paul may teach elsewhere (Schreiner 2010: 258–59).

In this verse Paul rounds off the discussion he began in verse 7 by bringing together the key point of the section: those who belong to Christ—Jew or Gentile—belong to Abraham's seed; they are full members of God's people (Schlier 1989: 176; Matera 1992: 153). Because complete provision for their standing with God and within his people is provided in Christ, no other requirement, such as obedience to the law, can be added. The verse also anticipates the direction of Paul's argument by tying the promise to being an "heir."

3:29

The δέ (*de*) that opens the verse has a weak continuative significance (thus "and" [most versions] or untranslated [NIV]). It introduces a logical argument stated in the form of a conditional sentence. The protasis summarizes the christological focus of verses 26–28: εἰ . . . ὑμεῖς Χριστοῦ (*ei . . . hymeis Christou*). The genitive (of Christ) is probably broadly possessive (Mussner 1988: 266); hence, "if you belong to Christ" (NIV, NRSV, NLT, NAB, NET, CEB). It is simply another way of stating the idea of being "in Christ." The apodosis of the conditional sentence is introduced by ἄρα (*ara*, therefore; cf. BDF §451.2) and returns to the language of 3:16, 19 and to the conceptual categories of 3:7. The promises, Paul claims in verse 16, were "spoken to Abraham and to his seed." In that verse, Paul interprets "seed" (σπέρμα, *sperma*) in its singular sense, referring to Christ. But Christ is a corporate person. By faith one can enter into union with Christ and be counted, with him, as the "seed" to whom the promises were made. At the same time being the "seed" of Abraham is equivalent to being his "sons," or "children" (3:7). And so the argument comes full circle. Those who have faith are "Abraham's sons" (3:7) because faith unites us with Christ, who is the ultimate "seed" and "son" of Abraham. "Being 'in' Christ enables them to be 'in' Abraham" (Hodge 2007: 103).

In addition to being Abraham's "seed," Paul finally affirms that we are also κατ' ἐπαγγελίαν κληρονόμοι (*kat' epangelian klēronomoi*): "heirs according to the promise." In a passage with several parallels to this one, Paul uses the idea of the "heir" to describe the eschatological realities that will follow on our present enjoyment of sonship (Rom. 8:14–17). But his logic here seems to be different. In the following paragraph, Paul contrasts the "child," waiting for the inheritance, with sonship, now experienced in Christ. Hence, being an "heir" apparently here focuses on what has already been inherited rather than on an inheritance for which one is still waiting (contra Kwon 2004: 86–92). The NLT, while not following the Greek structure, nevertheless captures the idea well: "You are his heirs, and God's promise to Abraham belongs to you."

Additional Note

3:28. The opposing pairs that characterize Gal. 3:28; 1 Cor. 12:13; and Col. 3:11 have rough ancient parallels. Philo (*Spec. Laws* 1.211), for instance, invites thanks not only for the "unity" "of human beings" (ἀνθρώπων, *anthrōpōn*) but also for the unity "of species" (εἰδῶν, *eidōn*): "for men and women, for Greeks and barbarians, for dwellers on the mainland and those whose lot is cast in the islands" (see Grant 1997: 7–12). Betz (1979: 188–92) summarizes the evidence for a widespread ancient longing for a breaking down of racial or social barriers and the creation of a new unity among human beings. Paul, of course, may well have been familiar with such traditions, and they could then have exerted some influence on his claim that in Christ—and only in Christ—is the longed-for unity among humans achieved. Other scholars (e.g., Bruce 1982b: 187; R. Longenecker 1990: 157) note the well-known rabbinic saying attributed to Rabbi Judah b. Elai: "There are three Benedictions which one must say every day: 'Blessed be He who did not make me a Gentile'; 'Blessed be He who did not make me a woman'; 'Blessed be He who did not make me an uneducated man'" (*t. Ber.* 7.18). But the date of the evidence for the saying makes it unclear if it would have been available for Paul (Paulsen 1980: 85). Less likely is that Paul's saying has anything to do with other ancient ideas about the creation of an androgynous human—that is, a human combining male and female (Betz [1979: 196–200] is open to this connection; but see, convincingly, to the contrary, esp. Gundry-Volf 1997). Many scholars suppose that these sayings all reflect a common baptismal liturgy of the early church. But this is not clear (Dautzenberg 1982: 182–83), and it is possible that Paul has first formulated the principle here in Galatians.

4. From Slaves to Sons of God (4:1–7)

Where this paragraph fits in the progress of Paul's argument is unclear. With the claim that belonging to Abraham's seed takes place through union with Christ, a union that the Galatian Gentile Christians have experienced through faith (3:26–29), a key conclusion in Paul's argument has been reached. We may then expect that this next paragraph would inaugurate a new phase in Paul's argument (as some think: e.g., Matera 1992: 153). Yet significant connections between this paragraph and the immediately preceding argument in 3:23–29 are evident, as the table below shows (see also Dunn 1993a: 210):

Galatians 3:23–29	Galatians 4:1–7
Now before faith came, we were guarded under the law, confined until the faith that was about to be revealed. (v. 23)	Now I say, as long as the heir is underage, he is no different than a slave. (v. 1) When we were children, we were enslaved under the elements of the world. (v. 3) . . . Until the time set by his father, (v. 2)
The law became our guardian until Christ. (v. 24)	he is under guardians and trustees. (v. 2)
But since faith has come, we are no longer under a guardian. (v. 25)	When the fullness of the time came, God sent his Son, born of a woman, born under the law, to redeem those under the law (vv. 4–5)
For in Christ Jesus you are all sons of God through faith. (v. 26)	in order that we might receive sonship. (v. 5) You are no longer a slave but a son. (v. 7)
You are the seed of Abraham, heirs according to the promise. (v. 29)	You are also an heir, through God. (v. 7)

Each of these paragraphs is dominated by a temporal contrast between a time of confinement and a time of freedom/inheritance, cast in terms of the maturation of a child. These parallels suggest that 4:1–7 is an elaboration of this key salvation-historical contrast in 3:23–29 (see, e.g., Lightfoot 1881: 165; R. Longenecker 1990: 161; Mussner 1988: 266). But 4:1–7 adds a significant feature not found in 3:23–29: the Spirit (v. 6). With this reminder of the Galatians' experience of the Spirit, Paul returns to the place where he began his argument in 3:1–5 (Hays 2000: 280).

The paragraph falls into two parts: a reminder of common inheritance procedure (vv. 1–2) and the application of that procedure to the experience of the Galatian Christians (vv. 3–7).

Exegesis and Exposition

¹Now I say, as long as the heir is underage, he is no different than a slave, even though he is the owner of everything. ²But he is under guardians and trustees until the time set by his father. ³In the same way, when we were children, we ⌜were⌝ enslaved under the elements of the world. ⁴But when the fullness of the time came, God sent his Son, born of a woman, born under the law, ⁵to redeem those under the law, in order that we might receive sonship. ⁶And because you are sons, God sent the Spirit of his Son into ⌜our⌝ hearts, crying "Abba, Father." ⁷So you are no longer a slave but a son. And if you are a son, you are also an heir, ⌜through God.⌝

4:1   The phrase λέγω δέ (*legō de*, now I say) probably functions to introduce the material that follows as an elaboration and clarification of what has just been said (the phrase functions like this also in 1 Cor. 1:12; cf. also Gal. 5:16; 1 Cor. 7:8 [cf. vv. 6, 10, 12]; and see λέγω οὖν [*legō oun*, then I ask] in Rom. 11:1, 11). The connection is especially with the *paidagōgos* (guardian) imagery in 3:24–25. As the child is "under" the *paidagōgos* until a certain age, so an heir is "under" legal guardians until the time stipulated for the inheritance to be received. Both situations illustrate the position of Israel (and by extension, the Galatians) before Christ, when they were "under the law." Here again we notice the linking-word mechanism that Paul has employed so often in this section of the letter: "heir" (κληρονόμος, *klēronomos*) in verse 1 picks up the final word in the previous paragraph (κληρονόμοι). In verses 1–2 Paul describes the typical situation of the heir who has not yet entered into his inheritance. "As long as" (ἐφ' ὅσον χρόνον, *eph' hoson chronon*; on the phrase, see BDAG 367.18.c.β; Rom. 7:1; 1 Cor. 7:39) the "heir" is "underage," that heir is "no different than a slave" (διαφέρει δούλου, *diapherei doulou*; Wallace [1996: 111] notes that this verb often takes the genitive of separation) "even though" (ὤν [*ōn*] is concessive) he[1] is "owner [see BDAG 577.1 for this meaning of κύριος, *kyrios*] of everything." The translation "underage" (NIV, NJB; "not of age" in NAB; cf. "minor(s)" in NRSV, NET, CEB) reflects the definition for νήπιος (*nēpios*) in BDAG (671.2), which suggests that it here is a technical legal term meaning "one who is not yet of legal age, *minor, not yet of age.*" This translation makes good sense in a context focused on legal status and avoids the possible confusion that the usual translation, "child, infant," would create with the contrasting term υἱός (*huios*, son) that Paul uses later (vv. 6, 7; cf. v. 5). We should note that Paul here adds an emphasis not found in his earlier comparison, the idea that the underage heir is no better than a "slave."

4:2   The ἀλλά (*alla*, but) that introduces this verse contrasts the end of verse 1 with verse 2: even though the heir is "owner of everything," he nevertheless "is under guardians and trustees" (ὑπὸ ἐπιτρόπους ἐστὶν καὶ οἰκονόμους, *hypo*

---

1. We follow, e.g., the NIV, in using masculine language throughout this paragraph in order to bring out Paul's appeal to ancient laws of inheritance, which applied exclusively to males (see, e.g., Hodge 2007: 69).

epitropous estin kai oikonomous). And this subservient status lasts "until the time set by his father" (ἄχρι τῆς προθεσμίας τοῦ πατρός, *achri tēs prothesmias tou patros*; προθεσμία means "determined in advance," with ἡμέρα [*hēmera*, day] to be supplied [BDAG 869–70; BDF §241.2]; the word προθεσμία is common in the papyri [*NewDocs* 2:95]). Paul's portrayal of the heir's legal status has stimulated considerable discussion. The word ἐπίτροπος can be used of any "manager" or "steward" (Matt. 20:8; Luke 8:3) but is also used particularly of a "guardian" (e.g., 2 Macc. 11:1; 13:2; 14:2). But the second word Paul uses to describe those who are over the underage heir, οἰκονόμος, is apparently never used in this way elsewhere. The word refers to a steward or manager of property (Luke 12:42; 16:1, 3, 8; of a city, in Rom. 16:23; metaphorically, of the "mysteries of God," in 1 Cor. 4:1, 2; of a household, in Titus 1:7; of the grace of God, in 1 Pet. 4:10). Even more problematic is Paul's reference to a time set by the father, since ancient inheritance law did not generally allow the father to stipulate the time when his child would inherit. These difficulties have created questions about what specific form of ancient inheritance law Paul might be referring to: Roman (Lyall 1984: 112–14; Bruce 1982b: 192), Hellenistic (Burton 1921: 213–15; Mussner 1988: 266–67), or local laws influenced by the Seleucids (Ramsay 1900: 391–93; J. Scott [1992: 3–13] provides a quick overview)?

These difficulties, along with other textual clues, have led J. Scott (1992: 122–45) to take a different direction entirely in the interpretation of this passage. Paul, he argues, is alluding not to ancient inheritance practice but to the foundational "adoption" event in the history of Israel: the people's liberation from their taskmasters in Egypt (the "guardians and trustees") at the time determined by God, a liberation that led to their "inheritance" (the promised land). The Galatians, along with other believers in Christ, have experienced a similar "liberation leading to sonship" (see also, with some modifications, Hafemann 1997: 333–51). J. Scott's interpretation rightly highlights the significance of salvation history in this part of Galatians, but it finally lacks clear-enough connections with the exodus narrative to be compelling. Yet Scott is right to claim that none of the suggested legal backgrounds can adequately explain the situation that Paul describes in these verses. What this means, however, is that Paul has allowed his statement of the illustration to be affected by his intended application. Paul describes a situation with sufficient analogies to the experience of his readers in order for the illustration to be effective and meaningful, but takes liberties with some of the details of that experience in order to facilitate its application to their spiritual situation (Betz 1979: 203, 204; R. Longenecker 1990: 163–64). Paul therefore may use οἰκονόμος as a rough synonym for ἐπίτροπος (R. Longenecker 1990: 163–64), or if a difference is intended, οἰκονόμος may denote the person in charge of the property of the heir, and ἐπίτροπος may refer to the one who supervises the person of the heir (Bruce 1982b: 192). And "the time set by the father," while possibly having some basis in ancient Roman practice (see esp. Bruce 1982b: 192), is probably a backreading of the application into the illustration: God has determined in "the fullness of time" to send his Son to bring about liberation from sin and instatement to the full rights of sonship (vv. 4–5).

4:3   Paul now applies his illustration from inheritance practice to the situation of believers in Christ (οὕτως καὶ ἡμεῖς, *houtōs kai hēmeis*, so also we). His choice of the first-person plural pronoun raises once again the question of intended referent. And, once again, many interpreters think that Paul refers to his fellow Jews (e.g., R. Longenecker 1990: 164; Bruce 1982b: 193 [both, however, add "primarily"]; Hafemann 1997: 340–41; Bergmeier 2010: 61–64). But, as we have argued elsewhere (see the comments on 3:14), it is very difficult to find any consistent pattern in Paul's use of pronouns in Galatians; rhetorical concerns and context seem to be the more important issues. In this case, Paul's application of the situation he describes to the Galatian Christians in 4:8 makes it likely that the ἡμεῖς refers to Christians generally (e.g., Lightfoot 1881: 166–67; Burton 1921: 215; Byrne 1979: 176–78; J. Scott 1992: 155–57).[2] Paul claims that before coming to Christ, people were like the underage heir in Paul's illustration (νήπιοι, *nēpioi*, underaged), living in a state of slavery (ἤμεθα δεδουλωμένοι, *ēmetha dedoulōmenoi*; the construction, a pluperfect periphrastic, suggests the idea of a past state of affairs that has now come to an end: see, e.g., Wallace 1996: 585).

This verse therefore continues the use of slavery imagery from the illustration (v. 2) to connote the pre-Christian condition, imagery that the language of 3:22–25 has prepared us for (συνεκλείω [*synekleiō*, confine] in 3:22–23 and the ὑπό [*hypo*, under] language in 3:22–23, 25). In contrast to this earlier text, however, the power under which humans are enslaved is no longer sin (v. 22) or the law (vv. 23–25), but "the elements of the world" (τὰ στοιχεῖα τοῦ κόσμου, *ta stoicheia tou kosmou*). The meaning of this phrase is disputed. It occurs here and again, in abbreviated form, in verse 9 (τὰ ἀσθενῆ καὶ πτωχὰ στοιχεῖα, *ta asthenē kai ptōcha stoicheia*, the weak and miserable elements) as well as in Col. 2:8, 20. The particular problem in Gal. 4 is to find a lexically supported meaning that also fits the context. The word στοιχεῖον (*stoicheion* [singular]) has a "formal" sense, meaning "fundamental component" or "element," and thus can take on a wide variety of specific senses, depending on the context in which it is used.[3] It can, for instance, refer to the letters of the alphabet, the notes of a musical scale, or the propositions of geometry. But three meanings (or applications) of the word are particularly relevant to the interpretation of the phrase here in Galatians (and in Colossians):

1. In Paul's day (and afterward), the word was most often used to denote the "fundamental components" of the universe, the "elements" from

---

2. The suggestion that ἡμεῖς refers to Gentile Christians only (Dalton 1990: 40–41; Hodge 2007: 71) has little to commend it.

3. See esp. Bandstra 1964: 31–46. As Wink (1984: 68, referring to Bandstra) summarizes: "It [*stoicheion*] denotes merely an irreducible component; what it is an irreducible component of must be supplied by the context in which it is used."

which all matter was composed—usually identified as air, earth, fire, and water.[4] The word is used in this sense in its three LXX occurrences (4 Macc. 12:13; Wis. 7:17; 19:18), in most of its occurrences in Philo, Josephus, and the apostolic fathers, and in two of the seven NT occurrences (2 Pet. 3:10, 12).[5]

2. The word was also used in the sense of the "essential principles" of a particular area of study.[6] This meaning is also found in the NT, in Heb. 5:12, where the author refers to "the elementary truths [τὰ στοιχεῖα τῆς ἀρχῆς] of God's word."

3. Finally, στοιχεῖα came to be used for spiritual beings. The word is never given this application in any pre-Christian writing; its first extant use in this way comes in the post-NT period, as in the Testament of Solomon.[7] But many scholars are convinced that the word was being used this way in Paul's day.

Traditionally, scholars have preferred either the second or the third meaning for the phrase here in Galatians. The phrase will therefore indicate either "the elementary principles of the world" (NRSV, ESV; cf. NLT, NJB; cf. Burton 1921: 510–18; Belleville 1986: 64–69; R. Longenecker 1990: 165–66) or "the elemental spirits of the universe" (NIV: "elemental spiritual forces"; cf. NAB; cf. Bruce 1982b: 202–4; B. Longenecker 1998: 47–53; Arnold 1996: 57–72; Adams 2000: 228–30). The elementary-principles meaning appears to make good sense of the relationship that Paul appears to suggest between the law and "the elements." Moreover, it also fits well with the dominant metaphor of the maturation of a child. Israel (and people in general) under the law is like a child who has not yet received the expected inheritance. It would thus be very natural for Paul to describe the law and its peculiar requirements—circumcision, abstinence from certain foods, the celebration of holy days (see 4:10)—as "elementary principles" that have now been put aside in the new era of salvation history. The spiritual-powers interpretation, on the other hand, appears to have strong contextual support in 4:8–9: "Formerly, when you did not know God, you were slaves to *those who by nature are not gods*. But now that you know God, or rather are known by God, how is it that you are turning back to those *weak and miserable* στοιχεῖα? Do you wish to be enslaved by them all over again?" On this view, Paul would be suggesting that the agitators, by insisting that

4. This is also the usual meaning in Philo and Josephus. As an example of this meaning, see Sib. Or. 2.206–7: "And then all the elements of the world will be bereft—air, land, sea, light, vault of heaven, days, nights."

5. This meaning is also the most common among the early fathers of the church (Riches 2008: 223).

6. See, e.g., Xenophon, *Mem.* 2.1.1: "How would you educate them? If you wish, let us consider it, beginning with food, as one of the elementary issues" (AT).

7. In T. Sol. 8.2; 18.2 the στοιχεῖα are called "the cosmic rulers of darkness." This work is difficult to date (first–third centuries AD), but is certainly post-NT.

their Gentile converts place themselves under the authority of the Mosaic law, are in effect forcing them back into an earlier stage of their religious experience, when the various spirits of this world dominated their existence. Both these interpretations work well also in Colossians—an important consideration, since the rarity of the phrase makes it likely that it has the same meaning in both books.

Nevertheless, recent scholarship has shown a tendency to gravitate toward the first meaning of the phrase, taking it to refer to the basic material elements of the world (see esp. Martyn 1997: 393–406; and also J. Scott 1992: 157–60; Hays 2000: 282–83; Hafemann 1997: 346–48; Thielman 1989: 80–83; de Boer 2007; 2011: 252–56). The reason for this is lexical. This was by far the dominant meaning of the word στοιχεῖα in Paul's day. Moreover, every instance of the phrase [τὰ] στοιχεῖα [τοῦ] κόσμου from Paul's general time period apparently has this meaning.[8] And, although at first sight this meaning may not seem to fit the context as well as the others, two considerations suggest that it actually could fit very well. First, an important component of the agitators' program is a preoccupation with rules or issues relating to the physical world: circumcision (2:3; 5:2–12; 6:12–15), rules concerning food (2:11–14), and the observance of religious festivals marked by the movement of the heavenly bodies (4:10). Second is the ancient worldview that lies behind Paul's reference to physical elements. The material components of the universe were often associated with spiritual beings or the gods (see the second additional note on 4:3). In light of this background, then, a reference to the material elements of the universe would almost certainly include some reference to the deities or spirits who were so closely associated with the elements.[9] In this sense, those who suggest that the phrase is a general way of describing the situation of humans before and outside of Christ are not far off the mark (e.g., Bruce 1982b: 204; Dunn 1993a: 213).[10]

Paul therefore may use the στοιχεῖα language in order to associate the situation of the Gentile Galatians in their preconversion state with that of the Jews before Christ. As we have seen, Paul, on the one hand, views the law in Galatians (and in his other writings) as peculiarly given to Israel: it is the *torah*, the law of Moses. On the other hand, he also in some manner associates Gentiles apart from Christ with the sin-producing and death-dealing effects of the law. By introducing the στοιχεῖα, Paul is able further to associate the

8. See the summary of a TLG search by Rusam 1992: 119–25. He finds nine occurrences, in addition to the eleven that Blinzler (1963) had already discovered.

9. For this view in general, see esp. Blinzler 1963; Rusam 1992; Schweizer 1970. Bandstra's (1964: 68–72) view, often categorized with the "principial" interpretation (στοιχεῖα as basic principles), may ultimately fit better in this category: the στοιχεῖα as the "elementary forces" of flesh and the law.

10. Some object to the "material" interpretation of the phrase on the basis that it does not retain the pejorative sense of the word κόσμος (see esp. Bandstra 1964: 57). However, Paul often uses κόσμος to mean "the universe," "all creation" (Rom. 1:20; 1 Cor. 3:22 (?); 4:9; 7:31; 8:4; Eph. 1:4; Phil. 2:15), while only a minority of Paul's uses of κόσμος have the pejorative sense (e.g., Gal. 6:14).

situation of Jews under the law and the Gentiles outside of Christ. Paul does not equate the law with the στοιχεῖα; nor does he even suggest that the law is a subset of the στοιχεῖα (contra, e.g., Donaldson 1986: 103–4; Schreiner 2010: 269). But the close connection of verses 3 and 4–5 shows that he does associate them in some way.[11] Perhaps, if our view of στοιχεῖα is right, he wants to suggest that Gentiles under the στοιχεῖα share with Jews under the law the same condition of living under a religious regimen involving rules relating to material realities—and that together these religious realities are all outmoded with the coming of Christ.[12] Paul, of course, never gives up his conviction that the law comes from God and is, as he puts it in Romans, "holy, righteous and good" (7:12). However, in that same context in Romans, Paul also shows how the law has been used by sin to produce death. Here in Galatians he is pulling out all the rhetorical stops to try to convince the Galatians not to put themselves under that law by suggesting that, while quite different in basic ways from the pagan religions under which the Galatians once lived, the law, like those religions, belongs to a stage of religious experience that has been brought to an end with the coming of Christ.

Paul uses the inheritance illustration primarily to illuminate the dire condition of the Galatians in their pre-Christian state (v. 3). But the illustration hints also at the change that occurs when the underage boy enters into his inheritance. In verses 4–5, Paul applies this side of the illustration, although abandoning for now (see v. 7) the specific language of the illustration. In other words, we might have expected Paul to match the language of his illustration by describing how the Galatians have entered into their inheritance at the time set by God. The latter idea has some parallel in verse 4 ("the fullness of time" = "the time set by his father" [v. 2]), but the contrast "underage/heir" is dropped in favor of a claim about "sonship." This shift in language creates a certain tension between illustration and application, for the underage child, the minor of the illustration, is of course already a "son." This dissonance between illustration and application may be due simply to Paul's decision to leave his illustration behind. But Paul does so at least partly in order to bring into his argument a widespread early Christian tradition. This tradition, recognized in many parts of the NT, focuses on the idea of God "sending" his Son "in order to" accomplish his beneficial purposes in the world (for this tradition, see esp. Schweizer 1966; R. Longenecker 1990; 166–70). This language is particularly common in the Johannine literature (e.g., John 3:16; 1 John 4:9), but perhaps the closest parallels to Gal. 4:4–7 occur in Rom. 8:1–17:[13]

4:4

---

11. If the στοιχεῖα refer to spiritual beings, then the point of comparison might be with the angels, involved in mediating the law (3:19; cf. Reicke 1951: 259–63).

12. Witulski (2000: 84–152) argues that the phrase connotes pagan deities, and especially the divinized Augustus and other cultic gods.

13. For a similar table, see Bergmeier 2010: 65. He also cites a number of wider connections between the language of this section and Rom. 8:18–25.

Galatians 4:4–7	Romans 8:1–17 (AT)
ὅτε δὲ ἦλθεν τὸ πλήρωμα τοῦ χρόνου, (*hote de ēlthen to plērōma tou chronou*, But when the fullness of the time had come,)	
ἐξαπέστειλεν ὁ θεὸς τὸν υἱὸν αὐτοῦ, (*exapesteilen ho theos ton huion autou*, God sent forth his Son,)	ὁ θεὸς τὸν ἑαυτοῦ υἱὸν πέμψας (*ho theos ton heautou huion pempsas*, God, sending his own son [v. 3])
γενόμενον ἐκ γυναικός, γενόμενον ὑπὸ νόμον, (*genomenon ek gynaikos, genomenon hypo nomon*, born of a woman, born under the law,)	ἐν ὁμοιώματι σαρκὸς ἁμαρτίας καὶ περὶ ἁμαρτίας (*en homoiōmati sarkos hamartias kai peri hamartias*, in the likeness of sinful flesh and as a sin offering [v. 3])
⁵ἵνα τοὺς ὑπὸ νόμον ἐξαγοράσῃ, (*hina tous hypo nomon exagorasē*, in order to redeem those under the law,)	
ἵνα τὴν υἱοθεσίαν ἀπολάβωμεν. (*hina tēn huiothesian apolabōmen*, in order that we might receive sonship.)	ἐλάβετε πνεῦμα υἱοθεσίας (*elabete pneuma huiothesias*, you received the spirit of sonship [v. 15])
⁶Ὅτι δέ ἐστε υἱοί, ἐξαπέστειλεν ὁ θεὸς τὸ πνεῦμα τοῦ υἱοῦ αὐτοῦ εἰς τὰς καρδίας ἡμῶν κρᾶζον· Αββα ὁ πατήρ. (*hoti de este huioi, exapesteilen ho theos to pneuma tou huiou autou eis tas kardias hēmōn krazon: Abba ho patēr*, and because you are sons, God sent forth the Spirit of his Son into our hearts, crying, "Abba, Father.")	οὗτοι υἱοὶ θεοῦ εἰσιν (v. 14) ἐν ᾧ κράζομεν· Αββα ὁ πατήρ (v. 15) (*houtoi huioi theou eisin* [v. 14], these are the sons of God [v. 14]) (*en hō krazomen: Abba ho patēr* [v. 15], in which we cry, "Abba, Father" [v. 15])
⁷ὥστε οὐκέτι εἶ δοῦλος ἀλλὰ υἱός· (*hōste ouketi ei doulos alla huios*, so that you are no longer a slave but a son;)	οὐ γὰρ ἐλάβετε πνεῦμα δουλείας (*ou gar elabete pneuma douleias*, for you did not receive a spirit of slavery [v. 15])
εἰ δὲ υἱός, καὶ κληρονόμος διὰ θεοῦ. (*ei de huios, kai klēronomos dia theou*, and if a son, then also an heir through God.)	εἰ δὲ τέκνα, καὶ κληρονόμοι (*ei de tekna, kai klēronomoi*, and if children, then also heirs [v. 17])

Among these parallels, particular mention should be made of the similarities between the language of Gal. 4:4–5 and the "sending" formula in Rom. 8:3–4: "For what the law was powerless to do because it was weakened by the flesh, *God* did by *sending his own Son* in the likeness of sinful *flesh* to be a sin offering. And so he condemned sin in the flesh, *in order that* the righteous requirement of the law might be fully met in us, who do not live according to the flesh but according to the Spirit" (NIV, emphasis added). Both texts refer to God's sending (πέμπω [*pempō*] in Rom. 8:3; ἐξαποστέλλω [*exapostellō*] in Gal. 4:6)[14] his Son, to the Son's humanity ("born of a woman" in Gal. 4:4; "in

14. It is not clear why Paul uses the verb ἐξαποστέλλω, which he uses only here in 4:4, 6 (elsewhere in the NT, the verb is confined to Luke [Luke 1:53; 20:10, 11; Acts 7:12; 9:30; 11:22; 12:11; 13:26; 17:14; 22:21]). But the verb has the connotation of send to a different locality, on a

the likeness of sinful flesh" in Rom. 8:3), to the problem of the law, and to the purpose of that sending (see Dunn 1993a: 214). The parallel is all the more striking when we take note of the further parallels in the context. The extent of these parallels suggests that Paul here in Gal. 4 is citing an association of ideas that, while originally perhaps built on an early Christian "sending" formula, has become a distinctly Pauline way of presenting the work of Christ. The way in which ideas that are concentrated in Gal. 4:4–7 are scattered throughout Rom. 8:1–17 also makes it unlikely that Paul is quoting a set piece of early Christian teaching here in Galatians.

God sent his Son when "the fullness of time" (τὸ πλήρωμα τοῦ χρόνου, *to plērōma tou chronou*) came (4:4). This phrase loosely corresponds to "the time set by the father" in the illustration (v. 2) and refers to that moment in salvation history when God deemed it appropriate to initiate the work of redemption by sending his Son into the world (see the roughly parallel Eph. 1:10: the mystery of God's will was "to be put into effect when the times reach their fulfillment" (τοῦ πληρώματος τῶν καιρῶν, *tou plērōmatos tōn kairōn*).[15] Speculation about what made this particular "time" appropriate for the sending of the Son is fruitless; we can only know that God determined it to be the "right" time. Many interpreters think that this "sending" may suggest the preexistence of Christ (Lightfoot 1881: 168; Burton 1921: 216–17; Bruce 1982b: 195; Mussner 1988: 272; Gathercole 2006: 28–29). The language need not have this sense; the focus could be simply on God's sending Christ on a mission (e.g., R. Longenecker 1990: 170): Dunn (1980: 38–44) claims that "God sent [Jesus] to Golgotha—not Bethlehem" (also, e.g., Peppard 2011: 99). The verb ἐξαπέστειλεν (*exapesteilen*, sent) is used in this sense in Acts 9:30; 11:22; 17:14; 22:21 (Paul uses it only here in Gal. 4:4, 6). If this is what Paul intends, then the two parallel participial qualifiers of the verb "sent"—γενόμενον ἐκ γυναικός, γενόμενον ὑπὸ νόμον (*genomenon ek gynaikos, genomenon hypo nomon*, born of a woman, born under the law)—would provide background information: God sent one who *had* been born in this manner. But the unusual nature of these two qualifiers suggests, rather, that the participial clauses describe the nature of the sending, a sending that involved *taking on* the state of being human and Jewish (see below). As Fee puts it, "the fact that both γενόμενος phrases emphasize the Son's *human* condition seems to suggest that the sending word *presupposes*

---

mission (see BDAG 345.1), so it is certainly appropriate in this context. Schweizer (1966) suggests that the sending formula in Gal. 4:4–5 and Rom. 8:3 may have its antecedent in the traditions about wisdom (see also E. Schweizer, *TDNT* 8:374–76). See especially the parallelism between the sending of wisdom and the sending of the Spirit in Wis. 9:10, 17. For a critical evaluation of Schweizer's proposal, see Dunn 1988: 277–79.

15. Paul uses the word χρόνος (*chronos*) in Gal. 4:4, which, in distinction from καιρός (*kairos*, proper time), denotes "general" time as opposed to a distinct time, or "moment." Paul seems often, though not always, to preserve this distinction; contrast, for instance, "the law rules over a person for as much time as [ἐφ' ὅσον χρόνον, *eph' hoson chronon*] they live" (Rom. 7:1 AT) with, e.g., "at just the right time [κατὰ καιρόν, *kata kairon*], . . . Christ died for the ungodly" (Rom. 5:6; and cf. BDAG 497–98, 1092).

a prior existence that was not human" (Fee 2007b: 214–15). Preexistence is probably implied.

The two parallel participial clauses, then, describe the condition into which the Son was "sent." The former, γενόμενον ἐκ γυναικός, refers simply to human birth: γίνομαι (*ginomai*) is sometimes virtually equivalent to γεννάω (*gennaō*, give birth; see, e.g., Sir. 44:9; John 8:58; Rom. 1:3; BDAG 197.1).[16] What the second phrase means is more difficult to know. As we have seen (see the additional note on 3:23), many think the phrase ὑπὸ νόμον is shorthand for "under the curse of the law" (Hong 2002: 360–70; Wilson 2007: 35–36). The phrase could certainly have this sense here since, as Paul says explicitly in 3:13, Christ "became a curse for us" (using the same form of the same verb as occurs here: γενόμενος). However, the parallelism of the phrases in verse 4 suggests that γενόμενος means that Christ was "born" under the law. And this makes it unlikely that the phrase means "under the curse of the law," since Christ voluntarily took on himself that curse. Probably, then, the phrase here again means "subject to the rule of the law."

4:5 The sentence that Paul began in verse 4 continues in this verse, with a chiastic structure evident: God sent his *Son* (A) . . . born *under the law* (B) in order that he might redeem *those under the law* (B′), in order that we might receive *the adoption as sons* (A′). The sequence of two purpose clauses not separated by a conjunction is very similar to the clauses in 3:14; indeed, the whole context is quite similar:

Galatians 3:13–14	Galatians 4:4–5
Χριστὸς ἡμᾶς ἐξηγόρασεν ἐκ τῆς κατάρας τοῦ νόμου . . . (*Christos hēmas exēgorasen ek tēs kataras tou nomou* . . . , Christ redeemed us from the curse of the law . . .)	ἐξαπέστειλεν ὁ θεὸς τὸν υἱὸν αὐτοῦ . . . (*exapesteilen ho theos ton huion autou* . . . , God sent his Son . . .)
ἵνα εἰς τὰ ἔθνη ἡ εὐλογία τοῦ Ἀβραὰμ γένηται ἐν Χριστῷ Ἰησοῦ, (*hina eis ta ethnē hē eulogia tou Abraam genētai en Christō Iēsou*, in order that the blessing of Abraham might come to the Gentiles in Christ Jesus,)	ἵνα τοὺς ὑπὸ νόμον ἐξαγοράσῃ, (*hina tous hypo nomon exagorasē*, in order that those under the law might be redeemed,)
ἵνα τὴν ἐπαγγελίαν τοῦ πνεύματος λάβωμεν διὰ τῆς πίστεως. (*hina tēn epangelian tou pneumatos labōmen dia tēs pisteōs*, in order that we might receive the promise of the Spirit through faith.)	ἵνα τὴν υἱοθεσίαν ἀπολάβωμεν. (*hina tēn huiothesian apolabōmen*, in order that we might receive the adoption as sons.)

Both passages use the verb ἐξαγοράω (*exagoraō*, redeem; although at different points in the structure). Both emphasize redemption in terms of the law: "from the curse of the law," "those under the law." Both use the double

---

16. The phrase γίνομαι + ἐκ with woman/women as object also occurs in this sense: 1 Esd. 4:16; Tob. 8:6; Josephus, *Ant.* 2.216; see Dunn 1993a: 215; Bruce 1982b: 195; contra, e.g., Byrne 1979: 181.

ἵνα structure. And both shift to first-person plural forms in the last clause: "in order that we might receive the promise of the Spirit through faith," "in order that we might receive the adoption as sons." We argued that the two purpose clauses in 3:14 are coordinate. However, as we noted, this decision is contextually based, since there is no clear pattern in Paul's syntax on this point. The issue in Gal. 4:5 is complicated by the difficulty of determining the relationship between "those under the law" in the first clause and the "we" implied in the verb ἀπολάβωμεν in the second clause. Most interpreters think that both phrases denote all believers (e.g., Burton 1921: 219–20; Bruce 1982b: 197; Martyn 1997: 390; Byrne 1979: 182; J. Scott 1992: 173–74). In this case, the second clause should probably be seen as an "enriching explication" of the first (Martyn 1997: 390). Others, however, think that only Jews can be said to be "under the law": the law is clearly the Mosaic law (see 3:17), and that law was given exclusively to Israel (see esp. the contrasts in Rom. 2:12; 3:19; 1 Cor. 9:20).[17] Those who understand the phrase in this restricted sense divide over the scope of "we" in the second clause. Some think Paul continues to focus on Jewish Christians (e.g., R. Longenecker 1990: 172; Witherington 1998: 288–89), others that it refers to Gentile Christians (e.g., Matera 1992: 156; Hays 2000: 284; Donaldson 1986: 96–99), and still others that it means all believers (Betz 1979: 208; Dunn 1993a: 216–17). Deciding among these options is difficult. On the one hand, Paul elsewhere seems to use the phrase "under the law" to refer to Jews in distinction from Gentiles (see esp. 1 Cor. 9:20). On the other hand, in some texts Paul also implies that being "under the law" is a condition that applies to Gentiles as well as Jews (Rom. 6:14–15), and we have argued that this kind of implicit extension of the reference from Jews and Gentiles best explains the argument of Gal. 3:22–4:3. This last argument finally tilts the balance of the argument ever so slightly toward the majority view: Paul has in view Christians generally throughout verse 5.

The verb ἐξαγοράσῃ, as in 3:13, connotes liberation from enslavement, involving the payment of a price: the price of Christ's death (Ridderbos 1975: 195–97). This language corresponds nicely with the condition of enslavement that Paul has depicted in verse 3. In an example of what Morna Hooker (1971) has labeled "interchange in Christ," Christ becomes a slave to the law so that those who are enslaved under that law might be set free. Many again think that the redemption here consists of being set free from the curse of the law (Wilson 2007: 35), but redemption from bondage under the law, conceived as a ruling power of the old age, is more likely the sense. The idea of interchange is carried into the second clause, as Christ, the Son, becomes human so that humans can become sons. Specifically, Paul refers to believers receiving υἱοθεσίαν, a word that means, as J. Scott (1992: 13–57) has shown, "adoption as a son." The word is found only in the Letters of Paul in the NT (see also Rom. 8:15, 23; 9:4; Eph. 1:5) and never in the LXX. It has a distinctly Greco-Roman flavor

---

17. Jerome argued that only Jews needed to be "redeemed" from the law, although all people needed to be freed from it (cf. Edwards 1999: 54).

and undoubtedly alludes to the Greek and/or Roman practice of adoption, which stresses the legal rights and privileges that are conferred on the man who is adopted. Paul therefore uses this word to highlight the status enjoyed by believers, heirs of all that God has promised his own people. Believers, whether male or female, attain the status reserved in the ancient world for the one specially chosen "son." But υἱοθεσία contains a further nuance. Although the legal practice of adoption has no real precedent in the OT or Judaism, the concept of being God's son, or sons, is deeply rooted in the OT (see esp. J. Scott 1992; also Ridderbos 1975: 197–99). In Exod. 4:22 God claims that "Israel is my firstborn son" (see also, e.g., Jer. 31:20 [38:20 LXX]). Paul himself, significantly, uses the word υἱοθεσία to describe the status of the people of Israel (Rom. 9:4); and in 2 Cor. 6:18 he elaborates the promise of God about a Davidic descendant in 2 Sam. 7:14—"I will be his father, and he will be my son"—in terms of all Christians: "I will be a Father to you, and you will be my sons and daughters, says the Lord Almighty" (again see J. Scott 1992: 187–213). In claiming that Christians enjoy υἱοθεσία, then, Paul is claiming not only that we believers become his adopted children, with all the rights and privileges pertaining to that status, but also that we have become his own people, inheriting the status and blessings promised to his people Israel.

4:6 Verse 6 builds on the claim at the end of verse 5 that Christians have received the status of "adoption as sons" and reintroduces into Paul's discussion the critical argument about the reception of God's Spirit (see 3:2, 5, 14). The initial ὅτι (hoti, because) is most naturally taken in a causal sense, and this also fits the sequence of Paul's argument: we have received the adoption as sons, and because we are now sons, we also have the Spirit. The only problem with this interpretation is that the claim that possession of the Spirit proceeds from the status of sonship appears to contradict Paul's usual sequence, which is just the opposite. Especially important is Rom. 8:14–17, a passage with many obvious similarities to Gal. 4:4–6 (see the chart in the comments on 4:4):

> For all who are led by the Spirit of God are sons of God. [15]For you did not receive the spirit of slavery to fall back into fear, but you have received the Spirit of adoption as sons, by whom we cry, "Abba! Father!" [16]The Spirit himself bears witness with our spirit that we are children of God, [17]and if children, then heirs—heirs of God and fellow heirs with Christ, provided we suffer with him in order that we may also be glorified with him. (ESV)

Further, earlier in Galatians Paul has assumed that the Spirit marks the beginning of Christian experience (3:3). For these reasons, some interpreters suggest that this initial ὅτι might have a "declarative" function and depend on an implied assertion such as "to prove that"; see NAB: "As proof that you are children, God sent the spirit of his Son into our hearts, crying out, 'Abba, Father!'" (see also Lietzmann 1932: 25; Dunn 1993a: 219; Moule 1959: 147; Rohde 1989: 173). However, this is not the obvious way to understand ὅτι, and it is doubtful if we need to introduce such a reading in order to preserve Pauline consistency. A careful reading of Rom. 8:14–17 shows that Paul is not clearly arguing for a sequence of Spirit—sonship. Having the Spirit means that one is a "son"; but Paul is not clearly saying that the Spirit confers sonship. Nor does Paul's claim that the Spirit marks the "beginning" of Christian experience (3:3) mean that the Spirit must be absolutely prior to all other Christian blessings. Paul wants to associate the status of sonship with the gift of the Spirit, but claiming that Paul teaches a strict temporal or logical sequence between them would be overreading this text and others (see, e.g., R. Longenecker 1990: 173; Martyn 1997: 391; Schreiner 2010: 272).[18] The "sequence" of sonship and Spirit in various texts in Paul is thus probably dictated more by rhetorical than theological concerns.

Paul parallels God's sending of the Spirit with the sending of his Son: these two verses are the only places where Paul uses the verb ἐξαποστέλλω (*exapostellō*, send).[19] But Paul brings these assertions together in a more significant way by claiming that it is "the Spirit *of his Son*" whom God has sent. This language echoes other Pauline texts that associate the Spirit and the Son: see especially Rom. 8:9, "the Spirit of Christ," and Phil. 1:19, "the Spirit of Jesus Christ." We should not try to pin down the specific function of the Spirit that Paul has in mind. His point is general: the Spirit whom God gives is defined by and experienced in terms of God's Son, Jesus Christ. The eschatological ministry of the Spirit to which the prophets looked forward (see esp. Ezek. 36:26–27) is experienced not in the context of the torah but through union with Christ by faith (on this point see esp. Dunn 1993a: 220–21). In this passage, one might also notice the incipient trinitarianism that occasionally marks NT texts: *God* sends the *Spirit* of his *Son* (see the similar Rom. 8:9–11; Fee 1994: 400). The place to which the Spirit is sent—εἰς τὰς καρδίας ἡμῶν (*eis tas kardias hēmōn*, into our hearts)—continues the allusion to the prophetic expectation of the ministry of God's Spirit: "I will give you a new heart and put a new spirit in you; I will remove from you your heart of stone and give you a heart of flesh. And I will put my Spirit in you [LXX: ἐν ὑμῖν, *en hymin*; MT: בְּקִרְבְּכֶם, *bĕqirbĕkem*, in your inner being] and move you to follow my decrees and be careful to keep my laws" (Ezek. 36:26–27; see also Jer. 31:31–34). The ministry of the Spirit, as Paul will argue explicitly in 5:13–6:10, is what enables God's people in the new covenant to "follow his

---

18. Some interpreters try to solve the apparent contradiction by positing an "objective" and "subjective" sonship. A person, perhaps in baptism (see esp. Schlier 1989: 200), becomes a son of God in reality, followed by the gift of the Spirit and subjective experience of sonship (Calvin 1854: 78; Burton 1921: 221). Ridderbos (1975: 200–201), on the other hand, appears to suggest that the sonship to which Paul refers in v. 6 is, in keeping with Rom. 8:23, the final status given at the resurrection.

19. The verb ἐξαπέστειλεν (*exapesteilen*, he sent [out]) is a "collective historical aorist," referring (in 4:6) to "the successive bestowals of the Spirit on individuals" (Burton 1921: 223). Fee (2007b: 214) suggests that Paul may allude to Ps. 104:30a: "When you send [ἐξαποστελεῖς, *exaposteleis*] your Spirit, they [creatures in general] are created" (103:30a LXX). Beale (2005: 11), on the other hand, thinks an allusion to Isa. 48:16d may be present: "And now the Sovereign LORD has sent me, endowed [ἀπέσταλκεν, *apestalken*] with his Spirit." Neither allusion is likely.

laws": no longer, however, to fulfill the will of God as found in torah, but as found in the eschatological torah, the "law of Christ" (6:2). Paul's shift from the second-person plural ἐστε (este, you are) to the first-person plural ἡμῶν (hēmōn, our) is not because he shifts referent but because of rhetorical considerations. "You are" explicitly applies Paul's argument to the Galatians; then with "our," Paul moves naturally and probably unconsciously into confessional Christian style (on the textual issue regarding ἡμῶν, see the additional note).

The Spirit given to us, Paul claims, "cries out, 'Abba, Father.'" The form of the participle, κρᾶζον (krazon, crying), shows that it is the Spirit who "cries out," although Paul undoubtedly thinks of the Spirit crying out through our own voices; see the parallel Rom. 8:15: "The Spirit you received brought about your adoption to sonship. And by him we cry, 'Abba, Father.'" Interpreters discuss the specific situation in which this "cry" might be heard: as the community speaks in tongues, in normal prayer, and so forth. But this question might be inappropriate: Paul perhaps uses a word picture to convey the deep and emotional reaction within the believer's heart to the joyful conviction, brought by God's Spirit, that we are, indeed, God's sons. Paul uses not only the Greek ὁ πατήρ (ho patēr, Father; the nominative is used for the vocative) but also the Aramaic Αββα (אַבָּא, Abba, Father—an emphatic form of Hebrew/Aramaic אַב that was also used as a vocative).[20] The term was often (though not always) used in the context of the family and is not attested for this period within Palestinian Judaism as an address to God.[21] There is reason to think that this way of addressing God, while not necessarily unique to Jesus, was distinctive of his way of speaking to the Father (Mark 14:36). It was probably because the Aramaic word conveyed this distinctive sense of the intimate relationship to God that it was preserved among Greek-speaking Christians, especially in emotional responses such as we find here and in the closely parallel Rom. 8:15.[22]

4:7   The ὥστε (hōste, so that) marks this verse as a conclusion from the preceding; and the content of the verse suggests that it harks back to all of verses 1–6 (Lightfoot 1881: 170; Schreiner 2010: 272; it is unlikely that it concludes all the argument from 3:1–4:6, as R. Longenecker [1990: 175] suggests). The contrast between δοῦλος (doulos, slave) and υἱός (huios, son) picks up the fundamental contrast in the paragraph between the state of being no better than a "slave" (δοῦλος, doulos; v. 1), placed "under guardians and trustees" (v. 2), and indeed "enslaved" (δεδουλωμένοι, dedoulōmenoi) "under the stoicheia of the world"

20. Augustine suggested that the occurrence of both terms was intended to signal that God was father of both Gentiles and Jews (cf. Edwards 1999: 54–55).

21. The term abba is found once in the Babylonian Talmud as an address to God (b. Ta'an. 23b), but as Bruce (1982b: 199) points out, it occurs here only because of a play on words with reference to an earthly father.

22. The classic work on abba is Jeremias 1966, which, however, made certain claims about the uniqueness of the term and of its use among small children that were later shown to be overstated (see, e.g., the later work of Jeremias himself [1971: 61–68]; and also Barr 1988; Vermès 1981: 130–40; see esp. M. Thompson 2000: 21–34 for a judicious review of the question).

(v. 3)—and the state of being a "son" (vv. 5–6). In this verse Paul shifts from the plural forms of verses 5–6 to the singular (εἶ, *ei*, you are) in order to bring home this point to each of the Galatian Christians. The second part of the verse, building on the first part, also harks back to a key idea in this paragraph: inheritance. If "you are a son," Paul claims, then you are also an "heir, through God" (κληρονόμος, *klēronomos*, heir; see v. 1 and also 3:29). This last and very clipped phrase (διὰ θεοῦ, *dia theou*) is the subject of some debate. Scribes had problems with it and so provided a number of variant readings (see the additional note on 4:7). But it is just the difficulty of the brief phrase that testifies to its originality. The preposition διά usually denotes instrument, an idea that seems inappropriate with God as the object. But the preposition can also at times denote ultimate cause, or author (BDF §223), and that meaning is undoubtedly intended here (Wallace 1996: 433–34; Schlier 1989: 199; Mussner 1988: 277). The phrase means, then, that God is the Creator, or bestower of the inheritance (see NLT, "God has made you his heir"). Paul may add this phrase to suggest the security we enjoy: God himself has made us heirs! (R. Longenecker 1990: 175); but the argument of the letter may make it more likely that the focus is on grace: "heir not by virtue of birth, or through merits of your own" (Lightfoot 1881: 170; see also Burton 1921: 225).

Additional Notes

4:3. The MSS vary in the form of the verb between ἦμεν (A B C D¹ Ψ 1739 1881 𝔐) and ἤμεθα (𝔓⁴⁶ ℵ D* F G, etc.). Since the former form of the verb is more common in the NT, the second should probably be preferred as the more difficult reading (see, e.g., BDF §98). No difference in meaning is involved.

4:3. The association between the material "elements" of the universe and various kinds of religions and gods was widespread in the ancient world. Philo (*Decalogue* 53) comments: "Some nations have made divinities of the four elements, earth and water, and air and fire. Others, of the sun and moon, and of the other planets and fixed stars. Others, again, of the whole world." This tendency to "spiritualize" or "divinize" the material elements was a strong cultural current that the people of God had to fight against. The Lord, for instance, warns the Israelites: "And when you look up to the sky and see the sun, the moon and the stars—all the heavenly array—do not be enticed into bowing down to them and worshiping things the Lᴏʀᴅ your God has apportioned to all the nations under heaven" (Deut. 4:19). The characterization of pagan religion as involving worship of physical elements as well as warnings against it are found throughout Jewish and early Christian apologetics. The first-century BC Jewish book Wisdom of Solomon furnishes a typical example: "For all people who were ignorant of God were foolish by nature; and they were unable from the good things that are seen to know the one who exists, nor did they recognize the artisan while paying heed to his works; but they supposed that either fire or wind or swift air, or the circle of the stars, or turbulent water, or the luminaries of heaven were the gods that rule the world" (13:1–2). See also Philo, *Contempl.* 3, who mentions people who "honor the elements, earth, water, air, and fire." Among the Christian apologists, see, e.g., The Preaching of Peter; Tertullian, *Idol.* 4; Arist. 2–6; Clement of Alexandria, *Exhort.* 5 (commenting on Col. 2:8).

4:6. The one variant worthy of comment in this verse is the variation in pronoun after εἰς τὰς καρδίας. This variant is one of the more common ones found in the NT, the difference being of only one letter, with both pronouns often making perfectly good contextual sense. The earliest and best MSS (𝔓⁴⁶ ℵ

B et al.) read the first-person plural ἡμῶν, "into our hearts." But other MSS (𝔐 along with D², Ψ, 33) have the second-person plural ὑμῶν, "into your hearts." In addition to having the stronger external support, the former reading, because it involves a shift in person in midverse—"because *you* are sons, God sent the Spirit of his Son into *our* hearts"—is the more difficult reading. It is rather clear, then, that it should be preferred (Metzger 1994: 526; for the contrary opinion, see Witherington 1998: 289–90).

4:7. The clipped διὰ θεοῦ at the end of the verse, as well as the possible difficulty of thinking that the believer's inheritance comes "through" God, has led to a number of relatively poorly attested variants: (1) διὰ θεόν, "because of God" (F G et al.); (2) διὰ Χριστοῦ, "through Christ" (81 630); (3) διὰ Ἰησοῦ Χριστοῦ, "through Jesus Christ" (1739ᶜ); θεοῦ διὰ ['Ιησοῦ P 6 326 1505 et al.] Χριστοῦ, "[heirs] of God, through [Jesus] Christ" (ℵ² C³ D 0278 𝔐); (4) κληρονόμος μὲν θεοῦ, συγκληρονόμος δὲ Χριστοῦ, "heir through God, fellow heir with Christ" (Ψ et al.). Only the third has enough support to be seriously considered, but it is suspect as a harmonization with Rom. 8:17. The text, διὰ θεοῦ, attested in 𝔓⁴⁶ ℵ* B C* 33 1739*ᵛⁱᵈ, should be retained.

C. Appeal (4:8–31)

Paul occasionally addresses the Galatians in the argument of 3:7–4:7 (γινώσκετε [ginōskete, you know] in 3:7; ἀδελφοί [adelphoi, brothers and sisters] in 3:15); in this section he undoubtedly intends to include the Galatians in his second-person pronouns and verbal forms and, though more indirectly, in some of the first-person pronouns and verbal forms. But he has not referred to them specifically since his rebuke in 3:1–6. Beginning in 4:8, this changes. As he has done earlier in the letter (1:6; 3:1–5), he expresses his consternation about their strange infatuation with the agitators and addresses them in direct and personal terms. This shift probably marks a fundamental move within the letter, as Paul moves from argument (3:7–4:7) to appeal (4:8–31; e.g., de Boer 2011: 269–70). Other interpreters argue that this basic transition occurs in 4:12 (see esp. G. Hansen 1989: 44–50; R. Longenecker 1990: 184; Dahl 2002: 134; Hansen and Longenecker, reading the letter against the background of ancient rhetoric, find a shift here from "forensic" rhetoric to "deliberative" rhetoric). It is true that 4:8–11 has important contacts with 4:1–7 in particular (Burchard 1999: 41–42); it is something of a transitional unit. But we think the tone of exhortation begins in verse 8.

Exhortations or implied exhortations punctuate this part of the letter: "How is it that you are turning back to those weak and miserable elements? Do you wish to be enslaved all over again?" (4:9). "Become as I am" (4:12). "I fear . . . that I have wasted my efforts on you" (4:20). "You who want to be under the law, do you not hear the law?" (4:21). "Cast out the slave woman" (4:30). Paul's appeal falls into three distinct sections. The first two are distinguished by a focus on the past, as Paul implicitly and explicitly urges the Galatians to halt their dalliance with the law by reminding them of their own past (4:8–11) and of Paul's relationship with them (4:12–20). In 4:21–31, Paul uses Scripture to remind them of their present status and urges them to resist the agitators on this basis.

1. Looking at the Past: The Galatians' Slavery (4:8–11)

Central to this unit is Paul's consternation over the Galatians' initial moves to abandon the freedom they have in the gospel for slavery under the "elements of the world" from which they have been rescued. In this paragraph, Paul's appeal finds its basis in a consideration of the Galatians' past. As we argue in the introduction to 4:8–31, we think this paragraph initiates a new section of the letter in which Paul appeals to the Galatians. But there are also key points of continuity with the argument that has preceded it. This paragraph continues the distinctive vocabulary and key themes from the preceding verses. In verse 9 especially notice Paul's expression of amazement that the Galatians might be turning back to "the weak and miserable elements," becoming "enslaved" to them again, and compare that with verse 3: "We were enslaved under the elements of the world." The characterization of the pre-Christian state in terms of slavery is indeed a key motif of 4:1–7, occurring at both its beginning (v. 1) and end (v. 7) as well as in verse 3; and, of course, "elements" (στοιχεῖα, *stoicheia*) is rare in Paul (occurring only in these verses in Galatians and in Col. 2:8, 20). This close relationship could suggest that 4:8–11 concludes 4:1–7 (as Hays 2000: 280 suggests). At the same time, the imagery of 4:1–7 brings to a climax some of the key themes of 3:7–4:7 as a whole: the inability of the law to secure Abrahamic inheritance (3:6–9, 14, 15–18; cf. the connection of "heir" in 4:1, 7 with Abraham via 3:29); the consequent need for redemption from the curse of the law (3:13; 4:5); the pre-Christian state as one of bondage to the law (3:22–25; "under the law" in 4:5); and the gift of sonship in Christ (3:26; 4:5–7). Therefore, as the initial paragraph in Paul's appeal to the Galatians, 4:8–11 applies the wider argument of which 4:1–7 is the conclusion: not only 3:23–4:7 (Fung 1988: 167) or 3:15–4:7 (Schreiner 2010: 275) but, more broadly, 3:7–4:7 (R. Longenecker 1990: 178–79; G. Hansen 1994: 124–25).

Exegesis and Exposition

[8]But at one time, when you did not know God, you were enslaved to those who by nature are not gods. [9]Now, however, having come to know God—or rather, having come to be known by God—how can you consider turning again to the weak and impotent elements? Do you want to become enslaved to them all over again? [10]You are observing days and months and seasons and years. [11]I fear that I may have labored over you in vain.

The ἀλλά (*alla*, but) at the beginning of the verse may signal a broad contrast   **4:8**
between the argument in the preceding section and the appeal that now follows (de Boer 2011: 269). But more likely it has a narrower focus, contrasting
Paul's claim about Christians being "sons of God" in 4:1–7 with their former
life. (Only a minority of the English translations explicitly translate this ἀλλά,
probably because it is awkward to have adversatives in both vv. 8 and 9.) Paul
portrays this situation in stark terms: the Galatians were formerly (τότε, *tote*,
at one time) people who, "not knowing God" (οὐκ εἰδότες θεόν, *ouk eidotes
theon*),[1] were "enslaved to those who by nature are not gods" (ἐδουλεύσατε τοῖς
φύσει μὴ οὖσιν θεοῖς, *edouleusate tois physei mē ousin theois*). "Not knowing God" is a way of describing non-Christians and especially Gentile non-
Christians (2 Thess. 1:8; Titus 1:16; note 1 Thess. 4:5, "the pagans [ἔθνη, *ethnē*]
who do not know God"), with the verb "know" (whether οἶδα [*oida*], as here,
or γινώσκω [*ginōskō*]) taking on the typical OT sense of intimate knowledge
or relationship. Paul's claim that the Galatians were once "enslaved" picks up
key language from 4:1–7 and echoes more distantly the earlier language about
being "confined under the law" (3:23) or "under a *paidagōgos*" (παιδαγωγός,
guardian; 3:24, 25). The confining or enslaving power is now, however, not the
law or the elements of the world (4:3) but false gods. It is not clear how Paul
views these beings who, he claims, are not "by nature gods." Is he suggesting
that those to whom the Galatians were once enslaved do not actually exist?
Or is he implying that the Galatians were once worshiping beings that exist
but are not actually gods, as they once may have thought them to be? The latter is probably to be preferred; see especially Paul's claim in 1 Cor. 10:19–20:
"Do I mean then that food sacrificed to an idol is anything, or that an idol is
anything? No, but the sacrifices of pagans are offered to demons, not to God,
and I do not want you to be participants with demons."[2]

The "but now" (νῦν δέ, *nyn de*) in this verse contrasts with the τότε of verse   **4:9**
8, as Paul completes one of his typical "once/but now" contrasts between the
old era/person and the new (see also Rom. 6:19, 21–22; 7:5–6; 11:30; Gal. 1:23;
Eph. 2:12–13; 5:8; Col. 1:21–22; 3:7–8; Philem. 11). The contrast is stark: the
Galatians have moved from the state of "not knowing God" to "knowing
God" (γνόντες θεόν, *gnontes theon*; the shift from the verb οἶδα in verse 8 to
γινώσκω here is difficult to explain but probably conveys no change in meaning; cf. Bruce 1982b: 202). The force of the aorist γνόντες may be inceptive;
see RSV: "You have come to know God" (also NRSV, ESV, NASB, NET, NJB,
NAB; cf. Fung 1988: 189; R. Longenecker 1990: 180). As "*not* knowing God"
denotes non-Christians, so "knowing God" is standard NT language for being

---

1. The use of the negative οὐ/οὐκ (instead of μή [*mē*]) with the participle is rare in the NT but
follows the practice in classical Greek (BDF §430). Mussner (1988: 291) suggests that the participle
may be causal: "because" the Galatians did not know God, they were enslaved to false gods.
2. Betz 1979: 215. Witherington (1998: 297–98) and Witulski (2000) argue that Paul may have
in view the cult of the emperor. But it is not certain that the emperor cult was popular enough
in Asia Minor when Paul wrote Galatians for him to have it in view here.

in relationship with God (the language is especially common in 1 John: 1 John 2:3, 4, 14; 3:6; 4:6, 7, 8; cf. also Heb. 8:11 [= Jer. 31:34]; Paul uses the language in a weakened sense in Rom. 1:21 to denote people who know something about God). Interestingly, however, Paul immediately "corrects" this way of putting the matter by adding, in a somewhat parenthetical aside, "rather, having come to be known by God" (μᾶλλον δὲ γνωσθέντες ὑπὸ θεοῦ, *mallon de gnōsthentes hypo theou*). "Know" here has the sense of intimate relationship or even election that the language frequently has in the Bible (e.g., Gen. 18:19 KJV; Amos 3:2; Jer. 1:5). Paul obviously does not intend his second clause as a replacement of the former but rather as a second and, he implies, more fundamental way of expressing the relationship between God and his people (see the similar 1 John 4:10: "This is love: not that we loved God, but that he loved us and sent his Son as an atoning sacrifice for our sins"). Humans do indeed come to know God, but they do so only because God first determines to "know" us in Christ. In this context Paul may want to stress the divine initiative to highlight God's grace as the foundation for the Galatians' relationship to Christ and the foolishness of turning away from the rich experience of that grace (see, e.g., Martyn 1997: 412–13).[3]

Yet, Paul says, that is just what the Galatians are in danger of doing. Of course, they do not see it this way. For them, following the agitators' agenda by adopting adherence to the law and adding that to their faith in Christ would mean "completing" their relationship with God (cf. 3:3). But, as Paul has made clear throughout his argument, such a step of addition is in fact subtraction, implicitly calling into question the adequacy of God's provision in Christ. Granted all this, Paul is amazed that the Galatians are contemplating a return to "those weak and impotent elements." His use of πῶς (*pōs*, how) to introduce his question suggests his consternation: "How is it possible that" you are "returning" (ἐπιστρέφετε, *epistrephete*; Burton 1921: 230–31). The present tense of the verb emphasizes the imminent danger: "You are in process of returning" (A. Robertson 1934: 879) or "You are trying to return" (a conative idea; see Dunn 1993a: 225–26). There may be deliberate irony in the choice of a verb that is often used for conversion "from . . . worthless things to the living God" (Acts 14:15; also 3:19; 9:35; 11:21; 15:19; 26:18, 20; 2 Cor. 3:16; 1 Thess. 1:9; 1 Pet. 2:25).

The close connection between the argument of verses 1–7 and the warning of verses 8–11 is again evident in Paul's reference to the "elements" (στοιχεῖα, *stoicheia*), clearly the same "elements of the world" under which "we were once enslaved" (v. 3) and under which, astonishingly, the Galatians apparently want to be enslaved again. Emphasizing just how foolish such a move would be, Paul characterizes these elements as ἀσθενῆ (*asthenē*, weak) and πτωχά (*ptōcha*). Some of the English translations, following BDAG (896.4), translate the latter as "miserable" (e.g., NIV), but it might be better

---

3. On contextual grounds, Rosner (2008: 217–18) argues that being "known by God" here refers to adoption as his children.

to classify the word here under another meaning in BDAG (896.3): "lacking in spiritual worth"; hence our translation "impotent" (Martyn 1997: 411; cf. "worthless" in NASB, ESV, NET; NLT: "useless"; NAB: "destitute"). The Galatians are threatening to reverse their initial religious conversion, when they "turned [ἐπεστρέψατε, *epestrepsate*] to God from idols to serve the living and true God" (1 Thess. 1:9). As we noted in our comments on verse 3, the στοιχεῖα are probably the basic material building blocks of the universe, the "elements" that were often associated with various forms of idolatrous worship in the ancient world. The word therefore refers to the religions the Galatians practiced in their pre-Christian past. The Galatians, however, were not seeking to return to their earlier religious beliefs and practices; they were being tempted to place themselves under the Mosaic law. For Paul's warning to "work," then, it appears as if he must think of the law as a subset of the "elements." This is an incredibly bold claim. Barrett (1985: 61) claims that we find here "as extraordinary a statement as is to be found anywhere in [Paul's] letters. . . . Here in Galatians he virtually equates Judaism with heathenism. To go forward into Judaism is to go backward into heathenism." Some interpreters, however, take this too far, claiming that Paul in effect demonizes the law, putting its observance in the same category as the pagan religions of his day (see esp. Hübner 1984: 33–34). So strong a conclusion, however, goes too far. Paul is pulling out all the rhetorical stops to convince the Galatians not to take what he views as a disastrous step. To accomplish this, he implies that putting themselves under the law, since the era of the law has ended with the coming of the promised Seed, is akin to returning to their impotent pagan religions.[4]

Paul's claim that the Galatians "are observing days and months and seasons and years" appears to intrude rather abruptly. But a close connection with verse 9 may be recognized. The religious observances that Paul mentions here are governed by the movements of the heavenly bodies: precisely those "elements" that Paul has mentioned in verse 9. Rather than identifying the "elements" with "those who are by nature not gods" in verse 8 (e.g., Arnold 1996: 57–72; Adams 2000: 228–30), it makes better sense to identify them with the astronomically governed religious observances in this verse (R. Longenecker 1990: 181; Dunn 1993a: 228–29; Witherington 1998: 297; de Boer 2007: 216–22; Wink 1984: 67–77). The present-tense verb Paul uses, παρατηρεῖσθε (*paratēreisthe*), may signify "you are on the verge of observing."[5] But more probably, like ἐπιστρέφετε in verse 9, it has the sense "you are in process of observing" (e.g., Bruce 1982b: 205; R. Longenecker 1990: 182–83; the middle voice may suggest the special interest of the subject: you are observing for yourself [Wallace 1996: 421]). This verb occurs with reference to observing traditions or religious

4:10

---

4. S. Elliott (2003) suggests that Paul may be implying a relationship between circumcision and the ritual castration practiced by certain Anatolian religions.

5. Interpreting the present tense to refer generally to the observances of scrupulous religious people (Betz 1979: 217) is far less likely.

customs only here in the Bible, but is used in this sense in extrabiblical Greek (Josephus, *Ant.* 3.91; 11.292; cf. BDAG 771.3).

The language Paul uses for these observances seems to be deliberately vague and open-ended. Since it is the law of Moses that the Galatians are being urged to adopt, the language undoubtedly has some reference to Jewish religious observances. "Days" (ἡμέρας, *hēmeras*) probably, then, denotes the Sabbath and perhaps other festival days, such as the Day of Atonement (Dunn 1993a: 227).[6] "Months" (μῆνας, *mēnas*) is more difficult to pin down but may refer to new-moon festivals (BDAG [668–69] refers to Col. 2:16, where Paul uses νεομηνία [*neomēnia*]; cf. Num. 28:11–15). "Seasons" (καιρούς, *kairous*) probably has in view the Jewish festivals, which usually span a number of days (such as the Festival of Unleavened Bread).[7] "Years" (ἐνιαυτούς, *eniautous*) probably refers to "sabbatical years" (Lev. 25; see, e.g., Luke 4:19, ἐνιαυτὸν κυρίου δεκτόν [*eniauton kyriou dekton*], "the year of the Lord's favor"). The sequence of words is similar to that found in some Jewish texts, as in Jub. 2.9: "And the Lord set the sun as a great sign upon the earth for days, sabbaths, months, feast (days), years, sabbaths of years, jubilees, and for all the appointed times of the years." At the same time, however, it is striking that Paul's list of terms contains no "technical" references to Jewish religious celebrations (in this respect, contrast the very similar Col. 2:16, "Therefore do not let anyone judge you by what you eat or drink, or with regard to a religious festival, a New Moon celebration or a Sabbath day"). Paul may therefore choose a rather vague way of referring to the Jewish observances to tie them as closely as possible to the "elements" (Hays 2000: 288) and perhaps also to the religious observances in the Galatians' pagan past (see esp. Martin 1996, who thinks the reference is explicitly to pagan days of religious observance; and also Betz 1979: 217–18; de Boer 2011: 276). The language may also reflect the creation account in Gen. 1 (see v. 14 NIV: "And God said, 'Let there be lights in the vault of the sky to separate the day from the night, and let them serve as signs to mark sacred times, and days and years'") as a way of emphasizing the relationship between the observance of holy days and the created world (Bruce 1982b: 205; Martyn 1997: 416–17; Schreiner 2010: 279).

4:11   Paul wraps up his warning on a note of personal concern that anticipates the tone of the next paragraph: "I fear that I may have labored over you in vain" (φοβοῦμαι ὑμᾶς μή πως εἰκῇ κεκοπίακα εἰς ὑμᾶς, *phoboumai hymas mē pōs eikē kekopiaka eis hymas*).[8] (The first ὑμᾶς need not be explicitly represented in translation [RSV, NRSV, ESV, NJB], since it anticipates the one to follow

---

6. When ἡμέρα (*hēmera*) denotes a Jewish religious "day" in the NT, it is followed by a genitive noun denoting the particular day (e.g., σαββάτων, "day of the Sabbath" [as in Luke 4:16]). But ἡμέρα is used absolutely in Rom. 14:5 to refer (probably) to Sabbath observance.

7. See Lev. 23:4: "These are the Lᴏʀᴅ's appointed festivals, the sacred assemblies you are to proclaim at their appointed times [ἐν τοῖς καιροῖς αὐτῶν, *en tois kairois autōn*]." Here again it is clear that καιρός (*kairos*, appointed time) in itself does not designate a holy day, nor is there any place in Scripture that it does.

8. The use of πως with μή accentuates the note of anxiety (BDF §370).

in the subordinate clause [prolepsis; cf. BDF §476.3]). Paul frequently uses the verb κοπιάω (*kopiaō*) to describe the "work" of ministry (Rom. 16:6, 12; 1 Cor. 15:10; 16:16; Col. 1:29; 1 Thess. 5:12; 1 Tim. 4:10; 5:17). And, as here, he also worries elsewhere about that ministry proving to be "in vain" (1 Cor. 15:14; Gal. 2:2; Phil. 2:16; 1 Thess. 3:5, all using a form of κενός [*kenos*, empty, without purpose]); or similarly, peoples' faith to be "in vain" (1 Cor. 15:2 [εἰκῇ], 14 [κενός]). Here Paul may intend to evoke particularly Gal. 3:4, where, at the beginning of this section of the letter, he asks the Galatians, "Have you experienced so much in vain [εἰκῇ]?" The various expressions of the Galatians' commitment to Christ along with Paul's ministry among them will prove to be "empty," "without purpose," if the Galatians should succumb to the message of the agitators by submitting to the law.

2. Looking at the Past: Paul and the Galatians (4:12–20)

If the Galatians' past slavery under the "elements of the world" should deter them from giving up the gospel in favor of the law, so should the lessons learned from their past relationship with Paul. This new paragraph is cast in even more personal terms than verses 8–11 but also shares key features with it (Witherington 1998: 303–4). We note especially the similarity between verse 9, "How can you consider turning again to the weak and impotent elements?"—and verses 15 and 16: "Where, then, is your blessing of me now?" "Have I now become your enemy by telling you the truth?"

It is Paul's fear about having ministered in vain among the Galatians (v. 11) that draws his attention back to the time when he first brought the gospel to the communities there. In the paragraph that follows, then, he reflects very personally on his first experience with the Galatians as the basis for a renewed plea to resist the agitators and remain committed to his gospel. The tone of these verses is characteristic of the ancient rhetorical device called "pathos," by which a speaker seeks to move the audience by appealing to the emotions and to shared personal experience (see esp. Witherington 1998: 295–96, 305–7).[1] Paul has provided the Galatians with a complex and, he hopes, convincing theological argument (3:1–4:7). Now he hopes to move them to response by building on his appeal to their minds and adding an appeal to their hearts.[2] By its nature, this style of speaking or writing is not oriented toward a logical development of ideas. Hence this paragraph falls into no easily discerned structure. It is framed by direct appeals to the Galatians—"brothers and sisters" in verse 12; "my children" in verse 19—with which Paul explicitly (v. 12) or implicitly (vv. 19–20) calls on his readers to change course and return to their adherence to Paul and the gospel that he preaches. The focus on returning to an earlier state of close personal relationship continues in verses 12b–16, as Paul contrasts the response he received when he first came among them with their attitude toward him now. In verses 17–18, Paul contrasts the badly directed zeal of the agitators with the zeal for Paul and his gospel that the Galatians should consistently exhibit.

---

1. As Witherington (1998: 295–96, 305–7) notes, if we classify Paul's rhetoric in one of the ancient categories, vv. 12–20 would probably fit the "deliberative" type better than the "forensic" type (see also R. Longenecker 1990: 184).

2. The importance of this appeal to the emotions makes it impossible to relegate vv. 12–20 to the status of a parenthesis (contra Mussner 1988: 305).

Exegesis and Exposition

¹²I plead with you, brothers and sisters: become like me, for I have become like you. You did me no wrong. ¹³Now you know that it was because of a weakness of the flesh that I first proclaimed the gospel to you. ¹⁴Yet though ⌜my condition was a source of temptation for you⌝, you did not reject me or despise. Rather, you received me as an angel of God, as Christ Jesus. ¹⁵Where, then, is your blessing? For I testify that, if it were possible, you would have gouged out your eyes and given them to me. ¹⁶So have I now become your enemy by telling you the truth?

¹⁷These people are zealous for you, but for no good. They want to exclude you, in order that you might be zealous for them. ¹⁸It is always good ⌜to be zealous⌝ in a good cause, and not only when I am with you.

¹⁹My ⌜dear children⌝, for whom I am again in the pains of childbirth until Christ is formed in you—²⁰I could wish to be present with you now and to change my voice, because I am perplexed about you.

The verse begins abruptly with an imperative verb addressed to the Galatians: **4:12**
γίνεσθε ὡς ἐγώ, *ginesthe hōs egō*, become like me. The sequence of the words in Greek, in which the main verb, δέομαι (*deomai*, I plead),[3] and the vocative address, ἀδελφοί (*adelphoi*, brothers and sisters), come later in the verse, highlights this imperative. As we noted in the introduction to this section, this is the first imperative in the letter that calls on the Galatians to take action. Just what Paul wants the Galatians to do, however, is not clear. In other texts where Paul calls on his readers to imitate him, the context usually indicates what Paul has in view (see 1 Cor. 4:16; 11:1; Phil. 3:17; 2 Thess. 3:7, 9; cf. 1 Thess. 1:6). But the following causal clause and the context of the letter point to what Paul has in mind. The Galatians are to become like Paul, he says, "because I have become like you" (ὅτι κἀγὼ ὡς ὑμεῖς, *hoti kagō hōs hymeis*). In light of Paul's claim that he "died to the law" (2:19) and so is no longer "under the law" (3:23–25), along with the clear hint in his autobiography that he has left "his way of life in Judaism" (1:13), his becoming like the Gentiles will mean that he has abandoned the law as the way by which righteousness before God is to be pursued.[4] The verb to be supplied in the second clause is therefore undoubtedly ἐγενόμην (*egenomēn*), which could be translated into English either as a simple past, "I became" (NIV, HCSB)—or perhaps better as a perfect (R. Longenecker 1990: 189), "I have become" (RSV, NRSV, ESV, NLT, NAB, NET, NASB, CEB). A parallel to this claim, though probably involving a more comprehensive relationship to the law, is found in the famous 1 Cor. 9:21: "To those not having the law I became like one not having the law (though I am not free from God's law but am under Christ's law), so as

---

3. "Plead" is a good English rendering, connoting the strength of this verb (see *NewDocs* 6:146).

4. See, e.g., Gaventa 1986, on the relationship between Paul's autobiography in Gal. 1–2 and his imperative here.

to win those not having the law."[5] Paul has exchanged his life under the law for a life under the dominion of Christ, an existence no longer determined by the law. How foolish for the Galatians, then, to be contemplating the opposite exchange, to put the law in place of Christ (see 5:2). This appeal is the key point of the paragraph, and its orientation toward Paul's own experience sets the tone for the rest of the paragraph.

The final clause in this verse is introduced just as abruptly as the opening imperative: οὐδέν με ἠδικήσατε (ouden me ēdikēsate, you did me no wrong).[6] The aorist form of the verb most naturally refers to past time, and that past time is likely to be when Paul had first preached the gospel in Galatia. A plausible sequence of thought then emerges if we identify the action of "not doing wrong" to Paul as not criticizing or rejecting him because of the law-free lifestyle that he exhibited among them (e.g., Mussner 1988: 306). It is less clear whether Paul implies a contrast in what he says, such as, "You did not wrong me then, but you are wronging me now" (Hays 2000: 293).

4:13   In verses 13–14, which form one sentence in Greek, Paul continues to remind the Galatians of the good relationships that they enjoyed when Paul first ministered among them. He reminds them specifically of (1) the reason why he first evangelized among them (v. 13); (2a) how they did *not* respond to him (v. 14a); and (2b) how they *did* respond to him (v. 14b).

It was because of ἀσθένειαν τῆς σαρκός (astheneian tēs sarkos) that Paul first preached the gospel in Galatia. Identifying what Paul means by this "weakness of the flesh" is very difficult. Most interpreters rightly argue that Paul's famous "thorn in the flesh" (σκόλοψ τῇ σαρκί, skolops tē sarki), given him to keep him humble (2 Cor. 12:7), refers to the same situation.[7] A few interpreters think Paul in 2 Cor. 12:7 may be referring to opponents of his, since Paul's stance vis-à-vis such people is a prominent theme in 2 Cor. 10–13. It is possible that ἀσθένειαν τῆς σαρκός here in Galatians could also refer to opposition (Güttgemanns 1966: 173–77) or perhaps to the results of opposition: the scars Paul bore on his body as a result of physical punishment (see Gal. 6:17; Hays 2000: 293–94; Eastman 2007: 100–109; Goddard and Cummins 1993: 101–7).[8] However, most interpreters rightly think that a reference to some kind of persistent or periodically severe physical problem is probably intended. Paul

5. Other interpreters argue that Paul's reference here is broader, including the way Paul has committed himself to the gospel after having been in subjection to the "elements of this world" (e.g., B. Longenecker 1999: 100; Eastman 2007: 40).

6. The οὐδέν, which is technically not needed, is a "cognate accusative of the inner object" (A. Robertson 1934: 482).

7. Witherington (1998: 309) argues that they are not the same because the "thorn in the flesh" was given to Paul "fourteen years" before he wrote 2 Corinthians (see 2 Cor. 12:2), that is, around AD 42–43, whereas Paul first visited the Galatians at the earliest in AD 46–47. But in 2 Cor. 12:7 the present tenses of the verbs ὑπεραίρωμαι (hyperairōmai, becoming conceited) and κολαφίζῃ (kolaphizē, torment) imply that the thorn was a persistent condition (e.g., Harris 2005: 857).

8. The idea that the "flesh" could refer to the Galatians—i.e., their fleshly nature—is unlikely (contra Martin 1999b).

does use ἀσθένεια to refer to physical illness in one other text (1 Tim. 5:23), and the Gospels and Acts use the word exclusively in this sense (Matt. 8:17; Luke 5:15; 8:2; 13:11, 12; John 5:5; 11:4; Acts 28:9). And σάρξ often means "body" in Paul (e.g., Rom. 2:28; 2 Cor. 4:11; Eph. 2:11). However, Paul's one other use of the phrase ἀσθένειαν τῆς σαρκός has another meaning (mental or spiritual incapacity; cf. Rom. 6:19). Identifying the physical problem from which Paul suffered has been a long-standing and ultimately insoluble puzzle (for an excellent survey of options and the evidence to be considered in making a decision, see Harris 2005: 857–59). The best guess—and it can be little more than that—is some kind of eye problem, perhaps hinted at in verses 14 and 15 (see our comments there; see, e.g., Dunn 1993a: 234, 236; Witherington 1998: 309–10). Whatever the condition, it was "because of it" (διά with the accusative) that Paul first preached to the Galatians. The particular construction that Paul uses here probably cannot be watered down to mean simply that Paul was ill when he first preached in Galatia (NLT, HCSB); the "weakness" was the *reason* Paul preached there (so, e.g., NIV, ESV). Why Paul's physical problem led him to evangelize in Galatia simply cannot be known.[9]

Paul's claim that it was because of this "weakness of the flesh" that he "first" preached the gospel in Galatia has also drawn a lot of attention. The word Paul uses here, πρότερον (*proteron*), originally meant specifically "the former of two" (as a comparative form). If this were what Paul meant, then it might be possible, by tracing Paul's movements in the book of Acts, to pinpoint the time at which he wrote Galatians. Unfortunately, Acts does not really settle the matter. Luke refers to the "Galatian" country twice, in Acts 16:6 and 18:23, during, respectively, Paul's second and third missionary journeys; and some interpreters are convinced that these must be the visits to which Paul alludes in verse 13 (e.g., Lightfoot 1881: 174–75; Mussner 1988: 306–7; Schlier 1989: 209–10). If so, Galatians must have been written on the third missionary journey (fitting the traditional North Galatian view of the churches of Galatia). Other interpreters, however, argue that "Galatia" is the geographic term that best encompasses all the cities Paul visited on the first missionary journey (Acts 13–14), and that Paul here in verse 13 refers to his initial evangelizing visit and to his follow-up visit (see Acts 14:21–22). If this were so, then Paul must be writing before his third visit (Acts 16:6), and the churches he addresses must be in South Galatia. However, the assumption that both these views rest upon, that πρότερος means here "the first of two," must be questioned. In the Greek of Paul's day, comparative adjectives and adverbs were being used somewhat loosely, often losing their strict "former of two" meanings. Paul himself tends to use the word to mean simply "formerly," "earlier" (BDF §62; Turner 1965: 90–91; see 2 Cor. 1:15; Eph. 4:22; 1 Tim. 1:13; cf. also John 6:62; 7:50; 9:8; Heb. 4:6; 7:27; 10:32; 1 Pet. 1:14). In this text, then, Paul probably intends simply

9. Ramsay (1900: 417–22) used this language famously to claim that Paul suffered from malaria, an illness that would have been tempered by a move to the higher elevations of the Galatian plateau.

to contrast his "former" or "earlier" relationships with the Galatians to the situation that "now" prevails (see v. 16; Betz 1979: 224; Bruce 1982b: 209; R. Longenecker 1990: 190; Martyn 1997: 420; de Boer 2011: 279).

4:14 Although the second clause of the sentence that spans verses 13–14 is linked very generally to the first (καί, *kai*, and), it is reasonable to suspect that there is a relationship between Paul's "weakness of the flesh" and the "temptation . . . in my flesh" (πειρασμόν . . . ἐν τῇ σαρκί μου, *peirasmon . . . en tē sarki mou*) that Paul refers to here in this clause. The textual tradition is unclear about whether the pronoun following πειρασμόν is ὑμῶν or μου (see the additional note on 4:14). Though I favor the former as the original text, the difference between the two may not be very great: in one case Paul would be saying "the trial you experienced" (objective genitive), and in the other "the trial I caused" (subjective genitive). In either case, we must supply, as the occasion of the trial, Paul's "weakness in the flesh," an idea that the English versions rightly introduce into this clause. Another problem is how to understand πειρασμόν, a word that in the NT refers either to "trial" (an outward circumstance) or "temptation" (an inner enticement to evil). Paul uses the word in only two other places: in one verse it rather clearly means "temptation" (1 Tim. 6:9), but in the other it might mean either "trial" or "temptation" (1 Cor. 10:13). In our text it might be slightly preferable to render it as "temptation" since Paul's point is that there was something in his physical condition that might have tempted the Galatians to reject him rather than to receive him (NLT; cf. NET: "put you to the test"; Fung 1988: 198). The whole phrase πειρασμὸν ὑμῶν ἐν τῇ σαρκί μου can then be unpacked: "the temptation caused you by my bodily condition" (see BDAG 793.2.b and 352.1–2).

Despite the temptation that Paul's "weakness of the flesh" created for them, the Galatians did not "reject" (ἐξουθενήσατε, *exouthenēsate*) or "despise" (ἐξεπτύσατε, *exeptysate*) him. The first verb, used seven other times by Paul (Rom. 14:3, 10; 1 Cor. 1:28; 6:4; 16:11; 2 Cor. 10:10; 1 Thess. 5:20), is quite straightforward. But the second, used only here in Biblical Greek, is more striking. The verb originally meant "spit, spit out"; and since spitting out was a sign of contempt, it came to be used to mean simply "despise" or "scorn" (as the English versions here translate; and cf. R. Longenecker 1990: 192; Goddard and Cummins 1993: 107). However, the verb continued to be used specifically to refer to the act of spitting as a means of avoiding the "evil eye" (see BDAG 309), and it is tempting to think that Paul might have this connotation in view here (Dunn 1993a: 234; Martyn 1997: 421; Witherington 1998: 311). As we have seen, the verb βασκαίνω (*baskainō*) in 3:1 may have the idea of "bewitched by means of the evil eye." What Paul could be saying here, then, is that his physical condition might have been one that tempted the Galatians to view him as possessed by a demon or as evil in some way.[10]

---

10. Hafemann (1997: 354–55), reading this whole context in Galatians against the background of the Deuteronomic tradition, suggests that the Galatians had been encouraged by the agitators to view Paul's physical condition as a sign that he was under a curse.

And it is further tempting to think that it might have been a condition affecting Paul's eyes that led them to view him in just this way (J. Elliott 1990: 268–69).

Far from rejecting Paul, the Galatians, Paul reminds them, "welcomed him as an angel of God, as Christ Jesus." Paul uses the verb δέχομαι (dechomai, receive) in a variety of ways, but he can elsewhere speak of the "welcome" extended to a Christian envoy (2 Cor. 7:15; Col. 4:10). It is not clear why Paul compares the welcome he received to what might be extended to an angel. If Paul is, as we think, writing to churches planted on the first missionary journey, he might be referring specifically to the incident in Lystra, when the people there mistook Paul for the god Hermes (Acts 14:12; cf. Dunn 1993a: 235). But the response to Paul in Lystra was one that the apostle, naturally, strongly disavowed (Acts 14:14–18), and it would be unusual for Paul to use the incident positively here. Paul's comparison may, then, be intended to highlight the way the Galatians not only received him as a person but also the way they responded positively to the message that he brought—for a major function of angels in Scripture is to bring divine messages. But Paul makes the point even more strongly: they received Paul "as Christ Jesus." A few interpreters think that the phrase ἄγγελον θεοῦ (angelon theou) might refer to "*the* angel of the Lord," the figure who appears in the OT as an apparent preincarnate Christ (see Fee 2007b: 230–31; Wallace 1996: 252; cf. Turner 1963: 180). In this case, ὡς Χριστόν Ἰησοῦν (hōs Christon Iēsoun) could be a simple appositive: "as the angel of God, that is, as Christ Jesus." But this interpretation is quite unlikely. If this is what Paul intends, it is hard to know why he does not use κυρίου (kyriou, of the Lord) rather than θεοῦ. More likely, then, as in 1:8, Paul refers to an angel as an exalted messenger, to be received with all due reverence. "As Christ Jesus" thus is ascensive: "You welcomed me as an angel of God, indeed, as if I were Christ Jesus himself" (see NIV; Mussner 1988: 308).[11]

Paul's focus shifts from the initial reception that he enjoyed among the Galatians to the present situation. Following the English versions, we should assume that Paul intends his opening rhetorical question to be filled out with a present-tense verb: "Where, then, *is* your blessing?" (ποῦ οὖν ὁ μακαρισμὸς ὑμῶν; pou oun ho makarismos hymōn?). It is not clear what Paul means by μακαρισμός here, as the variety of renderings in English translations reveal: "your blessing of me" (NIV); "the blessing you felt" (ESV); "the good will you felt" (NRSV); "sense of happiness" (NET). Interpreters suggest other options: "state of blessedness" or "happiness" (LN 302.25.118; B. Longenecker 1999: 103), "praise" (Betz 1979: 227) or "congratulations" (Bruce 1982b: 227). Two factors suggest the direction we should take in interpreting the word. First, in contrast to εὐλογία (eulogia, blessing), μακαρισμός usually has the sense "pronounce a blessing" (see Rom. 4:6, 9, where the only other

4:15

11. This apparently ascensive function makes it unlikely that Paul is hinting at a relationship between his sufferings and the sufferings of Christ (contra Hafemann 2000: 136).

occurrences of the word in Biblical Greek are found).[12] Second, the previous (vv. 13–14) and following (v. 15b) context focuses on the Galatians' relationship with Paul. This latter factor suggests that μακαρισμός will probably not refer to the spiritual state of the Galatians in general (e.g., "blessedness," "happiness," "the blessing you felt," etc.), but to the relationship between themselves and Paul. Granted the probable lexical sense of the word, then, the best option is to take the phrase to mean "the blessing you pronounced on me" (Hays 2000: 294; cf. NIV), and this would certainly fit the context (Hays 2000: 294).

Paul now expands on (γάρ, *gar*, for) the nature of the "blessing" that the Galatians pronounced on Paul: so positively did they feel toward him that "if it were possible [εἰ δυνατόν, *ei dynaton*; a contrary-to-fact condition without ἄν; cf. BDF §360], you would have gouged out your eyes and given them to me." (The circumstantial participle ἐξορύξαντες [*exoryxantes*, gouging out] is appropriately translated as a finite verb in English; for similar uses of the verb ἐξορύσσω [*exoryssō*], see Judg. 16:21; 1 Sam. 11:2.) Paul clearly intends to stress the degree of personal regard, affection—even love—that the Galatians demonstrated on his first visit. There is some evidence from ancient sources that giving one's eyes was a metaphor for self-sacrificing love; and this may be all that Paul intends here (see Lucian, *Tox.* 40–41; and, e.g., Fung 1988: 199; R. Longenecker 1990: 193; Martyn 1997: 421). But one wonders why Paul would have chosen this particular metaphor, which was not widespread. It may, then, be possible that the Galatians expressed a willingness to give Paul their eyes because it was his eyes that were badly affected by his "weakness in the flesh" (v. 13; cf. Schlier 1989: 211; Dunn 1993a: 236).

4:16   Paul reverts back to the present situation: "So have I now become your enemy by telling you the truth?" The inferential ὥστε at the beginning of this clause ("and so," "accordingly"; cf. Moule 1959: 144) is an unusual, though not unprecedented, way of introducing a rhetorical question.[13] It signifies that Paul is using this question to sum up the current state of affairs between him and the Galatians. The English versions, correctly enough, translate the verbal ἀληθεύων (*alētheuōn*) "telling [you] the truth" (the verb is relatively rare in Biblical Greek, with only seven occurrences). Yet it is not simply truth telling that is involved, but more fundamentally, truth proclaiming: namely, the "truth of the gospel" that is at stake in Galatia (Gal. 2:5, 14; 5:7). The central component of this truth is not that the gospel has opened the way for Gentiles to be included (as important as that is), but that the gospel is offered freely by grace and is to be accepted and lived out by means of faith alone (cf. Bruce 1982b: 211; contra Dunn 1993a: 237). Paul is fighting for that

12. The fact that Paul uses μακαρισμός here but εὐλογία (*eulogia*, blessing) in 3:14 makes it unlikely that he here refers back to the "blessing of Abraham" from that verse (contra Dunn 1993a: 235).

13. A few interpreters think that the opening clause may be a statement (R. Longenecker 1990: 193; Witherington 1998: 313), but a rhetorical question makes better sense.

truth and is willing to jeopardize his close relationship with the Galatians for the sake of that truth—even if it means that he becomes their "enemy" (ἐχθρός, *echthros*; probably used in an active sense: Paul was being viewed by the Galatians as their enemy [cf. Lightfoot 1881: 176; Fung 1988: 199]). It is difficult to know when this "truth telling" has taken place. Lightfoot (1881: 176) suggests that Paul refers to warnings he gave the church during his second visit to them (which he identifies with Acts 18:23). But it is more likely that Paul is being accused of being the Galatians' "enemy" by the agitators, who are trying to convince the Galatians that Paul proclaimed to them a defective gospel (Martyn 1997: 421–22).

As we noted in the introduction to this paragraph, a neat logical sequence is difficult to find. And this is certainly not unexpected in a passage that appeals to the Galatians on the basis of emotion and past "friendship" (on this theme, see esp. Betz 1979: 221, et al.) rather than on the basis of compelling reasoning. But nowhere in the paragraph is the movement of thought more abrupt than here, where Paul turns suddenly to the motives of the agitators. And yet, as we have suggested, verse 16 has prepared for this shift of focus since it was probably the agitators who were portraying Paul as the Galatians' enemy.

4:17

Paul is so caught up in the moment that he does not even bother explicitly to identify the subjects of his third-person plural verbs: ζηλοῦσιν (*zēlousin*, they are zealous), θέλουσιν (*thelousin*, they wish). English versions exhibit a range of approaches to this lack of subject, some simply using the pronoun "they" (NRSV, ESV, NASB, NET); others "those people" (NIV); and still others, more interpretatively, "those false teachers" (NLT). There can be no doubt, however, that it is the agitators that he has in view. When ζηλόω has a personal object, the verb means "be deeply interested in someone, court someone's favor, make much of" (BDAG 427.1.b): as in the NIV, the agitators "are zealous to win you over."[14] Yet their enthusiasm for the Galatians is not for the good (οὐ καλῶς, *ou kalōs*, "directed toward the bad," "for no good purpose" [NRSV]), in direct contrast to the attitude toward the Corinthians that the apostle expresses in 2 Cor. 11:2 (AT): "I am zealous for you with a godly zeal" (ζηλῶ γὰρ ὑμᾶς θεοῦ ζήλῳ, *zēlō gar hymas theou zēlō*). Rather (ἀλλά, *alla*) than having a sincere concern for the Galatians, the agitators want to "exclude" (ἐκκλεῖσαι, *ekkleisai*) them. Paul may be referring to the effect that the agitators, in drawing the boundaries of the covenant so tightly in terms of torah obedience, have on those who do not measure up to this standard (Dunn 1993a: 238; Hays 2000: 295). But the purpose clause that depends on this statement, ἵνα αὐτοὺς ζηλοῦτε (*hina autous zēloute*, in order that you might be zealous for them), suggests rather that the issue is more focused on gaining disciples: the agitators want to exclude the Galatians from the orbit of Paul's ministry and gospel so that the Galatians might "have zeal

---

14. Dunn (1993a: 237) thinks that the verb may have connotations of typically Jewish "zeal" (see 1:14), but this is unlikely (Bruce 1982b: 211).

for," attach themselves to, the agitators (Bruce 1982b: 212; R. Longenecker 1990: 194; Fung 1988: 200; Smiles 1998: 66–67; Wilson 2007: 55).[15]

4:18 As Paul's attention shifts back to the Galatians, the use of the verb ζηλόω is the point of continuity from verse 17. The most likely reading (see the additional note on 4:18) has the infinitive ζηλοῦσθαι (zēlousthai), which could be either middle (with an active sense) or passive. The form is unusual: no other examples of a middle or passive of this verb are found among its sixty Biblical Greek occurrences. But the difficulty of explaining why Paul shifts from the active to the middle forms if he intends an active sense in verse 18 (Lightfoot 1881: 177) strongly favors a passive sense (as almost all the English versions and commentators assume or argue). The unusual form of the verb along with the lack of clear tie-in with the context suggests that Paul may be quoting a proverbial saying (e.g., Betz 1979: 231; R. Longenecker 1990: 194), to be translated something like "It is good to be courted in a good cause (or for a good purpose)." Paul then applies the proverb by emphasizing that it should "always" (πάντοτε, pantote) pertain and not only when he is present with the Galatians. Bruce (1982b: 212) well summarizes the resulting sense (bringing in v. 17 as well): "It is always good . . . to be courted with honourable intentions, as you were 'courted' by me when I was present with you; but as it is, no sooner has my back been turned than you let someone else come and 'court' you with *dis*honourable intentions!"

4:19 In yet another abrupt transition, Paul concludes this paragraph with a direct appeal to the Galatians. This appeal maintains the intensely personal flavor of the paragraph as Paul compares the Galatians to his children and himself to their mother, struggling as if in birth pains to bring them into conformity with Christ (v. 19), and expressing how much he would like to restore the warm relationship they once enjoyed together (v. 20).

While the transition from verse 18 to verse 19 is indeed abrupt (with no conjunction to mark the connection), there is a general conceptual continuity.[16] In contrast to the agitators' zeal for the Galatians, which is "not for the good" and oriented toward their personal aggrandizement, Paul's concern for the Galatians is deep and oriented toward their welfare (Eastman 2007: 96). His address to them as "my dear children" (τεκνία μου, teknia mou; see the additional note on 4:19 for my choice of τεκνία over τέκνα) suggests this kind of relationship. But the point is made even more clearly by his following description of the Galatians: οὓς πάλιν ὠδίνω (hous palin ōdinō, for whom I am again in the pains of childbirth [the masculine accusative οὓς after the neuter-plural τεκνία is an example of "construction according to the sense"; cf. BDF §296]). The verb ὠδίνω means "to be in the pains of childbirth," "to be in labor" (cf. 4:27; Rev. 12:2 and, e.g., Isa. 26:17; Jer. 4:31); it is an example

---

15. Dunn (1993a: 238–39) suggests again that it is specifically zeal for the covenant that is in view here, but this interpretation does not satisfactorily explain the personal focus (αὐτούς).

16. A few interpreters think that v. 19 continues the sentence from v. 18 (Lightfoot 1881: 178; Burton 1921: 248; as does ESV).

of the way Paul can use maternal as well as paternal imagery to describe his relationship with his churches (see also 1 Thess. 2:7–8). The "again" (πάλιν) in this clause shows that Paul thinks of his initial evangelization of the Galatians in these terms, as he proclaimed the gospel to them, hoping thereby to bring them to the "new birth" or regeneration. There is an implicit rebuke, then, in Paul's claim that he feels himself to be back in that position, suffering such "birth pains" all over again on their behalf. The imagery also reveals how strongly Paul feels about his converts and how much it pains him when they are not thriving spiritually.

Indeed, Paul says, he continues to labor and suffer with and for the Galatians, "until Christ is formed in you" (μέχρις οὗ μορφωθῇ Χριστὸς ἐν ὑμῖν, *mechris hou morphōthē Christos en hymin*). The metaphor shifts again, with the implication that the Galatians are the ones in whom gestation is occurring (μορφόω is sometimes used to describe the formation of an embryo; cf. BDAG 659–60).[17] The imagery of Christ being "formed" within the Galatians suggests that Paul will not be content until Christ so dominates their lives that there can be no possible change from a settled spiritual condition. While this is the only place Paul uses this particular verb, he uses several cognate words to express this sense of "conformity" to Christ (see esp. Rom. 8:29; also Phil. 3:10, 21). It is not clear whether Paul thinks of Christ as being "formed" within each of the Galatians (Bruce 1982b: 212; R. Longenecker 1990: 195; Witherington 1998: 315–16), within the community of the Galatians (Martyn 1997: 424–25; Hays 2000: 296), or perhaps both (Betz 1979: 235; Mussner 1988: 313; Schreiner 2010: 290). But the first option seems better to respect the imagery and the way Paul applies it here.

Verse 19 consists of a vocative address and then a relative clause that depends on that address ("my children"). Some translations take verse 20 as the continuation of this sentence (NASB, NRSV, NIV, NJB), while others have Paul starting over in verse 20, leaving verse 19 as a sentence fragment (most clearly in NASB; see also NAB; yet NET, NLT, and HCSB turn the Greek relative clause in verse 19 into an independent clause; for this latter reading, see, e.g., Mussner 1988: 313; Schlier 1989: 213). The issue does not substantially affect our interpretation, but the latter approach is probably better (the δέ at the beginning of v. 20 makes a continuation of the sentence from v. 19 difficult). In verse 18, Paul encouraged the Galatians to remain constant to him even when he is not "present" (παρεῖναι, *pareinai*) with them. Now he expresses the wish that he could, indeed, be "present" (παρεῖναι) with them again. Perhaps more important than his presence with the Galatians, however, is Paul's wish that he could "change my voice" (ἀλλάξαι τὴν φωνήν μου, *allaxai tēn phōnēn mou*).

4:20

17. Gaventa (1990) argues that the language Paul uses in this verse—esp. ὠδίνω—picks up apocalyptic motifs associated with the "new birth" of Israel as the people whom God would once again embrace as his own. Paul's suffering, then, becomes an important part of the apocalyptic "woes" that will usher in the new creation (see also Garlington 2003: 189–92; Eastman 2007: 111–21).

The imperfect form of the verb that governs both these infinitives (ἤθελον, *ēthelon*, I was wishing) suggests that Paul knows his wish cannot be fulfilled (Wallace 1996: 551; BDF §359; Dunn 1993a: 241; cf. NASB: "I could wish"; NIV: "How I wish"). He would very much like to be with the Galatians and using the tone of voice appropriate to the friendship that has characterized their previous relations. But the circumstances force him to address them otherwise, using argument and a rebuking tone to bring them back to submission to the "truth of the gospel."

Until then, however, Paul remains puzzled by their failure to understand and appreciate the benefits of the gospel he has preached to them: "I am perplexed about you" (ἀποροῦμαι ἐν ὑμῖν, *aporoumai en hymin*; forms of ἀπορέω [*aporeō*, be perplexed] occur also in Mark 6:20; Luke 24:4; John 13:22; Acts 25:20). The Galatians have experienced the blessing of Abraham (3:14) and the powerful ministry of the Spirit (3:2–5): how can they turn their backs on these? As he ended the previous paragraph, in 4:11, here Paul ends this one also on a note of perplexity and deep concern about the Galatians.

Additional Notes

4:14. We find several variations in wording following πειρασμόν in the MS tradition:

ὑμῶν (ℵ* A B C² D* F G 33)
ὑμῶν τόν (several minuscules)
τόν (ℵ², several minuscules)
μου (𝔓⁴⁶)
μου τόν (C*ᵛⁱᵈ D¹ Ψ 075 0150, many minuscules, 𝔐)

The article is added in some MSS to ease the transition to the prepositional phrase. The more important issue is whether to read the second-person plural—"your trial or temptation"—or the first-person singular—"my trial or temptation." The former has strong external support and is arguably the more difficult reading (see Metzger 1994: 527). Only the NKJV among modern versions (following, of course, KJV) uses "my" here.

4:18. In place of the accepted reading ζηλοῦσθαι, some MSS have τὸ ζηλοῦσθαι (D F G 𝔐), which yields the same meaning, while others have ζηλοῦσθε, "you are zealous" / "you are being courted" (ℵ B 33). The infinitive, which has wide support (A C 062 0278, et al.) and is the more difficult reading, is widely adopted as original.

4:19. The MS tradition is split between τέκνα (children; ℵ* B D* F G 062 and a few minuscules) and τεκνία (a diminutive form, either "little children" or "dear children"; ℵ² A C D¹ Ψ 0278 33 1739 1881 𝔐). The UBS⁴ and NA²⁸ texts both read τέκνα (and see Burton 1921: 249; Betz 1979: 233), but several versions, judging from their translations, read τεκνία (KJV, NIV, NRSV, ESV, NLT), and this reading receives some support from scholars (Lightfoot 1881: 178; R. Longenecker 1990: 195; Witherington 1998: 315). External evidence is fairly evenly divided, and it could be argued that τεκνία, a word Paul never uses elsewhere, would more easily have been changed to the common τέκνα (thirty-nine times in Paul; several [4:25, 27, 28, 31] in this context).

4:20. Calvin (1854: 87) comments on Paul's wish that he could "change his voice":

He [Paul] was prepared most cheerfully to assume a variety of forms, and even if the case required it, to frame a new language. This is a course which pastors ought most carefully to follow. They must not be entirely guided by their own inclinations, or by the bent of their own genius, but must accommodate themselves, as far as the case will allow, to the capacity of the people—with this reservation, however, that they are to proceed no farther than conscience shall dictate, and that no departure from integrity shall be made, in order to gain the favor of the people.

3. Looking at the Present: Children of the Promise (4:21–31)

This new paragraph shares with 4:8–11 and 4:12–20 direct appeals to the Galatians: "Tell me, you who want to be under the law . . ." (v. 21). "Cast out the slave woman with her son" (quoting Gen. 21:10). These appeals lead into 5:1: "Stand, therefore, and do not again be burdened by a yoke of slavery." This imperative mode, however, is mixed with a strong indicative mode. Paul returns to the argument about what it means to be the "children of Abraham" that was so important in 3:7–29 (Dunn 1993a: 246). Now, however, the issue is taken a step further as Paul distinguishes two lines of descent from Abraham, one stemming from the "slave woman" Hagar and the other from the "free woman" Sarah. The Galatians, Paul argues, belong to this second line of descent, children of Spirit, born through the promise, just as Isaac was. Paul bases this argument on Scripture, citing the story of Sarah and Hagar in Gen. 16–21 (cf. γέγραπται [gegraptai, it is written] in v. 22) and Isaiah's prophecy (54:1) about the reversal of fortunes experienced by a barren woman in verse 27 (γέγραπται again).

This mixture of argument and exhortation makes it difficult to know whether 4:21–31 should be viewed basically as a return to scriptural argument after the hortatory section of 4:8–20 (e.g., Martyn 1997: 432; Witherington 1998: 321) or basically as a continuation of the exhortation focus of 4:8–20 (e.g., R. Longenecker 1990: 199; Rohde 1989: 204). The best response to this debate is to sidestep it by insisting that Paul mixes argument with appeal. To be sure, his argument from Scripture takes a different form in this new paragraph. Rather than citing a series of texts, as he did in 3:6–14, he draws parallels, using what he calls an "allegorical" approach, between the narrative of Gen. 16–21 and the situation of his own day. Many interpreters think that Paul's argument here may be defensive, a response to the agitators who were using this story in their own propaganda (see esp. Barrett 1976; and also, e.g., Calvert-Koyzis 2004: 88; Bruce 1982b: 218; G. Hansen 1994: 140–41; R. Longenecker 1990: 207–8; Dunn 1993a: 243; Hays 2000: 300; de Boer 2011: 286). They surmise such a scenario partly because of this unusual way of appropriating Scripture and partly also because the story of Sarah and Hagar is not, on the surface, a natural place for Paul to make his own case for the law-free gospel. Other interpreters, however, think that Paul is himself responsible for turning our attention to this passage since it serves to make two points connected with what he has argued earlier (e.g., Cosgrove 1988: 223; Watson 2004: 207). First, the appeal to the Sarah and Hagar narrative enables Paul to develop and to refine his basic argument from 3:7–29 that those who belong to Christ are the sons/seed of Abraham. What is implicit in that earlier argument becomes explicit here: it is not biological descent from Abraham that marks the true children of Abraham but descent through the line of promise. Paul therefore anticipates the argument that will become more explicit in his Letter to the Romans (9:6b–13). Second, by focusing on the women who give birth to the two contrasting sets of children, Paul more allusively returns to the theme of Jerusalem that served as the key reference point in his own autobiography (1:18–2:10). Without contesting the importance of the church in Jerusalem or the apostles who are located there, Paul nevertheless shows that appeal to Jerusalem per se no longer carries much weight: for "the present Jerusalem" "is in slavery with her children" (v. 25).

Although a decision about these issues is not easy, we slightly prefer to think that Paul's argument in this paragraph is defensive, a response to the agitators' use of these same texts, and that it belongs with 4:8–11 and 4:12–20 as part of the "appeal" section of the letter. The concern with the past in these two paragraphs is replaced now with a focus on the present status of the Galatian believers and exhortations based on that status. However, while an important argument and not a mere add-on (contra, e.g., Burton 1921: 251; Schlier 1989: 216; Garlington 2003: 193), this paragraph is not the climax of the letter (contra Boyarin 1993: 62; Harmon 2010: 173).

The agitators, as we have noticed before, are following a strongly continuous reading of salvation history. God's people are those who descend from Abraham, through Isaac, and then the patriarchs, from whom comes the nation of Israel. And Israel is given the law, which then becomes the means by which God's people are to identify themselves and live out their elect status. Therefore we can well imagine the agitators arguing that promise and law are correlative, that only by submitting to the law can one claim to be truly descended from Isaac and therefore from Abraham. Only law-observant people can be children of Sarah. Paul counters this argument by developing his own understanding of salvation history. Key to his argument is the contrast between slavery and freedom. This contrast is the leitmotif of this paragraph:

"The slave woman" [differs from] "the free woman" (v. 22–23).
"[Hagar] bears children for slavery" (v. 24b).
"The present Jerusalem . . . is enslaved with her children" (v. 25).
"The Jerusalem above is free" (v. 26).
"The son of the slave woman will not inherit with the son of the free woman" (v. 30).
"We are children not of the slave woman but of the free woman" (v. 31).

The importance of the slave/free contrast, then, dominates the paragraph. Moreover, Paul's interest in this contrast is made even clearer when we consider that he is the one who has brought the language of "freedom" into the story: Sarah is never designated as a "free" woman in the OT.

Earlier in Galatians, Paul has prepared the way for his deployment of this language here. The contrast is first found in 2:4, where Paul contrasts the "freedom we have in Christ Jesus" with the "slavery" that the "false brothers" were trying to impose with their insistence on circumcision. Here slavery is implicitly associated with the imposition of law obedience, and this becomes clearer as Paul's argument unfolds. The language of "under the law" / "under the *paidagōgos* (guardian)" / "under the elements of the world" (3:23, 24, 25; 4:2, 5) suggests the idea of slavery. And in 4:3, 7, 8, and 9, Paul characterizes the Galatians' past situation as one of slavery and argues that they would return to this status if they were to submit to the law. "Freedom" drops out of Paul's vocabulary after 2:4 but resurfaces in 4:21–31 as the keynote of his argument.

It is the characterization of Hagar as a "slave woman" (παιδίσκη, *paidiskē*) in the key OT narrative under dispute that provides Paul with the toehold to develop this contrast. As Paul's own claim about "speaking allegorically" (v. 24a) implies, he is not arguing from the plain sense of the OT narrative. Rather, his reading is based on his conviction about the direction that salvation history has taken and is mediated by his appropriation of Isa. 54:1 (see esp. Harmon 2010: 173–85; Willitts 2005). Paul knows that Christ is the climax of salvation history and that access to Christ is given by faith (alone!) and through the eschatological gift of the Spirit (see esp. 3:1–5; 5:5). It is therefore by faith in Christ that the "many children" Isaiah has promised to eschatological Zion/Jerusalem have been born. Moreover, it is Israel's failure to obey the law that has led the people into their current "barrenness" (Jobes 1993: 313). The move from the two stages in the existence of Jerusalem in Isa. 54:1 to Sarah and Hagar is based on Paul's broader reading of the OT and of Isa. 49–54. The "barren woman" who rejoices, clearly Jerusalem in 54:1, alludes to Sarah, the "barren woman" who ultimately gives birth par excellence (51:1–2); and the association of Hagar with the current barren state of Jerusalem follows from this identification. It is therefore Paul's christological reading of Isaiah that provides him the scriptural basis to align Sarah with the law-free gospel that has given birth to the "Jerusalem above"; contrariwise, Hagar becomes associated with subjection to the law.

Paul's interpretation of the story about Sarah and Hagar, while not by any means a straightforward reading of the narrative, is not an arbitrary reading either. It is informed by Paul's hermeneutical axioms: his basic convictions about Christ as the fulfillment and culmination of salvation history, informed by and influenced by his, and other early Christians', actual experience of God's working in their midst. Of course, all NT appropriations of the OT are governed by such hermeneutical axioms. Nevertheless, Paul's interpretation of the Sarah/Hagar story seems to go further in the direction of an imposition of a preconceived scheme onto a text than is typical of NT interpretation of the OT. And this impression is strengthened by Paul's explicit claim in Gal.

4:24 that he is "speaking allegorically" (ἀλληγορούμενα, *allēgoroumena*). What are we to make of this claim? How should we characterize what Paul is doing with Scripture in this text?

First, we should recognize that in Paul's day this term "allegory" did not have the technical sense often associated with the word in later centuries. It simply refers to an interpretation that would today be called "figurative": a reading of a text or narrative in terms of some "other" issue or reality. As Lincoln (1981: 13) notes, "Literally, ἀλληγορέω [*allēgoreō*] need only mean 'to speak with another meaning' and theoretically the means by which this was done could involve what we would now term either analogy or typology or allegory." Which of these best describes Paul's "contemporizing" of Scripture here? Observing that Paul is comparing two sets of historical experiences (the story of Sarah and Hagar alongside the story of the church and Judaism), many scholars insist that Paul's interpretation rightly belongs in the category of typology. See Chrysostom (*Comm. Gal.* on 4:24 [*NPNF*[1] 13:34]): "Contrary to usage, he calls a type an allegory; his meaning is as follows; this history not only declares that which appears on the face of it, but announces somewhat farther, whence it is called an allegory" (also see Hanson 1974: 93–103; Bruce 1982b: 217; Silva 2007: 808). Others, however, insist that while Paul's interpretation is not "allegory" in quite the same sense as, for instance, many of the scriptural applications found in Philo or Origen, what he is doing can properly be called "allegory" since he does not, as would usually be the case in typology, identify an OT person (type) with a NT person (antitype), but rather OT people are identified with biblical institutions or places (e.g., Sarah and Hagar = covenants; Hagar = Mount Sinai; see, e.g., Hays 1989a: 116; R. Longenecker 1990: 209; Witherington 1998: 322–23; Dunn 1993a: 247–48). But perhaps a majority of contemporary interpreters would categorize Paul's interpretation neither as "typology" nor as "allegory," but as a mixture of the two (Betz 1979: 239; Lincoln 1981: 13–14; Goppelt 1982: 139; Mussner 1988: 320; Martyn 1997: 436; Drane 1975: 41–43; Schreiner 2010: 293); yet still others bypass the debate by using other designations (e.g., "trope" [Jobes 1993; Harmon 2010: 174], "analogy" [Fung 1988: 218]).

The matter is complicated by the lack of clear and agreed-upon definitions of "typology" and "allegory"; and Hays (1989a: 116) is undoubtedly right in claiming that Paul would not likely have distinguished between the two. If allegory is understood as a technique that plays down or rejects the historicity of the narrative, then "allegory" is not the right word for what Paul is doing: there is every reason to think that Paul viewed the narrative about Sarah and Hagar from Genesis as historical.[1] We may want to continue to use "allegory" in this restricted sense; and, of course, we have every right

---

1. Many evangelical interpreters want to avoid calling what Paul is doing "allegory" because of this issue or because they define allegory in terms of the particular way that Philo uses the approach (see Silva 1987: 69–75; Bray 2005: 34). Treier (2005: 825) proposes a useful distinction between allegory and typology in terms of a contrast between an "iconic" approach, which preserves narrative coherence, and a "symbolic" approach, which "arbitrarily imposes a

to do so. But one might make a case that this definition of allegory is too narrow, failing to acknowledge how what we often call allegory was actually being practiced in the history of the church. Used in a more general sense, then, "allegory" might not be the worst way to characterize what Paul is doing in this paragraph.[2] Whatever name we give it, however, what is most important is to recognize that Paul's interpretation cannot fairly be accused of "willful distortions" of the text or of engaging in "sheer Hellenistic midrash speculation" (as Schoeps 1959: 238 claims). Rather, as we have argued above, Paul grounds his reading of the Sarah and Hagar narrative in an important pattern of OT salvation-historical movement, a reading, to be sure, enhanced by his hermeneutical axioms. He gives to the narrative before him in Genesis, without denying its intended historical sense, an additional or added meaning in light of these hermeneutical axioms.[3] What is important to note is that any contemporizing reading of the OT, whether that found in the Dead Sea Scrolls or in the rabbis or in early Christianity, is inevitably the product of some set of extratextual hermeneutical axioms.

The paragraph divides naturally into three basic parts: an introduction (v. 21), the interpretation of the narrative of Sarah and Hagar (vv. 22–27), a section marked out by the two occurrences of γέγραπται (vv. 22, 27); and the application and appeal (4:28–31; see Matera 1992: 174).

Exegesis and Exposition

[21]Tell me, you who want to be under the law, do you not hear the Law?

[22]For it is written that Abraham had two sons, one of the slave woman and one of the free woman. [23]But the one of the slave woman was born according to the flesh, while the one of the free woman was born through ⌜promise⌝. [24]These things are being taken allegorically. For these women represent two covenants, one from Mount Sinai that bears children for slavery, which is Hagar. [25]⌜Now the Hagar⌝ Sinai mountain is in Arabia. But it corresponds to the present Jerusalem, for she is enslaved with her children. [26]But the Jerusalem above is free, which is ⌜our mother⌝. [27]For it is written,

⌜Be glad, barren woman who has not born a child;
　shout for joy, you have not been in birth pains;
because more are the children of the desolate woman
　than of her who has a husband.⌝

---

thoroughly ahistorical connection." I certainly don't think Paul's approach is "arbitrary"; but is it ahistorical? Does it preserve narrative coherence? These questions are not easy to answer.

2. Gignilliat (2008) indeed suggests that typology be viewed as one form of allegory.

3. Witherington (1998: 330) is right, then, to argue that Paul gives the text not a "deeper sense" but a "secondary referent." See also Gignilliat (2008: 145): "A Christian reading of the OT is, therefore, a reading that takes seriously the literal sense of the text in its unique temporal setting coupled with the reality of this unique temporal setting being caught up in another realm of divinely ordered sequence in which figure and fulfillment mutually correspond to one another and inform one another in an eschatological reality."

²⁸Now ⌜you⌝, brothers and sisters, are, like Isaac, children of promise. ²⁹But just as at that time the one born according to the flesh persecuted the one born according to the Spirit, so now. ³⁰But what does the Scripture say? "Cast out the slave woman and her son. For the son of the slave woman will not inherit with the son of the free woman." ³¹Therefore, brothers and sisters, we are not children of the slave woman but of the free woman.

The new paragraph is marked by the vocative address, "you who want to be **4:21** under the law" (οἱ ὑπὸ νόμον θέλοντες εἶναι, *hoi hypo nomon thelontes einai*), and by the imperative λέγετε (*legete*), "tell [me]."[4] The phrase ὑπὸ νόμον has occurred earlier in Galatians (3:23; 4:4, 5), along with phrases expressing a similar idea: ὑπὸ παιδαγωγόν (*hypo paidagōgon*, under a guardian; 3:24, 25); and ὑπὸ τὰ στοιχεῖα τοῦ κόσμου (*hypo ta stoicheia tou kosmou*, under the elements of the world; 4:3). To be "under the law," we have argued, means to be under the ruling authority of the Mosaic law, a situation that, if no other factors apply, leads (at least according to Paul) to condemnation ("the curse of the law"; cf. 3:13).[5] The phrase therefore invokes the idea of subjection or slavery that is the key motif of this paragraph. (And note that Paul unpacks the phrase "under the elements of the world" in 4:3 with the language of slavery in 4:9.) While the agitators are not yet explicitly in view, it is clear that it is their propaganda that has led the Galatian Christians to consider placing themselves under the law of Moses. Only by doing so, Paul's opponents were apparently arguing, could the Galatians be sure of inheriting the Abrahamic blessing (see 3:7–9).

In an obvious play on words, Paul then challenges the Galatians, who want to be "under the law," to "hear the Law." Paul mostly uses νόμος (*nomos*, law) to denote the body of commandments given by God to Israel through Moses; but in keeping with Jewish usage, he also uses the word in a "canonical" sense, to denote the Pentateuch (as here; cf. also Rom. 3:21b; 1 Cor. 9:8, 9; 14:34[?]), or sometimes the entire OT (Rom. 3:19a; 1 Cor. 9:8, 9; 14:21; see Moo 1983: 75–90). The verb ἀκούω (*akouō*, hear) probably has the sense of the Hebrew שָׁמַע (*šama*ʿ, hear), used in conjunction with the law: not just "hearing" or "listening" but also "attentive hearing," a "listening that leads to understanding and obedience" (Mussner 1988: 317). Paul wants the Galatians to "learn" what the Law is saying.

With his customary introductory formula, γέγραπται (*gegraptai*, it is written), **4:22** Paul now introduces the "Law" that he wants the Galatians to understand. In the first of many unusual features in Paul's handling of the OT in this paragraph, γέγραπται does not introduce an OT quotation but a brief synopsis of

4. The "you" in English translation reflects Paul's clear intention to address the Galatians here (a ὑμεῖς [*hymeis*] can be inferred; cf. Mussner 1988: 317).

5. The fact that the Galatians *want* to be "under the law" makes it unlikely that the phrase in itself denotes "under the curse of the law." Wilson (2007: 40–42) seeks to avoid this problem by suggesting that Paul is speaking ironically. However, while irony is not easy to detect in written form, we don't think the evidence he marshals for an ironic tone here is convincing.

an OT narrative. The narrative is found in Gen. 16–21, and Paul selects one element from that narrative: the birth of two sons of Abraham, "one [born to] the slave woman and one [born to] the free woman" (ἕνα ἐκ τῆς παιδίσκης καὶ ἕνα ἐκ τῆς ἐλευθέρας, *hena ek tēs paidiskēs kai hena ek tēs eleutheras*).[6] The articles with παιδίσκης and ἐλευθέρας suggest reference to the well-known "slave woman" and "free woman": well-known characters from the biblical narrative to which Paul refers (Wallace 1996: 225). The reference, of course, is to Hagar and Sarah, but Paul signals his interpretive approach to the story by characterizing them rather than naming them. Hagar is called a παιδίσκη ("[female] slave") in Gen. 21 (vv. 10, 12, 13; the Hebrew, אָמָה [*'āmâ*] is roughly equivalent). Paul never uses the name "Sarah" anywhere in his exposition, instead referring to her throughout as the "free woman" (vv. 30, 31; the "barren woman," by inference, in v. 27). Paul's concern with this motif is revealed by the fact that the OT never uses the language of freedom to characterize Sarah—although the contrast with Hagar does not mean that Paul has read this idea into the text (Watson 2004: 208). Thus the "two sons" of Abraham are Ishmael and Isaac. Again, however, Paul never uses the name "Ishmael" in this text and names "Isaac" only once, almost in passing (v. 28). In Gal. 3:7–4:7, we might say, Paul's concern is with paternity and takes the form of a positive argument: people who by faith attach themselves to Christ are the children of Abraham. In this passage, Paul's concern is with maternity, and the argument proceeds by oppositions: believers are the children of the free woman and not the children of the slave woman.

4:23 The oppositions that characterize Paul's exposition in this paragraph continue in this verse as Paul contrasts the manners of birth of the two sons: the one (Ishmael, from the "slave woman") κατὰ σάρκα (*kata sarka*, according to the flesh), the other (Isaac, from the "free woman") δι' ἐπαγγελίας (*di' epangelias*, through the promise). The ἀλλ' (*all'*, but) that introduces this verse may suggest a contrast between Paul's use of the story and the way the agitators were using it (Martyn 1997: 434), but more likely it functions to highlight a further difference between the two sons. Each was born to a different kind of woman (v. 22), *but* in addition, each was born in a different manner. Paul uses the perfect tense of the verb here (γεγέννηται, *gegennētai*, was born) to indicate that "the OT event . . . still retains its (exemplary) meaning" (BDF §342.5; Wallace 1996: 582). The real difficulty in this verse is to determine the meaning of the opposition "flesh/promise." The latter term reflects the importance of God's promise in the birth of Isaac. Sarah, old and barren, is promised by God that she will give birth to a son who will become Abraham's heir (see esp. Gen. 17:15–16; 18:10–15; 21:1: "The Lord did for Sarah what he had promised"). So the son born to her can be said to have been born "through promise." The διά in this phrase could indicate "attendant circumstances": Isaac was born

---

6. Paul's claim that "Abraham had two sons" technically contradicts the OT claim that Abraham and Keturah had several more sons after Sarah's death (Gen. 25:1–6). But Paul's focus is on the sons of Abraham who might have a role as his heirs.

"in conjunction with" or "as a result of" (cf. NIV, HCSB) the promise. But since God's promise about the child that Sarah would have does necessarily carry with it God's purpose to intervene and cause the birth, it is better to think that διά retains its usual instrumental sense (Harris 2012: 152) and that Paul wants to accentuate the divine agency in Isaac's birth: "the son of the freeborn wife was born as God's own fulfillment of his promise" (NLT; see Dunn 1993a: 247; Mussner 1988: 319; Fung 1988: 206; Watson 2004: 206–7). In contrast, then, κατὰ σάρκα draws attention to the strictly human agency that led to the birth of Ishmael. In this case, not only was there no divine promise or any indication of special divine intervention; but the birth also was the result of the (overly hasty?) decision of Abraham and Sarah to seek an heir by marrying Abraham to their female slave (Gen. 16; 17:18). The word σάρξ (*sarx*, flesh) is one of the most difficult words to understand in Paul, but it generally connotes a sense of "strictly/narrowly human." *Sarx* does not necessarily have an explicitly negative connotation, but by virtue of its generally implicit contrast with Spirit or something of the sort, it tends to take on the nuance of at least a limited or restricted perspective. Here, therefore, the idea may be captured well by TNIV: "as the result of human effort"; compare also the slightly more negative (and very expansive!) NLT: "in a human attempt to bring about the fulfillment of God's promise." Some interpreters think there may be a further allusion to the agitators' program, which focused on "works of the law" and circumcision and which Paul has earlier associated with the flesh (3:3; see Dunn 1993a; 246–47; Martyn 1997: 435–36); but this is not clear.

What Paul has said about the OT narrative of Abraham's two wives and their children in verses 22–23 straightforwardly summarizes that story—albeit with an interpretive overlay in the "flesh/promise" language. Now, however, Paul signals that his interpretation is taking a different direction: "These things are being taken allegorically" (ἅτινά ἐστιν ἀλληγορούμενα, *hatina estin allēgoroumena*). The indefinite relative pronoun ἅτινα (which, as is often the case in NT Greek, is equivalent to the definite relative ἅ [Bruce 1982b: 217; contra Lightfoot 1881: 180]) refers to the two women of verses 22–23, "the slave woman" and "the free woman." The participle ἀλληγορούμενα (which functions here with ἐστιν as a present periphrasis [BDF §353.4]), is derived from the verb ἀλληγορέω, which can mean either "speak allegorically" or "explain allegorically" (F. Büchsel, *TDNT* 1:260). The verb does not occur elsewhere in Biblical Greek, but it is used (once) in Josephus (*Ant.* 1.24; the cognate occurs in *Ag. Ap.* 2.255), while Philo, who is well known for his strongly "allegorical" approach to the interpretation of the OT, uses it twenty-five times, both in the sense "speak allegorically" (e.g., *Leg.* 2.5) and "interpret allegorically" (e.g., *Leg.* 3.238; Philo uses cognate nouns and adjectives seventeen times). Since Paul here refers to the women in the narrative rather than to the narrative itself, it is probable that he uses it in the sense "interpret allegorically": "Now this may be interpreted allegorically" (ESV; see, e.g., R. Longenecker 1990: 209–10; de Boer 2011: 295; contra, e.g., NASB, "This is allegorically speaking"; and

4:24

see Sellin 1999: 67). As we noted above in the introduction to this paragraph, Paul's claim to be giving an "allegorical" interpretation means simply that he is using one set of realities (the narrative of Sarah and Hagar) to speak of another set of realities ("to speak" [ἀγορεύω] of "other things" [ἄλλα]). Philo employs the method in a distinctive manner to contemporize the scriptural narrative in the direction of a Platonizing and moralizing meaning. But the "allegorical" approach in the ancient world was quite broad, and it would be a mistake to think that Paul is claiming to do what Philo was doing. Paul gives no indication that he is calling into question the initial historical referentiality of this narrative. What he is doing is showing how that narrative can be seen to foreshadow the realities of the new covenant that he is defending. If, then, we label Paul's method of interpretation at this point as "allegory," it is allegory "tempered fundamentally by typology" (Martyn 1997: 436).

Paul now elaborates (γάρ, *gar*, for) the manner in which he is giving the two women allegorical significance. They "represent" (surely what εἰσιν must mean here; cf. NIV) "two covenants," one of those covenants being "from Mount Sinai" and "bearing children for slavery" (εἰς δουλείαν γεννῶσα, *eis douleian gennōsa*); and this covenant (ἥτις [*hētis*] probably refers to διαθήκη [Schreiner 2010: 301]) is Hagar. In this paragraph Paul's argument, as above, proceeds via a series of contrasts; it indeed is probable that he explicitly suggests these dualities with the verb συστοιχεῖ (*systoichei*, corresponds to) in verse 25 (see our comments on 4:25). A table is a useful way to chart these contrasts:

verse 22	Ἀβραὰμ δύο υἱοὺς ἔσχεν (*Abraam dyo huious eschen*, Abraham had two sons)	
verse 22	ἕνα ἐκ τῆς παιδίσκης (*hena ek tēs paidiskēs*, one from the slave woman)	καὶ ἕνα ἐκ τῆς ἐλευθέρας (*kai hena ek tēs eleutheras*, and one from the free woman)
verse 23	κατὰ σάρκα γεγέννηται (*kata sarka gegennētai*, born according to the flesh)	[γεγέννηται] δι' ἐπαγγελίας ([*gegennētai*] *di' epangelias*, [born] through promise)
verse 24	μία [διαθήκη] μὲν ἀπὸ ὄρους Σινᾶ εἰς δουλείαν γεννῶσα (*mia [diathēkē] men apo orous Sina eis douleian gennōsa*, one [covenant] from Mount Sinai bearing children for slavery)	
verses 25–26	τῇ νῦν Ἰερουσαλήμ, δουλεύει γὰρ μετὰ τῶν τέκνων αὐτῆς (*tē nyn Ierousalēm, douleuei gar meta tōn teknōn autēs*, the present Jerusalem, for she is enslaved with her children)	ἡ δὲ ἄνω Ἰερουσαλὴμ ἐλευθέρα ἐστίν (*hē de anō Ierousalēm eleuthera estin*, but the Jerusalem above is free)
verse 27 [Isa. 54:1]	πολλὰ τὰ τέκνα τῆς ἐρήμου (*polla ta tekna tēs erēmou*, many are the children of the desolate one)	μᾶλλον ἢ τῆς ἐχούσης τὸν ἄνδρα (*mallon ē tēs echousēs ton andra*, more than the one who had a husband)

verse 29	ὁ κατὰ σάρκα γεννηθεὶς (*ho kata sarka gennētheis*, the one born according to the flesh)	τὸν [γεννηθέντα] κατὰ πνεῦμα (*ton [gennēthenta] kata pneuma*, the [one born] according to the Spirit)
verse 30	ὁ υἱὸς τῆς παιδίσκης (*ho huios tēs paidiskēs*, the son of the slave woman)	τοῦ υἱοῦ τῆς ἐλευθέρας (*tou huiou tēs eleutheras*, the son of the free woman)
verse 31	οὐκ ἐσμὲν παιδίσκης τέκνα (*ouk esmen paidiskēs tekna*, We are not children of the slave woman)	ἀλλὰ [τέκνα] τῆς ἐλευθέρας (*alla [tekna] tēs eleutheras*, but children of the free woman)

As the chart reveals, Paul never identifies the covenant that contrasts with the covenant of Mount Sinai. By introducing his reference to this Mount Sinai covenant with a μέν, he suggests that he intends to continue his sentence with a corresponding δέ clause in which he would identify this covenant. But his audacious claim that Hagar represents this Mount Sinai covenant derails him, and he never returns to complete the comparison. How should we fill in this blank? With a glance at 2 Cor. 3, many interpreters think that Paul would have contrasted the Mount Sinai covenant with the "new covenant" (Lincoln 1981: 16; Rohde 1989: 195; R. Longenecker 1990: 21; J. Meyer 2009: 115–37). However, within the argument of Galatians, it is more likely that Paul would be thinking of the Abrahamic covenant. To be sure, Paul does not explicitly label the Abrahamic promise arrangement as a "covenant," but the logic of Gal. 3:15 makes clear that he thinks of the Abrahamic promise arrangement as a covenant. And, of course, the OT speaks explicitly of such a covenant (Gen. 17; cf. Acts 7:8; and note Paul's references to "covenants" in Rom. 9:4 and Eph. 2:12). However, if we do identify this second covenant as the Abrahamic covenant, we must also follow Paul's lead and speak of the Abrahamic covenant as christologically defined (this is the majority view; see, e.g., Hays 2000: 302; Harmon 2010: 230–31; Garlington 2003: 198; de Boer 2011: 296).[7]

Paul's focus on Mount Sinai implicitly identifies the covenant associated with Hagar as the Mosaic covenant. This being the case, we would naturally think of those children "who are being born into slavery" as unbelieving Jews generally; and this has been the usual interpretation. However, Martyn has made a case for identifying these "children" as those being "begotten" by the agitators' version of the gospel. The key contrast in this paragraph is not, then, between Christianity and Judaism in general, but specifically between Paul's law-free gospel and the "other gospel" that the agitators are propagating. Martyn (1997: 437, 451–54) buttresses his case here by noting the present tense of the participle γεννῶσα (see also Witherington 1998: 331; Hays 2000: 302). However, the tense could as easily refer to the ongoing birth of Jews generally (Dunn 1993a: 250). We will need to track Martyn's interpretation

7. Dunn (1993a: 249–50) argues that the contrast may be between two different interpretations of the Abrahamic covenant. However, as Witherington (1998: 330) pertinently remarks, "It is the argument of the agitators, not Paul, that the Mosaic covenant is an extension of the Abrahamic covenant."

as it unfolds in the following verses, but anticipating this discussion, we can say that we ultimately find his view unsatisfactory.

4:25 The first clause of this verse is very difficult to integrate into the flow of Paul's argument, a problem evidently felt by the early scribes, who supply several different readings. With the majority of commentators and versions, I take the original reading to be thus: τὸ δὲ Ἀγὰρ Σινᾶ ὄρος ἐστὶν ἐν τῇ Ἀραβίᾳ (to de Hagar Sina oros estin en tē Arabia), "now the Hagar Sinai mountain is in Arabia." This translation reflects my very tentative decision about the meaning of this difficult clause. Five issues require attention. First is the decision about where to place the equivalent of the copulative ἐστιν. Most of the versions and commentators think it is to be placed between "Hagar" and "Sinai mountain": "Now Hagar stands for Mount Sinai in Arabia" (NIV; cf. also ESV, NRSV, NASB, NET, HCSB, NAB). This interpretation fits the way Paul in this paragraph regularly identifies elements of the Sarah/Hagar story with other realities, often with a form of εἰμί (vv. 24, 26). However, (1) Paul usually lines up OT realities with NT counterparts; and (2) Paul has already tacitly, if not explicitly, identified Hagar with Sinai in verse 24. Second, the new (and at first sight surprising) information in this clause is the reference to Arabia. These first two points combine to suggest that it might be better to place the copula between "Hagar Sinai mountain" and "in Arabia" (as our translation above reflects). The third issue to consider is the use of the neuter article τό before Ἀγὰρ. This is usually explained as a not uncommon use of a neuter article to focus on the word itself: the "word Hagar" in this text means . . . (cf. Hays 2000: 302; cf. BDF §267.1; Borgen 1995: 157). However, it is also possible to take the article with ὄρος, a neuter noun. This would have the effect of turning both "Hagar" and "Sinai" into quasi-adjectives; hence "the Hagar Sinai mountain"; that is, "the mountain that is named Sinai and which I have associated (v. 24) with Hagar." This interpretation would fit with a fourth circumstance to be noted in this text. The words Σινᾶ and ὄρος occur together twenty other times in Biblical Greek. But everywhere else (as in v. 24), the order is ὄρος Σινᾶ.

Fifth, and ultimately most important, is the point Paul is making in this clause and its integration into its context. Some scholars suggest that Paul's purpose is to identify Hagar with Mount Sinai, either on the basis of a linguistic similarity or on the basis of geographical knowledge.[8] But these suggestions have difficulties, not the least of them being how the Galatians would have had any access to this rather esoteric information. Hays (2000: 303) argues that the clause functions to identify Hagar with Sinai (cf. E. Lohse, *TDNT* 7:285–86), but as we have seen, Paul has already made this identification in

---

8. For instance, some interpreters think that Paul is playing on the Arabic word *ḥajar*, which sounds a bit like "Hagar" and means "stone," and which is used in various geographic names associated with Sinai (BDAG 7; McNamara 1978; R. Longenecker 1990: 212). Others suggest that Paul is locating Sinai and (by inference) the law in the land traditionally associated with Hagar and the Ishmaelites (e.g., Martyn 1997: 438).

verse 24, and this view is unable to explain the reference to Arabia. Unable to identify a specific function for the clause, most interpreters resort to viewing the reference as an "afterthought," supplying geographic information (Fung 1988: 208). However, a key benefit of our reading of the syntax is that the clause can be seen to supply a clear link in Paul's argument. This general view has been argued by Mussner (1988: 322–24) and Ridderbos (1953: 177–78) on the basis of the "shorter text" that omits Hagar, but it works also if, as we think, Hagar is part of the original text (cf. Dunn 1993a: 251; Lincoln 1981: 15–16). On this view, verse 25a acknowledges a well-known geographic fact as preparation for the point that Paul is going to make in verse 25b. Verses 25a and 25b will therefore be in adversative relationship; so we can paraphrase: "Now the mountain that is Sinai and that is represented by Hagar is, to be sure, in Arabia; nevertheless [δέ, *de*] she [or it] represents the present Jerusalem." We think the ability to explain this clause in its context outweighs the objection that this is not the most natural reading of the τὸ Ἁγὰρ Σινᾶ ὄρος sequence.

If we are right about our interpretation of verse 25a, then the δέ that joins verse 25b to verse 25a is adversative, and the subject of the verb may be "the Hagar Sinai mountain" rather than (as most versions assume), Hagar. Hence we translate, "but it corresponds to the present Jerusalem" (συστοιχεῖ δὲ τῇ νῦν Ἰερουσαλήμ, *systoichei de tē nyn Ierousalēm*).[9] The verb συστοιχέω (*systoicheō*) is often said to provide an important clue to the way Paul argues in this paragraph (see esp. Martyn 1997: 438–39, 449–50). For the verb often refers to the "lining up" of items in two columns, exactly the sort of thing that Paul does in this paragraph as he places in separate columns the spiritual realities associated with Hagar (the Mosaic covenant, Sinai, children for slavery, present Jerusalem) and Sarah (the Abrahamic/Christ covenant, Zion, children for freedom, the Jerusalem above). The paucity of evidence (the verb is not found elsewhere in Biblical Greek or in Josephus or Philo) makes it hard to be sure if this meaning was a "live" one for Paul, but it makes good sense in this context (see also Lightfoot 1881: 181; Dunn 1993a: 252; Hays 2000: 302–3). The "present Jerusalem," "lined up" with Hagar and Mount Sinai, is most naturally taken as a reference to the Judaism of Paul's day, which focused on the law given at Sinai as the mark of its special identity. And this has been the usual interpretation of the phrase.[10] However, a number of scholars have recently suggested that this identification may be too general and may miss the

---

9. In 4:25–26 Paul uses the form Ἰερουσαλήμ, in contrast to the form Ἰεροσόλυμα (*Hierosolyma*, Jerusalem) that he used in 1:17, 18; 2:1, probably because the former has a more "religious" connotation (as used in the LXX, where there is a Hebrew equivalent; see, e.g., Bruce 1982b: 220; R. Longenecker 1990: 213). The use of the adverb νῦν with a noun such as Ἰερουσαλήμ in virtually an adjectival sense—"the 'now' Jerusalem"—has precedents in NT usage (see A. Robertson 1934: 547).

10. Willitts (2005: 204) argues that "the present Jerusalem" refers to the city of the former Mosaic covenant. However, while reference to a previous Jerusalem can make sense in the context of Paul's salvation-historical framework, it is doubtful that the reference can be confined to the past in light of the language Paul uses here: νῦν and the present tense, δουλεύει (*douleuei*, is enslaved).

sharp point Paul is making in this paragraph. His exhortation to the Galatians in verse 30 to "cast out the slave woman" suggests that the people he has in mind are not Jews in general but the Judaizing Christians, the agitators, who have infiltrated the Galatian churches and need to be thrown out. The "present Jerusalem," then, refers not to Judaism generally but to the particular configuration of Jewish Christianity that the agitators were claiming represented what the "mother church" in Jerusalem truly stood for (see esp. Martyn 1997: 439; and also Mussner 1988: 325; Brawley 2002: 114–15; de Boer 2004: 380–82; 2011: 300–301; Schreiner 2010: 302). However, we doubt that the text justifies narrowing the focus in this way. The language of verse 30, to be sure, seems to fit the agitators better than Judaism in general. But the language Paul uses there is constrained by the text of the OT that he is quoting. The rest of the paragraph, with its references to the two sons of Abraham, dueling covenants, and the "flesh/Spirit" contrast, suggests that Paul is engaged in a more fundamental contrast of two readings of salvation history, one focusing on the law as the continuing qualification for the people of God, and the other focusing on the law-free gospel. Certainly this contrast is at the heart of Paul's earlier argument (3:15–4:7). The "present" Jerusalem, then, is Paul's way of speaking of the Judaism of his day, a Judaism that continues to rely on the law and ignore or not give adequate place to Christ (Harmon 2010: 175). The language of Jerusalem suggests that he is already influenced by the Isa. 54:1 text that he will cite in verse 27, a text that presumes the reality of Israel's exile for its sin and disobedience to the law (see esp. Starling 2011: 23–60).

The final clause in verse 25 supplies a missing element in Paul's logic. How can he identify Hagar with Sinai (vv. 24–25)? This is quite an audacious move on Paul's part, and there is little in the OT to back up his identification. But it may be the theme of "slavery" that, for Paul, justifies the identification. As we have seen, the "free/slave" contrast is fundamental to the argument of this paragraph. Hagar, of course, is identified explicitly by the OT text as a "slave woman" (see vv. 22–23). Now, Paul claims, the "present Jerusalem" is also "enslaved with her children" (δουλεύει . . . μετὰ τῶν τέκνων αὐτῆς, *douleuei . . . meta tōn teknōn autēs*). The γάρ (*gar*) that introduces this clause may, then, be causal: "the Hagar Sinai mountain represents the present Jerusalem, *because* it (like Hagar) is in slavery."

4:26　In contrast to (δέ, *de*) the present Jerusalem, enslaved with her children, "the Jerusalem above is free" (ἡ . . . ἄνω Ἰερουσαλήμ ἐλευθέρα ἐστίν, *hē . . . anō Ierousalēm eleuthera estin*). In the spiritual geography of early Judaism and Christianity, "above" means "heavenly" (see Acts 2:19 NIV, "in the heavens above" [ἐν τῷ οὐρανῷ ἄνω, *en tō ouranō anō*]; John 8:23; Phil. 3:14; Col. 3:1, 2; and on this theme in Paul, see esp. Lincoln 1981). "The Jerusalem above" is therefore equivalent to "the heavenly Jerusalem" (BDAG 471.3) or the "new Jerusalem" and taps into a widespread OT and Jewish tradition. This tradition, especially prominent in apocalyptic, pictures the perfected eschatological Jerusalem to come as already existing in the heavenly sphere and anticipates the time when this city will be established on the earth (Ps. 87:1–3; Ezek. 40–48; 2 Esd. [4 Ezra] 7:26; 13:36; 2 Bar. 4.2–6; Heb. 11:10, 14–16; 12:22; 13:14; Rev. 3:12; 21:2). The Jewish tradition focused on a literal renewed and perfected Jerusalem, but the imagery functions in early Christianity as a way of referring to "the new age depicted in spatial terms and the anticipation of the full life of this new age now present in the church" (Lincoln 1981: 21). In light of the temporal marker in verse 25, "the present Jerusalem," we might have expected a contrasting temporal reference here. But a moment's reflection reveals that such a temporal indication here would simply not work. The only option would be to say "the Jerusalem to come." But, of course, it is fundamental to Paul's argument here, and to NT teaching in general, to claim that the eschatological realities to which the image of "new Jerusalem" refers have, in fact, entered into history in the work of Christ: the "fullness of the time" has arrived (4:4). He therefore produces a combination of the spatial (explicit) and temporal (implicit) categories in a way typical of some streams of NT teaching (particularly some found in Hebrews).

Picking up a key motif from this paragraph, Paul affirms that this new Jerusalem, like Sarah (vv. 22, 23), is "free." This assertion of freedom undoubtedly has some allusion to "freedom from the law," since subjection and even slavery to the law has been a prominent theme in 3:23–4:11 and is hinted at here in the association of Sinai and slavery. This is confirmed by the summary of this text in 5:1, which calls on believers to stand "in freedom" and not to submit again to a "yoke of slavery," a clear reference to the law (see 5:2–4). At the same time, slavery to the law points to and leads to slavery to sin (3:22), and it is this fundamental spiritual condition that ultimately characterizes the present Jerusalem, along with all her "children."[11] Apart from Christ, Jewish people live under a state of condemnation into which subjection to the law has led them. In contrast, Paul affirms, the "Jerusalem above . . . is our mother."[12] The eschatological realities symbolized by the Jerusalem above are giving birth to people who share in its freedom from the law and from sin. The imagery of motherhood, birth, and children arises from the dual influences of the Sarah/Hagar story (vv. 22–23) and the Isa. 54:1 text, which Paul quotes in verse 27.

Paul's quotation of Isa. 54:1 in this verse follows the LXX exactly, and the LXX faithfully renders the Hebrew (see the additional note). Isaiah calls on a "barren woman, who does not bear a child" (στεῖρα, ἡ οὐ τίκουσα, *steira, hē ou tikousa*) and "is not in labor" (ἡ οὐκ ὠδίνουσα, *hē ouk ōdinousa*) to "be glad" (εὐφράνθητι, *euphranthēti*) and to "break forth in a shout" (ῥῆξον καὶ

4:27

---

11. See Thielman 1989: 84, although we do not agree with his denial that slavery to the law is involved here.

12. Paul again uses an indefinite relative pronoun (ἥτις, *hētis*) with the sense of a definite relative pronoun (ἥ, *hē*, who; see v. 24). Paul's claim that Christians have the Jerusalem above as their mother may counter the agitators' claims to represent the "mother city" (Martyn 1997: 441); an allusion to Isa. 1:26 LXX, μετὰ ταῦτα κληθήσῃ πόλις δικαιοσύνης, μητρόπολις πιστὴ Σιων (*meta tauta klēthēsē polis dikaiosynēs, mētropolis pistē Siōn*, after these things you will be called the City of Righteousness, the Faithful Mother-City Zion), is also possible (Jobes 1993: 310).

βόησον, *rhēzon kai boēson*).[13] She is to do so because "more are the children of the desolate woman than of the woman who has a husband" (ὅτι πολλὰ τὰ τέκνα τῆς ἐρήμου μᾶλλον ἢ τῆς ἐχούσης τὸν ἄνδρα, *hoti polla ta tekna tēs erēmou mallon ē tēs echousēs ton andra*).[14] The two women in the text have been variously identified, but it makes best sense to think that they both refer to Jerusalem/Zion, at different stages of its existence (Keil and Delitzsch 1969b: 312; Goldingay and Payne 2006: 337; Willitts 2005: 195–97; Starling 2011: 44–46; contra Oswalt 1998: 413; Motyer 1993: 445). Jerusalem or Zion is mentioned repeatedly in the preceding context (51:3, 9 [LXX only], 11, 16, 17; 52:1, 2, 7, 8, 9), and the following context makes explicit this identification (54:11–14). All of Isa. 54 celebrates the time when God would reverse the situation of his exiled people, apparently abandoned by their God, and call them back to their own land once again. The contrast in 54:1, then, is between the "present" Jerusalem, apparently "barren" and "desolate," and this same city renewed and repopulated by God's own intervention on behalf of his people.

As we have argued in our introduction to this paragraph and in comments on verses 22–26 (and vv. 25–26 in particular), Paul's quotation of Isa. 54:1 in this verse provides the lens through which he interprets and applies the narrative about Hagar and Sarah. That being the case, the introductory formula, γέγραπται γάρ (*gegraptai gar*, for it is written), may introduce the quotation as a ground or explanation of all of verses 22–26 (Harmon 2010: 177). And this makes good sense if, indeed, we realize that Paul is associating the "barren woman" who eventually produces many children with Sarah, and the "one who has a husband" with Hagar. The former identification finds solid basis in the OT and in the immediate context of the Isaiah text. The theme of a barren woman who, by God's intervention, is able to have children is a motif found at several points in the OT (see Goldingay and Payne 2006: 341; Jobes 1993: 306–7), but Sarah is surely the most prominent example of this pattern. And reference to Sarah in this regard is picked up elsewhere in the NT (Rom. 4:18–21; Heb. 11:11–12). Particularly relevant is the explicit reference to Sarah in a text related contextually to Isa. 54:1, namely, Isa. 51:1–3:

> Listen to me, you who pursue righteousness and who seek the LORD: Look to the rock from which you were cut and to the quarry from which you were hewn; [2]look to Abraham, your father, and to Sarah, who gave you birth. When I called him he was only one man, and I blessed him and made him many. [3]The LORD will surely comfort Zion and will look with compassion on all her ruins; he

13. The participles τίκτουσα and ὠδίνουσα are probably gnomic, justifying the translation "who has never given birth" and "who was never in birth pains." The phrase ῥῆξον καὶ βόησον (break forth and shout) is probably a hendiadys; hence "break into a joyful shout" (NLT). Eastman (2007: 157) suggests that here the verb ὠδίνω to some extent alludes to the use of that verb in v. 19 and that Paul may thus be alluding to his own gospel preaching as the means by which children are being born into the new Jerusalem. But we suspect that connection is accidental rather than deliberate.

14. The Greek πολλά . . . μᾶλλον is awkward because it reproduces the Hebrew מִ . . . רַבִּים.

will make her deserts like Eden, her wastelands like the garden of the LORD. Joy and gladness will be found in her, thanksgiving and the sound of singing.

This is the only place in the OT where Sarah is mentioned outside the Genesis narrative.[15] And this text also has many points of contact with Isa. 54:1: the bearing-children metaphor, the feminine imagery in verse 3, and the celebratory language. The identification of the other woman in Isa. 54:1, τῆς ἐχούσης τὸν ἄνδρα, is not as clear. The Greek phrase can mean either "have a man," in the sense of "have sexual relations" (e.g., 1 Cor. 7:2) or "have a husband" (John 4:17; cf. BDAG 420.2.a). However, the underlying Hebrew (a participle from the verb בָּעַל) means "married" (*HALOT* 142). Paul may be exploiting the ambiguity to connote both a woman who is married and who is engaging in sexual relations (Harmon 2010: 180–81). In any case, it is not difficult to see how Paul could have identified this woman "who has a man" as Hagar, since she is presented in Genesis as one who both has sex with Abraham and who marries him; see Gen. 16:3: "Sarai his wife took her Egyptian servant Hagar and gave her to her husband to be his wife [ἔδωκεν αὐτὴν Ἀβραμ τῷ ἀνδρὶ αὐτῆς αὐτῷ γυναῖκα, *edōken autēn Abram tō andri autēs autō gynaika*]."

However, Isa. 54:1 enables Paul to do much more than simply contrast Sarah and Hagar (a move that is, after all, evident in the Genesis text itself). What is more important is that it enables Paul to line up Sarah with the "Jerusalem above" and Hagar with the "present Jerusalem." In Isaiah, therefore, Sarah is lined up with the "new" Jerusalem, while Hagar is implicitly identified with the present city. Here Isaiah combines Abrahamic covenant language with the tradition of the restoration of Zion and return from exile (Harmon 2010: 178–79). The text portrays two parallel reversals, as "the barren and desolate woman becomes a joyful mother and the ravaged city becomes a nurturing metropolis overflowing with inhabitants" (Eastman 2007: 129). Paul is convinced, of course, that the "new Jerusalem," representing the age to come, has come into being and that it is through his Spirit-empowered preaching of the gospel that this new Jerusalem is being populated. And this gospel, Paul is convinced, is only truly the gospel if it is a matter of a freely offered gift, apart from any human contribution.[16] Thus Paul's gospel-oriented reading of Isa. 54:1, in its context, convinces him that Sarah represents the new age, made available to humans by the life-giving gospel. With the preaching and response to that gospel, "the exiles have returned to inhabit their glorified city"

15. Jewish tradition made the same move: the Targum of Isaiah mentions Jerusalem explicitly in 54:1 while Pesiq. Rab. 32.2 associates Sarah with the rebuilding of Jerusalem, citing Isa. 54:1 (cf. R. Longenecker 1990: 215).

16. Hays (2000: 304), noting the prominence of Gentile inclusion in Isa. 40–66, suggests this as the emphasis that Paul may have in view here. But this theme is not actually prominent in Isa. 54. What is emphasized is God's own gracious intervention to enable his own people to recover from their own sin-induced desolate condition. Divine versus human action is therefore hinted at in these texts (Watson 2004: 205–8).

(Garlington 2003: 204). Hagar, on the other hand, must therefore represent the old age, with its outmoded and futile focus on doing the law. (And as the OT makes clear, it was disobedience to the law that led to Jerusalem's barren and desolate condition.) Paul may intend a further allusion: An important element of the OT story, which is emphasized in its NT appropriation, is the fact that Sarah's barren condition was reversed by a special life-giving intervention of God. It was "the God who gives life to the dead," in whom Abraham believed, who enabled him and Sarah to produce offspring (Rom. 4:17). Such a life-giving intervention of God must come into play to transform the barren "present" Jerusalem into the joyful and fecund "Jerusalem above": and any Christian would readily identify the resurrection of Christ as that life-giving event (see esp. Jobes 1993: 316–18). Finally, of course, Isa. 54:1 follows immediately the great fourth Servant Song, which celebrates the redeeming death of the Servant of God. It is no stretch at all, then, to think that Paul would have read Isa. 54:1 as a celebration of the new state of affairs brought about by the death and resurrection of Christ.

4:28   With the clinching quotation from Isa. 54:1, which, as we have seen, provides so much of the hermeneutical justification for Paul's application of the Sarah and Hagar narrative, Paul is now in position to apply to the Galatians the conclusions he wants to draw from his interpretation (Bonnard 1972: 99; Harmon 2010: 181). Verses 28 and 31 frame this conclusion, with similar assertions: "You are children of the promise." "We are children of the free woman." In verses 29–30, Paul raids the Genesis narrative one more time to suggest a parallel between the Galatians and the agitators/Jews, on the one hand, and Isaac and Ishmael, on the other; on the basis of this comparison, he calls on his readers to take action (v. 30).

The turn to application in this verse suggests that the δέ (*de*) should be translated "now," as in most of the English versions. The shift from exposition to application may also be suggested by the direct address of the readers: ὑμεῖς, . . . ἀδελφοί (*hymeis, . . . adelphoi*, you, . . . brothers and sisters; see Runge 2010: 117–22). The language of "sons" (υἱοί, *huioi*, in v. 22), "children" (τέκνα, *tekna*, in vv. 25 and 27), and childbearing (γεννάω, *gennaō*, in vv. 23 and 24) knits this passage together; so it is not surprising to find Paul applying his exposition in these terms: the Galatian Christians, Paul affirms, are κατὰ Ἰσαὰκ ἐπαγγελίας τέκνα (*kata Isaak epangelias tekna*). The word τέκνα occurs in the previous verse, in the quotation of Isa. 54:1, but we have last heard the word ἐπαγγελία in verse 23. The word is probably a qualitative genitive, loosely characterizing the Galatians as children who are somehow related to the promise (Burton 1921: 265). Paul's earlier association of promise with grace, and contrast of promise with the law (3:15–18), suggests what this means: that Christians owe their status as children not to a natural process (as was the case of the children of Hagar; cf. "according to the flesh" in v. 23) but to the supernatural intervention of God. When God promises, he pledges himself to carry out what he has promised. Obedience to the law, because of human frailty and sinfulness, will always fail to secure the promise. It is only those who grasp what is promised in faith who are certain to inherit the blessing (3:7–9, 29; and cf. Rom. 4:13–14).

Paul's claim that Christians are children κατὰ Ἰσαάκ makes a similar point. Isaac is not named in Paul's earlier exposition, but readers would have no trouble identifying Isaac as the child of Abraham born to the "free woman" "through a promise" in verses 22–23. The κατά therefore means "like," "just as" (BDAG 513.5.b.α), "in the pattern of" (Martyn 1997: 444; Witherington 1998: 338; Hays 2000: 305): "Just as Isaac was, so you also are children born as a result of and in conjunction with the promise of God." This likeness includes both the means ("as God graciously does what he has promised") but also perhaps the outcome ("as God gave life to Sarah's 'dead' body, so in conjunction with the resurrection of Christ, he gives life to people 'dead in trespasses and sins'"; Eph. 2:1; see Rom. 4:17–21). Of course, this line of argument would have been especially significant for the Galatians, as Gentiles. They had no claim to be children of Abraham in any natural sense; only by God's gracious promise could they hope to be included among his children. As children of Abraham, they are also children of God (3:26).

Before Paul can continue to apply his exposition of Sarah and Hagar and their respective children to the Galatians, he must revert once more to the story to make a further comparison. Since Paul then seems to be adding another comparison to his list, it may be that the ἀλλά (alla, but) introducing the verse should be given a continuative force (Betz 1979: 249; R. Longenecker 1990: 216; Schreiner 2010: 305). But it is better to retain the usual adversative meaning of ἀλλά, assuming a bit of an ellipsis: "You have the benefit of being children of promise (v. 28); but do not think that this exempts you from suffering; rather you are undergoing persecution just as Isaac once did" (Mussner 1988: 329). In the OT story "at that time [τότε, tote] the one born according to the flesh persecuted the one born according to the Spirit, so now." The "one born according to the flesh" (ὁ κατὰ σάρκα γεννηθείς, ho kata sarka gennētheis) is Ishmael, the son of Hagar (see v. 23), while the "one born according to the Spirit" (τὸν [γεννηθεὶς] κατὰ πνεῦμα, ton [gennētheis] kata pneuma) is Isaac, the son of Sarah. The additional comparison has probably been sparked by Paul's explicit mention of Isaac in verse 28. This is the first time in this paragraph that we find the typical Pauline "flesh/Spirit" contrast; in verse 23 Paul has contrasted "flesh" with "promise." Since Paul usually associates the Spirit with new-covenant realities (see 3:14), some interpreters think that κατὰ πνεῦμα actually belongs with the clause that follows, "and so also now," with Paul's elliptical style of writing causing it to appear with Isaac (Burton 1921: 266). But this is not the most natural way of reading the verse. The preposition κατά probably here indicates "the nature, kind, peculiarity or characteristics" of the births of Ishmael and Isaac (BDAG 513.5.b.β). As we noted in verse 23, Ishmael's birth "according to the flesh" suggests that he was born in the natural way and by the power of human decision. In contrast, then, Isaac's

4:29

birth "according to the Spirit" would be a birth characterized by the work of the Spirit, which may in this context mean "took place by the power of the Spirit" (NIV, NLT; Dunn 1993a: 257; Martyn 1997: 444).

Paul's claim that Ishmael "persecuted" (ἐδίωκεν, ediōken) Isaac does not, at first sight, have a basis in the Genesis narrative. Probably, however, he alludes to Gen. 21:9, the verse just before the one that Paul quotes in Gal. 4:30. Genesis 21:8–10 reads:

> The child grew and was weaned, and on the day Isaac was weaned Abraham held a great feast. [9]But Sarah saw that the son whom Hagar the Egyptian had borne to Abraham was mocking, [10]and she said to Abraham, "Get rid of that slave woman and her son, for that woman's son will never share in the inheritance with my son Isaac."

Ishmael's mockery is not directed specifically at Isaac in the Hebrew text, but the LXX does say that Ishmael was "playing with Isaac" (παίζοντα μετὰ Ισαακ, paizonta meta Isaak). This "play" or "mockery" could be construed as a form of persecution, and it is particularly significant that later Jewish tradition took it in exactly this sense (for references, see esp. R. Longenecker 1990: 217). Probably, then, it is this verse, in light of its traditional interpretation, that is the basis for Paul's claim about persecution (so most commentators; see, e.g., Lightfoot 1881: 183; Bonnard 1972: 99; Dunn 1993a: 256).

As it was in the time of Isaac and Ishmael, claims Paul, so now (οὕτως καὶ νῦν, houtōs kai nyn): the children "according to the Spirit" are being persecuted by the children "according to the flesh." As we noted in our comments on verse 25, several interpreters argue that the key contrast in this passage is not between "Christianity" and "Judaism" but between the Christian mission as Paul understands it and the Christian mission of the agitators. So in this verse, it is argued, Paul is referring to the way the agitators are "persecuting" the Gentiles in Galatia by trying to impose the burden of the law on them and suggesting that, if they do not submit, they will lose their position in the people of God (see esp. Martyn 1997: 444–45; and also, e.g., Mussner 1988: 330–31; Matera 1992: 173–74; Witherington 1998: 337–38). In favor of this interpretation is the natural reading that can be given to verse 31. However, this benefit is offset by the difficulty of thinking of the agitators' program as, in any natural sense of the word, "persecution" (Wilson 2007: 83–84; cf. the verb διώκω [diōkō, persecute] in Gal. 1:13, 23; 5:11; 6:12). We also think that the contrast between the "present Jerusalem" and the "Jerusalem above" better fits the fundamental salvation-historical contrast between Judaism as a whole, which is continuing to find its basic identity in a view of election that is tied up with law observance—and the emerging Christian movement, which insists on the presence of eschatological realities and orients its view of election to the person of Christ. To be sure, Paul would view the agitators as representatives of the former movement because, in his view, their insistence on law observance for Gentiles puts them into that camp. But his purview in this paragraph moves beyond the agitators to the more basic law-observing perspective that they represent. Paul does not think the agitators are wrong simply to insist on law observance for Gentiles. More fundamentally, he identifies them with a failed program of election and salvation that, sadly, typifies the majority of Jewish people in his day. Of course, elsewhere the NT speaks about Jewish persecution of the nascent Christian movement; and, as we have seen, Gal. 3:4 probably alludes to their suffering, perhaps at the hands of Jewish unbelievers (see our comments on 3:4 and the references to Acts there).

"But what does the Scripture say?" is strongly reminiscent of the question that opens this paragraph, "Do you not hear the Law?" In some ways, then, the exhortation in this verse is the climax of the paragraph, taking words from the scriptural narrative that forms the basis of Paul's extended commentary and using them to summarize what is expected of the Galatians in light of this commentary.[17] As is usually the case in Paul, γραφή (*graphē*, Scripture) refers to a single text from the OT, in this case Gen. 21:10. Paul modifies the wording of this text a bit, mainly because he is lifting it out of its original context, in which Sarah is speaking to Abraham about Hagar. But Paul's reference at the end of the quotation to "the free woman" (τῆς ἐλευθέρας, *tēs eleutheras*) is more significant, as he again emphasizes what for him is a key point of application for his readers in the story of Sarah and Hagar. The quotation of the OT text serves two purposes for Paul. First, by again introducing the language of "inheritance" (3:29; 4:1–2, 7), Paul makes explicit what the defining issue is between Isaac and Ishmael, and all those "descended" from them. Both are "sons" (v. 22); both will be the progenitors of nations (on Ishmael, see Gen. 17:20; 21:13); but only one is an "heir," to whom is promised all of God the Father's spiritual blessings. Second, by omitting any reference to Sarah as the original speaker in the OT text, Paul is able to cite scriptural warrant for the action he expects the Galatians to take: they are to "cast out the slave woman and her son" (ἔκβαλε τὴν παιδίσκην καὶ τὸν υἱὸν αὐτῆς, *ekbale tēn paidiskēn kai ton huion autēs*). Paul preserves the singular form of the OT text, perhaps simply because he is disinclined to change the text, perhaps because he wants to individualize the command: each of the Galatians is to take responsibility.[18]

The language of this text—which, as we have seen, many think is the climax of this paragraph—provides a good basis for interpreting the basic contrast of this paragraph in terms of the Pauline law-free mission and the agitators' law-focused mission (see our comments on 4:25 and 29 for this view). For the command to "cast out the slave woman and her son" is exactly what we might imagine Paul would want the Galatian Christians to do with the agitators who

4:30

---

17. R. Longenecker (1990: 217) speculates that the agitators may themselves have used this text to insist that the Galatians "cast out" Paul and his teaching; but there is little evidence to back this up.

18. Eastman (2007: 133) argues that the second-person singular form of the verb stands in contrast to Paul's pattern of addressing the Galatians with plural verbs and indicates that he probably does not direct this command to them. But the fact that he is quoting a text robs this point of much of its strength.

have infiltrated their churches with the false gospel (again, see Martyn 1997: 446). However, while some reference to the agitators may be present, we think the evidence of the paragraph shows that Paul views the "slave woman and her son" as representing a much more fundamental reality: the Judaism of his day that has rejected Christ and insists on law observance as essential for righteousness (Betz 1979: 250–51; Dunn 1993a: 258). But what would Paul's command to "cast out" "law-observant Judaism" mean? Some interpreters argue that the command in the verse, since it is a quotation, is not directed to the Galatians but embodies a more general truth: "by taking the line they had, they [the Judaizers] had excluded themselves not simply from the Church but from the eternal inheritance of the people of God" (Barrett 1985: 29; similar interpretations in Bruce 1982b: 225; Eastman 2007: 133). Obviously the wording does not originate from Paul but from the text he quotes. This observation simply raises another question: why quote this text? The answer is that, for whatever reason (see the introduction to this section), Paul has decided to use the Sarah/Hagar narrative to teach and exhort the Galatians at this point in the letter. And the command in Gen. 21:10, based on the inheritance issue, provides the best text from this narrative for the application Paul wants to draw. The Galatians will "cast out the slave woman" by refusing to have anything to do with those who continue to insist on law observance as necessary for righteousness and by distancing themselves from the theology of the "present Jerusalem," with its continuing insistence on reading the Abrahamic promise covenant in the context of the Mosaic law covenant (Dunn 1993a: 258); they should "exclude" those who are trying to "exclude" them (see v. 17; Lincoln 1981: 28–29).

4:31 The διό (*dio*, therefore) and the direct address (ἀδελφοί, *adelphoi*, brothers and sisters) that introduce this verse indicate that it brings to a conclusion the argument of this paragraph (Lietzmann 1923: 32).[19] Dunn (1993: 259) compares it to Gal. 3:29, "If you belong to Christ, then [ἄρα, *ara*] you are Abraham's seed, and heirs according to the promise." In Gal. 3:7–29, Paul argued that Christians are, in Christ, the true "seed" of Abraham, heirs to the promises he was given. In this paragraph he has shown that Christians are the "children of the free woman," Sarah, and thus like Isaac are heirs of all the promises that God gave to Isaac and his descendants. Believers can trace their privileged status to both their paternity and their maternity. However, as the antithetical form of this conclusion reveals—"children of the free woman, *not* of the slave woman"[20]—Paul's use of the Sarah argument enables him to do something else as well: to contrast the children of Abraham and Sarah with

---

19. Others suggest that it may serve to conclude the whole argument from 3:1 onward (e.g., George 1994: 348). But the distinctive contrast between "slave" and "free" echoes the focus on this particular paragraph.

20. Paul's decision to use the article with ἐλευθέρας but not with παιδίσκης (in 4:31) may be because he wants to accentuate the qualitative force of the latter relationship (Burton 1921: 267) or because he wants to refer to any "slave woman" (Lightfoot 1881: 185). But equally it may simply be a stylistic variant.

the children of Abraham and Hagar. By means of this contrast, he is able to distinguish more clearly what he badly needs to distinguish: a version of salvation history insisting on law obedience as essential to defining the people of God and opposed to Paul's own version, in which faith in Christ, "the seed" of Abraham, is fully sufficient to guarantee the inheritance. As Ebeling (1981: 319) comments, the "either/or" of this verse expresses "the basic theological teaching of Galatians" (AT).

Additional Notes

4:22. The line of descent from Abraham through Isaac was naturally a common source of comment among Jewish writers, who often traced their special status as God's people to Isaac. See, for example, Jub. 16.16b–18:

> And through Isaac a name and a seed would be named for [Abraham]. And all of the seed of his sons would become nations. And they would be counted with the nations. But from the sons of Isaac one would become a holy seed and he would not be counted among the nations because he would become the portion of the Most High . . . so that he might become a people (belonging) to the LORD, a (special) possession from all people, and so that he might become a kingdom of priests and a holy people. (O. S. Wintermute, *OTP* 2:88)

In this sense, a contrast between Israel, descended from Isaac, and other nations that traced their descent from Ishmael is also common (Ishmael is often said to be the progenitor of Arabs [Jub. 20.13; Josephus, *Ant.* 1.221; Pesiq. Rab. 21.2–3; Pirqe R. El. 41; Lam. Rab. 3.1] and sometimes of Gentiles generally [Gen. Rab. 45.8]; for a survey of Jewish interpretation, see esp. R. Longenecker 1990: 200–206). We can well imagine, then, the agitators arguing that the true children of Abraham are traced through Sarah and Isaac and that these children, the people of Israel, were given circumcision to mark their status and were expected to obey the law that God gave Israel.

4:23. The textual tradition is divided between the reading δι' ἐπαγγελίας ($\mathfrak{P}^{46}$ ℵ A C Ψ and several minuscules) and διὰ τῆς ἐπαγγελίας (B D F G 062 0278 𝔐). The former is usually preferred on the grounds that it matches better the contrasting κατὰ σάρκα (Burton 1921: 253).

4:25. Several variations of the opening words of v. 25 are found in the MSS: the two main issues are whether to read Ἁγάρ and what the connecting conjunction is:

> τὸ γὰρ Σινᾶ ὄρος (for the Sinai mountain) (ℵ C F G, etc.)
> τὸ δὲ Σινᾶ ὄρος (but/and/now the Sinai mountain) ($\mathfrak{P}^{46}$)
> τὸ γὰρ Ἁγάρ Σινᾶ ὄρος (for the Hagar Sinai mountain) (K L P Ψ 062 𝔐, etc.)
> τὸ δὲ Ἁγάρ Σινᾶ ὄρος (but/and/now the Hagar Sinai mountain) (A B D 0278, etc.)

A few English translations (NJB, NLT) and interpreters choose a reading that omits Hagar, either with the δέ (NJB, NLT; Betz 1979: 244–45 [possibly]; Mussner 1988: 322–24) or with the γάρ (Lightfoot 1881: 181). But most versions and interpreters argue, we think correctly, that the presence of the word Ἁγάρ is by far the more difficult reading and that δέ should be read because it has much stronger external support than γάρ (e.g., Martyn 1997: 437–38; Witherington 1998: 332–33). Metzger (1994: 527) further suggests that the scribes may have accidently omitted Ἁγάρ once the very similar γάρ had been introduced into the tradition.

4:26. Some MSS add πάντων between μήτηρ and ἡμῶν ("mother of all of us"; ℵ² A C³ 0261^vid 𝔐). But external evidence for the omission is stronger ($\mathfrak{P}^{46}$ ℵ* B C* D F G Ψ and several minuscules), and it is the shorter reading.

4:27. Paul's quotation of Isa. 54:1 follows the LXX exactly, which, in turn, translates the Hebrew quite straightforwardly:

Isa. 54:1 MT:

רָנִּי עֲקָרָה לֹא יָלָדָה
פִּצְחִי רִנָּה וְצַהֲלִי לֹא־חָלָה
כִּי־רַבִּים בְּנֵי־שׁוֹמֵמָה
מִבְּנֵי בְעוּלָה

Isa. 54:1 LXX:

εὐφράνθητι στεῖρα ἡ οὐ τίκτουσα,
ῥῆξον καὶ βόησον, ἡ οὐκ ὠδίνουσα,
ὅτι πολλὰ τὰ τέκνα τῆς ἐρήμου
μᾶλλον ἢ τῆς ἐχούσης τὸν ἄνδρα

Gal. 4:27:

εὐφράνθητι, στεῖρα ἡ οὐ τίκτουσα,
ῥῆξον καὶ βόησον, ἡ οὐκ ὠδίνουσα·
ὅτι πολλὰ τὰ τέκνα τῆς ἐρήμου
μᾶλλον ἢ τῆς ἐχούσης τὸν ἄνδρα.

Second-temple Jewish interpreters continued to look for the fulfillment of the prophecy of Isa. 54:1. Such expectation indicates that, although there were various viewpoints on the question, many Jews in Paul's day did not think that the return of many Jews to Israel after the deportations in the eighth and sixth centuries BC had truly ended the exile. Until the prophetic promises about full restoration and spiritual renewal were fulfilled, the "exile," in a certain sense, continued (this point has received considerable emphasis in the work of N. T. Wright, probably to the point of exaggeration [see Seifrid 1994; Bryan 2002: 8–12; and see the mediating view of Hafemann 1997: 368–70]). However, although Second Temple Jews hoped for the restoration of Zion, their expectation did not include an influx of Gentiles (see Starling 2011: 30–35).

4:28. In place of the second-person pronoun found in the text of NA[28] and assumed in most of the modern English translations (ὑμεῖς, with the verb ἐστέ at the end of the verse), some MSS, including 𝔐 (and hence the "we" in KJV and NKJV), read ἡμεῖς (with ἐσμέν). The variation between these two words is one of the most common in the NT textual tradition, and a decision between the two is not always easy. In this case, however, while the external evidence is fairly evenly split (in favor of ὑμεῖς . . . ἐστέ: 𝔓[46] B D* F G 0261[vid] 0278 and a number of minuscules; in favor of ἡμεῖς . . . ἐσμέν: ℵ A C D² Ψ 062, in addition to 𝔐), internal considerations favor ὑμεῖς, since assimilation to the first-person plural pronouns in vv. 26 and 31 would have happened easily (see Metzger 1994: 528; and almost all the commentators).

4:30. Paul's quotation of Gen. 21:10 generally follows the LXX; the LXX in turn accurately renders the Hebrew:

Gen. 21:10 MT:

גָּרֵשׁ הָאָמָה הַזֹּאת וְאֶת־בְּנָהּ כִּי לֹא יִירַשׁ בֶּן־הָאָמָה הַזֹּאת עִם־בְּנִי עִם־יִצְחָק:

Gen. 21:10 LXX:

ἔκβαλε τὴν παιδίσκην ταύτην καὶ τὸν υἱὸν αὐτῆς· οὐ γὰρ κληρονομήσει ὁ υἱὸς τῆς παιδίσκης ταύτης μετὰ τοῦ υἱοῦ μου Ισαακ.

Gal. 4:30:

ἔκβαλε τὴν παιδίσκην καὶ τὸν υἱὸν αὐτῆς· οὐ γὰρ μὴ κληρονομήσει ὁ υἱὸς τῆς παιδίσκης μετὰ τοῦ υἱοῦ τῆς ἐλευθέρας.

There are several minor differences among these texts. Paul, in contrast to both MT and LXX, has no demonstrative adjective (this) with either of the references to the "slave woman." Paul may omit it because, in contrast to the OT text, Hagar has not been explicitly mentioned since v. 25.

Paul uses the compound negative οὐ μή in place of the LXX οὐ (Heb. לֹא). This double negation, which often occurs, as here, with future verbs, is often thought to be emphatic (BDF §365; Dunn 1993a: 258; see NIV: "will never share in the inheritance"). If so (and there is some question whether the compound has begun losing any particular emphasis; see Zerwick 1963: §444), Paul may be strengthening the claim that the child of the slave woman would not inherit.

"My son Isaac" in the LXX and MT is replaced by Paul with "the son of the free woman." To some extent, of course, this change is required because Paul introduces the verse simply as what Scripture says, whereas in the OT it is Sarah who is speaking. But the unnecessary addition of "the free woman" signals Paul's concern with this theme throughout this paragraph.

D. Exhortation and Warning: Faith, Spirit, and Righteousness (5:1–12)

The two paragraphs that compose this section (vv. 1–6, 7–12) form the rhetorical climax of Paul's Letter to the Galatians (Heiligenthal 1984: 45–46; I. Scott 2006: 252; Boyce 2000: 133–34). Some interpreters argue that these paragraphs introduce the last major section of the letter, a section that focuses on exhortation (e.g., Betz 1979: 254; G. Hansen 1989: 79–82). The many parallels between these verses and the passionate introductory rebuke of the Galatians in 1:6–10 (see esp. R. Longenecker 1990: 221–22) could support this reading of the structure. However, it seems better to view 5:1–12 as the hortatory conclusion to the great central section of the letter (R. Longenecker 1990: 222; Dunn 1993a: 261; Hays 2000: 306). Paul here returns to many of the same themes found in the opening paragraph of the section (3:1–6), so 3:1–6 and 5:1–12 bracket the argument in this part of the letter. Both sections make allusive reference to the agitators: compare "Who [τίς, *tis*] has bewitched you?" (3:1) with "Who [τίς] cut in on you?" (5:7). And as the former passage opens with a reference to the cross (3:1), so this one ends with such a reference (5:11). More significantly, both passages highlight the central importance of faith and the Spirit (3:2, 3, 5, 6; 5:5), in contrast to the law (3:2, 5; 5:2–4) and stress the complete sufficiency of faith (and the Spirit) as the means of righteousness (3:6; 5:5).

In the first paragraph of this section, Paul brings together the key theological themes of the letter[1] to issue a stark warning to the Galatians: they must choose between Christ, as Paul has presented him to them in his gospel, or the law, which the agitators are insisting the Galatians must observe. The issue is also clear: "justification" (v. 4) and "righteousness" (v. 5). The heat of Paul's rhetoric here and elsewhere in Galatians is occasioned by the fact that the believers' ultimate issue of eternal destiny is at stake. The matter involves not only how the Galatians are to live out their Christian identity (a "nomistic" vs. "Christic" lifestyle) but also whether that manner of living will eventuate in acceptance before God: "righteousness." As he has so often done in Galatians, Paul lines up and contrasts two sets of entities: law (vv. 3, 4) and circumcision (vv. 2, 3) on the one side, and Christ (v. 4), grace (v. 4), faith (v. 5), and the Spirit (v. 5) on the other.

---

1. In vv. 4–5, Paul brings together in close relationship much of the key vocabulary of his earlier argument (as, e.g., Engberg-Pedersen [2000: 135] notes): "justify" (5:4; see 2:16 [3x], 17; 3:8, 11, 24); "righteousness" (5:5; see 2:21; 3:6, 21); "faith" (5:5, 6; see 1:23; 2:16 [2x], 20; 3:2, 5, 7, 8, 9, 11, 12, 14, 22, 23 [2x], 24, 25, 26; 5:22; 6:10); "grace" (5:4; see 1:3, 6, 15; 2:9, 21; 6:18); "Spirit" (5:5; see 3:2, 3, 5, 14; 4:6, 29; 5:16, 17 [2x], 18, 22, 25 [2x]; 6:1, 8 [2x], 18).

The second paragraph builds on the argument of the first. Here Paul issues a strongly worded warning about the false teachers and urges the Galatians in very personal terms to continue on the good gospel road that they had begun traveling. Galatians 5:1–12 therefore resembles, in its movement from theological summary to personal pleas and warnings, the sequence of argument in 4:1–20.

1. Justified by Faith and Not by the Law (5:1–6)

After the transitional summarizing imperative in verse 1a, these verses reveal a shift in key vocabulary from the freedom/slavery nexus of 4:21–31 to the law/faith/Spirit/justification nexus typical of 2:16–4:7. After the personal exhortation of 4:12–20 and the (mainly defensive) scriptural argument of 4:21–31, Paul now weaves together the threads of his theological argument into a clear and pointed expression of his key concern in the letter.

This paragraph falls into two parts. In the last part of verse 1, Paul warns against submitting again to a yoke of slavery, and he unpacks this general warning in three roughly parallel warnings in verses 2–4: if the Galatians are circumcised or seek justification via the law, "Christ will be of no benefit to them" (v. 2), they will need to do all the law (v. 3), and they will be cut off from grace (v. 4). The second part of the paragraph (vv. 5–6) picks up the positive part of Paul's exhortation in verse 1b: "stand." The new focus is marked by the shift from the second-person formulation in verses 2–4 to the first-person language in verses 5–6: Christians have secure expectation of being justified on the final day, through the Spirit and through their faith, a faith that produces works pleasing to God. This paragraph occupies a key place of transition in the letter. It succinctly reasserts the central theological truth of 2:16–4:7: "justification" is by faith. At the same time, with the emphasis on the Spirit and love, it anticipates the key emphases of the argument in 5:13–6:10. The phrase "in Christ Jesus" at the beginning of verse 6 sounds again the keynote of christological inclusion, an underappreciated theological basic in Paul's argument in the letter.

Although Paul has hinted that circumcision might be an issue in the Galatian churches (2:3), this is the first time that Paul mentions it as a key point of contention. Withholding this pivotal matter until now is a common rhetorical strategy (Witherington 1998: 364) and gives it special prominence. God gave circumcision to Abraham and his descendants as a "sign of the covenant" (Gen. 17:11–12), and it took on special importance as a "marker" of Jewishness in the pluralistic Greco-Roman first-century world. The agitators therefore were probably insisting on circumcision as a necessary step for the Galatian Christians to be considered as belonging to the covenant people and therefore to be found "righteous" on the day of judgment. To counter this claim, Paul brings to bear the theology of the law that he has developed in great detail in 2:16–4:31. In common with Jews of his day, he associates circumcision closely with law obedience. Indeed, in apparent contrast to what the agitators themselves were saying, he makes clear that circumcision is bound up with a commitment to obey the entire law (5:3). If they become circumcised, therefore, the Galatians would tie themselves to a law that is outmoded (3:15–18; 4:1–3), demanding works that sinful humans cannot adequately produce (cf. 3:10, 12) and therefore subjecting its "doers" to a curse (3:10, 13; 4:4–5).

Exegesis and Exposition

¹⌐It is for freedom that Christ has set us free. Stand therefore⌐ and do not become burdened again by a yoke of slavery.

²Notice that I, Paul, am the one saying this to you: if you undergo circumcision, Christ will be of no benefit to you. ³Now I testify again to every man who wants to be circumcised that he is obligated to do the whole law. ⁴You who are seeking to be justified by the law have been alienated from Christ; you have fallen away from grace. ⁵For we, by the Spirit, by faith, are eagerly awaiting the hope of righteousness. ⁶For in Christ Jesus neither circumcision nor uncircumcision matters, but faith working through love.

The place of this verse in the movement of Paul's argument is debated. On the one hand, the verse may be the conclusion of 4:21–31. Paul's self-reference and the verb of speaking in verse 2 could suggest that a new section begins only with that verse. And the key motif of 4:21–31, the contrast between slavery and freedom, is found again in verse 1 (e.g., Bruce 1982b: 226; Martyn 1997: 432; and see NRSV, CEB, NLT).[1] On the other hand, 5:1 seems to make a new beginning by virtue of both its style and content. The verse lacks any explicit connection with what precedes (asyndeton). The introduction of the person of Christ (absent entirely from the exposition in 4:21–31) suggests a shift of emphasis; and the warning about "again" succumbing to slavery reminds us of 4:1–11 (see esp. vv. 3 and 9; see, e.g., Burton 1921: 269; Mussner 1988: 333; Betz 1979: 255; Dunn 1993a: 261; and see NIV, ESV, NKJV, HCSB, NET, NJB). Moreover, the way both this verse and 5:13 pick up the theme of freedom as a basis for further teaching suggests that in both places Paul initiates a new focus by means of this central theme in 4:21–31. As most interpreters agree, then, 5:1a is a Janus, looking both backward and forward, but we think it looks forward a bit more than it looks backward. The verse catches up the key idea of 4:21–31 and uses it as the launching pad for the exhortations that follow in 5:1b–4.

The verse opens with an indicative summary of the key idea of freedom for which Paul has been arguing throughout 4:21–31. Paul puts the term τῇ ἐλευθερίᾳ (*tē eleutheria*, for freedom) first in the sentence, thereby emphasizing it (an emphasis brought out in the NIV: "It is for freedom that Christ has set us free"; cf. also NASB). The dative form of the word could indicate

5:1

---

1. Boyce (2000: 293) argues that the verse is basically independent, not clearly connected with what precedes or what follows.

instrument: "by (bestowing) the freedom (spoken of above) Christ has made us free" (Burton 1921: 271; see also Bruce 1982b: 226). But, along with all the modern translations and most interpreters, it is better to take the dative as indicating "destination" or "purpose": "for the sake of, or with the goal of freedom, Christ has set us free" (Coppins 2009: 110–12; e.g., R. Longenecker 1990: 224; Martyn 1997: 447). In 2:4 Paul refers to "the freedom we have in Christ," and in this context, it is clear that the freedom involves not being bound by the demand of circumcision. The language of redemption in 3:13 and 4:5 is conceptually similar to freedom; in both these texts redemption is from a situation having to do with the law: "the curse of the law" in 3:13, and "those under the law" in 4:5. And now in 5:1, Paul goes on to warn about a yoke of slavery, language that almost certainly refers to the law. (Note that freedom and the law are closely related again in 5:13–15.) All this makes it likely that "freedom" refers to "freedom from the law's binding authority." However, it is possible that, while focused on the issue of the law in this context, the freedom that Paul celebrates ultimately includes being free from all those powers of the old age (see 1:4) from which believers in Christ are set free: sin (see 3:22), death/curse (3:13), "the elements of this world" (4:3; see Rom. 6:18, 22; 8:2, 21–22; 2 Cor. 3:17; and, e.g., H. Schlier, *TDNT* 2:497–99; Coppins 2009: 112–15; Vollenweider 1989: 285–321 [who argues that freedom is the product of new creation]). This opening assertion has a bit of an ironic quality to it: Christ has set us "free": don't you realize that it is "freedom" (not slavery) that being free leads to?

In a typical NT mixture of indicative and imperative, Paul now calls on his readers to "stand" (στήκετε, *stēkete*) in the freedom that Christ has won for them. Paul elsewhere uses this verb to exhort Christians to hold fast to the privileges and blessings they enjoy in the new realm of salvation (Phil. 1:27; 4:1; 1 Thess. 3:8; 2 Thess. 2:15). It has a military flavor: the rendering "stand firm," found in many of the English versions, is quite justified. This positive command is matched by a negative, which draws attention to the specific threat to freedom that Paul combats in this letter: "Do not become burdened again by a yoke of slavery" (μὴ πάλιν ζυγῷ δουλείας ἐνέχεσθε, *mē palin zygō douleias enechesthe*). The imperative ἐνέχεσθε could be middle, with a "direct" middle sense, "Do not submit yourselves," but it is more likely passive, "Do not let yourselves be burdened." The verb ἐνέχω has the sense "be subject to," "be loaded down with" (BDAG 336.2; it does not occur in this form elsewhere in Biblical Greek except as a variant reading in 2 Thess. 1:4, but it occurs with this sense in 3 Macc. 6:10: "Even if our lives have become entangled [ἐνέσχηται, *eneschētai*] in impieties in our exile, rescue us from the hand of the enemy, and destroy us, Lord, by whatever fate you choose"). The phrase "yoke of slavery" plays on the widespread Jewish use of the imagery of the yoke to describe the law (e.g., *m. 'Abot* 3.5; cf. Acts 15:10; Matt. 11:29–30). Of course, Jewish teachers would never have called the law a "yoke of slavery": this is Paul's summary of the effect that submission to the law would have for the Galatian Gentile believers. The "again" reflects the way that Paul has described the Galatian Gentiles' previous subjection to "the elements of the world" (4:3, 9) and associated that with subjection to the law.

The verse begins with a strong personal emphasis: ἴδε ἐγὼ Παῦλος (*ide egō*   **5:2** *Paulos*, see I Paul). The word ἴδε, a second-person singular imperative of ὁράω (*horaō*), literally meaning "see," "look" (e.g., ESV), often, as here, takes on the sense "take notice of" (LN 355.30.45), "pay special attention to" (see NIV "mark my words" [R. Longenecker 1990: 225]; Dunn [1993a: 263] suggests that it might reflect the Hebrew *hinneh*). Paul draws attention to himself as the one who addresses the Galatians. His purpose might be to remind the Galatians of his authority as an apostle (so most interpreters, such as Betz 1979: 258). But the more intimate relationship between Paul and the Galatians that he has alluded to in 4:12–20 might suggest rather that his intent is to bring that relationship into play here: "'This is Paul speaking to you'—Paul whom you know, Paul your friend and father in Christ" (Bruce 1982b: 229).[2] From a larger discourse perspective, this kind of unnecessary "metacomment" draws attention to what Paul is about to say (Runge 2010: 101–17).[3]

The content of what Paul is saying (ὅτι, *hoti*, that) and to which he draws attention is urgent: ἐὰν περιτέμνησθε, Χριστὸς ὑμᾶς οὐδὲν ὠφελήσει (*ean peritemnēsthe, Christos hymas ouden ōphelēsei*, if you undergo circumcision, Christ will be of no benefit to you).[4] As we noted above, the fact that circumcision surfaces here as a key issue for the first time does not mean it is of only minimal importance in the Galatian situation. On the contrary, it emerges as the key "presenting" issue. In keeping with standard Jewish theology, the agitators were insisting that the Gentile Galatians needed to undergo circumcision in order to secure their identification as children of Abraham, recipients of the blessings promised to him and his descendants. The present tense in 4:10—"You *are observing* days and months and seasons and years"—suggests that the Galatians have already taken the first steps toward law observance. The agitators are urging that they take the next and decisive step.[5] If they do so, however, Paul warns, Christ will "be of no benefit to you."[6] Paul may use

---

2. Dunn (1993a: 264) suggests that Paul may be referring to the distortions of his view that others have introduced (see v. 11). It is unlikely, however, that the personal focus is intended as a contrast with what Scripture has said (as Martyn 1997: 469 suggests).

3. John White (1972: 60–63) argues that ἴδε ἐγὼ Παῦλος marks the beginning of the "body closing" (he cites Rom. 15:14 and Philem. 19 as parallels).

4. Whether the verb περιτέμνησθε is middle (Bruce 1982b: 229) or passive (BDAG 807.a) makes little difference to its meaning here. The sense is "allow yourselves to be circumcised."

5. As Dunn (1993a: 264–65) points out, circumcision, because it was both painful and scorned by most Gentiles, was often the last and highest hurdle for Gentiles interested in converting to Judaism. And in his survey of Jewish attitudes toward Gentiles in the first century, Donaldson (2007: 488–90, summary) has shown that circumcision was widely considered an essential step in conversion to Judaism.

6. In this clause (5:2b) each of the two accusatives has its own function, ὑμᾶς being the direct object of the verb while οὐδέν is, as A. T. Robertson (1934: 482) says, "a cognate accusative of the inner object." The infinitive ποιῆσαι (in 5:3b) depends on the substantive ὀφειλέτης ("debtor"; BDF §393).

a future tense of the verb ὀφείλω because the "no profit" would logically follow the circumcision (e.g., Burton 1921: 273; R. Longenecker 1990: 226). But a temporal force is more likely: Paul warns the Galatians that accepting circumcision will mean that Christ will be no benefit to them on the day of judgment (Betz 1979: 259). Martyn (1997: 468–69) rightly draws attention to the future focus that characterizes this entire paragraph.

In a stark portrayal of the options typical of Paul's rhetoric in this letter, he insists that circumcision and Christ cannot mix. One cannot choose circumcision *and* Christ: it is circumcision *or* Christ. "What the Galatians perceive to be a necessary supplement to their faith Paul views as a radical break with faith" (Beker 1980: 53). Of course, Paul's flat prohibition of circumcision is contextually determined. He is unalterably opposed to requiring Gentiles to be circumcised in order to qualify them for full membership in the people of God. He has nothing against circumcision of Jews when it is not a matter of a requirement for salvation; he is therefore quite happy for Timothy, whose Jewish mother qualified him as a Jew, to be circumcised (Acts 16:1–3). Nor would Paul have any quarrel with the modern practice of circumcising male babies for (debated) health reasons. He means what he says in verse 6: "neither circumcision nor uncircumcision has any significance." It is not the physical act as such that Paul opposes; it is its ritual significance within the first-century Jewish context that is the issue.

5:3   Paul makes just this point about the significance of circumcision in the Galatian situation in this next verse. He draws attention to what he says by using the verb μαρτυρέω (*martyreō*, testify, bear witness; see also Eph. 4:17). Shifting from the second-person plural of direct address in verse 2, Paul now uses the third-person singular to state a general principle. The man who is circumcised, Paul affirms, is "obligated to do the whole law" (ὀφειλέτης ἐστὶν ὅλον τὸν νόμον ποιῆσαι, *opheiletēs estin holon ton nomon poiēsai*). Circumcision is bound up with doing the law. This assertion explains (the δέ [*de*, now] is explanatory; see Mussner 1988: 347) Paul's claim in verse 2: the person who is circumcised will receive no benefit from Christ because circumcision entails obedience to the entire law of God—and as Paul has made clear earlier in the letter (3:11, 21–22) and says again in verse 4, no person can be justified in the law. Hays (2000: 312) puts it well: "If [the Galatians] choose to be circumcised, they are crossing a border into an occupied territory where the Law rules." The πάλιν (*palin*, again) is probably functioning, then, to mark verse 3 as a kind of restatement of verse 2 (Bruce 1982b: 229; R. Longenecker 1990: 226; Martyn 1997: 469; de Boer 2011: 313). The repetition of the "owe" or "obligation" language (ὠφελήσει in v. 2; ὀφειλέτης in this verse) emphasizes this relationship. To be sure, granted the similarities (on which see below) between this verse and what Paul has said in 3:10, it is tempting to think that Paul draws attention to that earlier text (Gundry 1985: 26; Barclay 1988: 64; Bergmeier 2005: 162; Schreiner 2010: 314). But an analysis of Paul's use of πάλιν in similar contexts shows that he almost always draws a connection with an immediately preceding point (Rom. 15:10, 11, 12; 1 Cor. 3:20; 12:21; 2 Cor. 11:16; Gal. 1:9; Phil. 4:4).[7]

Just what Paul intends to say by claiming that a man who undergoes circumcision is obliged to obey the whole law is not clear. Two issues call for comment: First, why does Paul need to make this point to the Galatians? Most interpreters think that Paul insists on the connection between being circumcised and doing the whole law because the agitators themselves had withheld this point from the Galatians. They would agree with Paul that circumcision entails obedience to the whole law, but they were hoping to bring the Galatians along by a policy of gradualism, only after the fact making clear just what circumcision really means (e.g., Bruce 1982b: 229; Jewett 1970–71: 207–8; Mussner 1988: 347–48; R. Longenecker 1990: 226–27; Martyn 1997: 470). However, there are serious problems with this explanation (see esp. Barclay 1988: 60–65). As Dunn (1993a: 264–65) notes, circumcision was usually the last and most difficult step for Gentiles in their taking on the obligations of the law. Furthermore, the breadth of the language Paul uses throughout Gal. 2:16–4:7 suggests that the agitators were demanding—and the Galatians understood—that submission to the law very broadly conceived was being required (see esp. the phrase "under the law" [e.g., 4:21]). In addition, the view that the law must be treated as a unity, that all its commandments must be undertaken, was the standard view in the Judaism of Paul's day. Justin, writing a bit later than Paul, summarizes the standard Jewish view: "If, then, you are willing to listen to me . . . , first be circumcised, then observe what ordinances have been enacted with respect to the Sabbath, and the feasts, and the new moons of God; and, in a word, do all the things which have been written in the Law" (*Dial.* 8; see also, e.g., *m. 'Abot* 2.1; 4.2; 4 Macc. 5:20–21; Sir. 7:8; 1QS 1.14; James 2:10). It is very unlikely, then, that Paul is telling the Galatians anything new. Rather, he is pointing out to them something whose significance they have not yet fully appreciated (Betz 1979: 260–61; Barclay 1988: 64; Fung 1988: 222; Hays 2000: 313).

Second, all this raises the larger issue: what is the logic of Paul's argument here? Some interpreters think that Paul is simply warning the Galatians that their decision to be circumcised will mean that they will be committed to the "total Jewish way of life." As Sanders (1983: 29) puts it, "Paul may very well simply have been reminding his converts that, if they accepted circumcision, the consequence would be that they would have to begin living their lives according to a new set of rules for daily living." Why would embracing the Jewish way of life be a problem? Dunn (2008c: 314), in keeping with his general reading of the letter, thinks the problem is ethnic exclusivity: "For them to accept the necessity of circumcision shifted the grounds for their redemption to membership of a people and made their previous commitment to Christ (in baptism) a pointless rite" (see also Dunn 1993a: 266–67). However, in this

---

7. This same point makes it unlikely that Paul is referring to an earlier occasion when he taught the Galatians (as Burton [1921: 274–75] suggests).

verse Paul refers to doing the law, not to "membership in a people." Only if Paul had prepared his readers to identify "law-doing" with "people member-ship" earlier in the letter would it be legitimate to find this latter issue in this verse; and we are not convinced that Paul has done so.

Another way to interpret the logic is, in effect, to deny that there is any logic: Paul simply rules out the law because he is convinced that Christ and Christ only is able to save (Bruce 1982b: 230–31). But this begs the question: why is the law unable to save? The argument of 3:15–25 might suggest one answer: the law belongs to the epoch before Christ, and to place oneself under the law via circumcision would be, in effect, to deny that Christ has come, and thus such a person would fail to find the justification that only Christ can provide in this new age. But if this were Paul's point here, why does he not simply say, "Every man who receives circumcision places himself under the law"? Paul's focus in this verse on *doing* the law, and especially on doing the *whole* law, suggests another possibility.

In 3:10–11 Paul argues that the law does not justify, instead claiming that those who seek justification by doing the law ("the works of the law") fall under the curse. And the reason this is so, Paul says, quoting Deut. 27:26 (and related texts), is because the curse falls on "everyone who does not remain in all that is written in the book of the law to do [the commandments of the law]." The similarities with 5:3–4 are obvious: both passages deny that justi-fication can come "in the law" (ἐν νόμῳ, *en nomō* [3:11; 5:4]); both focus on "doing" (ποιέω); and both emphasize the need to do "all" the law. We argued that 3:10 makes the best sense if Paul is assuming that no person is actually able satisfactorily to "do" the law. We should see the same logic at work in this verse. If the Galatians decide to be circumcised, they will be condemn-ing themselves because the power of sin prevents them from doing the whole law—which they must obey if they are to find justification in the law (see, e.g., Schreiner 1985: 266–68; Thielman 1989: 53; van Dülmen 1968: 57–58; Baugh 2009: 271–75). Part of the logic informing Paul's warning is explicitly formulated in the Letter of James (2:10), which, because of its early date and atmosphere, may be taken as representative of Judaism at the time: "Whoever keeps the whole law and yet stumbles at just one point is guilty of breaking all of it" ("the whole law" translates ὅλον τὸν νόμον [*holon ton nomon*], one of two texts in the LXX and NT, in addition to Gal. 5:3, that uses this phrase [see also Matt. 22:40]).

Of course, the Jewish view was that the guilt incurred by breaking even one commandment could be atoned for by means of the law's own provisions. In this sense one can say that Jews viewed the law as able to be fulfilled (see esp. "The Logic of Paul's Response" in the introduction). But in the new age inaugurated by Christ's death and resurrection, the old sacrifices no longer have validity. Two, and only two, options remain open for the sinner in the Christian era: to find justification in Christ by faith; or find justification through doing, whether that doing be defined by the law of Moses or by some other law, code, or moral impulse. But human "doing," because of the power of sin over people, is always inadequate to secure justification. Assuming this point in the logic of Gal. 5:2–4 fits very well in this context. The parallelism that is evident among verses 2, 3, and 4 makes clear that obligation to do the whole law is somehow related to being "separated from Christ" (v. 2) and having "fallen away from grace" (v. 4). Obligation to do the whole law brings a person into the sphere of a works-oriented approach to justification that in itself is fruitless and in turn fundamentally denies the meaning of grace. It therefore separates a person from Christ, who benefits people only by means of grace. Why else would Paul put so much stress on the need to do the *whole* law? As Das (2001: 168) puts it, "The only way 5:3 can function as a technique of *dissuasion* is if obeying the whole law is difficult or impossible" (see also van Dülmen 1968: 57–58). In contrast to many interpreters in the modern era,[8] then, we think that the Reformers were right to find in Paul's condemnation of circumcision and the law certain broader anthropological and theological implications. Though obviously focused in Galatians on a particular issue having to do with first-century Judaism, Paul's argument reaches beyond that historical issue to embrace the more fundamental and universal issues of doing versus believing. (For more detailed argument, see the section "The Logic of Paul's Response" in the introduction.)

In verse 2, Paul warned that if the Galatians become circumcised, Christ would be "of no benefit" to them. He now reiterates that warning. Paul makes clear why circumcision is so decisive a step by making clear that it involves "seeking to be justified by the law." As we noted in our comments on verse 2, circumcision signifies the intention to put oneself under the law of Moses and therefore (and this is the point that Paul is driving home to the Galatians) to seek to secure one's status with God in terms of that law. As most interpreters recognize, the present tense verb δικαιοῦσθε (*dikaiousthe*) has a conative force, justifying the translation "seeking to be justified" (or equivalent renderings) that is found in most of the English versions (and see BDF §319; Wallace 1996: 535). Only this interpretation of the verb makes sense of Paul's unqualified claim elsewhere that the law cannot justify; for example, "It is clear that no one can be justified before God by the law [ἐν νόμῳ, *en nomō*]" (3:11). As in 3:11, the ἐν before νόμῳ is probably instrumental rather than local ("by the law," as in most of the English versions; cf. BDF §195.2).

In the Greek text, Paul's description of what the Galatians are, in effect, seeking to do is bracketed by two strong warnings: "You have been separated from Christ"; "You have fallen away from grace." The positioning of these warnings draws attention to them (R. Longenecker 1990: 228). Our past-tense translation, mirrored in the English versions, reflects the aorist form of the verbs in each of these clauses (κατηργήθητε, *katērgēthēte*, you have been separated; ἐξεπέσατε, *exepesate*, you have fallen away). The tenses may be gnomic, used to state a generally valid truth (Schreiner 2010: 314), but

5:4

---

8. E.g., Watson (2007: 130): Paul opposes circumcision "because it is the rite of entry into the Jewish people, *and for that reason alone*" (with original emphasis); cf. also Barclay 2010: 39–42.

perhaps it is more suitable to view them in terms of the rhetoric of the verse. "The relative clause has a conditional sense 'if you seek justification in the law' and the aorist as it were dramatically represents the consequence as a historical fact" (Zerwick 1963: §257). In place of the conditional form that Paul used in verse 2 ("*if* you are circumcised"), Paul here uses the indefinite relative pronoun in a generic sense (οἵτινες, *hoitines*; see Wallace 1996: 344) to make his point: "those who fall into the category of seeking to be justified by the law." This kind of construction is naturally completed with a simple assertion of the results that would stem from this attempt at justification by the law (and we must, in any case, remember not to assume too much temporal significance in the aorist tense).

The verb καραργέω, which is used especially often by Paul in the NT (twenty-five of twenty-seven occurrences), means generally "abolish" or "render powerless," but in this context, because it is followed by the preposition ἀπό (*apo*, from), denoting separation, it means "alienate from," "sever from." Paul uses this combination of verb and preposition in only one other context. In Rom. 7:1–6, Paul employs the marriage relationship as an analogy for the believer's transfer from one binding relationship to another (see v. 2). We believers, once bound to the law, have been "released from [κατηργήθημεν ἀπό, *katērgēthēmen apo*]" the law in order to be joined to Christ and serve in the new way of the Spirit (vv. 5–6). Tragically, the Galatians are flirting with the possibility of reversing this situation: binding themselves to the law and becoming alienated from Christ. This alienation from Christ entails also a "falling away" from grace (τῆς χάριτος, *tēs charitos*, with the phrase occurring first in the clause for emphasis [and perhaps to set up a neat bracketing with the two verbs of warning at opposite ends of the verse]). Christ and grace are intimately connected in NT thinking. "Grace and truth" came in Christ (John 1:17), and Paul can use the word "grace" to summarize the "state of being a Christian" (e.g., Rom. 5:1–2). Paul has used the word in this sense earlier in the letter (2:21; cf. also 1:3, 6, 15; 2:9; 6:18). In this verse the article probably focuses attention on the particular manifestation of grace that is associated with Christ's work on our behalf (Burton 1921: 276–77; R. Longenecker 1990: 228). However, this appropriate acknowledgment of the referent of grace in this verse should not be allowed to obscure the significance of Paul's choice of this particular word in this context (contra, e.g., Barclay 2010). Grace in Paul reflects his conviction that God is free and unconstrained and that all that he does for his created beings is therefore given freely and without conditions (see esp. Rom. 4:4–5). By using this word, therefore, Paul suggests that the Galatians' flirtation with the law as a means of justification is wrong not only because the law has been set aside in the new era or because the law acts as a barrier to keep Gentiles out of the kingdom. Pursuing the law is wrong also, or even mainly, because the pursuit of the law as a means of justification involves an attempt to find security with God by means of human effort, a "doing" of the law (cf. v. 2) that, with whatever attitude it is pursued, introduces into the divine-human relationship a nexus of obligation that is incompatible with the nature of our gracious God.

A rhetorical shift occurs with verse 5. Paul shifts from the second-person address of verses 2 and 4: "Christ will be of no benefit to *you*"; "*You* will be alienated from Christ"; "*You* have fallen from grace." Now in verse 5 he uses first-person forms: "*We* . . . eagerly await." Paul draws attention to this shift by beginning his assertion with the (unnecessary) nominative pronoun ἡμεῖς (*hēmeis*, we). As we have argued earlier (see the first additional note on 3:13), Paul chooses his pronouns in Galatians for rhetorical more than for substantive reasons. In this case, Paul is not referring to Gentiles (in contrast to Jews; as, e.g., R. Longenecker [1990: 229] suggests); rather, he is using a "confessional" style that invites the Galatians to join with him in taking ownership of the truth he states here (e.g., Dunn 1993a: 269; Fee 1994: 418; Schewe 2004: 69–72).[9] Those who seek justification by the law will be cut off from Christ, because (γάρ, *gar*) *we* understand, by contrast, that righteousness is attained through the Spirit by faith. While cast in indicative form, then, verse 5 functions effectively as an exhortation.[10] This "indicative exhortation" is the climax of Paul's argument in the letter, bringing together (when we add the closely related v. 6) most of the key emphases of the letter: righteousness, faith, and the Spirit as the means by which that righteousness is attained and maintained, and love as the expression and embodiment of faith (cf. de Boer 2011: 315).

The verb in verse 5, ἀπεκδεχόμεθα (*apekdechometha*), is intensive: we "are eagerly awaiting." Paul uses this verb five other times, in each case referring to eschatological anticipation (Rom. 8:19, 23, 25; 1 Cor. 1:7; Phil. 3:20; cf. also Heb. 9:28; 1 Pet. 3:20). What we anticipate, Paul says, is ἐλπίδα δικαιοσύνης (*elpida dikaiosynēs*, hope of righteousness). While a few interpreters think that δικαιοσύνη might refer to ethical righteousness or to a mixture of ethical and forensic righteousness (e.g., Burton 1921: 278; Ziesler 1972: 179–80), the term should be taken in a purely forensic sense (in keeping with δικ- language throughout the letter; see "Justification/Righteousness" in the introduction; Moo 2011). But is the forensic status of righteousness something that already exists or something that believers are still awaiting? The answer to the question depends on how we understand the relationship between the two words in the phrase ἐλπίδα δικαιοσύνης. This phrase may mean "the hope that is based on righteousness" (a source genitive) or "the hope that is righteousness" (an epexegetic or appositional genitive). No major English translation explicitly adopts the former interpretation, but it is held by a number of scholars (e.g., Fung 1988: 226; Matera 1992: 182; George 1994: 361; Ziesler 1972: 179;

9. As we noted in our comments on 3:13, the pattern of pronominal forms in Galatians makes it impossible systematically to assign particular forms to one group or another.

10. Horrell (2005: 94) notes that Paul's "indicative" often functions this way, providing a critical bridge to his imperatives: "The apparently paradoxical nature of the Pauline indicative-imperative formulations can, then, be resolved when the indicatives in question are seen not as statements which can be held to be either 'true' or not but as identity-descriptors and group norms which need to be constantly affirmed."

Eckstein 1996: 142; Fee 1994: 419). This understanding of the phrase is certainly linguistically possible,[11] and it is often advocated on the grounds that it creates a better fit with Paul's teaching elsewhere, since he tends to present forensic righteousness as given to the believer at the moment of conversion.[12]

Nevertheless, as we have argued earlier (see again the introduction and Moo 2011), a future element of forensic righteousness is not incompatible with what Paul teaches about righteousness elsewhere. And there are good reasons to think that the word here does indicate the content of Christian hope. Linguistically, an appositional or objective genitive is in keeping with most comparable Pauline phrases.[13] But more important is the context. If "righteousness" in this verse refers to the believer's "past" justification, then Paul would be saying that "we eagerly await" the "hope," in the sense of "what we hope for." But after the verb ἀπεκδεχόμεθα we expect a more specific object than this. "We are eagerly awaiting what we hope for" would make sense if Paul had defined this hope in the context. But he does not. This is the first reference to Christian hope in any form in Galatians. An equally significant contextual indicator is the antithetical parallel between verse 5 and verse 4. In the latter verse, Paul refers to the Galatians as "trying to be justified by the law." The Galatians have already experienced new life in Christ. The problem is that they are in danger of being convinced that they can maintain their status of righteousness only by adding torah obedience to their faith in Christ. The rhetorical situation is clearly revealed in 3:1–6, where Paul argues *from* the good start that the Galatians have made *to* the need to continue as they began. The situation requires that Paul emphasize how the Galatians are to *maintain* their status of righteousness and how they can expect to be found to be in the "right" in the judgment.

But Paul's real concern in 5:5 is not to tell us something new about justification or righteousness but to insist that our right standing with God is finally confirmed for us through the Spirit and by means of faith. To be sure, πνεύματι

11. See τῆς ἐλπίδος τοῦ εὐαγγελίου (*tēs elpidos tou euangeliou*) in Col. 1:23, where NRSV's "the hope promised by the gospel" captures Paul's intent.

12. George (1994: 361) summarizes the point: "Paul was not saying, of course, that we must wait until the second coming of Christ either to receive justification or to be assured of it. The whole burden of Paul's doctrine of justification is that divine righteousness is imparted here and now through faith in Jesus Christ." Baugh (2007: 150–56) explicitly grounds his opposition to a future element of justification in Paul on this point.

13. In addition to Gal. 5:5 and Col. 1:23, Paul uses a genitive (other than a pronoun or verbal clause) after ἐλπίς (*elpis*, hope) eight other times. Two appear to be subjective: Eph. 1:18: ἡ ἐλπὶς τῆς κλήσεως αὐτοῦ (*hē elpis tēs klēseōs autou*, the hope to which he has called you); Eph. 4:4: μιᾷ ἐλπίδι τῆς κλήσεως ὑμῶν (*mia elpidi tēs klēseōs hymōn*, one hope when you were called). But six others appear to be objective/epexegetical: Rom. 5:2: ἐλπίδι τῆς δόξης τοῦ θεοῦ (*elpidi tēs doxēs tou theou*, hope of [sharing] the glory of God); Col. 1:27: ἡ ἐλπὶς τῆς δόξης (*hē elpis tēs doxēs*, the hope of [sharing] glory); 1 Thess. 1:3: τῆς ἐλπίδος τοῦ κυρίου ἡμῶν Ἰησοῦ Χριστοῦ (*tēs elpidos tou kyriou hēmōn Iēsou Christou*, hope in our Lord Jesus Christ); 1 Thess. 5:8: ἐλπίδα σωτηρίας (*elpida sōtērias*, the hope that we will be saved [AT]); Titus 1:2 and 3:7: ἐλπίδι/ἐλπίδα ζωῆς αἰωνίου (*elpidi/elpida zōēs aiōniou*, the hope that we will have eternal life [AT]).

(*pneumati*, through/by the Spirit) and ἐκ πίστεως (*ek pisteōs*, by faith) modify the verb,[14] but it is clear that the means of expecting is also the means of attaining the goal of that expectation. Paul signals his basic concern by putting πνεύματι and ἐκ πίστεως toward the front of the verse. In the earlier part of the letter, the *experience* of the Spirit is what Paul emphasizes: his presence among the Galatians marks them out as the recipients of God's new covenant blessing (3:2, 5, 14). In 5:13–6:10, on the other hand, Paul focuses on the *work* of the Spirit. Paul is undoubtedly thinking ahead to this argument in his brief reference to the Spirit in 5:5. It is by appropriating and living out of the power of the Spirit that believers confidently wait for the ultimate confirmation of their righteous status before God. Reflecting a common Pauline view, our text puts the Spirit in the role of the ἀρραβών (*arrabōn*, pledge; cf. 2 Cor. 1:22; 5:5; Eph. 1:14), the guarantee that what God has begun in us he will bring to completion. A deep-seated confidence in the Spirit's power to transform believers lies at the heart of Paul's teaching about Christian obedience; that confidence in the Spirit should be a hallmark of any faithful teaching about the nature of the Christian life. The tight connection between righteousness and faith is critical to Paul's argument in Galatians. The phrase ἐκ πίστεως here echoes the eight earlier occurrences of this phrase (direct in 2:16; 3:8, 11, 24; indirect in 3:7, 9; see also 3:12, 22). The importance of the connection between faith and righteousness in Gal. 5:5 should not be overlooked. If righteousness here indeed refers to a future dimension of justification, then Paul affirms quite clearly that faith is the means not only of entering into relationship with God, but also of maintaining that relationship and of confirming that relationship on the day of judgment.[15]

In verse 6 Paul explains (γάρ, *gar*, for) why the Spirit and faith, and not the law, are the means of finding acceptance with God: "neither circumcision nor uncircumcision matters" (οὔτε περιτομή τι ἰσχύει οὔτε ἀκροβυστία, *oute peritomē ti ischyei oute akrobystia*).[16] Or more exactly, the verse highlights the significance of faith, suggesting that, without minimizing the Spirit's significance in the new life, it is faith (as the argument of 2:16–4:7 makes clear) that is the key matter. The claim that circumcision is irrelevant to standing with God (ἰσχύει has the sense of "have meaning, be valid, be in force" [BDAG

5:6

---

14. Since in Gal. 3 (vv. 2, 5, 14) Paul suggests that it is by faith that we experience the Spirit, it is possible that we should connect ἐκ πίστεως with πνεύματι, rendering something like "through the Spirit, which you have received by faith" (Cosgrove 1988: 152). But it is more likely that ἐκ πίστεως parallels πνεύματι, both referring to the means through which we wait for the final verdict of righteousness. A few interpreters think that in this verse πίστις (*pistis*, faith) refers to Christ's faithfulness or fidelity (Choi 2005; D. Campbell 2009: 887–92; de Boer 2011: 316–17), but this is improbable.

15. Hence Rainbow's (2005: 194) claim that Paul never suggests that the final judgment will be based on faith, while perhaps linguistically valid, is conceptually erroneous. Indeed, he seems to contradict his own claim two pages later, where he refers to "the sort of faith which is active will withstand the judgment" (196).

16. Whether or not we assume the phrase εἰς δικαιοσύνην (*eis dikaiosynēn*, for righteousness) as Burton (1921: 279) wants to do, it is clear that ἰσχύει has justification in view (see vv. 4 and 5).

484.4]) makes perfect sense in light of the concern that Paul expresses in verses 2–4. But what is surprising is his mention of "uncircumcision" as well. His reference to both fundamental religious states (see the similar "neither Jew nor Greek" in 3:28; and also 1 Cor. 7:19) suggests that Paul is implicitly appealing to a fundamental theological conviction that undergirds the argument of Galatians: the fact that a new world has come into existence, a "new creation" so radically new that all human claims and status cease to have significance (see esp. Martyn 1997: 472–73). This perspective is continued by the appearance of similar language in 6:15: "Neither circumcision nor uncircumcision means anything; what counts is the new creation." And in keeping with the importance of inclusive Christology throughout Galatians, it is, of course "in Christ Jesus" (ἐν . . . Χριστῷ Ἰησοῦ, en . . . Christō Iēsou) that this new creation is to be found.

What does "have value" in this new creation, by contrast (ἀλλά, alla, but), is πίστις δι᾽ ἀγάπης ἐνεργουμένη (pistis di' agapēs energoumenē, faith working through love). This phrase has been a focal point of controversy since at least the time of Augustine.[17] It was the subject of especially intense debate during the time of the Reformation and immediately afterward, as Protestants and Roman Catholics disputed the relationship between love, which might be seen as shorthand for works, and faith. Protestants generally insisted that this verse stresses the need (and indeed the inevitability) for true faith to manifest itself in works through love but that love in no way qualifies faith, as if love is necessary before faith can be justifying. Roman Catholics, on the other hand, tended to insist on the idea of faith as being "formed by" love. The theological issue is related to, though not necessarily solved by, the linguistic issue of the mood of the participle ἐνεργουμένη. By form, this participle could be passive or middle. If passive is chosen, the phrase would mean something like "faith that is energized or produced by love" (Witherington 1998: 370; and see esp. the excursus on this matter in J. Robinson 1903: 241–47). However, as Bruce (1982b: 232) judiciously puts it, "In every NT occurrence of a form of ἐνεργέω which might be either middle or passive, a good case can be made out for taking it as middle" (see Rom. 7:5; 2 Cor. 1:6; 4:12; Eph. 3:20; Col. 1:29; 1 Thess. 2:13; 2 Thess. 2:7; James 5:16; and see also Piper 2007: 203–6). Almost all the translations and a large majority of commentators also take the participle as middle. It could then modify the verb ἰσχύει (which must be inferred here from the previous clause): "faith is valid as/when it works through love." But it is more likely to qualify the word πίστις itself, as recognized by the usual English rendering: "faith working through love" (= faith that works through love). In this case, Paul is claiming not that faith has power only when and if it results in love but rather that the faith that expresses itself, working itself out in acts of love, is the faith that is valid, or counts, for justification. Calvin's

---

17. Augustine used the phrase to reconcile Paul and James (cf. James 2) and therefore, as D. Wright (2006: 63) puts it, "influentially bequeathed to Western theology a prominent role for Galatians 5:6."

expression of the point is classic: "It is not our doctrine that the faith which justifies is alone; we maintain that it is invariably accompanied by good works; only we contend that faith alone is sufficient for justification" (1854: 132). Faith and love must be distinguished; but with this clause Paul emphasizes that the two, while separate, are inseparable. The verse classically expresses Paul's understanding of faith as an active and powerful quality, showing his close alignment with James on this point at least ("These words . . . bridge over the gulf which seems to separate the language of St. Paul and St. James" [Lightfoot 1881: 205]).

In terms of the movement of thought within the letter, this concluding phrase acts as something of an anticipatory bridge between the central and concluding sections of the letter. "Faith" plays a key role in 2:16–4:31, while "love" is a prominent theme in 5:13–6:10. "Faith expressing itself through love" thus forges a strong link between the so-called theological section of the letter and the so-called ethical section.[18] Paul's argument may thus be more continuous than we have sometimes recognized: throughout the letter he focuses on the sufficiency of the Spirit and faith for the "righteousness" that counts before God (Barclay 1988: 95–96). Those who are "in Christ" by faith need to live by faith, a faith that produces works of love pleasing to God through the Spirit; and it is by living in this way that people can have a sure hope of righteousness.

Additional Note

5:1. The opening part of this verse is found in quite a variety of forms in the MS tradition. These forms boil down to two basic options:

A formulation with two independent verbs, requiring us to put a major stop before the imperative:

τῇ ἐλευθερίᾳ ἡμᾶς Χριστὸς ἠλευθέρωσεν· στήκετε οὖν ("Christ has set us free for freedom; therefore stand!")—ℵ* A B D* (omits οὖν) P and a few minuscules; ℵ² C* Ψ and some minuscules have this same text, with ἡμᾶς and Χριστός reversed; H and a few minuscules also have this basic text, substituting στῆτε for στήκετε.

A formulation with a dependent relative clause dependent on the imperative:

τῇ ἐλευθερίᾳ οὖν ᾗ Χριστὸς ἡμᾶς ἠλευθέρωσεν, στήκετε ("therefore in the freedom with/for which Christ has set us free, stand")—D¹ 075 (with minor variations in D² and some other minuscules); a number of other minuscules follow this basic reading but include οὖν in the first clause.

Metzger (1994: 528) argues that the first reading, with good external support, should be accepted: the variant readings reflect the perceived difficulty of the sequence τῇ ἐλευθερίᾳ . . . ἠλευθέρωσεν.

---

18. As Fee (1994: 420) puts it, vv. 5–6 "encapsulate the two major theological agendas of this letter, that righteousness in terms of right standing with God is predicated on the work of Christ alone, and that righteousness in terms of righteous behavior is a necessary corollary of faith in Christ Jesus." This anticipatory nature of v. 6 makes clear that "love" in v. 6 must refer to believers' love, not Christ's (contra de Boer 2011: 318–19).

2. Resisting the Agitators (5:7–12)

Paul wraps up the central argument of the letter (3:1–5:12) with a final paragraph of exhortation. This exhortation, however, is more implicit than explicit. Paul's language takes a decided shift from the theological (5:2–6) to the personal. He describes and condemns the agitators (vv. 7b–9, 10b, 12), refers to his own ministry (v. 11), and implicitly appeals to the Galatians to "stay the course" (vv. 7a, 10a). A telling clue to the style of the paragraph is the general omission of conjunctions and particles: only verses 10b, 11a, and 11b are explicitly linked to their context. Commentators regularly note the rambling style of the paragraph, as Paul moves rapidly from rhetorical questions to aphorisms to scathing sarcasm; Dunn (1993a: 273) refers to "a series of abrupt expostulations, like snorts of indignation." Yet the style, while different from the logical progression of, for instance, verses 2–6, has its own power and matches rhetorical patterns of Paul's day (see esp. Betz [1979: 253–55, 264], who labels the paragraph as "diatribe"; Witherington 1998: 263–64). Apart from the somewhat parenthetical verse 11, Paul makes two closely related points: (1) the agitators are unworthy and should not be listened to; they are, in fact, under condemnation; and (2) the Galatians, Paul is confident, will agree with Paul and maintain the good gospel course they have already embarked on. With this last point, Paul has moved full circle in his rhetoric back to where he began in 3:1–6, where his concern also was to encourage the Galatians to "finish" their course as they had begun it (see 3:3). At the same time, the concerns of this paragraph reach all the way back to the opening substantive paragraph of the letter (1:6–9; see Engberg-Pedersen 2000: 135).

Exegesis and Exposition

[7]You were running well. Who has cut in on you to keep you from obeying ⌜the⌝ truth? [8]This persuasion is not from the one who calls you. [9]"A little leaven leavens the whole batch of dough." [10]I am confident in the Lord that you will think in no other way. But the one who is troubling you will bear their judgment, whoever they may be. [11]Brothers and sisters, if I am ⌜still⌝ preaching circumcision, why then am I being persecuted? In that case, the scandal of the cross would be removed. [12]I could even wish that the people who are agitating you ⌜would emasculate⌝ themselves.

5:7 The paragraph opens abruptly (no particle or conjunction connects it to what has preceded) with a renewed affirmation of the Galatians' previous strong spiritual condition (1:6; 3:1–5): "You were running well" (ἐτρέχετε καλῶς, *etrechete kalōs*). The running race, a competition popular among the Greeks and featured in the Isthmian and Olympic games, was one of Paul's favorite metaphors to depict the Christian life (1 Cor. 9:24; cf. Heb. 12:1) and his own ministry (1 Cor. 9:26; Gal. 2:2; Phil. 2:16; cf. 2 Tim. 2:5; see Pfitzner 1967). Paul reminds the Galatians of the benefits that their Spirit-filled, faith-governed way of living out the Christian life has brought to them. Why, Paul implicitly asks, should you depart from that good course?

Race-course imagery continues in the rhetorical question in the second part of the verse: τίς ὑμᾶς ἐνέκοψεν [τῇ] ἀληθείᾳ μὴ πείθεσθαι; (tis hymas enekopsen [tē] alētheia mē peithesthai? Who has cut in on you to keep you from obeying the truth?). To be sure, the verb ἐνκόπτω can mean simply "hinder" (Acts 24:4; Rom. 15:22; 1 Thess. 2:18; 1 Pet. 3:7), but the general notion of hindrance is rooted in the imagery of an obstacle in a race; and in a context in which a race has been explicitly mentioned, it is likely that Paul intends us to "hear" this connotation (G. Stählin, *TDNT* 3:855–56; R. Longenecker 1990: 230; Dunn 1993a: 274).[1] The aorist form of the verb may suggest that the agitators have already managed to "cut in" on the Galatians (R. Longenecker 1990: 230): thus the question is how the Galatians will react to their attempt to put an obstacle in the way of their spiritual progress. A number of commentators think that the indefinite τις might hint at a reference to Satan (e.g., Mussner 1988: 355); see 1 Thess. 2:18, where Paul says that he wanted to visit the Thessalonians but that "Satan hindered [ἐνέκοψεν, enekopsen] us" (RSV). But there is no good reason to read this text in light of 1 Thess. 2:18. In keeping with the style of the paragraph (see v. 10), Paul uses indefinite and allusive language to force the Galatians themselves to identify the people who might be "cutting in" on their successful spiritual run. This "cutting in" has the purpose of preventing the Galatians from obeying the truth. "The truth" is shorthand for "the truth of the gospel" (2:5, 14; cf. Silva 2000: 57). The verb that Paul uses in this question, πείθω, in the middle or passive form, has the connotation "obey" (BDAG 792.3.b; Wallace 1996: 416); so the English translations that choose this English rendering are accurate enough. Yet the verb may also have the connotation of an obedience that comes as a result of persuasion: Paul will use this same verb or its cognate noun twice again in this paragraph with such a connotation (vv. 8, 10).

As we noted above, verse 8 is tied closely to the rhetorical question in verse 7b by a play on words: the verb πείθω, "to obey as a result of persuasion" (in the middle/passive form) is picked up in its cognate noun, πεισμονή (peismonē, persuasion). The English versions indicate this backward reference by rendering "*this* persuasion" (RSV, ESV, HCSB, NET), "*such* persuasion" (NRSV), or "this *kind of* persuasion" (NIV). (The article with the word, then, is anaphoric; see BDF §488.1: "obey no one in such a way as to disobey the truth; *that* [sort of] obedience is not from him who calls you.") It is hard to know whether this rare noun (it may occur here for the first time in Greek) refers to

5:8

---

1. Hays (2000: 314–15) suggests that there may be a further allusion to the "cutting" of circumcision, but the meaning of the verb does not naturally suggest such a connotation.

the Galatians ("your state of being persuaded") or to the agitators ("their act of persuading"). But the connection with verse 7 favors the latter (Mussner 1988: 356; Dunn 1993a: 275; contra Lightfoot 1881: 206; Bruce 1982b: 234). The attempt of the agitators to persuade the Galatians, Paul warns, is "not from the one who calls you" (οὐκ ἐκ τοῦ καλοῦντος ὑμᾶς, *ouk ek tou kalountos hymas*). "The one who calls" them is God. As often in Paul, "call" has the sense of God's effectual call, his powerful reaching out to bring people into relationship with himself. The Galatians were initially "called" to live in God's grace (1:6); the attempts of the agitators to persuade the Galatians do not arise from that God who initially called them.

5:9   Paul reinforces his implicit warning about the agitators in verse 8 by citing an aphorism in this verse (the NIV encloses the verse in quotation marks to signal the fact that Paul is quoting a well-known saying): "A little leaven leavens the whole batch of dough" (μικρὰ ζύμη ὅλον τὸ φύραμα ζυμοῖ, *mikra zymē holon to phyrama zymoi*). As with many aphorisms, this one plays on universally understood daily experience; we can be quite sure that Paul is quoting such a saying because we find an identical saying in 1 Cor. 5:6: "Your boasting is not good. Don't you know that a little leaven leavens the whole batch of dough?" (AT; οὐκ οἴδατε ὅτι μικρὰ ζύμη ὅλον τὸ φύραμα ζυμοῖ; *ouk oidate hoti mikra zymē holon to phyrama zymoi?*). Leaven (yeast) was used to cause fermentation in bread; in the ancient world a small piece of fermented dough from an earlier batch of bread was often used (Vanderkam, *NIDB* 3:627). The prohibition of leaven in some key Jewish rituals, such as Passover and the Feast of Unleavened Bread (Exod. 12:14–20; Deut. 16:3–8), as well as on other occasions (e.g., Lev. 2:11; Num. 6:15, 17, 19; 2 Kings 23:9), resulted in leaven being used to symbolize something negative. Thus Jesus warns about "the leaven of the Pharisees [and Sadducees]" (Matt. 16:6, 11, 12; Mark 8:15; Luke 12:1). But leaven does not necessarily symbolize something evil; in Matt. 13:33 its power is used to describe a feature of the kingdom of heaven (using the verb ζυμόω [*zymoō*]). In Gal. 5:9, while the aphorism refers to something evil, the aphorism per se is simply picturing the extensive effects that something small and/or hidden could have. In this case the "leaven" may be the doctrine taught by the false teachers (e.g., Burton 1921: 283), but considering the personal focus of this paragraph, it more likely refers to the false teachers themselves (Lightfoot 1881: 206). See, explicitly, NLT: "But it takes only one wrong person among you to infect all the others—a little yeast spreads quickly through the whole batch of dough!"

5:10   The focus again shifts abruptly, as Paul expresses his personal (note the emphatic ἐγώ [*egō*, I]) confidence in the Galatians. The verb Paul uses to express this confidence is πέποιθα, a perfect form with present meaning (BDF §341) that means "be convinced," "trust" (BDAG 792.2.a). Since Paul has used this same verb in verse 7 and its cognate noun in verse 8, it is possible that he is using a key word to link some of these ideas. While impossible to maintain in English translation (and no version tries to do so), we might paraphrase "Who has cut in on you with the purpose of *persuading* you not to follow the truth? Such *persuasion* is not from God. . . . I myself, however, am *persuaded* about you that . . ." Both the prepositional phrases in this clause modify the verb, the first one, εἰς ὑμᾶς (*eis hymas*, with respect to you), indicating the people with reference to whom Paul has confidence; and the second, ἐν κυρίῳ (*en kyriō*, in the Lord), specifying the sphere in which, and derivatively the reason why, Paul has the confidence that he expresses here (R. Longenecker 1990: 231–32).

This confidence is, specifically, that the Galatians will "think nothing other" (οὐδὲν ἄλλο φρονήσετε, *ouden allo phronēsete*). The verb φρονέω refers to the possession of a certain mind-set; note especially Phil. 2:2, 5, where Paul uses the verb to refer to the mind-set he wants the Philippians to have (the verb is a favorite of Paul's: twenty-three of the twenty-six NT occurrences are in his letters). In this text the verb has a narrower focus, however, referring to the "opinion" or "viewpoint" that Paul expects the Galatians to have: hence the translation "take no other view" found in many of the versions (e.g., NIV, RSV, ESV; cf. also NASB, NET, HCSB). What is this "no other view," or to put it positively, "the same view" that Paul expects to find among the Galatians? Burton (1921: 284) thinks the reference is to verse 9, while Lightfoot (1881: 206) thinks Paul alludes to the viewpoint that the Galatians had before the false teachers arrived. This last point is surely generally true, but the context suggests that Paul is referring more specifically to the view he has of the false teachers: their persuasive speech is not from God (v. 8), and they stand condemned before God (v. 10b). Paul's expression of confidence is undoubtedly sincerely meant. Yet rhetorically this expression functions also to motivate the Galatians to live up to the confidence that Paul has in them. In 4:19 Paul addresses the Galatians as his children and uses parental imagery to speak of his role with them. Here also he speaks like a parent who hopes to motivate the children to do the right thing by expressing confidence in their own values and decision-making ability.

The focus shifts back to the agitators: "But the one who is troubling you will bear their judgment, whoever they may be" (ὁ δὲ ταράσσων ὑμᾶς βαστάσει τὸ κρίμα, ὅστις ἐὰν ᾖ, *ho de tarassōn hymas bastasei to krima, hostis ean ē*). The δέ is adversative: "I have confidence in you, *but* as for the one who is troubling you . . ." (NRSV, NASB, NET, HCSB; contra RSV, ESV). The singular substantival participle ὁ ταράσσων could refer to a particular individual, perhaps the leader of the agitators, whom Paul does not want to name explicitly (e.g., Betz 1979: 267–68; Martyn 1997: 475). But the singular is more likely generic (cf. 1:7; 5:12): note the indefinite ὅστις at the end of the verse (e.g., Burton 1921: 285; Mussner 1988: 358; R. Longenecker 1990: 232). Rhetorical considerations again probably dictate the form of the accusation: Paul wants to allow the Galatians themselves to identify the specific individual or individuals who fit the profile he presents. Paul's choice of ταράσσω to describe the agitators focuses, in keeping with the style of this paragraph, on the personal rather than the doctrinal. The verb refers to being disturbed in one's mental state (often in the Gospels) and can refer, as here (and in 1:7; Acts 15:24), to the state of being distressed or troubled by false teaching. People who so "trouble" others, says Paul, will "pay the penalty" (BDAG 171.2.b.β; cf. NIV, NET, HCSB). The word for "penalty" is κρίμα, which can refer to condemnation in the eschatological judgment of God (e.g., Rom. 2:2, 3; 3:8; 5:16; 13:2 [probably]; 1 Tim. 5:12). This is almost certainly what Paul intends (e.g., R. Longenecker 1990: 232; Hays 2000: 315, thinking it might also refer to the Galatians' excluding the agitators). The unnecessary addition of the phrase "whoever it may be" (see BDF §303 for this translation) may suggest that prominent leaders are involved in the false teaching (Fung 1988: 238).

5:11 The progress of this paragraph follows, as we have seen, a rhetorical rather than a logical sequence. Despite this, one can easily make sense of the train of thought in verses 7–10. But one is hard pressed to fit verse 11 neatly into the flow of thought. Why would Paul suddenly bring up the issue of his own alleged preaching of circumcision? The answer is almost certainly that Paul thinks he needs to respond to an accusation made by the agitators and well known to the Galatians. The NLT brings this out by inserting the clause "as some say I do" midway through the opening rhetorical question.

Paul signals a shift in focus with his emphatic reference to himself at the beginning of the verse, ἐγὼ δέ (egō de, now as for me), and the direct address of his readers: ἀδελφοί (adelphoi, brothers and sisters). His rhetorical question suggests that his still being persecuted makes it illogical to think that he is "still" (ἔτι, eti) preaching circumcision. The ἔτι (eti, still) makes it clear that Paul had once "preached circumcision." But when? Some interpreters think his opponents are seizing on practices that Paul continued to advocate as a Christian. For instance, at the beginning of the second missionary journey, he had Timothy, who would be considered Jewish by virtue of his Jewish mother, circumcised (Acts 16:1–3; Hays 2000: 316). It is unlikely that this incident is specifically in view since that incident in Acts probably took place after Galatians was written. However, Paul may have done something like this on other occasions; and in any case, working out the implications of his conviction that "neither circumcision nor uncircumcision means anything" (v. 6), Paul was not opposed to circumcising Jews (Bruce 1982b: 236–37; Dunn 1993a: 278–79; in a stronger form, Kinzer 2005: 73). However, this view does not fit the logic of Paul's question very well. The question takes the form of a conditional sentence, with εἰ (ei, if) introducing the protasis, or "if" clause (taking this form because the reality of the situation is presumed for the sake of argument), and the second ἔτι introducing the apodosis (e.g., see BDAG 400.3 for this meaning of ἔτι: it should therefore be translated "then"). The logic thus is "I am being persecuted, and that demonstrates that I am no longer preaching circumcision." This makes clear that "preaching circumcision" is something that Paul is no longer doing. Probably, then, as indeed we might expect, "preaching circumcision" means the kind of insistence on circumcision for one's standing with God that typifies the Jewish viewpoint. It was just this viewpoint, of course, that Paul held before his conversion; hence he must be referring to this preconversion phase of his life (Burton 1921: 286; R. Longenecker 1990: 233 [?]). The only difficulty with this view is the use of the verb κηρύσσω, which might imply missionary proclamation of the Jewish way of life, for which we have little evidence in Paul's past. However, "preaching circumcision" could mean, more loosely, "insisting on circumcision" in one's teaching.

The last statement in the verse depends not on the apodosis of the previous sentence, but the protasis (Baarda 1992). If Paul really were still preaching circumcision, "then" (ἄρα, ara) "the scandal of the cross would be removed" (κατήργηται τὸ σκάνδαλον τοῦ σταυροῦ, katērgētai to skandalon tou staurou). And this would, of course, also explain why Paul would *not* be persecuted. The word σκάνδαλον, very rare in secular Greek, was used in the LXX to denote a trap or snare (Lev. 19:14; Ps. 140:5 [139:6 LXX]) and, derivatively, an obstacle that can cause stumbling and eventual ruin (Ps. 119:165 [118:165]). The NT uses the word, along with its cognate verb, σκανδαλίζω (skandalizō), to refer to something that might cause one to fall into sin or in some way to bar one's way to God (G. Stählin, *TDNT* 7:339–58). (Paul uses the noun in Rom. 9:33 [= Isa. 8:14]; 11:9 [= Ps. 69:22 = 68:23 LXX]; 14:13; 16:17; 1 Cor. 1:23; and the verb in 1 Cor. 8:13 [2x]; 2 Cor. 11:29.) The English word "offense," used by many English versions here and in parallel NT texts, conveys the idea accurately. The genitive in the phrase is probably appositional: the σκάνδαλον is the cross (Fung [1988: 240] suggests a genitive of definition). An important parallel is 1 Cor. 1:23, where Paul claims that "Christ crucified" is a σκάνδαλον for the Jews. The "offense" of Christ's crucifixion is usually explained in terms of the claim of Deut. 21:23, that a person who is "hung" on a cross is accursed by God (cf. Gal. 3:13). Yet without ignoring the importance of this notion, it is possible that the opposition between circumcision and the cross has another idea in view. Circumcision signifies a way of salvation that focuses on doing the law (5:2–4), while for Paul, Christ's crucifixion signifies a way of grace and faith (2:21; 3:1–6; 5:5). The "offense" of the cross, then, may include the need for human beings to give up any means by which they might by their own efforts secure their status before God (G. Stählin, *TDNT* 7:354; Bruce 1982b: 238; Schreiner 2010: 327).[2]

The paragraph ends with a final powerful and sarcastic blast against the agitators. Paul now labels them οἱ ἀναστατοῦντες (hoi anastatountes), "trouble-makers" (NLT) or "agitators" (NIV, NET; the verb identifies the action of a political rebel in Acts 21:38, and in Acts 17:6 it describes the upsetting effect that the apostolic preaching is having on the whole world). He expresses a wish (ὄφελον, ophelon): "would that" (NAB)[3] these agitators would "get themselves emasculated" (ἀποκόψονται, apokopsontai; see BDF §317 on this specific connotation of the middle form of the verb). The verb ἀποκόπτω (apokoptō) means

5:12

2. Dunn's claim (1993a: 281) that the cross symbolizes here the unity of Jew and Gentile does not have good basis in the context.

3. The word ὄφελον should probably be interpreted as a participle with ἐστιν to be supplied (BDAG 743; BDF §67.2). The word connotes an unattainable wish (Moule 1959: 137).

simply "cut off" or "cut away" (see Mark 9:43, 45; John 18:10, 26; Acts 27:32), but it is sometimes used absolutely with "private parts" implied (BDAG 113.a; see Deut. 23:1 [23:2 LXX]). At least since Chrysostom (*Comm. Gal.* on 5:12 [*NPNF*[1] 13:39]), then, the verb here has been understood to refer to castration (so most modern commentators). Paul's disgust for the agitators and the effect they are having on his beloved converts overflows in a desire that they would go far beyond their preoccupation with cutting off a small piece of flesh from the penis and cut off the whole organ (NIV gets this ascensive idea in its rendering: "As for those agitators, I wish they would go the whole way and emasculate themselves!" The καί provides some basis for this ascensive emphasis). Some interpreters protest that Paul would never have indulged in such blunt sarcasm (e.g., Ramsay 1900: 437–40). But ancient authors frequently used language that today would be considered overbold, and it should also be recognized that self-castration was a more widespread phenomenon in Paul's day. Especially relevant is the self-castration practiced by the priests of the goddess Cybele. This cult had its epicenter in central Asia Minor, and many interpreters suspect that Paul may be alluding to these priests here (e.g., Lightfoot 1881: 206; Burton 1921: 289; Betz 1979: 270).[4] Such an allusion would be particularly appropriate if the Galatians lived in this part of Asia Minor. Even if (as we think) they did not, they could well have been familiar with the cult and its practices. But whether there is an allusion to a specific contemporary practice or not, we must appreciate the strength of Paul's rhetoric. He treats almost sarcastically one of the cardinal defining rituals of the Jewish faith in which he was reared. (Phil. 3:2 [AT], with its warning about "the mutilation of the flesh" [τὴν κατατομήν, *tēn katatomēn*], is somewhat similar.) Some interpreters think that another idea may be implied here also. In Deut. 23:1 [23:2 LXX], which uses the verb that occurs here, those who are emasculated are forbidden from entering the assembly of the Lord. In wishing that they would get themselves emasculated, then, Paul might also be wishing that the agitators would separate themselves from the Christian community (Fung 1988: 242).

Additional Notes

5:7. Some early and good witnesses omit the article before ἀληθείᾳ. It should probably be read, but it makes little difference to the sense.

5:11. Some, mainly Western witnesses, omit the first ἔτι in the verse. This omission is suspect because it eases a difficult text.

5:12. In place of the future indicative ἀποκόψονται, a few MSS read the aorist subjunctive ἀποκόψωνται. The word ὄφελον is invariably followed by the indicative rather than the subjunctive in Biblical Greek. This could, of course, argue for the subjunctive as the more difficult reading. But the witnesses are too few to make this likely, and the consideration of what Paul was most likely to have written therefore takes precedence. In either case, there is little difference in meaning.

4. Dunn (1993a: 283), agreeing that an allusion to the Cybele cult is present, thinks that Paul may be implying that these agitators might as well become pagans.

IV. The Life of the Gospel (5:13–6:10)

The third main part of Paul's Letter to the Galatians can be identified by a shift in vocabulary and thus in subject matter.[1] The word groups that are central to the argument of the second part of the letter ([2:15 and] 3:1–5:12)—"faith/believe," "righteousness/justify," and "son/child/seed"—are almost entirely absent in 5:13–6:20 (the only exception is πίστις [pistis, faith], which occurs twice [5:22; 6:10]). In place of these words, two others dominate this new section: "Spirit" and "love." The Spirit is mentioned ten times, and especially characteristic of the section is the opposition between the Spirit and the flesh (5:17, 19/22, 24–25; 6:8). The noun "love" is lexically represented only twice (5:13, 22) but is thematically a key motif (see also 5:14 [the verb]; 6:1–2, 9–10). The Spirit and love do not appear on the scene here for the first time. The Spirit has been mentioned at critical points (3:2, 5, 14; 4:6; 5:5) and in contrast to the flesh (3:3; 4:29). The centrality of love in the Christian life is also introduced earlier (5:6 [and note the reference to divine love in 2:20]). One topic carries over as a key concern from the earlier discussion: the law (5:14, 18, 23; 6:2). The basic argument of this section is that the Spirit enables believers to overcome the continuing power of the flesh and, by stimulating love for others, provides for the true fulfillment of the law.

But this section stands out even more by a shift in focus. Galatians has featured imperatives and exhortations (esp. 4:12–20; 5:7–12), but these are related to the basic theological issue of the letter. The exhortations, prohibitions, and warnings in 5:13–6:10 are much more general, treating basic elements of Christian conduct. Such sections of exhortation are often called "paraenesis," which Gammie (1990: 51) defines as "a form of address which not only commends, but actually enumerates precepts or maxims which pertain to moral aspiration and the regulation of human conduct." Calling it the "ethical" section of the letter is not incorrect, as long as "ethics" is understood in its broadest, theological sense.[2] Paul does, indeed, give specific practical advice, particularly in 5:25–6:6. But his more basic concern is to lay the theological

---

1. The majority of Galatians interpreters agree that 5:13–6:10 is the third major part of the letter. But there are dissenters. Some think that 5:1, or 5:2, marks the beginning of this third main section (see the introduction to 5:1–12). Others divide the letter into two basic parts, argument and exhortation, with exhortation beginning at 4:12; thus 5:13–6:10 would be either the second basic part of this exhortation section (R. Longenecker 1990: 235) or simply a continuation of it (Dahl 2002: 134; Schreiner 2010: 330). Still others think that only with v. 16 does a major transition occur, with vv. 13–15 being a continuation of vv. 2–12 (Witherington 1998: 375).

2. As long as theology itself is seen as (at least significantly) shaping and ordering human life, theology inevitably bleeds over into practice (see, e.g., Horrell 2005: 84–85). Yet in the letter the focus does shift from the question of standing before God (2:16–5:12) to living for God (5:13–6:10).

groundwork for the life of the believer. The indicatives in this passage "are identity-descriptors and group norms which need to be constantly affirmed" (Horrell 2005: 94; see also Esler 1998: 216–18). In keeping with this focus is the relative paucity of imperatives in the first part of the section (only in 5:13, 14, 16). As Martyn (1997: 482) puts it, "Paul is intent on describing the real world, the world that has been made what it is by God's sending into it Christ and his Spirit." This "ethical" section of the letter is therefore not an add-on but constitutes a vital part of Paul's argument against the agitators: presenting the life governed by God's Spirit in Christ as a powerful and compelling alternative to that espoused by the agitators, a life governed by the law (Engberg-Pedersen 2000: 136).

How does this concern with the sufficiency of the Spirit advance the argument of the letter? And what specific issue within the Galatian situation does it address? The idea that in 5:13 Paul might be turning to a "libertine" group within the community (after his focus on "legalists" earlier in the letter) is now almost universally abandoned.[3] Barclay (1988) argues that 5:13–6:10 must be integrated with the argument of the letter; he claims this can be done once it is recognized that the question addressed in this section—How should Christians live?—is in fact a concern throughout the letter.[4] Membership in the people of God and behavior are, Barclay argues, intimately connected; and 5:13–6:10 continues key themes from the earlier part of the letter. This part of Galatians does not turn to a new group or to a new problem, and Paul fashions his argument specifically for the Galatian situation. Barclay's general approach is on target. A concern with living by the Spirit surfaces earlier in Galatians (3:3; cf. 3:14), and the section must surely be integrated with the message of the letter and the situation in Galatia. None of this changes the fact that a shift from the tone and emphases of the earlier part of the letter occurs here.

Throughout this section references to the law are particularly significant for understanding its function within the letter.[5] Betz (1979: 273) suggests that Paul's concern to show that life in the Spirit meets the demands of the law may be directed to a concern that the Galatians had before the agitators arrived: they were looking for assurance about a moral basis for their lives, an assurance the agitators were happy to give by putting them under the law. Paul, on the other hand, argues that the Spirit is quite sufficient. Betz's reconstruction makes a certain amount of sense granted the concern that the Galatians may have felt about a lack of obvious religious ritual or structure

3. The idea that Galatians fights a "two-front" war against two distinct groups was argued especially by Lütgert (1919) and Ropes (1929) and was suggested also by Lightfoot (1881: 208); R. Longenecker (1990: 238), while not recognizing a distinct group of opponents, suggests that Paul now addresses a "libertine tendency" in Galatia.

4. Kwon (2004: 184–212) goes further, arguing that the fundamental issue in Galatia was the moral one that Paul addresses in this section.

5. For a survey of options for explaining the focus on the law in this section, see Wilson 2007: 4–16. Wilson himself thinks that Paul's concern is with the curse pronounced by the law and that his purpose is to show how the Spirit provides for redemption from that curse.

in their experience of Paul's gospel (Lull 1980: 25–43; Barclay 1988: 70–72). Yet it is also possible that the agitators themselves awakened this concern among the Galatians. Paul's version of the gospel, they may have argued, provides insufficient means to fight the tendency to sin within people. People need the clear and detailed prescriptions of the law of Moses to combat the power of sin. On this reading of the section, Paul is not so much continuing an argument begun earlier in the letter as responding to a possible objection to that argument. The Spirit-filled life, Paul is saying, is not only fully adequate to maintain and confirm one's status of righteousness before God; the Spirit also provides fully for the life of righteousness that God expects of his people. The sinful impulse ("the flesh") is conquered not by the law but by the Spirit (for this general approach, see B. Longenecker 1998: 80–81; Fung 1988: 243; Hays 2000: 320–21).

Most interpreters divide the passage into two parts: 5:13–24 and 5:25–6:10 (or 5:13–26 and 6:1–10). But a division into four parts more accurately tracks the movement of thought. In 5:13–15 Paul introduces two ideas that will dominate the passage: the danger posed to Christian living by the "flesh" and the importance of love for one another in Christian community. He then introduces the key "actor" in the drama of Christian living: the Spirit, who is entirely sufficient to subdue the impulses of the flesh and meet all the demands of the law (5:16–24). After stressing the need to "live" by the Spirit (cf. v. 16), Paul then spells out some specific ways in which believers can "keep in step" with the Spirit (5:25–6:6; cf. 5:25). The section ends appropriately with a reminder of the importance of Christian obedience for the eschatological judgment and a final call to love all people, but especially "the family of believers" (6:7–10).

A. The Basic Pattern of the New Life: Serving One Another in Love (5:13–15)

Throughout 5:13–6:10 Paul is concerned with relationships between believers. To this extent, then, verses 13–15 state the basic theme of what is to follow (Fee 1994: 205; Kertelge [1989: 335–36] compares 5:13–14 to Rom. 12:1–2). Paul creates a transition to his new topic by picking up the idea of "freedom" from 5:1 and warning his readers about allowing that freedom to become corrupted as an excuse for selfish and sinful conduct. Instead, Paul urges them, in a call that sets the agenda for much of what follows, "in love act as slaves to one another." Love can be singled out for such special emphasis, Paul goes on to explain, because it "fulfills the whole law." Only by such love will the Galatian Christians escape the community-destroying selfishness that may already be rearing its head among them.

Exegesis and Exposition

13Now you, my brothers and sisters, were called to freedom. However, do not use this freedom as an opportunity for the flesh. Rather, in love act as slaves toward one another. 14For the whole law ⌜is fulfilled⌝ in this one command: "Love your neighbor as yourself." 15But if you bite and devour one another, be careful that you are not destroyed by one another."

5:13 The γάρ (*gar*, for) that introduces this verse is often given its normal causal or explanatory sense (so most English versions imply by translating "for"). It is thought that verse 13 provides the basis for verse 12 (Burton 1921: 291) or for verses 1–12 (Schlier 1989: 241) or for verses 2–10 (Hays 2000: 320). But none of these connections makes very good sense. It is far better, then, to understand the γάρ as simply introducing the next stage in the argument (hence untranslated in the NIV and CEB; see Betz 1979: 272; this function of γάρ is well attested [Zerwick 1963: §47]). The opening statement of the verse, ὑμεῖς γὰρ ἐπ᾽ ἐλευθερίᾳ ἐκλήθητε, ἀδελφοί (*hymeis gar ep᾽ eleutheria eklēthēte, adelphoi*, now you were called to freedom, brothers and sisters),[1] picks up the important capstone summary of the Hagar and Sarah allegory from 5:1: Τῇ ἐλευθερίᾳ ἡμᾶς Χριστὸς ἠλευθέρωσεν (*Tē eleutheria hēmas Christos ēleutherōsen*, It is for

1. The verb ἐκλήθητε (from καλέω, *kaleō*) refers to God's effectual "call" to sinners to enter into relationship with himself (see 1:6, 15; 5:8; it functions as a divine passive, with God as the implicit agent). As with the dative in v. 1 (τῇ ἐλευθερίᾳ, *tē eleutheria*, for freedom), ἐπ᾽ (from ἐπί, *epi*) in this verse probably has the sense of result or purpose (BDAG 366.16; BDF §235.4; "movement ending in a definite spot" [Moule 1959: 53]).

freedom that Christ has set us free). Paul uses the theme of freedom effectively to create a transition into the ethical concerns that dominate 5:13–6:10. For freedom, as we know from our day, can mean very different things to different people. In the context of this letter, freedom means liberation from the powers of the old age: sin, the "elements of the world," false gods, and especially the law (cf. 3:22–25; 4:3, 8–9, 24–31; cf. Beker 1980: 269–71). What freedom is emphatically *not*, either here or elsewhere in Scripture, is that autonomy, the "free to be and do whatever we want" attitude, which governs much modern thinking. The freedom that Christ has won for us (v. 1) and to which we have been called by God (v. 13) is a freedom to be what God originally made us to be. And as Paul will explain, God has called his people to live in loving, sacrificial service with one another.

But before Paul makes this positive point, he issues a warning: "However, do not use this freedom as an opportunity for the flesh" (μόνον μὴ τὴν ἐλευθερίαν εἰς ἀφορμὴν τῇ σαρκί, *monon mē tēn eleutherian eis aphormēn tē sarki*). The adverb μόνον functions here as an adversative conjunction (see also Phil. 1:27; 2 Thess. 2:7) and, as elsewhere (1 Cor. 7:39; Gal. 2:10; 6:12), the verb is elided (BDF §481 suggests ἔχετε [*echete*, you have], which could be translated with the common English rendering here of "use" [verb]). "On this word, as on a hinge, the thought of the epistle turns from freedom to . . . the danger of abusing freedom" (Burton 1921: 291). The freedom that Paul has been talking about (the article with ἐλευθερίαν is anaphoric) must not become an "occasion" (ἀφορμήν) for the flesh—that is, "a base or circumstance from which other action becomes possible" (BDAG 158) for the flesh.[2]

"Flesh" translates σάρξ (*sarx*), one of the most challenging words in Paul's theological vocabulary. This is not the place to enter into the extensive discussions and debates about the religious milieu from which Paul has drawn the word or the nuance the word takes on in its various occurrences.[3] Yet in brief, Paul's uses of the word may be tracked on a spectrum from the physical/neutral to the spiritual/negative. On the physical/neutral end of the spectrum are places where the word refers to the soft tissues of the human body (1 Cor. 15:39; with specific reference to circumcision in Rom. 2:28; Gal. 6:12, 13; Eph. 2:11; Phil. 3:3, 4 [?]; Col. 2:13) or to the human body as a whole (1 Cor. 5:5 [?]; 6:16; 2 Cor. 7:1; 12:7; Gal. 4:13; Eph. 5:31). From this usage, and in accordance with the OT use of בָּשָׂר (*bāśār*, flesh) in this sense, σάρξ then is broadened to refer to the human being as a whole (e.g., Gal. 2:16: "no human

---

2. The word ἀφορμή (*aphormē*) is sometimes used to denote the resources necessary to carry out a military expedition (BDAG 158), and Martyn (1997: 485; cf. also Hays 2000: 321) thinks the word may here have this connotation, for he argues that the entire context pictures an apocalyptic war between the Spirit and the flesh. But there are probably not enough distinctly military words or metaphors to justify this way of reading the passage, and Paul's other uses of ἀφορμή (Rom. 7:8, 11; 2 Cor. 5:12; 11:12 [2x]; 1 Tim. 5:14) do not suggest military imagery.

3. For some orientation to this discussion, see, e.g., Sand 1967; Brandenburger 1968; Stacey 1956: 154–73; Jewett 1971: 49–94; E. Schweizer, *TDNT* 7:99–124; Ridderbos 1975: 64–68, 93–95; Bultmann 1951: 239–46; Dunn 1998: 62–73; Russell 1997; Scornaienchi 2008.

being"; sometimes with αἷμα [*haima*, blood], as in Gal. 1:16; 1 Cor. 15:50). This usage then morphs subtly into another, where the reference is to the general condition of being human, but without regard for sin. Paul can therefore speak of Jesus having come "in the σάρξ" or of being "according to the σάρξ" or of having σάρξ (e.g., Rom. 1:3; 8:3; 9:5; Eph. 2:15; 1 Tim. 3:16). Even in these references, however, σάρξ carries a hint of limitation, of a concept that does not tell the whole story: thus, for instance, to recognize that Jesus has taken on flesh without at the same time recognizing that he has also become the powerful Son of God in the realm of the Spirit (Rom. 1:4) or indeed "God over all, forever praised!" (Rom. 9:5) is to miss something essential about him (see esp. Dunn 1973 for this point). Thus the so-called neutral use of the word easily leads to the other end of the spectrum, where σάρξ denotes the limitations of the human condition that have been imposed by sin.

By a natural movement, σάρξ meaning "human beings distinct from God" comes to mean "human beings in opposition to God" (Laato 1991: 95; as Jewett [1971: 103] puts it, "Everything aside from God in which one places his final trust"). This is the sense that the word has in this part of Galatians (5:16, 17 [2x], 19, 24; 6:8). In each of these texts, σάρξ is placed in opposition to the Spirit, and their relationship is described in terms of a struggle between two powers (see 5:17 esp.). It is debated to what extent σάρξ in these verses takes on the notion of a power or realm.[4] This usage is clear in Rom. 7–8, where, for instance, Paul speaks of Christians as no longer being "in the flesh" (7:5; 8:8–9). But it is not clear that Paul has made that final step here in Galatians. The specialized and almost technical sense of σάρξ in Paul makes it slightly preferable to choose the simple translation "flesh" for the word in these contexts (so most versions; contra "sinful nature" in NIV 1984 [changed in NIV 2011] and NLT; "self-indulgence" in NJB; "selfish impulses" in CEB).[5]

Christian freedom can easily be abused and become a platform for all kinds of sinful behavior. As Martyn (1997: 485) puts it, "Because there is no such thing as an autonomously free will, 'freedom from' easily becomes nothing more than a transfer from one form of slavery to another." In fact, Christian freedom, Paul goes on to say, should lead to a particular Christian form of

---

4. The notion of σάρξ as demonic power—"Flesh" (capped) in opposition to Spirit—is emphasized especially by Martyn (1997: 526–36; see also Hays [2000: 321]: "a quasi-personified hostile power"). In these kinds of contexts, it is notoriously difficult to determine when personification has become personalization; when a picturesque way of speaking about the human propensity to sin has become a description of a more-than-human entity. Jewett (1971: 103) argues for two related perspectives: "On the one hand man's concrete bodily flesh constitutes the source of sensual desires, and on the other hand it acts independent of man to oppose the spirit" (and see also 114–15). Russell (1997) argues that σάρξ has a temporal/material sense in Galatians, with a focus on the law and its demand for circumcision as part of the old era, now ended in Christ.

5. This is a change in position from my earlier view (Moo 2003); and it should also be stressed that the claim that "flesh" should be preferred as the "literal" translation of σάρξ betrays an all-too-widespread fallacy about the way words work. The Greek word σάρξ has a spectrum of meanings, not all of which can be rendered by a single English word—as all modern translations recognize (none tries to translate all occurrences of σάρξ with "flesh").

slavery: "in love act as slaves toward one another" (διὰ τῆς ἀγάπης δουλεύετε ἀλλήλοις, *dia tēs agapēs douleuete allēlois*). We translate the present, durative δουλεύετε awkwardly with "act as a slave" to highlight the paradoxical point that Paul makes: as Luther famously put it, "A Christian is a perfectly free lord of all, subject to none. A Christian is a perfectly dutiful servant of all, subject to all" (*The Freedom of a Christian*; see Dillenberger 1961: 53).[6] Paul has painted slavery in very negative tones throughout the letter (4:1–7, 21–31; cf. 5:1), so his claim that Christians are to become like slaves to one another is quite striking. Two words that are important indicators of the direction this section takes are used here in 5:13: "love" (5:14, 22; conceptually elsewhere) and "one another" (vv. 15 [2x], 17, 26 [2x]; 6:2; nowhere else in Galatians). Love demands a reciprocal concern for others in the community that the pronoun ἀλλήλοις brings out. The διά that governs ἀγάπης is usually translated and interpreted as instrumental ("through" in most English versions). But "love" is not so much the means through which we serve others as the motivation for the service (R. Longenecker [1990: 241] refers to a "conditioning cause"). Love is both the reason why we serve others and the manner in which we serve others (perhaps this διά is best classified under the category "attendant circumstance" [for which see BDAG 224.3.c; and Harris 2012: 77–80] and best translated "in" [NIV, NLT]). "Love," as we noted earlier, was significantly introduced in 5:6 as the virtue through which faith finds its expression (some accordingly think the article with ἀγάπης refers back to this occurrence [Bruce 1982b: 240], but it is probably too far away; the article is often used with abstract nouns [Wallace 1996: 226–27]).

The reason (γάρ, *gar*, for) it is important for believers to act as slaves toward one another in love is because love fulfills the law. Or, to stick more closely to Paul's actual wording, the love commandment from Lev. 19:18 fulfills the law: ὁ γὰρ πᾶς νόμος ἐν ἑνὶ λόγῳ πεπλήρωται, ἐν τῷ· ἀγαπήσεις τὸν πλησίον σου ὡς σεαυτόν (*ho gar pas nomos en heni logō peplērōtai, en tō: agapēseis ton plēsion sou hōs seauton*, for the whole law is fulfilled in this one command: "Love your neighbor as yourself"). The word λόγος has a general sense, "a communication whereby the mind finds expression" (BDAG 599.1), and refers to all kinds of specific types of communications. Here it refers to a "command" (thus NIV, NLT; "commandment" in NRSV, NET).[7] The command

5:14

---

6. The NRSV translates "become slaves" (and see also Hays 2000: 321), but the present tense of the imperative makes it more likely that the command is to continually act as a slave toward others rather than entering into the condition of slavery (for which the aorist might have been more appropriate).

7. Hays (2000: 324) argues, however, that Paul uses λόγος (*logos*, word/command) to refer to the promise of Christ that the Spirit would enable love for the other. In the OT, the "Ten Commandments" are called "words" (Exod. 20:1; 34:28; Deut 10:4; in each case, Hebrew: הַדְּבָרִים, *haddĕbārîm*; LXX: λόγους, *logous*); and see also Philo, *Heir* 168; *Decalogue* 32; Josephus, *Ant.* 3.138; and λόγος is used elsewhere in the NT to refer to commands: Luke 4:36; 2 Thess. 3:14; 2 Pet. 3:5, 7. The phrase ἐν τῷ immediately before the quotation picks up the earlier reference to ἐν ἑνὶ λόγῳ; the article goes with (introduces) the quotation (BDF §267.1): "The whole law

is an exact quotation from the LXX of Lev. 19:18 (which in turn faithfully renders the Hebrew). This command was singled out by Jesus as one of the two greatest commandments in the law (Matt. 22:39//Mark 12:31//Luke 10:27; cf. also Matt. 5:43; 19:19), and since Judaism gave no special attention to the command, it is undoubtedly the influence of Jesus's teaching that has led NT letter writers to highlight the command (Rom. 13:9; James 2:8; and see also the "new command" of John 13:34; 1 John 2:7, 8 [cf. 1 John 3:23; 4:21]; see esp. Dunn 1993a: 291 on this point). Paul therefore places himself firmly within the early Christian teaching, stemming from Jesus himself, that made love for "the neighbor / one another" central to the Christian life. In the OT, the "neighbor" is one's fellow Israelite (the עֵרַ, rēʿa), and Paul's emphasis on "one another" in both verses 13 and 15 could suggest that he intends also to restrict the scope of love in this instance to fellow believers (Witherington 1998: 384; de Boer 2011: 350). But the final verse in this larger section, which may serve with verses 13–14 as something of a bookend around this passage, urges believers to "do good to all people, especially to the family of faith" (6:10). Here the "doing good" that matches and fleshes out love is extended to everyone. And this more universal interpretation of "neighbor" in this text is all the more likely if, as seems likely, Paul is aware of Jesus's expansion of the meaning of "neighbor" (Luke 10:25–37; and see Calvin 1854: 109).

Paul's main purpose in this verse is clear enough: to encourage the kind of selfless, loving service to others that he has called for in verse 13. What is not clear is how the love command "fulfills the whole law." As we have noted in the introduction to 5:13–6:10, a concern with the way Christian love and the life of the Spirit relate to the law is a recurring motif (see also 5:18, 23; 6:2). And we further suggested that Paul carries over this focus on the law from earlier in the letter because he needs to assure the Galatians that the Christian life as Paul understands it is fully able to provide that conformity to the will of God that the agitators were apparently claiming could be found only by submission to the law of God. But what specifically is Paul saying here about the relationship of the love command to the law? Two matters require comment.

First, what does Paul mean by ὁ πᾶς νόμος? In verse 3, Paul uses a similar phrase, insisting that the man who receives circumcision is obliged to obey "the whole law" (ὅλον τὸν νόμον, *holon ton nomon*). A few interpreters argue that the two phrases refer to different conceptions of the law, but this reads far too much into the shift in wording. The particular phrasing that Paul uses may put some emphasis on the "wholeness" of the law (BDF §275.7; and see the second additional note on 5:14), but the difference from the phrase in verse 3 is slight—if indeed there is any difference at all.[8]

---

is fulfilled in this one command: that is, in the 'You shall love your neighbor as yourself' command." It is unlikely that "word" refers to Scripture generally (contra de Boer 2011: 342–50).

8. Hübner (1984: 36–37; cf. 1975) has argued the strongest (and strangest!) version of this view, insisting that v. 14 can only be reconciled with v. 3 and with Paul's teaching about the law elsewhere in Galatians if ὁ πᾶς νόμος is interpreted as an ironical comment on the Jewish insistence on doing all the law. Hübner's view rests on a misinterpretation of both v. 3 (he thinks

The second matter of significance for the meaning of this clause is πεπλήρωται. This perfect passive form is from a verb that is widely and importantly used in the NT to denote the "fulfillment" of the OT in Christ (in addition to the many occurrences in formulas introducing a quotation, see esp. Matt. 5:17; Mark 1:15; Luke 24:44; Rom. 8:4; 13:8). Many interpreters argue that the verb is a rough synonym for other words that Paul uses to speak about "doing" the law (e.g., ποιέω [poieō, do; Gal. 3:10; 5:3], πράσσω [prassō, practice; Rom. 2:25]). This text may then teach that Christians are to "do" the law by obeying the love command (the law is "reduced" to this one command; see, e.g., Räisänen 1983: 26–28; Thielman 1994: 140) or to keep the law truly by making love preeminent in their broader "doing" of the law (George 1994: 379–81).[9] But the distinctive theological significance of this verb in the NT suggests that it is not referring simply to obedience to the law, but to an eschatological completion of the law. This word, or its cognates, has this salvation-historical sense in the other texts where Paul speaks of "fulfilling" the law (Rom. 8:4; 13:8, 10 [πλήρωμα, plērōma]; Gal. 6:2 [ἀναπληρόω, anaplēroō]).[10] The passive form of the verb, in turn, suggests that the statement has a retrospective viewpoint: Paul is not enjoining obedience to the law; he is claiming that, in some sense, the love command results in the law's being fulfilled (see esp. Westerholm 1986 [summarized in 2004: 434–37]; cf. also Betz 1979: 275; Barclay 1988: 137–41; Witherington 1998: 381–83; Mussner 1988: 390; Hays 2000: 322).

How, then, is it "fulfilled"? To answer this question, we might better ask, "By whom is it fulfilled?" The implied agent of the passive verb is usually assumed to be the believer, and the reference to the "one command" is expanded to mean obeying that command; as Lightfoot (1881: 209) puts it, "ἐν ἑνὶ λόγῳ, 'in one maxim or precept,' means 'in the observance of one maxim or precept'" (cf. NIV: "in keeping this one command"). Christians bring the whole law to its conclusive and intended "end" by loving others (see, e.g., Mussner 1988: 370). This interpretation matches the way Paul uses similar language about the law in Rom. 13:8–10: "for whoever loves others has fulfilled [πεπλήρωκεν, peplērōken] the law" (v. 8); "therefore love is the fulfillment [πλήρωμα] of the law" (v. 10). The whole law aims at "doing good" to others, and if one loves

---

the "upshot" of the verse is that "one is *not to obey the whole law*," whereas Paul's point is that one should not undertake circumcision because one would then need to obey the whole law) and 5:14 (he mistakenly thinks the verse claims that "it is *incumbent on Christians to fulfill the whole law*" [emphasis in original]). For critiques of Hübner, see esp. Sanders 1983: 96–97. Other interpreters suggest that v. 14 refers to the spirit of the law, or the general principle in or behind the law (Bruce 1982b: 241; Martyn 1997: 502–14; Thurén 2000: 75–76), but these views likewise have inadequate linguistic basis (see the second additional note on 5:14) and seek to handle supposed contradictions that are not really present.

9. Several interpreters puzzlingly speak of this verse as enjoining obedience to the law (e.g., Schreiner 1993b: 38, 110). Those who advocate this general interpretation usually take the perfect to be a gnomic perfect, stating a general truth.

10. See Moo 1996: 482–84, 813–15; 1993: 359–60.

truly and consistently, all that the law is aiming at is also accomplished.[11] But another interpretation, one that sticks closer to the actual wording of the text, should also be considered. On this view, the implied agent of the passive verb is Jesus Christ, who "fulfills" the whole law in his teaching by highlighting love for the neighbor as the true and ultimate completion, or "filling up," of the law—and in his life by going to the cross as the ultimate embodiment and pattern of sacrificial love (see esp. Hays 2000: 322–24; also Martyn 1997: 480–90; Eastman 2007: 173; Suh 2012).[12] The fact that Paul refers to the "law of Christ" later in this section (6:2) would fit well with this focus on Christ's own teaching; and this interpretation would also dovetail nicely with the claim Jesus makes in Matt. 5:17 about the "fulfillment" of "the law and the prophets."[13]

Each of these interpretations does justice to πεπλήρωται, the wording of the text, and the context. But we think the latter interpretation has slightly more to be said for it in this context. In keeping with the central theme of the letter, Paul once again emphasizes that Christ has inaugurated a new era, an era in which "observing the law" takes on a new, christological form. The Galatians are to serve one another "in love" precisely because love is the true meaning and "fulfillment" of the law in this new era. Paul's wider concern is to assure the Galatians that their new life in Christ does indeed provide them with the direction (love) and power (Spirit) that they need to live godly lives.[14] Indeed, it is only with the coming of Christ and the gift of his Spirit that true "completion" of the law has become possible. But that completion does not take the form of obedience to the many commands of the law. Rather, it happens as Christians love others—with a love possible only for those who are in Christ and walk according to the Spirit.[15]

5:15 Paul now contrasts (adversative δέ [*de*, but]) the love for others that he has urged in verse 13 with the opposite kind of behavior: "If you bite and devour one another, be careful that you are not destroyed by one another." The verse is a conditional sentence with the apodosis (or "then" clause) taking the form of a warning. (βλέπετε [*blepete*] in these contexts means "watch" or "beware of" [BDAG 179.5], while μή [*mē*, not] introduces a negative purpose clause.)

---

11. As is his habit, Paul focuses on the law in its "horizontal" dimension, on its demands for our relationship with other human beings (see also Rom. 13:8–10).

12. On this view, the perfect may (but need not have) the sense of a past act (Christ's teaching) with enduring results (Hays 2000: 322–23). This view is similar to those who argue that πεπλήρωκεν has a meaning similar to ἀνεκεφαλαιοῦται (*anekephaloioutai*) in Rom. 13:9: the whole law is "summed up" (NRSV, NLT, NET) in the love command (Furnish 1973: 97; Dunn 1993a: 289).

13. Elsewhere we argue that in Matt. 5:17 Jesus is claiming that his own teaching brings the OT law to its intended eschatological completion (Moo 1984: 17–28).

14. Wilson (2007: 105–12, 116) argues that Christians are enabled by the Spirit to fulfill the law and thereby escape the curse of the law. But we think that this view underplays the determinative significance of Jesus's death as the means by which the curse is removed from all who belong to him (3:13).

15. On the question of whether Paul leaves open a continuing authority for the Mosaic law in directing Christian conduct, see the additional note on 6:2.

Most interpreters, since at least Chrysostom (*Comm. Gal.* on 5:15 [*NPNF*[1] 13:40]), argue that Paul is here using the imagery of animals biting and then devouring one another: "The comparison describes mad beasts fighting each other so ferociously that they end up killing each other" (Betz 1979: 277). The key words, to be sure, do not point all that clearly to such imagery. The first verb in the protasis, δάκνω (*daknō*, bite), is mostly used of the bite of snakes (see BDAG 211.1), not animals, while the second, κατεσθίω (*katesthiō*, consume), is widely used in Biblical Greek for destruction caused by all manner of things (to be sure, including animals: e.g., Gen. 37:20; 41:20; Rev. 12:4). The verb in the apodosis, ἀναλίσκω (*analiskō*), means "destroy," and is most often applied to the results of fire (Joel 1:19; 2:3; Ezek. 15:4, 5; 19:12; 2 Macc. 1:31; 2:10, 11; Luke 9:54; only Prov. 30:14 in Biblical Greek uses the verb with animals). Nevertheless, an allusion to animal behavior probably makes the best sense of the progression in the verse. Only by positing a difference between κατεσθίετε in the protasis and ἀναλωθῆτε (*analōthēte*, are destroyed) in the apodosis does Paul's warning in the last part of the verse make sense. The former verb may mean, then, "tear to pieces," Paul using animal behavior to picture partisan strife (BDAG 532.2.d). Bickering and infighting among believers, Paul warns, can lead to destruction—presumably the destruction of the health and witness of the Christian community (Fee 2007a: 206).

Most interpreters also think that the form of the protasis, using εἰ (*ei*, if) with present-tense verbs, shows that Paul knows of this kind of internecine strife already occurring in the Galatian churches—perhaps because the Galatians are deeply divided over the agitators and their message (e.g., Burton 1921: 297; Bruce 1982b: 242). However, this is not immediately clear (Betz 1979: 277; Dunn 1993a: 293). The grammar certainly does not require this interpretation. The use of εἰ with indicative in a protasis does not indicate that the condition is real, only that it is being presented as if it were real. And the present tense in such clauses does not necessarily have the force of continuing an action already engaged in—"keep on biting and devouring"—but more generally of a continuous action: "if you are always biting and devouring one another" (NLT). This being said, we must also ask the contextual question: why does Paul bring up this matter here? And the best answer to this question might be, indeed, that he knows of such a problem within the Galatian churches. This conclusion receives support from the way Paul focuses on sins that involve dissensions in his list of "the works of the flesh" in verses 19–21 (see esp. "dissensions" and "factions" at the end of v. 20).

Additional Notes

5:14. Highlighting specific commandments as particularly significant within the law takes place in various Jewish traditions as well (Str-B 1:907–8). Perhaps the most famous comes from *b. Šabb.* 31a:

> On another occasion it happened that a certain heathen came before Shammai and said to him, "Make me a proselyte, on condition that you teach me the whole Torah while I stand on one foot." Thereupon he repulsed him with the builder's cubit that was in his hand. When he went before Hillel, he said to him,

"What is hateful to you, do not to your neighbor: that is the whole Torah, while the rest is the commentary thereof; go and learn it."

Hillel does not cite Lev. 19:18, but Tg. Ps.-J. on Lev. 19:18 includes Hillel's "negative golden rule" as found in this passage (R. Longenecker 1990: 243–44). What is important to note, however, is that the Jewish traditions involve identification of commands that are particularly important within the law or those from which other commands can be deduced; no idea of "reducing" the law or "replacing" laws with a single command is countenanced (Urbach 1979: 349). This more technical focus on the essence or center of the law seems quite far from Paul's conception of fulfillment (contra, e.g., Schnabel 1995: 272).

5:14. Paul frequently uses the sequence πᾶς + article + substantive (over thirty times in the singular and forty times in the plural; the other predicative sequence, article + substantive + πᾶς, occurs six times). But the sequence we find in Gal. 5:14, article + πᾶς/ἅπας + substantive occurs in only two other verses in Paul (2 Cor. 5:10: τοὺς γὰρ πάντας ἡμᾶς φανερωθῆναι δεῖ ἔμπροσθεν τοῦ βήματος τοῦ Χριστοῦ; 1 Tim. 1:16: ἀλλὰ διὰ τοῦτο ἠλεήθην, ἵνα ἐν ἐμοὶ πρώτῳ ἐνδείξηται Χριστὸς Ἰησοῦς τὴν ἅπασαν μακροθυμίαν πρὸς ὑποτύπωσιν τῶν μελλόντων πιστεύειν ἐπ᾽ αὐτῷ εἰς ζωὴν αἰώνιον). A pattern similar to the NT emerges in the LXX with the same words as in Gal. 5:14, but in the sequence πᾶς + article + νόμος, which occurs seven times in the LXX (Lev. 19:37 [2x]; Num. 5:30; Deut. 4:8; 24:8; 27:8; 2 Kings 23:25); yet the sequence article + πᾶς + νόμος is not found. Why Paul has chosen such an unusual sequence of words is not clear. Most grammars argue that the unusual attributive pattern emphasizes the "wholeness," contrasting the whole with the parts (Turner 1963: 200–201; BDF §275.7), and this view is taken up in most of the commentaries. However, the distinction between ὁ πᾶς νόμος and πᾶς ὁ νόμος should probably not be pressed. And in this case, a linguistic basis for distinguishing vv. 3 and 14 disappears, for there seems to be no substantive difference in Paul between ὅλος + article + substantive and πᾶς + article + substantive (compare ὅλῳ τῷ κόσμῳ in Rom. 1:8 with πᾶς ὁ κόσμος in Rom. 3:19, and ὅλον τὸ σῶμα in 1 Cor. 12:17 with πᾶν τὸ σῶμα in Eph. 4:16).

5:14. A number of MSS, including 𝔐, have the present tense πληροῦται in place of the perfect πεπλήρωται, while a few other MSS, in obvious assimilation to Rom. 13:9, have ἀνακεφαλαιοῦται. If the present tense were read, it would give more credence to the view that sees a reference to believers' fulfilling the law. But it has too little support to be the original reading.

B. Implementing the New Life: Walking by the Spirit (5:16–24)

In verse 13 Paul warns of the danger of giving any toehold to the flesh, that orientation toward this world that exerts a continuing influence on believers and must be resisted. In this new section, Paul continues to talk about the flesh and its dangers. But as the keynote of the section, the opposing power of the Spirit is brought onto the scene. Paul's purpose is both to warn and to assure believers. He warns them that Christians find themselves in the midst of a continuing battle between these two powers (see esp. vv. 17, 21). But, more importantly, he assures believers that, because we are in Christ (v. 24), the Spirit is now the dominant power and provides the believer with victory over the flesh (vv. 16, 24) and release from any threat that the law may pose (vv. 18, 23b). This last point reveals again the continuing concern to counter the agitators' claim that submission to the law is necessary in order to resist and overcome the influence of the flesh (Hays 2000: 325; Fee 2007a: 201–2). In this section, the focus on the Spirit elaborates important allusions to the significance of the Spirit earlier in the letter. Paul now goes into detail about the Spirit's role in enabling believers to finish what they have begun (3:3), providing for the ultimate verdict of righteousness (5:5; stated negatively in our paragraph: "those who do [the works of the flesh] will not inherit the kingdom of God" [v. 21b]). And the Spirit whom Paul now celebrates as the power of the new life is nothing other than that Spirit whom the prophets predicted would take possession of God's people in the eschatological age, providing for that wholehearted obedience to the Lord that the law could not secure ("the promise of the Spirit" in 3:14; see, e.g., Jer. 31:31–34; Ezek. 36:24–28; Joel 2:28–32).

The passage falls into three paragraphs (e.g., Schreiner 2010: 339). Verses 16–18 are framed by references to "walking" and "being led" by the Spirit and focus on the power of the Spirit to overcome the flesh and the law. Verse 16, with its promise that those who walk by the Spirit will overcome the flesh, is the theme verse for all that follows. The second paragraph of the section contrasts the effects of the flesh with those of the Spirit (vv. 19–23). Verse 24 concludes the section with a final assurance that the people who belong to Christ have been given a new freedom from the power of the flesh. As Dunn (1993a: 295) points out, the section also displays something of a concentric structure:

> A Assurance about the flesh (vv. 16–17)
>   B Those led by the Spirit are not under the law (v. 18)

> C The "works" of the flesh (vv. 19–21)
> C′ The fruit of the Spirit (vv. 22–23a)
> B′ No law stands against the fruit of the Spirit (v. 23b)
> A′ Assurance about the flesh (v. 24)

After beginning with an imperative, "walk by the Spirit," Paul uses indicative verbs in the rest of this section. This mixture of imperative and indicative is typical of Paul's paraenesis. He is, of course, not shy about prescribing the behavior that should characterize those who know Christ. But he is especially intent on describing the new reality that has dawned with Christ: everyone who belongs to Christ is taken up into that new reality. Such descriptions remind us of who we are but also are identity-forming concepts in their own right—and importantly, community-forming teachings as well. For the focus in this section, emerging especially clearly from the works of the flesh and the fruit of the Spirit that Paul chooses to mention, continues to be very much on relationships among believers.

Exegesis and Exposition

¹⁶So I say, walk by the Spirit, and you will not gratify the desire of the flesh. ¹⁷For the flesh desires what is contrary to the Spirit, and the Spirit what is contrary to the flesh. ⌜For⌝ these are in conflict with each other, so that you do not do whatever you want. ¹⁸But if you are led by the Spirit, you are not under the law.

¹⁹The works of the flesh are obvious, which are: ⌜sexual immorality⌝, impurity, debauchery, ²⁰idolatry, sorcery, enmities, ⌜discord⌝, ⌜jealousy⌝, fits of rage, rivalries, dissensions, divisions, ²¹⌜envy⌝, drunkenness, orgies, and things like these. As I told you before, I say again: those who do such things will not inherit the kingdom of God. ²²But the fruit of the Spirit is love, joy, peace, patience, kindness, goodness, faithfulness, ²³gentleness, self-control. Against such things there is no law.

²⁴Those who belong to Christ ⌜Jesus⌝ have crucified the flesh with its passions and desires.

5:16   The introductory λέγω δέ (legō de, now I say) suggests that the following section elaborates an earlier point in a new direction (Oepke 1973: 173; see 1 Cor. 1:12; 7:8; Gal. 4:1). As we suggested, this earlier point is the warning about the influence of the flesh in verse 13. To counter this influence, Paul now brings onto the stage, front and center, the Spirit. "Walk by the Spirit, and you will not carry out the desire of the flesh" (πνεύματι περιπατεῖτε καὶ ἐπιθυμίαν σαρκὸς οὐ μὴ τελέσητε, pneumati peripateite kai epithymian sarkos ou mē telesēte). As R. Longenecker (1990: 244) points out, this command is the theme of the whole larger section that follows: it is elaborated in verses 17–24, restated in verse 25, and applied to the Galatians in 5:26–6:10. The use of the verb "walk" (περιπατέω, peripateō) to depict Christian conduct is common in the NT (thirty times in Paul), although this is its only occurrence in Galatians. The NT usage reflects the common use of the Hebrew הָלַךְ (hālak, walk) in this way, depicting a way of life as a particular way or road to be followed. See, for example, Exod. 18:20: "and you shall warn them about the statutes and the laws, and make them know the way in which they must walk [Heb. הלך; LXX πορεύομαι, *poreuomai*, go] and what they must do" (ESV).[1] (This way of speaking is also common in rabbinic literature.) The present tense of the verb probably connotes continuous action: "be always walking by the Spirit," "be a person characterized by walking by the Spirit." The imperative περιπατεῖτε is qualified by the dative πνεύματι, which comes first in the clause, probably for emphasis. This dative is one of those many that defy simple classification. The use of "by" to translate the idea in most English versions could suggest a dative of agency or instrumental dative (Wallace 1996: 166), but the Spirit is not simply the "means" by which we "walk"; as the "fruit of the Spirit" illustrates, the Spirit also gives direction to that walk (Mussner [1988: 375] therefore suggests a dative of manner; Russell [1997: 126–30] labels it a dative of "rule or direction"). The "walk" of the believer is determined by the Spirit, who both directs and empowers Christian living. Probably, then, the dative construction has a sense similar to other constructions that Paul uses with this verb.[2]

The second part of the verse indicates the result that will follow from walking by the Spirit: one will not "gratify the desire of the flesh" (RSV and NRSV take this clause as a second imperative, but it is almost certainly a result clause). "Gratify" (NIV, ESV, NRSV, NAB) is an appropriate contextual translation of τελέσητε, from τελέω (*teleō*), "complete" or "accomplish" (in Paul elsewhere: Rom. 2:27; 13:6; 2 Cor. 12:9; 2 Tim. 4:7). The word "desire" (ἐπιθυμία) can have a neutral sense (Phil. 1:23; 1 Thess. 2:17), but usually in the NT, as here, it refers to sinful passion or desire (see the plural of this word in v. 24). The somewhat unexpected singular ἐπιθυμίαν focuses attention on the single basic direction that characterizes the "desire" or "intent" of the flesh (probably a subjective genitive; see NLT "what your sinful nature craves"). The singular may also reflect the widespread Jewish conception of the *yēṣer hāraʿ*, the "impulse to evil" that wars with the *yēṣer haṭṭôb*, "the impulse to good" within human beings (Hays 2000: 326). Philo (*Migr.* 92), as Bruce points out (1982b: 243), describes circumcision as the "cutting off of pleasure and all passion," and it is possible that the agitators were putting forth circumcision as the means by which sinful passion could be overcome. In contrast, Paul insists that it is the Spirit, the Spirit of the new age inaugurated by Christ, who overcomes all sinful passion.

The introductory γάρ (*gar*, for) suggests that verse 17 explains or provides some kind of basis for the promise that people who walk by the Spirit will not be

5:17

---

1. Dunn (1993a: 295) thinks that Paul may be making a deliberate play on such OT texts: the Spirit, not the law, now governs the "walk" of God's people.

2. Other constructions use περιπατέω (walk) with κατά ("*according to* the Spirit" [Rom. 8:4]; "*according to* the tradition" [2 Thess. 3:6 NRSV]) and with ἐν ("*in* newness of life" [Rom. 6:4 NRSV]; "*in* them [good works]" [Eph. 2:10]; "*in* . . . love" [Eph. 5:2]; "*in* him [Christ Jesus the Lord]" [Col. 2:6]; "*in* wisdom" [Col. 4:5 KJV]).

enslaved to sinful passion. Just how verse 17 grounds verse 16 depends, however, on the difficult decision about how to interpret the overall thrust of this verse. Four clauses make up the verse. The first two are parallel coordinate clauses affirming that "desires" of the flesh are antithetical to desires of the Spirit. The third summarizes this conflict, while the fourth is either a final (purpose) clause or a result clause that refers to the frustration of human wishing.

The unusual combination of the verb ἐπιθυμεῖ (*epithymei*, desires) plus the preposition κατά (*kata*, against)—which occurs only here in Biblical Greek—reflects Paul's intent to carry over the language of verse 16 (ἐπιθυμίαν) into this verse. While awkward, the sense is clear enough in both Greek and English: the intent/purpose of the flesh is contrary to the intent/purpose of the Spirit. The verb ἐπιθυμεῖ is probably to be carried over into the second clause (e.g., Dunn 1993a: 297; contra Lightfoot 1881: 210), where Paul makes the same point from the perspective of the Spirit. Paul makes a similar point about the conflict between Spirit and flesh in Rom. 8:5–6: "Those who live according to the flesh have their minds set on what the flesh desires; but those who live in accordance with the Spirit have their minds set on what the Spirit desires. The mind governed by the flesh is death, but the mind governed by the Spirit is life and peace." In contrast to the anthropological element in this passage, however, verse 17 is framed as a conflict between two powers, a conflict in which human beings are caught up. The conflict is not between tendencies/natures within human beings (although "flesh" cannot be entirely cut loose from anthropology); it is a conflict between God's Spirit and the impulse to sin, an impulse that no longer rules in the believer but still exerts influence that must be resisted. Paul brings to our attention the fundamental spiritual battle that Christians must be aware of so that we will take with the utmost seriousness Paul's command that we "walk by the Spirit."

The third clause summarizes the situation that Paul has described in the first two clauses: ταῦτα γὰρ ἀλλήλοις ἀντίκειται (*tauta gar allēlois antikeitai*, for these are opposed to one another). The γάρ (*gar*, for) introducing it may be causal: the flesh desires what is contrary to the Spirit, and the Spirit desires what is contrary to the flesh, *because* they are opposed to one another. But it is also possible that the γάρ loses its causal sense and simply marks the beginning of a new sentence, or even an inference from the previous two clauses: the flesh desires what is contrary to the Spirit and the Spirit what is contrary to the flesh; *so [we see that]* they are opposed to one another (see BDAG 189.2 and LN 811.91.1 for these meanings of γάρ generally).

The crux of the difficulty in this verse comes in the final clause: ἵνα μὴ ἃ ἐὰν θέλητε ταῦτα ποιῆτε (*hina mē ha ean thelēte tauta poiēte*). A relatively "literal" translation reads: "in order that / so that whatever you might want, these things you are not doing."[3] Two intertwined issues are particularly important: the meaning of ἵνα and the kind of "wishing" or "willing" intended

---

3. The relative pronoun ἅ is the object of θέλητε, while ταῦτα, referring back to this pronoun, is the object of ποιῆτε. The μή negates the main verb, ποιῆτε.

with the verb θέλητε. The conjunction ἵνα usually indicates purpose, "in order that," but it can sometimes denote result, or consequence ("with the result that"; see, e.g., Moule 1959: 142–43). The verb θέλητε, in turn, might refer to a "willing" to do what the Spirit desires, a "willing" to do what the flesh desires, or simply to "willing" that remains under the control of humans. As Barclay (1988: 113–14) notes, decisions about these two issues combine to generate three general directions of interpretation:

1. The willing could be willing to do what the Spirit wants, with ἵνα indicating result: the Spirit and the flesh are so opposed to each other that you are not able to do the good that you wish to do (e.g., Augustine; see Plumer 2003: 209; Calvin 1854: 143; Ridderbos 1953: 203–4; Morris 1996: 169; George 1994: 387–88).[4] The NLT reflects this interpretation: "The sinful nature wants to do evil, which is just the opposite of what the Spirit wants. And the Spirit gives us desires that are the opposite of what the sinful nature desires. These two forces are constantly fighting each other, so you are not free to carry out your good intentions." Advocates of this view sometimes appeal to Rom. 7:14–25 as a parallel passage in which Paul bemoans his failure, as a Christian, to do the good that, at one level, he really wants to do. The interpretation of this passage in Romans, however, is too uncertain to render this parallel very helpful; moreover, even if Rom. 7 is referring to Christian experience (which we doubt; see Moo 1996: 442–51), the absence of any reference to the Spirit renders it a very imperfect parallel to Gal. 5:17. There are two other main problems with this view. First, one must wonder why Paul would choose the indefinite construction ἐὰν θέλητε to denote "the good things the Christian wants to do." Second, while not as serious an objection as some have made it, the fit between a negative statement in verse 17 as a ground for the positive promise in verse 16 is not good (e.g., Barclay 1988: 112; Witherington 1998: 394).

2. The willing could be a willing to follow the flesh. On this view, the ἵνα could express purpose: the Spirit opposes the intention of the flesh with the purpose that you not do the fleshly things that you are still tempted to do (Chrysostom ad loc.; Witherington 1998: 395). It is also possible to take ἵνα as indicating result and give the main verb an imperatival thrust: "so that you are not to do whatever you want" (NIV); that is, "you are not to do whatever your flesh might be prompting you to do (Fee 1994: 436; 2007a: 209–10; de Boer 2011: 354–55). On this view, while Paul has given the flesh and the Spirit equal billing in the first part of the verse, the implicit subject of the final clause is the Spirit. This view provides a better grounding for verse 16, but suffers from one minor and one major problem. The minor problem is again the reason why Paul has used the indefinite ἐὰν θέλητε. In this case, however, it could perhaps be argued that "whatever you want" suggests a kind of unbridled, uncontrolled willing that could fit with a reference to evil behavior.

---

4. Lutjens (1990) supports this general view, arguing that the final clause depends on the first clause, while the second and third clauses form a parenthesis that emphasizes the power of the Spirit to overcome the flesh.

The major problem is why, granted the precisely equal attention that Paul has given to the flesh and the Spirit earlier in the verse, the implied subject of the last clause should be the Spirit.

3. The willing could be an autonomous willing (both good and evil), with ἵνα being consecutive: the flesh and the Spirit are fighting each other, and their power and influence determine the direction of one's life; as a result, you cannot do what you yourselves want (but only what the flesh or the Spirit wants). This is probably the most popular interpretation among modern scholars (see, e.g., Barclay 1988: 113–14; Dunn 1993a: 299; Engberg-Pedersen 2000: 162–63; Mussner 1988: 377–78; R. Longenecker 1990: 246 [who, however, takes the ἵνα as final]). In this case the emphasis is on the transpersonal power of the flesh and the Spirit as those entities that exert control over the Christian. Believers lose any autonomy because of the influences of these opposing forces, preventing them from doing "whatever" they might want. Only by allowing the Spirit to take control, then, can the believer experience victory in this battle. This view has the advantage of doing justice to the equivalent place that Paul gives to both the flesh and the Spirit; and it explains the indefinite ἐὰν θέλητε. It also suffers from two main problems: Would Paul want to go so far as to say that believers can do nothing they want to do? And does this assertion of the frustration of all human willing adequately support the promise of verse 16?

None of these views can claim to explain all the difficulties in this verse. On the whole, and reluctantly, we think the third has perhaps the fewest problems. Paul insists that the new position of believers, "in Christ" and controlled by the Spirit, has put them into an entirely new relationship to flesh and to sin, a relationship that will be manifested in and vindicated by the fruit of the Spirit in that person's life (5:24; Rom. 6:1–11; 8:9–11). But his purpose in this verse is to remind believers of the warfare between the powers that is ultimately determinative of this relationship. Christians should not think they have the choice to do "whatever they want"; whether conscious of it or not, their actions at every point are governed by either the flesh or the Spirit.

5:18 As suggested by the almost universal translation in English versions, "but," the δέ (*de*) that introduces this verse is adversative (Martyn 1997: 495; contra R. Longenecker 1990: 246). In contrast to what could be understood as an equal battle between the flesh and the Spirit (v. 17), Paul now stresses that the Spirit is the victor for the Christian. At the beginning of this short paragraph, Paul urged Christians to "walk by the Spirit" (v. 16). Now he speaks of their being "led by the Spirit" (πνεύματι ἄγεσθε, *pneumati agesthe*).[5] Paul speaks in the same manner about the influence of the Spirit in Rom. 8:14: "For those who are led by the Spirit of God [πνεύματι θεοῦ ἄγονται, *pneumati theou agontai*] are the children of God." In neither verse does "led by" mean what it sometimes does in popular Christian parlance: a specific "leading" of the Spirit to do something. The verb (in the present tense) suggests the idea of

---

5. The word πνεύματι is often taken as dative of agent. Wallace (1996: 163–66) objects, claiming that this sense of the dative is very rare. He prefers a dative of means.

being continually influenced by and directed by the Spirit.[6] As people outside of Christ can be "led" (ἤγεσθε, ēgesthe) by mute idols (1 Cor. 12:2)—that is, have their whole being determined by these false gods—so Christians are people who are under the influence of the Spirit.

Paul does not simply assert that Christians are led by the Spirit. Using a form that presents the matter as "true for the sake of argument" (εἰ [ei, if] + indicative), Paul claims that those who are led by the Spirit "are not under the law" (οὐκ ἐστὲ ὑπὸ νόμον [ouk este hypo nomon]). The "law," as almost always in Galatians, refers to the law of Moses; and the phrase "under the law" is one that Paul has used earlier (3:23; 4:4, 5, 21). Some interpreters think that here Paul refers to the fact that Spirit-led believers are set free from the condemnation on sin pronounced by the law (e.g., Ridderbos 1975: 282–83; Wilson 2007: 117–20). But, as we have argued elsewhere (see esp. the additional note on 3:23), the phrase "under the law" is better understood as connoting "subject to the rule of the law." Christ was himself, as a member of the people of Israel, born "under the law" (4:4); and he was sent to redeem "those under the law" (4:5; see 3:23). The Galatians, as Gentiles not naturally "under the law," are being tempted by the agitators to subject themselves to that law (4:21). If "subject to the law" is what the phrase means here also, then Paul's point is that Christians, precisely because they are under the influence of the Spirit, are members of the new-covenant era in which the law of Moses no longer has binding authority (R. Longenecker 1990: 246; Schreiner 2010: 345).[7] The power of the Spirit means that there is no longer need for such a law (Engberg-Pedersen 2000: 163). Here, then, is another implicit appeal to the Galatians to reject the message of the agitators: "You are under the powerful influence and direction of God's Spirit, so why try to put yourself under the law?" At the same time, however, Paul is pursuing a theme that surfaces repeatedly in this part of the letter: the utter effectiveness of the Spirit to provide the power and ethical guidance that the agitators are claiming only the law can supply.

At the center of verses 16–24 are two contrasting lists: the "works of the flesh" (vv. 19–21) and "the fruit of the Spirit" (vv. 22–23). Paul emphasizes the parallelism between the lists by adding a concluding comment at the end of each.

5:19

"The works of the flesh"

List of fifteen of those "works"

"Those who do such things [τοιαῦτα, toiauta] will not inherit the kingdom of God."

---

6. In Luke 4:1, "led by the Spirit" (ἤγετο ἐν τῷ πνεύματι, ēgeto en tō pneumati), in the context of Jesus's experience of temptation in the wilderness, has a more physical element. Beale (2005) has argued that here Paul alludes to Isa. 63:11–15, a passage that speaks of the Lord's "leading" (ἄγω, agō) the people of Israel from Egypt as a parallel to his new leading of his people to deliverance (see also Harmon 2010: 222–25).

7. Dunn (1993a: 301) again suggests that there may be some allusion to the power of the law to keep Gentiles out of the kingdom of God.

"The fruit of the Spirit"

List of nine of those "fruits"

"Against such things [τοιούτων, *toioutōn*] there is no law."

To some extent these contrasting lists elaborate verse 17a–b: here are specifics about what the "flesh desires" and what "the Spirit desires." But more generally Paul simply provides specifics about the contrast between flesh and Spirit that dominates this paragraph. The δέ (*de*) that introduces verse 19 is resumptive, best translated "now" (NRSV, ESV, NET, HCSB, NAB, NASB) or left untranslated (NIV, CEB; see Burton 1921: 303; R. Longenecker 1990: 252).

Ancient authors often listed vices and virtues in these ways, and the form was taken up in the NT ("vice lists": Rom. 1:29–31; 1 Cor. 5:9–11; 6:9–10; Gal. 5:19–21; Eph. 4:31; 5:3–5; Col. 3:5; 1 Tim. 1:9–10; 6:4–5; 2 Tim. 3:2–4; Titus 1:7; 1 Pet. 4:3; Rev. 21:8; 22:15; and "virtue lists": Eph. 6:14–17; Phil. 4:8; Col. 3:12; 1 Tim. 3:2–3; 6:11; Titus 1:7–8; James 3:17; 2 Pet. 1:5–8; see the additional note on 5:19–23).

Paul notes that the "works of the flesh" (τὰ ἔργα τῆς σαρκός, *ta erga tēs sarkos*) are "manifest" or "obvious" (φανερά, *phanera*): they are well known to the Galatians from their pagan background. Paul reminds his readers about them so that they will have a clear-eyed understanding of just what the "passion of the flesh" that the Spirit will help them avoid looks like. Paul introduces the list with an indefinite relative pronoun (ἅτινα [*hatina*]: "which" in AT [cf. NASB]; it is left untranslated in most English versions). Paul probably uses the indefinite pronoun to signal that his list is far from exhaustive (Lightfoot 1881: 210). Why, then, has he chosen these particular manifestations of the flesh to mention? And is the sequence in which they are listed significant? One focus that emerges from the list is a concentration on sins that involve community relationships: the sixth ("hatred/enmities") through the thirteenth ("envy") all touch on relationships with others. This focus is in keeping with Paul's paraenesis throughout 5:13–6:10, which begins with the call to "serve one another in love" and ends with a plea to "do good to all, especially those in the household of the faith." Some interpreters argue that the sequence of sins follows a random pattern that matches the random and uncontrolled nature of the flesh (Betz 1979: 283; Martyn 1997: 498). But this ignores the obvious focus on sins involving relationships that we have just noted. Most interpreters divide the list into four parts: (1) three sins of sensuality ("sexual immorality, impurity, debauchery"); (2) two associated with pagan religions ("idolatry, sorcery"); (3) eight having to do with relationships ("hatred" through "envy"); (4) two involving dissipated living ("drunkenness, orgies"; e.g., Lightfoot 1881: 210; the NIV signals this division by interspersing commas and semicolons).[8]

---

8. Witherington (1998: 398–99) suggests a simpler, chiastic arrangement, with the first five items and the last two focusing on sins of the pagan past, and the middle eight items on community relations.

"Sexual immorality" (πορνεία, *porneia*) refers to sexual sins of any kind. The Greco-Roman world in which Paul was proclaiming the gospel was noted for considerable "openness" in sexual matters, and so he and the other early Christian evangelists specially emphasized that conversion means a fundamental new orientation to sexual habits. See, for example, 1 Thess. 4:3: "It is God's will that you should be sanctified: that you should avoid sexual immorality" (and also 1 Cor. 5:1; 6:13–18).

"Impurity" translates ἀκαθαρσία (*akatharsia*), a word that looks at sin from the standpoint of Jewish purity concerns (the Greek word can mean simply "uncleanness"; cf. 1 Macc. 13:48; 14:7; 3 Macc. 2:17; Matt. 23:27). The word can, then, denote any kind of sinful behavior (Rom. 6:19; 1 Thess. 4:7). But it occurs with other words for sexual sin in Paul's "vice lists": with πορνεία in Eph. 5:3 and Col. 3:5, and with both πορνεία and ἀσέλγεια (*aselgeia*) in 2 Cor. 12:21 (and in a context with ἀσέλγεια in Eph. 4:19; the related form πορνός [*pornos*], "immoral person," occurs with ἀκάθαρτος [*akathartos*], "unclean person," in Eph. 5:5). These associations suggest that the word connotes sexual misbehavior in general.

The third sin, ἀσέλγεια, is defined by BDAG (141) as "lack of self-constraint which involves one in conduct that violates all bounds of what is socially acceptable" (cf. Lightfoot [1881: 210]: "an open and reckless contempt of propriety"). In some Jewish texts (3 Macc. 2:26) as well as in the NT (Rom. 13:13; 1 Pet. 4:3), it is associated with wild living, the kind of lifestyle we would today associate with the "party animal" (see also Mark 7:22; Eph. 4:19; 2 Pet. 2:2, 7, 18; Jude 4).

The next two works of the flesh describe the pagan religions from which the Galatians have emerged. "Idolatry" (εἰδωλολατρία, *eidōlolatria*) is a general word for the worship of anything apart from the one true God. The word itself is rare (only four times in Biblical Greek: see also 1 Cor. 10:14; Col. 3:5; 1 Pet. 4:3), but the idea it connotes is very widespread, touching on perhaps the fundamental sin that humans commit (see esp. Rom. 1:18–32; and the cognate adjective, εἰδωλολάτρης [*eidōlolatrēs*], idolater, occurs in 1 Cor. 5:10, 11; 6:9; 10:7; Eph. 5:5; Rev. 21:8; 22:15).

5:20

"Sorcery" translates the word φαρμακεία (*pharmakeia*), whose similarity to our English "pharmacy" reveals its basic meaning of dispensing drugs for medicinal purposes. In the Greek of our literature, however, it has a negative sense, referring either to the administration of poison (in Josephus [e.g., *Ant.* 15.47]) or to the use of drugs in magical practices and, by extension, to those practices themselves (the word is used of the "secret arts" of the Egyptian magicians [Exod. 7:11, 22; 8:3, 14]; see also Isa. 47:9, 12; Rev. 18:23 [the only other NT occurrence]).

The sixth manifestation of the flesh begins a series of eight that are especially harmful to good community relationships, a special concern of Paul's in this context. "Hatred" actually translates a plural word, ἔχθραι (*echthrai*). Greek uses plural forms of abstract nouns more readily than does English, and it is not always clear that a genuine plural meaning is intended (as BDAG 625 notes, with reference to the plural μέθαι [methai] in verse 21; Jdt. 13:15 uses its plural to refer to "the drunken stupor" of Holofernes). However, BDF notes that the Greek also uses the plurals of abstract nouns to denote "concrete phenomena" (BDF §142). Thus if (though not always) possible, it might be preferable to reflect this sense in English. "Enmities/hostilities/hatreds" (NRSV, NASB, NET, HCSB, NAB) is not very natural English, but the idea could perhaps be captured in a phrase such as "expressions of hatred." "Hatred," "hostility," or "enmity" (all possible renderings of the Greek) can exist between humans and God (e.g., Rom. 8:7; James 4:4), and R. Longenecker (1990: 255) thinks that the word may have this reference here. But the context argues strongly for a human-against-human hatred. The term is very general, but it is unlikely that it denotes a fundamental attitude that manifests itself in some of the more specific sins that follow in the list (contra Lightfoot 1881: 211).

"Discord" (NIV), or "strife" (NRSV, ESV, NASB, NET, HCSB), or "quarreling" (NLT) translate ἔρις (eris), a word that characterizes the unprofitable and self-oriented bickering that erupts between rival factions (1 Cor. 1:11; 3:3; cf. Phil. 1:15; 1 Tim. 6:4; Titus 3:9; cf. also 2 Cor. 12:20 [a vice list]).

The next word in the list, ζῆλος (zelos), can refer positively to the "jealousy" or "zeal" that God has for his own person and his people (e.g., Isa. 26:11; Ezek. 16:42; Heb. 10:27) and that his people should have, in return, for him or his representatives (John 2:17; Rom. 10:2; 2 Cor. 7:7, 11; 9:2). Earlier in Galatians, Paul has used the cognate verb "be zealous" in this positive sense to refer to those who seek the spiritual good of the Galatians (4:17, 18) and, in a usage particularly prominent in Paul's Jewish world, to his passionate commitment to the "traditions of his fathers" (1:14, using the cognate adjective). However, in a list of the "works of the flesh," ζῆλος obviously has its other sense, the sinful jealousy of others. The word ζῆλος occurs together with ἔρις elsewhere with this sense (Rom. 13:13; 1 Cor. 3:3; 2 Cor. 12:20).

The next word is another plural in the Greek (θυμοί, thymoi), probably best translated as "fits of rage" (NIV) or "outbursts of anger" (NET; the plural is also used in the vice list in 2 Cor. 12:20, a list with many parallels to the Galatians text). The word θυμός often refers (frequently along with ὀργή [orge], whose meaning overlaps with θυμός) to God's wrath or anger, but here again, obviously, the reference is to human anger (as also in Luke 4:28; Acts 19:28; Eph. 4:31; Col. 3:8; Heb. 11:27).

Returning to the focus on factional bickering suggested with ἔρις (and to some extent with ζῆλος), Paul now mentions "selfish ambition" (ἐριθεῖαι, eritheiai). This translation, from the NIV, captures the sense of this word, which is rare yet was used by Aristotle in his work on Politics (5.3) to criticize the factional and self-oriented infighting among rival political parties in his day (the word occurs in the NT also in Rom. 2:8; 2 Cor. 12:20 [again!]; Phil. 1:17; James 3:14, 16 [in these last two texts it is paralleled with ζῆλος]). The plural form of the word may again connote various manifestations of this attitude as "rivalries."

Next on Paul's list is "dissensions" (so most English versions), a word that particularly clearly highlights what seems to be Paul's basic focus in this part of the list. The Greek word, διχοστασία (*dichostasia*), is relatively rare (only 1 Macc. 3:29 and Rom. 16:17 elsewhere in Biblical Greek), and it occurs here again in the plural.

The distinction between these "dissensions" and the "factions" listed next is not entirely clear, but the latter (αἵρεσις, *hairesis*) may suggest a more formally organized "party" (Luke uses the word to refer to the "parties" of the Sadducees and Pharisees [Acts 5:17; 15:5; 26:5] as well as to the nascent Christian "movement" or "sect" [24:5, 14; 28:22]). In later years the word was used to denote the "heresies" of the church (see 2 Pet. 2:1). Neither of these last two sins are mentioned in any other NT "vice list," suggesting, as Dunn (1993a: 305) notes, that these must have had particular relevance to the situation in Galatia (see 5:15).

Paul's concern with infighting in the community surfaces in one more word: **5:21**
φθόνοι (*phthonoi*), which means "envy." The word is again plural, but in this case the NAB is the only translation that tries to carry this over ("occasions of envy"; the plural also occurs in 1 Pet. 2:1). The meaning of this word is difficult to distinguish from ζῆλος when the latter is used in a negative way. It often occurs with ἔρις in the NT (Rom. 1:29; Phil. 1:15; 1 Tim. 6:4), revealing the close relationship between the attitude of envy and the "strife" to which envy naturally leads.

With the final two words of the list, Paul returns to sins characteristic of the Gentile world of his day. "Drunkenness" (μέθαι, *methai*) may refer simply to inebriation, but as BDAG (625) notes, the proximity of this word with κῶμοι (*kōmoi*, orgies) both here and in Rom. 13:13 may suggest the more specific nuance of "drinking bout" (the plural has a singular sense).

This last word (κῶμοι) originally referred to a festal procession in honor of a Greek god and then came to be used more broadly for a feast or banquet. In Biblical Greek, however, the word always has the negative sense of "excessive feasting," always involving too much drinking and often sexual liberties. A text from 2 Maccabees describing the activities of Greeks who desecrated the Jerusalem temple gives a sense of the word: "For the temple was filled with debauchery and reveling [κώμων] by the Gentiles, who dallied with prostitutes and had intercourse with women within the sacred precincts, and besides brought in things for sacrifice that were unfit" (2 Macc. 6:4; see also Wis. 14:23; Rom. 13:13; 1 Pet. 4:3). The plural form is again used, with "wild parties" (NLT) perhaps catching the idea fairly well (NIV and ESV "orgies" is too specifically sexual). Peter uses this word, along with two others that Paul lists in this context, to describe the pagan lifestyle characteristic of Gentiles before conversion: "For you have spent enough time in the past doing what pagans choose to do—living in debauchery [ἀσέλγεια], lust, drunkenness, orgies, carousing [κώμοις] and detestable idolatry [εἰδωλολατρίαις]" (1 Pet. 4:3).

As he did at the beginning of the list (see ἅτινα), so Paul now makes clear again that the vices he has enumerated are representative of "the works of the flesh": there are other "things like these" (τὰ ὅμοια τούτοις, *ta homoia toutois*). In passing, he makes the same point in the next sentence by referring to "such things" (τοιαῦτα, *toiauta*): "As I told you before, I say again: those who do such things will not inherit the kingdom of God." We are not sure when Paul had previously warned the Galatians about these works of the flesh and their danger. Some think it was on his second visit to them (Lightfoot 1881: 212), but the importance of a warning like this for converts from a Gentile background suggests that Paul might have issued such a warning during his initial visit (R. Longenecker 1990; 258; Martyn 1997: 487).

Vice lists in the NT often end with a warning (Rom. 1:32a; Col. 3:6; Rev. 21:8). Particularly apropos to Gal. 5:21 are the following:

> 1 Cor. 6:9–11: Or do you not know that wrongdoers will not inherit the kingdom of God? Do not be deceived: Neither the sexually immoral nor idolaters nor adulterers nor men who have sex with men [10]nor thieves nor the greedy nor drunkards nor slanderers nor swindlers will inherit the kingdom of God. [11]And that is what some of you were. But you were washed, you were sanctified, you were justified in the name of the Lord Jesus Christ and by the Spirit of our God.

> Eph. 5:5: For of this you can be sure: No immoral, impure or greedy person—such a person is an idolater—has any inheritance in the kingdom of Christ and of God.

As do these texts, Gal. 5:21 also warns that "those who do" (πράσσοντες, *prassontes*) such things "will not inherit the kingdom of God" (βασιλείαν θεοῦ οὐ κληρονομήσουσιν, *basileian theou ou klēronomēsousin*). In contrast to the Gospels, where the language is ubiquitous, Paul does not often refer to the "kingdom of God" (only thirteen times). In contrast to the claims made by some scholars, Paul's references to the kingdom exhibit the typical inaugurated-eschatology framework found also in the Gospels: the kingdom is both present (Rom. 14:17; 1 Cor. 4:20; 15:24; Col. 1:13; 4:11) and future (1 Cor. 6:9, 10; 15:50; Eph. 5:5; 2 Tim. 4:1, 18; present or future is unclear in 1 Thess. 2:12 and 2 Thess. 1:5). The reference here is to the future manifestation of the kingdom. "Inherit" language is used in the OT to describe what God has promised his people and, derivatively, to the people themselves as the Lord's "inheritance" (e.g., Isa. 19:25; Jer. 10:16). It often refers to the land that God has promised to Israel as their inheritance (e.g., 1 Kings 8:36) and that the people are urged to "take possession" of or inherit (again and again in Deuteronomy, as in 1:8). The NT follows the OT in using inheritance language to refer to what God has promised his people (Heb. 6:12; 1 Pet. 3:9; Rev. 21:7). Hays (2000: 327; cf. Dunn 1993a: 307) plausibly suggests that the inheritance language might have a polemical thrust against the agitators:

> The missionaries have taught that circumcision is necessary to inherit the kingdom. Paul, by contrast, indicates that one is excluded from the inheritance

by these flesh-driven, community-splitting behaviors—precisely the outcomes produced, in his view, by the politics of the circumcision faction (2:11–14; 4:17; 5:15, 26; 6:13).

As we note from the texts quoted above, Paul uses the language of "inheriting the kingdom" to describe the believer's eschatological hope. In keeping with these other texts, the warning here in Galatians underscores an important element in Paul's view of this inheritance. While promised by God and therefore secured apart from the law by our faith and through the Spirit's provision (3:18; 4:28–31; cf. 5:2–5), the inheritance of God's kingdom will not come to those who continue to manifest "the works of the flesh" in their lives. In light of NT teaching elsewhere and Paul's own blunt appraisal of continuing sinfulness among the holy people of God, this does not mean that the kingdom is reserved only for the sinless. But it does mean that a consistent preoccupation with these sins resulting in a life marked by them rather than by the fruit of the Spirit reveals that such a person is not "being led by the Spirit." Clear NT warnings of the necessity of putting away sin in order to gain eternal life (see also esp., Rom. 8:12–13) must not be swept under the carpet by a one-sided and unbiblical understanding of "justification by faith alone."

In contrast to the "works of the flesh" is "the fruit of the Spirit." The shift from the plural ἔργα (*erga*, works) to the singular καρπός (*karpos*, fruit) is often thought to signal two emphases: that what "the flesh *demands*, . . . the Spirit *produces*" (Dunn 1993a: 308, with original emphasis)—and that the infinite variety of fleshly deeds stands in contrast to the "inner connection and single source" of the virtues the Spirit produces (Schlier 1989: 256).[9] Neither point is entirely clear. As R. Longenecker (1990: 259) points out, Paul can use the language of "fruit" for evil deeds as well as Spirit-induced deeds (Rom. 6:21); on the other hand, "works" can refer to activities pleasing to God (e.g., Eph. 2:10). Nevertheless, the preponderance of Paul's usage and the nature of the contrast in this passage suggest that the shift to "fruit" might, indeed, accentuate the manner in which the Spirit works to bring out these virtues in the believer. The shift from plural to singular is less likely to be significant. While the plural of καρπός is not uncommon in Biblical Greek (45 among almost 200 total occurrences), Paul uses the plural only once, and then in a special sense (as a partitive genitive: πρῶτον τῶν καρπῶν [*prōton tōn karpōn*, "first of the crops"] in 2 Tim. 2:6 TNIV). The singular is Paul's normal speech, so there is no good reason to think that he is making a special point by using the singular form here (Fee 2007a: 217; and note the parallel "fruit of the light" [ὁ καρπὸς τοῦ φωτός, *ho karpos tou phōtos*] in Eph. 5:9).[10]

5:22

9. Wallace (1996: 105–6) goes so far as to classify the genitive τοῦ πνεύματος (*tou pneumatos*, of the Spirit) here as a "genitive of production" (perhaps an overly specific categorization?).

10. De Boer (2011: 362) suggests that the singular "fruit" may suggest that love is *the* fruit of the Spirit, with the other virtues flowing from it. Beale (2005) has argued that the fruit-of-the-Spirit passage echoes two related passages in Isaiah: 32:15–18 and 57:15–16 (see also Barclay 1988: 120–21). The texts refer to the sending of God's Spirit on the land to bring about

As in the case of the "works of the flesh," there is discussion about the grouping and sequence of the nine "fruits" of the Spirit that Paul enumerates. In this case, however, a rationale for their sequence or any divisions among them is lacking. Lightfoot (1881: 212) indeed suggests that we find three virtues of the mind, three relating to human relations, and then three relating to conduct, but these categories are by no means clear. The one significant matter in the sequence is the fact that "love" comes first as the primary and foundational "fruit" (Schreiner 2010: 348; see 5:13–14).[11]

The headline placement of "love" (ἀγάπη, *agapē*) in the list of the Spirit's fruit is due both to the centrality of love within new-covenant ethics (see vv. 6, 13–14; Rom. 13:8–10; 1 Cor. 13) and because it is the most important bulwark against the factional infighting that seems to be racking the Galatian churches (see v. 15). It is interesting in this regard that love occurs in only one other NT virtue list, and then in fourth position (1 Tim. 6:11). Of course, this does not diminish its importance, since love is often singled out for special attention in the contexts where these lists occur (compare the list in Col. 3:12 with verse 14: "And over all these virtues put on love, which binds them all together in perfect unity"). The noun ἀγάπη is not found in classical Greek, which uses three other words for "love": φιλία (*philia*), a general word; ἔρως (*erōs*), mainly sexual love; and στοργή (*storgē*), usually the love among family members. The word ἀγάπη does occur about twenty times in the LXX, although with no special meaning. The noun comes into its own in the NT, where it occurs almost 120 times (seventy-five of these in Paul). Many have speculated about why this noun rose to such prominence in the NT, but the reasons are not clear; nor is it useful to think that ἀγάπη in itself denotes a special kind of "Christian love" (Barr 1987). What gives ἀγάπη its distinctive Christian flavor are the concepts associated with it, not the word itself. This noun, along with its cognate verb, denotes the love that God and Christ have for us (e.g., Rom. 5:5, 8; 8:35) as well as our love for God and Christ (2 Cor. 5:14 [?]) and (esp. common in Paul) our love for one another.

"Joy" (χαρά, *chara*) occurs only here in the NT virtue lists but is prominent elsewhere. In the Greco-Roman world generally, "joy" is an emotion closely related to pleasure (ἡδονή [*hēdonē*]; H. Conzelmann, *TDNT* 9:359–62). In Paul, however, "joy" is a settled state of mind that arises from a sense of God's love for us, produced by the Spirit (1 Thess. 1:6) and that exists even in the face of difficulties and trials (2 Cor. 7:4; 1 Thess. 1:6).

"Peace" (εἰρήνη, *eirēnē*) also occurs in no other NT virtue list (though cf. "peaceful" [εἰρηνική, *eirēnikē*] in James 3:17), but it is paired with "joy" twice elsewhere in Paul (Rom. 14:17; 15:13). Peace can mean "peace with God": the objective state that follows our deliverance from the hostility that characterizes

---

fruitfulness not only for the land but also, morally, for the people of God (see also Harmon 2010: 214–21).

11. Some find significance in both the first and the last (love and self-control; R. Longenecker 1990: 260; Hays 2000: 328).

our natural relationship with God because of sin (Rom. 5:1; Eph. 2:17; probably both other occurrences in Galatians: 1:3; 6:16). But "peace" can also denote the harmonious and loving relationships with other believers that are the natural outcome of the peace we have with God (Rom. 14:19; Eph. 2:14, 15). It is this attitude toward fellow believers to which Paul probably refers here.

"Patience" (μακροθυμία, *makrothymia*) is also an attitude that both God the Father and Christ display toward sinful creatures (Rom. 2:4; 9:22; 1 Pet. 3:20; 1 Tim. 1:16; 2 Pet. 3:15) and that we, as his people, should display toward one another (2 Cor. 6:6; Gal. 5:22; Eph. 4:2; Col. 1:11; 3:12; 2 Tim. 3:10; 4:2; Heb. 6:12; James 5:10). Both "peace" and "patience" are related to love, as Eph. 4:1–3 makes clear:

> I therefore, a prisoner for the Lord, urge you to walk in a manner worthy of the calling to which you have been called, ²with all humility and gentleness, with patience [μετὰ μακροθυμίας, *meta makrothymias*], bearing with one another in love [ἐν ἀγάπῃ, *en agapē*], ³eager to maintain the unity of the Spirit in the bond of peace [τῆς εἰρήνης, *tēs eirēnēs*]. (ESV)

The Greek word translated "kindness" in all major English versions (χρηστότης, *chrēstotēs*) is employed only by Paul in the NT. He often uses it to denote God's gracious response to his rebellious creation (Rom. 2:4; 11:22; Eph. 2:7; Titus 3:4; cf. Pss. 31:19; 68:10; 119:68 [LXX: 30:20; 67:11; 118:68]), but also, as here, the kindness that humans show toward one another (2 Cor. 6:6; Col. 3:12; in Rom. 3:12, quoting Ps. 14:3 [13:3 LXX], it means "goodness"). This virtue is related to "patience" (Rom. 2:4; Col. 3:12), to love (Titus 3:4, using φιλανθρωπία [*philanthrōpia*]), and to both patience and love (2 Cor. 6:6).

Most English versions also agree on "goodness" as the translation for ἀγαθωσύνη (*agathōsynē*; NRSV, agreeing with BDAG 4.b, has "generosity"). This word is also confined to Paul in the NT (Rom. 15:14; Eph. 5:9; 2 Thess. 1:11).

The seventh fruit of the Spirit is the only one in the list that poses any real question of meaning. The Greek word πίστις (*pistis*) can mean either "faith," in the sense of the act or state of believing (in) someone or something, or "faithfulness," "the state of being someone in whom complete confidence can be placed" (LN 377.31.88). Paul, of course, has used πίστις frequently in Galatians in the former sense (twenty times before this verse), and so it is possible that he intends the same meaning in 5:22 (Dunn 1993a: 311–12 [who suggests it might have elements of both meanings here]). Paul certainly views faith as a divine gift and as closely related to the work of the Spirit (3:2–5; 5:5), so a reference to human believing would make sense. Yet the context suggests that, like the other virtues in this list, πίστις denotes an attitude or response that we have toward other people, and especially other Christians (see also 1 Tim. 6:11, where the word occurs in such a list along with ἀγάπη).

In keeping with his focus on those manifestations of the Spirit that are particularly foundational for a harmonious community life, "gentleness" (πραΰτης

5:23

[*praytēs*]) is now mentioned. In defining this word, BDAG (861) expansively but helpfully has "the quality of not being overly impressed by a sense of one's self-importance." The model for this attitude is Jesus, who claimed to be "gentle [πραΰς, *prays*] and humble in heart" (Matt. 11:29; cf. 21:5; 2 Cor. 10:1). The NT letters frequently call on Christians to follow Christ's example in this self-giving mode. Note especially the presence of this word in the passage we have noted several times, Eph. 4:1–3, and Paul's return to this concern when he applies his general paraenesis to the Galatians (6:1; see also Col. 3:12; 2 Tim. 2:25; Titus 3:2; James 1:21; 3:13; 1 Pet. 3:16).

Some interpreters (e.g., Burton 1921: 318) suggest that Paul might intend the final fruit of the Spirit, "self-control" (ἐγκράτεια, *enkrateia*), to be a deliberate contrast with the final two "works of the flesh," "drunkenness and carousing." Whether intended by Paul or not, the contrast is certainly evident. "Self-control" was prized by some of the Greek philosophers (Socrates considered it one of the cardinal virtues, and Aristotle gives much attention to it in his *Ethics*), but it barely appears in the LXX (only 4 Macc. 5:34). It does figure more prominently in some of the Hellenistic Jewish writings. The NT, however, follows the OT in mentioning the virtue rarely (Acts 24:25; 1 Pet. 1:6 [2x]; the cognate adjective occurs in Titus 1:8).

The importance of this list of the fruit of the Spirit (as in the case of "the works of the flesh") lies not so much in the individual virtues as in their cumulative effect. While Paul has undoubtedly chosen some of the terms because of their inherent importance to the Christian ethic ("love," esp.), it would be a mistake to assume that this list provides a fundamental or comprehensive blueprint for the shape of the Christian life. Paul has chosen the particular virtues he includes here with an eye on the apparently quarrelsome Galatians. Hence his list of the fruit of the Spirit might have looked a bit different if it had come in a different context.

In this last part of the letter, Paul's continued concern with the basic issue in Galatia is revealed again in the end of verse 23. As in verses 14 and 18, he relates his paraenetic teaching to the law: κατὰ τῶν τοιούτων οὐκ ἔστιν νόμος (*kata tōn toioutōn ouk estin nomos*, against such things there is no law). The pronoun τοιούτων could be masculine ("against such people"; Oepke 1973: 183), but it is more likely neuter ("against such things"), as in most of the English versions. As the translation "no law" suggests, νόμος (*nomos*) refers to "law" in general, but in the context of Galatians it must have in view especially the law of Moses.[12] Just what Paul wants to say about the relationship between the fruit of the Spirit and the law is debated.

The most straightforward reading is that Paul is simply claiming that no law forbids the virtues that Paul has just listed. This point may appear to be

---

12. One could also translate with a more direct reference to the Mosaic law: "The law [of Moses] is not against such things." No major English version presents a translation like this, but it appears to be unobjectionable. The οὐκ could modify ἔστιν, "is not," as easily as νόμος, "no law," and the presence or lack of the article with νόμος, as is now generally recognized, provides no guidance to the referent of the word.

a truism, but it might make sense as an ad hominem riposte to the kinds of claims the agitators are making for the law (Barclay 1988: 122–24). Barrett (1985: 77) paraphrases, "You want to observe the law, don't you? You will not find any law that forbids these things" (see also Mussner 1988: 389; Räisänen 1983: 114–15). Furthermore, implied in Paul's negative point might be a positive one: the Spirit can be relied on never to lead believers against the true intent of the law (Martyn 1997: 500).

A second, though related, understanding of this claim is that no law, including the law of Moses, condemns such virtues (or such people; Ridderbos 1953: 208; Fung 1988: 273; Garlington 2003: 259; R. Campbell 1996). Interpreted this way, the finale on the "fruit of the Spirit" passage would match the one that ends the "works of the flesh" list: as those works keep a person from "inheriting the kingdom," so this fruit enables a person to avoid the curse of the law and enter the kingdom.

Third, Paul might be saying that "when these qualities [the fruit of the Spirit] are in view we are in a sphere with which law has nothing to do" (Bruce 1982b: 255; cf. also Matera 1992: 211). Bruce, with other interpreters (e.g., R. Longenecker 1990: 264), supports this interpretation by citing a passage from Aristotle's *Politics* (3.13) that is remarkably close to the Greek of Gal. 5:23. In this passage, Aristotle refers to people who are so led by "virtue" that they are "above the law"; as he puts it, "against such people there is no law" (κατὰ δὲ τῶν τοιούτων οὐκ ἔστι νόμος, *kata de tōn toioutōn ouk esti nomos*; AT).

A decision between these interpretations is difficult. But we think that Paul's significant claim about love as the fulfillment of the law in verse 14 should probably govern the sense of this clause. If so, the second view is probably to be preferred: the Spirit produces fruit in the lives of believers and thereby provides for all that the law itself requires.

Paul ends this paragraph by returning to the point where he began. In verse 16, he exhorted believers to "walk by the Spirit" so that they might not "carry out the desire of the flesh" (ἐπιθυμίαν σαρκός, *epithymian sarkos*). Now he claims that "those who belong to Christ Jesus have crucified the flesh with its passions and desires" (οἱ δὲ τοῦ Χριστοῦ ['Ἰησοῦ] τὴν σάρκα ἐσταύρωσαν σὺν τοῖς παθήμασιν καὶ ταῖς ἐπιθυμίαις, *hoi de tou Christou [Iēsou] tēn sarka estaurōsan syn tois pathēmasin kai tais epithymiais*). Calling believers οἱ τοῦ Χριστοῦ reminds us again of the inclusive Christology that is so central to Paul's theology in Galatians (see esp. 3:26–29). This same point is underscored by the verb ἐσταύρωσαν, an aorist form that probably refers to Christ's own crucifixion, in which the believer, by God's decree, shares (see esp. Rom. 6:6; cf. Bruce 1982b: 256; Dunn 1993a: 314). When Paul refers to this conception, however, the verb is usually in the passive, as in Gal. 2:19, "I have been crucified with Christ," and 6:14, "the world has been crucified to me and I to the world." The active form of the verb may put more stress on the decision to accept the benefits of this cocrucifixion (e.g., Mussner 1988: 390; Schreiner 2010: 351; some refer specifically to baptism [e.g., Schlier 1989: 263–64]).

5:24

Perhaps, however, we should not make too much of the active form here, which can simply signify the fact that something has happened. The crucifixion of the flesh does not mean that it is totally destroyed but that it is definitely judged and its power decisively broken (see the parallel with the crucifixion of the "old self" in Rom. 6:6; and Moo 1996: 372–76). By adding the phrase σὺν τοῖς παθήμασιν καὶ ταῖς ἐπιθυμίαις, Paul emphasizes this totality as well, perhaps referring to the inner dispositions that are affected (R. Longenecker 1990: 264; for παθήμασιν, which usually refers to "sufferings" in the NT, see Rom. 7:5; on ἐπιθυμίαις, see the comments on 5:16).[13]

The similarities between verses 16 and 24 are matched, of course, by a significant difference: the definitive defeat of the flesh is conditioned on the response of believers. This combination of "indicative" (what God has done) and "imperative" (what we must do) is typical of Paul's presentation of the Christian life. A concentration on either to the neglect of the other leads to an imbalance. Either the believer is lulled into passivity by assuming that God automatically does all we need apart from the response of our own will—or the believer, thinking it all falls on their own shoulders, lapses into a "works" mentality that breeds anxiety.

Additional Notes

5:17. In place of the second γάρ, which is found in only a few MSS, but early and good ones (e.g., 𝔓⁴⁶ ℵ* B), a wide variety of witnesses read δέ. The γάρ has the stronger external support.

5:19. A good number of MSS (including 𝔐; see the KJV) add the word μοιχεῖα, "adultery," before πορνεία. It has almost certainly been added on the basis of parallel texts (the plural in Matt. 15:19; Mark 7:22).

5:19–23. Lists of vices (often with contrasting virtues) are first found in Aristotle and became especially popular among the Stoics, from whom a number of scholars think Paul has borrowed this "form" (e.g., Easton 1932). But Jewish writers use similar lists, borrowing perhaps from the widespread OT tradition of the "two ways" (e.g., Ps. 1). It must also be noted that (1) the lists of vices and virtues in the NT take a variety of specific contextually oriented forms; and (2) such lists are to some extent a rather natural way to refer to ethical conduct. For studies of NT vice-and-virtue lists and their background, see esp. Vögtle 1936; Kamlah 1964; Wibbing 1959; Suggs 1972; and on Galatians particularly, Betz 1979: 281–83; Witherington 1998: 403–6.

5:20. In place of the singular ἔρις, which finds solid external support in the combination of ℵ, A, and B, 𝔐 and a few other MSS read the plural ἔρεις (see again the NKJV). Paul varies singular and plural forms rather indiscriminately in this context (see the next variant), so it is difficult to know which he would have intended. But the singular has better support.

5:20. The plural ζῆλοι appears in some MSS (many of which also read the plural ἔρεις [see the previous note]).

---

13. J. Thompson (2011: 142–43) suggests that Paul may be responding to a Jewish tradition that viewed the law as the means to combat "passions."

5:21. A good spread of MSS add the word φόνοι (murders) after φθόνοι. The similarity in appearance and sound of these two words may mean that φόνοι was accidentally omitted due to homoeoteleuton (similar endings; see Lightfoot 1881: 212). The UBS committee, however, noted the possibility that the word was added by assimilation to Rom. 1:29 (Metzger 1994: 529). The omission also has strong MS support ($\mathfrak{P}^{46}$ ℵ B).

5:24. The evidence for including Ἰησοῦ is slightly stronger than the evidence for omitting it (see Lightfoot 1881: 213). On the other hand, the combination article + Χριστὸς Ἰησοῦς does not have an unquestioned parallel in Paul (it is a variant reading also in Eph. 3:1).

C. Some Specific Parameters of the New Life (5:25–6:6)

"If we live by the Spirit, let us keep in step with the Spirit" (v. 25) could well signal the conclusion of the previous section. Its language is very similar to the language of verse 16, "walk by the Spirit," and could therefore function as the second member of an inclusio, which would bracket the material in between (Fee 2007a: 228). In this case, verse 26 might initiate a new stage in Paul's argument (e.g., Mussner 1988: 395). But verse 26 should probably be kept with verse 25, so the new section might begin rather with 6:1 (note the direct address: "brothers and sisters"; see, e.g., R. Longenecker 1990: 268–71; and most English Bibles). But it is better to place a weak transition at verse 25. "If we live by the Spirit" summarizes what Paul has spelled out about believers and the Spirit in verses 16–24. With verse 25, then, he advances the argument a step further: those who "live" by the Spirit (v. 16), who are "led by the Spirit" (v. 18), should be people also who "stay in step with the Spirit." While somewhat transitional, then (cf. Parsons 1995: 240), verse 25 introduces the next section, in which Paul will spell out some of the ways believers are to manifest the reality of the Spirit (so most commentators; e.g., Dunn 1993a: 316). "Paul's admonitions . . . are practical (but generalized) examples that demonstrate what a community is to look like when the Spirit of God is at work within its members" (B. Longenecker 1998: 82 [with reference to 6:1–10]).

    The internal structure of this section is also not clear. Some interpreters think that Paul has followed an alleged Greco-Roman paraenetic style and simply throws together various gnomic sayings somewhat at random.[1] However, at the risk of imposing a structure that Paul never intended, we may discern three general parts. The call to "stay in step with the Spirit" (v. 25) is the general exhortation that Paul elaborates in the rest of the section (see Harnish 1987: 292). A concern for appropriate relationships within the community dominates 5:26–6:5, expressed negatively with warnings about undue pride (5:26; 6:3–5) and positively with exhortations to restore people caught in sin (6:1) and carry the burdens of others (6:2). The concluding

---

1. See esp. Betz 1979: 291–93; and also Rohde 1989: 257. Understanding "paraenesis" as a collection of traditional, loosely organized, general maxims goes back especially to the work of M. Dibelius (1976: 1–11, conveniently laying out his approach in his commentary on James). Betz (1979) also argues that Paul takes many of these maxims from Greco-Roman moral teaching. Several of the exhortations in this section are indeed similar to common Greco-Roman teaching, but Paul has set them in a new context that often quite significantly changes their meaning and application (see esp. Barclay 1988: 170–77).

exhortation to support those who minister the word generally follows this theme, but it is more of an independent saying loosely attached to 6:5.[2] The importance of love, probably alluded to in the reference to the "law of Christ" in 6:2, undergirds all these exhortations, showing how these verses continue to explicate the basic command to "serve one another in love" (5:13; see Dunn 1993a: 316). This language of "one another" is prominent (twice) in verse 26, which sets the agenda for what follows. A concern about community discord is again very evident in the section, although whether this dissension is the result of differing reactions to the agitators is difficult to say.[3] Dunn (1993a: 317) neatly summarizes the heart of Paul's teaching in these verses: "Fundamental to v.25–vi.6 is the thought that the order of the Spirit is marked both by sympathy towards others and readiness to criticize oneself—not the other way round!"

Exegesis and Exposition

[5:25]If we live by the Spirit, let us keep in step with the Spirit. [26]Let us not be conceited, provoking one another, envying ⌜one another⌝. [6:1]Brothers and sisters, if ⌜someone⌝ should be overtaken by a transgression, you who are Spirit people should restore that person in a spirit of gentleness. But watch yourself so that you are not also tempted. [2]Bear one another's burdens, and in this way you ⌜will fulfill⌝ the law of Christ. [3]For if anyone thinks they are something when they are not, they are deceiving themselves. [4]Each one should test their own work, and then they will have reason to boast in themselves and not in the other person. [5]For each should carry their own load. [6]But let the one who is taught the word share all good things with the one who is teaching.

Essential to Christian existence, Paul has argued, is the Spirit. The Spirit fulfills God's promise that he will transform the hearts of his people in the eschatological age (3:14), producing among them those character traits that please God and build up his people (5:22–23a). The Spirit is the power that inaugurates Christian existence (3:3) and brings it to completion (5:5). The Spirit "leads" believers (5:18), and believers are, in turn, obliged to "walk by the Spirit" (v. 16). When Paul now says "If we live by the Spirit," he is summing up in one succinct clause this Spirit-dominated existence that fundamentally characterizes believers who live in the age of fulfillment (for a similar emphasis, see Rom. 8:4–13). This clause, the protasis ("if" clause) of a conditional sentence, uses the so-called first-class form of εἰ (*ei*, if) plus an indicative verb (ζῶμεν, *zōmen*, we live). This form should not be translated "since" (as do

5:25

---

2. Barclay (1988: 149–50) discerns a more complicated structure. He thinks that, after the heading in 5:25–26, the passage 6:1–10 follows a responsibility (vv. 1a, 2, 6, 9–10) and accountability (vv. 1b, 3–5, 7–9) scheme, with the two chiastically arranged. Barclay is right to see these two issues throughout, and there is some plausibility to his identifications.

3. Brinsmead (1982: 164–92) has argued that, at least in 6:1ff., Paul is directly confronting the agitators. But it is more likely that the disputes implied in this passage are the indirect result of the agitators' teaching. See the full discussion in Barclay 1988: 150–68.

NIV, HCSB, NLT, NJB) because such a translation robs the construction of its rhetorical power. Paul does not want his readers to sit back contentedly thinking, "Yes, I am indeed living by the Spirit." By using a conditional construction, he wants them to ask of themselves "Is this really true of me?" (see esp. Wallace 1996: 692–93).

In the Greek word order, the second clause in the verse is the mirror image of the first one: "If we live by the Spirit, with the Spirit let us also stay in step." If "living by the Spirit" is simply another way of saying "being led by the Spirit" or "walking by the Spirit," the second clause in the verse, πνεύματι καὶ στοιχῶμεν (*pneumati kai stoichōmen*), must be saying something different, for otherwise the verse would make no sense. The verb στοιχέω originally had the sense of to "be drawn up in line" (BDAG 946; MM 591) and was sometimes used in military contexts to mean "stay in line with." It came to be used metaphorically to mean "fall into line with," as in Polybius (*Hist.* 28.5.6): "After these speeches, Gaius and his colleague, seeing that the populace disliked the idea of having garrisons, and wishing to follow the line [στοιχεῖν, *stoichein*] of policy marked out by the Senate, expressed their adherence to the view of Diogenes." All four of the other NT usages have this general sense (Acts 21:24; Rom. 4:12; Gal. 6:16; Phil. 3:16), and this might be all that is intended in verse 25 (G. Delling, *TDNT* 7:668–69; Mussner 1988: 391). But Rom. 4:12, with specific reference to the "footsteps" of Abraham, may preserve the more specific sense of "stay in step with," and the other Pauline occurrences could have a similar nuance.[4] At the risk, then, of attributing an overly specific meaning to the verb, we think that "keep in step with" (NIV) is a good contextual translation of the word. Dunn (1993a: 317–18) suggests that it connotes "a sense of order imposed by an external authority or in accord with a recognized standard"; BDAG (946) proposes the meaning "to be in line with a pers. or thing considered as standard for one's conduct." This being the case, the dative πνεύματι will probably not indicate means, "by the Spirit" (most interpreters), but association, as a derivative of the verb it goes with (as in the three other Pauline occurrences). Indeed, the shift in meaning of the dative contributes something of the rhetorical force to the verse: "if we are working out our Christian existence by means of the Spirit's power, let us keep in step with what the Spirit desires."[5] This combination of indicative ("we live by the Spirit") and imperative ("we must keep in step with the Spirit") is typical of Paul's two-age eschatological perspective: "The simultaneous existence of the old 'evil' aeon determined by the flesh and the newly inaugurated

4. A few interpreters (Witherington 1998: 413; Hays 2000: 328–29; Schreiner 2010: 356–57) think that the verb στοιχῶμεν may play on the cognate noun, στοιχεῖον (*stoicheion*, element), that Paul has used in 4:3, 9: the "order" imposed by the pagan gods is replaced by the "order" created by the Spirit. But these verses are rather distant from 5:26.

5. See, e.g., Beker (1980: 222), who distinguishes between "living by the Spirit," a specific condition, and staying in step with the Spirit, "a walk, activity, manifestation of life that is commensurate with it." See also Schnelle (2009: 322), who paraphrases, "Live in harmony with the Spirit."

aeon of the new creation determined by the Spirit establishes the situation of the believer 'between the ages.' This salvation-historical tension explains why the indicative and the imperative appear side by side" (Schnabel 1995: 274).

In a natural transition, Paul now warns against behavior that is *not* consistent with "keeping in step with the Spirit." He urges his readers not to be κενόδοξοι (*kenodoxoi*, conceited) and then elaborates on what he means by this with two parallel participial constructions: ἀλλήλους προκαλούμενοι, ἀλλήλοις φθονοῦντες (*allēlous prokaloumenoi, allēlois phthonountes*, provoking each other, envying each other). Etymology is rarely a sure guide to word meaning, but in the case of κενόδοξος it points us in the right direction. It is composed of κενός (*kenos*), "empty," and δόξα (*doxa*), "praise," "renown" (note KJV: "vain glory"). It connotes the attitude of persons who think they have a right to praise and renown when, in fact, they have no such right: hence "conceited" (most English versions). The word occurs only here in Biblical Greek, but its cognate noun, κενοδοξία (*kenodoxia*) occurs in Phil. 2:3: "Do nothing out of selfish ambition or vain conceit [κενοδοξίαν]. Rather, in humility value others above yourselves." Paul prohibits conceit with a hortatory subjunctive, μὴ γινώμεθα (*mē ginōmetha*), which could mean either "Let us not *become* conceited" (so most versions) or simply "Let us not *be* conceited" (γίνομαι is often equivalent in meaning to εἰμί [*eimi*, I am], esp. in the imperative and subjunctive moods; cf. RSV, NAB, NJB).

The two participle clauses that follow the initial prohibition are modal (Betz 1979: 294), explaining how "conceit" operates in interpersonal relationships. The word ἀλλήλους (*allēlous*, "one another") occurs in first position in both clauses for emphasis. The verb προκαλέω (*prokaleō*) means, in this kind of context, to provoke or challenge (only here in the NT; in this sense, see, e.g., Josephus, *Ant.* 6.177, where Goliath "challenges" the Israelites). An attitude of conceit, of thinking more of oneself than a person should, will often manifest itself in aggressive challenges to others and their views. This first participle focuses on the active manifestation of conceit; the second draws attention to the passive motivation: envy.[6] Paul has already singled out "envy" as one of the "works of the flesh" (v. 21): the noun (φθόνος, *phthonos*) occurs there and the cognate verb φθονέω (*phthoneō*, envy) here (only here in the NT).

The direct address, "brothers and sisters" (ἀδελφοί, *adelphoi*), may signal a new stage in Paul's argument. However, as we have argued above, the section break is better placed between 5:24 and 5:25. Paul may, then, use the direct address to signal a move from the generalized command and prohibition of 5:25–26 to the more specific exhortations of 6:1–6. The familial flavor of this address, though somewhat formalized in Paul, is nevertheless probably important here: "[Paul] wants the members of the Galatian churches to see themselves not as rivals competing to see who can be the most devout (5:26),

5:26

6:1

---

6. Lightfoot (1881: 214) suggests that "conceit" leads to "provoking" and "provoking" to "envy," but the sequence is not logically clear.

but rather as brothers and sisters, . . . supporting one another as they walk through perilous times of spiritual warfare" (Hays 2000: 331).

One way in which brothers and sisters can support one another is by seeking to bring those who have committed a sin back into the fellowship of the community. To be sure, Paul refers to the person committing this sin with the general ἄνθρωπος (anthrōpos, human being), but he clearly has in view a member of the Christian community. Paul is evidently not thinking of a specific circumstance but of a possible situation that might arise anytime. He uses the so-called third-class conditional form, ἐάν (ean) plus the subjunctive, a form that indicates a possible yet not immediate condition (the καί [kai, and] following the particle emphasizes this hypothetical quality; "even if" [cf. BDR §374]). His language suggests a situation in which a brother or sister has somewhat unexpectedly found oneself to be committing a sin. The verb προλαμβάνω (prolambanō, used here in the third-person singular aorist subjunctive) might mean "caught by [someone else]" or "caught in" a sin. A few interpreters argue for the former (Schlier 1989: 270; Dunn 1993a: 319 [probably]), but the latter, implied by most of the English versions and most commentators, is more likely.[7] Paul's use of παράπτωμα (paraptōma, transgression) instead of ἁμαρτία (harmatia, sin) may accentuate the mild nature of the failing (such a difference between the two words might be present in Pss. Sol. 3.7; 13.6–10). But this is not clear; the two words are often near synonyms (see Rom. 4:25; Col. 2:13; Paul may sometimes use παράπτωμα to denote a specific sin and ἁμαρτία to mean "sin as a power" [see Rom. 5:15–20; 2 Cor. 5:19–20; a distinction is hard to maintain in Eph. 2:1 [cf. 2:5]).[8]

When such a circumstance arises, "You who are Spirit people should restore such a person in a spirit of gentleness." "You who are Spirit people" is a cumbersome attempt to carry over into English translation what Paul means by οἱ πνευματικοί (hoi pneumatikoi). It is generally agreed that the word is not intended to single out a particular segment within the Galatian churches, a "spiritual" or "Spirit-filled" group of believers distinguished from a less-than-spiritual group (see esp. Fee 1994: 461; contra Dunn 1993a: 319–20). To be sure, Paul may use this word to imply a distinction among Christians in 1 Cor. 3:1 (where it is contrasted with σάρκινος [sarkinos, fleshly]), but the nature and significance of this contrast are not clear. No such contrast is evident in his other uses of the word (Rom. 1:11; 7:14; 15:27; 1 Cor. 2:13 [2x], 15; 9:11; 10:3, 4 [2x]; 12:1; 14:1, 37; 15:44 [2x], 46 [2x]; Eph. 1:3; 5:19; 6:12; Col. 1:9; 3:16). Thus Paul's intention here is to characterize all the Christians he addresses as people who are "led by" the Spirit (5:18) and "live by" the Spirit (5:25). Perhaps he is also giving an implicit reminder to those who have determined to "walk by the Spirit" (5:16) and to "stay in step with the Spirit" (5:25)—as

---

7. The verb προλαμβάνω occurs in the active in the NT in Mark 14:8 and 1 Cor. 11:21 with the sense "do something before"; only here in Biblical Greek does the verb occur in the passive with a following ἐν (en, in).

8. R. Longenecker (1990: 272) suggests that Paul uses παράπτωμα, by etymology meaning a "false step," to match his command to "stay in step" (στοιχέω, stoicheō) with the Spirit in v. 25.

Lightfoot (1881: 215) paraphrases, "Ye who have taken my lesson to heart, ye who would indeed be guided by the Spirit."

These "Spirit people" are to be active in "restoring" a wayward brother or sister. The verb καταρτίζω (*katartizō*) has a wide range of meanings: "prepare" (Matt. 21:16; Rom. 9:22; Heb. 10:5); "supply" (1 Thess. 3:10; Heb. 13:21); "put in order," as used of the "mending" of nets (Mark 1:19; Matt. 4:21), is relevant here (see also 1 Pet. 5:10). To "restore" the offender is to put matters in order by integrating them back into full fellowship with the Lord and with their brothers and sisters. This restoring work (and the present tense of the verb suggests a process) is to be done "in a spirit of gentleness" (ἐν πνεύματι πραΰτητος, *en pneumati praytētos*). "Spirit" might have some reference to the Holy Spirit; Fee (1994: 462), characteristically, wants to translate "S/spirit" (see also Betz 1979: 297). And "gentleness" (πραΰτης, *praytēs*) is one of the fruits of the Spirit (5:23); as Chrysostom comments, "[Paul] says not 'in meekness,' but, 'in a spirit of meekness,' signifying thereby that this is acceptable to the Spirit, and that to administer correction with mildness is a spiritual gift" (*Comm. Gal.* on 6:1 [*NPNF*[1] 13:43]). However, πνεῦμα in this kind of phrase is more naturally taken as a reference to the human spirit; with the following noun, the term simply means "in gentle manner" (e.g., Mussner 1988: 398). See 1 Cor. 4:21: "Shall I come to you with a rod of discipline, or shall I come in love and with a gentle spirit? [ἐν ἀγάπῃ πνεύματί τε πραΰτητος; *en agapē pneumati te praytētos?*]" Certain kinds of sins and certain kinds of sinners (esp. those who remain unrepentant) must be dealt with seriously, even to the point of excluding them from Christian fellowship (1 Cor. 5:1–5; 1 Tim. 1:20). But many brothers and sisters, whose sin is more inadvertent and who may already be feeling shame, will be brought to forgiveness and restoration to fellowship through gentleness and humility. Harshness may simply drive them further away.

Barclay (1988: 149–50) notes that 6:1–10 is characterized by an alternation between responsibility and accountability. Paul has begun with our responsibility to restore others. Now he reminds us that as we do so, we are accountable. In this clause the accountability is enhanced by Paul's shift from the plural forms earlier in the verse to the singular (σκοπῶν [*skopōn*, watching], σεαυτόν [*seauton*, yourself], πειρασθῇς [*peirasthēs*, be tempted]). "Watch yourself," he says, "so that you may not also be tempted." This reminder is attached to the main verb "restore" with a participle, σκοπῶν, which becomes virtually a second imperative (Betz 1979: 298; Mussner 1988: 397). This same verb is used in Phil. 2:3–4, in a passage that has many parallels with 6:1: "Do nothing out of selfish ambition or vain conceit [κενοδοξίαν]. Rather, in humility value others above yourselves, not looking [σκοποῦντες, *skopountes*] to your own interests but each of you to the interests of the others." But what would the people who are restoring a sinner be tempted to do? Three possibilities seem likely: (1) anger at the offender (Garlington 2003: 266); (2) self-righteousness/pride (Bruce 1982b: 260; Matera 1992: 214); (3) the same sin that has overtaken the offender (Dunn 1993a: 321). The continuation of the general line of thought in 6:3–4 favors the second of these options.

6:2   Paul does not connect this verse to the previous context via a particle or conjunction, so it is left to the reader to infer the relationship of the verses. Probably the "burdens" (βάρη, *barē*) that Paul calls on us to bear in this verse are related to the process of restoring the sinner in verse 1. Bringing back into the fellowship of Christ a brother or sister who has strayed will often mean entering into their lives with empathy and a concern to take on ourselves whatever of their own sorrows and difficulties that we can. However, while undoubtedly including and perhaps even focused on the particular situation of the sinner in verse 1, the burdens probably extend more broadly to include all those problems that afflict our brothers and sisters (R. Longenecker 1990: 274–75; Dunn 1993a: 322).[9] The verb "bear" (βαστάζω, *bastazō*) is a natural one to use with βάρος (*baros*, burden): they are found together also in Matt. 20:12. The present tense of the imperatival verb probably stresses the need to make burden bearing a constant practice. "One another" (ἀλλήλων, *allēlōn*), coming first in the clause for emphasis, picks up a word that reverberates throughout this context (5:13, 15 [2x], 17, 26 [2x]).

By means of this burden bearing (οὕτως [*houtōs*, in this way]), Paul claims, "you will fulfill the law of Christ." The verb in this clause could be an imperative (followed apparently by the NLT: "and in this way obey the law of Christ") but is probably a future indicative: ἀναπληρώσετε (*anaplērōsete*, you will fulfill; on the textual issue, see the additional note). The use of the compound verb (ἀνα + πληρόω) may signify emphasis (you will truly, or really, fulfill [Lightfoot 1881: 216]) or repetition (you will follow Christ [see 5:14] in fulfilling the law [Martyn 1997: 547–48; Hays 2000: 333]). But compound verbs in NT Greek often lose any particular emphasis or nuance relative to the simple verb, so we should probably not think the verb means anything more than the simple πληρόω (*plēroō*, which occurs in 5:14).

The "law of Christ" (τὸν νόμον τοῦ Χριστοῦ, *ton nomon tou Christou*) that believers fulfill by bearing one another's burdens has been variously identified. Two general directions of interpretation can be identified:

1. The law is the law of Moses, the torah, as fulfilled by, or interpreted by, or focused on, Christ.[10]
2. The law is a law distinct from the law of Moses, either
   a. the love command, singled out by Christ as the center of the law;[11]
   b. the ethical teaching of Christ in general (C. Dodd 1968);

9. Strelan (1975; and to a lesser extent, Witherington [1998: 419–20]) suggests that the burdens here are particularly financial burdens. However, he reads back into this whole paragraph, without adequate linguistic basis, the financial focus that is (probably) evident in 6:6.

10. In his survey of interpretation, Wilson (2006) notes that this interpretation has become especially popular in recent years. See esp. A. Chester 2007: 537–601; and, e.g., Ridderbos 1975: 284–85; Barclay 1988: 126–41; Kertelge 1984: 389–90; Schreiner 1993b: 158–59; Sanders 1983: 97–98; Matera 1992: 219–21; Stanton 1996: 115–16; J. Thompson 2011: 126–27; Thielman 1994: 141 (the "law of Christ" is both "something new" yet also "a reference to Christ's summary of the Mosaic law"); Wilson 2007: 100–104; Dunn 1993a: 323 ("that law [the torah] as interpreted by the love command in the light of the Jesus-tradition and the Christ-event").

11. Furnish 1968: 60–64; Mussner 1988: 399; Schrage 1996: 183–88.

c. the example of Christ;[12]
d. or some combination of these.[13]

In favor of the first direction of interpretation is the fact that Paul has up to this point in Galatians used νόμος almost exclusively to refer to the law of Moses (5:23 may be an exception). Furthermore, 6:2 has obvious reference back to 5:14. "Bearing one another's burdens" is a form of love, and both passages refer to the "fulfillment" of the law. Yet 5:14 refers explicitly to a command from the law of Moses (Lev. 19:18). In addition, a concern with fulfilling the law of Moses (albeit in some altered form because of Christ) is said to be manifest in other passages in Paul in which he apparently expects his readers to obey commandments from that law (see esp. 1 Cor. 7:19 and Eph. 6:2).

Nevertheless, the arguments in favor of the second direction of interpretation are a bit more compelling. First, the genitive qualifier Χριστοῦ most naturally identifies this law as the law "belonging to" or "stemming from" Christ, a kind of deliberate counterpart to the "law of Moses," the law "belonging to" or "stemming from" Moses (van Dülmen 1968: 66–67; Garlington 2003: 269). As Lightfoot (1881: 216) paraphrases the idea, "If you must observe a law, let it be the law of Christ." Second, τὸν νόμον τοῦ Χριστοῦ has a close parallel in 1 Cor. 9:20–21:

> To the Jews I became like a Jew, to win the Jews. To those under the law [ὑπὸ νόμον, *hypo nomon*] I became like one under the law (though I myself am not under the law), so as to win those under the law. [21]To those not having the law [ἀνόμοις, *anomois*] I became like one not having the law [ἄνομος] (though I am not free from God's law [ἄνομος θεοῦ] but am under Christ's law [ἔννομος Χριστοῦ]), so as to win those not having the law.

As Feuillet (1980) has shown, Paul in this text breaks the broad "law of God" into two parts: (1) the law that was valid for Jews and that Paul is no longer "under"; (2) and the law of Christ, to which Paul is obligated. In other words, Paul distinguishes the law of Christ (to be sure, in slightly different words) from the law of Moses.

Since Paul is using "law of Christ" as a kind of rhetorical counterpart to the law of Moses, we should not insist that "law" will have precisely the same form as it does with reference to the law of Moses. Certainly the love command, for reasons explained above, must be part of what Paul intends.

12. Hays 1987; Schürmann 1974; Horrell 2005: 222–31; Fee 1994: 463–64; Witherington 1998: 423–25.

13. Vouga 1998: 95; R. Longenecker 1990: 275–76; 1964: 190; van Dülmen 1968: 66–68; Thurén 2000: 86–87; Deidun 1981: 210; Davies 1948: 11–46; Bruce 1982b: 261; Garlington 2003: 269; Fung 1988: 287. A few interpreters suggest that, as a rhetorical counterpart to the Mosaic law, "law of Christ" has no real content (see esp. Winger 2000; and also Räisänen 1983: 77–80). De Boer (2011: 378–80) argues that "law" refers to the scriptural promise of the coming of Christ.

But it is arguable that Paul includes more than the love command in "the law of Christ." Precisely because the phrase serves as the new covenant counterpart to the "law of Moses," we should expect the reference to include all those teachings and commandments set forth by Christ and by his inspired apostles—including Paul. Dunn (1997: 654–55) makes a strong case for including Jesus's example, or pattern of life, within the law of Christ. He notes that Paul follows a pattern in Romans that seems to parallel what Paul says here in Galatians. Paul moves from the fulfilling of the law in terms of love (13:8–10) to a reference to "bearing" the failings of the weak and doing good to the neighbor, a command undergirded by appeal to the example of Christ (15:1–3). The distance between the passages in Romans raises some question about this argument, but the pattern to which Dunn refers has some basis in Galatians also (see 2:20 esp.).[14]

At the risk, then, of "having one's cake and eating it twice" (or three or four times), we think Paul's phrase "the law of Christ" refers, in direct counterpart to "the law of Moses," to the broadly ethical demand of the gospel. R. Longenecker (1990: 275–76) summarizes it especially well: "prescriptive principles stemming from the heart of the gospel (usually embodied in the example and teachings of Jesus), which are meant to be applied to specific situations by the direction and enablement of the Holy Spirit, being always motivated and conditioned by love." (On this point, also see Moo 1996: 367–70.)

6:3 Verses 3–5, while not tied closely together, have a certain coherence in their focus on the need for self-examination (Barclay 1988: 159). Reflective of this emphasis is a shift from the pronoun ἀλλήλους (allēlous, one another, in 5:26; 6:2) to ἕκαστος (hekastos, each, in vv. 4, 5) and ἑαυτόν (heauton, himself, in vv. 3, 4). Each believer, Paul argues, should avoid the pride that comes when they do not truly understand themselves (v. 3). Any sense of pride should be based on critical self-reflection and not on a comparison with others (v. 4). This is because, on the day of judgment, each believer will need to answer for themselves alone (v. 5). This summary of verses 3–5 rests on a certain interpretation of some disputed texts, which will be explained below (see the comments on 6:4–5). For now, it is important to explain why Paul moves into this general issue at this point in his paraenesis. One possibility is given explicit recognition in the NLT translation of verse 3: "If you think you are too important to help someone, you are only fooling yourself. You are not that important." "To help someone" represents nothing specific in the Greek text but introduces what the translators consider to be the implications of the γάρ (gar, for [v. 3]): "Bear one another's burdens" (v. 2); *and you should not refrain from doing so* because you think too highly of yourself" (for a connection with v. 2, see R. Longenecker 1990: 276). Another option is to relate verse 3 to the warning in

14. Older interpreters sometimes argued that with the phrase "law of Christ," Paul was picking up a Jewish tradition that Messiah would establish his own torah. But most contemporary interpreters are not convinced that this is what the relevant Jewish sources are teaching (see Urbach 1979: 302; P. Schäfer 1974: 198–213).

verse 1 that those who restore a sinner should be careful that they do not fall into temptation (the temptation to think too much of themselves; Lightfoot 1881: 216; cf. also Betz 1979: 301). But perhaps the best option is to take verses 3–5 as a further discrete development of the warning about "conceit" (κενόδοξοι) in verse 26 (Mussner 1988: 400; cf. Hays 2000: 334). As we noted, verses 25–26 serve as a kind of heading for what follows, so it is natural to think that verses 3–5 would return to elaborate on one of the key concerns in those verses.

Verse 3 is an implicit warning in the form of a conditional sentence. The protasis, in a "considered true for the sake of argument" form (εἰ [*ei*, if] + indicative δοκεῖ [*dokei*, thinks]), refers to a believer who, "while being nothing" (μηδὲν ὤν [*mēden ōn*]) "thinks they are something" (τι [*ti*]). Such people, Paul argues, are "deceiving themselves" (φρεναπατᾷ ἑαυτόν [*phrenapata heauton*]).[15] This verb occurs for the first time here in extant Greek, but its meaning is clear from this context and from its cognate adjective (φρεναπάτης, *phrenapatēs*) in Titus 1:10. Paul's claim that believers "are nothing" must, of course, be carefully qualified. There is no intention to dismiss the biblical teaching about the worth of human beings as created in the image of God (e.g., James 3:9). Paul's concern is the tendency for believers to take credit for their own accomplishments without recognizing their absolute dependence on God's grace and Spirit for anything useful that is done for the Lord.

In contrast, then, to a superficial and deceptive view of themselves as more than they really are (the δέ [*de*] is adversative: "but"),[16] every believer should "test their own work" (τὸ . . . ἔργον ἑαυτοῦ δοκιμαζέτω, *to . . . ergon heautou dokimazetō*). The singular ἔργον is a collective, picturing the many actions of a person as a totality. In light of Pauline usage, one could argue that this "work" might refer specifically to the work of ministry (1 Cor. 3:13–15; 9:1; 16:10; Eph. 4:12; Phil. 2:30; 1 Thess. 5:13; 2 Tim. 4:5). And the clear reference to ministry in verse 6 could provide some contextual basis for this interpretation. But the near context does not suggest such a restriction; verses 5 and 7–8 appear to be more general in their focus. Probably, then, the word ἔργον refers generally to all that a believer does (as in Rom. 2:7; 1 Cor. 15:58; 1 Thess. 1:3; and so virtually all interpreters). We are again reminded that Paul does not oppose works in principle but only when those works are thought to be the basis for God's justifying verdict and therefore undercut the primacy and absolute nature of grace.[17] The verb δοκιμάζω (*dokimazō*) means "examine to test genuineness," and the self-testing that Paul calls for echoes widespread Greco-Roman teaching about the importance of "knowing oneself" (Betz 1979: 302). Paul elsewhere stresses the importance of believers' engaging in

6:4

---

15. Following the trend of modern English, here we use "themselves" after the singular "someone" (τις, *tis*) in a distributive, or singular, sense (see a synopsis of the Collins Study of Gender Language at http://www.niv-cbt.org/information/collins-corpus-report/; and note NIV).

16. Some interpreters (Burton 1921: 332; R. Longenecker 1990: 277) connect v. 4 with vv. 1–2.

17. Contra, e.g., Dunn (1993a: 325), who thinks that the opposition is between "works of the law" and "works" in general.

this kind of self-assessment, but a self-assessment that now takes into account the reality of God's standard and grace (see esp. 1 Cor. 4:3–5; 2 Cor. 13:5; and also 1 Cor. 11:28).

The result (καὶ τότε, *kai tote*, and then) of this self-examination is stated in the second half of the verse. The key point comes in the contrast between εἰς ἑαυτὸν μόνον (*eis heauton monon*, unto oneself alone) and εἰς τὸν ἕτερον (*eis ton heteron*, unto the other). "The other" (ἕτερον) is another person: "someone else" (NIV). Based on Rom. 13:8 ("the one who loves the other [ἕτερον] has fulfilled the law" [AT]) and some other texts, it is possible that ἕτερον here is equivalent to πλησίον (*plēsion*); hence the translation "neighbor" in RSV, NRSV, ESV (and see Burton 1921: 333). The nature of the contrast in these antithetical phrases is not clear, the interpretation hinging on two issues: the meaning of καύχημα (*kauchēma*) and the force of the twice-used preposition εἰς. (1) The word καύχημα might mean "act of boasting" (as in 1 Cor. 5:6; 2 Cor. 5:12; 9:3; Phil. 1:26; 2:16), and the preposition εἰς could have its usual "directional" sense. The contrast in this case would be between one who makes boasts to others and one who boasts only to oneself. Any sense of accomplishment that might arise from self-examination should be kept to oneself and not brought up before others (e.g., Barclay 1988: 160–61; Martyn 1997: 550; Hays 2000: 334). (2) On the other hand, καύχημα might refer to the cause or the basis for boasting: "that which constitutes a source of pride" (BDAG 537.1; cf. Rom. 4:2; 1 Cor. 9:16; 2 Cor. 1:14). The preposition εἰς would then mean "with reference to" or "in regard to." Two specific options for interpretation emerge from this general reading. (a) Paul might mean that every believer should find a reason to boast in their own work and not take pride in the work of another (NRSV, ESV, HCSB, NAB, NASB; Witherington 1998: 428). (b) Paul might mean that a believer should view one's own work alone as a cause for boasting, without having to engage in comparisons with the work of someone else (see esp. NIV, NET, NLT; Betz 1979: 302–3; Dunn 1993a: 325). The pattern of Pauline usage with regard to prepositions after this noun or its cognate verb may slightly favor view 1,[18] but the context seems strongly to favor some form of view 2. For Paul goes on to stress the fact that each believer will need to stand before God in the judgment on the basis of what they have done (v. 5). A further decision between views 2a and 2b is difficult, but we slightly favor the latter: one's cause of boasting should rest solely on self-scrutiny without involving comparison with what others are doing. If, as we think, the future

---

18. When Paul specifies the thing, or person, "with regard to which" one boasts (using either καύχημα or its cognate verb καυχάομαι [*kauchaomai*, boast]), he normally uses ἐν (*en*, in; e.g., Rom. 2:17; 5:11; 1 Cor. 1:31; Phil. 3:3) and occasionally ἐπί (*epi*, in; Rom. 5:2) or ὑπέρ (*hyper*, in; 2 Cor. 5:12; 9:3). However, in one text (2 Cor. 11:10) he does use εἰς after a cognate noun (καύχημα) to denote the person with regard to which he boasts: ἔστιν ἀλήθεια Χριστοῦ ἐν ἐμοὶ ὅτι ἡ καύχησις αὕτη οὐ φραγήσεται εἰς ἐμὲ ἐν τοῖς κλίμασιν τῆς Ἀχαΐας (*estin alētheia Christou en emoi hoti hē kauchēsis hautē ou phragēsetai eis eme en tois klimasin tēs Achaias*, as the truth of Christ is in me, this boasting with respect to me will not be stopped in the regions of Achaia [AT]).

judgment is in view in verse 5, the future verb ἕξει (*hexei*, will have) in verse 4 may have a similar focus (Mussner 1988: 401). In any case, Paul's purpose is to discourage self-congratulation that rests on a comparison with others (R. Longenecker 1990: 277). We can always find people who are doing worse than we are in matters of the Spirit and take confidence from that comparison. But when we look at ourselves honestly and in light of God's word and his expectations of us, the result will often be quite different.

6:5

This verse flows naturally from our interpretation of verse 4: as believers put their work "of faith" to the test, they should find cause for boasting in *their own work* (and not through comparison with others' work) *because* (γάρ, *gar*) "each person will carry their own load" (ἕκαστος . . . τὸ ἴδιον φορτίον βαστάσει, *hekastos . . . to idion phortion bastasei*)—that is, on the day of judgment, each person will need to answer to the Lord for their conduct. We therefore follow those interpreters who find in the future verb βαστάσει an allusion to the eschatological judgment (e.g., Matera 1992: 222; Hays 2000: 335; Schreiner 2010: 362). Other interpreters suggest that the saying is gnomic in character, with the future tense functioning simply to state what is usually true (see Betz 1979: 304; translations that render the future verb as "should" or "must" carry [NIV, NRSV; cf. NJB] may reflect this interpretation). What Paul says about individual responsibility on the day of judgment finds an echo in 2 Esd. (4 Ezra) 7:104–5:

> The day of judgment is decisive and displays to all the seal of truth. Just as now a father does not send his son, or a son his father, or a master his servant, or a friend his dearest friend, to be ill or sleep or eat or be healed in his place, [105]so no one shall ever pray for another on that day, neither shall anyone lay a burden on another; for then all shall bear their own righteousness and unrighteousness.

This eschatological interpretation removes any possible conflict between this verse and verse 2a, for they are referring to different matters. When Paul urges the Galatians to "bear one another's burdens," he intends for them to enter empathetically into the problems and cares of fellow believers. When he now warns that "each will bear their own burden," he reminds them that it is the total conduct of their own lives alone that will be evaluated by God on the day of judgment. The word φορτίον normally has the somewhat negative nuance of "burden" (eight LXX occurrences and Matt. 11:30; 23:4; Luke 11:46 [2x]; Acts 27:10), and some interpreters therefore think that it might here refer to the "daily struggle of life" (Betz 1979: 304). But the word is probably chosen for its natural resonance with the verb "carry," "bear" (βαστάζω) and refers to the ἔργον of the believer (v. 4): the sum total of one's conduct and service to the Lord (Martyn 1997: 550).[19] Nevertheless, the slightly negative nuance of the whole expression should not be missed: even for believers who

---

19. Witherington (1998: 429), on the other hand, thinks the term might refer to finances (see the comments on 6:2 and the first footnote there).

are confident in their justification, the judgment of God is a solemn prospect (Eastman 2007: 167).

6:6   Paul now encourages "the one who receives instruction" (ὁ κατηχούμενος, *ho katēchoumenos*) in the "word" or "message" (τὸν λόγον, *ton logon*) of the gospel to "share" (κοινωνείτω, *koinōneitō*) with "their teacher" (τῷ κατηχοῦντι, *tō katēchounti*) "in all good things" (ἐν πᾶσιν ἀγαθοῖς, *en pasin agathois*). Two interpretations of this injunction are possible, depending on whether we understand the imperative κοινωνείτω in an active or passive sense. If passive, Paul would be encouraging the person who is being taught to "be sharing *in* all the good things" that the teacher is imparting in the instruction. These "good things" would then be spiritual in nature; and a close parallel would be Rom. 15:27, where Paul refers to Gentiles who "share [ἐκοινώνησαν, *ekoinōnēsan*] in the spiritual blessings of the Jews" (AT). On the other hand, if active, Paul's point would be that the one who is being taught is responsible to "share *with*" the "one who is teaching" "all good things." In this case, "all good things" would be material in nature, and Phil. 4:15 would furnish a parallel: "Moreover, as you Philippians know, in the early days of your acquaintance with the gospel, when I set out from Macedonia, not one church shared with me [μοι ... ἐκοινώνησεν, *moi ... ekoinōnēsen*] in the matter of giving and receiving, except you only." A few interpreters favor the former view, spiritual sharing (Oepke 1973: 191–93); but the overwhelming majority of interpreters favor the latter, material sharing (e.g., Mussner 1988: 403; R. Longenecker 1990: 278–79). And indeed, the latter view is to be preferred, since it better explains why Paul puts the responsibility on the one being taught rather than on the one who is teaching (Dunn 1993a: 327).

If this is what Paul means, we can next ask about how it is related to its context. It is possible, indeed, that the injunction stands on its own with little thematic connection with its context (see Betz 1979: 304; the NRSV and NLT make v. 6 its own paragraph). But it is also possible to find some contextual connection. On the one hand, Paul might be encouraging believers to share with their teachers in light of the fact that they will reap what they sow (v. 7)—a connection rendered plausible by the way Paul uses the metaphor of sowing and reaping elsewhere with reference to finances (2 Cor. 9:6). Most English Bibles suggest such a connection by attaching the verse to what follows (ESV, CEB, NKJV, HCSB, NET). Other translations, however, attach the verse to what precedes (NIV). The specific connection might then be with verse 2: sharing with others is a form of burden bearing (Lightfoot 1881: 217). But we think a more likely connection is with the immediately preceding verses. Paul has just put a strong emphasis on individual responsibility, arguing that believers should find cause for boasting in their own work (v. 4) and that they will need to answer for their own conduct on the day of judgment (v. 5). This emphasis on self-reliance could, Paul realizes, easily be misinterpreted as a reason to hold back from supporting those who teach. Here he therefore heads off any such incorrect inference from his principle of self-examination (see Barclay 1988: 162–63; Dunn 1993a: 326).

The importance of supporting Christians who are active in teaching the word is founded in the words of Jesus (Luke 10:7; cf. 1 Cor. 9:14). The word that Paul uses for both the "one teaching" and "the one being taught" is κατηχέω (*katēcheō*), a quasi-technical word in the NT for gospel instruction (Luke 1:4; Acts 18:25; 21:21, 24; 1 Cor. 14:19; cf. Rom. 2:18); the word "catechesis" ("catechetical"), later used to denote formal instruction in the rudiments of the Christian faith, is derived from it. We have little knowledge of the situation in Galatia that might have given rise to this particular injunction. Some have speculated that the reference might be to the collection for the saints in Jerusalem, with the "instructor" perhaps being the Jerusalem or Jewish church, and the "one being instructed" being the Gentile churches of Galatia (e.g., Hurtado 1979: 53–57; Mussner 1988: 402–3; cf. Borse 1972: 37–38; and note the Rom. 15:27 text cited earlier). But the language Paul uses here is hardly amenable to such an application (Martyn 1997: 552). We simply have no data on which to suppose anything more than what this verse plainly indicates: that there was in the Galatia churches a recognized group of people engaged in gospel instruction, and that it was incumbent on those taught by these people to provide the instructors with financial support.

Additional Notes

5:26. In the last clause of the verse, the MS tradition varies between the accusative ἀλλήλους and the dative ἀλλήλοις. Either is grammatically possible, but the accusative is suspect of assimilation to the accusative form of the same word earlier in the verse (e.g., Burton 1921: 324; contra Lightfoot 1881: 214).

6:1. After ἄνθρωπος, a few MSS add ἐξ ὑμῶν. The addition no doubt reflects the correct interpretation, specifying that the person is "from among" the Galatians, but it has slim external support.

6:2. The verb in the second half of the verse is a future indicative (ἀναπληρώσετε) in many MSS (e.g., B) and an aorist imperative (ἀναπληρώσατε) in others (e.g., ℵ), including 𝔐 (note KJV: "and so fulfill"). A change from one to the other would have been very easy since the difference consists in only one letter. The UBS committee gave slight preference to the future (a "C" rating) on the basis of diversified external support and the suspicion that scribes might have conformed an original future indicative to the imperatives found in the context (Metzger 1994: 530; for the opposite conclusion, see Burton 1921: 330).

D. The Urgency of Living the New Life (6:7–10)

The fourth and final section in the paraenetic part of the letter falls into two parts. In the first (vv. 7–8), Paul seeks to motivate his readers to action by warning that their conduct will have consequences for the eschatological judgment. Appeal to the prospect of a divine assessment in the last day is a natural and typical way for Paul to conclude his paraenesis (see esp. Rom. 13:11–14 within 12:1–13:14; and also Phil. 3:12–21). Paul returns to the flesh-Spirit antithesis, which he made central in his description of the Christian life in 5:13–25. The second part of the paragraph (vv. 9–10) summarizes Paul's paraenesis in a final exhortation to his readers to be fully and consistently engaged in "doing good."

Exegesis and Exposition

[7]Do not be deceived: God is not mocked. For whatever a person sows, that they will also reap. [8]For the one who sows to his own flesh will reap destruction from that flesh. But the one who sows to the Spirit will reap eternal life from that Spirit. [9]Let us not become weary in doing good, for at just the right moment we will reap a harvest if we do not give up. [10]Therefore, as we ⌜have⌝ time, let us ⌜do⌝ good to everyone, and especially to the household of faith.

6:7   The opening clause, "Do not be deceived" (μὴ πλανᾶσθε, *mē planasthe*), does not indicate that Paul thinks the Galatians are in danger of being tempted to mock God; it is a rhetorical device to draw attention to what Paul is about to say (note NAB: "Make no mistake"; see also 1 Cor. 6:9; 15:33 [both, interestingly, in eschatological contexts]; James 1:16). The verb translated "mocked" (μυκτηρίζεται, *myktērizetai*) has the etymological sense of "turn up one's nose at" (μυκτήρ, *myktēr*, means "nose"; see BDAG 660). It occurs only here in the NT (although the compound form, ἐκμυκτηρίζω, *ekmyktērizō*, is found in Luke 16:14; 23:35) but is used sixteen times in the LXX. Particularly relevant is 2 Chron. 36:16: "But they [the unfaithful priests and people] mocked [μυκτηρίζοντες, *myktērizontes*] God's messengers, despised his words and scoffed at his prophets until the wrath of the LORD was aroused against his people and there was no remedy." Paul, similarly, is concerned that believers may "mock" God by not taking seriously his word of warning about the judgment to come.

But before he gives the substance of this warning (v. 8), Paul prepares the way by introducing the particular word picture that he will use to make his point. Especially in societies dominated by agriculture, the use of the imagery of "sowing" and "reaping [a harvest]" is a natural way to speak of cause and consequence. This language had become proverbial, found in the wider Greco-Roman world (see F. Hauck, *TDNT* 3:132–33), in the OT (see esp. Job 4:8; Ps. 126:5; Prov. 22:8; Jer. 12:13; Hosea 8:7), in Judaism (e.g., Sir. 7:3), and elsewhere in the NT (1 Cor. 9:11; 2 Cor. 9:6; cf. also John 4:36–38). In texts such as 2 Cor. 9:6 (see the comments on 6:6 above), Paul's application of this imagery to financial giving has led some interpreters to think that the proverb is intended to support Paul's plea for the support of teachers in Gal. 6:6 (e.g., Hurtado 1979: 53; Witherington 1998: 431; Schreiner 2010: 368). But the obvious connection is with verse 8, where Paul picks up the proverb to encourage Christian obedience in light of the coming judgment.

Paul now fills out the terms of the proverb; the ὅτι (*hoti*) is not causal ("because," as in HCSB) but explanatory: "that is [the application in this instance is]:" (see Schreiner 2010: 368). Paul emphasizes the similarity between the two instances of sowing and reaping by maintaining a close parallelism between the two clauses, even to the point of keeping the same order of words and phrases in the Greek: **6:8**

ὁ σπείρων εἰς τὴν σάρκα ἑαυτοῦ ἐκ τῆς σαρκὸς θερίσει φθοράν,
ὁ δὲ σπείρων εἰς τὸ πνεῦμα ἐκ τοῦ πνεύματος θερίσει ζωὴν αἰώνιον.

ho speirōn eis tēn sarka heautou ek tēs sarkos therisei phthoran,
ho de speirōn eis to pneuma ek tou pneumatos therisei zōēn aiōnion.

The one who sows to their own flesh will reap destruction from that flesh,
but the one who sows to the Spirit will reap eternal life from that Spirit.

One difference, however, is apparent: the reflexive pronoun in the first clause—"their own [ἑαυτοῦ] flesh"—has no counterpart in the second clause, where Paul refers simply to "the Spirit." "Spirit" is rightly capitalized in English versions (a puzzling exception is the NAB): Paul refers to the Holy Spirit, given to all believers as the mark of the new age (3:3) and both the power (5:16) and standard (5:25b) by which they are to live for the Lord within that new age. The contrast between this Spirit and the flesh is central to Paul's presentation of the Christian life. The Spirit has taken control of believers (5:18), both enabling and compelling them to an obedience not possible before. But in this time between the two "appearances" of Christ (Titus 2:12–13), believers continue to be affected by the "flesh," their rootedness by virtue of being fallen human beings in the things of this world. Why, then, does Paul speak in this verse of "their own flesh"? One option is that he alludes to the physicality of each person's flesh, reminding the Galatians that they are faced with the choice of continuing their Christian walk by means of the Spirit—or succumbing to circumcision and all that it entails (see esp. 5:2–4; and see Matera 1992:

216; Hays 2000: 336).[1] Paul makes the connection between circumcision and the flesh explicit later in chapter 6 (vv. 12–13). Yet, while perhaps an allusion to circumcision cannot be ruled out, "flesh" must refer to much more than circumcision in light of its obvious reference back to the language of 5:13–26. Probably, then, Paul refers to "their own" flesh because, unlike God's Spirit, "flesh" is something that belongs innately to fallen human beings. The source of temptation, as James reminds us, lies within each person (1:13–15).

"Sowing" refers to the actions or conduct of a person, while "reaping" refers to the consequences of those actions and particularly to the consequences that will come about on the day of judgment. "Reaping" or "harvesting" alludes to the judgment elsewhere in Scripture (Jer. 12:13; Matt. 13:24–30, 36–43; Rev. 14:15–16). Paul's use of an everyday, natural phenomenon such as sowing and reaping to illuminate a spiritual matter inevitably puts a strain on the language. Only in three other texts in the Greek Bible (Judg. 9:45 [B]; Matt. 13:22//Mark 4:18; all three in a physical sense) do we find the combination of the verb σπείρω (speirō, sow) and the preposition εἰς. The preposition probably has a sense similar to the dative of advantage (see BDAG 290.4.g on this), signifying the person or thing "for whom" the sowing is done. Sowing "to please" (NIV) or "to satisfy" (NLT) the flesh/Spirit, then, is close to the idea (contra Dunn 1993a: 330). To emphasize the parallel between cause and consequence, Paul uses a second set of prepositional phrases with the verb θερίσει: ἐκ τῆς σαρκός / τοῦ πνεύματος. Paul pictures the flesh and the Spirit as, in a sense, "paying back" people for the service they render them, the flesh with φθορά and the Spirit with ζωὴ αἰώνιος. The word φθορά can mean either "corruption" (most English versions; cf. Rom. 8:21; 1 Cor. 15:42, 50; Col. 2:22; 2 Pet. 1:4; 2:19) or "destruction" (NIV). Some favor the former meaning here in light of the word picture Paul is using, with φθορά referring to rotten or decaying crops (e.g., Lightfoot 1881: 219). But the parallel between φθοράν and ζωὴν αἰώνιον shows that Paul has moved beyond the figure of speech and is considering the spiritual realities to which the figure points. Probably, then, φθοράν refers to the ultimate "corruption" that is eternal death, the negative verdict in God's judgment (cf. 2 Pet. 2:12 [albeit in a metaphor]; and so most commentators). "Destruction" is an adequate translation, always remembering that, when applied to the eternal state in the NT, this kind of language refers not to annihilation but to eternal judgment (see, e.g., Moo 2004). And since Paul uses φθορά elsewhere to describe the "body of corruption," in contrast to the "incorruptible," resurrection body, "eternal life" may allude particularly to the life of resurrection (Dunn 1993a: 331).

While Paul uses the generic language of "one who sows" in this verse, it is clear from the reference to the Spirit and from the context that he is referring to people from within the community of faith. And reference to "destruction" and "eternal life" shows that he refers not to degrees of reward that believers may look forward to in the next life (contra, e.g., G. Vos 1972: 269–79), but to

---

1. Dunn (1993a: 330) typically finds an allusion to ethnic exclusiveness in the word "flesh."

that life itself: salvation. Human effort, Paul makes clear (as he does elsewhere, e.g., Rom. 8:12–13), is required if a believer expects to attain ultimate salvation. This insistence on the indispensability of human works for the attaining of eternal life must, of course, be integrated with Paul's equally clear insistence in Galatians that our ultimate justification rests on our faith and the work of the Spirit (see 5:5 and our comments there). Paul himself highlights the importance of the Spirit in this verse: it is "from the Spirit" that believers will reap eternal life. Faith is not explicitly mentioned here. But we can hardly have forgotten that just a chapter earlier Paul has insisted that it is "faith working through love" that counts (5:6). We thus cannot be accused of imposing an alien dogmatic edifice on Paul if we seek to read all these texts in harmony with one another. Human works that please the Spirit are indeed necessary for final salvation, and the very fact that Paul sets forth two options before his readers makes clear that he does not assume that all those he addresses will necessarily produce those works. But Paul's teaching elsewhere in this very letter justifies our claiming that these works are the effect of faith and are produced in and through the Spirit.[2] Nevertheless, we must be careful lest our insistence on "faith alone" leave insufficient space for responsible human activity. It might be accurate to follow the Reformation tradition in labeling works the "evidence" of faith. But we must also finally do justice to the fact that this evidence is something we are commanded to produce.[3]

Paul wraps up the paraenetic section of the letter with a general call for believers to be "doing good" (καλὸν ποιοῦντες, *kalon poiountes*, in verse 9; ἐργαζώμεθα τὸ ἀγαθόν [*ergazōmetha to agathon*, let us do good] in v. 10). The δέ (*de*) that connects these two verses to the previous context marks discourse development (Runge 2010: 28–36). In this case the development involves both a kind of inference from verse 7—you must "sow to the Spirit," *therefore* "do good" (cf. NLT, HCSB)—and a general summary of 5:13–6:8. "So then," found in many English versions (RSV, NRSV, ESV, NAB, NASB, NET, NJB), expresses the relationship well. A connection with verse 8 is evident also in the continuation in this verse of the harvest imagery; as Dunn (1993a: 331–32) puts it, the allusion is to "the sustained hard work required of the farmer between sowing and reaping if the harvest . . . is to be won."

6:9

But Paul does not simply exhort his readers to do good; rather, "Let us not grow weary in doing good" (τὸ δὲ καλὸν ποιοῦντες μὴ ἐγκακῶμεν, *to de kalon poiountes mē enkakōmen*).[4] And at the end of the verse Paul returns to reinforce

2. Some recent writers have failed to integrate these perspectives as well as they might have (e.g., Yinger 1999; Rainbow 2005; and esp. VanLandingham 2006: 208–10, on this passage).

3. Calvin (1854: 179) typically acknowledges the biblical use of the language of "reward," yet he attributes the reward entirely to grace: "The undeserved kindness of God appears in the very act of honouring the works which his grace has enabled us to perform, by promising to them a reward to which they are not entitled."

4. The participle ποιοῦντες "supplements" the hortatory subjunctive ἐγκακῶμεν, which is otherwise an incomplete thought (BDF §414.2; Wallace 1996: 646). The verb ἐγκακέω (*enkakeō*),

this same point: "if we do not give up" (μὴ ἐκλυόμενοι, *mē eklyomenoi*).[5] Why express the point in this negative way? R. Longenecker (1990: 281), in accordance with his general reading of this part of the letter, suspects that Paul is countering libertine influence. It is also possible that the divisions apparently created by the agitators and the different reception given to them within the Galatian churches might have created lassitude about active engagement in Christian work. On the other hand, such lassitude may have arisen simply through the passing of time (Betz 1979: 309). This latter interpretation finds some basis in 2 Thess. 3:13, which is remarkably similar to our verse: "Never tire of doing what is good" (μὴ ἐγκακήσητε καλοποιοῦντες, *mē enkakēsēte kalopoiountes*). By using the general language of "doing good" to depict Christian responsibility, Paul not only summarizes all the various specific things he has exhorted believers to do in this context; he is also able to show how that duty extends to matters that may not be so obviously related to faith.[6]

The reason (γάρ, *gar*, for) why believers should not grow weary in doing good is because "at just the right moment we will reap a harvest" (καιρῷ ... ἰδίῳ θερίσομεν, *kairō ... idio therisomen*). The language of "reaping" is carried over from verses 7–8 and thus refers to the final judgment. The phrase καιρῷ ἰδίῳ means, strictly, "in one's own time." But in such contexts ἴδιος comes to mean "appropriate" (e.g., Acts 1:25; 1 Cor. 3:8; 15:23). In this context, then, it probably means "at the time that is appropriate for the harvest." The resulting sense could be "whenever the harvest is gathered" (e.g., Lightfoot 1881: 220), but in light of the evident reference to the judgment with the harvest language in verse 8, it probably means the appointed time of eschatological evaluation (see Matt. 13:30; the plural καιροὶ ἴδιοι occurs in the Pastoral Epistles to denote definitive moments of God's intervention [1 Tim. 2:6; 6:15; Titus 1:3; cf. 1 Cor. 4:5]; for this interpretation see, e.g., Wallace 1996: 157; Bruce 1982b: 265).

6:10   Verse 10 has much in common with verse 9: in both verses the central call is to "do good," and this doing good is related to an "appropriate time" (καιρός). But Paul also sets off this verse from verse 9 with the strong doubled inferential ἄρα οὖν (*ara oun*, now therefore). With this final call to do good, then, Paul is concluding at least all of 6:1–10 and perhaps all of 5:13–6:10 (R. Longenecker 1990: 282). Paul uses ἀγαθός (*agathos*) to denote the "good" that believers are to be "doing" (ἐργαζώμεθα, *ergazōmetha*, a durative present), a different word than the one he used for the same idea in verse 9 (καλός, *kalos*). It is sometimes possible to find a semantic distinction between these words, but in this context they are synonymous (as also in Rom. 7:18 and 1 Tim. 5:10 in a similar sense). We are, Paul says, to be engaged in this doing good "as we have time/opportunity" (ὡς καιρὸν ἔχομεν, *hōs kairon echomen*). The word

---

"to grow weary," "to become discouraged," "to lose heart," is a late Greek word, appearing in the NT also in Luke 18:1; 2 Cor. 4:1, 16; Eph. 3:13; 2 Thess. 3:13.

5. The participle is conditional (Wallace 1996: 633).

6. "Doing good" could, then, include financial support, but (contra, e.g., Schreiner 2010: 370) it is unlikely that it is specially singled out.

καιρός could again (as in v. 9) refer to "any opportunity one might have" (R. Longenecker 1990: 282; the "whenever" in several translations [NRSV, NLT, NET] seems to signal this meaning), but, as in verse 9, it probably has a more theological sense: "as long as the appointed time before the end lasts" (the word has this sense in Rom. 3:26; 8:18; 13:11; 1 Cor. 7:29; 2 Cor. 6:2; 2 Tim. 3:1 [plural]; see, e.g., Betz 1979: 310).

The general call to do "good" fits with the people for whom that good is to be done: "everyone" (πάντας, pantas). As the next phrase makes clear, this "all" is without boundaries, including unbelievers as well as believers. Amid the vital theological issue with which they are wrestling and the internal divisions this issue has created, the Galatian Christians are to continue to manifest the love of Christ and grace of God to all the people they come into contact with.[7] When Paul then adds, "especially to the household of faith" (μάλιστα δὲ πρὸς τοὺς οἰκείους τῆς πίστεως, malista de pros tous oikeious tēs pisteōs), this is meant "not as a narrowing of the general obligation, but as the most immediate way of giving it effect" (Dunn 1993a: 333). Calling the fellowship of believers a "household" has OT roots ("the house of Israel" [e.g., Lev. 10:6; Num. 20:29; Judg. 2:1 LXX]) and brings to expression one of the key NT images of the church, an extended spiritual family (see οἰκεῖος in Eph. 2:19; and οἶκος in 1 Tim. 3:15; 1 Pet. 2:5; 4:17; Heb. 3:6; and, of course, the ubiquitous address "brothers and sisters"). Paul may choose this particular expression in order deliberately to mark out the church as the new covenant counterpart to Israel (see 6:16; Dunn 1993a: 333; Garlington 2003: 279; the objection of Hays [2000: 337] rests too much on lexical difference between οἶκος [in the OT] and οἰκεῖος). The language also provides the community with a status that they would readily recognize and that would enable them to confirm their identity as a cohesive group within their culture (Esler 1998: 224–25, 233–34). It is also no accident that Paul uses the word "faith" to characterize this new spiritual family. As he has argued throughout Galatians, faith (in Christ)[8] is the fundamental and transforming mark of God's new covenant people.

Additional Notes

6:10. Some very good MSS (e.g., ℵ and B) read the hortatory subjunctive ἔχωμεν—"let us have [or enjoy]"—in place of the better attested indicative (ἔχομεν). The confusion of the two words was easy, involving a difference between two vowels that sound a lot alike (see also Rom. 5:1). The indicative is virtually required by the context (with ὡς).

6:10. A second variant in v. 10 involves exactly the same issue: a difference between the vowels omicron (o) and omega (ω) that signals a difference between an indicative (ἐργαζόμεθα) and a subjunctive (ἐργαζώμεθα; there are also two other less attested variants). Solid external attestation and context favor the (hortatory) subjunctive (Metzger 1994: 530), "Let us do good."

---

7. B. Longenecker (2010: 141–42) sees a particular focus on helping the poor.
8. Not the "faith/faithfulness" of Christ, as D. Campbell (2009: 894) thinks.

V. Closing: Cross and New Creation (6:11–18)

The title of Jeff Weima's book (1994) on the conclusions of the Pauline Letters, *Neglected Endings*, makes an important point. Too often we move rapidly through or even ignore the endings of these letters, thinking that what Paul really wanted to communicate has now been concluded. But this is a mistake, and in no letter of Paul is this more of a mistake than in Galatians. Various studies, some of which compare Paul's Letters with letters in the wider Greco-Roman world, have shown that Paul's letter endings fall into a clear pattern, marked by certain standard features (see the additional note on 6:11–18). The ending of Galatians, however, omits some of these standard features, such as greetings of other believers, requests to greet others, notification of travel plans, requests for prayer, and doxologies. In their place, Paul has included a final rebuke of the agitators (vv. 12–13) and significant theological comment on the situation and status of his readers: with Paul (implied), they have been "crucified to the world" and "the world to them" (v. 14); they live in the new creation (v. 15), and they constitute the "new Israel" (v. 16). It is not hard to figure out why the ending of Galatians takes this different form. As was the case with the introduction to the letter, the urgency of the situation in Galatia leads Paul to dispense with some of the usual "polite" formulas and to cut right to the heart of the life-and-death issue confronting the churches (see esp. Weima 1994: 159–60).

The ending of the letter matches the introduction in another respect also: both set the situation in Galatia and Paul's response to it in their appropriate eschatological context (B. Longenecker 1998: 36–46). Rescue from the "present evil age" (1:4) is matched in 6:14 by Paul's claim to have been separated from "the world" by means of his cocrucifixion with Christ. Positively, Paul wants the Galatians to recognize and take to heart the reality of the "new creation" in which they now live (v. 15). Christ's death has broken the power of the old age, the world, and inaugurated God's all-embracing work of making the universe new. Recognizing that Christians by faith are participants in this eschatological project should go a long way to helping them resist the claims of the agitators, bound as they are, according to Paul, to a past age and a world already in principle judged by God. Granted the importance of these conceptions, then, it is only a slight exaggeration to claim that the ending of the letter provides "the hermeneutical key to the intentions of the Apostle" (as Betz [1979: 313] puts it; see also Weima 1994: 160–61; 1993: 93–94). Paul uses this ending both to sum up the central concern of his argument and to move his readers to action (Witherington 1998: 443–45).

The structure of the passage is concentric. The reference to Paul's own "signature" in verse 11 and the grace wish in verse 18 provide a formal frame around the passage. Paul's rebuke of the agitators in verses 12–13 is matched by his plea that such people no longer "give him trouble" in verse 17. And at the center of the passage are the key theological images—crucifixion to the world; new creation; and believers as the "Israel of God," maintaining this new-creation perspective—that should reorient the mind-set of the Galatian Christians. The passage is characterized throughout, as Weima (1994: 161) has noted, by antitheses between the agitators and Paul: they are motivated by selfish considerations while Paul is motivated by Christ's cross; they focus on the physical mark of circumcision, Paul on the "marks" of Jesus; they are bound to this world, and Paul is bound to the next world (see also Witherington 1998: 445). And the creator of all these antitheses is the cross of Christ (vv. 12, 14).

Exegesis and Exposition

[11]See with what large letters I write to you in my own hand! [12]As many as want to make a good showing in the flesh, these are trying to force you to be circumcised— only they want to avoid ⌜being persecuted⌝ because of the cross of ⌜Christ⌝. [13]For not even ⌜the circumcised⌝ themselves are keeping the law, but they want you to be circumcised in order that they might boast in your flesh. [14]But as for me, may I never boast in anything except the cross of our Lord Jesus Christ, though which the world has been crucified to me and I to the world. [15]For ⌜ ⌝ neither circumcision nor uncircumcision ⌜means⌝ anything, but the new creation. [16]And peace and mercy be upon as many as ⌜stay in step⌝ with this rule—even to the Israel of God. [17]From now on, let no one give me any trouble, for I bear in my body the marks of ⌜Jesus⌝. [18]The grace of our Lord Jesus Christ be with your spirit, brothers and sisters. Amen.

The letter closing opens with an "autograph," Paul's "signature," as it were. **6:11** He asks his readers to "notice" (the NLT rendering of ἴδετε [*idete*, see]) that he writes with "such large letters" (πηλίκοις . . . γράμμασιν, *pēlikois . . . grammasin*) and "in my own hand" (τῇ ἐμῇ χειρί, *tē emē cheiri*). "I write" (ἔγραψα, *egrapsa*), with the specific reference to letters, refers not to authorship in a general sense but to the physical act of "writing down" (see BDAG 207.2.b). How much of the letter is Paul referring to? The verb "write" is in the aorist tense, which could refer to what Paul has already written. Chrysostom (*Comm. Gal.* on 6:12 [*NPNF*[1] 13:46]), therefore, thought that Paul was claiming to have written all of Galatians in his own hand. But this would be unusual. Most ancient letter writers entrusted the actual writing down of a letter to an amanuensis; and Rom. 16:22—"I, Tertius, who wrote down this letter"—shows that Paul was no exception (on the use of an amanuensis in the ancient world and in the NT, see esp. R. Longenecker 1974; Richards 1991). Probably, then, ἔγραψα in Gal. 6:11 is an epistolary aorist, referring not to a past but a present action, and what Paul himself "wrote down" is only 6:11–18 (so the vast majority of scholars; virtually all the English versions so translate [the exception being NKJV, following here the KJV]). We cannot know who Paul's amanuensis was; but at this point Paul takes up the stylus reed to add his signature as a kind of authentication of the letter. See especially 2 Thess. 3:17: "I, Paul, write this greeting in my own hand, which is the distinguishing mark in all my letters. This is how I write" (and also Philem. 19).

Scholars love to speculate on what cannot be known; and so it is regarding the reason why Paul claims he is writing "such large letters." Three suggestions are worth mentioning: (1) Paul was unskilled in writing and so wrote letters much larger than a trained amanuensis was able to do (Deissmann 1903: 348–49); (2) Paul's failing eyesight (see 4:13–15 and the comments on those verses) was at fault (Witherington 1998: 441; du Toit 2007: 166); or (3) Paul wanted to emphasize what he is saying by using the ancient equivalent of a bold font (so the large majority of scholars). There is some evidence from ancient writing that large letters were sometimes used for emphasis, so this third option is certainly viable. But Witherington (1998: 441) is right to ask why Paul does not, then, draw attention to large letters elsewhere when he wants to make an important point. At the end of the speculation, we cannot know why the letters here are large.

6:12 In verses 12–13 Paul turns to the agitators, focusing on two basic points. First, he briefly describes their agenda and their personal failings: they "are trying to force you to be circumcised" (v. 12b), "they want you to be circumcised" (v. 13b), and "they are not themselves keeping the law" (v. 13a). Second, he analyzes their motives: they "want to make a good showing in the flesh" (v. 12a), they want to avoid being persecuted because of the cross of Christ (v. 12c), and they "want to boast in your flesh" (v. 13c). The agitators' concern with "flesh" thus brackets these verses (Martyn 1997: 561). In a context that focuses on circumcision, σάρξ is likely to have a physical connotation, and this is borne out by the contexts in which Paul uses it. The agitators are trying to "make a good showing in the flesh" (ἐν σαρκί, *en sarki*) and are "boasting in your flesh" (ἐν τῇ ὑμετέρᾳ σαρκί, *en tē hymetera sarki*). But σάρξ figures prominently in 5:13–26 (cf. also 6:7–8), where it has a theological sense, depicting human weakness and proneness to sin. Some reference to this theological nuance may be present here (e.g., Schlier 1989: 280; Hays 2000: 342). Paul indulges in a bit of sarcasm: you agitators are bragging in a matter of the flesh, little understanding that you are actually thereby revealing your enslavement to the narrowly human and un-Spiritual.

Following the pattern of the letter as a whole (see also 1:8–9; 3:1; 4:17; 5:7, 10, 12), Paul identifies the agitators only allusively: "as many as," "those who" (ὅσοι, *hosoi*). He first accuses them of wanting to "make a good showing" (εὐπροσωπῆσαι, *euprosōpēsai*). The verb is rare, found only once before Paul (in a papyrus manuscript). Its etymology ("good + face") and cognate adjective (εὐπρόσωπος, *euprosōpos*; see Gen. 12:11 LXX) show that it means "to have a good face." "Face" (πρόσωπον) can often have the sense of "(mere) outward appearance," and that is clearly the case here. The agitators are trying to "make a good impression" (cf. NIV) in the flesh of their converts.[1] They are doing this by "trying to force you to be circumcised" (ἀναγκάζουσιν ὑμᾶς περιτέμνεσθαι, *anankazousin hymas peritemnesthai*). The verb ἀναγκάζουσιν is a conative present (BDF §319; Wallace 1996: 535), justifying the translation "trying to compel" (NIV, NAB; cf. NASB, NET). This verb has been used twice earlier in the letter to refer to the same general issue that we find in this verse. In 2:3–4, Paul refers to false brothers at the Jerusalem conference who wanted to "compel" Titus, a Gentile, to be circumcised. And in 2:14 he quotes himself scolding Peter about wanting to "force" Gentiles to live like Jews. In all three of the situations, Jews are putting pressure on Gentiles to be circumcised or to submit generally to the authority of the law of Moses.

We have seen that a biblical-theological argument could be mustered for the agitators' insistence on circumcision and torah obedience. God did give the law of Moses to his people as the means by which they should live under his lordship, and one could argue that the arrival of the Messiah and the inclusion of Gentiles should not have changed this requirement. However, Paul does not mention the theological rationale of the agitators (a matter that he has dealt with at great length in 2:15–4:7). His focus here is more personal and polemical: *their* purpose, he claims, is to avoid being persecuted "because of the cross of Christ" (τῷ σταυρῷ τοῦ Χριστοῦ, *tō staurō tou Christou*; the dative is probably causal [BDF §196; Wallace 1996: 168]). Some versions (e.g., NIV) translate in such a way as to suggest that this is the "only" reason for the agitators to insist on circumcision (following here BDAG 659.2.d, who translate "solely in order that"). This might not be right, however. The adverb μόνον (*monon*, only) might rather function as a linking word that adds a qualification to what Paul has just said (see Gal. 1:23; 2:10; 5:13). As Lightfoot (1881: 222) puts it, "Only (their object in doing this is) that . . ." If this is right, Paul is not claiming quite so strongly that the only reason the agitators are insisting on circumcision is to avoid persecution.

But how would insisting on circumcision enable them to avoid being persecuted? The answer is almost certainly that anyone proclaiming the Messiah without insisting that converts be circumcised and follow the law would be criticized, ostracized, and perhaps even physically punished by Jews (so most scholars). As Jewett (1970–71) has noted, the Zealot movement, with its (sometimes violent) resistance to any compromise with Gentiles, was gaining ground at just this period of time. It was this kind of pressure, as we have seen, that was probably being brought to bear on Peter and other Jewish

---

1. Hardin (2008: 89–91) follows Winter (1994: 137–42; 2002) in arguing that the verb εὐπροσωπέω (*euprosōpeō*) alludes to "making a good standing" with Rome. He therefore thinks that the key issue in these verses is the fear of losing standing with the Roman authorities. But neither the words in this passage nor the larger argument of Galatians suggests that a concern about imperial standing was an issue.

Christians in Antioch (2:11–14; and see the comments on that passage). It was not, then, simply for proclaiming the cross of Christ that persecution might come; it was for preaching the cross of Christ as Paul understood it, as the sole basis for acceptance with God, that would have sparked the resistance (Dunn 1993a: 336–37).

6:13   With a γάρ (*gar*, for) Paul introduces a further elaboration of the false motives of the agitators. However, it is not initially clear that Paul is referring to the agitators at all in the first clause of this verse. He identifies the people he is talking about with the substantival participle (οἱ) περιτεμνόμενοι (*[hoi] peritemnomenoi*). The present tense of this participle could refer to people "who are being circumcised" (if the participle is passive) or "who are receiving circumcision" (if the participle is middle). In either case, it would be natural to identify these people as Gentiles who are in the process of receiving circumcision—either Gentile converts (e.g., Burton 1921: 252–53) or the agitators (who on this view are actually Gentiles rather than Jews: see Munck 1959: 87–90; Schoeps 1959: 65). But the first option does not make much sense in this context, which focuses so much on the agitators, while the second is forced to ignore too much rather clear evidence from elsewhere in the letter indicating that the agitators were Jews. So it is preferable, with most scholars, to understand the participle as stressing not the process of "being circumcised" but the fact of circumcision (a common function of the present tense): "the circumcised" (NRSV); "those who belong to the circumcision party" (R. Longenecker 1990: 292).

What is Paul's point, then, in claiming that the agitators do not "themselves keep the law" (αὐτοὶ νόμον φυλάσσουσιν, *autoi nomon phylassousin*)? He might mean simply that their distance from Jerusalem is preventing them from keeping many of the sacrificial laws (there is a reference to such a situation in Justin [*Dial.* 46]). However, as Lightfoot (1881: 222) points out, the polemical context suggests that it is the insincerity, not the impossibility, of obedience that is Paul's focus. Another option, then, is that the agitators were not very rigorous about their own adherence to the law (R. Longenecker 1990: 293; Hays 2000: 343). Paul's insistence in 5:3 that accepting circumcision requires a person to "do the whole law" is often thought to indicate that the agitators were not making clear to their converts that they needed to obey the entire law; so perhaps what they were failing to preach they were also failing to practice. Yet another option is that the agitators were not keeping the law in terms of its ultimate meaning, its pointing forward to Christ (Jewett 1970–71: 201–2; Garlington 2003: 284; cf. Nanos 2002: 226–33). But the best option is to read this clause in light of the longer (albeit later) discussion in Rom. 2, where Paul accuses Jewish people of failing to "do" the law that they take so much pride in possessing (most scholars adopt a view similar to this). This is a critique found frequently in the OT and elsewhere in the NT (Acts 7:53). Paul's point would then be similar to the one that he has made in the passages earlier in the letter that touch on the same point (3:10; 5:3): accepting circumcision puts people under an obligation—to do "the whole law"—that they are unable to fulfill. The agitators themselves exhibit this fundamental problem.[2]

In the last part of verse 13, Paul returns to where he began in verse 12, with a focus on the motivation of the agitators in terms of the flesh. The agitators "want to circumcise you" (θέλουσιν ὑμᾶς περιτέμνεσθαι, *thelousin hymas peritemnesthai*) "so that they might boast in your flesh" (ἵνα ἐν τῇ ὑμετέρᾳ σαρκὶ καυχήσωνται, *hina en tē hymetera sarki kauchēsōntai*). As we noted above, σάρξ (*sarx*) refers to the flesh of the Galatians ("your flesh") that will be affected by circumcision: "flesh which was cut off in circumcision" (Jewett 1971: 96). Paul's rivals "want to display the foreskins of the Galatians as trophies of their own triumphant persuasive power" (Hays 2000: 343). While the physical sense of σάρξ is clearly dominant here, a reference to the theological sense of the word may also be present: the agitators, in taking pride in physical flesh, are also and ironically allying themselves with the power of the old age.[3]

In stark contrast to the object in which the agitators boast is the focus of Paul's own boasting: "the cross of our Lord Jesus Christ." The δέ (*de*) at the beginning of the verse is therefore adversative, and the ἐμοί (*emoi*, me) comes first in the sentence for emphasis: "but as for me . . ." (HCSB, NJB; cf. NLT). Paul's passion for the centrality and exclusivity of the cross finds expression elsewhere in Galatians in strong assertions of his own perspective (see esp. 2:18–21 and 5:11); and these kind of assertions occur elsewhere in his letters (most famously in 1 Cor. 2:1–5). Yet Paul's remarks are not narrowly autobiographical. He presents his own perspective as exemplary for all believers. Paul expresses this perspective in the form of a "wish" using (a rare) optative (μὴ γένοιτο, *mē genoito*). He often uses this combination absolutely to express a strong negation ("May it never be!"; cf. Gal. 2:17; 3:21) but only here in combination with another verb (καυχᾶσθαι, *kauchasthai*): "May it not be with respect to me to boast . . ." (see BDF §409.1). The idea of boasting in the cross of Christ probably does not strike modern readers (particularly modern Christian readers) as particularly unusual. But the notion would have been strange and even bizarre for ancient readers, for whom crucifixion would have connoted violent and shameful death—something people did not talk about in polite society (see esp. Hengel 1977). In Paul's day taking pride in the cross would be something like taking pride in the guillotine or the electric chair today. Of course, it is not crucifixion per se in which Paul boasts, but the crucifixion of "our Lord Jesus Christ" (Paul adds solemnity with the piling up of titles [R. Longenecker 1990: 294]). The singular event of Christ's crucifixion, where God was "reconciling the world to himself" (2 Cor. 5:19), is what transforms the cross for Paul.

---

2. Hardin (2008: 89), in keeping with his reading of this text as concerned with standing before Roman authorities, argues that the idea is preserving the law from being disregarded among the Galatians.

3. Dunn (1993a: 339–40) again finds in σάρξ an allusion to "ethnic identity and prerogative."

In the second part of the verse, Paul explains just how significant the cross has been for him (the relative pronoun οὗ [*hou*, which] refers to the cross rather than to Christ; so almost all the English versions). Paul again stresses the first-person pronoun by putting it early in the clause: "*to me* the world has been crucified, and I to the world" (ἐμοὶ κόσμος ἐσταύρωται κἀγὼ κόσμῳ, *emoi kosmos estaurōtai kagō kosmō*). In each of these clauses, the precise force of the datives is hard to determine: what is the sense of the world being "crucified" to me (ἐμοί) and I to the world (κόσμῳ)? While the exact language is different, we might compare 2:19–20: "For through the law I died to the law [νόμῳ ἀπέθανον, *nomō apethanon*] so that I might live for God [θεῷ, *theō*]; I have been crucified with [συνεσταύρωμαι, *synestaurōmai*] Christ. I no longer live, but Christ lives in me." As we noted in our comments on that text, the datives probably express a general "reference" idea, the precise force being determined by the meanings of the words and the concepts to which they point. In 6:14, the point seems to be that Paul's crucifixion means a decisive separation between the world and himself: he stands in a wholly new relationship to it (see also 5:24: believers have "crucified" the flesh). Paul often uses κόσμος to describe, neutrally, the world of human beings or the cosmos in an all-encompassing sense (e.g., Rom. 1:20; 4:13; Col. 1:6; Phil. 2:15). But the term also functions within Paul's apocalyptically colored worldview to denote the spatiotemporal realm of sin, death, and evil (the world that is "passing away" [1 Cor. 7:31]; cf. Adams 2000: 225–27, 240–42). This is the sense that the word has here, occupying the same general semantic space as the "present evil age" in 1:4. Paul's choice of the imagery of crucifixion along with the parallel text in 2:19–20 makes clear that, as Betz (1979: 318) puts it, Paul's boasting "cannot simply be based upon 'what happened to me,' but must be based upon 'what happened through Christ to me.'" Christ's crucifixion is a redemptive-historical event in which believers participate (see the σύν [*syn*, with] language in Gal. 2:19–20; Rom. 6:1–6). Through their cocrucifixion with Christ, Paul and other believers are definitively freed from the baneful influence of this world, and they no longer owe that world their allegiance (Minear 1979). Christ's crucifixion is "the transformative event that ended the old order of things" (Hays 2000: 344).

6:15 Verse 15 explains verse 14 (γάρ, *gar*, for) by rephrasing it (Dunn 1993a: 342). The first and negative part of the sentence elaborates "world" in verse 14, and "new creation" in the second part describes what has taken the place of the world. "Neither circumcision nor uncircumcision is anything" (οὔτε . . . περιτομή τί ἐστιν οὔτε ἀκροβυστία, *oute . . . peritomē ti estin oute akrobystia*) echoes a formula that occurs earlier in Galatians and (later) in 1 Corinthians:

For in Christ Jesus neither circumcision nor uncircumcision has any value, but [ἀλλά] faith working through love. (Gal. 5:6)

Circumcision is nothing and uncircumcision is nothing, but [ἀλλά] keeping God's commands. (1 Cor. 7:19 AT)

In each case, Paul dismisses any value in circumcision or uncircumcision and contrasts this lack of value with the very great value of something else. We are justified, then, in speaking of a kind of Pauline slogan here, with "circumcision and uncircumcision" standing for those "worldly" valuations that no longer matter in the new age. In a move typical of Paul's polemics in Galatians, he dares to associate God's old-covenant requirement of circumcision with this worldly system of values that has now been judged by Christ's death and resurrection. Significantly, it is not only circumcision that has no value in this new "world," but uncircumcision as well. Paul has chosen these particular terms for specific mention here in Galatians because this contrast is at the heart of the issue in Galatia. In light of that situation, the claim that circumcision has no value makes perfect sense. But by adding "uncircumcision," Paul broadens the idea to embrace all matters of purely worldly significance—an idea that comes to more particular expression in 3:28, with its reference to "Jew or Gentile," "slave or free," "male and female." These texts together assert that the coming of Christ introduces a whole new state of affairs in the world. Distinctions of ethnicity, social class, and gender that are determinative for this world—they no longer matter (see esp. Martyn 1985a). All "simply human" factors become meaningless in the face of God's world-transforming work in his Son Jesus Christ. The old state of affairs is ended.

The other half of the contrast is stated very compactly: simply "new creation" (καινὴ κτίσις, *kainē ktisis*). The phrase occurs once elsewhere in Paul, in similarly brief form: "Therefore, if anyone is in Christ, new creation [καινὴ κτίσις]! The old has gone, the new is here!" (2 Cor. 5:17 AT). The word κτίσις can mean either "creature" (Rom. 1:25; 8:39 KJV) or "creation" (Rom. 8:19, 20, 21, 22; Col. 1:15 [probably]; 1:23 ESV [probably]).[4] Many interpreters either opt for "creature" (Gal. 6:15 KJV) or argue that, even if we translate "new creation," the reference is to the individual believer, renewed by God's transforming grace (see esp. Hubbard 2002; and also Lightfoot 1881: 224; Burton 1921: 355; R. Longenecker 1990: 296; Reumann 1973: 97–98). Some think there is special attention to the community. But most interpreters think "new creation" refers generally to the new state of affairs that Christ's death and resurrection has inaugurated (see esp. G. Vos 1972: 46–49; Stuhlmacher 1967; Hoch 1995: 155–66; Jackson 2010: esp. 90–95; Dunn 1993a: 342–43; Hays 2000: 344–45). Since lexicography, as we have seen, cannot solve this question, we must turn to possible antecedents of the language and to context.

The phrase "new creation" itself never occurs in the OT, but its equivalent is found in several Jewish texts (see esp. Jub. 1.29; 4.26; 1 En. 72.1; 1QS 4.25; 2 Bar. 44.12 ["new world"]).[5] As in the Pauline texts, "new creation" is introduced in these Jewish texts without explanation, but the concept seems to denote the

---

4. For a survey of usage, see Lampe 1964; Adams 2000: passim; Wischmeyer 1996; and for a broader overview of this term and related cosmological terms in the NT, see Pennington and McDonough 2008.

5. Some scholars think that 2 Esd. (4 Ezra) 7:75 and 2 Bar. 32.6 should also be included.

final state of affairs after God's climactic intervention on behalf of his people (for surveys of the background, see Stuhlmacher 1967; Mell 1989; Adams 2000: 225–28; Joel White 2008: 90–106). Of course, we must check more than this handful of linguistic parallels when considering the possible background to Paul's "new creation." Isaiah, especially in chapters 40–55, makes extensive use of creation language to compare and contrast God's original "creation" of Israel at the time of the exodus with his re-creation of the people after the exile (see esp. Isa. 43:15–19, alluded to in 2 Cor. 5:17; and see on this esp. Stuhlmueller 1970). And this vision of re-creation ultimately expands to include the whole cosmos: a "new heavens and earth" (Isa. 65:17–22; cf. 66:22–24). Other Jewish texts give "creation" language a more personal focus. Jeremiah and Ezekiel, for instance, predict that God will overcome Israel's failure to follow God's laws by giving his people a new heart (e.g., Ezek. 36:26). *Joseph and Aseneth* (e.g., 12.1–4) uses creation language to describe conversion from paganism to Judaism (see esp. Hubbard 2002: 11–76). And there is some evidence that the rabbis used "new creation" language to describe inner renewal and forgiveness (Schwantes 1962: 26–31; Chilton 1978: 312; Lightfoot 1881: 224). Yet on the whole the evidence from the background suggests, in the words of Adams (2000: 226), that "the expression 'new creation' was an established, technical term in Jewish apocalypticism, referring to the new or transformed creation expected to follow the destruction or renewal of the world."

The context bears out this interpretation. "New creation" most naturally functions, in contrast to the "world" (v. 14) and the "present evil age" (1:4), as a designation of the new state of affairs that the cross signifies and inaugurates. Strictly speaking, as Theodoret notes (Edwards 1999: 98), *"new creation* is the transformation of all things which will occur after the resurrection of the dead." But, in a move fundamental to NT eschatology, Paul announces the inauguration of that new creation in the death and resurrection of Christ. Foundational to this new state of affairs, of course, is the conversion of individuals; and central to it is the new community of Jew and Gentile (see Gal. 3:28 and the argument of Eph. 2:11–22). But "new creation," while implicitly including these, is a wider concept, embracing the entire transforming work of God, a work that will ultimately have cosmic reverberations (for further detail on "new creation" and its cosmic scope, see Moo 2006; 2010a; and for an argument that 2 Cor. 5:17 also refers to this all-embracing "new creation," see Moo 2010a: 51–58). Paul again draws a contrast between the more modest "newness" advocated by the agitators and the sweeping and all-embracing "newness" that Paul thinks is the outcome of Christ's death and resurrection.

6:16 Many of Paul's letter endings include a promise using the word peace in some form (Rom. 15:33; 16:20; 2 Cor. 13:11; Eph. 6:23; Phil. 4:9; 1 Thess. 5:23; 2 Thess. 3:16). Galatians again reveals its distinctiveness by mentioning both "peace" (εἰρήνη, *eirēnē*) and "mercy" (ἔλεος, *eleos*)—no other Pauline concluding promise mentions "mercy"—and by making the promise conditional: it is only for those "who follow this rule" (ὅσοι τῷ κανόνι τούτῳ στοιχήσουσιν, *hosoi tō kanoni toutō stoichēsousin).*[6] Yet this latter feature fits very well with the nature of this letter. Just as Paul cannot include his usual thanksgiving for his addressees in the introduction, so he cannot promise peace to his readers. Rather, the entire letter stands between the conditional curse of 1:8–9 and the conditional blessing of 6:16 (Betz 1979: 321; Hays 2000: 345). The situation in Galatia is too dire and the reaction of the Galatians too uncertain to allow for such unqualified promises.

Thus verse 16 becomes, in effect, an exhortation: you Galatians, Paul is saying, must join the unbounded group (ὅσοι) who will experience God's peace and mercy. This group is composed of those who will follow "this rule" (τῷ κανόνι τούτῳ). "Rule" is the translation of κανόνι in most English versions, although NLT has "principle" and HCSB "standard." The Greek word refers to a "rod," and such a rod could be used as a standard of measurement (like our yardstick)—hence a "standard" or "rule" (see 4 Macc. 7:21, which refers to "the rule of philosophy" [τὸν τῆς φιλοσοφίας κανόνα, *ton tēs philosophias kanona*]; the word occurs elsewhere in the NT only in 2 Cor. 10:13, 15, 16, with a slightly different sense). In later Christian times, of course, the word denoted the "rule" of faith, the standard by which orthodoxy could be determined; from this sense came our use of "canon" to describe a set of documents that meet the standard of orthodoxy. But what is the "rule" or "standard" in this context? The τούτῳ suggests a reference to something that Paul has just said, so the reference might be to the whole of verse 15 (Betz 1979: 321; R. Longenecker 1990: 296–97). But it is more likely that the "rule" has to do with "new creation" in verse 15b (e.g., Bruce 1982b: 273; Kwon 2004: 173). As we have noted, "new creation" is a big idea, incorporating within it all those elements of the new era that Christ has inaugurated. Specifically, "new creation," as Paul has stressed throughout the letter, will prominently feature the work of the Spirit, faith, and the love to which faith gives birth (5:6)—three key ideas of the letter that otherwise go unmentioned in the letter ending. That we are on the right track is confirmed by Paul's use here of the verb στοιχέω (*stoicheō*, follow, stay in step with), which he uses in 5:25 with reference to the Spirit: "Since we live by the Spirit, let us keep in step with [στοιχῶμεν, *stoichōmen*] the Spirit." In a typical linkage of "indicative" and "imperative," the reality of the new creation carries with it its own rule or standard of living. The old age—"the present evil age" (1:4), the "world" (6:14), the spatiotemporal state of affairs condemned at the cross—has its own set of values: flesh, circumcision, the law; the new creation carries its own values: the Spirit, faith, and love. Believers will experience God's peace and mercy only as they align themselves with these values.

This conditional promise of blessing raises several issues in its own right. "Peace" (εἰρήνη) is frequently featured as a key blessing of the new-covenant

---

6. The verb στοιχήσουσιν is future, and some English versions therefore use a future form (NRSV, NET, NASB). Yet the future could be gnomic (on the category, see Wallace 1996: 571), justifying the present translation found in most versions.

era. It is often paired with "grace" in the salutations of Paul's Letters (as in Gal. 1:3) and, as we noted above, in promises found in his letter endings (e.g., "Peace to the brothers and sisters, and love with faith from God the Father and the Lord Jesus Christ" [Eph. 6:23]). "Peace" can sometimes have a subjective sense (an experience of well-being; cf. Phil. 4:7), but more often it denotes the objective state of reconciliation with God (Rom. 5:1; cf. Rom. 5:11) and with others (Eph. 2:15–17) that the gospel brings. In this sense, the concept is rooted in the OT prophetic hope for an era of שָׁלוֹם (šālôm, peace), when God's people would be delivered from their enemies and enjoy both physical and spiritual well-being (Isa. 52:6–10; and also texts such as Isa. 9:7; 26:3, 12; 27:5; 52:7; 55:12; 66:12; Jer. 29:11; 30:10; 33:6, 9; 46:27; Ezek. 34:29; 37:26; Mic. 5:5; Hag. 2:9; Zech. 9:10). "Mercy" (ἔλεος) is much less common in Paul, occurring apart from this text only nine times (Rom. 9:23; 11:31; 15:9; Eph. 2:4; 1 Tim. 1:2; 2 Tim. 1:2, 16, 18; Titus 3:5).[7] The two words ἔλεος and εἰρήνη are associated in several OT and Jewish texts (Ps. 85:10 [84:11 LXX]; Isa. 54:10; Tob. 7:12 [א]; 2 Bar. 78.2)[8] and in four NT passages: with χάρις (charis, grace) in 1 Tim. 1:2; 2 Tim. 1:2; and 2 John 3; and with ἀγάπη (agapē, love) in Jude 2. The pairing of εἰρήνη and ἔλεος (on their own) is, then, somewhat unusual, and so is the order in which they are listed: in the four other NT passages where they are found together, ἔλεος comes first in what many think is the more natural progression: it is the bestowal of God's mercy that creates peace.

However, the pairing of terms and the order in which they occur is not the only unusual feature of this conditional blessing. What is even more striking is the word order, with εἰρήνη and ἔλεος being separated by a prepositional phrase: εἰρήνη ἐπ' αὐτοὺς καὶ ἔλεος (eirēnē ep' autous kai eleos, peace upon them and mercy). It is rather clear that the αὐτούς must have as its antecedent "as many as follow this rule." But the rest of the syntax is quite controversial. It will be useful to set out these syntactical options first:

1. The two prepositional phrases could express two related, or identical, objects of the dual blessing of "peace" and "mercy." The καί before the last prepositional phrase could then be
   a. epexegetic, in which case "the Israel of God" is identical to "all who follow this rule"—"Peace and mercy to all who follow this rule—to the Israel of God" (NIV; cf. also NLT); or
   b. conjunctive, in which case "the Israel of God" might be a separate, or overlapping, group with respect to "all who follow this rule"—"And as for all who walk by this rule, peace and mercy be upon them, and upon the Israel of God" (ESV; see also NAB).

7. Requests to God to bestow "peace" or "mercy" on Israel are found in several Jewish texts (for the former, see 11QPs[a] 23.11; for the latter, Pss. Sol. 13.12; 16.6; 17.45; 18.5; see Dunn 1993a: 344).

8. Beale (1999) thinks that Isa. 54:10 (with its blessing of God's חֶסֶד [ḥesed, loving-kindness] and שָׁלוֹם [šālôm, peace]) has particularly influenced Paul's language here, since the context of that verse (Isa. 40–66) speaks of the restoration of Israel in terms of the language of a new creation.

2. The first prepositional phrase could be dependent on εἰρήνη and the second on ἔλεος. In this case the καί before ἔλεος would be conjunctive ("and") and the καί before the final prepositional phrase adverbial ("also"): "May peace come to all those who follow this standard, and mercy [also] to the Israel of God!" (HCSB).

The reason why these syntactical decisions are so fraught is because they impinge on the controversial issue of what Paul means by "the Israel of God" (τὸν Ἰσραὴλ τοῦ θεοῦ, *ton Israēl tou theou*). If we adopt option 1a, "the Israel of God" is another way of referring to "as many who follow this rule." And since the latter clearly refers to Christians (or at least to faithful Christians), "Israel of God" would then refer to the new-covenant people of God. This is, in fact, the most common interpretation of the verse (see esp. Köstenberger 2001; Dahl 1950; and also, e.g., Chrysostom, *Comm. Gal.* on 6:15–16 [*NPNF*[1] 13:47]; Calvin 1854: 186; Luther 1964: 142; Lightfoot 1881: 224–25; Oepke 1973: 204–5; Barclay 1988: 98; Schlier 1989: 283; Fung 1988: 311; Garlington 2003: 292–93; Hays 2000: 345–46; R. Longenecker 1990: 297–98; Martyn 1997: 574–77; Schreiner 2010: 381–83; Beale 1999; Ridderbos 1975: 336).

However, options 1b and 2 suggest that "Israel of God" refers to a group different from "all who follow this rule." And this falls into line with the many interpreters who insist that "Israel of God" must refer to a strictly Jewish group: (1) the people of Israel as a whole (Bachmann 2008; Dunn 1993a: 345 [the covenant people of God as redefined in Gal. 2–4]); (2) Jewish Christians (Schrenk 1949; 1950; Betz 1979: 322–23);[9] (3) the Israel destined for salvation (see Rom. 11:26; Richardson 1969: 74–84; Bruce 1982b: 274–75; Mussner 1988: 416–17; S. Johnson 1986); or (4) a combination of views 2 and 3 (Burton 1921: 357–58). Options 1b and 2 more naturally suggest this sense of the debated phrase.

Three matters must be considered in evaluating these options: the syntax of the sentence, the referent of "Israel" elsewhere in Paul and in the NT, and the context of Galatians. Syntax favors either view 1b or 2. An epexegetic use of καί is certainly possible. Turner (1963: 335) and BDAG (495.1.c) mention a dozen NT examples, and there may be many more (see esp. Titrud 1993: 247–48; and also Zerwick 1963: §455γ). A clear instance, for example, is Acts 5:21: "At daybreak they entered the temple courts, as they had been told, and began to teach the people. When the high priest and his associates arrived, they called together the Sanhedrin and the full assembly of the elders of Israel [τὸ συνέδριον καὶ πᾶσαν τὴν γερουσίαν τῶν υἱῶν Ἰσραήλ, *to synedrion kai pasan tēn gerousian tōn huiōn Israēl*] and sent to the jail for the apostles" (AT). The Sanhedrin and the "assembly," or *gerousia*, of Israel are identical, so the καί joining them must be epexegetic (as signaled in most English versions; on this text and its relevance for Gal. 6:16, see esp. Köstenberger 2001:

---

9. De Boer (2011: 405–8) thinks the reference is to "Jewish believers in Christ who remain fully law observant."

9–10). Yet καί does not often function epexegetically; all other things being equal, we might expect it rather to be conjunctive ("peace and mercy be upon them *and* on the Israel of God") or adverbial ("Peace be upon them and mercy *also* upon the Israel of God"). Another syntactical factor to consider is word order. Note the symmetry:

εἰρήνη ἐπ' αὐτούς	*eirēnē ep' autous*
καὶ	*kai*
ἔλεος καὶ ἐπὶ τὸν Ἰσραὴλ τοῦ θεοῦ	*eleos kai epi ton Israēl tou theou*

This order of words might suggest that there are two separate blessings on, presumably, two separate entities (as in option 2). Moreover, as we noted above, the sequence of peace-mercy seems unusual if both blessings are being conferred on the same people. Nevertheless, while the syntactical evidence favors interpreting "the Israel of God" as an entity separate from "those who follow this rule," the other option is certainly possible. As we have seen, the "blessing" in this verse is conditional, and Paul puts that condition up front in a "hanging nominative" clause that he then refers back to with the preposition αὐτούς: "and as many as follow this rule—peace be upon them [αὐτούς]." This particular sequence is very unusual, and its awkwardness could easily have led to a comparatively unusual sequence of words and phrases in the rest of the verse.

In an influential study, P. Richardson (1969) argues that "Israel" was not used to refer to the church until AD 160, in the writings of Justin Martyr. Everywhere in the NT, then, he argues, "Israel" denotes ethnic Jews. This pattern of usage, if borne out, obviously favors interpreting "the Israel of God" as a Jewish entity separate from "all who follow this rule." In fact, however, the data are disputed. No one doubts that Israel refers to an ethnic/national entity in the vast majority of its NT occurrences. But two occurrences of the word in Rom. 9–11 are in dispute. In 9:6b, Paul distinguishes between two "Israels": "For not all who are descended from Israel are Israel." It is not clear whether the second refers to a (Jewish) "Israel" within Israel or to an "Israel" that extends beyond ethnic Israel to embrace the whole new-covenant people of God (see 9:24–25). Famously in dispute is the referent of Israel in Rom. 11:26, "and in this way all Israel will be saved": a significant minority of contemporary scholars insist that the reference is to all the elect of God, Jew and Gentile alike. In our view, the reference in both verses is to ethnic Israel (see Moo 1996: 573–74, 719–26), but in any case, the meaning of these passages is so debated that they can shed no certain light on the meaning of Gal. 6:16. On the one hand, then, the preponderant NT usage of "Israel" suggests a reference to ethnic Israel. On the other hand, however, two texts in Paul suggest that Paul could use the word in a more theological sense. One is Rom. 9:6 (cited above), where, on any view of the passage, Paul distinguishes ethnic Israel from some other (spiritual) "Israel." The second is 1 Cor. 10:18, where Paul's reference to "Israel according to the flesh" (AT) implies the existence of an "Israel according to the Spirit." It is fundamental to Paul's theology that the Spirit in this new age is creating a people that extends beyond any ethnic boundaries.

This latter point leads to the third issue, the context of Galatians. Scholars who think that "Israel of God" must be coextensive with "all who follow this rule" and include believing Gentiles as well as Jews cite this issue as by far the most significant. Throughout Galatians, Paul has argued strenuously that the old barriers distinguishing Jews and Gentiles, circumcision and the law, have been removed. In Christ, there is no longer a distinction between "Jew" and "Gentile/Greek" (3:28): both have equal access to God through faith. Moreover, Paul redefines the "seed of Abraham," insisting that his heirs consist of all who believe (3:7–29) and that the Gentile Galatians are "like Isaac, children of promise" (4:28). Granted this central and critical argument, it is inconceivable, so it is argued, that Paul would here at the end of his letter suddenly reerect ethnic considerations by pronouncing a blessing on an "Israel" distinct from Christian believers in general.

While the data do not all point in one direction, we think this last point is decisive in favoring interpretation 1a above: "the Israel of God" is another way of referring to "all who follow this rule." By speaking of an "Israel *of God*" (language found only here in the NT), Paul tacitly recognizes the existence of an ethnic/national Israel, but he insists that the Israel that counts before God, the Israel that will receive the blessings of peace and mercy, is constituted on different grounds.[10]

In verses 14–16 Paul sets forth the vision that should exercise controlling influence over believers in Christ. We are to view ourselves as people who (1) have been definitely removed from the controlling influence of this world; (2) participate in the new creation, God's (ultimately cosmic) restoration project; and (3) belong to God's people, now redefined around Jesus the Messiah. Everything, Paul is saying, has been reconstituted in light of the cross, and believers must live out of this fundamental, world-changing reality (v. 16a).

After this positive presentation of the believer's situation in Christ, Paul returns (see vv. 12–13) to a concern with the agitators. As in verse 14, he speaks of

6:17

---

10. Betz (1979: 322–23) appropriately notes the contentious debates among Jews in this era over just who constituted the "true" Israel, the Israel that would inherit God's promises. It is also possible that the conception and possibly the wording of Gal. 6:16 have been influenced by the nineteenth of the well-known Shemoneh Esreh (the Amidah, or The Eighteen Benedictions), a series of prayer requests regularly recited by Jews in Sabbath services and on other occasions. This final benediction begins: "Grant peace, welfare, blessing, grace, loving-kindness and mercy unto us and unto all Israel, Your people." Note that, as in Gal. 6:16, "peace" precedes "mercy," and that there is a distinction between "us" and "all Israel." Paul may have adapted this well-known language for his own purposes, changing the wording to indicate that the Galatian believers are themselves "the Israel of God." However, this nineteenth benediction is included only in some forms of the Shemoneh Esreh (hence the variety of titles), and its date is uncertain. Sherwood (2012: 224–31) argues that "new creation" (interpreted in a cosmological sense) and "Israel of God" stem from the same OT/Jewish tradition that focuses on the nations joining Israel in the last days.

himself, but unlike verse 14, what he says here has reference only to himself. Clearly, as 4:12–20 and 5:12 also make clear, the Galatian crisis has taken a personal toll on the apostle. The transitional phrase τοῦ λοιποῦ (*tou loipou*) could simply introduce the next subject: "as far as the rest is concerned," or "finally" (e.g., R. Longenecker 1990: 299; see Eph. 6:10; the accusative [τὸ] λοιπόν is often used this way [1 Cor. 7:29; 2 Cor. 13:11; Phil. 3:1; 4:8; 1 Thess. 4:1; 2 Thess. 3:1]). But the phrase is more likely to be temporal, as the English versions recognize: "from now on" (Moule 1959: 161). Paul puts his request in the third-person imperative because he is addressing the agitators, not the Galatians: "Let no one cause me trouble" (κόπους μοι μηδεὶς παρεχέτω, *kopous moi mēdeis parechetō*). The word κόπος usually means "work" or "toil," but in combination with παρέχω it means "trouble" (as in Sir. 29:4; Matt. 26:10; Mark 14:6; Luke 11:7; 18:5). However, while directed to the agitators, this request might be implicitly directed to the Galatians themselves. Paul can't do much to stop the agitators from their preaching and teaching heresy. But they will not "trouble" Paul if Christians for whom he feels spiritual responsibility, such as the Galatians, stop paying attention to them.

Paul grounds his request (γάρ, *gar*, for) in an intriguing personal remark: "I bear the marks of Jesus on my body" (ἐγώ . . . τὰ στίγματα τοῦ Ἰησοῦ ἐν τῷ σώματί μου βαστάζω, *egō . . . ta stigmata tou Iēsou en tō sōmati mou bastazō*). "Marks" translates the Greek word στίγματα, which, transliterated, is used to describe the marks of Jesus's crucifixion that some mystics claim to have on their own bodies. The word occurs only once else in Biblical Greek, with uncertain meaning (Song 1:11), but it was used in the ancient world to refer to the "brand" that masters sometimes used to mark ownership of slaves and to religious tattoos worn by some devotees of various religions. Explicit reference to his "body" makes clear that Paul is referring to physical marks of some sort, but just what they were or what they signified is debated (for a history of interpretation, see Güttgemanns 1966: 126–35). Some have thought that the reference might be to a mark on his body deliberately made to show his allegiance to Christ (such as the cross in our day; see Dinkler 1954: 93). Most interpreters, however, think that the reference is to scars and other marks on Paul's body that are the result of his persecution on behalf of Christ; he may refer to these in 2 Cor. 4:10: "We always carry around in our body the death of Jesus, so that the life of Jesus may also be revealed in our body." Some then suppose that Paul views them as signs of his dedication to God (reference is made to Gen. 4:15; Ezek. 9:4; Rev. 7:2–4; see, e.g., Lightfoot 1881: 225). Others suggest that the marks may indicate that Paul is the slave of the Lord Jesus (e.g., Bruce 1982b: 275–76). Of course, these two ideas are very close, if not overlapping, so it is probably not necessary (or possible) to choose between them. In either event, Paul probably intends these physical scars to stand in contrast to the physical mark of circumcision. As Eastman (2007: 109) paraphrases Paul's point, "'You want something to brag about? You want identity markers? I'll give you identity markers! You see these scars? I'm branded for Jesus. Become like me!'"

Paul concludes his letter with a "grace" wish, a standard literary feature **6:18** that marks the endings of all Paul's Letters (Rom. 16:20b; 1 Cor. 16:23; 2 Cor. 13:14 NIV; Eph. 6:24; Phil. 4:23; Col. 4:18c; 1 Thess. 5:28; 2 Thess. 3:18; 1 Tim. 6:21b; 2 Tim. 4:22b; Titus 3:15b; Philem. 25). With it, he circles back to the more formal focus with which this ending began (v. 11). As in this passage, the grace is usually defined in terms of "the Lord Jesus Christ" (τοῦ κυρίου ἡμῶν Ἰησοῦ Χριστοῦ, *tou kyriou hēmōn Iēsou Christou*), the genitive being one of those hard-to-categorize ones simply indicating that grace "has to do" with Christ. The wish that this grace be with "your spirit" (μετὰ τοῦ πνεύματος ὑμῶν, *meta tou pneumatos hymōn*) is found elsewhere only in 2 Tim. 4:22. But appearing nowhere else in these concluding Pauline grace wishes is a reference to "brothers and sisters" (ἀδελφοί, *adelphoi*). Perhaps Paul has added it to emphasize one last time that the Gentile Galatian believers, along with Jewish believers such as Paul, belong to one spiritual family.

This "grace wish" serves, among other things, to signify just what Galatians has been all about. As Martyn (1997: 559) puts it, "With the blessings of 6:16 and 6:18 and with the final 'Amen,' Paul makes clear to the Galatians that, in listening to his letter, they have been dealing not simply with him but also and fundamentally with God."

Additional Notes

6:11–18. The closing sections of the Letters of Paul typically include certain standard elements. To be sure, there is considerable variation (as, e.g., Doty 1973: 39 points out), but even so, the ending of Galatians stands out by virtue of the number of common elements not found here:

Paul's Travel Plans		Rom. 15:14–29; 1 Cor. 16:1–9
Request for Prayer		Rom. 15:30–32; Eph. 6:18–20; Col. 4:3–4; 1 Thess. 5:25; 2 Thess. 3:1–2; Philem. 22
Prayer-Wish for Peace	Gal. 6:16	Rom. 15:33; 2 Cor. 13:11c; Eph. 6:23; Phil. 4:9; 1 Thess. 5:23; 2 Thess. 3:16
Paul's Associates		Rom. 16:1–2; 1 Cor. 16:10–12, 15–18; Eph. 6:21–22; Col. 4:7–9; 2 Tim. 4:20
Exhortation to Greet One Another		Rom. 16:3–15; 1 Cor. 16:20b; 2 Cor. 13:12; Phil. 4:21a; (Col. 4:15); 1 Thess. 5:26; 2 Tim. 4:19; Titus 3:15b
The "Holy Kiss"		Rom. 16:16a; 1 Cor. 16:20; 2 Cor. 13:12a; 1 Thess. 5:26
Autograph	Gal. 6:11	2 Thess. 3:17; Philem. 19
Warning/Exhortation	Gal 6:12–15, 17	Rom. 16:17–19; 1 Cor. 16:13–14, 22; 2 Cor. 13:11b; Eph. 6:10–17 (?); Col. 4:17
Eschatological Wish/Promise	Gal. 6:16	Rom. 16:20a; 1 Cor. 16:22b; 1 Thess. 5:24
Concluding "Grace"	Gal. 6:18	Rom. 16:20b; 1 Cor. 16:23; 2 Cor. 13:14; Eph. 6:24; Phil. 4:23; Col. 4:18c; 1 Thess. 5:28; 2 Thess. 3:18; 1 Tim. 6:21b; 2 Tim. 4:22b; Titus 3:15b; Philem. 25

Greetings from Paul's Associates	Rom. 16:16b, 21–23; 1 Cor. 16:19–20a; 2 Cor. 13:13; Phil. 4:21b–22; Col. 4:10–14; 2 Tim. 4:21b; Titus 3:15a; Philem. 23–24
Doxology	Rom. 16:25–27; Phil. 4:20

6:12. A number of MSS have the indicative form of the verb, διώκονται, in place of the subjunctive, διώκωνται. An indicative after ἵνα μή would be unprecedented in NT Greek, and is probably an early textual corruption (BDF §369.6).

6:12. A few MSS add Ἰησοῦ after Χριστοῦ, but "cross of Christ" is good Pauline language and is probably what he wrote (Burton 1921: 350).

6:13. The MS tradition is divided between a present participle, περιτεμνόμενοι, and a perfect participle, περιτετμημένοι. The present participle is the more difficult reading, since it could suggest that the people referred to were in process of being circumcised—a reference that sits awkwardly in a context focusing on the agitators, who were advocating circumcision. Most scholars are inclined, because of the difficulty (which is not insuperable; see the commentary on 6:13), to think that the present form of the verb is original (e.g., Lightfoot 1881: 223).

6:15. At the beginning of the verse, a significant number of MSS read ἐν γὰρ Χριστῷ Ἰησοῦ οὔτε, but the addition is rather clearly an assimilation to the similar 5:6 (Metzger 1994: 530).

6:15. Another assimilation to 5:6 is the reading ἰσχύει in place of ἐστιν.

6:16. The MS tradition is divided over the form of the verb in the first clause, some reading the future indicative (στοιχήσουσιν), others a present (στοιχοῦσιν), and still others an aorist subjunctive (στοιχήσωσιν). The future indicative has strongest support.

6:17. The MS tradition offers several options for the name to be read after τὰ στίγματα τοῦ: (1) Ἰησοῦ; (2) Χριστοῦ; (3) κυρίου Ἰησοῦ; (4) κυρίου ἡμῶν Ἰησοῦ Χριστοῦ. The choice lies between the first and the second readings, the others being suspect because of the multiplication of names. The first has strong external support and is usually adopted (Metzger 1994: 530).

Works Cited

Aasgard, R.
2004   *"My Beloved Brothers and Sisters!":*
          Christian Siblingship in Paul. Journal
          for the Study of the New Testament:
          Supplement Series 265. London: T&T
          Clark.

ABD   *The Anchor Bible Dictionary.* Edited by
          D. N. Freedman et al. 6 vols. New York:
          Doubleday, 1992.

Achtemeier, P. J., J. B. Green, and M. M. Thompson
2001   *Introducing the New Testament: Its*
          Literature and Theology. Grand Rap-
          ids: Eerdmans.

Adams, E.
2000   *Constructing the World: A Study of*
          Paul's Cosmological Language. Studies
          of the New Testament and Its World.
          Edinburgh: T&T Clark.

Aland, K.
1956   "Wann starb Petrus? Ein Bemerkung
          zu Gal 2:6." *New Testament Studies*
          2:267–75.

Alexander, T. D.
1989   "From Adam to Judah: The Signifi-
          cance of the Family Tree in Genesis."
          Evangelical Quarterly 61:5–19.
1997   "Further Observations on the Term
          'Seed' in Genesis." *Tyndale Bulletin*
          48:363–67.

Allaz, J., et al.
1987   *Chrétiens en Conflit: L'Épître de Paul*
          aux Galates. Geneva: Labor et Fides.

Allison, D.
1992   "Cephas and Peter: One and the
          Same." *Journal of Biblical Literature*
          111:489–95.

Andersen, F. I.
2001   *Habakkuk: A New Translation with*
          Introduction and Commentary. Anchor
          Bible Commentary 25. New York:
          Doubleday.

Anderson, R. D., Jr.
1999   *Ancient Rhetorical Theory and Paul.*
          Rev. ed. Contributions to Biblical

Exegesis and Theology 18. Louvain:
          Peters.

ANRW   *Aufstieg und Niedergang der römischen*
          Welt. Edited by H. Temporini and W.
          Haase. Part 2: *Principat.* Berlin: de
          Gruyter, 1972–.

Arnold, C. E.
1996   "Returning to the Domain of the
          Powers: *Stoicheia* as Evil Spirits in Ga-
          latians 4:3, 9." *Novum Testamentum*
          38:55–76.
2005   "'I Am Astonished That You Are So
          Quickly Turning Away' (Gal 1.6): Paul
          and Anatolian Folk Belief." *New Testa-
          ment Studies* 51:429–49.

Aus, R. D.
1979   "Three Pillars and Three Patriarchs:
          A Proposal concerning Gal 2:9."
          Zeitschrift für die neutestamentliche
          Wissenschaft und die Kunde der älteren
          Kirche 70:252–61.

Avemarie, F.
2005   "Paul and the Claim of the Law ac-
          cording to the Scripture: Leviticus 18:5
          in Galatians 3:12 and Romans 10:5."
          Pp. 125–48 in *The Beginnings of Chris-
          tianity: A Collection of Articles.* Edited
          by J. Pastor and M. Mor. Jerusalem:
          Yad Ben-Zvi Press.

Baarda, T.
1992   "Τί ἔτι διώκομαι in Gal 5:11: Apodo-
          sis or Parenthesis?" *Novum Testamen-
          tum* 34:250–56.

Baasland, E.
1984   "Persecution: A Neglected Feature in
          the Letter to the Galatians." *Studia*
          theologica 38:135–50.

Bachmann, M.
1992   *Sünder oder Übertreter: Studien zur*
          Argumentation in Gal 2,15ff. Wissen-
          schaftliche Untersuchungen zum Neuen
          Testament 2/59. Tübingen: Mohr
          Siebeck.

1998 "4QMMT und Galaterbrief, מעשי התורה und ΕΡΓΑ ΝΟΜΟΥ." Zeitschrift für die neutestamentliche Wissenschaft und die Kunde der älteren Kirche 89:91–113.

2003 "Gal 1,9: 'Wie Wir Schon Früher Gesagt Haben, So Sage Ich Jetzt Erneut.'" Biblische Zeitschrift 47:112–15.

2005 "Keil oder Mikroskop? Zur jüngeren Diskussion um den Ausdruck 'Werke des Gesetzes.'" Pp. 69–134 in Lutherische und neue Perspektive: Beiträge zu einem Schüsselproblem der gegenwärtigen exegetischen Diskussion. Edited by M. Bachmann. Tübingen: Mohr Siebeck.

2008 "The Church and the Israel of God: On the Meaning and Ecclesiastical Relevance of the Benediction at the End of Galatians." Pp. 101–23 in Anti-Judaism in Galatians? Exegetical Studies on a Polemical Letter and on Paul's Theology. Grand Rapids: Eerdmans.

Bammel, E.
1960 "Gottes ΔΙΑΘΗΚΗ (Gal. III.15–17) und das jüdische Rechtsdenken." New Testament Studies 6:313–19.

Bandstra, A. J.
1964 The Law and the Elements of the World: An Exegetical Study in Aspects of Paul's Teaching. Kampen: Kok.

Barclay, J. M. B.
1987 "Mirror-Reading a Polemical Letter: Galatians as a Test Case." Journal for the Study of the New Testament 31:73–93.

1988 Obeying the Truth: Paul's Ethics in Galatians. Edinburgh: T&T Clark.

2010 "Paul, the Gift and the Battle over Gentile Circumcision: Revisiting the Logic of Galatians." Australian Biblical Review 58:36–56.

Barnett, P.
1999 Jesus and the Rise of Early Christianity: A History of New Testament Times. Downers Grove, IL: InterVarsity.

2000 "Galatians and Earliest Christianity." Reformed Theological Review 59:112–29.

2008 Paul: Missionary of Jesus. Grand Rapids: Eerdmans.

Barnikol, E.
1931 Der nichtpaulinische Ursprung des Parallelismus der Apostel Paulus und Petrus (Galater 2:7–9). Keil: Mühlau.

Barr, J.
1987 "Words for Love in Biblical Greek." Pp. 3–18 in The Glory of Christ in the New Testament. Edited by L. D. Hurst and N. T. Wright. Oxford: Clarendon.

1988 "'Abba' Isn't 'Daddy.'" Journal of Theological Studies 39:28–47.

Barrett, C. K.
1976 "The Allegory of Abraham, Sarah, and Hagar in the Argument of Galatians." Pp. 1–16 in Rechtfertigung: Festschrift für Ernst Käsemann zum 70. Geburtstag. Edited by J. Friedrich, W. Pöhlmann, and P. Stuhlmacher. Göttingen: Vandenhoeck & Ruprecht.

1985 Freedom and Obligation: A Study of the Epistle to the Galatians. Philadelphia: Westminster.

1998 A Critical and Exegetical Commentary on the Acts of the Apostles. 2 vols. International Critical Commentary. Edinburgh: T&T Clark.

Bassler, J. M.
2007 Navigating Paul: An Introduction to Key Theological Concepts. Louisville: Westminster John Knox.

Bauckham, R.
1979 "Barnabas in Galatians." Journal for the Study of the New Testament 2:61–70.

1990 Jude and the Relatives of Jesus in the Early Church. Edinburgh: T&T Clark.

1995 "James and the Jerusalem Church." Pp. 415–80 in The Book of Acts in Its Palestinian Setting. Edited by R. Bauckham. Grand Rapids: Eerdmans.

2004 "James, Peter and the Gentiles." Pp. 91–142 in The Missions of James, Peter and Paul: Tensions in Early Christianity. Edited by B. Chilton and C. Evans. Leiden: Brill.

Baugh, S. M.
2007 "The New Perspective, Mediation, and Justification." Pp. 137–63 in Covenant, Justification, and Pastoral Ministry: Essays by the Faculty of Westminster Seminary California. Edited by R. Scott Clark. Phillipsburg, NJ: P&R.

2009 "Galatians 5:1–6 and Personal Obligation: Reflections on Paul and the Law." Pp. 259–82 in The Law Is Not of Faith: Essays on Works and Grace in the Mosaic Covenant. Edited by B. Estelle, J. Fesko, and D. VanDrunen. Phillipsburg, NJ: P&R.

Baumert, N., and J. Meissner
2010 "Nomos bei Paulus." Pp. 9–245 in *Nomos und andere Vorarbeiten zur Reihe Paulus neu gelesen*. Edited by N. Baumert. Würzburg: Echter.

BDAG *A Greek-English Lexicon of the New Testament and Other Early Christian Literature*. By W. Bauer, F. W. Danker, W. F. Arndt, and F. W. Gingrich. 3rd ed. Chicago: University of Chicago Press, 2000.

BDF *A Greek Grammar of the New Testament and Other Early Christian Literature*. By F. Blass and A. Debrunner. Translated and revised by R. W. Funk. Chicago: University of Chicago Press, 1961.

BDR *Grammatik des neutestamentlichen Griechisch*. By F. Blass, A. Debrunner, and F. Rehkopf. Göttingen: Vandenhoeck & Ruprecht, 1984.

Beale, G. K.
1999 "Peace and Mercy upon the Israel of God: The Old Testament Background of Galatians 6,16b." *Biblica* 80:204–23.
2004 *The Temple and the Church's Mission: A Biblical Theology of the Dwelling Place of God*. Downers Grove, IL: InterVarsity.
2005 "The Old Testament Background of Paul's Reference to 'the Fruit of the Spirit' in Galatians 5:22." *Bulletin for Biblical Research* 15:1–38.

Beasley-Murray, G. R.
1962 *Baptism in the New Testament*. Grand Rapids: Eerdmans.

Beker, J. C.
1980 *Paul the Apostle: The Triumph of God in Life and Thought*. Philadelphia, Fortress.

Belleville, L. L.
1986 "'Under Law': Structural Analysis and the Pauline Concept of Law in Galatians 3:21–4:11." *Journal for the Study of the New Testament* 26:53–78.

Bergmeier, R.
2005 "Vom Tun der Tora." Pp. 161–81 in *Lutherische und neue Paulusperspektive: Beiträge zu einem Schlüsselproblem der gegenwärtigen exegetischen Diskussion*. Wissenschaftliche Untersuchungen zum Neuen Testament 182. Edited by M. Bachmann and J. Woyke. Tübingen: Mohr Siebeck.

2010 *Gerechtigkeit, Gesetz und Glaube bei Paulus: Der judenchristliche Heidenapostel im Streit um das Gesetz und seine Werke*. Biblisch-theologische Studien 115. Neukirchen-Vluyn: Neukirchener Theologie.

Betz, H. D.
1975 "The Literary Composition and Function of Paul's Letter to the Galatians." *New Testament Studies* 21:353–79.
1979 *Galatians: A Commentary on Paul's Letter to the Churches in Galatia*. Minneapolis: Fortress.

Billings, J. T.
2007 *Calvin, Participation, and the Gift: The Activity of Believers in Union with Christ*. Changing Paradigms in Historical and Systematic Theology. Oxford: Oxford University Press.

Bird, M.
2006 "Justification as Forensic Declaration and Covenant Membership: A Via Media between Reformed and Revisionist Readings of Paul." *Tyndale Bulletin* 57:109–30.
2007 *The Saving Righteousness of God: Studies on Paul, Justification, and the New Perspective*. Paternoster Biblical Monographs. Waynesboro, GA: Paternoster.

Bird, M., and P. M. Sprinkle (eds.)
2009 *The Faith of Jesus Christ: Exegetical, Biblical, and Theological Studies*. Peabody, MA: Hendrickson.

Bligh, J.
1969 *Galatians: A Discussion of St. Paul's Epistle*. London: St. Paul Publications.

Blinzler, J.
1963 "Zur Auslegung von I Kor 7,14." Pp. 23–41 in *Neutestamentliche Aufsätze: Festschrift für Josef Schmid*. Edited by J. Blinzler. Regensburg: Friedrich Pustet.

Blocher, H.
2004 "Justification of the Ungodly (*Sola Fide*): Theological Reflections." Pp. 465–500 in *Justification and Variegated Nomism*, vol. 2: *The Paradoxes of Paul*. Edited by D. A. Carson, P. T. O'Brien, and M. A. Seifrid. Tübingen: Mohr Siebeck / Grand Rapids: Baker Academic.

Blomberg, C., and M. Kamell
2008 *James*. Zondervan Exegetical Commentary on the New Testament. Grand Rapids: Zondervan.

Blommerde, A. C. M.

1975 "Is There an Ellipsis between Galatians 2,3 and 2,4?" *Biblica* 56:100–102.

Bockmuehl, M.

2000 *Jewish Law in Gentile Churches: Halakah and the Beginning of Christian Public Ethics*. Edinburgh: T&T Clark.

Boer, M. C. de

2004 "Paul's Quotation of Isaiah 54.1 in Galatians 4.27." *New Testament Studies* 50:370–89.

2005 "Paul's Use and Interpretation of a Justification Tradition in Galatians 2.15–21." *Journal for the Study of the New Testament* 28:189–216.

2007 "The Meaning of the Phrase Τὰ Στοιχεῖα τοῦ Κόσμου in Galatians." *New Testament Studies* 53:204–24.

2011 *Galatians: A Commentary*. New Testament Library. Louisville: Westminster John Knox.

2012 "Salvation History in Galatians? A Response to Bruce W. Longenecker and Jason Maston." *Journal for the Study of Paul and His Letters* 2:105–14.

Boers, H.

1994 *The Justification of the Gentiles: Paul's Letters to the Galatians and Romans*. Peabody, MA: Hendrickson.

2006 *Christ in the Letters of Paul: In Place of a Christology*. Beihefte zur Zeitschrift für die neutestamentliche Wissenschaft 140. Berlin: de Gruyter.

Bonnard, P.

1972 *L'épitre de saint Paul aux Galates*. 2nd ed. Commentaire du Nouveau Testament 9. Neuchâtel: Delachaux & Niestlé.

Borgen, P.

1995 "Some Hebrew and Pagan Features in Philo's and Paul's Interpretation of Hagar and Ishmael." Pp. 151–64 in *New Testament and Hellenistic Judaism*. Edited by P. Borgen and S. Giversen. Aarhus: Aarhus University Press.

2000 *Early Christianity and Hellenistic Judaism*. London: T&T Clark.

Borse, U.

1972 *Der Standort des Galaterbriefes*. Cologne: Peter Hanstein.

Bouttier, M.

1976 "Complexio Oppositorum: Sur les formules de I Cor 12:13; Gal 3:26–8; Col 3:10, 11." *New Testament Studies* 23:1–19.

Boyarin, D.

1993 "Was Paul an 'Anti-Semite'? A Reading of Galatians 3–4." *Union Seminary Quarterly Review* 47:47–80.

Boyce, J. L.

2000 "The Poetry of the Spirit: Willing and Doing in Galatians 5 and 6." *Word and World* 20:290–98.

Brandenburger, E.

1962 *Adam und Christus: Exegetisch-religionsgeschichtliche Untersuchung zu Rom 5,12–21 (1 Kor 15)*. Wissenschaftliche Monographien zum Alten und Neuen Testament 7. Neukirchener: Neukirchener Verlag.

1968 *Fleisch und Geist: Paulus und die dualistische Weisheit*. Neukirchen Vluyn: Neukirchener.

Braswell, J. P.

1991 "'The Blessing of Abraham' Versus 'The Curse of the Law': Another Look at Gal 3:10–13." *Westminster Theological Journal* 53:73–91.

Braude, W. G. (trans.)

1968 *Pesikta Rabbati: Discourses for Feasts, Fasts, and Special Sabbaths*. 2 vols. New Haven: Yale University Press.

Brawley, R. L.

2002 "Contextuality, Intertextuality, and the Hendiadic Relationship of Promise and Law in Galatians." *Zeitschrift für die neutestamentliche Wissenschaft und die Kunde der älteren Kirche* 93:99–119.

2005 "Meta-Ethics and the Role of Works of Law in Galatians." Pp. 135–59 in *Lutherische und neue Perspektive: Beiträge zu einem Schlüsselproblem der gegenwärtigen exegetischen Diskussion*. Edited by M. Bachmann. Tübingen: Mohr Siebeck.

Bray, G. L.

2005 "Allegory." Pp. 34–36 in *Dictionary for the Theological Interpretation of Scripture*. Edited by K. J. Vanhoozer. Grand Rapids: Baker Academic.

2009 *Ambrosiaster: Commentaries on Galatians–Philemon*. Ancient Christian Texts. Downers Grove, IL: InterVarsity.

Breytenbach, C.

1996 *Paulus and Barnabas in der Provinz Galatien: Studien zu Apostelgeschichte 13f.; 16.6; 18,23 und den Adressanten des Galaterbriefes*. Arbeiten zur Geschichte des antiken Judentums und des Urchristentums 38. Leiden: Brill.

Bring, R.
1961   *Commentary on Galatians.* Philadelphia: Muhlenberg.
1969   *Christus und das Gesetz: Die Bedeutung des Gesetzes des Alten Testaments nach Paulus und sein Glauben an Christus.* Leiden: Brill.

Brinsmead, B. H.
1982   *Galatians: Dialogical Response to Opponents.* Chico, CA: Scholars Press.

Brown, R. E.
1997   *An Introduction to the New Testament.* New York: Doubleday.

Bruce, F. F.
1952   *The Acts of the Apostles: The Greek Text with Introduction and Commentary.* 2nd ed. Grand Rapids: Eerdmans.
1974   *Paul: Apostle of the Heart Set Free.* Grand Rapids: Eerdmans.
1982a   "The Curse of the Law." Pp. 27–36 in *Paul and Paulinism: Essays in Honour of C. K. Barrett.* Edited by M. G. Hooker and S. G. Wilson. London: SPCK.
1982b   *The Epistle to the Galatians: A Commentary on the Greek Text.* New International Greek Testament Commentary. Grand Rapids: Eerdmans.
1983   *Philippians.* San Francisco: Harper & Row.
1988   *The Book of Acts.* Rev. ed. New International Commentary on the New Testament. Grand Rapids: Eerdmans.
1993   "Habakkuk." Vol. 2 / pp. 831–96 in *The Minor Prophets: An Exegetical and Expository Commentary.* Edited by T. E. McComiskey. Grand Rapids: Baker.

Brueggemann, W.
1982   *Genesis.* Atlanta: John Knox.

Bruno, C. R.
2010   "'God Is One': The Function of ΕΙΣ Ο ΘΕΟΣ as a Ground for Gentile Inclusion in Paul's Letters." PhD diss., Wheaton College.

Bryan, S. M.
2002   *Jesus and Israel's Traditions of Judgement and Restoration.* Society for New Testament Studies Monograph Series 117. Cambridge: Cambridge University Press.

Bryant, R. A.
2001   *The Risen Crucified Christ in Galatians.* Atlanta: Society of Biblical Literature.

Buck, C. H.
1951   "The Date of Galatians." *Journal of Biblical Literature* 70:113–22.

Bultmann, R. K.
1951   *Theology of the New Testament,* vol. 1. New York: Charles Scribner's Sons.

Burchard, C.
1998   "Noch Ein Versuch zu Galater 3,19 und 20." Pp. 184–202 in *Studien zur Theologie, Sprache und Umwelt des Neuen Testaments.* Edited by D. Sänger. Tübingen: Mohr Siebeck.
1999   "Zu Galater 4,1–11." Pp. 41–58 in *Das Urchristentum in seiner literarischen Geschichte: Festschrift für Jürgen Becker zum 65. Geburtstag.* Edited by U. Mell and U. B. Müller. Berlin: de Gruyter.

Burge, G. M., L. H. Cohick, and G. L. Green
2009   *The New Testament in Antiquity.* Grand Rapids: Zondervan.

Burton, E. de W.
1898   *Syntax of the Moods and Tenses of New Testament Greek.* 3rd ed. Chicago: University of Chicago Press.
1921   *A Critical and Exegetical Commentary on the Epistle to the Galatians.* International Critical Commentary. Edinburgh: T&T Clark.

Byrne, B.
1979   *"Sons of God"—"Seed of Abraham": A Study of the Idea of the Sonship of God of All Christians in Paul against the Jewish Background.* Analecta biblica 83. Rome: Pontifical Biblical Institute.

Callan, T.
1980   "Pauline Midrash: The Exegetical Background of Gal 3:19b." *Journal of Biblical Literature* 99:549–67.

Calvert-Koyzis, N.
2004   *Paul, Monotheism and the People of God: The Significance of Abraham Traditions for Early Judaism and Christianity.* Journal for the Study of the New Testament: Supplement Series 273. London: T&T Clark.

Calvin, J.
1854   *Commentaries on the Epistles of Paul to the Galatians and Ephesians.* Edinburgh: Thomas Clark.
Institutes   *Institutes of the Christian Religion.* Edited by John T. McNeill. Translated by Ford L. Battles. 2 vols. Library of Christian Classics 20–21. Philadelphia: Westminster, 1960.

Campbell, C. R.
2012   *Paul and Union with Christ: An Ex-egetical and Theological Study.* Grand Rapids: Zondervan.

Campbell, D. A.
2005   *The Quest for Paul's Gospel: A Suggested Strategy.* London: T&T Clark.
2009   *The Deliverance of God: An Apocalyptic Reading of Justification in Paul.* Grand Rapids: Eerdmans.

Campbell, R. A.
1996   "'Against Such Things There Is No Law'? Galatians 5:23b Again." *Expository Times* 107:271–72.

Caneday, A.
1989   "'Redeemed from the Curse of the Law': The Use of Deut 21:22–23 in Gal 3:13." *Trinity Journal* 10:185–209.
2009   "The Faithfulness of Jesus Christ as a Theme in Paul's Theology in Galatians." Pp. 185–205 in *The Faith of Jesus Christ: Exegetical, Biblical, and Theological Studies.* Edited by M. F. Bird and P. M. Sprinkle. Peabody, MA: Hendrickson.

Carson, D. A.
1986   "Pauline Inconsistency: Reflections on 1 Corinthians 9:19–23 and Galatians 2:11–14." *Churchman* 100:6–45.

Carson, D. A., and D. J. Moo
2005   *An Introduction to the New Testament.* 2nd ed. Grand Rapids: Zondervan.

Carson, D. A., P. T. O'Brien, and M. A. Seifrid (eds.)
2001   *Justification and Variegated Nomism,* vol. 1: *The Complexities of Second Temple Judaism.* Tübingen: Mohr Siebeck / Grand Rapids: Baker Academic.

Cavallin, H. C. C.
1978   "'The Righteous Shall Live by Faith': A Decisive Argument for the Traditional Interpretation." *Studia theologica* 32:33–43.

Chapman, D. W.
2008   *Ancient Jewish and Christian Perceptions of Crucifixion.* Wissenschaftliche Untersuchungen zum Neuen Testament 2/244. Tübingen: Mohr Siebeck.

Charlesworth, J. H. (ed.)
2010   *The Old Testament Pseudepigrapha.* 2 vols. New York: Doubleday, 1983–85. Reprinted Peabody, MA: Hendrickson.

Chester, A.
2007   *Messiah and Exaltation: Jewish Messianic and Visionary Traditions and New Testament Christology.* Wissenschaftliche Untersuchungen zum Neuen Testament 207. Tübingen: Mohr Siebeck.

Chester, S. J.
2003   *Conversion at Corinth: Perspectives on Conversion in Paul's Theology and the Corinthian Church.* Studies of the New Testament and Its World. London: T&T Clark.
2008   "When the Old Was New: Reformation Perspectives on Galatians 2:16." *Expository Times* 119:320–29.
2009   "It Is No Longer I Who Live: Justification by Faith and Participation in Christ in Martin Luther's Exegesis of Galatians." *New Testament Studies* 55:315–37.
2011   "Paul and the Galatian Believers." Pp. 63–78 in *The Blackwell Companion to Paul.* Edited by S. Westerholm. Chichester: Wiley-Blackwell.

Chibici-Revneanu, N.
2008   "Leben im Gesetz: Die paulinische Interpretation von Lev 18:5 (Gal 3:12; Röm 10:5)." *Novum Testamentum* 50:105–19.

Childs, B. S.
1985   *Old Testament Theology in a Canonical Context.* Philadelphia: Fortress.
2008   *The Church's Guide for Reading Paul: The Canonical Shaping of the Pauline Corpus.* Grand Rapids: Eerdmans.

Chilton, B.
1978   "Galatians 6:15: A Call to Freedom before God." *Expository Times* 89:311–13.

Chilton, B. (ed.)
1987   *The Isaiah Targum: Introduction, Translation, Apparatus and Notes.* The Aramaic Bible, vol. 11. Wilmington, DE: Michael Glazier.

Choi, H.-S.
2005   "ΠΙΣΤΙΣ in Galatians 5:5–6: Neglected Evidence for the Faithfulness of Christ." *Journal of Biblical Literature* 124:467–90.

Ciampa, R. E.
1998   *The Presence and Function of Scripture in Galatians 1 and 2.* Wissenschaftliche Untersuchungen zum Neuen Testament 2/102. Tübingen: Mohr Siebeck.
2010   "Abraham and Empire in Galatians." Pp. 153–68 in *Perspectives on Our Father Abraham: Essays in Honor of Marvin R. Wilson.* Edited by S. A. Hunt. Grand Rapids: Eerdmans.

Collins, C. J.
2003 "Galatians 3:16: What Kind of Exegete Was Paul?" *Tyndale Bulletin* 54:75–86.

Colson, F. H. (trans.)
1935 *Philo: De Vita Mosis*. Loeb Classical Library 289. Cambridge, MA: Harvard University Press.
1939 *Philo: De Virtutibus*. Loeb Classical Library 341. Cambridge, MA: Harvard University Press.

Colson, F. H., and G. H. Whitaker (trans.)
1929 *Philo: On Creation*. Loeb Classical Library 226. Cambridge, MA: Harvard University Press.

Cook, D.
1992 "The Prescript as Programme in Galatians." *Journal of Theological Studies* 43:511–19.

Coppins, W.
2009 *The Interpretation of Freedom in the Letters of Paul*. Wissenschaftliche Untersuchungen zum Neuen Testament 261. Tübingen: Mohr Siebeck.

Corley, B.
1997 "Interpreting Paul's Conversion: Then and Now." Pp. 1–17 in *The Road from Damascus: The Impact of Paul's Conversion on His Life, Thought, and Ministry*. Edited by R. N. Longenecker. Grand Rapids: Eerdmans.

Cosgrove, C.
1987 "Justification in Paul: A Linguistic and Theological Reflection." *Journal of Biblical Literature* 106:653–70.
1988 *The Cross and the Spirit: A Study in the Argument and Theology of Galatians*. Mercer, GA: Mercer University Press.

Craigie, P. C.
1976 *The Book of Deuteronomy*. New International Commentary on the Old Testament. Grand Rapids: Eerdmans.

Cranfield, C. E. B.
1964 "St. Paul and the Law." *Scottish Journal of Theology* 17:43–64.
1975 *A Critical and Exegetical Commentary on the Epistle to the Romans*, vol. 1: *Introduction and Commentary on Romans I–VIII*. International Critical Commentary. Edinburgh: T&T Clark.
1991 "'The Works of the Law' in the Epistle to the Romans." *Journal for the Study of the New Testament* 43:89–101.

Cremer, H.
1899 *Die paulinische Rechtfertigungslehre im Zusammenhange ihrer geschichtlichen Voraussetzungen*. 2nd ed. Gütersloh: Bertelsmann.

Crüsemann, F.
1976 "Jahwes Gerechtigkeit (צדק/צדקה) im Alten Testament." *Evangelische Theologie* 36:427–50.

Cummins, S. A.
2001 *Paul and the Crucified Christ: Maccabean Martyrdom and Galatians 1 and 2*. Society for the Study of the New Testament Monograph Series 114. Cambridge: Cambridge University Press.

Dahl, N. A.
1950 "Der Name Israel: Zur Auslegung von Gal 6,16." *Judaica* 6:161–70.
1977 "Contradictions in Scripture." Pp. 159–77 in *Studies in Paul*. Minneapolis: Augsburg.
2002 "Paul's Letter to the Galatians: Epistolary Genre, Content, and Structure." Pp. 117–42 in *The Galatians Debate: Contemporary Issues in Rhetorical and Historical Interpretation*. Edited by M. D. Nanos. Peabody, MA: Hendrickson.

Dalton, W. J.
1990 "The Meaning of 'We' in Galatians." *Australian Biblical Review* 38:33–44.

Danby, H. (ed.)
1933 *The Mishnah: Translated from the Hebrew with Introduction and Brief Explanatory Notes*. Oxford: Oxford University Press.

Das, A. A.
1995 "Oneness in Christ: The *Nexus Indivulsus* between Justification and Sanctification in Paul's Letter to the Galatians." *Concordia Journal* 21:173–86.
2001 *Paul, the Law, and the Covenant*. Peabody, MA: Hendrickson.
2003 *Paul and the Jews*. Peabody, MA: Hendrickson.
2009 "Paul and Works of Obedience in Second Temple Judaism: Romans 4:4–5 as a 'New Perspective' Case Study." *Catholic Biblical Quarterly* 71:795–812.
2010 "Paul and the Law: Pressure Points in the Debate." Pp. 99–116 in *Paul Unbound: Other Perspectives on the Apostle*. Edited by M. D. Given. Peabody, MA: Hendrickson.

Dautzenberg, G.
1982 "'Da ist nicht männlich und weiblich': Zur Interpretation von Gal 3:28." *Kairos* 24:181–206.

Davidson, R. M.
1996 "The Meaning of *Niṣdaq* in Daniel 8:14." *Journal of the Adventist Theological Society* 7:107–19.

Davies, W. D.
1948 *Paul and Rabbinic Judaism: Some Rabbinic Elements in Pauline Theology.* London: SPCK.

Deidun, T. J.
1981 *New Covenant Morality in Paul.* Analecta biblica 89. Rome: Pontifical Biblical Institute.

Deissmann, A.
1901 "Prolegomena to the Biblical Letters and Epistles." Pp. 1–59 in *Bible Studies.* Edinburgh: T&T Clark.
1903 *Bible Studies.* 2nd ed. Edinburgh: T&T Clark.

Dibelius, M. (with H. Greeven)
1976 *A Commentary on the Epistle of James.* Hermeneia. Philadelphia: Fortress.

Dillenberger, J. (ed.)
1961 *Martin Luther: Selections from His Writings.* Garden City, NY: Doubleday.

Dinkler, E.
1954 "Jesu Wort vom Kreuztragen." Pp. 110–29 in *Neutestamentliche Studien für Rudolf Bultmann.* Edited by W. Eltester. Beihefte zur Zeitschrift für die neutestamentliche Wissenschaft 21. Berlin: de Gruyter.
1967 "Der Brief an die Galater: Zum Kommentar von Heinrich Schlier." Pp. 270–82 in *Signum Crucis: Aufsätze zum Neuen Testament und zur christlichen Archäologie.* Tübingen: Mohr Siebeck.

Dodd, B. J.
1996 "Christ's Slave, People Pleasers and Galatians 1.10." *New Testament Studies* 42:90–104.
1999 *Paul's Paradigmatic "I": Personal Example as Literary Strategy.* Sheffield: Sheffield Academic Press.

Dodd, C. H.
1937 *The Apostolic Preaching and Its Developments.* London: Hodder & Stoughton.
1952 *According to the Scriptures: The Sub-Structure of New Testament Theology.* London: Collins.
1968 "Ἔννομος Χριστοῦ." Pp. 134–48 in *More New Testament Studies.* Manchester: Manchester University Press.

Donaldson, T.
1986 "The 'Curse of the Law' and the Inclusion of the Gentiles: Galatians 3:13–14." *New Testament Studies* 32:94–112.
1997 *Paul and the Gentiles: Mapping the Apostle's Convictional World.* Minneapolis: Fortress.
2007 *Judaism and the Gentiles: Jewish Patterns of Universalism (to 135 CE).* Waco: Baylor University Press.

Doty, W. G.
1973 *Letters in Primitive Christianity.* Guides to Biblical Scholarship: New Testament Series. Philadelphia: Fortress.

Downs, D. J.
2008 *The Offering of the Gentiles: Paul's Collection for Jerusalem in Its Chronological, Cultural, and Cultic Contexts.* Wissenschaftliche Untersuchungen zum Neuen Testament 248. Tübingen, Mohr Siebeck.

Drane, J. W.
1975 *Paul: Libertine or Legalist? A Study in the Theology of the Major Pauline Epistles.* London: SPCK.

Dülmen, A. van
1968 *Die Theologie des Gesetzes bei Paulus.* Stuttgart biblische Monographien 5. Stuttgart: Katholisches Bibelwerk.

Dumbrell, W.
1992 "Justification in Paul: A Covenantal Perspective." *Reformed Theological Review* 51:91–101.
2000 "Abraham and the Abrahamic Covenant in Galatians 3:1–14." Pp. 19–31 in *The Gospel to the Nations: Perspectives on Paul's Mission; In Honour of P. T. O'Brien.* Edited by P. Bolt and M. Thompson. Downers Grove, IL: InterVarsity.

Dunn, J. D. G.
1970 *Baptism in the Holy Spirit.* Studies in Biblical Theology 15. London: SCM.
1973 "Jesus—Flesh and Spirit: An Exposition of Romans I.3–4." *Journal of Theological Studies* 24:44–51.
1980 *Christology in the Making: A New Testament Inquiry into the Origins of the Doctrine of the Incarnation.* Philadelphia: Westminster.
1983 "The Incident at Antioch (Gal 2:11–18)." *Journal for the Study of the New Testament* 18:3–57.
1985 "Works of the Law and the Curse of the Law (Galatians 3:10–14)." *New Testament Studies* 31:523–42.

1988	*Romans*, vol. 1: *Romans 1–8*; vol. 2: *Romans 9–16*. Word Biblical Commentary 38A–B. Dallas: Word.
1990	*Jesus, Paul, and the Law: Studies in Mark and Galatians*. Louisville: Westminster John Knox.
1991	"The Theology of Galatians: The Issue of Covenantal Nomism." Pp. 125–46 in *Pauline Theology*, vol. 1: *Thessalonians, Philippians, Galatians, Philemon*. Edited by J. M. Bassler. Fortress: Minneapolis.
1993a	*The Epistle to the Galatians*. Peabody, MA: Hendrickson.
1993b	*The Theology of Paul's Letter to the Galatians*. Cambridge: Cambridge University Press.
1995	"Was Paul against the Law? The Law in Galatians and Romans: A Test-Case of Text in Context." Pp. 455–75 in *Texts and Contexts: Biblical Texts in Their Textual and Situational Contexts*. Edited by T. Fornberg and D. Hellholm. Oslo: Scandinavian University Press.
1997a	"4QMMT and Galatians." *New Testament Studies* 43:147–53.
1997b	"Once More, ΠΙΣΤΙΣ ΧΡΙΣΤΟΥ." Pp. 61–81 in *Pauline Theology*, vol. 4: *Looking Back, Pressing On*. Edited by E. E. Johnson and D. M. Hay. Atlanta: Society of Biblical Literature.
1998	*A Theology of Paul the Apostle*. Grand Rapids: Eerdmans.
2005a	*The New Perspective on Paul: Collected Essays*. Wissenschaftliche Untersuchungen zum Neuen Testament 185. Tübingen: Mohr Siebeck.
2005b	"Noch einmal 'Works of the Law': The Dialogue Continues." Pp. 407–21 in *The New Perspective on Paul: Collected Essays*. Wissenschaftliche Untersuchungen zum Neuen Testament 185. Tübingen: Mohr Siebeck.
2008a	"Ἐκ Πίστεως: A Key to the Meaning of *Pistis Christou*." Pp. 351–66 in *The Word Leaps the Gap: Essays on Scripture and Theology in Honor of Richard B. Hays*. Edited by J. R. Wagner, K. C. Rowe, and K. Grieb. Grand Rapids: Eerdmans.
2008b	"Jesus the Judge: Further Thoughts on Paul's Christology and Soteriology." Pp. 395–412 in *The New Perspective on Paul: Collected Essays*. Rev. ed. Grand Rapids: Eerdmans.
2008c	"Neither Circumcision nor Uncircumcision, but . . . (Gal 5.2–12; 6.12–16; cf. 1 Cor 7.17–20)." Pp. 313–37 in *The New Perspective on Paul: Collected Essays*. Rev. ed. Grand Rapids: Eerdmans. Reprinted from Pp. 79–110 in *La foi agissant par l'amour (Galates 4.12–6.16)*. Edited by A. Vanhoye. Rome: Benedictina.
2008d	"The New Perspective on Paul: Whence, What, Whither?" Pp. 1–97 in *The New Perspective on Paul: Collected Essays*. Rev. ed. Grand Rapids: Eerdmans.
2008e	"Paul and the Torah: The Role and Function of the Law in the Theology of Paul the Apostle." Pp. 447–68 in *The New Perspective on Paul: Collected Essays*. Rev. ed. Grand Rapids: Eerdmans.
2009	*Christianity in the Making*, vol. 2: *Beginning from Jerusalem*. Grand Rapids: Eerdmans.
2010	*Did the First Christians Worship Jesus? The New Testament Evidence*. Louisville: Westminster John Knox.

du Toit, A.

| 2007 | "Alienation and Re-identification as Pragmatic Strategies in Galatians. Pp. 149–69 in *Focusing on Paul: Persuasion and Theological Design in Romans and Galatians*. Edited by C. Breytenbach and D. S. du Toit. Beihefte zur Zeitschrift für die neutestamentliche Wissenschaft 151. Berlin: de Gruyter. |

Eastman, S.

| 2001 | "The Evil Eye and the Curse of the Law: Galatians 3.1 Revisited." *Journal for the Study of the New Testament* 83:69–87. |
| 2007 | *Recovering Paul's Mother Tongue: Language and Theology in Galatians*. Grand Rapids: Eerdmans. |

Easton, B. S.

| 1932 | "New Testament Ethical Lists." *Journal of Biblical Literature* 51:1–12. |

Ebeling, G.

| 1981 | *Die Wahrheit des Evangeliums: Eine Lesehilfe zum Galaterbrief*. Tübingen: Mohr Siebeck. |

Eckert, J.

| 1971 | *Die Urchristliche Verkündigung im Streit zwischen Paulus und seinen Gegnern nach dem Galaterbrief*. Regensburg: Friedrich Pustet. |

Eckey, W.

| 2010 | *Der Galaterbrief: Ein Kommentar*. Neukirchener-Vluyn: Neukirchener Verlag. |

Eckstein, H.-J.
1996   *Verheissung und Gesetz: Eine exegetische Untersuchung zu Galater 2,15–4,7.* Wissenschaftliche Untersuchungen zum Neuen Testament 86. Tübingen: Mohr Siebeck.

Edwards, M. J.
1999   *Galatians, Ephesians, Philippians.* Ancient Christian Commentary: New Testament 8. Downers Grove, IL: InterVarsity.

Ehrman, B.
1990   "Cephas and Peter." *Journal of Biblical Literature* 109:463–74.

Eisenbaum, P.
2009   *Paul Was Not a Christian: The Original Message of a Misunderstood Apostle.* New York: HarperOne.

Elliott, J. H.
1990   "Paul, Galatians, and the Evil Eye." *Currents in Theology and Mission* 17:262–73.

Elliott, M. W.
2009   "Πίστις Χριστοῦ in the Church Fathers and Beyond." Pp. 277–89 in *The Faith of Jesus Christ: Exegetical, Biblical, and Theological Studies.* Edited by M. F. Bird and P. M. Sprinkle. Peabody, MA: Hendrickson.

Elliott, N.
1994   *Liberating Paul: The Justice of God and the Politics of the Apostle.* Minneapolis: Fortress.

Elliott, S.
2003   *Cutting Too Close for Comfort: Paul's Letter to the Galatians in Its Anatolian Cultic Context.* Journal for the Study of the New Testament: Supplement Series 248. London: T&T Clark.

Ellis, E. E.
1978   "Midrash Pesher in Pauline Hermeneutics." Pp. 173–81 in *Prophecy and Hermeneutic in Early Christianity: New Testament Essays.* Wissenschaftliche Untersuchungen zum Neuen Testament 18. Grand Rapids: Eerdmans.

Elmer, I. J.
2009   *Paul, Jerusalem and the Judaizers: The Galatians Crisis in Its Broadest Historical Context.* Wissenschaftliche Untersuchungen zum Neuen Testament 2/258. Tübingen, Mohr Siebeck.

Engberg-Pedersen, T.
1995   "Galatians in Romans 5–8 and Paul's Construction of the Identity of Christ Believers." Pp. 477–505 in *Texts and Contexts: Biblical Texts in Their Textual and Situational Contexts.* Edited by T. Fornberg and D. Hellholm. Oslo: Scandinavian University Press.
2000   *Paul and the Stoics.* Louisville: Westminster John Knox.

Enns, P.
2005   *Inspiration and Incarnation: Evangelicals and the Problem of the Old Testament.* Grand Rapids: Baker Academic.

Epstein, I. (ed.)
1935–52 *The Babylonian Talmud: Translated into English with Notes, Glossary, and Indices.* 35 vols. London: Soncino.

Esler, P. F.
1995   "Making and Breaking an Agreement Mediterranean Style: A New Reading of Galatians 2:1–14." *Biblical Interpretation* 3:285–314.
1998   *Galatians.* London: Routledge.

Estelle, B. D.
2009   "Leviticus 18:5 and Deuteronomy 30:1–14 in Biblical Theological Development: Entitlement to Heaven Foreclosed and Proffered." Pp. 109–46 in *The Law Is Not of Faith: Essays on Works and Grace in the Mosaic Covenant.* Edited by B. D. Estelle, J. V. Fesko, and D. VanDrunen. Phillipsburg, NJ: P&R.

Evans, C. A.
2005   "Paul and 'Works of the Law' Language in Late Antiquity." Pp. 201–26 in *Paul and His Opponents.* Edited by S. E. Porter. Pauline Studies (Past) 2. Leiden: Brill.

Evans, W. B.
2008   *Imputation and Impartation: Union with Christ in American Reformed Theology.* Studies in Christian History and Thought. Eugene, OR: Wipf & Stock.

Farmer, W. R.
1999   "James the Lord's Brother, according to Paul." Pp. 133–53 in *James the Just and Christian Origins.* Edited by B. D. Chilton and C. A. Evans. Supplements to Novum Testamentum 98. Leiden: Brill.

Fee, G. D.
1994   *God's Empowering Presence: The Holy Spirit in the Letters of Paul.* Peabody, MA: Hendrickson.
2007a   *Galatians.* Pentecostal Commentary. Blandford Forum, UK: Deo.

2007b   *Pauline Christology: An Exegetical/ Theological Study.* Peabody, MA: Hendrickson.

Feuillet, A.
1980   "Loi de Dieu, loi du Christ et loi de l'esprit d'après les epîtres Pauliniennes: Les rapports de ces trois avec la loi Mosaique." *Novum Testamentum* 22:29–63.

Fitzmyer, J.
1981   "Habakkuk 2:3–4 and the New Testament." Pp. 236–45 in *To Advance the Gospel: New Testament Studies.* New York: Crossroad.
1998   "Crucifixion in Ancient Palestine, Qumran Literature, and the New Testament." Pp. 125–46 in *To Advance the Gospel: New Testament Studies.* 2nd ed. Grand Rapids: Eerdmans. Originally published in *Catholic Biblical Quarterly* 40 (1978): 493–513.
2006   "Justification by Faith in Pauline Thought: A Catholic View." Pp. 77–94 in *Rereading Paul Together: Protestant and Catholic Perspectives on Justification.* Edited by D. E. Aune. Grand Rapids: Eerdmans.

Fredriksen, P.
1991   "Judaism, the Circumcision of Gentiles, and Apocalyptic Hope: Another Look at Galatians 1 and 2." *Journal of Theological Studies* 42:532–64.

Fuller, D. P.
1975–76   "Paul and 'The Works of the Law.'" *Westminster Theological Journal* 38:28–42.
1980   *Gospel and Law: Contrast or Continuum? The Hermeneutics of Dispensationalism and Covenant Theology.* Grand Rapids: Eerdmans.
1992   *The Unity of the Bible: Unfolding God's Plan for Humanity.* Grand Rapids: Zondervan.

Fung, R. Y. K.
1988   *The Epistle to the Galatians.* New International Commentary on the New Testament. Grand Rapids: Eerdmans.

Furnish, V. P.
1968   *Theology and Ethics in Paul.* Nashville: Abingdon.
1973   *The Love Command in the New Testament.* London: SCM.

Gaechter, P.
1958   *Petrus und seine Zeit: Neutestamentliche Studien.* Innsbruck: Tyrolia.

Gaffin, R. B., Jr.
2006   *"By Faith, Not by Sight": Paul and the Order of Salvation.* Waynesboro, GA: Paternoster.

Gager, J. G.
1983   *The Origins of Anti-Semitism: Attitudes towards Judaism in Pagan and Christian Antiquity.* New York: Oxford University Press.
2000   *Reinventing Paul.* Oxford: Oxford University Press.

Gammie, J. G.
1990   "Paraenetic Literature: Toward the Morphology of Secondary Genre." *Semeia* 50:41–77.

Garcia, M. A.
2008   *Life in Christ: Union with Christ and Twofold Grace in Calvin's Theology.* Studies in Christian History and Thought. Milton Keynes: Paternoster.

García Martínez, F., and E. J. C. Tigchelaar
1997–98   *The Dead Sea Scrolls Study Edition.* 2 vols. Leiden: Brill.

Garlington, D. B.
1994   *Faith, Obedience, and Perseverance: Aspects of Paul's Letter to the Romans.* Wissenschaftliche Untersuchungen zum Neuen Testament 79. Tübingen: Mohr Siebeck.
1997   "Role Reversal and Paul's Use of Scripture in Galatians 3.10–13." *Journal for the Study of the New Testament* 65:85–121.
2003   *An Exposition of Galatians: A New Perspective/Reformational Reading.* Eugene, OR: Wipf & Stock.
2008   *Studies in the New Perspective on Paul: Essays and Reviews.* Eugene, OR: Wipf & Stock.
2009   "'Even We Have Believed': Galatians 2:15–16 Revisited." *Criswell Theological Review* 7:3–28.

Gaston, L.
1987   *Paul and the Torah.* 2nd ed. Vancouver: University of British Columbia Press.

Gathercole, S. J.
2002a   "A Law unto Themselves: The Gentiles in Romans 2.14–15 Revisited." *Journal for the Study of the New Testament* 85:27–49.
2002b   *Where Is Boasting? Early Jewish Soteriology and Paul's Response in Romans 1–5.* Grand Rapids: Eerdmans.
2004a   "Justified by Faith, Justified by His Blood: The Evidence of Romans 3:21–4:25." Pp. 147–84 in *Justification*

and Variegated Nomism, vol. 2: *The Paradoxes of Paul*. Edited by D. A. Carson, P. T. O'Brien, and M. A. Seifrid. Tübingen: Mohr Siebeck / Grand Rapids: Baker Academic.

2004b   "Torah, Life, and Salvation: Leviticus 18:5 in Early Judaism and the New Testament." Pp. 126–45 in *From Prophecy to Testament: The Function of the Old Testament in the New*. Edited by C. A. Evans. Peabody, MA: Hendrickson.

2005   "The Petrine and Pauline *Sola Fide* in Galatians 2." Pp. 309–27 in *Lutherische und neue Paulusperspektive*. Edited by M. Bachmann. Tübingen: Mohr Siebeck.

2006   "The Doctrine of Justification in Paul and Beyond: Some Proposals." Pp. 219–41 in *Justification in Perspective: Historical Developments and Contemporary Challenges*. Edited by B. L. McCormack. Grand Rapids: Baker Academic/Edinburgh: Rutherford House.

Gaventa, B. R.

1986   "Galatians 1 and 2: Autobiography as Paradigm." *Novum Testamentum* 28:309–26.

1990   "The Maternity of Paul: An Exegetical Study of Galatians 4:19." Pp. 189–201 in *The Conversation Continues: Studies in Paul and John in Honor of Louis Martyn*. Edited by R. T. Fortna and B. R. Gaventa. Nashville: Abingdon.

1991   "The Singularity of the Gospel: A Reading of Galatians." Pp. 147–59 in *Pauline Theology: Thessalonians, Philippians, Galatians, Philemon*. Edited by J. M. Bassler. Minneapolis: Fortress.

George, T.

1994   *Galatians*. New American Commentary. Nashville: Broadman & Holman.

Gignac, A.

1994   "Citation de Lévitique 18,5 en Romains 10,5 et Galates 3,12: Deux lectures différentes des rapports Christ-Torah?" *Église et Théologie* 25:367–403.

Gignilliat, M.

2008   "Paul, Allegory, and the Plain Sense of Scripture: Galatians 4:21–31." *Journal of Theological Interpretation* 2:135–46.

GKC   *Gesenius' Hebrew Grammar*. Edited and enlarged by E. Kautzsch. Revised by A. E. Cowley. 2nd English ed. Clarendon: Oxford, 1910.

Goddard, A. J., and S. A. Cummins

1993   "Ill or Ill-Treated? Conflict and Persecution as the Context of Paul's Original Ministry in Galatia (Galatians 4.12–20)." *Journal for the Study of the New Testament* 52:93–126.

Goldingay, J., and D. F. Payne

2006   *A Critical and Exegetical Commentary on Isaiah 40–55*. 2 vols. International Critical Commentary. London: T&T Clark.

Goppelt, L.

1982   *Typos: The Typological Interpretation of the Old Testament in the New*. Grand Rapids: Eerdmans.

Gordon, T. D.

2009   "Abraham and Sinai Contrasted in Galatians 3:6–14." Pp. 240–58 in *The Law Is Not of Faith: Essays on Works and Grace in the Mosaic Covenant*. Edited by B. D. Estelle, J. V. Fesko, and D. VanDrunen. Phillipsburg, NJ: P&R.

Gorman, M. J.

2004   *Apostle of the Crucified Lord: A Theological Introduction to Paul and His Letters*. Grand Rapids: Eerdmans.

2009   *Inhabiting the Cruciform God: Kenosis, Justification, and Theosis in Paul's Narrative Soteriology*. Grand Rapids: Eerdmans.

Grabner-Haider, A.

1968   *Paraklese und Eschatologie bei Paulus: Mensch und Welt im Anspruch der Zukunft Gottes*. Neutestamentliche Abhandlungen. Münster: Aschendorff.

Grant, R. M.

1997   "Neither Male nor Female." *Biblical Research* 37:5–14.

Grüneberg, K. N.

2003   *Abraham, Blessing and the Nations: A Philological and Exegetical Study of Genesis 12:3 in Its Narrative Context*. Beihefte zur Zeitschrift für die Alttestamentliche Wissenschaft 332. Berlin: de Gruyter.

Gundry, R. H.

1985   "Grace, Works, and Staying Saved in Paul." *Biblica* 66:15–32.

Gundry-Volf, J.

1997   "Christ and Gender: A Study of Difference and Equality in Gal 3,28." Pp. 439–77 in *Jesus Christus als die Mitte der Schrift: Studien zur Hermeneutik des Evangeliums*. Edited by C. Landmesser, H.-J. Eckstein, and H. Lichtenberger.

Beihefte zur Zeitschrift für die neutestamentliche Wissenschaft 86. Berlin: de
Gruyter.

Guthrie, D.
1990   *New Testament Introduction.* 4th ed.
Downers Grove, IL: InterVarsity.

Güttgemanns, E.
1966   *Der Leidende Apostel und Sein Herr:
Studien zur Paulinischen Christologie.*
Forschungen zur Religion und Literatur
des Alten und Neuen Testaments 90.
Göttingen: Vandenhoeck & Ruprecht.

Haacker, K.
1986   "Paulus und das Judentum im Galaterbrief." Pp. 95–111 in *Gottes Augapfel.*
Edited by E. Brocke and J. Seim. Neu-
kirchener-Vluyn: Neukirchener Verlag.

Haenchen, E.
1971   *The Acts of the Apostles: A Commentary.* Philadelphia: Westminster.

Hafemann, S. J.
1997   "Paul and the Exile of Israel in Galatians 3–4." Pp. 329–71 in *Exile: Old
Testament, Jewish, and Christian Conceptions.* Edited by J. M. Scott. Leiden:
Brill.
2000   "'Because of Weakness' (Galatians
4:13): The Role of Suffering in the Mission of Paul." Pp. 131–46 in *The Gospel
to the Nations: Perspectives on Paul's
Mission in Honour of P. T. O'Brien.*
Edited by P. Bolt and M. Thompson.
Downers Grove, IL: InterVarsity.

Hahn, F.
1971   "Genesis 15:6 im Neuen Testament."
Pp. 90–107 in *Probleme Biblischer
Theologie: Gerhard von Rad zum 70.
Geburtstag.* Edited by H. W. Wolff.
Munich: Kaiser.

Hahn, S. W.
2005   "Covenant, Oath, and the Aqedah
(Διαθήκη) in Galatians 3:15–18."
Catholic Biblical Quarterly 67:79–100.
2009   *Kinship by Covenant: A Canonical
Approach to the Fulfillment of God's
Saving Promises.* New Haven: Yale
University Press.

Hall, R. G.
1987   "The Rhetorical Outline for Galatians:
A Reconsideration." *Journal of Biblical
Literature* 106:277–87.

HALOT   *The Hebrew and Aramaic Lexicon of
the Old Testament.* By L. Koehler, W.
Baumgartner, J. J. Stamm, and M. E.
Richardson. 5 vols. Leiden: Brill, 2000.

Hamilton, V. P.
1990   *The Book of Genesis: Chapters 1–17.*
New International Commentary on
the Old Testament. Grand Rapids:
Eerdmans.

Hansen, B.
2010   *All of You Are One: The Social Vision
of Galatians 3.28, 1 Corinthians 12.13
and Colossians 3.11.* Library of New
Testament Studies 409. London: T&T
Clark.

Hansen, G. W.
1989   *Abraham in Galatians: Epistolary and
Rhetorical Contexts.* Journal for the
Study of the New Testament: Supplement Series 29. Sheffield: JSOT.
1994   *Galatians.* IVP New Testament Commentary Series 9. Downers Grove, IL:
InterVarsity.

Hanson, A. T.
1974   *Studies in Paul's Technique and
Theology.* Grand Rapids: Eerdmans.

Hardin, J. K.
2008   *Galatians and the Imperial Cult: A
Critical Analysis of the First-Century
Social Context of Paul's Letter.* Wis-
senschaftliche Untersuchungen zum
Neuen Testament 237. Tübingen, Mohr
Siebeck.

Harland, P. A.
2005   "Familial Dimensions of Group Identity: 'Brothers' (ΑΔΕΛΦΟΙ) in Associations of the Greek East." *Journal of
Biblical Literature* 124:491–513.

Harmon, M.
2010   *She Must and Shall Go Free: Paul's Isa-
ianic Gospel in Galatians.* Beihefte zur
Zeitschrift für die neutestamentliche
Wissenschaft 168. Berlin: de Gruyter.

Harnish, J. A.
1987   *Jesus Makes the Difference! The Gospel in Human Experience.* Nashville:
Upper Room.

Harris, M. J.
1999   *Slave of Christ: A New Testament
Metaphor for Total Devotion to Christ.*
New Studies in Biblical Theology 8.
Downers Grove, IL: InterVarsity.
2005   *The Second Epistle to the Corinthians.*
New International Greek Testament
Commentary. Grand Rapids: Eerdmans.
2012   *Prepositions and Theology in the
Greek New Testament.* Grand Rapids:
Zondervan.

Harrisville, R. A., III
1992   *The Figure of Abraham in the Epistles of St. Paul*. San Francisco: Mellen University Research Press.
1994   "Πίστις Χριστοῦ: The Witness of the Fathers." *Novum Testamentum* 36:233–41.

Hartman, L.
1993   "Galatians 3:25–4:11 as Part of a Theological Argument on a Practical Issue." Pp. 127–58 in *The Truth of the Gospel (Galatians 1:11–4:11)*. Edited by J. Lambrecht. Rome: Benedictina.

Hays, R. B.
1983   *The Faith of Jesus Christ: An Investigation of the Narrative Substructure of Galatians 3:1–4:11*. Society of Biblical Literature Dissertation Series 56. Chico, CA: Scholars Press.
1987   "Christology and Ethics in Galatians: The Law of Christ." *Catholic Biblical Quarterly* 49:268–90.
1989a   *Echoes of Scripture in the Letters of Paul*. New Haven: Yale University Press.
1989b   "'The Righteous One' as Eschatological Deliverer: A Case Study in Paul's Apocalyptic Hermeneutics." Pp. 191–215 in *Apocalyptic and the New Testament: Essays in Honor of J. Louis Martyn*. Edited by J. Marcus and M. L. Soards. Journal for the Study of the New Testament: Supplement Series 24. Sheffield: Sheffield Academic Press.
2000   "The Letter to the Galatians: Introduction, Commentary, and Reflections." Vol. 11 / pp. 181–348 in *The New Interpreter's Bible*. Edited by L. E. Keck et al. Nashville: Abingdon.
2002   *The Faith of Jesus Christ: The Narrative Substructure of Galatians 3:1–4:11*. 2nd ed. Grand Rapids: Eerdmans.

Heckel, U.
2002   *Der Segen im Neuen Testament*. Wissenschaftliche Untersuchungen zum Neuen Testament 2/150. Tübingen: Mohr Siebeck.

Heiligenthal, R.
1984   "Soziologische Implikationen der paulinischen Rechtfertigungslehre in Galaterbrief am Beispiel der 'Werke des Gesetzes.'" *Kairos* 26:38–53.

Heliso, D.
2007   *Pistis and the Righteous One: A Study of Romans 1:17 against the Background of Scripture and Second Temple Jewish Literature*. Wissenschaftliche Untersuchungen zum Neuen Testament 235. Tübingen: Mohr Siebeck.

Hemer, C.
1976   "The Adjective 'Phrygia.'" *Journal of Theological Studies* 27:122–26.
1989   *The Book of Acts in the Setting of Hellenistic History*. Edited by C. Gempf. Wissenschaftliche Untersuchungen zum Neuen Testament 49. Tübingen: Mohr Siebeck.

Hengel, M.
1977   *Crucifixion in the Ancient World and the Folly of the Message of the Cross*. Translated by J. Bowden. Philadelphia: Fortress.

Hengel, M., and A. M. Schwemer
1997   *Paul between Damascus and Antioch: The Unknown Years*. Louisville: Westminster John Knox.

Heussi, K.
1955   *Die römische Petrustradition in kritischer Sicht*. Tübingen: Mohr Siebeck.

Hill, D.
1967   *Greek Words with Hebrew Meanings: Studies in the Semantics of Soteriological Terms*. Society for the Study of the New Testament Monograph Series 5. Cambridge: Cambridge University Press.

Hoch, C. B.
1995   *All Things New: The Significance of Newness for Biblical Theology*. Grand Rapids: Baker.

Hodge, J.
2007   *If Sons, Then Heirs: A Study of Kinship and Ethnicity in the Letters of Paul*. New York: Oxford University Press.

Hofius, O.
1984   "Gal 1:18 : ἱστορῆσαι Κηφᾶν." *Zeitschrift für die neutestamentliche Wissenschaft und die Kunde der älteren Kirche* 75:73–85.
2006   "'Werke des Gesetzes': Untersuchungen zu der paulinischen und johanneischen Theologie und Literatur." Pp. 271–310 in *Paulus and Johannes: Exegetische Studien zur paulinischen und johanneischen Theologie und Literatur*. Edited by D. Sänger and U. Mell. Wissenschaftliche Untersuchungen zum Neuen Testament 198. Tübingen: Mohr Siebeck.

Holl, K.
1928   "Der Kirchenbegriff des Paulus in seinem Verhältnis zu dem der Urgemeinde." Pp. 44–67 in *Gesammelte*

Aufsätze zur Kirchengeschichte, vol. 2. Tübingen: Mohr Siebeck.

Hong, I.-G.
1993   *The Law in Galatians.* Journal for the Study of the New Testament: Supplement Series 81. Sheffield: JSOT Press.
1994   "Does Paul Misrepresent the Jewish Law? Law and Covenant in Gal 3:1–14." *Novum Testamentum* 36:164–82.
2002   "Being 'under the Law' in Galatians." *Evangelical Review of Theology* 26:354–72.

Hooker, M. D.
1971   "Interchange in Christ." *Journal of Theological Studies* 22:349–61.

Horrell, D. G.
2005   *Solidarity and Difference: A Contemporary Reading of Paul's Ethics.* London: T&T Clark.

Horton, M. S.
2007   *Covenant and Salvation: Union with Christ.* Louisville: Westminster John Knox.

Hove, R.
1999   *Equality in Christ? Galatians 3:28 and the Gender Dispute.* Wheaton: Crossway.

Howard, G.
1973–74   "'The Faith of Christ.'" *Expository Times* 85:212–14.
1979   *Paul: Crisis in Galatia; A Study in Early Christian Theology.* Society for the Study of the New Testament Monograph Series 35. Cambridge: Cambridge University Press.

Hubbard, M. B.
2002   *New Creation in Paul's Letters and Thought.* Society for the Study of the New Testament Monograph Series 119. Cambridge: Cambridge University Press.

Hübner, H.
1975   "Das Ganze und das eine Gesetz: Zum Problemkreis Paulus und die Stoa." *Kerygma und Dogma* 21:239–56.
1984   *Law in Paul's Thought: A Contribution to the Development of Pauline Theology.* Studies of the New Testament and Its World. Edinburgh: T&T Clark.

Hultgren, A. J.
1980   "The *Pistis Christou* Formulation in Paul." *Novum Testamentum* 22:248–63.
2006   "The Scriptural Foundations for Paul's Mission to the Gentiles." Pp. 21–44 in

Paul and His Theology. Edited by S. E. Porter. Pauline Studies 3. Leiden: Brill.

Humphrey, E.
2009   "On Probabilities, Possibilities and Pretext: Fostering a Hermeneutics of Sobriety, Sympathy and Imagination in an Impressionistic and Suspicious Age." Pp. 256–76 in *Translating the New Testament: Text, Translation, Theology.* Edited by S. E. Porter and M. J. Boda. Grand Rapids: Eerdmans.

Hunn, D.
2006   "*Pistis Christou* in Galatians 2:16: Clarification from 3:1–6." *Tyndale Bulletin* 57:23–33.
2009   "Habakkuk 2.4b in Its Context: How Far Off Was Paul?" *Journal for the Study of the Old Testament* 34:219–39.
2010   "Christ versus the Law: Issues in Galatians 2:17–18." *Catholic Biblical Quarterly* 72:537–55.

Hurtado, L. W.
1979   "The Jerusalem Collection and the Book of Galatians." *Journal for the Study of the New Testament* 5:46–62.

Hyldahl, N.
2000   "Gerechtigkeit durch Glauben: Historische und theologische Beobachtungen zum Galaterbrief." *New Testament Studies* 46:425–44.

Institutes   *Institutes of the Christian Religion.* By John Calvin. Edited by John T. McNeill. Translated by Ford L. Battles. 2 vols. Library of Christian Classics 20–21. Philadelphia: Westminster, 1960.

Jackson, T. R.
2010   *New Creation in Paul's Letters: A Study of the Historical and Social Setting of a Pauline Concept.* Wissenschaftliche Untersuchungen zum Neuen Testament 2/272. Tübingen: Mohr Siebeck.

Jeremias, J.
1958   "Chiasmus in den Paulusbriefen." *Zeitschrift für die neutestamentliche Wissenschaft und die Kunde der älteren Kirche* 49:145–56.
1966   *Abba: Studien zur neutestamentlichen Theologie und Zeitgeschichte.* Göttingen: Vandenhoeck & Ruprecht.
1971   *New Testament Theology: The Proclamation of Jesus.* New York: Scribner's Sons.

Jewett, R.
1970–71   "The *Agitators* and the Galatian Congregation." *New Testament Studies* 17:198–212.

1971   *Paul's Anthropological Terms: A Study of Their Use in Conflict Settings.* Arbeiten zur Geschichte des antiken Judentums und des Urchristentums 10. Leiden: Brill.

1979   *A Chronology of Paul's Life.* Philadelphia: Fortress.

Jobes, K. H.
1993   "Jerusalem, Our Mother: Metalepsis and Intertextuality in Galatians 4:21–31." *Westminster Theological Journal* 55:299–320.

Johnson, H. W.
1987   "The Paradigm of Abraham in Galatians 3:6–9." *Trinity Journal* 8:179–99.

Johnson, L. T.
1982   "Rom 3:21–26 and the Faith of Jesus." *Catholic Biblical Quarterly* 44:77–90.

Johnson, S. L.
1986   "Paul and 'The Israel of God': An Exegetical and Eschatological Case-Study." Pp. 183–94 in *Essays in Honor of J. Dwight Pentecost.* Edited by S. Toussaint and C. Dyer. Chicago: Moody.

Jones, S. F.
1987   *"Freiheit" in den Briefen des Apostels Paulus: Eine historische, exegetische, und religionsgeschichtliche Studie.* Göttinger theologischer Arbeiten 34. Göttingen: Vandenhoeck & Ruprecht.

Jüngel, E.
2001   *Justification: The Heart of the Christian Faith; A Theological Study with Ecumenical Purpose.* Edinburgh: T&T Clark.

Kaiser, W. C., Jr.
1971   "Leviticus 18:5 and Paul: 'Do This and You Shall Live (Eternally?).'" *Journal of the Evangelical Theological Society* 14:19–28.

1994   "The Book of Leviticus." Vol. 1 / pp. 983–1191 in *The New Interpreter's Bible.* Edited by L. E. Keck et al. Nashville: Abingdon.

Kamlah, E.
1964   *Die Form der katalogischen Paränese im Neuen Testament.* Wissenschaftliche Untersuchungen zum Neuen Testament 7. Tübingen: Mohr Siebeck.

Karlberg, M. W.
2000   *Covenant Theology in Reformed Perspective.* Eugene, OR: Wipf & Stock.

Käsemann, E.
1969   "The Righteousness of God in Paul." Pp. 168–82 in *New Testament Questions of Today.* Edited by E. Käsemann. Philadelphia: Fortress.

Kautzsch, E.
1881   *Über die Derivate des Stammes צדק im alttestamentlichen Sprachgebrauch.* Tübingen: Mohr Siebeck.

Keil, C. F., and F. Delitzsch
1969a   *Commentary on the Old Testament: The Pentateuch.* Grand Rapids: Eerdmans.

1969b   *Commentary on the Old Testament: The Prophecies of Isaiah.* Grand Rapids: Eerdmans.

Kennedy, G. A.
1984   *New Testament Interpretation through Rhetorical Criticism.* Chapel Hill: University of North Carolina.

Kern, P. H.
1998   *Rhetoric and Galatians: Assessing an Approach to Paul's Epistle.* Society for New Testament Studies Monograph Series 101. Cambridge: Cambridge University Press.

Kertelge, K.
1984   "Gesetz und Freiheit im Galaterbrief." *New Testament Studies* 30:382–94.

1989   "Freiheitsbotschaft und Liebesgebot im Galaterbrief." Pp. 326–37 in *Neues Testament und Ethik: Für Rudolf Schnackenburg.* Edited by H. Merklein. Freiburg: Herder.

Kibbe, M.
2012   "'The Obedience of Christ': A Reassessment of τὴν Ὑπακοὴν τοῦ Χριστοῦ in 2 Corinthians 10:5." *Journal for the Study of Paul and His Letters* 2:41–56.

Kilpatrick, G. D.
1954   "Gal. 2:14: ὀρθοποδοῦσιν." Pp. 269–74 in *Neutestamentliche Studien für Rudolf Bultmann zu seinem siebzigsten Geburtstag am 20. Aug. 1954.* Edited by W. Eltester. Beihefte zur Zeitschrift für die neutestamentliche Wissenschaft 21. Berlin: Töpelmann.

1959   "Galatians 1.18: ΙΣΤΟΡΗΣΑΙ ΚΗΦΑΝ." Pp. 144–49 in *New Testament Essays: Studies in Memory of T. W. Manson.*

Edited by A. J. B. Higgins. Manchester: Manchester University Press.

1983   "Peter, Jerusalem and Galatians 1:13–2:14." *Novum Testamentum* 24:318–26.

Kim, S.

2002   *Paul and the New Perspective: Second Thoughts on the Origin of Paul's Gospel.* Grand Rapids: Eerdmans.

2008   *Christ and Caesar: The Gospel and the Roman Empire in the Writings of Paul and Luke.* Grand Rapids: Eerdmans.

2011   "Paul as Missionary Herald." Pp. 9–24 in *Paul as Missionary: Identity, Activity, Theology, and Practice.* Edited by T. J. Burke and B. S. Rosner. Library of New Testament Studies 420. London: T&T Clark.

Kinzer, M. S.

2005   *Post-Missionary Messianic Judaism: Redefining Christian Engagement with the Jewish People.* Grand Rapids: Baker Academic.

Klein, G.

1960   "Galater 2:6–9 und die Geschichte der Jerusalemer Urgemeinde." *Zeitschrift für Theologie und Kirche* 57:275–95.

Kline, M. G.

2000   *Kingdom Prologue: Genesis Foundations for a Covenantal Worldview.* Overland Park, KS: Two Age.

Koch, D. A.

1985   "Der Text von Hab 2 4b in der Septuaginta und im Neuen Testament." *Zeitschrift für die neutestamentliche Wissenschaft und die Kunde der älteren Kirche* 76:68–85.

1986   *Die Schrift als Zeuge des Evangeliums: Untersuchungen zur Verwendung und zum Verständnis der Schrift bei Paulus.* Beiträge zur historischen Theologie 69. Tübingen: Mohr Siebeck.

1999   "Barnabas, Paul und die Adressaten des Galaterbriefs." Pp. 85–106 in *Das Urchristentum in seiner literarischen Geschichte: Festschrift für Jürgen Becker zum 65. Geburtstag.* Edited by U. Mell and U. B. Müller. Berlin: de Gruyter.

Köstenberger, A.

2001   "The Identity of the ΙΣΡΑΗΛ ΤΟΥ ΘΕΟΥ (Israel of God) in Galatians 6:16." *Faith and Mission* 19:3–24.

Kruse, C.

1996   *Paul, the Law and Justification.* Leicester, UK: Inter-Varsity.

Kuhn, H. W.

1994   "Die Bedeutung der Qumrantexte für das Verhältnis des Galaterbriefes." Pp. 169–221 in *New Qumran Texts and Studies.* Edited by G. J. Brooke. Leiden: Brill.

Kümmel, G. K.

1975   *Introduction to the New Testament.* 2nd ed. London: SCM.

Kuula, K.

1999   *The Law, the Covenant and God's Plan,* vol. 1: *Paul's Polemical Treatment of the Law in Galatians.* Publications of the Finnish Exegetical Society 72. Göttingen: Vandenhoeck & Ruprecht.

Kuyper, L. J.

1977   "Righteousness and Salvation." *Scottish Journal of Theology* 3:233–52.

Kwon, Y. G.

2004   *Eschatology in Galatians: Rethinking Paul's Response to the Crisis in Galatia.* Wissenschaftliche Untersuchungen zum Neuen Testament 183. Tübingen: Mohr Siebeck.

Laato, T.

1991   *Paulus und das Judentum: Anthropologische Erwägungen.* Abo: Abo Academy.

2004   "Paul's Anthropological Considerations: Two Problems." Pp. 343–59 in *Justification and Variegated Nomism,* vol. 2: *The Paradoxes of Paul.* Edited by D. A. Carson, P. T. O'Brien, and M. A. Seifrid. Tübingen: Mohr Siebeck / Grand Rapids: Baker Academic.

Lagrange, M.-J.

1918   *Saint Paul: Épître aux Galates.* Paris: Gabalda.

Lake, K.

1933   "Paul's Route in Asia Minor." Vol. 5 / pp. 224–39 in *The Beginnings of Christianity,* part 1: *The Acts of the Apostles.* Edited by F. J. Foakes-Jackson and K. Lake. London: Macmillan.

Lambrecht, J.

1978   "Line of Thought in Gal. 2:14b–21." *New Testament Studies* 24:484–95.

1987   "Once Again Gal 2:17–18 and 3:21." *Ephemerides theologicae lovanienses* 63:148–53.

1991   "Transgressor by Nullifying God's Grace: A Study of Gal 2,18–21." *Biblica* 72:217–36.

1996   "Paul's Reasoning in Galatians 2:11–21." Pp. 53–74 in *Paul and the Mosaic*

Law. Edited by J. D. G. Dunn. Tübingen: Mohr Siebeck.

Lampe, G. W. H.
1964   "The New Testament Doctrine of *Ktisis*." *Scottish Journal of Theology* 17:457–58.

Lee, C.-C.
2009   "The Blessing of Abraham and the Promise of the Spirit: The Influence of the Prophets on Paul in Galatians 3:1–14." PhD diss., Wheaton College.

Lee, G. M.
1970   "The Aorist Participle of Subsequent Action (Acts 16,6)." *Biblica* 51:235–57.

Légasse, S.
2000   *L'épître de Paul aux Galates*. Lectio Divina Commentaries 9. Paris: Cerf.

LEH   *Greek-English Lexicon of the Septuagint*. Compiled by J. Lust, E. Eynikel, and K. Hauspie. Rev. ed. Stuttgart: Deutsche Bibelgesellschaft, 2003.

Leithart, P. J.
2007   "Adam the Catholic? Faith and Life in the Adamic Covenant." Chap. 4 in *A Faith That Is Never Alone: A Response to Westminster Seminary California*. Edited by P. Andrew Sandlin. La Grange, CA: Kerygma.

Lemmer, H. R.
1992   "Mnemonic Reference to the Spirit as a Persuasive Tool." *Neotestamentica* 26:359–88.

Letham, R.
2011   *Union with Christ: In Scripture, History, and Theology*. Phillipsburg, NJ: P&R.

Levy, I. C.
2011   *The Letter to the Galatians*. The Bible in Medieval Tradition. Grand Rapids: Eerdmans.

Lietzmann, H.
1923   *An die Galater*. 2nd ed. Handbuch zum Neuen Testament 10. Tübingen: Mohr Siebeck.

Lightfoot, J. B.
1881   *Saint Paul's Epistle to the Galatians: A Revised Text with Introduction, Notes, and Dissertations*. 7th ed. London: Macmillan.

Lim, T. H.
1997   *Holy Scripture in the Qumran Commentaries and Pauline Letters*. Oxford: Clarendon.

Lincoln, A. T.
1981   *Paradise Now and Not Yet: Studies in the Role of the Heavenly Dimension in Paul's Thought with Special Reference to His Eschatology*. Society for the Study of the New Testament Monograph Series 43. Cambridge: Cambridge University Press.

Lindars, B.
1961   *New Testament Apologetic: The Doctrinal Significance of the Old Testament Quotations*. London: SCM.

LN   *Greek-English Lexicon of the New Testament: Based on Semantic Domains*. By J. P. Louw and E. A. Nida. 2nd ed. New York: United Bible Society, 1999.

Longenecker, B. W.
1998   *The Triumph of Abraham's God: The Transformation of Identity in Galatians*. Edinburgh: T&T Clark.
1999   "'Until Christ Is Formed in You': Suprahuman Forces and Moral Character in Galatians." *Catholic Biblical Quarterly* 61:92–108.
2010   *Remember the Poor: Paul, Poverty, and the Greco-Roman World*. Grand Rapids: Eerdmans.
2012   "Salvation History in Galatians and the Making of a Pauline Discourse." *Journal for the Study of Paul and His Letters* 2:65–87.

Longenecker, R. N.
1964   *Paul, Apostle of Liberty: The Origin and Nature of Paul's Christianity*. Grand Rapids: Baker.
1974   "Ancient Amanuenses and the Pauline Epistles." Pp. 281–97 in *New Dimensions in New Testament Study*. Edited by M. C. Tenney and R. N. Longenecker. Grand Rapids: Zondervan.
1983   "On the Form, Function, and Authority of the New Testament Letters." Pp. 101–14 in *Scripture and Truth*. Edited by D. A. Carson and J. D. Woodbridge. Grand Rapids: Zondervan.
1990   *Galatians*. Word Biblical Commentary. Dallas: Word.
1997   *The Road from Damascus: The Impact of Paul's Conversion on His Life, Thought, and Ministry*. Grand Rapids: Eerdmans.

Lowe, B. A.
2009   "James 2:1 in the Πίστις Χριστοῦ Debate: Irrelevant or Indispensable?" Pp. 239–58 in *The Faith of Jesus Christ: Exegetical, Biblical, and Theological*

Studies. Edited by M. F. Bird and P. M. Sprinkle. Peabody, MA: Hendrickson.

LSJ   *A Greek-English Lexicon*. By H. G. Liddell, R. Scott, and H. S. Jones. 9th ed. Oxford: Oxford University Press, 1940.

Lüdemann, G.
1984   *Paul, Apostle to the Gentiles: Studies in Chronology*. Philadelphia: Fortress.

Lull, D. J.
1980   *The Spirit in Galatia: Paul's Interpretation of Pneuma as Divine Power*. Society of Biblical Literature Dissertation Series 49. Atlanta: Scholars.

Lütgert, W.
1919   *Gesetz und Geist: Eine Untersuchung zur Vorgeschichte des Galaterbriefes*. Gütersloh: Bertelsmann.

Luther, M.
1963   *Lectures on Galatians 1535, Chapters 1–4*. Luther's Works 26. Saint Louis: Concordia.
1964   *Lectures on Galatians 1535, Chapters 5–6, and Lectures on Galatians 1519, Chapters 1–6*. Luther's Works 27. Saint Louis: Concordia.

Lutjens, R.
1990   "'You Do Not Do What You Want': What Does Galatians 5:17 Really Mean?" *Presbyterion* 16:103–17.

Lyall, F.
1984   *Slaves, Citizens, Sons: Legal Metaphors in the Epistles*. Grand Rapids: Zondervan.

Lyons, G.
1985   *Pauline Autobiography: Toward a New Understanding*. Society of Biblical Literature Dissertation Series 73. Atlanta: Scholars Press.

Malherbe, A. J.
1980   "MH ΓΕΝΟΙΤΟ in the Diatribe and Paul." *Harvard Theological Review* 73:231–40.

Marchant, E. C., and G. W. Bowersock (trans.)
1968   *Xenophon: Agesilaus*. Loeb Classical Library 183. Cambridge, MA: Harvard University Press.

Marchant, E. C., and O. J. Todd (trans.)
1923   *Xenophon: Memorabilia*. Loeb Classical Library 168. Cambridge, MA: Harvard University Press.

Marcus, J.
2001   "'Under the Law': The Background of a Pauline Expression." *Catholic Biblical Quarterly* 63:72–83.

Marcus, R. (trans.)
1943   *Josephus: Antiquities, Books XII–XIII*. Loeb Classical Library 365. Cambridge, MA: Harvard University Press.

Martin, T. W.
1996   "Pagan and Judeo-Christian Time-Keeping Schemes in Gal 4.10 and Col 2.16." *New Testament Studies* 42:105–19.
1999a   "The Ambiguities of a 'Baffling Expression' (Gal 4:12)." *Filologia Neotestamentaria* 12:123–38.
1999b   "Whose Flesh? What Temptation? (Galatians 4.13–14)." *Journal for the Study of the New Testament* 74:65–91.
2003   "The Covenant of Circumcision (Genesis 17:9–14) and the Situational Antitheses in Galatians 3:28." *Journal of Biblical Literature* 122:111–25.

Martyn, J. L.
1985a   "Apocalyptic Antinomies in Paul's Letter to the Galatians." *New Testament Studies* 31:410–24.
1985b   "A Law-Observant Mission to Gentiles: The Background of Galatians." *Scottish Journal of Theology* 38:307–24.
1997   *Galatians: A New Translation and Introduction with Commentary*. Anchor Bible 33A. New York: Doubleday.

Maston, J.
2012   "The Nature of Salvation History in Galatians." *Journal for the Study of Paul and His Letters* 2:89–103.

Matera, F. J.
1992   *Galatians*. Sacra pagina 9. Collegeville, MN: Liturgical Press.
1993   "The Death of Christ and the Cross in Paul's Letter to the Galatians." *Louvain Studies* 18:283–96.

Matlock, R. B.
1996   *Unveiling the Apocalyptic Paul: Paul's Interpreters and the Rhetoric of Criticism*. Journal for the Study of the New Testament: Supplement Series 127. Sheffield: Sheffield Academic Press.
2000   "Detheologizing the ΠΙΣΤΙΣ ΧΡΙΣΤΟΥ Debate: Cautionary Remarks from a Lexical Semantic Perspective." *Novum Testamentum* 42:1–23.
2002   "The Arrow and the Web: Critical Reflections on a Narrative Approach to Paul." Pp. 44–57 in *Narrative Dynamics in Paul: A Critical Assessment*. Edited by B. W. Longenecker. Louisville: Westminster John Knox.

2007 "The Rhetoric of *Pistis* in Paul: Galatians 2.16, 3.22, Romans 3.22, and Philippians 3.9." *Journal for the Study of the New Testament* 30:173–203.

2009a "Helping Paul's Argument Work? The Curse of Galatians 3.10–14." Pp. 154–79 in *The Torah in the New Testament: Papers Delivered at the Manchester-Lausanne Seminar of June 2008*. Edited by M. Tait and P. Oakes. London: T&T Clark.

2009b "Saving Faith: The Rhetoric and Semantics of Πίστις in Paul." Pp. 73–89 in *The Faith of Jesus Christ: Exegetical, Biblical, and Theological Studies*. Edited by M. F. Bird and P. M. Sprinkle. Peabody, MA: Hendrickson.

McCartney, D.
2009 *James*. Baker Exegetical Commentary on the New Testament. Grand Rapids: Baker Academic.

McComiskey, T. E.
1985 *The Covenants of Promise*. Grand Rapids: Baker.

McDonald, L. M., and S. E. Porter
2000 *Early Christianity and Its Sacred Literature*. Peabody, MA: Hendrickson.

McKnight, S.
1991 *Light among the Gentiles: Jewish Missionary Activity in the Second Temple Period*. Minneapolis: Fortress.
1995 *Galatians*. NIV Application Commentary. Grand Rapids: Zondervan.
2000 "The Ego and 'I': Galatians 2:19 in New Perspective." *Word and World* 20:272–80.

McNamara, M.
1978 "'To de (Hagar) Sina oros estin en tē Arabia' (Gal 4:25a): Paul and Petra." *Milltown Studies* 2:24–41.

Meiser, M.
2007 *Galater*. Novum Testamentum Patristicum. Göttingen: Vandenhoeck & Ruprecht.

Mell, U.
1989 *Neue Schöpfung: Eine traditionsgeschichtliche und exegetische Studie zu einem soteriologischen Grundsatz paulinischer Theologie*. Beihefte zur Zeitschrift für die neutestamentliche Wissenschaft 56. Berlin: de Gruyter.
2006 "Der Galaterbrief als urchristlicher Gemeindeleitungsbrief." Pp. 353–80 in *Paulus und Johannes: Exegetische Studien zur paulinischen und johanneischen Theologie und Literatur*. Edited by D. Sänger and U. Mell. Wissenschaftliche Untersuchungen zum Neuen Testament 198. Tübingen: Mohr Siebeck.

Metzger, B. M.
1994 *A Textual Commentary on the Greek New Testament*. 2nd ed. Stuttgart: Deutsche Bibelgesellschaft.

Meyer, H. A. W.
1873 *Critical and Exegetical Handbook to the Epistle to the Galatians*. New York: Scribner, Welford & Armstrong.

Meyer, J. C.
2009 *The End of the Law: Mosaic Covenant in Pauline Theology*. NAC Studies in Bible and Theology 6. Nashville: B&H Academic.

Miller, J. C.
2011 "Paul and His Ethnicity: Reframing the Categories." Pp. 37–50 in *Paul as Missionary: Identity, Activity, Theology, and Practice*. Edited by T. J. Burke and B. S. Rosner. Library of New Testament Studies 420. London: T&T Clark.

Minear, P.
1979 "The Crucified World: The Enigma of Galatians 6:14." Pp. 395–407 in *Theologia Crucis—Signum Crucis: Festschrift für Erich Dinkler zum 70. Geburtstag*. Edited by C. Andresen and G. Klein. Tübingen: Mohr Siebeck.

Mitchell, S.
1993 *Anatolia: Land, Men, and Gods in Asia Minor*. Oxford: Clarendon.

MM *The Vocabulary of the Greek Testament: Illustrated from the Papyri and Other Non-literary Sources*. By J. H. Moulton and G. Milligan. Reprinted Grand Rapids: Eerdmans, 1976.

Moo, D. J.
1983 "'Law,' 'Works of the Law,' and Legalism in Paul." *Westminster Theological Journal* 45:73–100.
1984 "Jesus and the Authority of the Mosaic Law." *Journal for the Study of the New Testament* 20:3–49.
1986 "The Problem of Sensus Plenior." Pp. 179–211, 397–405 in *Hermeneutics, Authority, and Canon*. Edited by D. A. Carson and J. D. Woodbridge. Grand Rapids: Zondervan.
1993 "The Law of Christ as the Fulfillment of the Law of Moses: A Modified Lutheran View." Pp. 319–76 in *The Law, the Gospel, and the Modern Christian: Five Views*. Grand Rapids: Zondervan.

1996   *The Epistle to the Romans.* New International Commentary on the New Testament. Grand Rapids: Eerdmans.

2000   *The Letter of James.* Pillar New Testament Commentary. Grand Rapids: Eerdmans.

2003   "'Flesh' in Romans: A Problem for the Translator." Pp. 365–79 in *The Challenge of Bible Translation: Communicating God's Word to the World; Essays in Honor of Ronald F. Youngblood.* Edited by G. S. Scorgie, M. L. Strauss, and S. M. Voth. Grand Rapids: Zondervan.

2004   "Israel and the Law in Romans 5–11: Interaction with the New Perspective." Pp. 185–216 in *Justification and Variegated Nomism,* vol. 2: *The Paradoxes of Paul.* Edited by D. A. Carson, P. T O'Brien, and M. A. Seifrid. Tübingen: Mohr Siebeck / Grand Rapids: Baker Academic.

2006   "Nature in the New Creation: New Testament Eschatology and the Environment." *Journal of the Evangelical Theological Society* 49:449–88.

2008   *The Letter to the Colossians.* Pillar New Testament Commentary. Grand Rapids: Eerdmans.

2010a   "Creation and New Creation." *Bulletin for Biblical Research* 20:39–60.

2010b   Review of *The Deliverance of God: An Apocalyptic Rereading of Justification in Paul,* by Douglas A. Campbell. *Journal of the Evangelical Theological Society* 53:143–50.

2011   "Justification in Galatians." Pp. 160–95 in *Understanding the Times: New Testament Studies in the 21st Century; Essays in Honor of D. A. Carson on the Occasion of His 65th Birthday.* Edited by A. Köstenberger and R. Yarbrough. Wheaton: Crossway.

Morales, R. J.
2009   "The Words of the Luminaries, the Curse of the Law, and the Outpouring of the Spirit in Gal 3,10–14." *Zeitschrift für die neutestamentliche Wissenschaft* 100: 269–77.

Morris, L. L.
1984   *The Apostolic Preaching of the Cross.* Grand Rapids: Eerdmans.

1996   *Galatians: Paul's Charter of Christian Freedom.* Downers Grove, IL: InterVarsity.

Motyer, A.
1993   *The Prophecy of Isaiah: An Introduction and Commentary.* Downers Grove, IL: InterVarsity.

Moule, C. F. D.
1959   *An Idiom Book of New Testament Greek.* Cambridge: Cambridge University Press.

1967   "Obligation in the Ethic of Paul." Pp. 389–406 in *Christian History and Interpretation: Studies Presented to John Knox.* Edited by W. R. Farmer, C. F. D. Moule and R. R. Niebuhr. Cambridge: Cambridge University Press.

1970   "Death 'to Sin,' 'to the Law,' and 'to the World': A Note on Certain Datives." Pp. 367–75 in *Mélanges bibliques en hommage au R. P. Béda Rigaux.* Edited by A. Descamps and A. de Halleux. Gembloux: Duculot.

Moulton, J. H.
1908   *Prolegomena.* Vol. 1 of *A Grammar of New Testament Greek.* Edinburgh: T&T Clark.

Munck, J.
1959   *Paul and the Salvation of Mankind.* London: SCM.

Mundle, W.
1977   *Der Glaubensbegriff des Paulus: Eine Untersuchung zur Dogmengeschichte des ältesten Christentums.* Darmstadt: Wissenschaftliche Buchgesellschaft.

Murphy-O'Connor, J.
1993   "Paul in Arabia." *Catholic Biblical Quarterly* 55:732–37.

1995   *Paul the Letter-Writer: His World, His Options, His Skills.* Collegeville, MN: Liturgical Press.

1996   *Paul: A Critical Life.* Oxford: Clarendon.

Murray, J.
1957   *Principles of Conduct: Aspects of Biblical Ethics.* Grand Rapids: Eerdmans.

Mussner, F.
1988   *Der Galaterbrief.* 5th ed. Herders theologischer Kommentar zum Neuen Testament 9. Freiburg: Herder.

NA[28]   *Novum Testamentum Graece.* Edited by Eberhard Nestle, Erwin Nestle, B. Aland, K. Aland, J. Karavidopoulos, C. M. Martini, and B. M. Metzger. 28th ed. Stuttgart: Deutsche Bibelgesellschaft, 2012.

Nanos, M. D.
2002   *The Irony of Galatians: Paul's Letter in First-Century Context.* Minneapolis: Fortress.

2005   "Intruding 'Spies' and 'Pseudo-brethren': The Jewish Intra-group Politics of Paul's Jerusalem Meeting (Gal 2:1–10)."

Pp. 59–97 in *Paul and His Opponents.* Edited by S. E. Porter. Leiden: Brill.

2010   "Paul and Judaism: Why Not Paul's Judaism?" Pp. 117–60 in *Paul Unbound: Other Perspectives on the Apostle.* Edited by M. D. Given. Peabody, MA: Hendrickson.

NETS   *A New English Translation of the Septuagint.* By the International Organization for Septuagint and Cognate Studies. New York: Oxford University Press, 2007.

NewDocs   *New Documents Illustrating Early Christianity.* Edited by G. H. R. Horsley and S. R. Llewelyn. North Ryde, NSW: Ancient History Documentary Research Centre, Macquarie University, 1980–98.

Newman, C. C.
1992   *Paul's Glory-Christology: Tradition and Rhetoric.* Supplements to Novum Testamentum 69. Leiden: Brill.

New Pauly   *Brill's New Pauly: Encyclopedia of the Ancient World.* Edited by H. Cancik, H. Schneider, and M. Landfester. 20 vols. Leiden: Brill, 2002–11.

Neyrey, J. H.
1988   "Bewitched in Galatia: Paul and Cultural Anthropology." *Catholic Biblical Quarterly* 50:72–100.

Ngewa, S.
2010   *Galatians.* Africa Bible Commentary Series. Nairobi: Hippo.

NIDB   *The New Interpreter's Dictionary of the Bible.* Edited by K. D. Sakenfeld. 5 vols. Nashville: Abingdon, 2009.

NIDNTT   *New International Dictionary of New Testament Theology.* Edited by C. Brown. 4 vols. Grand Rapids: Zondervan, 1975–85.

Niebuhr, K.-W.
1992   *Heidenapostel aus Israel: Die jüdische Identität des Paulus nach ihrer Darstellung in seinen Briefen.* Wissenschaftliche Untersuchungen zum Neuen Testament 2/62. Tübingen: Mohr Siebeck.

Noth, M.
1966   "'For All Who Rely on Works of the Law Are under a Curse.'" Pp. 118–31 in *The Laws in the Pentateuch and Other Essays.* Edinburgh: Oliver & Boyd.

NPNF¹   *Nicene and Post-Nicene Fathers of the Christian Church.* Edited by P. Schaff. 1st series. 14 vols. Reprinted Grand Rapids: Eerdmans, 1952–57.

O'Brien, K. S.
2006   "The Curse of the Law (Galatians 3.13): Crucifixion, Persecution, and Deuteronomy 21.22–23." *Journal for the Study of the New Testament* 29:55–76.

O'Brien, P. T.
1992   "Justification in Paul and Some Crucial Issues of the Last Two Decades." Pp. 69–95 in *Right with God: Justification in the Bible and the World.* Edited by D. A. Carson. Grand Rapids: Baker.

2004a   "Was Paul a Covenantal Nomist?" Pp. 249–96 in *Justification and Variegated Nomism,* vol. 2: *The Paradoxes of Paul.* Edited by D. A. Carson, P. T. O'Brien, and M. A. Seifrid. Tübingen: Mohr Siebeck / Grand Rapids: Baker Academic.

2004b   "Was Paul Converted?" Pp. 361–91 in *Justification and Variegated Nomism,* vol. 2: *The Paradoxes of Paul.* Edited by D. A. Carson, P. T. O'Brien, and M. A. Seifrid. Tübingen: Mohr Siebeck / Grand Rapids: Baker Academic.

O'Donovan, O.
1994   *Resurrection and Moral Order: An Outline for Evangelical Ethics.* 2nd ed. Grand Rapids: Eerdmans.

Oegema, G. S.
1999   *Für Israel und die Völker: Studien zum Alttestamentlich-Jüdischen Hintergrund der Paulinischen Theologie.* Supplements to Novum Testamentum 95. Leiden: Brill.

Oeming, M.
1983   "Ist Genesis 15 ein Beleg für die Anrechnung des Glaubens zur Gerechtigkeit?" *Zeitschrift für die alttestamentliche Wissenschaft* 95:182–97.

Oepke, A.
1973   *Der Brief des Paulus an die Galater.* Theologischer Handkommentar zum Neuen Testament. Berlin: Evangelische Verlagsanstalt.

Orchard, B.
1973   "The Ellipsis between Galatians 2,3 and 2,4." *Biblica* 54:469–81.

1976   "Once Again the Ellipsis between Gal. 2,3 and 2,4." *Biblica* 57:254–55.

Ortlund, D. C.
2009   "Justified by Faith, Judged according to Works: Another Look at a Pauline Paradox." *Journal of the Evangelical Theological Society* 52:323–39.

2012 *Zeal without Knowledge: The Concept of Zeal in Romans 10, Galatians 1, and Philippians 3.* Library of New Testament Studies 472. London: T&T Clark.

Oswalt, J. H.
1998 *Isaiah 40–66.* New International Commentary on the Old Testament. Grand Rapids: Eerdmans.

OTP *The Old Testament Pseudepigrapha.* Edited by J. H. Charlesworth. 2 vols. Garden City, NY: Doubleday, 1983–85.

Owen, P. L.
2007 "The 'Works of the Law' in Romans and Galatians: A New Defense of the Subjective Genitive." *Journal of Biblical Literature* 126:553–77.

Parsons, M.
1995 "Being Precedes Act: Indicative and Imperative in Paul's Writing." Pp. 217–47 in *Understanding Paul's Ethics: Twentieth Century Approaches.* Edited by B. S. Rosner. Grand Rapids: Eerdmans. Reprinted from *Evangelical Quarterly* 60 (1988): 99–127.

Pate, C. M.
2000 *The Reverse of the Curse: Paul, Wisdom, and the Law.* Wissenschaftliche Untersuchungen zum Neuen Testament 2/114. Tübingen: Mohr Siebeck.

Patterson, R. D.
1991 *Nahum, Habakkuk, Zephaniah.* Wycliffe Exegetical Commentary. Chicago: Moody.

Paulsen, H.
1980 "Einheit und Freiheit der Söhne Gottes—Gal 3:26–29." *Zeitschrift für die neutestamentliche Wissenschaft* 71:74–95.

Pennington, J. T., and S. M. McDonough (eds.)
2008 *Cosmology and New Testament Theology.* Library of New Testament Studies 355. London: T&T Clark.

Peppard, M.
2011 "Adopted and Begotten Sons of God: Paul and John on Divine Sonship." *Catholic Biblical Quarterly* 73:92–110.

Perkins, P.
2003 *Abraham's Divided Children: Galatians and the Politics of Faith.* Harrisburg, PA: Trinity Press International.

Perrin, B. (trans.)
1916 *Plutarch: Life of Pericles.* Loeb Classical Library 65. Cambridge, MA: Harvard University Press.

Peterson, D. G.
2009 *The Acts of the Apostles.* Pillar New Testament Commentary. Grand Rapids: Eerdmans.

Pfitzner, V. C.
1967 *Paul and the Agōn Motif: Traditional Athletic Imagery in the Pauline Letters.* Supplements to Novum Testamentum 16. Leiden: Brill.

Piper, J.
1983 *The Justification of God: An Exegetical and Theological Study of Romans 9:1–23.* Grand Rapids: Baker.
2007 *The Future of Justification.* Wheaton: Crossway.

Plumer, E. A. (trans.)
2003 *Augustine's Commentary on Galatians: Introduction, Text, Translation and Notes.* Oxford: Oxford University Press.

Pollmann, I.
2012 *Gesetzeskritische Motive im Judentum und die Gesetzeskritik des Paulus.* Novum Testamentum et Orbis Antiquus/Studien zur Umwelt des Neuen Testaments 98. Göttingen: Vandenhoeck & Ruprecht.

Porter, S. E.
1989 *Verbal Aspect in the Greek of the New Testament, with Reference to Tense and Mood.* Studies in Biblical Greek 1. New York: Peter Lang.
1992 *Idioms of the Greek New Testament.* Biblical Language: Greek 2. Sheffield: Sheffield Academic Press.

Porter, S. E., and S. A. Adams (eds.)
2011 *Paul and the Ancient Letter Form.* Leiden: Brill.

Porter, S. E., and A. W. Pitts
2009 "Πίστις with a Preposition and Genitive Modifier: Lexical, Semantic, and Syntactic Considerations in the Πίστις Χριστοῦ Discussion." Pp. 33–53 in *The Faith of Jesus Christ: Exegetical, Biblical, and Theological Studies.* Edited by M. F. Bird and P. M. Sprinkle. Peabody, MA: Hendrickson.

Przybylski, B.
1980 *Righteousness in Matthew and His World of Thought.* Society for the Study of the New Testament Monograph Series 41. Cambridge: Cambridge University Press.

Rad, G. von
1951   "Die Anrechnung des Glaubens zur Gerechtigkeit." *Theologische Literaturzeitung* 76: cols. 129–32.

Rainbow, P. A.
2005   *The Way of Salvation: The Role of Christian Obedience in Justification.* Waynesboro, GA: Paternoster.

Räisänen, H.
1983   *Paul and the Law.* Tübingen: Mohr Siebeck.

Ramsay, W.
1893   *The Church in the Roman Empire before A.D. 170.* New York: Putnam's Sons.
1900   *A Historical Commentary on St. Paul's Epistle to the Galatians.* New York: Putnam's Sons.
1920   *St. Paul the Traveller and Roman Citizen.* 14th ed. London: Hodder & Stoughton.

Reed, J. T.
1993   "Using Ancient Rhetorical Categories to Interpret Paul's Letters: A Question of Genre." Pp. 292–324 in *Rhetoric and the New Testament: Essays from the 1992 Heidelberg Conference.* Edited by S. Porter and T. H. Olbricht. Journal for the Study of the New Testament: Supplement Series 90. Sheffield: JSOT.

Refoulé, F.
1988   "Date de l'Épître aux Galates." *Revue biblique* 95:161–83.

Reicke, B.
1951   "The Law and This World according to Paul: Some Thoughts concerning Gal 4:1–11." *Journal of Biblical Literature* 70:259–76.

Reumann, J.
1973   *Creation and New Creation: The Past, Present, and Future of God's Creative Activity.* Minneapolis: Augsburg.
1982   *"Righteousness" in the New Testament: "Justification" in the United States Lutheran-Roman Catholic Dialogue.* Philadelphia: Fortress.

Richards, R.
1991   *The Secretary in the Letters of Paul.* Wissenschaftliche Untersuchungen zum Neuen Testament 2/42. Tübingen: Mohr Siebeck.

Richardson, P.
1969   *Israel in the Apostolic Church.* Society for the Study of the New Testament Monograph Series 10. Cambridge: Cambridge University Press.
1980   "Pauline Inconsistency: 1 Corinthians 9:19–23 and Galatians 2:11–14." *New Testament Studies* 26:347–62.

Riches, J.
2008   *Galatians through the Centuries.* Oxford: Blackwell.

Ridderbos, H. N.
1953   *The Epistle of Paul to the Churches of Galatia: The English Text with Introduction, Exposition and Notes.* New International Commentary on the New Testament. Grand Rapids: Eerdmans.
1975   *Paul: An Outline of His Theology.* Grand Rapids: Eerdmans.

Riesner, R.
1998   *Paul's Early Period: Chronology, Mission Strategy, Theology.* Grand Rapids: Eerdmans.

Robertson, A. T.
1934   *A Grammar of the Greek New Testament in the Light of Historical Research.* Nashville: Broadman.

Robertson, O. P.
1980   "Genesis 15:6: New Covenant Exposition of an Old Covenant Text." *Westminster Theological Journal* 42:259–89.
1990   *The Books of Nahum, Habakkuk, and Zephaniah.* New International Commentary on the Old Testament. Grand Rapids: Eerdmans.

Robinson, D. W. B.
1970   "'Faith of Jesus Christ'—A New Testament Debate." *Reformed Theological Review* 29:71–81.

Robinson, J. A.
1903   *St. Paul's Epistle to the Ephesians.* London: James Clarke.

Rohde, J.
1989   *Der Brief des Paulus an die Galater.* Theologischer Handkommentar zum Neuen Testament 9. Berlin: Evangelische Verlagsanstalt.

Roo, J. C. R.
2007   *Works of the Law at Qumran and in Paul.* New Testament Monographs 13. Sheffield: Sheffield Phoenix.

Ropes, J. H.
1929   *The Singular Problem of the Epistle to the Galatians.* Cambridge, MA: Harvard University Press.

Rosner, B.
2008 "'Known by God': The Meaning and Value of a Neglected Biblical Concept." *Tyndale Bulletin* 59:207–30.

Runge, S. E.
2010 *Discourse Grammar of the Greek New Testament: A Practical Introduction for Teaching and Exegesis.* Peabody, MA: Hendrickson.

Rusam, D.
1992 "Neue Belege zu den *Stoicheia tou Kosmou* (Gal 4,3.9, Kol 2,8.20)." *Zeitschrift für die neutestamentliche Wissenschaft und die Kunde der älteren Kirche* 83:119–25.

Russell, W. B.
1997 *The Flesh/Spirit Conflict in Galatians.* Lanham, MD: University Press of America.

Sailhamer, J. H.
2009 *The Meaning of the Pentateuch: Revelation, Composition and Interpretation.* Downers Grove, IL: InterVarsity.

Sampley, J. P.
1977 "'Before God, I Do Not Lie' (Gal 1:20): Paul's Self-Defense in the Light of Roman Legal Praxis." *New Testament Studies* 23:477–82.
1985 "Romans and Galatians: Comparison and Contrast." Pp. 315–39 in *Understanding the Word: Essays in Honour of Bernhard W. Anderson.* Edited by J. T. Butler, E. W. Conrad, and B. C. Ollenburger. Journal for the Study of the Old Testament: Supplement Series 37. Sheffield: JSOT Press.

Sand, A.
1967 *Der Begriff "Fleisch" in den paulinischen Hauptbriefen.* Regensburg: Pustet.

Sanders, E. P.
1977 *Paul and Palestinian Judaism: A Comparison of Patterns of Religion.* Philadelphia: Fortress.
1983 *Paul, the Law, and the Jewish People.* Minneapolis, Fortress.
1990 "Jewish Association with Gentiles and Galatians 2:11–14." Pp. 170–88 in *The Conversation Continues: Studies in Paul and John in Honor of J. Louis Martyn.* Edited by R. Fortna and B. Gaventa. Nashville: Abingdon.

Sandnes, K. O.
1991 *Paul—One of the Prophets? A Contribution to the Apostle's Self-Understanding.* Wissenschaftliche Untersuchungen zum Neuen Testament 43. Tübingen: Mohr Siebeck.

Sänger, D.
1994 *Die Verkündigung des Gekreuzigten und Israel: Studien zum Verhältnis von Kirche und Israel bei Paulus und im frühen Christentum.* Wissenschaftliche Untersuchungen zum Neuen Testament 2/75. Tübingen: Mohr Siebeck.

Schäfer, P.
1974 "Die Torah der messianischen Zeit." *Zeitschrift für die neutestamentliche Wissenschaft* 65:27–42.

Schäfer, R.
2004 *Paulus bis zum Apostelkonzil: Ein Beitrag zur Einleitung in den Galaterbrief, zur Geschichte der Jesusbewegung und zur Pauluschronologie.* Wissenschaftliche Untersuchungen zum Neuen Testament 179. Tübingen: Mohr Siebeck.

Schauf, S.
2006 "Galatians 2:20 in Context." *New Testament Studies* 52:86–101.

Schewe, S.
2004 *Der Galater Zurückgewinnen: Paulinische Strategien in Galater 5 und 6.* Forschungen zur Religion und Literatur des Alten und Neuen Testaments 208. Göttingen: Vandenhoeck & Ruprecht.

Schlatter, A.
1998 *The Theology of the Apostles: The Development of New Testament Theology.* Grand Rapids: Baker.

Schlier, H.
1989 *Der Brief an die Galater.* 15th ed. Kritisch-exegetischer Kommentar über das Neue Testament (Meyer-Kommentar) 7. Göttingen: Vandenhoeck & Ruprecht.

Schliesser, B.
2007 *Abraham's Faith in Romans 4: Paul's Concept of Faith in Light of the History of Reception of Genesis 15:6.* Wissenschaftliche Untersuchungen zum Neuen Testament 2/224. Tübingen: Mohr Siebeck.

Schmid, H. H.
1968 *Gerechtigkeit als Weltordnung: Hintergrund und Geschichte des alttestamentlichen Gerechtigkeitsbegriffes.* Beiträge zur historischen Theologie 40. Tübingen: Mohr Siebeck.
1980 "Gerechtigkeit und Glaube: Genesis 15,1–6 und sein biblisch-theologischer Kontext." *Evangelische Theologie* 40:396–420.

Schnabel, E. J.

1995 "How Paul Developed His Ethics: Motivations, Norms and Criteria of Pauline Ethics." Pp. 267–97 in *Understanding Paul's Ethics: Twentieth Century Approaches*. Edited by B. S. Rosner. Grand Rapids: Eerdmans.

2004 *Early Christian Mission*, vol. 2: *Paul and the Early Church*. Downers Grove, IL: InterVarsity.

Schnelle, U.

2005 *Apostle Paul: His Life and Theology.* Grand Rapids: Baker Academic.

2009 *Theology of the New Testament.* Grand Rapids: Baker Academic.

Schoeps, H. J.

1959 *Paul: The Theology of the Apostle in the Light of Jewish Religious History.* Philadelphia: Westminster.

Schrage, W.

1996 "Probleme paulinischer Ethik anhand von Gal 5,25–6,10." Pp. 155–94 in *La foi agissant par l'amour (Galates 4,12–6,16)*. Edited by A. Vanhoye. Rome: Abbaye de S. Paul.

Schreiner, T. R.

1984 "Is Perfect Obedience to the Law Possible? A Re-examination of Galatians 3:10." *Journal of the Evangelical Theological Society* 27:151–60.

1985 "Paul and Perfect Obedience to the Law: An Evaluation of the View of E. P. Sanders." *Westminster Theological Journal* 47:245–78.

1993a "Did Paul Believe in Justification by Works? Another Look at Romans 2." *Bulletin for Biblical Research* 3:131–58.

1993b *The Law and Its Fulfillment: A Pauline Theology of Law.* Grand Rapids: Baker.

2010 *Galatians.* Zondervan Exegetical Commentary on the New Testament. Grand Rapids: Zondervan.

Schrenk, G.

1923 *Gottesreich und Bund im älteren Protestantismus, vornehmlich bei Johannes Cocceius.* Gütersloh: Bertelsmann.

1949 "Was bedeutet 'Israel Gottes'?" *Judaica* 5:81–94.

1950 "Der Segenwunsch nach der Kampfepistel." *Judaica* 6:170–90.

Schürmann, H.

1974 "Das Gesetz des Christus" (Gal 6,2): Jesu Verhalten und Wort als letztgültige sittliche Norm nach Paulus." Pp. 282–300 in *Neues Testament und Kirche*. Edited by J. Gnilka. Freiburg: Verlag Herder.

Schütz, J. H.

2007 *Paul and the Anatomy of Apostolic Authority.* New Testament Library. Reprinted Louisville: Westminster John Knox. Originally published in 1975 by Cambridge University Press.

Schwantes, H.

1962 *Schöpfung und Endzeit: Ein Beitrag zum Verständnis der Auferweckung bei Paulus.* Arbeiten zur Theologie 12. Stuttgart: Calwer.

Schweitzer, A.

1931 *The Mysticism of Paul the Apostle.* London: Black.

Schweizer, E.

1966 "Zum religionsgeschichtlichen Hintergrund der Sendungsformel." *Zeitschrift für die neutestamentliche Wissenschaft und die Kunde der älteren Kirche* 57:199–210.

1967–68 "Dying and Rising with Christ." *New Testament Studies* 14:1–14.

1970 "Die 'Elemente der Welt' Gal 4,3 9; Kol 2,8 20." Pp. 245–59 in *Verborum Veritas*. Wuppertal: Brockhaus Verlag.

Scobie, C. H. H.

2003 *The Ways of Our God: An Approach to Biblical Theology.* Grand Rapids: Eerdmans.

Scornaienchi, L.

2008 *Sarx und Soma bei Paulus: Der Mensch zwischen Destruktivität und Konstruktivität.* Novum Testamentum et Orbis Antiquus 67. Göttingen: Vandenhoeck & Ruprecht.

Scott, I. W.

2006 *Implicit Epistemology in the Letters of Paul: Story, Experience and the Spirit.* Wissenschaftliche Untersuchungen zum Neuen Testament 205. Tübingen: Mohr Siebeck.

2007 "Common Ground? The Role of Galatians 2:16 in Paul's Argument." *New Testament Studies* 53:425–35.

2008 *Paul's Way of Knowing: Story, Experience, and the Spirit.* Grand Rapids: Baker Academic.

Scott, J. M.

1992 *Adoption as Sons: An Exegetical Investigation into the Background of ΥΙΟΘΕΣΙΑ in the Pauline Corpus.* Wissenschaftliche Untersuchungen zum Neuen Testament 2/48. Tübingen: Mohr Siebeck.

1993 "'For as Many as Are of Works of the Law Are under a Curse' (Galatians

3:10)." Pp. 187–221 in *Paul and the Scriptures of Israel*. Edited by C. A. Evans and J. A. Sanders. Journal for the Study of the New Testament: Supplement Series 83. Sheffield: JSOT Press.

Seifrid, M. A.

1994   "Blind Alleys in the Controversy over the Paul of History." *Tyndale Bulletin* 45:73–96.

2001   "Righteousness Language in the Hebrew Scriptures and Early Judaism." Pp. 415–42 in *Justification and Variegated Nomism*, vol. 1: *The Complexities of Second Temple Judaism*. Edited by D. A. Carson, P. T. O'Brien, and M. A. Seifrid. Tübingen: Mohr Siebeck / Grand Rapids: Baker Academic.

2003   "Paul, Luther, and Justification in Gal 2:15–21." *Westminster Theological Journal* 65:215–30.

2004   "Paul's Use of Righteousness Language against Its Hellenistic Background." Pp. 39–74 in *Justification and Variegated Nomism*, vol. 2: *The Paradoxes of Paul*. Edited by D. A. Carson, P. T. O'Brien, and M. A. Seifrid. Tübingen: Mohr Siebeck / Grand Rapids: Baker Academic.

2009   "The Faith of Christ." Pp. 129–46 in *The Faith of Jesus Christ: Exegetical, Biblical, and Theological Studies*. Edited by M. F. Bird and P. M. Sprinkle. Peabody, MA: Hendrickson.

Sellin, G.

1999   "Hagar und Sara: Religionsgeschichtliche Hintergründe der Schriftallegorese Gal 4,21–31." Pp. 59–84 in *Das Urchristentum in seiner literarischen Geschichte: Festschrift für Jürgen Becker zum 65. Geburtstag*. Edited by U. Mell and U. B. Müller. Berlin: de Gruyter.

Sherwood, A.

2012   *Paul and the Restoration of Humanity in Light of Ancient Jewish Traditions*. Arbeiten zur Geschichte des antiken Judentums und des Urchristentums 82. Leiden: Brill.

Siber, P.

1971   *Mit Christus Leben: Eine Studie zur paulinischen Auferstehungshoffnung*. Abhandlungen zur Theologie des Alten und Neuen Testaments 61. Zurich: Theologischer Verlag.

Silva, M.

1987   *Has the Church Misread the Bible? The History of Interpretation in the Light of Current Issues*. Grand Rapids: Zondervan.

2000   "The Truth of the Gospel: Paul's Mission according to Galatians." Pp. 51–61 in *The Gospel to the Nations: Perspectives on Paul's Mission*. Edited by P. Bolt and M. Thompson. Downers Grove, IL: InterVarsity.

2001   *Interpreting Galatians: Explorations in Exegetical Method*. 2nd ed. Grand Rapids: Baker Academic.

2003   Unpublished Manuscript on Galatians 1:1–2:16a.

2004   "Faith versus Works of Law in Galatians." Pp. 217–48 in *Justification and Variegated Nomism*, vol. 2: *The Paradoxes of Paul*. Edited by D. A. Carson, P. T. O'Brien, and M. A. Seifrid. Tübingen: Mohr Siebeck / Grand Rapids: Baker Academic.

2007   "Galatians." Pp. 785–812 in *Commentary on the New Testament Use of the Old Testament*. Edited by G. K. Beale and D. A. Carson. Grand Rapids: Baker Academic.

Smedes, L.

1970   *All Things Made New: A Theology of Man's Union with Christ*. Grand Rapids: Eerdmans.

Smiles, V. M.

1998   *The Gospel and the Law in Galatia: Paul's Response to Jewish-Christian Separatism and the Threat of Galatian Apostasy*. Collegeville, MN: Liturgical Press.

2008   "The Blessing of Israel and 'the Curse of the Law': A Study of Galatians 3:10–14." *Studies in Christian-Jewish Relations* 3:1–17.

Smith, R. S.

2001   *Justification and Eschatology: A Dialogue with "the New Perspective on Paul."* Reformed Theological Review Supplement Series 1. Doncaster, Australia: Reformed Theological Review.

Snaith, N. H.

1946   *The Distinctive Ideas of the Old Testament*. Philadelphia: Westminster.

Sprinkle, P. M.

2008   *Law and Life: The Interpretation of Leviticus 18:5 in Early Judaism and in Paul*. Wissenschaftliche Untersuchungen zum Neuen Testament 241. Tübingen: Mohr Siebeck.

2009   "Why Can't 'the One Who Does These Things Live by Them'? The Use of

Leviticus 18:5 in Galatians 3:12." Pp. 126–37 in *Early Christian Literature and Intertextuality*, vol. 2: *Exegetical Studies*. Edited by C. A. Evans and H. D. Zacharias. London: T&T Clark.

Stacey, D.

1956   *The Pauline View of Man: In Relation to Its Judaic and Hellenistic Background*. London: Macmillan.

Stanley, C. D.

1990   "'Under a Curse': A Fresh Reading of Galatians 3:10–14." *New Testament Studies* 36:481–511.

1992   *Paul and the Language of Scripture: Citation Techniques in the Pauline Epistles and Contemporary Literature*. Society for the Study of the New Testament Monograph Series 74. Cambridge: Cambridge University Press.

2004   *Arguing with Scripture: The Rhetoric of Quotations in the Letters of Paul*. London: T&T Clark.

Stanton, G. N.

1996   "The Law of Moses and the Law of Christ: Galatians 3:1–6:2." Pp. 99–116 in *Paul and the Mosaic Law*. Edited by J. D. G. Dunn. Wissenschaftliche Untersuchungen zum Neuen Testament 89. Tübingen: Mohr Siebeck.

Starling, D. I.

2011   *Not My People: Gentiles as Exiles in Pauline Hermeneutics*. Beihefte zur Zeitschrift für die neutestamentliche Wissenschaft 184. Berlin: de Gruyter.

Stowers, S. K.

1986   *Letter Writing in Greco-Roman Antiquity*. Philadelphia: Westminster.

Str-B   *Kommentar zum Neuen Testament aus Talmud und Midrasch*. By H. L. Strack and P. Billerbeck. 6 vols. Munich: Kessinger, 1922–61.

Strelan, J. G.

1975   "Burden-Bearing and the Law of Christ: A Re-examination of Galatians 6:2." *Journal of Biblical Literature* 94:266–76.

Strobel, A.

1961   *Untersuchungen zum eschatologischen Verzögerungsproblem auf Grund der spätjudisch-urchristlichen Geschichte von Habakuk 2,2ff*. Supplements to Novum Testamentum 2. Leiden: Brill.

Stuhlmacher, P.

1966   *Gerechtigkeit Gottes bei Paulus*. Forschungen zur Religion und Literatur des Alten und Neuen Testaments 87. Göttingen: Vandenhoeck & Ruprecht.

1967   "Erwägungen zum ontologischen Charakter der *kainē ktisis* bei Paulus." *Evangelische Theologie* 27:1–35.

1968   *Das Paulinische Evangelium*. Göttingen: Vandenhoeck & Ruprecht.

1986a   "The Apostle Paul's View of Righteousness." Pp. 68–93 in *Reconciliation, Law, and Righteousness: Essays in Biblical Theology*. Philadelphia: Fortress.

1986b   "The End of the Law: On the Origin and Beginnings of Pauline Theology." Pp. 134–54 in *Reconciliation, Law, and Righteousness: Essays in Biblical Theology*. Philadelphia: Fortress.

2001   *Revisiting Paul's Doctrine of Justification*. Downers Grove, IL: InterVarsity.

2005   *Biblische Theologie des Neuen Testaments*. 3rd ed. Göttingen: Vandenhoeck & Ruprecht.

Stuhlmueller, C.

1970   *Creative Redemption in Deutero-Isaiah*. Rome: Pontifical Biblical Institute.

Suggs, M. J.

1972   "The Christian Two Ways Tradition: Its Antiquity, Form, and Function." Pp. 60–74 in *Studies in the New Testament and Other Early Christian Literature: Festschrift für A. P. Wikgren*. Edited by D. E. Aune. Supplements to Novum Testamentum 33. Leiden: Brill.

Suh, M. K. W.

2012   "'It Has Been Brought to Completion': Leviticus 19:18 as Christological Witness in Galatians 5:14." *Journal for the Study of Paul and His Letters* 2:115–32.

Tannehill, R. C.

1967   *Dying and Rising with Christ: A Study in Pauline Theology*. Beihefte zur Zeitschrift für die neutestamentliche Wissenschaft 32. Berlin: Töpelmann.

TDNT   *Theological Dictionary of the New Testament*. Edited by G. Kittel and G. Friedrich. Translated and edited by G. W. Bromiley. 10 vols. Grand Rapids: Eerdmans, 1964–76.

TDOT   *Theological Dictionary of the Old Testament*. Edited by G. J. Botterweck, H. Ringgren, and H.-J. Fabry. Translated by J. T. Willis, G. W. Bromiley, D. E. Green, and D. W. Stott. 14 vols. Grand Rapids: Eerdmans, 1974–.

Thielman, F.

1989   *From Plight to Solution: A Jewish Framework for Understanding Paul's View of the Law in Galatians and*

Romans. Novum Testamentum Supplement 61. Leiden: Brill.

1994   *Paul and the Law: A Contextual Approach*. Downers Grove, IL: InterVarsity.

Thompson, J. W.

2011   *Moral Formation according to Paul: The Context and Coherence of Pauline Ethics*. Grand Rapids: Baker Academic.

Thompson, M. M.

2000   *The Promise of the Father: Jesus and God in the New Testament*. Louisville: Westminster John Knox.

Thrall, M.

1962   *Greek Particles in the New Testament: Linguistic and Exegetical Studies*. New Testament Tools and Studies 3. Grand Rapids: Eerdmans.

Thurén, L.

2000   *Derhetorizing Paul: A Dynamic Perspective on Pauline Theology and the Law*. Wissenschaftliche Untersuchungen zum Neuen Testament 124. Tübingen: Mohr Siebeck.

Thüsing, W.

1965   *Per Christum in Deum: Studien zum Verhältnis von Christozentrik und Theozentrik in den paulinischen Hauptbriefen*. Neutestamentliche Abhandlungen 1. Münster: Aschendorff.

Titrud, K.

1993   "The Function of Καί in the Greek New Testament and an Application to 2 Peter." Pp. 240–70 in *Linguistics and New Testament Interpretation: Essays on Discourse Analysis*. Edited by D. A. Black. Nashville: Broadman.

TLG   Thesaurus Linguae Graecae. Online digital library. Irvine: University of California, 2001–.

Tolmie, F.

2005   *Persuading the Galatians: A Text-Centered Rhetorical Analysis of a Pauline Letter*. Wissenschaftliche Untersuchungen zum Neuen Testament 190. Tübingen: Mohr Siebeck.

Torrance, T. F.

1956–57   "One Aspect of the Biblical Conception of Faith." *Expository Times* 68:111–14.

Treier, D. J.

2005   "Typology." Pp. 823–27 in *Dictionary for the Theological Interpretation of the Bible*. Edited by K. J. Vanhoozer. Grand Rapids: Baker Academic.

Trench, R. C.

1989   *Synonyms of the Greek New Testament*. 9th ed. Reprinted Grand Rapids: Baker Books.

Turner, N.

1963   *Syntax*. Vol. 3 of *A Grammar of New Testament Greek*, by J. H. Moulton. Edinburgh: T&T Clark.

1965   *Grammatical Insights into the New Testament*. Edinburgh: T&T Clark.

UBS⁴   *The Greek New Testament*. Edited by B. Aland et al. 4th rev. ed. Stuttgart: Deutsche Bibelgesellschaft, 1993.

Ulrichs, K. F.

2007   *Christusglaube: Studien zum Syntagma πίστις Χριστοῦ und zum paulinischen Verständnis von Glaube und Rechtfertigung*. Wissenschaftliche Untersuchungen zum Neuen Testament 227. Tübingen: Mohr Siebeck.

Urbach, E. E.

1979   *The Sages: Their Concepts and Beliefs*. 2 vols. Jerusalem: Magnes.

Usher, S. (trans.)

1974   *Dionysius of Halicarnassus: Isaeus*. Loeb Classical Library 465, vol. 8.1. Cambridge, MA: Harvard University Press.

Vanhoozer, K. J.

2011   "Wrighting the Wrongs of the Reformation? The State of the Union with Christ in St. Paul and Protestant Soteriology." Pp. 235–59 in *Jesus, Paul and the People of God: A Theological Dialogue with N. T. Wright*. Edited by N. Perrin and R. B. Hays. Downers Grove, IL: InterVarsity.

Vanhoye, A.

1993   "Pensèe thèologique et qualitè rhètorique in Galates 3,1–14." Pp. 91–114 in *The Truth of the Gospel (Galatians 1:1–4:11)*. Edited by J. Lambrecht. Rome: Benedictina.

VanLandingham, C.

2006   *Judgment and Justification in Early Judaism and the Apostle Paul*. Peabody, MA: Hendrickson.

Vermès, G.

1981   *Jesus the Jew*. Philadelphia: Fortress.

Verseput, D. J.

1993   "Paul's Gentile Mission and the Jewish Christian Community: A Study of the Narrative in Galatians 1 and 2." *New Testament Studies* 39:36–58.

Vickers, B.
2006   *Jesus' Blood and Righteousness: Paul's Theology of Imputation.* Wheaton: Crossway.

Vögtle, A.
1936   *Die Tugend- und Lasterkataloge im Neuen Testament, exegetisch, religions- und formgeschichtlich Untersucht.* Neutestamentliche Abhandlungen 16. Münster: Aschendorff.

Vollenweider, S.
1989   *Freiheit als neue Schöpfung: Eine Untersuchung zur Eleutheria bei Paulus und in seiner Umwelt.* Forschungen zur Religion und Literatur des Alten und Neuen Testaments 147. Göttingen: Vandenhoeck & Ruprecht.

Voorst, R. E.
2010   "Why Is There No Thanksgiving Period in Galatians? An Assessment of an Exegetical Commonplace." *Journal of Biblical Literature* 129:153–72.

Vos, G.
1972   *The Pauline Eschatology.* Reprinted Grand Rapids: Eerdmans.

Vos, J. S.
1992   "Die hermeneutische Antinomie bei Paulus (Galater 3:11–12, Römer 10:5–10)." *New Testament Studies* 38:254–70.
1993   "Die Argumentation des Paulus in Galater 1,1–2,10." Pp. 11–43 in *The Truth of the Gospel (Galatians 1:1–4:11).* Edited by J. Lambrecht. Rome: Benedictina.

Vouga, F.
1998   *An die Galater.* Handbook zum Neuen Testament. Tübingen: Mohr Siebeck.

Wakefield, A. H.
2003   *Where to Live: The Hermeneutical Significance of Paul's Citations from Scripture in Galatians 3:1–14.* Society of Biblical Literature Academia Biblica 14. Atlanta: Society of Biblical Literature.

Walker, W. O., Jr.
1997   "Translation and Interpretation of Ἐὰν Μή in Galatians 2:16." *Journal of Biblical Literature* 116:515–20.

Wallace, D. B.
1990   "Galatians 3:19–20: A Crux Interpretum for Paul's View of the Law." *Westminster Theological Journal* 52:225–45.
1996   *Greek Grammar beyond the Basics: An Exegetical Syntax of the New Testament.* Grand Rapids: Zondervan.

Wallis, I. G.
1995   *The Faith of Jesus Christ in Early Christian Traditions.* Society for the Study of the New Testament Monograph Series 84. Cambridge: Cambridge University Press.

Waltke, B. K.
2001   *Genesis: A Commentary.* Grand Rapids: Zondervan.
2007   *An Old Testament Theology: An Exegetical, Canonical, and Thematic Approach.* Grand Rapids: Zondervan.

Waltke, B. K., and M. P. O'Connor
1990   *An Introduction to Biblical Hebrew Syntax.* Winona Lake, IN: Eisenbrauns.

Walton, J.
2001   *Genesis.* The NIV Application Commentary. Grand Rapids: Zondervan.

Waters, G.
2006   *The End of Deuteronomy in the Epistles of Paul.* Wissenschaftliche Untersuchungen zum Neuen Testament 221. Tübingen: Mohr Siebeck.

Watson, F.
2002   "Is There a Story in These Texts?" Pp. 231–39 in *Narrative Dynamics in Paul: A Critical Assessment.* Edited by B. W. Longenecker. Louisville: Westminster John Knox.
2004   *Paul and the Hermeneutics of Faith.* Edinburgh: T&T Clark.
2006   "Construction and Antithesis: Pauline and Other Jewish Perspectives on Divine and Human Agency." Pp. 99–116 in *Divine and Human Agency in Paul and His Cultural Environment.* Edited by J. M. G. Barclay and S. Gathercole. Edinburgh: T&T Clark.
2007   *Paul, Judaism, and the Gentiles: Beyond the New Perspective.* Rev. ed. Grand Rapids: Eerdmans.
2009   "By Faith (of Christ): An Exegetical Dilemma and Its Scriptural Solution." Pp. 147–63 in *The Faith of Jesus Christ: Exegetical, Biblical, and Theological Studies.* Edited by M. F. Bird and P. M. Sprinkle. Peabody, MA: Hendrickson.

Watts, R. E.
1999   "'For I Am Not Ashamed of the Gospel': Romans 1:16–17 and Habakkuk 2:4." Pp. 3–25 in *Romans and the People of God: Essays in Honor of Gordon D. Fee on the Occasion of His 65th Birthday.* Edited by S. K. Soderlund and N. T. Wright. Grand Rapids: Eerdmans.

Weima, J. A. D.
1993   "Gal 6:11–18: A Hermeneutical Key to the Galatian Letter." *Calvin Theological Journal* 28:90–107.
1994   *Neglected Endings: The Significance of the Pauline Letter Closings.* Journal for the Study of the New Testament: Supplement Series 101. Sheffield: Sheffield Academic Press.

Welles, C. B. (trans.)
1963   *Diodorus Siculus: Library of History Books XVI.66–XVII.* Loeb Classical Library 422. Cambridge, MA: Harvard University Press.

Wenham, D.
1993   "Acts and the Pauline Corpus II. The Evidence of Parallels." Pp. 215–58 in *The Book of Acts in Its First Century Setting,* vol. 1: *The Book of Acts in Its Literary Setting.* Edited by B. W. Winter and A. D. Clarke. Grand Rapids: Eerdmans.

Wenham, G. J.
1979   *The Book of Leviticus.* New International Commentary on the Old Testament. Grand Rapids: Eerdmans.
1987   *Genesis 1–15.* Word Biblical Commentary 1. Nashville: Nelson.

Westerholm, S.
1986   "On Fulfilling the Whole Law (Gal 5:14)." *Svensk Exegetisk Årsbok* 51–52:229–37.
2004   *Perspectives Old and New on Paul: The "Lutheran" Paul and His Critics.* Grand Rapids: Eerdmans.

Westermann, C.
1995   *Genesis 12–36.* Continental Commentary. Minneapolis: Fortress.

White, Joel
2008   "Paul's Cosmology: The Witness of Romans, 1 and 2 Corinthians, and Galatians." Pp. 90–106 in *Cosmology and New Testament Theology.* Edited by J. Pennington and S. McDonough. Library of New Testament Studies 355. London: T&T Clark.

White, John L.
1972   *The Form and Function of the Body of the Greek Letter: A Study of the Letter–Body in the Non-literary Papyri and in Paul the Apostle.* Missoula, MT: Society of Biblical Literature.

Wibbing, S.
1959   *Die Tugend- und Lasterkataloge im Neuen Testament und ihre Traditionsgeschichte unter besonderer Berücksichtigung der Qumran-Texte.* Beihefte zur Zeitschrift für die neutestamentliche Wissenschaft 25. Berlin: Töpelmann.

Wilcox, M.
1977   "Upon the Tree: Deut 21:22–23 in the New Testament." *Journal of Biblical Literature* 96:85–99.

Wiles, M. F.
1967   *The Divine Apostle: The Interpretation of St. Paul's Epistles in the Early Church.* Cambridge: Cambridge University Press.

Wilk, F.
1998   *Die Bedeutung des Jesajabuches für Paulus.* Forschungen zur Religion und Literatur des Alten und Neuen Testaments 179. Göttingen: Vandenhoeck & Ruprecht.

Williams, S. K.
1987   "Justification and the Spirit in Galatians." *Journal for the Study of the New Testament* 29:91–100.
1989   "Promise in Galatians: A Reading of Paul's Reading of Scripture." *Journal of Biblical Literature* 107:709–20.

Willitts, J.
2003   "Context Matters: Paul's Use of Leviticus 18:5 in Galatians 3:12." *Tyndale Bulletin* 54:105–22.
2005   "Isa 54,1 in Gal 4,24b–27: Reading Genesis in Light of Isaiah." *Zeitschrift für die neutestamentliche Wissenschaft und die Kunde der älteren Kirche* 96:188–210.

Wilson, T. A.
2006   "The Law of Christ and the Law of Moses: Reflections on a Recent Trend in Interpretation." *Currents in Biblical Research* 5:123–44.
2007   *The Curse of the Law and the Crisis in Galatia: Reassessing the Purpose of Galatians.* Wissenschaftliche Untersuchungen zum Neuen Testament 225. Tübingen: Mohr Siebeck.

Winger, M.
1992   *By What Law? The Meaning of Νόμος in the Letters of Paul.* Society of Biblical Literature Dissertation Series 128. Atlanta: Scholars Press.
2000   "The Law of Christ." *New Testament Studies* 46:537–46.

Wink, W.
1984   *Naming the Powers: The Language of Power in the New Testament.* Philadelphia: Fortress.

Winter, B. W.
1994   *Seek the Welfare of the City: Christians as Benefactors and Citizens*. First Century Christianity in the Graeco-Roman World. Grand Rapids: Eerdmans.
2002   "The Imperial Cult and Early Christians in Roman Galatia (Acts XIII 13–50 and Gal VI 11–18)." Pp. 67–75 in *Actes du 1er Congrès International sur Antioche de Pisidie*. Edited by T. Drew-Bear, M. Tashalan, and C. M. Thomas. Lyon: Kocaeli.

Wischmeyer, O.
1996   "ΦΥΣΙΣ und ΚΤΙΣΙΣ bei Paulus: Die paulinische Rede von Schöpfung und Natur." *Zeitschrift für Theologie und Kirche* 93:352–75.

Wisdom, J. R.
2001   *Blessing for the Nations and the Curse of the Law*. Wissenschaftliche Untersuchungen zum Neuen Testament 133. Tübingen: Mohr Siebeck.

Witherington, B., III
1998   *Grace in Galatia: A Commentary on Paul's Letter to the Galatians*. Grand Rapids: Eerdmans.
1999   *Jesus the Seer: The Progress of Prophecy*. Peabody, MA: Hendrickson.

Witulski, T.
2000   *Die Adressaten des Galaterbriefes: Untersuchungen zur Gemeinde von Antiochia ad Pisidiam*. Göttingen: Vandenhoeck & Ruprecht.

Wrede, W.
1908   *Paul*. Boston: American Unitarian Association.

Wright, D. F.
2006   "Justification in Augustine." Pp. 55–72 in *Justification in Perspective: Historical Developments and Contemporary Challenges*. Edited by B. L. McCormack. Grand Rapids: Baker Academic.

Wright, N. T.
1991   *The Climax of the Covenant: Christ and the Law in Pauline Theology*. Minneapolis: Fortress.
1994   "Gospel and Theology in Galatians." Pp. 222–39 in *Gospel in Paul: Studies on Corinthians, Galatians and Romans for Richard N. Longenecker*. Edited by L. A. Jervis and P. Richardson. Sheffield: Sheffield Academic Press.

1996   "Paul, Arabia, and Elijah (Galatians 1:17)." *Journal of Biblical Literature* 115:683–92.
1997   *What Saint Paul Really Said: Was Paul of Tarsus the Real Founder of Christianity?* Grand Rapids: Eerdmans.
2000   "The Letter to the Galatians: Exegesis and Theology." Pp. 205–36 in *Between Two Horizons: Spanning New Testament Studies and Systematic Theology*. Edited by J. B. Green and M. Turner. Grand Rapids: Eerdmans.
2002   "The Letter to the Romans: Introduction, Commentary, and Reflections." Vol. 10 / pp. 393–770 in *The New Interpreter's Bible*. Edited by L. E. Keck et al. Nashville: Abingdon.
2005   *Paul in Fresh Perspective*. Minneapolis: Fortress.
2009   *Justification: God's Plan and Paul's Vision*. Downers Grove, IL: InterVarsity.
2011   "Justification: Yesterday, Today, and Forever." *Journal of the Evangelical Theological Society* 51:49–64.

Yeung, M. W.
2002   *Faith in Jesus and Paul: A Comparison with Special Reference to "Faith That Can Remove Mountains" and "Your Faith Has Healed/Saved You."* Wissenschaftliche Untersuchungen zum Neuen Testament 2/147. Tübingen: Mohr Siebeck.

Yinger, K. L.
1999   *Paul, Judaism, and Judgment according to Deeds*. Society for the Study of the New Testament Monograph Series 105. Cambridge: Cambridge University Press.

Zahn, E.
1907   *Der Brief des Paulus an die Galater*. Leipzig: Deichert.

Zerwick, M.
1963   *Biblical Greek Illustrated by Examples*. Translated by J. Smith. Scripta Pontificii Instituti Biblici 114. Rome: Pontifical Biblical Institute Press.

Ziesler, J. A.
1972   *The Meaning of Righteousness in Paul: A Linguistic and Theological Enquiry*. Society for the Study of the New Testament Monograph Series 20. Cambridge: Cambridge University Press.

Index of Subjects

Index of Authors

Index of Greek Words

Index of Scripture and Other Ancient Writings

Old Testament

Genesis

1 278
1–2 254
1:14 278
1:27 254
4:10 244
4:15 404
6:9 49
12 189
12:1–3 199, 228
12:2 199
12:3 195, 198–200, 218
12:7 228
12:11 LXX 392
13:15 228
15 198
15:1–5 228
15:4 188, 198
15:6 17, 18, 22, 38,
    47n57, 48, 51, 54,
    160, 187–91, 198,
    200, 207, 220, 224
15:8 230
15:13 245
15:18 228
16 299
16–21 292, 298
16:3 307
17 229, 301
17:1–8 228–30
17:1–14 22
17:1–21 230
17:8 228

17:9–14 224
17:11–12 318
17:15–16 298
17:18 299
17:20 311
18:10–15 298
18:18 195, 199–200,
    200n5, 218
18:19 276
21 298
21:1 298
21:8–10 310
21:9 310
21:10 292, 298, 311,
    312, 314, 315
21:12 298
21:13 298, 311
22 188, 216
22:15–18 228
22:16–18 200n5, 228n7
22:17–18 244
22:18 199–200, 215n23,
    218, 228, 244
24:7 228
25:1–6 298n6
26:1–5 228
26:4 199–200, 218
26:5 188, 216, 224
28:4 215, 231
28:13–15 228
28:14 199n5, 218
35:11–12 228
37:20 349

38:26 50
41:20 349
44:16 50

Exodus

4:22 250, 268
7:11 359
7:22 359
8:3 359
8:14 359
12:14–20 334
12:40 245
13:21–22 136
14:31 189
15:13 51n65, 52n65
15:26 183
18:20 353
19:5 183
20:1 345n7
23:7 50
23:21 147n3
23:22 183
32:8 76–77
34:28 345n7
34:29 235

Leviticus

2:11 334
7:18 190
10:6 389
18:1–5 208, 208n14

18:5 17, 60n79, 158,
    195, 208, 208n14,
    209, 209n15, 220–21
18:6–23 208
18:24–30 208
18:29 208n14
19:14 337
19:18 18, 345, 346, 350,
    377
19:36 49
19:37 LXX 350
23:4 278n7
25 278
26:46 235

Numbers

5:30 350
6:15 334
6:17 334
6:19 334
14:11 189
18:30 190
20:12 189
20:29 389
21:3 80
25:6–15 101
25:11 101
25:13 101
28:11–15 278

Deuteronomy

1:8 362
1:17 147n3

New Testament

Romans

Old Testament Apocrypha

Old Testament Pseudepigrapha

Rabbinic Writings

On the Migration of Abraham	On the Preliminary Studies	On the Special Laws	Who Is the Heir?
92 353	86–87 221	1.211 256	168 345n7

On the Virtues

63 67n2

Classical Writers

Aristotle

Ethics

in toto 366

Politics

3.13 367
5.3 360

Rhetoric

3.1.1358a 63n84

Diodorus Siculus

Library of History
17.116.4 105n11

Dionysius of Halicarnassus

De Isaeo
14.26 163n9

Lucian of Samosata

Toxaris
40–41 286

Plato

Lysis
208c 243

Plutarch

Cicero
7.5, 864C 151

Life of Pericles
15.5 43n50

Polybius

Universal History
28.5.6 372

Quintilian

Education of the Orator
in toto 63n84

Xenophon

Agesilaus
3.4.2–3 163n9

Memorabilia
2.1.1 261n6

Church Fathers

Aristides the Apologist

2–6 271

Clement of Alexandria

Exhortation to the Greeks

5 271

Ignatius of Antioch

To the Magnesians
10.3 100, 151

John Chrysostom

Commentary on the Epistle of St. Paul the Apostle to the Galatians

in toto 355
1:1 65
1:16 104
2:1–2 125n8
2:11–12 145, 146
2:17 28n37
2:19 28n37
3:2 28n37
3:10 28n37, 202
3:12 28n37

3:20 235
3:27 252n6
4:24 295
5:2 28n37
5:12 338
5:15 349
6:1 375
6:12 391
6:15–16 401

Justin Martyr

Dialogue with Trypho
8 323
46 394

Origen

Commentary on the Gospel of John
32.17 67

Preaching of Peter

in toto 271

Tertullian

On Idolatry
4 271